grant

CURRICULUM

FOUNDATIONS, PRINCIPLES, AND ISSUES

THIRD EDITION

ALLAN C. ORNSTEIN

Loyola University of Chicago

FRANCIS P. HUNKINS

University of Washington, Seattle

ALLYN AND BACON

Boston   London   Toronto   Sydney   Tokyo   Singapore

Senior Editor: Virginia Lanigan
Editorial Assistant: Kris Lamarre
Senior Marketing Manager: Kathy Hunter
Editorial Production Service: Raeia Maes, Maes Associates
Manufacturing Buyer: Megan Cochran
Cover Administrator: Linda Knowles

Copyright © 1998, 1993, 1988 by Allyn & Bacon
A Viacom Company
160 Gould Street
Needham Heights, MA 02194

Internet: www.abacon.com
America Online: keyword: College Online

Library of Congress Cataloging-in-Publication Data
Ornstein, Allan C.
    Curriculum—foundations, principles, and issues / Allan C.
Ornstein, Francis P. Hunkins. — 3rd ed.
        p.   cm.
    Includes bibliographical references and indexes.
    ISBN 0-205-27702-0
    1. Curriculum planning—United States.   2. Curriculum evaluation—
United States.   I. Hunkins, Francis P.   II. Title.
LB2806.15.O76   1998
375'.001'0973—dc21   97-24347
                                                                CIP

Printed in the United States of America

10   9   8   02

Brief Contents

Contents

PART II
PRINCIPLES OF CURRICULUM

CURRICULUM TIPS

PREFACE

Curriculum: Foundations, Principles, and Issues, Third Edition, is a book for researchers, theoreticians, and practitioners of curriculum. It is a basic text for those studying curriculum development, design and/or planning, as well as a reference for teachers, supervisors, and administrators who participate in curriculum making.

The book is a comprehensive and documented overview of the foundations, principles, and issues of curriculum: *foundations* are the areas of study outside curriculum that affect the field; *principles* refer to the means and methods used in reflecting about the totality of curriculum and for developing, designing, implementing, and evaluating curriculum; *issues* address the theories and trends that influence the field.

The book consists of a one-chapter introduction to the field plus three major parts: foundations, principles, and issues. Part I, Foundations of Curriculum, has five chapters: one each on the philosophical, historical, psychological, social, and theoretical foundations of curriculum. Part II, Principles of Curriculum, comprises five chapters: curriculum development; curriculum design; aims, goals, and objectives; curriculum implementation; and curriculum evaluation. Part III, Issues of Curriculum, includes two chapters that discuss present issues and trends and future directions.

This book differs from other curriculum texts in several ways. Most texts tend to focus on either theory or practice; we try to blend both aspects of curriculum. Most curriculum writers emphasize either the foundations, principles, or issues of curriculum; the majority focus on principles, and many others focus on foundations. We have attempted to balance all three areas of curriculum. Most texts take a particular philosophical or theoretical position; we, however, have tried to present various philosophies and theories. We provide readers with alternatives and choices for formulating their own views and values on curriculum foundations, principles, and issues.

We have also attempted to maintain a foot in the past while keeping our eyes and ears open to the future by combining traditional concepts of philosophy, history, and sociology with emerging and futuristic perspectives of the field. We have analyzed several competing theories, models, and paradigms, and we have recommended several practical guidelines. In short, we have supplied a mix of material to help researchers, theoreticians, and practitioners develop their own interpretations of past, present, and future curriculum domains.

In this third edition of the book, we have maintained three instructional and learning tools: curriculum tips, focusing questions, and overview tables. *Curriculum tips* are designed to give practical meaning to the research and insights into the curriculum process. The *focusing questions* at the beginning of each chapter are designed to orient the reader and set the stage for the main ideas in the chapter. The *overview tables* are incorporated in each chapter to make learning more meaningful and to provide summaries of the major concepts and principles conveyed in the chapter.

The creation of any textbook results from engagement with numerous people. We are continually influenced by our respective mentors of curriculum: Virgil Clift, Hilda Grobman, and O. L. Davis, Jr. We are most appreciative of those individuals who reviewed the manuscript: Dennis C. Buss, Rider University; Sam Evans, Western Kentucky University; and Billie McElroy, Oklahoma City University.

We also want to acknowledge the contributions of Virginia Lanigan, senior editor at Allyn and Bacon, and Kris Lamarre in the production of the book. Their efforts are much appreciated. Special thanks to William O. Thomas, who copyedited the manuscript, and to Raeia Maes, the editorial production supervisor.

A.C.O.
F.P.H.

1

THE FIELD OF CURRICULUM

Focusing Questions

1. How would you characterize the field of curriculum?
2. Why is it so necessary to understand the field of curriculum?
3. What approach to curriculum do most educators adopt? Why?
4. How do you define curriculum?
5. Why do most theorists define curriculum in terms of generic principles or processes, not specific subject matter?
6. What fundamental questions guide the field of curriculum?
7. How do the foundations of education influence curriculum? Which foundation areas are more important? Why?
8. What are the differences between curriculum development and design?
9. How can theory and practice be integrated into the planning of curriculum?
10. How do you define the role of the principal (teacher) in curriculum planning?
11. What influences on the field of curriculum are the reconceptualists and postmodernists having?

Curriculum as a field of study has been characterized as elusive, fragmentary, and confusing. Certainly, the field at times can be all that, but we must realize that curriculum as a field of study is crucial to the health of not only schools but the total society. Whether we consider curriculum narrowly as a listing of subjects to be taught in schools or broadly as experiences that individuals require for full and authentic participation in society, there is no denying that curriculum affects us all, both those within the field, the educators and curricularists of various stripes, and those in the general society.

After all the books, articles, and treatises that have been written about curriculum, many persons in this field feel frustrated because we still exhibit confusion. However, we would argue that the reasons for studying the field of curriculum are not to arrive at precise answers—to arrive at certainty, but to increase our understanding of the complexities, the paradigm shifts, of this realm of intellectual and practical activities. We need to realize that curriculum results from social activity. Curriculum is designed for both deliberate and emerging human purposes.[1] Society, especially today, is dynamic, with its members often exhibiting uncertainty and confusion. It is not surprising that the field of curriculum also reflects these characteristics. Ideally, as we investigate and participate in this field, we will develop comfort in processing the dynamics of the field within an environment of uncertainty. We think that what many define as confusion is in reality dynamism, the exuberance of the many voices within the field.

What we mean by curriculum, what it involves, and who is involved and served by the curriculum are best understood by analyzing the concept of curriculum in a broad context. We thus look at curriculum in terms of approach (an orientation or perspective) and definition. We consider, also, the relationships and differences between the foundations and domains of curriculum, the theory and practice of curriculum, and the roles of those who participate in the realm of curriculum. We present this broad brush to curriculum realizing that we as authors and you as readers do not stand outside the field of curriculum, but are well immersed within this dynamic system.

CURRICULUM APPROACHES

An individual's approach to curriculum reflects that person's view of the world, including what the person perceives as reality, the values he or she deems important, and the amount of knowledge he or she possesses. A curriculum approach reflects a *holistic* position or a *metaorientation,* encompassing the foundations of curriculum (the person's philosophy, view of history, view of psychology and learning theory, and view of social issues), domains of curriculum (common and important knowledge within the field), and the theoretical and practical principles of curriculum. An approach expresses a viewpoint about the development and design of curriculum, the role of the learner, teacher, and curriculum specialist in planning curriculum, the goals and objectives of the curriculum, and the important issues that need to be examined.

A curriculum approach reflects our views of schools and society; to some extent it may even become an all-encompassing outlook if we feel strongly about these views. By understanding one's curriculum approach, and the prevailing curriculum approach of the school or school district in which one works, it is possible to conclude whether one's professional view conflicts with the formal organizational view.

Although schools, over time, tend to become committed to a particular curriculum approach,

many educators are not strongly committed to one approach. Many of them do not have a single or pure approach; rather, in some situations they emphasize one approach, and in other cases they advocate several approaches. In still other cases, they fail to recognize that they even reflect a particular attitudinal or behavioral curriculum approach, or that they are in fact influenced by many approaches. They need to recognize that curriculum textbook writers sometimes adhere to more than one curriculum approach. Moreover, curriculum specialists, even curriculum students, need to examine their approaches.

Curriculum approaches can be viewed from a technical and nontechnical, or scientific and nonscientific, perspective. (Note that the terms *nontechnical* and *nonscientific* do not suggest a negative or disparaging approach; rather, these two terms denote a contrast.) Technical-scientific approaches coincide with traditional theories and models of education and reflect established and formal methods of schooling.

Many of these approaches are considered within the positivist or modern camp. Nontechnical and nonscientific approaches have evolved as part of avant-garde and experimental philosophies and politics of education; they tend to challenge established and formalized practices of education. Furthermore, nontechnical approaches reflect the views of postpositivists or postmodernists. These approaches are more fluid and emergent.

The remainder of this section outlines five curriculum approaches. The first three may be classified as technical or scientific, the latter two as nontechnical and/or nonscientific.

Behavioral Approach

Rooted in the University of Chicago school (from Bobbitt and Charters to Tyler and Taba), this is the oldest and still the major approach to curriculum.[2] As a means-ends approach it is logical and prescriptive. It relies on technical and scientific principles, and includes paradigms, models, and step-by-step strategies for formulating curriculum. Usually based on a plan, and sometimes called a blueprint or document, goals and objectives are specified, content and activities are sequenced to coincide with the objectives, and learning outcomes are evaluated in relation to the goals and objectives.

This curriculum approach, which has been applied to all subjects for more than two-thirds of this century, constitutes a frame of reference against which other approaches to curriculum are compared. Other names that have been used to identify this approach—including logical-positivist, conceptual-empiricist, experientalist, rational-scientific, and technocratic[3]—suggest that the approach is also technical and scientific and that it deals with principles for theoreticians and practitioners.

The behavioral approach started with the idea of efficiency, influenced by business and industry, and the scientific management theories of Frederick Taylor, who analyzed factory efficiency in terms of time and motion studies and concluded that each worker should be paid on the basis of his or her individual output, as measured by the number of units produced in a specified period of time. Efficient operation of the schools (and other social systems), sometimes called **machine theory** by its critics, became a major goal in the 1920s.

Often ensuring efficiency in schools meant eliminating small classes, increasing student-teacher ratios, hiring few administrators, cutting costs in teacher salaries, maintaining or reducing operational costs, and so on, and then preparing charts and graphs to show the resultant lower costs. Raymond Callahan later branded this idea the "cult of efficiency."[4] The goals or effects were to make schools in general and curriculum making more scientific, at least more precise, and to reduce teaching and learning to precise behaviors with corresponding activities that could be measured.

Franklin Bobbitt described the problems as he set out to organize a course of studies for the elementary grades. "We need principles of curriculum making. We did not know that we should first determine objectives from a study of social needs. . . . We had not learned that [plans] are means, not ends."[5]

Bobbitt developed his objectives and activities approach in the early 1920s in *How to Make a Curriculum*. In the book, he outlined more than 800 objectives and related activities to coincide with predetermined student needs. These activities ranged from the "ability to care for [one's] teeth . . . eyes . . . nose, and throat; . . . to keep home appliances in good working condition; . . . to spelling and grammar."[6] Bobbitt's methods

were quite sophisticated for the day, but taken out of context, his list of hundreds of objectives and activities, along with the machine or factory analogy that he advocated, was easy to criticize.

It was left to Ralph Tyler, who took a number of courses with Bobbitt at the University of Chicago, to recognize the need for behavioral objectives that were not so tiny or lockstep; instead, basic techniques of curriculum, instruction, and evaluation were combined in a simple plan. His idea was to use the philosophy of the school (or school district) "in making decisions about objectives." Thus he provided greater latitude and value judgments for those responsible for planning the curriculum. Tyler's approach combined behaviorism (objectives were an important consideration), and thus noted the influence of Thorndike, with progressivism (the emphasis on the needs of the learner), and the influence of Dewey, with the "scientific movement of curriculum [making] during the past thirty years" prior to his classic text.[7]

Today, there are few pure behaviorists. Behavioral research has evolved over the years to address the complexities of human learning. Behaviorism has even allowed for research that investigates the depths of the mind.[8] Most educators of this stripe realize that to obtain a more complete picture of how individuals learn the curriculum they, as researchers, must perceive individuals as cognitive functioning individuals within a social context.

Students will experience and respond to the same curriculum in unique ways, depending on their cultural interpretations and prior life activities. One stimulus does not elicit the same response from everyone. We can argue that this "enrichment" of our understanding of this approach to curriculum has further supported its popularity as a means of creating educational programs. Despite much conversation about paradigm shifts, the behavioral approach to curriculum, with its dependency on technical means of selecting and organizing curricula, is likely to continue to serve us well into the next century.

Managerial Approach

This approach considers the school as a social system, reminiscent of organizational theory, whereby groups of people such as students, teachers, curriculum specialists, and administrators interact according to certain norms and behaviors. Educators who rely on this approach plan the curriculum in terms of programs, schedules, space, resources and equipment, and personnel. This approach advocates, among other things, the need for selecting, organizing, communicating with, and supervising people involved in curriculum decisions. Consideration is given to committee and group processes, human relations, leadership styles and methods, and decision making.[9]

An offshoot of the behavioral approach, the managerial approach, also relies on a plan, rational principles, and logical steps, but not necessarily behavioral approaches. The managerial aspect tends to focus on the supervisory and administrative aspects of curriculum, especially the organizational and implementation process. See Curriculum Tips 1-1.

Advocates of this approach are interested in change and innovation, and in how curriculum specialists, supervisors, and administrators can facilitate these processes. The curriculum specialist and supervisor (sometimes the same person) is considered to be a practitioner, not a theoretician—a change agent, resource person, and facilitator. He or she reports to an administrator and follows the mission and goals of the school. If the school does not appreciate change, then the change role of the job is minimized. If the school is innovative or reform minded, then changes are expected and the school culture tends to create and sustain a culture for change.[10] However, if the school emphasizes the "three R's," then the curriculum specialist introduces plans accordingly. Most of the cues related to change or stability are communicated to subordinates (teachers) from managers through formal and informal (body language, conversations, and the like) communication networks.

The managerial approach is rooted in the organizational and administrative school models of the early 1900s—a period that combined a host of innovative plans involving curriculum and instruction that centered around individualization, departmentalization, nongrading, classroom grouping, and homeroom and work-study activities. It was an era when various school district plans were introduced by their respective superintendents in an attempt to modify the horizontal and vertical organization of the schools. The names of the plans were usually based either on the school district's name or organizational concept, such as the Batavia (New York) Plan, Denver (Colorado) Plan, Elizabeth (New Jersey) Plan, Pueblo (Colorado) Plan, Platoon (Gary, Indiana) Plan, Portland (Oregon) Plan, Santa Barbara (California) Plan, Study Hall (New York City) Plan, and Winnetka (Illinois) Plan. Superintendents and associate superintendents were very much involved in curriculum leadership, often developing a plan in one school district and being hired by another to implement the plan in the new district. Hence, there was a good deal of hopscotching around of administrators who combined managerial and curriculum leadership skills.[11]

The managerial approach became the dominant curriculum approach in the 1950s and 1960s. During this period, the notion of the principal as a curriculum leader and instructional leader was popularized and fused with the idea of general manager. It was in this era when Midwest school administrators and professors (with administrative backgrounds) dominated the field of curriculum in terms of setting policies and priorities, establishing the direction of change and innovation, and planning and organizing curriculum and instruction.

These administrators were very active politically. They used the supervisory and curriculum associations and their respective journals and yearbooks as platforms to publicize their ideas. Many, like Robert Anderson, Leslee Bishop, Gerald Firth, Arthur Lewis, and John McNeil, became curriculum professors at major universities; others became active as board directors and executive committee members of professional organizations that had major impact on curriculum, supervision, and administration. Many published curriculum books that expressed this managerial view.[12]

These school administrators were less concerned about content than about organization and implementation. And they were less concerned about subject matter, methods, and materials than about improving curriculum in light of policies, plans, and people on a system-wide basis. They envisioned curriculum changes and innovation as they administered the resources and restructured the schools.

Today, many of our "new" ideas of school reform and restructuring are rooted in the ideas of

---

Curriculum Tips 1-1

The Role of the Curriculum Supervisor

Regardless of the curriculum approach certain basic roles are performed by a curriculum supervisor or specialist. Such a person must perform many important tasks within the school or school district. Some of these follow.

1. Help develop the school's or community's *educational goals.*
2. *Plan curriculum* with students, parents, teachers, and support personnel.
3. Coordinate or evaluate *student needs survey.*
4. *Design programs* of study by grade level and/or subject.
5. Plan or *schedule classes;* plan school calendar.
6. Develop or help staff to write *behavioral objectives* in subject areas.
7. Prepare *curriculum guides* or teacher guides by grade level or subject area.
8. Formulate new (or revise) *resource units* and unit plans.
9. Help in the selection and evaluation of *textbooks.*
10. Organize, select, or order instructional *materials* and *media.*
11. Serve as a *resource agent* for teachers.
12. *Observe teachers* and hold pre- and post-observation conferences.
13. Help teachers to *implement curriculum* in the classroom.
14. Help redefine or *improve content.*
15. Work with staff in *writing grants.*
16. Encourage curriculum *innovation and change*; serve as a change agent.
17. *Conduct curriculum research* and/or work with curriculum consultants within the school.
18. Develop standards for curriculum and instructional *evaluation.*
19. Coordinate or *plan staff development* programs.
20. *Work with supervisors,* chairs, resource personnel, ed tech specialists, and teachers within the school (and school district).

---

change and innovation that characterized the 1950s and 1960s: then local control was a sacred cow, while today the state is playing a major role in reform. Many current plans related to school-based management and empowerment are based on the older career ladder and differential staffing models of this previous era. Much of the new legislative and administrative support for improving curriculum and instruction is based on the changing role of the superintendent and principal, as curriculum and instructional leaders, that blossomed during the 1950s and 1960s and is now shaping the profession again.

The Systems Approach

It was not far to leap from organizing people and policies, a managerial view, to organizing curriculum into a system. The systems aspect tends to view various units and subunits of the organization in relation to the whole, and organizational diagrams, flow charts, and committee structures are often diagrammed as the curriculum plan is introduced and monitored. Sometimes referred to as **curriculum engineering,** the approach includes the processes necessary to plan the curriculum by such *engineers* as superintendents, directors, coordinators, and principals: *the stages* (development, design, implementation, and evaluation) and *structures* (subjects, courses, unit plans, and lesson plans).

The systems approach to curriculum was influenced by systems theory, systems analysis, and systems engineering. These concepts, originally developed by social scientists in the 1950s and 1960s, are used or at least discussed widely by school managers as part of administrative and organizational theory. The largest users of the systems approach are the military, business, and industry, since it is critical that all learners master whatever tasks they perform (our nation's defense or a company's profits largely depend on people performing their jobs), and they can afford the start-up costs necessary to introduce the system.[13]

In the systems approach to curriculum, the parts of the total school district or school are closely examined in terms of their interrelatedness and influence on each other. Components like departments, personnel, equipment, and schedules are planned to create changes in people's behavior and expectations. Information is usually communicated to administrators who consider alternatives and choices.

One particular application of the systems approach was developed by Rand Corporation and has rapidly spread from government to business agencies. It is called Planning, Programming, Budgeting System (PPBS), and it brings together the components of planning, programming, and budgeting with the system's structure, functions, and capabilities. In our case, the system is curriculum.

Another well-known systems approach is the Program Evaluation and Review Technique (PERT), which was introduced by the Defense Department and subsequently spread to business and industry in the 1960s. Like PPBS, it has been introduced into education. Progress and interruptions of various facets of the program, in this case the curriculum, are computed, analyzed, and made available to administrators. Progress reports are continuously updated, reflecting changes in schedule, possible difficulties, and achievement rates. In both systems approaches, the curriculum is closely monitored by administrators; revisions and corrective action are introduced on a continuous basis.

Currently, many schools employ a systems approach known as *total quality control*. This approach, also drawn from industry, represents a paradigm shift emphasizing client priority, in our case students, the lack of hierarchy, self-monitoring and inspection, collaboration, horizontal communication, cooperation, and team responsibility.[14]

When applying total quality control to curriculum development and implementation, participants, as team players, realize that their function depends on the acquisition and application of what is called *profound knowledge*. Such knowledge is based on four components: systematic thinking, theory of variation, theory of knowledge, and knowledge of psychology. *Systematic thinking* enables the players to realize that their activities interact with the actions of others and that the total organization is a dynamic of interacting functions possessing many subprocesses. The *theory of variation* recognizes that in curriculum activity there are common and special causes and impacts. The environment of the school within which people create curricula is a community where people exhibit individual differences. Recognizing such variation allows educators to accept that no curriculum will be perfect, no learning complete. There can be no state of zero defects. For this reason, goals depicted as numerical scores are not feasible.

The *theory of knowledge* focuses the individual's attention on the fact that knowledge within the system and possessed by the players is essential to the success of the curricular game. Education within total quality management is concerned with prediction. For prediction to have validity, it must be based on knowledge. Schools must be able to predict results from student engagement with curriculum, and also must take the long view of the results of education. With a long-term perspective, schools are more likely to be successful in designing and delivering appropriate curricula. The *knowledge of psychology* supports total quality management in that this systems approach applies systematic thinking to the people involved by optimizing the participation and learning of all the players, that is, students and teachers. To employ this approach successfully, individuals must understand people and, more importantly, their differences. This approach is designed to free each person's potential so that all can soar.[15]

George Beauchamp described the first systems theory of curriculum. He divided theories of education into five major theories of equal importance: (1) administration, (2) counseling, (3) curriculum, (4) instruction, and (5) evaluation.[16] Many professors of education (outside of curriculum) do not accept this notion of equal theories, for they view their own field as their major system or area of study—and curriculum as a component or subsystem of the major system. For example, school administrators often delegate supervisors to take care of curriculum matters, especially if the administrators view their leadership role chiefly in terms of management. On the other hand, curriculum specialists usually view curriculum as the major system, and related fields such as teaching, instruction, and supervision are seen as subsystems that help implement the curriculum.[17]

However, what Beauchamp was trying to convey is that the five theories of education are applied realms of knowledge that draw their ideas from the foundations of education: psychology, sociology, history, philosophy, and so on. Rather than dispute what are the major systems or subsystems, it is more important to design procedures that are applicable to the real world and use whatever theory that can be helpful to the practitioner.

Curriculum specialists who value the systems approach take a macro or broad view of curriculum and are concerned with curriculum issues and questions that relate to the entire school or school system—not just in terms of particular subjects or grades. They are concerned with how the curriculum is related across different programs and content areas, to what extent the curriculum reflects the hierarchy or organizational arrangements of the school (or school system), the needs and training of the participants, and various methods for monitoring and evaluating results. Long-term planning is fused with short-range or incidental planning.

Academic Approach

Sometimes referred to as the traditional, encyclopedic, synoptic, intellectual, or knowledge-oriented approach, the academic approach attempts to analyze and synthesize major positions, trends, and concepts of curriculum. The approach tends to be historical or philosophical, and, to a lesser extent, social in nature. The discussion of curriculum making is usually scholarly and theoretical (not practical), and concerned with many broad aspects of schooling, including the study of education. This expansion of curriculum boundaries relative to the subject of schooling, and the treatment of curriculum as intellectual thought, are reflected in a good deal of background information and broad overview of events and people.

This approach is rooted in the philosophical and intellectual works of John Dewey, Henry Morrison, and Boyd Bode.[18] It became popular between the 1930s and 1950s. The influx of new topics related to curriculum during this period expanded the boundaries of the field to include a good number of trends and issues, and the integration of various instructional, teaching, learning, guidance, evaluation, supervision, and administrative procedures. The field became all-encompassing because the books published accumulated a great deal of curriculum knowledge and subject matter.

After the 1950s, major interest in curriculum centered around the structure of disciplines and qualitative methods. Thus the academic approach lost some of its glamor among curricularists. However, some of its appeal has returned in the focus on the nature and structure of knowledge as current curricularists address curriculum from a postmodern academic perspective. Attention is now on understanding how knowledge can be constructed, deconstructed, and then reconstructed and the implications of such activities for curriculum development and delivery.

Although the academic approach has usually been the primary concern of curriculum scholars and theorists, some scholars now urge practitioners to engage in the scholarly study and analysis of the field of curriculum. Indeed, William Pinar has noted that already this approach is achieving dominance as the field becomes more preoccupied with understanding. Pinar commented that we can no longer afford to be just technicians, people who carry out actions in unquestioning ways. All must strive, in both academe and the schools, to comprehend the phenomenon of curriculum and the dynamics of the field within which it exists.[19] It seems likely that this approach to curriculum will meld with the other approaches discussed in this section. We in curriculum activity must both study the field and also create curricula for students in an ever-increasing social dynamic.

The academic approach to curriculum broadens our focus much beyond subject matter and pedagogy. Academics cover numerous foundational topics (usually historical, philosophical, social, and political), thus presenting a general overview of curriculum. Currently, some academics state that the field of curriculum is rooted in and influenced by the entire world. Therefore, the field must address life in its totality, from birth to death. This broad-brush approach to the field brings in areas of study formally not included in curriculum deliberation and action, such as religion, psychotherapy, literary criticism, and linguistics. For many educators, such fields at first seem very foreign. However, educators are beginning to realize that it is increasingly necessary to perceive curriculum as diverse discourse, as varied text making. All involved in curriculum are in the "business" of words and ideas.[20]

Humanistic Approach

Some curriculum leaders reflect on the field and contend that the above approaches are too technocratic and rigid. They contend that in attempting to be scientific and rational, curricularists miss the personal and social aspects of curriculum and instruction; ignore the artistic, physical, and cultural aspects of subject matter; rarely consider the need for self-reflectiveness and self-actualization among learners; and, finally, overlook the sociopsychological dynamics of classrooms and schools.

This view is rooted in progressive philosophy and the child-centered movement of the early 1900s (first spearheaded at the University of Chicago when John Dewey, Charles Judd, and Francis Parker developed progressive methods of teaching, based on the student's natural development and curiosity).[21] In the 1920s and 1930s, the progressive movement moved east and was dominated by Teachers College, Columbia University, and by such professors as Frederick Bosner, Hollis Caswell, L. Thomas Hopkins, William Kilpatrick, Harold Rugg, and John Dewey (who had changed professional affiliations and was now at Columbia).[22] This approach gained further impetus in the 1940s and 1950s with the growth of child psychology (which deals with the needs and interests of children) and humanistic psychology (which deals with valuing, ego identity, psychological health, freedom to learn, and personal fulfillment).

From this approach, numerous curriculum activities have emerged, mainly at the elementary school level, including lessons based on life experiences, group games, group projects, artistic endeavors, dramatizations, field trips, social enterprises, learning and interest centers, and homework and tutoring stations (or corners). These activities include creative problem solving and active student participation; they emphasize socialization and life adjustment for students, as well as stronger family and school-community ties. They are representative of Parker, Dewey, Kilpatrick, and Washburne's ideal school and the kinds of curriculum activities they put into practice—and that are still practiced in the Parker School in Chicago, Dewey's lab school at the University of Chicago, Washburne's school district in Winnetka, Illinois, and Kilpatrick's Lincoln School of Teachers College, as well as in many other private and university lab schools and some school districts across the country.

Various developmental theories (Erikson, Havighurst, and Maslow) and child-centered methods (Frobel, Pestalozzi, and Neill) for curriculum are derived from the humanistic approach. The formal or planned curriculum is not the only curriculum to consider; the informal and hidden curricula are also worthwhile. Also, this approach considers the whole child, not only the cognitive dimension. Humanistic theories of learning are given equal billing, and sometimes greater emphasis, than behavioral and cognitive theories. Music, art, literature, health education, and the humanities are just as important as science and math (and other academic subjects).

Curriculum specialists who believe in this approach tend to put faith in cooperative learning, independent learning, small-group learning, and social activities, as opposed to competitive, teacher-dominated, large-group learning and only cognitive instruction. Each child, according to this approach, has considerable input in the curriculum and shares responsibility with parents, teachers, and curriculum specialists in planning classroom instruction. Curriculum leaders and supervisors tend to permit teachers more input in curriculum decisions, and the ideas of professional collegiality and mentor systems are more pronounced in the schools adopting this approach. Curriculum committees are *bottom up* instead of *top down,* and often students are invited into curriculum meetings to express their views on content and experiences related to curriculum development.[23]

The humanistic approach became popular again in the 1970s as relevancy, radical school reform, open education, and alternative education became part of the reform movement in education. Today, however, demands for educational excellence and academic productivity have resulted in emphasis on cognition, and not humanism, and on subjects such as science and math, and not art or music. The humanistic approach has usually represented a minority view among curriculum leaders in schools.

The humanistic approach will most likely continue to be challenged by those who argue for higher standards, assuming that, to be successful in the next century, students will require a good base in the academic core subjects. Many seem to believe that the next century will demand thinkers and not "feelers." However, the humanistic approach is not going to disappear. Indeed, it may actually gain more adherents as people come to realize the interdependence of cognition and affect.[24] Education must focus on both the personal and the interpersonal. This will require overcoming a long tradition of regarding cognition as something separate from feeling.

As Elliot Eisner points out, this view goes back to the time of Plato, who regarded knowledge of worth as knowledge that did not depend on the senses. The senses were untrustworthy. They could seduce a person from the clear track of coming to know the true. Thought should not be encumbered by feeling. Although Plato's ideas are still among us, increasing numbers of humanists refuse to be pushed aside. They advance strong arguments that it is the total person—the cognitive, the affective, and even the spiritual self—who is involved in gaining knowledge and working toward wisdom. The student's self-concept and self-esteem are essential factors in this journey.

Reconceptualists

For some curriculum scholars, the reconceptualists represent an approach to curriculum that is in large part an extension of the humanistic orientation. Others argue that the reconceptualists fail to

have an approach, in that they lack a model for developing and designing curriculum or for dealing with technical matters. However, this may be looking at the concept of approach too narrowly.

Reconceptualists do have an approach. They come to the field of curriculum with their attention centered on the larger ideological and moral issues of education (not only curriculum), and they strive to investigate and even influence the economic and political institutions of society (not only schools). Essentially, reconceptualists take an academic approach to curriculum, for they are more interested in studying curriculum in the abstract than in the practical application of knowledge to the creation of curriculum. They focus more on understanding than developing curriculum. Pinar has even gone so far as to state that the era of curriculum development is past.[25]

Some curricularists who at least associate with the reconceptualists camp urge the view that curriculum is postmodern. In developing a curriculum, one must embrace a new consciousness. There is no one precise and certain way to create curricula. Curriculum development is more like an open, interactive, communal conversation.[26] By participating in such an interactive conversation, people and the very process of curriculum development are transformed. A pattern of actions of curriculum development emerges from the apparent chaos. Curriculum development is not a closed system, but is ever open. To postmodernists, one requires open systems of action, for open systems transform, whereas closed systems transmit and transfer. If one still feels uncomfortable in saying that this is an approach to curriculum, one must at least realize that this is an attitude, a disposition to consider and act on curriculum matters in particular ways, with certain mind-sets.

Reconceptualists and postmodernists are interested in the interaction of curricula with political, economic, social, cultural, and even artistic forces. All influence the manner in which we create and design curricula.[27] Curricularists of this stripe argue that the school is not a system set unto itself, apart from the world. The school is in the world; it exists as an interacting peer system with the political, economic, and social systems. Since the school is very much in the world, an extension of society, its purpose is not to "fit" students into the world, into a static society, but rather to enable them to be transformed and to transform the society.

The purpose of the curriculum is emancipation. However, many reconceptualists posit that most current curricula are controlling and designed to preserve the existing order. A key assumption, and one that we would argue is flawed, is that the existing order is static and oppressive. The school and its curriculum must exist to change that. However, any society that is vital exists as an open system. That we have so much dialogue currently and that we are discussing postmodernism and paradigm shifts point to the vibrancy of the overall society. Certainly, there are problems; chaos exists. However, only a static, closed, unchanging society would have total harmony.

Those advocating the reconceptualist approach to curriculum have brought into curricular dialogue a greater range of voices. This is not the first time a request for such variety has been urged. Indeed, reconceptualism is rooted in the philosophy and social activism of such early reconstructionists as Counts, Rugg, and Benjamin.[28] These early scholars, as is true of our contemporary reconceptualists, urged curricularists to rethink, reconsider, and reconceptualize the curriculum.

Perhaps what really distinguishes many reconceptualists is the intensity of their political and ideological stances. Many are so convinced of the righteousness of their view that they fail to give any legitimacy to those who challenge them. Indeed, many reconceptualists have developed intellectual myopia, having been snared by a political, social metanarrative while saying that we should not ascribe to one.

DEFINITION OF CURRICULUM

What is curriculum? What is its purpose? How does it affect students and teachers? The way we define curriculum by and large reflects our approach to it. But the relationship between approach and definition is neither perfect nor mutually exclusive; approaches and definitions overlap. We can specify five basic views or definitions of curriculum. The first two, the most popular, delineate two extremes: specific and prescriptive versus broad and general.

A curriculum can be defined as a *plan* for action or a written document that includes strategies for achieving desired goals or ends. This position, popularized by Ralph Tyler and Hilda Taba, exemplifies a linear view of curriculum. The steps of the planner are sequenced in advance. The plan has a beginning and end, as well as a process (or means) so that the beginning can progress to an end. Most behavioral and some managerial and systems people today agree with this definition. For example, J. Galen Saylor defines curriculum "as a plan for providing sets of learning opportunities for persons to be educated."[29] Writes David Pratt, "Curriculum is an organized set of formal education and/or training intentions."[30] Jon Wiles and Joseph Bondi view "curriculum as a plan for learning [whereby] objectives determine what learning is important."[31]

Curriculum can, however, be defined broadly—as dealing with the *experiences* of the learner. This view considers almost anything in school, even outside of school (as long as it is planned) as part of the curriculum. It is rooted in Dewey's definition of experience and education, as well as in Caswell and Campbell's view, from the 1930s, that curriculum was "all the experiences children have under the guidance of teachers."[32]

Humanistic curricularists and elementary school curricularists subscribe to this definition, which, over the years, has been interpreted more broadly by textbook writers. State Shepherd and Ragan, "The curriculum consists of the ongoing experiences of children under the guidance of the school." It represents "a special environment . . . for helping children achieve self-realization through active participation within the school."[33] Eisner points out that the curriculum "is a program [the school] offers to its students." It consists of a "preplanned series of educational hurdles" and "an entire range of experiences a child has within the school."[34] Finally, Hass contends that "curriculum is all of the experiences that individuals have in a program of education . . . which is planned in terms of . . . theory and research or past and present professional practice."[35]

Three other definitions fall in between these two common, almost extreme definitions. Curriculum can be considered as a system for dealing with people and the processes or the organization of personnel and procedures for implementing that system. The system can be either linear or nonlinear. A linear system is a simple means-ends view of curriculum whereby a process or means is determined to achieve a desired end. A nonlinear system, however, permits the curriculum specialist to operate with flexibility and to enter at various points of the model, skip components or parts, reverse order, and work on more than one component at a time. Many managerial and systems curricularists adopt this definition.[36]

Curriculum can also be viewed as a *field of study,* comprising its own foundations and domains of knowledge, as well as its own research, theory, and principles and its own specialists to interpret this knowledge. The discussion of curriculum is usually scholarly and theoretical, not practical, and concerned with broad historical, philosophical, or social issues. Academics, such as McNeill, Schubert, and the Tanners, often subscribe to this view of curriculum.[37]

Finally, curriculum can be considered in terms of *subject matter* (mathematics, science, English, history, and so on) or content (the way we organize and assimilate information). We can also talk about subject matter or content in terms of different *grade levels.* Nonetheless, the emphasis from this viewpoint would be on facts, concepts, and generalizations of a particular subject or group of subjects, as opposed to generic concepts and principles of curriculum making that cut across the field of curriculum. There is no particular curriculum approach that adheres to this definition, and any curriculum approach could adopt this definition.

Beauchamp asserts that only definitions involving a plan, system, and field of study represent key or legitimate uses of the word curriculum.[38] But the other two definitions (dealing with experiences and subjects) are also consistent with good theory and practice. Surprisingly, there are no real curriculum advocates of subjects and grades. Because most school systems across the country develop curriculum in terms of different subjects and grades, it would seem that we need to view curriculum more in line with this definition than others. The fact that practitioners use this form of curriculum on a daily basis, whereas theoreticians rarely do (usually professing that they wish to examine generic concepts and principles

that are applicable to most subjects and grades) suggests that the two groups are not really talking to each other. Although many university curriculum departments offer courses in elementary and secondary school curriculum, they rarely offer curriculum courses by subjects—mathematics curriculum, science curriculum, and so on.

The Challenges of Definition

Numerous definitions of curriculum exist. To some, such variety creates confusion. However, we would argue that this is not necessarily a bad thing. The plethora of definitions demonstrates a dynamism of varied voices in the field. These voices introduce diverse interpretations by drawing on specific modes of thought, particular ideologies, diverse pedagogies, unique political experiences, and various cultural experiences. One could truly be concerned if such a cacophony of voices spoke with one voice, presented one paradigm, and agreed on one curriculum.

Definitional debates take time and energy from what some curricularists consider substantive problems and issues, from research and theoretical approaches that require attention. But the time consumed defining and redefining the concept of curriculum is well spent, for it engages us in the various dynamics of curriculum and the particular movements that affect it. To be sure, curricularists often have trouble communicating with each other. But the solution to communication problems is not establishing a simplistic language of key terms. Rather, we need to accept the various linguistic meanings of our terms. We must be "multidialectic" in our curricular conversations. We must be aware of and celebrate the fact that our curricular languages are neither philosophically or politically neutral.[39]

Our languages and use of terms also vary with regard to the scope and intent of meaning. By giving certain meanings to our terms, we simultaneously omit or de-emphasize other meanings.

The more precise one's definition of curriculum, and the more a person relies on a preconceived plan or document, the greater the tendency to omit, ignore, or miss relevant factors related to teaching and learning because they are not part of the written plan. As Doll points out, "Every school has a planned, formal acknowledged curriculum," but it also has "an unplanned, informal and hidden one" that must be considered.[40] The planned, formal curriculum focuses on goals, objectives, subject matter, and organization of instruction; the unplanned, informal curriculum deals with social-psychological interaction among students and teachers, especially their feelings, attitudes, and behaviors.

If we only consider the planned curriculum, the official curriculum evident in a written document, or if we are too prescriptive in our approach, in our delivery of instruction, we can ignore the numerous positive and negative consequences that can result. We may fail to realize the power of the hidden curriculum, that part of the curriculum that, while not written, will certainly be learned by students. The inclusion of certain content teaches that such knowledge is valued, at least by some. In defining the curriculum too narrowly we also fail to recognize what Eisner called the null curriculum and what students learn from it.[41] The *null curriculum* refers to those subject matters and/or experiences that are not taught or learned, but that students know, at least in a general way, exist. Students may infer from the null curriculum that what is left out is not considered of value or not within the purpose of schooling. Subjects such as dance and law are often left out, being replaced by the basic subjects—the sciences and the humanities. Students often construct more powerful learnings from the hidden and null curricula. They learn that their particular stories or cultures are not of equal worth. They frequently create false learnings about themselves. They may learn to dislike school not only for what is left out but for the manner in which included subjects are presented. Students may learn mathematics, but also learn to dislike it. The point is, we cannot be too rigid or close-ended, trying to fill in all the boxes.

There are too many gray areas in education, and too many human variables that we cannot control or plan for in advance. The curriculum must consider the smells and sounds of the classroom, the intuitive judgments and hunches of the teacher, and the needs and interests of the students that evolve and cannot always be planned by the student, teacher, or curriculum specialist.

On the other hand, a broad umbrellalike definition of curriculum as school experiences results in other problems. It assumes that almost everything that goes on in school can be classified or discussed in terms of curriculum. It even suggests that curriculum is synonymous with education. It also connotes that almost every field or discipline in schools of education has implications for curriculum or is part of the curriculum field. If nearly everything in schools and in the study of education is related to curriculum, classifying what is not curriculum is meaningless. When the content and scope of any field become all-encompassing, or so enlarged that they overlap with those of many other fields, then it becomes too difficult to delineate that field (say, curriculum) and separate it from other fields.

Background Issues for Defining the Field

Content or subject matter issues are relevant too. Is it appropriate to talk about a social studies or mathematics curriculum or about curriculum in general? Are there general principles of curriculum that apply to all subjects, or specific principles that apply to specific subjects? Should subject matter be organized around separate disciplines or based on interdisciplinary and core approaches? To what extent is subject a matter of student choice, professional choice, or parent choice? Should it be determined by the community, state, or nation? How should subjects be organized: around graded or nongraded approaches, behavioral objectives, student activities, social or community values, future jobs? What portion of subject matter should be classified as general, specialized, or elective? What is the appropriate mix of common subjects versus optional subjects? And what is the appropriate stress on facts, concepts, and principles of subject matter? As Beauchamp writes, "The posture . . . one assumes with respect to the content of a curriculum inevitably will be of great influence upon . . . theory and planning."[42] Actually, it has a major influence on everything that follows, from developing, designing, implementing, and evaluating the curriculum, from planning the policies and programs to determining the processes and products of the curriculum.

Other issues are related to people. Who are the major participants? To what extent should students, teachers, parents, and community members be involved in curriculum planning? Why are school administrators assuming greater roles in curriculum matters, and curriculum specialists assuming fewer roles? What are the roles and responsibilities of researchers and practitioners in curriculum making? And, how do we improve their communication?

Fundamental Questions

Asking the right questions is crucial for addressing basic concerns in curriculum and for determining the basic concepts, principles, and research methods of the field. If we ask the wrong questions, the discussions that follow (even the answers) are of little value. The danger in listing a host of fundamental questions, however, is that they tend to become translated as a set of principles or steps to be blindly followed. Indeed, appropriate questions can be used as a base for raising issues and problems that curriculum specialists need to address, whether they deal in theory or practice or both.

The first list of fundamental questions was formulated by a famous twelve-person committee on curriculum making, headed by Harold Rugg and organized in 1930 for the Twenty-Sixth Yearbook of the National Society for the Study of Education (NSSE). This group of curriculum specialists, perhaps the most prestigious ever convened to present a general system on the principles of curriculum making, started the second volume of the Yearbook with eighteen "fundamental questions" to serve as a basis for "viewing . . . the issues and problems of curriculum" for that era.[43] These questions are shown in column 1 of Table 1-1.

A more recent set of questions was presented more than 50 years later and is shown in column 2 of the same table. In general, the sets of both questions focus on the role of school in American society, the place and function of subject matter, the methods and materials for facilitating learning, the role of the curriculum specialist, and the relationship between curriculum, instruction, supervision, and governmental levels of curriculum making.

Most important, it can be argued that these fundamental questions help establish what Tyler called the "rationale" of curriculum, that later Say-lor, Alexander, and Lewis called the "purpose," and that Schubert more recently maintained was the "paradigm,"—which governs how inquiry in the field of curriculum may be established.[44] By asking these "what" and "how" questions, curriculum specialists can delineate important theories, concepts, and methods in the field.

FOUNDATIONS OF CURRICULUM

Debates continue on what is curriculum, and on how to outline the basic foundations (or boundaries) and domains (knowledge) of the field. An optimistic view would be that almost all, if not all, the knowledge concerning curriculum is available in the literature, but at present it is "widely scattered" and is either "unknown or unread" by a majority of those who teach or practice curriculum.[45] A pessimistic view is that the field lacks purpose and direction because it has extensively "adapted and borrowed subject matter from a number of [other] disciplines," including its major "principles, knowledge and skills."[46] This is basically the same criticism that Joseph Schwab made almost 30 years ago, when he complained that the field was "moribund [because] it has adopted theories from outside the field of education . . . from which to deduce . . . aims and procedures for schools and classrooms."[47]

Some argue that until these problems are resolved, curriculum as a field of study will be characterized by considerable confusion, conflict, and lack of coherence, and that it will continue to lack a well-organized professional and political constituency. A more optimistic view, however, considers this openness or lack of closure as a source of richness and challenge.

Major Foundations: Philosophy, History, Psychology, and Sociology

The foundations of curriculum set the external boundaries of the knowledge of curriculum and define what constitutes valid sources of information from which come accepted theories, principles, and ideas relevant to the field of curriculum.

The commonly accepted foundations of curriculum include the following knowledge areas: philosophical, historical, psychological, and social (sometimes cultural, political, or economical

TABLE 1-1 Fundamental Questions of Curriculum

18 QUESTIONS, 1930	15 QUESTIONS, 1987
1. What period of life does schooling primarily contemplate as its end?	1. How is curriculum defined?
2. How can the curriculum prepare for effective participation in adult life?	2. What philosophies and theories are we communicating, intentionally or not, in our curriculum?
3. Are the curriculum-makers of the schools obliged to formulate a point of view concerning the merits or deficiencies of American civilization?	3. What social and political forces influence curriculum? Which ones are most pertinent? Which constrain or impose limitations?
4. Should the school be regarded as a conscious agency for social improvement?	4. How does learning take place? What learning activities are most suitable for meeting the needs of our learners? How can these activities best be organized?
5. How shall the content of the curriculum be conceived and stated?	5. What are the domains of curriculum knowledge? What types of curriculum knowledge are essential?
6. What are the place and function of subject matter in the education process?	6. What are the essential parts of a curriculum?
7. What portion of education should be classified as "general" and what portions as "specialized" or "vocational" or purely "optional"? To what extent is general education to run parallel with vocational education, and to what extent is the latter to follow on the completion of the former?	7. Why do changes in curriculum take place? How does change affect the curriculum?
8. Is the curriculum to be made in advance?	8. What are the role's and responsibilities of the curriculum specialist?
9. To what extent is the "organization" of subject matter a matter of pupil-thinking and construction of, or planning by, the professional curriculum-maker as a result of experimentation?	9. How is the curriculum best organized?
10. From the point of view of the educator, when has "learning" taken place?	10. What are the roles and responsibilities of the teacher and student in organizing curriculum?
11. To what extent should traits be learned in their "natural" setting (that is, in a "life-situation")?	11. What are our aims and goals? How do we translate them into objectives?
12. To what degree should the curriculum provide for individual differences?	12. How do we define our educational needs? Whose needs? How do we prioritize these needs?
13. To what degree is the concept of "minimal essentials" to be used in curriculum construction?	13. What subject matter or content is most worthwhile? What are the best forms of content? How do we organize them?

(continued)

TABLE 1-1 Continued

18 QUESTIONS, 1930	15 QUESTIONS, 1987
14. What should be the form of organization of the curriculum? Shall it be one of the following or will you adopt others?	14. How do we measure or verify what we are trying to achieve? Who is accountable, for what, and to whom?

14. What should be the form of organization of the curriculum? Shall it be one of the following or will you adopt others?
    a. A flexibly graded series of suggestive activities with reference to subject matter which may be used in connection with the activities? Or,
    b. A rigidly graded series of activities with subject matter included with each respective activity? Or,
    c. A graded sequence of subject matter with suggestion for activities to which the subject matter is related? Or,
    d. A statement of achievements expected for each grade, a list of suggested activities, and an outline of related subject matter, through the use of which the grade object may be achieved? Or,
    e. A statement of grade objectives in terms of subject matter and textual and reference materials which will provide this subject matter without any specific reference to activities?
15. What, if any, use shall be made of the spontaneous interests of children?
16. What types of material (activities, reading, discussions problems and topics, group projects, and so on) should the curriculum-maker analyze [for] activities in which [students] actually engage?
17. How far shall methods of learning be standardized?
18. Administrative questions of curriculum-making.
    a. For what time units shall the curriculum be organized?
    b. For what geographic units shall the curriculum be made [national, state, school district, local school]? What is the optimal form in which to publish the course of study?

14. How do we measure or verify what we are trying to achieve? Who is accountable, for what, and to whom?

15. What is the appropriate relationship between curriculum and instruction? Curriculum and supervision? Curriculum and evaluation?

Source: Harold Rugg et al., "List of Fundamental Questions on Curriculum Making," in G. M. Whipple, ed., *The Foundations of Curriculum-making,* Twenty-sixth Yearbook of the National Society for the Study of Education, Part II (Bloomington, Ill.: Public School Publishing Co., 1930), p. 8; Allan C. Ornstein. "The Theory and Practice of Curriculum." *Kappa Delta Pi Record* (Fall 1987), p. 16.

foundations are included as part of or separate from the social foundations). Although curriculum writers generally agree on the foundation areas, few attempt to analyze or discuss these four areas in depth.

Of course, merely examining the foundation areas is insufficient. Curricularists need to show the relationship of the foundation areas and curriculum. They must analyze and synthesize what is known about each of the foundations and present implications that are relevant to curriculum. In this connection, Herbert Kliebard claims that the field of curriculum is a synoptic one. The specialist in curriculum brings perspectives from other fields to bear on curriculum. This means the curriculum person examines and uses the concepts, methods, and research tools of the philosopher, historian, psychologist, sociologist, economist, and political scientist.[48]

Regardless of their approach or their philosophical, historical, social, or psychological views, it is natural for curriculum people to rely on the foundation areas as a means of studying and practicing curriculum. This text examines four foundation areas (in four chapters) with the intention of presenting important sources of information from other fields that are pertinent to curriculum. It is important that the readers analyze and interpret the knowledge of foundations presented to establish and clarify the external boundaries of curriculum.

DOMAINS OF CURRICULUM

Whereas the foundations of curriculum represent the external boundaries of the field, the domains of curriculum define the internal boundaries, or accepted knowledge, of the field that can be derived from examining published textbooks, articles, and research papers. Although curriculum specialists generally agree on the foundation areas, they often do not agree on what represents the domains or common knowledge of curriculum. The latter problem suggests that the field is neither a disciplined body nor a full profession based upon a defined body of knowledge. Many efforts have been made to structure a matrix or map of the knowledge in curriculum so as to help conceptualize or set the boundaries within the field. According to some observers, the problem is

that the knowledge is diffused in several sources, many unrecognized as curriculum sources. In addition, many known sources are unread because there is so much literature to read.[49]

The lack of consensus of the domains of curriculum is illustrated by the experts themselves. For example, George Beauchamp divided curriculum knowledge into planning, implementation, and evaluation.[50] Fenwick English viewed curriculum in terms of ideological (or philosophical-scientific), technical (or design), and operational (or managerial) issues.[51] Finally, Edmund Short outlined the domains of curriculum into policy making, development, evaluation, change, decision making, activities or fields of study, and forms and language of inquiry (or theory).[52]

Linda Behar was the first to establish an empirical format for identifying *curriculum domains* (broad areas of knowledge based on the most influential curriculum textbooks over a 20-year period) and *curriculum practices* (precise activities teachers and curriculum specialists engage in while inquiring about, planning, or implementing the curriculum). As many as 49 curriculum practices were validated and then rated in importance by professors of curriculum across the nation. These practices were categorized into and used to define and support the existence of nine curriculum domains: (1) curriculum philosophy, (2) curriculum theory, (3) curriculum research, (4) curriculum history, (5) curriculum development, (6) curriculum design, (7) curriculum evaluation, (8) curriculum policy, and (9) curriculum as a field of study.[53] Although these curriculum domains vary from one theorist to another, so that a knowledge base in the field is difficult to agree upon, the reader might infer that Behar's work helps establish recommended content for a curriculum text.

Despite this lack of consensus, however, it is important to establish a framework for conceptualizing the domains of curriculum—that is, the significant and indispensable curriculum knowledge necessary to conduct research and make theoretical and practical decisions about curriculum. The problem is that few curriculum writers can agree on the domains of curriculum knowledge; in some cases, no framework exists that connotes curriculum as a distinct enterprise with its own boundaries, internal structures, relations, and activities. We maintain that, of all the domains of curriculum knowledge, the *development* and *design* of the curriculum—what some observers refer to as the theoretical aspects and what others call the technical aspects of curriculum—are crucial for any text.

Curriculum Development

Analyzing curriculum in terms of development is the traditional and most common approach to the field. The idea is to show how curriculum evolves or is planned, implemented, and evaluated, as well as what various people, processes, and procedures are involved in constructing the curriculum. Such development is usually examined in a logical step-by-step fashion, based on behavioral and managerial approaches to curriculum and rooted in scientific principles of education. In other words, the principles are generalizable. Many curriculum texts today use the terms *development* and *plan* in their titles—and thus reflect this thinking. See Curriculum Tips 1-2.

Saylor and others, for example, outline a concise four-step planning model, which includes goals and objectives, curriculum design (or specifications), curriculum implementation (or instruction), and curriculum evaluation. The planning model is influenced by several social forces and three social sources of curriculum—society, learners, and knowledge.[54] Another easy-to-understand approach is by Unruh and Unruh, who outline five developmental steps: goals and objectives, needs assessment, content, implementation, and evaluation.[55] Francis Hunkins has designed a systems model, in seven corresponding steps: curriculum conceptualization and legitimization, curriculum diagnosis, content selection, experience selection, curriculum implementation, curriculum evaluation, and curriculum maintenance.[56]

All these development models attempt to show the relationship of curriculum to various decisions, activities, and processes. They provide us with guideposts and structure to clarify our thinking. The models tend to be graphically or pictorially illustrated, and in terms of input, transformations, and output, they are sequential and rational, the curriculum is viewed as a total system, and all enterprises within the model are conceived as subsystems. The development models are also theoretical and scientific, and they are designed to increase understanding of facts, correlates, and relationships of curriculum. Finally, the models are conceived in technical terms—with the assumption that one must be knowledgeable of the field to fully appreciate and understand them.

Many curriculum textbook writers tend to formulate developmental models. However, some curricularists use the term *development* in their respective textbook titles without either formulating their own developmental models or even paying much attention to other models. But the emphasis on development is not without pitfalls. By basing their developmental models around scientific and technical terms, writers tend to overlook the human aspects of teaching and learning. By formulating steps that are concrete, prescriptive, and measurable, they tend to ignore processes that are not readily observable or measurable, that are not precisely consistent, or that are not applicable to a good deal of control. What they sometimes ignore are the personal attitudes, emotions, and feelings linked to teaching and learning, and the values and beliefs involved in curriculum making.

By adopting developmental models, curricularists tend to constrain curriculum choices and to limit flexibility in the various curriculum sequences or steps—from aims and objectives to evaluation of learning tasks and outcomes. They sometimes forget that the path to curriculum development is strewn with many concessions to social and political realities, qualitative judgments that require familiarity with teaching effectiveness and allowable choices in teaching methods and learning activities, and alternatives that recognize that one kind of curriculum may be more suitable and successful with one school (or with one population of students and teachers) than another.

However, adopting one or more of these developmental models does not prevent one from being mindful of these pitfalls. Some of the models' advocates would argue that by being systematic, they are able to consider students in all of their complexity and to manage the dynamics and decisions of curriculum activity; moreover, they might argue that their models consider multiple variables and permit choices.

Some curricularists argue that today more discussion about models of curriculum development

---

================= *Curriculum Tips 1-2* =================

Steps in Curriculum Planning

The following questions are based on three stages of curriculum planning: development, implementation, and evaluation. The questions presented are essential in the process leading to a new or revised curriculum. They are starting points or guides to help clarify curriculum planning in any subject area or grade level.

1. When the school system is developing a new curriculum:
   a. Who determines priorities?
   b. Who develops the time line?
   c. Who assigns members to curriculum committees?
   d. Who coordinates the efforts of curriculum committees?
   e. Who devises the curriculum development process?
2. After the curriculum has been approved and it is time to put it into place:
   a. Who decides on the materials and activities?
   b. Who determines how much money will be needed?
   c. Who decides what staff development will be offered to prepare teachers to use it?
3. Finally, to determine if the curriculum is meeting expectations:
   a. Who decides how the curriculum will be evaluated?
   b. Who is responsible for carrying out the evaluation?
   c. Who is responsible for reporting the results of the evaluation to teachers, administrators, school board members, and the public?

Source: Michael Campbell, Judy Carr, and Douglas Harris, "Board Members Needn't Be Experts to Play a Vital Role in Curriculum," *American School Board Journal* (April 1989) p. 30.

---

is unnecessary. We know how to do it. What we need is to understand the processes by which we bring the curriculum to life and the complexities by which students learn what is useful. Stating that we "know how to develop curricula" seems to be a misreading of the times. Certainly, we have the technical steps written down. However, even persons with a "technical stripe" realize that most procedures, however nice they look in graphic models, are not as neat in the real world.

Few advocates of employing models to guide curriculum deliberation accept that the models are grounded on ahistorical or universal principles. Models are not to be followed blindly as a metanarrative. Advocates of following models realize that players are more than technicians. In curriculum development in the current age, which some identify as postmodern, players must reflect on the meaning of knowledge, as reflected in the curriculum or types of test, and realize curriculum action as human relationships. As Slattery notes, curriculum development in a postmodern milieu will engage a community of "interpreters working together in mutually corrective and mutually collaborative efforts."[57]

In this textbook, considerable attention is given to nontechnical models. Some might consider them nonmodels. However, even these have some perceived sense built into them. William Doll notes that it is commonly heard among postmodernists that nothing is foundational; there are no universal principles. Everything is relational. Doll makes an interesting point in bringing into focus at least one concept that he believes foundational. This concept is *self-organization,* integral to the whole paradigm.[58]

Drawing on Doll, when people participate in curriculum creation, they engage each other in understanding the realms of knowledge and the lived experience and gain comprehension regarding what it means to exist as an individual alone and with others within the world. Under conditions of curriculum creation, people exhibit emerging actions such that curricula are generated, not specifically for all times, but for a particular period and for certain students. As time flows onward, these curricula will be deconstructed and reconstructed. Doll points out that a curriculum designed with self-organization as a basic assumption has challenge and perturbation as its *raison d'être*. This is in direct contrast to a curriculum that follows a narrow technical view. In a technical system, challenge and perturbation are viewed as disruptive and inefficient.[59]

Perhaps it would be more helpful to think of curriculum development as either an open or a closed system, rather than as a model or nonmodel. Open systems are dynamic and evolutionary. They require disruptions, or breakpoints, in order to function. Disruptions get open systems going. Closed systems are static and are actually headed toward dysfunction and termination or death. Closed systems cannot tolerate disruptions which are anathema to their functioning.

Perhaps all those involved should think of curriculum, the result of curriculum development, as an open system. By accepting this, teachers and students would celebrate the challenges, realizing that these are needed to disrupt their knowledge systems, in order for learning to occur and for personal transformation to occur.[60] Curriculum as an open system is a journey for all involved, a journey to be experienced with zest, not a destination to be arrived at and then stored and hoarded.

Curriculum Design

Curriculum design refers to the way we conceptualize the curriculum and arrange its major components (subject matter content, instructional methods and materials, learner experiences or activities) to provide direction and guidance as we develop the curriculum. Most curriculum writers do not have a single or pure design for curriculum; they tend to be influenced by many designs, as they are by many approaches, and they are likely to draw bits and pieces from different designs. Unless they are highly motivated or compelled by one curriculum approach or a set of values or tools for analyzing the world around them, they tend to use eclectic designs and to intermix ideas from several sources.

Nonetheless, the way someone designs a curriculum is partially rooted in his or her approach to and definition of curriculum. For example, those who view curriculum in behaviorist terms with a prescribed plan and set of learning outcomes and those who consider curriculum to be a system of managing people and organizing procedures will produce different curriculum designs. Those who have strong psychological views of teaching and learning will also present different designs for curriculum from those who have strong social or political views of schools. Whereas curriculum development tends to be technical and scientific, curriculum design is more varied, because it is based on curricularists' values and beliefs about education, priorities of schooling, and views of how students learn. Just asking questions such as what are schools for, what shall we teach, how shall we teach, and what learning theories should we stress evokes considerable controversy. The positions educators adopt on these questions, however, reflect their preferred designs in curriculum.

Questions such as these are not asked in isolation. Indeed, curricularists' views of the purpose of school and the curriculum are influenced by the curricularists' sense of the social–world context. How one perceives the world and its human and animal communities influences what one privileges in a curriculum design. If academic knowledge is viewed as paramount, the design most likely will stress disciplined knowledge. If one views the transformation of individuals as central to wise action, designs will be organized more to nurture the individual as a person and a member of various communities.

In general, a curriculum design should provide a basic frame of reference, a template if you wish, for planning what the curriculum will look like after one has engaged in curriculum development. If we liken a curriculum to a painting, design refers to how we want our artistic composition arranged. While a curriculum design is influenced to some extent by the writer's curriculum approach, just as a painting is influenced to some degree by the artist's approach, it is the writer's views of the world and his or her views of teaching, learning, and instruction that are key to design selection.

For most of the twentieth century, persons who have gone into teaching and have eventually become curriculum specialists have been content oriented. These persons have privileged a curriculum design that draws on the academic disciplines. Such prizing of content has been good, for most of the public looks to the schools to have curricula that allow students to learn content. This is not likely to change dramatically. However, there are those people, both within and outside education, who feel that we need designs that focus more on the human and less on the content. Many of these designs, within the liberal and humanistic camps, have been tried and have not gained major acceptance. It is not likely that schools in the immediate future will be more hospitable to novel and radical designs. This is not too surprising, for the schools in our society, and almost everywhere else, are given the traditional tasks of socializing students in accordance with the norms of society (a conservative function) and pursuing intellectual tasks (a cognitive function).

Other Domains of Curriculum

Those who study curriculum and who contribute to the professional literature must constantly deal with other domains of curriculum. Opinions about what curriculum knowledge is essential vary from one scholar to another and from one textbook writer to another. There appears to be more disagreement than agreement in the status and scope of remaining domains of curriculum. As Rosales-Dordelly and Short assert, "The status of the body of curriculum knowledge has been described by scholars in the field as amorphous, diffuse, incoherent, and fragmentary. . . . Few advances have been made in conceptualizing the field."[61]

Perhaps one reason for the confusion is that much of curriculum involves values, choices, and options, as well as personal reflection and various views (or perspectives) in different contexts. Presumably, we do not deliberately plan the curriculum or carry it out because it is required; we teach content and organize experiences in certain ways because of our personal and professional beliefs and because we understand the impact on our students. Hence our values, choices, and reflective processes lead to competing versions of the good curriculum and the appropriate domains of curriculum.

The minimum consensus for which we can strive is that a curriculum text include a discussion of development and design. Some might argue that it is important to include, also, discussions of curriculum foundations, curriculum change and innovation, curriculum research and inquiry, and other critiquing ways in which the field is understood. Behar's work comes closest for helping to establish recommended content for a curriculum text, since the domains she outlined were based on assessing the most influential texts in the field over a 20-year span.[62] Whatever other curriculum knowledge we can agree upon in the future as essential would facilitate theoretical and practical decisions in curriculum.

THEORY AND PRACTICE

A field of study basically involves theoretical and practical knowledge. By theory we mean the most advanced and valid knowledge available that can be generalized and applied to many situations. Theory often establishes the framework of the field and helps persons (researchers and practitioners) within the field analyze and synthesize data, organize concepts and principles, suggest new ideas and relations, and even speculate about the future. According to Beauchamp, theory may be defined as the knowledge and statements that "give functional meaning to a series of events [and] take the form of definitions, operational constructs, assumptions, postulates, hypotheses, generalizations, laws or theorems." In the case of curriculum theory, the subject matter involves "decisions about . . . the use of a curriculum, the development of curriculum, curriculum design and curriculum evaluation."[63] This definition suggests a scientific and technical approach that emphasizes the domain of knowledge that corresponds with curriculum development and also with most textbooks today.

Good theory in curriculum, or in education for that matter, describes and explains the various relationships that exist in the field. It also implies that there are elements of predictability, or that there are rigorous laws that yield high probability and control. Good theory should also prescribe actions to be taken; however, we do not always use theory productively in our practice or in education in general.

The more variable, complex, or unpredictable one views the teaching-learning process, the more one is compelled toward a belief that it is impossible to determine or agree upon generalizations or to obtain high predictability of outcomes. Curriculum, like other aspects of education, involves the use of judgments, hunches, and insights that are not always conducive to laws, principles, or even generalizations. A curriculum often does not emerge as a tightly regulated, predictable, or concise set of enterprises, or as a result of a single or theoretical mix of principles or processes; rather, it evolves as one act and one choice that lead to others, as interests emerge, and, finally, as educators reflect and quietly self-analyze their thinking.

Nonetheless, all curriculum texts should try to incorporate theory throughout the discussion to be systematic in their approach and to establish worthwhile practices. In fact, according to Taba, "any enterprise as complex as curriculum requires some kind of theoretical or conceptual framework of thinking to guide it."[64]

From Theory to Practice

The test of good theory is whether it can guide practice. In reverse, good practice is based on theory. By practice, we mean the procedures, methods, and skills that apply to the working world, where a person is on the job or actively involved in his or her profession. These procedures and methods are teachable and can be applied in different situations. When applied they should result in the practitioner being considered successful or effective.

Regardless of the theories discussed in any book, those who work with, shape, or formulate curriculum in one way or another have to deal with practice. Such people include administrators, supervisors, and teachers; curriculum developers and curriculum evaluators; textbook authors and test makers; and individuals assigned to curriculum committees, accrediting agencies, school boards, and local, regional, state, and federal edu-

cational agencies. The idea is to present theories that are workable for these practitioners, that make sense, and that can explain and be applied to the real world of classrooms and schools. See Curriculum Tips 1-3.

According to Elizabeth Vallance, "much ado [is] made about the split between theory and practice in the dialogues and concerns about professional curriculum workers." The crux of the matter is to provide "practical answers to very practical questions having to do with design, development, implementation, and evaluation of curricula." The distinctions between theory and practice are secondary to Vallance, because both aspects of curriculum focus on the "same curriculum problems."[65]

The problem is, however, that most curricularists, including those who write textbooks, have difficulty in fusing theory with practice. This is true even though many books in curriculum today emphasize "theory" and "practice"[66] or "principles" and "processes"[67] to reflect some form of theory and practice in their titles. Perhaps the reason curricularists have difficulty making the connection between theory and practice is that their methods of inquiry lend themselves more to theoretical discussions and less to practical matters. Also, good theory is recognized by professors of the field (and the research community in general) as a worthwhile endeavor; however, good practice is often misconstrued by theoreticians as a "cookbook" or as "do's and dont's" that are second rate or unimportant.

Decker Walker is more critical, noting the benefits of a theory in any field as being to provide a framework to conceptualize and clarify important problems and techniques. But "curriculum theories . . . that are correct and complete to serve as . . . a basis for practical decisions do not exist." Educators, including curricularists, tend to embrace "theory as an ideology," even though much of what they say is suspect and closes us to "other aspects of reality and other values."[68]

Most curriculum texts are more theoretical than practical, but so are education textbooks in general. Despite their claims, curricularists seem unable to make the leap from theory to practice, from the textbook and college course to the classroom and school (or other organizations). Good theory in curriculum (and in other fields of

---

===== *Curriculum Tips 1-3* =====

Translating Theory into Practice

Blending theory with practice is an old ideal. To make serious progress toward this goal in curriculum, we need to recognize certain basic steps.

1. *Read the literature.* Any attempt to relate theory and practice must be based on knowledge of the professional literature.
2. *Identify the major terms.* The need is for curriculum theorists and practitioners to identify and agree on the major constructs, concepts, and questions for discussion.
3. *Check the soundness of existing theories.* Existing theories need to be analyzed in terms of validity, evidence, accuracy, underlying assumptions, logic of argument, coherence, generalizability, values, and biases.
4. *Avoid fads.* New "fads" and "hot topics" must not be introduced to practitioners under the guise of a new theory or even as reform or innovation. When a new program or method is introduced into the professional literature, or at some professional conference, this is not the time to jump on the bandwagon, much less to call it "theory"; it is the time to pull back and wait for evaluations or complaints to surface.
5. *Align theory with practice.* Theory must be considered in context with the real world of classrooms and schools; it must be plausible, applicable, and realistic in terms of practice.
6. *Test theory.* If the theory is credible and makes common sense, then it must be empirically tested by trying it in practice and measuring the results It should be introduced first on a small scale, comparing experimental and control schools.
7. *Interpret theory.* The results must be tested and interpreted in terms of realistic conditions over realistic time periods. The theory must be evaluated in schools for a minimum of one year, and ideally over a three-year period to test for "fading out."
8. *Modify theory, reduce its complexity.* A theory is a generalizable construct supported by language or quantitative data. Nonetheless, theory must be modified from paper to practice, from the abstract to the concrete world, from complex concepts to lay terms. When we move theory to practice, we include many people (and resources) to make it work. Theory must fit with people (not mold people to theory) to move it from an idea to action.

---

education) often gets lost as practitioners (say, teachers) try to apply what they learned in college to the job setting in a search for practical solutions to common, everyday problems.

The problem of translating theory into practice is further aggravated by practitioners who feel that practical considerations are more worthwhile than theory; most teachers and principals view theory as unpractical and "how to do" approaches as helpful. In short, many theoreticians ignore the practitioners, and many practitioners ignore the theoreticians. Moreover, many theoretical discussions of curriculum are divorced from practical application in the classroom, and many practical

discussions of curriculum rarely consider theoretical relationships.[69]

Practice involves selecting strategies and rules that apply to various situations, like good theory, but all situations are not the same. This becomes especially evident when practitioners try to apply the theory they learn in their textbooks. Adopting the right method for the appropriate situation is not an easy task and involves a good deal of common sense and experience, which no one can learn from theoretical discussions. No matter how scientific we think our theories are, a certain amount of art is involved in the practice of curriculum—intuitive judgments and hunches that cannot be easily predicted or generalized from one situation to another, and this confounds theory.

Just what, then, does curriculum practice involve? The response is open to debate. But we might say that curriculum practice includes understanding the constraints and specifics operating within the school (or organization in which one is working) and comprehending the goals and priorities of the school and the needs of the students and staff. It also involves planning and working with procedures and processes that can be implemented in classrooms (or any formal group setting) and schools (or any formal organization). A successful practitioner in curriculum is capable of developing, implementing, and evaluating the curriculum; that is, he or she can select and organize (1) goals and objectives; (2) subject matter; (3) methods, materials, and media; (4) learning experiences and activities that are suitable for learners and then (5) assess these processes.

In the final analysis, it is up to the curriculum specialist to recognize that the theoretician and practitioner have different agendas and perceptions of what is important. The practitioner does not function as the mere user of the theoretician's or researcher's product, and the theoretician is often interested in knowledge that has little value to practitioners. One role for the curriculum specialist, what some educators call the "reflective practitioner," is to generate dialogue between the theoretician and practitioner and establish modes of collaboration that can benefit both groups.[70]

Curriculum Certification

The fact that curriculum lacks certification in most states (specified or professional requirements) adds to the problem of defining and conceptualizing the field and agreeing on curriculum courses at the college and university level. This lack of certification should be considered seriously, because we need competent people who can make wise curriculum decisions.

The closest thing to certification is an endorsement or license as a supervisor or principal. Curriculum making is a complicated procedure that cannot be left to just anyone or any group. We need people qualified to serve as generalists and specialists in curriculum, both as resource agents

and decision makers. And we need people who can maintain a curriculum balance in terms of goals, subject matter, and learning activities, given the numerous special-interest groups who wish to impose their brand of education on schools. Not only do minimum requirements for curriculum personnel vary among school systems within the same state, not to mention among states, but the programs in curriculum vary considerably among colleges and universities as well. Because there are no state or professional regulations, each school of education usually decides its own requirements and the courses it will use to meet these requirements. The result is a proliferation of elective courses in curriculum programs and a lack of specialized and general, agreed-upon courses. Even when curriculum course titles are similar, wide differences in content and level of instruction are common.

The irony is that there is great confusion about content and experiences in a field that should be very clear about its curriculum. Although there are many good curriculum programs at the university level, there is little guarantee that curricularists who graduate from a program know how to develop, implement, and evaluate a curriculum—or that they can translate theory into practice. Some curriculum students may not have taken courses in development, implementation, or evaluation (especially students in administration), whereas others may have taken several. And no test or screening device helps school systems or school board officials make choices about curriculum personnel and their expertise in curriculum. This also adds to the problem of defining who curriculum specialists or generalists are, and what their respective job titles, roles, and responsibilities, are. Is a supervisor a curriculum generalist or specialist? What about a principal who is supposed to be a curriculum and instructional leader? Is a resource teacher, consultant, or director a curriculum person? And what about the classroom teacher?

Professionals are certified in such other fields as teaching, counseling, school psychology, supervision, administration, and so on. Job descriptions and related course requirements are defined. Students can major in curriculum but they are at risk, because curriculum jobs are not well defined and there are few certification requirements or licenses that protect their jobs. Curriculum positions are definitely available in schools, universities, and local, regional, state, and federal education agencies, but without certification someone other than a curriculum person can obtain the same job.

The lack of certification weakens the role of curricularists in the schools and the influence of curricularists at the university level. It also encourages local and state policy makers and legislators to develop and design the school curriculum—to impose standards and approve programs in terms of goals, content, and subject matter. This is especially true in large states like California, Florida, Illinois, New York, and Texas, where standards and programs are often changed and influenced by pressure groups. Because the field lacks professional certification, the responsibilities of curriculum leaders are vague and diffuse, and a strong and organized constituency is lacking at the school and university levels.

THE ROLES OF THE CURRICULUM WORKER

Much has been written about the roles and responsibilities of the curriculum worker. Confusion exists for several reasons. First, the term is used interchangeably with curriculum supervisor, curriculum leader, curriculum coordinator, and curriculum specialist. A *curriculum worker* is a general term and includes various educators, from a teacher to a superintendent. Any person involved in some form of curriculum development, implementation, or evaluation is a curriculum worker. A *curriculum supervisor* is usually a chairperson, assistant principal, or principal; he or she usually works at the school level. A *curriculum leader* can be a supervisor or administrator—not only a chairperson or principal but also a director or associate superintendent of curriculum. A *curriculum coordinator* usually heads a program at the school district, regional, or state level; it may be a special government-funded program or a traditional subject area program involving math or English. A *curriculum specialist* is a technical consultant from the district level, regional or state department of education, or university. The person provides advice or in-service assistance, sometimes in the classroom but usually at meetings, conferences, or staff sessions. Most of the

terms, as well as the related responsibilities and functions of these people, depend on the philosophy and organization of the school district (or state education agency) and the personal preferences and views of the administration.

Another problem is the confusion on whether curriculum planning or development takes place at the local, state, or national level. In the past, emphasis on curriculum development was at the school or school district level; since the mid 1980s, the school reform movement has shifted some of the curriculum responsibilities to the state level, and there is serious talk of moving to the national level. (Bear in mind that most other nations have a national ministry of education with major curriculum responsibilities.)

Curriculum roles, in the past, have been defined at the local level, and decisions were made to develop curriculum leaders at the chair and principal's level. The majority of school districts depend on school people (teachers and supervisors) to develop curriculum and usually without pay, unless they meet in the summer; parents are also included in many curriculum committees at the school level. Staff limitations make unlikely the provision of curriculum specialists from the central office, and if such a person exists it is one person (possibly two) whose time is limited because of other responsibilities. Only large school districts can afford to have a curriculum department, with a full staff of specialists. In such school districts, most curriculum development takes place at the central level and teachers often complain that their professional input is minimal—relegated to implementing predetermined and prepackaged materials from the district office.

Responsibilities of the Curriculum Worker

What are the responsibilities of a curriculum worker? Assigned responsibilities within the school structure are important, but unclear, because different people (teachers, supervisors, principals, district personnel, and others) are usually expected to serve in the role of curriculum worker. Each position holder has different professional responsibilities, needs, and expectations. Adjustments must be made by each holder of a position. For example, teachers are usually expected among other things to provide instruction, but principals are expected to manage a school and provide assistance to teachers.

The curriculum worker has many different titles; nonetheless, the teacher is a member of the curriculum team and works with supervisors and administrators as part of the team. Early identification of teachers to serve in the capacity of a curriculum worker is essential for the growth of the teacher and vitality of the school (and school district). Where there is need or attention for clarifying the responsibilities of curriculum workers, consider the following:

1. Develop technical methods and tools to carry out curriculum planning in the school (or school district or state agency).
2. Blend theory building with practice; obtain curriculum knowledge and apply it in the real world of classrooms and schools.
3. Agree on what is involved in curriculum development and design, including the relationships that exist among the elements of curriculum.
4. Agree on the relationship between curriculum, instruction, and supervision, including the explicit language of each area and how each aids the work of the other.
5. Act as a change agent who considers schools in context with society; balance the demands and views of the local community with state and national goals and interests.
6. Create a mission or goal statement to provide direction and focused behavior within the organization.
7. Be open to new curriculum trends and thoughts; examine various proposals and suggest modifications, while not falling victim to fads and frills or to a particular pressure group.
8. Confer with various parental, community, and professional groups; have skills in human relations and in working with groups and individuals.
9. Encourage colleagues and other professionals to solve professional problems; innovate and become familiar with and use new programs and ideas.
10. Develop a program for continuous curriculum development, implementation, and evaluation.
11. Balance and integrate subject areas and grade levels into the total curriculum; pay close attention to scope and sequence by subject and grade level.
12. Understand current research in teaching and learning, as well as new programs that are relevant to target students for teaching and learning.

Other texts identify other responsibilities and duties of curriculum leaders. Table 1-2 shows the functions of curriculum leaders as purported by Doll in column 1 and Glatthorn in column 2. Those by Doll tend to be process oriented and diffuse; those by Glatthorn are task oriented and outcome based. Both lists are geared for the traditional curriculum leader, which excludes the teacher and emphasizes the school (school district) supervisor or administrator. Depending on one's philosophy and view of curriculum leadership, the reader may prefer one column over the other or borrow from both.

The authors' list of twelve responsibilities for the curriculum worker tends to be more theoretical and conceptual than the lists by Doll and Glatthorn, who tend to be more practical and action oriented. The authors' view implies curriculum workers, who may be teachers, supervisors, principals, and directors employed at the school, school district, or state level. Doll and Glatthorn examine the activities of curriculum leaders and connote a narrower view, which suggests a chair or principal operating at the school level. Finally, the authors' concept of the curriculum worker views the person in terms of broad responsibilities and the whole organization. Doll and Glatthorn zero in on explicit responsibilities or activities that are considered important for the curriculum leader—such as the school principal—and thus consider a limited part of the organization.

The Teacher and the Curriculum

Although Doll views the curriculum expert primarily as a chair or principal, he is concerned with the teacher's role in planning and implementing the curriculum at three levels: classroom, school, and district. In his opinion, the teacher should be involved "in every phase" of curriculum making, including the planning of "specific goals, . . . materials, content, and methods." Teachers should have a curriculum "coordinating body" to unify their work and develop "relationships

TABLE 1-2   Responsibilities and Activities of the Curriculum Leader

DOLL	GLATTHORN
1. Planning for improvement of the curriculum and of the curriculum development program	1. Determining the locus of planning decisions: differentiating between district and school planning responsibilities
2. Helping evaluate continuously both the appropriateness of the curriculum and the quality of the curriculum development program	2. Determining the organizational structures needed to facilitate planning and setting up those structures
3. Directing the formation of point of view, policies, and philosophy of education	3. Identifying leadership functions and allocating those functions properly
4. Directing the development of curriculum materials	4. Aligning the district's educational goals with appropriate curricular fields
5. Using ready-made research data and promoting local research	5. Developing a curriculum data base
6. Coordinating the activities of other special instructional personnel, supervisors or librarians, for example	6. Developing a planning calendar based on leader's assessments of organizational priorities
7. Working with guidance personnel to integrate curriculum and guidance functions	7. Conducting needs assessment in high-priority areas by using standardized tests, curriculum-referenced tests, and other measures and data sources; using assessment results to determine the need for curriculum development or improvement
8. Providing for lay participation in curriculum improvement	8. Organizing task forces to carry out development or improvement projects and monitoring their work
9. Arranging time, facilities, and materials for curriculum improvement	9. Evaluating development or improvement projects
10. Serving school personnel as technical consultant and advisor regarding curriculum problems	10. Making necessary organizational changes and provisions for effective implementation
11. Organizing and directing special in-service education projects	11. Securing resources needed for new or revised curricula
12. Interpreting the curriculum to the public and, in certain situations, to the board of education	12. Providing staff development needed for effective implementation
13. Encouraging articulation among levels of the school system	

Source: Adapted from Ronald C. Doll, *Curriculum Improvement: Decision Making and Process,* 8th ed. (Boston: Allyn and Bacon, 1992), pp. 494–496; Allan A. Glatthorn, *Curriculum Leadership* (Glenview, Ill.: Scott, Foresman, 1987), p. 144.

with supervisors [and] other teachers" involved in curriculum.[71]

Oliva adopts a broader view of the teacher's role. For him, teachers are seen as the "primary group in curriculum development." They constitute the "majority or the totality of the membership of curriculum committees and councils." Their role is to develop, implement, and evaluate curriculum. In his words, teachers work in committees and "initiate proposals, . . . review proposals, gather data, conduct research, make contact with parents and other lay people, write and create curriculum materials, . . . obtain feedback from learners, and evaluate programs."[72]

The views of Doll and Oliva suggest a *bottom-up* approach to curriculum, whereby the teacher has a major role to perform, a view popularized by Taba in her classic text on curriculum development,[73] but actually first introduced and elaborated by Harold Rugg, who argued that teachers needed to be released from all classroom duties "to prepare courses of study, and assemble materials, and develop outlines of the entire curriculum," and later by Caswell and Campbell, who envisioned teachers participating in curriculum committees at the school, district, and state levels during the summers and sometimes as a special assignment during the school year.[74]

Beane adopts a more moderate position for the teacher. Although teachers may emerge as curriculum leaders, the "major responsibility of administrative and supervisory personnel should be to provide leadership and assistance in curriculum development and implementation." Other aspects of curriculum work, such as "budget development, grant writing, and interaction with school boards," should be carried out by supervisors and administrators "in such a way as to facilitate curriculum planning." Nonetheless, the school district has the ultimate responsibility to employ support personnel who have skill in curriculum planning, and such personnel may include "teachers, school officials, and citizens."[75]

On the other side of the continuum, Glatthorn makes little provision for teacher input. He discusses the role of the "coordinators" at the district level and the principal, assistant principal, and chair at the school level. Only in elementary schools is he willing to recognize the role of a "teacher specialist" as a member of a subject or grade-level team and mainly confined to "reading and mathematics."[76]

Based on traditional theories of social organization and open systems and the latest we know about effective schools, our interpretation of the teachers' role in curriculum making is central. They are seen as part of a professional team, working with supervisors, administrators (and other colleagues) at all levels—at the school, district, and state level. In small and medium-sized school districts, teachers also work with parents where lay input is common in curriculum committees.

In our view, the teacher sees the curriculum as a whole and, at several points, serves as a resource and agent: developing it in committees, implementing it in classrooms, and evaluating it as part of a technical team. To guarantee continuity, integration, and unification of the curriculum, within and among subjects and grade levels, teachers must be actively involved in the curriculum. It is the experienced teacher who has a broad and deep understanding of teaching and learning, the needs and interests of students, and the content, methods, and materials that are realistic; therefore, it is the teacher (not the supervisor or administrator) who has the best chance of taking curriculum making out of the realm of theory or judgment and translating it into practice and utility. To be sure, the supervisor or administrator acts as a facilitator, lends support, coordinates, and communicates so that the mission can be achieved. But it is the teacher who should play a major role in planning, implementing, and evaluating the curriculum.

CONCLUSION

We have discussed curriculum in a variety of ways. We have tried to define it, to show the relationship between foundations and domains of curriculum, to illustrate how theory and practice interrelate with curriculum, and to describe the roles and responsibilities of the curriculum worker. In effect, we have told the reader that he or she can focus on approaches and definitions, foundations and domains, theory and practice, or curriculum and instruction. We feel that no one can fully integrate the entire field of curriculum. Eventually, each individual should choose an approach and definition, a school of philosophy and psychology, developmental and design models, theory and practice relationships, and curriculum responsibilities he or she wishes to promote. In this chapter, we outlined some options; we continue to do so in the remaining text.

ENDNOTES

1. Ivor F. Goodson, *Studying Curriculum* (New York: Teachers College Press, 1994).
2. Franklin Bobbitt, *The Curriculum* (Boston: Houghton Mifflin, 1918); W.W. Charters, *Curriculum Construction* (New York: Macmillan, 1923); Ralph W. Tyler, *Basic Principles of Curriculum and Instruction* (Chicago: University of Chicago Press, 1949); and Hilda Taba, *Curriculum Development: Theory and Practice* (New York: Harcourt Brace Jovanovich, 1962).
3. William Pinar, "Notes on the Curriculum Field," *Educational Researcher* (September 1978), pp. 5–12; William H. Schubert, *Curriculum Books: The First Eighty Years* (Lanham, Md.: University Press of America, 1980); and James T. Sears and J. Dan Marshall, eds., *Teaching and Thinking about Curriculum* (New York: Teachers College Press, Columbia University, 1990).
4. Raymond Callahan, *Education and the Cult of Efficiency* (Chicago: University of Chicago Press, 1962).
5. Bobbitt, *The Curriculum,* p. 283.
6. Franklin Bobbitt, *How to Make a Curriculum* (Boston: Houghton Mifflin, 1924), pp. 14, 28.
7. Tyler, *Basic Principles of Curriculum and Instruction,* p. 4.
8. Linda Darling-Hammond and Jon Snyder, "Curriculum Studies and the Traditions of Inquiry: The Scientific Tradition," in Philip W. Jackson, ed., *Handbook of Research on Curriculum* (New York: Macmillan Publishing Co., 1992), pp. 41–78.
9. Allan C. Ornstein, "The Field of Curriculum: What Approach?" *High School Journal* (April–May 1987), pp. 208–216.
10. See Matthew B. Miles and Karen Seashore Louis, "Mustering the Will and Skill for Change," *Educational Leadership* (May 1990), pp. 57–61; Allan C. Ornstein and Daniel U. Levine, "School Effectiveness and Reform: Guidelines for Action," *Clearing House* (November–December 1990), pp. 115–118.
11. Allan C. Ornstein, "Analyzing Curriculum," *NASSP Bulletin* (1993).
12. Leslee J. Bishop, *Staff Development and Instructional Improvement* (Boston: Allyn and Bacon, 1976); Gerald R. Firth and Richard Kimpston, *The Curriculum Continuum in Perspective* (Itasca, Ill.: Peacock, 1973); Robert S. Gilchrist, *Using Current Curriculum Developments* (Alexandria, Va.: Association for Supervision and Curriculum Development, 1963); Arthur J. Lewis and Alice Miel, *Supervision for Improved Instruction* (Belmont, Calif.: Wadsworth, 1972); John McNeil and William H. Lucio, *Supervision: A Synthesis of Thought and Action.* 2nd ed. (New York: McGraw-Hill, 1969); J. Lloyd Trump and Dorsey Baynham, *Focus on Change* (Chicago: Rand McNally. 1961); and Glenys G. Unruh and William A. Alexander, *Innovations in Secondary Education,* 2nd ed. (New York: Holt, Rinehart and Winston, 1971).
13. Walter Dick, "Instructional Design and the Curriculum Development Process," *Educational Leadership* (December–January 1987), pp. 54–56; Walter Dick and Robert A. Reiser, *Planning Effective Instruction* (Englewood Cliffs, N.J.: Prentice Hall, 1989); and Bruce Joyce, Marsha Weil, and Beverly Showers, *Models of Teaching,* 4th ed. (Boston: Allyn and Bacon, 1992).
14. Leo H. Bradley, *Total Quality Management for Schools* (Lancaster, Pa.: Technomic Publishing Co., 1993).
15. Ibid.
16. George A. Beauchamp, *Curriculum Theory,* 4th ed. (Itasca, Ill.: Peacock, 1981).
17. Allan C. Ornstein, "Curriculum, Instruction, and Supervision—Their Relationship and the Role of the Principal," *NASSP Bulletin* (April 1986), pp. 74–81.
18. John Dewey, *Democracy and Education* (New York: Macmillan, 1916); Henry C. Morrison, *The Practice of Teaching in the Secondary School* (Chicago: University of Chicago Press, 1926); and Boyd H. Bode, *Modern Educational Theories* (New York: Macmillan, 1927).
19. William F. Pinar, William M. Reynolds, Patrick Slattery, and Peter M. Taubman, *Understanding Curriculum* (New York: Peter Lang, 1995).
20. Ibid.
21. John Dewey, *The Child and the Curriculum* (Chicago: University of Chicago Press, 1902); Charles Judd, *The Evolution of a Democratic School System* (Boston: Houghton Mifflin, 1918); and Francis W. Parker, *Talks on Pedagogics* (New York: Kellogg, 1894).
22. Frederick G. Bosner, *The Elementary School Curriculum* (New York: Macmillan, 1920); Hollis L. Caswell, *Program Making in Small Elementary Schools* (Nashville, Tenn.: George Peabody College for Teachers, 1932); L. Thomas Hopkins and James E. Mendenhall, *Achievement at the Lincoln School* (New York: Teachers College Press, Columbia University, 1934); William H. Kilpatrick, *Foundations of Method* (New York: Macmillan, 1925); and Harold Rugg and Ann Shumaker, *The Child-centered School* (New York: World Books, 1928).
23. Allan C. Ornstein and Daniel U. Levine, "Urban School Effectiveness and Improvement," *Illinois School Research and Development* (Spring 1991), pp. 111–117; Ornstein and Levine, "School Effectiveness and Reform: Guidelines for Action."

24. Elliot W. Eisner, *Cognition and Curriculum Reconsidered* (New York: Teachers College Press, 1994).
25. Pinar et al., *Understanding Curriculum.*
26. William E. Doll, Jr., *A Post-Modern Perspective on Curriculum* (New York: Teachers College Press, 1993).
27. Yvonna S. Lincoln, "Curriculum Studies and the Traditions of Inquiry: The Humanistic Tradition," in Jackson, ed., *Handbook of Research on Curriculum,* pp. 79–97.
28. George S. Counts, *Dare the School Build a New Social Order?* (New York: John Day, 1932); Harold O. Rugg, ed., *Democracy and the Curriculum* (New York: Appleton-Century, 1939); Rugg et al., *American Life and the School Curriculum* (Boston: Ginn, 1936); and Harold Benjamin, *The Saber-tooth Curriculum* (New York: McGraw-Hill, 1939).
29. Saylor, Alexander, and Lewis, *Curriculum Planning for Better Teaching and Learning,* p. 10.
30. Pratt, *Curriculum: Design and Development,* p. 4.
31. Wiles and Bondi, *Curriculum Development: A Guide to Practice,* p. 131.
32. John Dewey, *Experience and Education* (New York: Macmillan, 1938); Caswell and Campbell, *Curriculum Development,* p. 69.
33. Shepherd and Ragan, *Modern Elementary Curriculum,* pp. 3–4.
34. Eisner, *The Educational Imagination,* p. 41.
35. Hass, *Curriculum Planning: A New Approach,* p. 54.
36. Doll, *Curriculum Improvement: Decision Making and Process*; Pajak, *The Central Office Supervisor and Curriculum and Instruction;* and Unruh and Unruh, *Curriculum Development: Problems, Process, and Progress.*
37. McNeil, *Curriculum: A Comprehensive Introduction;* Schubert, *Curriculum: Perspective, Paradigm, and Possibility;* and Tanner and Tanner, *Curriculum Development: Theory into Practice.*
38. Beauchamp, *Curriculum Theory,* 4th ed.
39. George J. Posner, *Analyzing the Curriculum* (New York: McGraw-Hill, 1992).
40. Doll, *Curriculum Improvement: Decision Making and Process,* p. 5.
41. Eisner, cited in Posner, *Analyzing the Curriculum.*
42. Beauchamp, *Curriculum Theory,* p. 81.
43. Harold Rugg, "Introduction," in G. M. Whipple, ed., *The Foundations of Curriculum Making,* Twenty-Sixth Yearbook of the National Society for the Study of Education, Part II (Bloomington, Ill.: Public School Publishing Co., 1930), p. 8.
44. Saylor, Alexander, and Lewis, *Curriculum Planning for Better Teaching and Learning;* Schubert, *Curriculum: Perspective, Paradigm, and Possibility;* and Tyler, *Basic Principles of Curriculum and Instruction,* Also see Charles P. McFadden, "Author-Publisher-Educator Relationships and Curriculum Reform," *Journal of Curriculum Studies* (January–February 1992), pp. 71–88.
45. Carmen L. Rosales-Dordelly and Edmund C. Short, *Curriculum Professors' Specialized Knowledge* (New York: Lanham, 1985), p. 23.
46. Oliva, *Developing the Curriculum,* p. 15.
47. Joseph J. Schwab, "The Practical: A Language of Curriculum," *School Review* (November 1969), p. 1.
48. Herbert Kliebard, "Curriculum Theory as Metaphor," *Theory into Practice* (Winter 1982), pp. 11–17; Kliebard, "Problems of Definition of Curriculum," *Journal of Curriculum and Supervision* (Fall 1989), pp. 1–5.
49. William M. Reynolds, "Comprehensiveness and Multidimensionality in Synoptic Curriculum Texts," *Journal of Curriculum and Supervision* (Winter 1990), pp. 189–193.
50. Beauchamp, *Curriculum Theory.*
51. Fenwick W. English, "Contemporary Curriculum Circumstances," in F. W. English, ed., *Fundamental Curriculum Decisions* (Alexandria, Va.: Association for Supervision and Curriculum Development, 1983), pp. 1–17.
52. Edmund C. Short, "Curriculum Decision Making in Teacher Education," *Journal of Teacher Education* (July–August 1987), pp. 2–12; Short, "Organizing What We Know about Curriculum," unpublished paper, 1984.
53. Linda Behar, "A Study of Domains and Subsystems in the Most Influential Textbooks in the Field of Curriculum 1970–1990," unpublished doctoral dissertation. Loyola University of Chicago, 1992.
54. Saylor et al., *Curriculum Planning for Better Teaching and Learning.*
55. Unruh and Unruh, *Curriculum Development: Problems, Processes, and Progress.*
56. Francis P. Hunkins, *Curriculum Development Program Improvement* (Columbus, Ohio: Merrill, 1980).
57. Patrick Slattery, *Curriculum Development in the Postmodern Era* (New York: Garland Publishing, Inc., 1995), p. 118.
58. Doll, *A Post-Modern Perspective on Curriculum.*
59. Ibid.
60. Ibid.
61. Rosales-Dordelly and Short, *Curriculum Professors' Specialized Knowledge,* p. 22.
62. Behar, "A Study of Domains and Subsystems in the Most Influential Textbooks in the Field of Curriculum 1970–1990."
63. Beauchamp, *Curriculum Theory,* p. 58.
64. Taba, *Curriculum Development: Theory and Practice,* p. 413.
65. Elizabeth Vallance, "Curriculum as a Field of Practice," in English, ed., *Fundamental Curriculum Decisions,* p. 155.

66. Miller and Seller, *Curriculum: Perspectives and Practice*; Tanner and Tanner, *Curriculum Development: Theory into Practice,* and Wiles and Bondi, *Curriculum Development: A Guide to Practice.*

67. Doll, *Curriculum Improvement: Decision Making and Process*; Unruh and Unruh, *Curriculum Development: Problems, Processes, and Progress.*

68. Walker, *Fundamentals of Curriculum,* p. 200.

69. Allan C. Ornstein and Francis P. Hunkins, "Theorizing about Curriculum Theory," *High School Journal* (December–January 1989), pp. 77–82.

70. Karen F. Osterman, "Reflective Practice: A New Agenda for Education," *Education and Urban Society* (February 1990), pp. 133–154; Donald A. Schon, *Educating the Reflective Practitioner* (San Francisco: Jossey-Bass, 1987); and Schon, "Critiques, Commentaries, Illustrations," *Journal of Curriculum and Supervision* (Fall 1989), pp. 6–9.

71. Doll, *Curriculum Improvement: Decision Making and Process,* p. 334.

72. Oliva, *Developing the Curriculum,* p. 120.

73. Taba, *Curriculum Development: Theory and Practice.*

74. Caswell and Campbell, *Curriculum Development*; Harold Rugg, "The Foundations of Curriculum Making," in G. Whipple, ed., *The Foundations of Curriculum Making,* Twenty-sixth Yearbook of the National Society for the Study of Education, Part II (Bloomington, Ill.: Public School Publishers, 1930), pp. 439–440.

75. Beane, Toepfer, and Alessi, *Curriculum Planning and Development,* pp. 355, 358.

76. Glatthorn, *Curriculum Leadership,* pp. 148–149.

2

PHILOSOPHICAL FOUNDATIONS OF CURRICULUM

Focusing Questions

1. How does philosophy influence curriculum workers?
2. In what way is philosophy the main curriculum source? Or only one of many curriculum sources?
3. What are the differences (in terms of knowledge and values) between idealism, realism, pragmatism, and existentialism?
4. What are the differences (in terms of content and methods) between perennialism, essentialism, progressivism, and reconstructionism?
5. Can schools promote the ideas of equality and excellence at the same time? Why? Why not?
6. In what ways are reconstructionists both realistic and idealistic? Mainstream and radical?
7. Which philosophical orientation is likely to have the major influence on the curriculum field in the future? Why do you think this to be so?
8. Which philosophical orientation appears the most critical of mainstream education?

Philosophy is central to curriculum because the philosophy advocated or reflected by a particular school and its officials influences the goals or aims and content, as well as the organization, of its curriculum. Usually, schools reflect several philosophies, which adds to the dynamics of the curriculum within the school. Studying philosophy not only allows us to better understand schools and their curricula, but also to deal with our own personal systems of perceptions, beliefs, and values—the way we perceive the world around us and how we define what is important to us. It helps us to understand who we are, why we are, and, to some extent, where we are going.

Philosophy deals with the larger aspects of life, the problems and prospects of living, and the way we organize our thoughts and facts. It is an effort to see life and its problems in full perspective. It requires looking beyond the immediate to causes and relationships and to future developments. It involves questioning one's own point of view as well as the views of others; it involves searching for defined and defensible values, clarifying one's beliefs and attitudes, and formulating a framework for making decisions and acting on these decisions.

Philosophical issues have always impacted and still do on schools and society. Contemporary society and the schools in it are changing fundamentally and rapidly, much more so than in the past. The special urgency that dictates continuous appraisal and reappraisal calls for a philosophy of

31

education. As William Van Til puts it, "Our source of direction is found in our guiding philosophy. . . . Without philosophy, [we make] mindless vaults into the saddle like Stephen Leacock's character who 'flung himself from the room, flung himself upon his horse, and rode madly off in all directions.' "[1] In short, our philosophy of education influences, and to a large extent determines, our educational decisions, choices, and alternatives.

PHILOSOPHY AND CURRICULUM

Philosophy provides educators, especially curriculum workers, with a framework or frameworks for organizing schools and classrooms. It helps them answer what schools are for, what subjects are of value, how students learn, and what methods and materials to use. It provides them with a framework for broad issues and tasks, such as determining the goals of education, the content and its organization, the process of teaching and learning, and in general what experiences and activities they wish to stress in schools and classrooms. It also provides them with a basis for dealing with precise tasks and for making such decisions as what textbooks to use, how to use them, what cognitive and noncognitive activities to utilize and how to utilize them, what homework to assign and how much of it, how to test students and how to use the test results, and what courses or subject matter to emphasize.

The importance of philosophy in determining curriculum decisions is expressed well by L. Thomas Hopkins:

> Philosophy has entered into every important decision that has ever been made about curriculum and teaching in the past and will continue to be the basis of every important decision in the future.
>
> When a state office of education suggests a pupil-teacher time schedule, this is based upon philosophy, either hidden or consciously formulated. When a course of study is prepared in advance in a school system by a selected group of teachers, this represents philosophy because a course of action was selected from many choices involving different values. When high school teachers assign to pupils more homework for an evening than any one of them could possibly do satisfactorily in six hours, they are acting on philosophy although they are certainly not aware of its effects. When a teacher in an elementary school tells a child to put away his geography and study his arithmetic she is acting on philosophy for she has made a choice of values . . . When teachers shift subject matter from one grade to another, they act on philosophy. When measurement experts interpret their test results to a group of teachers, they act upon philosophy, for the facts have meaning only within some basic assumptions. There is rarely a moment in a school day when a teacher is not confronted with occasions where philosophy is a vital part of action. An inventory of situations where philosophy was not used in curriculum and teaching would lead to a pile of chaff thrown out of educative experiences.[2]

Hopkins's statement reminds us how important philosophy is to all aspects of curriculum decisions, whether it operates overtly or covertly, whether we know that it is operating or not. Indeed, almost all elements of curriculum are based on philosophy. As John Goodlad points out, philosophy is the beginning point in curriculum decision making and is the basis for all subsequent decisions regarding curriculum.[3] Philosophy becomes the criterion for determining the aims, means, and ends of curriculum. The aims are statements of value, based on philosophical beliefs; the means represent processes and methods, which reflect philosophical choices; and the ends connote the facts, concepts, and principles of the knowledge or behavior learned, or what we feel is important to learning, which is also philosophical in nature.

Philosophy and the Curriculum Worker

The philosophy of the curriculum worker reflects his or her life experiences, common sense, social and economic background, education, and general beliefs about himself or herself and people. An individual's philosophy evolves and continues to evolve as long as he or she continues to grow and develop, and as long as he or she learns from experience. One's philosophy is a description, explanation, and evaluation of the world as seen from one's own perspective, or through what some social scientists call "social lenses."

Curriculum workers can turn to many sources, but no matter how many sources they may draw upon or how many authorities they may read or listen to, the decision is theirs to accept or reject the explanations and truths presented. Their decision is shaped by past and contemporary events and experiences that have affected them and the social groups with which they identify; it is based on values (attitudes and beliefs) that they have developed, and their knowledge and interpretation of causes, events, and their consequences. Philosophy becomes principles for guiding action.

No one can be totally objective in a cultural or social setting, but curriculum workers can broaden their base of knowledge and experiences, try to understand other people's sense of values, and analyze problems from various perspectives. They can also try to modify their own critical analyses and points of view by learning from their experiences and others. Curriculum workers who are unwilling to modify their points of view or compromise philosophical positions, when school officials or the majority of their colleagues lean toward another philosophy, are at risk of causing conflict and disrupting the school. Ronald Doll puts it this way: "Conflict among curriculum planners occurs when persons . . . hold positions along a continuum of [different] beliefs and . . . persuasions." The conflict may become so intense that "curriculum study grinds to a halt." Most of the time, the differences can be reconciled "temporarily in deference to the demands of a temporary, immediate task. However, teachers and administrators who are clearly divided in philosophy can seldom work together in close proximity for long periods of time."[4]

The more mature and understanding one is, and the less personally threatened and ego-involved one is, the more capable one is of reexamining or modifying his or her philosophy, or at least of being willing to appreciate other points of view. It is important for curriculum workers to consider their attitudes and beliefs as tentative— as subject to reexamination whenever facts or trends challenge them.

Equally dangerous for curriculum workers is the opposite: indecision or lack of any philosophy, which can be reflected in attempts to avoid commitment to sets of values. A measure of positive conviction is essential to prudent action, even though total objectivity is not humanly possible. Having a personal philosophy that is tentative or subject to modification does not lead to lack of

conviction or disorganized behavior. Curriculum workers can arrive at their conclusions on the best evidence available, and they can change when better evidence surfaces.

Philosophy as a Curriculum Source

The function of philosophy can be conceived as either (1) the base or starting point in curriculum development or (2) an interdependent function with other functions in curriculum development. John Dewey represents the first school of thought. He contended that "philosophy may . . . be defined as the general theory of education," and that "the business of philosophy is to provide" the framework for the "aims and methods" of schools. For Dewey, philosophy provides a generalized meaning to our lives and a way of thinking; it is "an explicit formulation of the . . . mental and moral habitudes in respect to the difficulties of contemporary social life."[5] Philosophy is not only a starting point for schools, it is also crucial for all curriculum activities. For Dewey, "education is the laboratory in which philosophic distinctions become concrete and are tested."[6]

In Ralph Tyler's framework of curriculum, philosophy is commonly one of five criteria for selecting educational purposes. The relationships between philosophy and the other criteria— studies of learners, studies of contemporary life, suggestions from subject specialists, and the psychology of learning—are shown in Figure 2-1. Although philosophy is not the starting point in Tyler's curriculum, but rather interacts on an equal basis with the other criteria, Tyler, highly influenced by Dewey, seems to place more importance on philosophy than other criteria for developing educational purposes. He writes, "The educational and social philosophy to which the school is committed can serve as the first screen for developing the social program." He concludes that "philosophy attempts to define the nature of the good life and a good society," and that the educational philosophies in a democratic society are likely "to emphasize strongly democratic values in schools."[7]

For John Goodlad, there can be no serious discussion about philosophy until we embrace the question of what education is. When we agree on what education is, we can ask what schools are

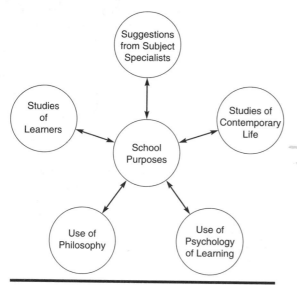

FIGURE 2-1   Tyler's View of Philosophy in Relationship to School Purposes

for. Then we can pursue the philosophy, aims, and goals of curriculum. According to Goodlad, the school's first responsibility is to the social order, what he calls the "nation-state," but in our society the sense of individual growth and potential is paramount, too.[8] This duality—society versus the individual—has been a major philosophical issue in western society for centuries, and was very important in Dewey's works. As the latter claimed, we not only wish "to make [good] citizens and workers," but also we ultimately want "to make human beings who will live life to the fullest."

This duality—allegiance to the nation and fulfillment of the individual—is a noble aim that should guide all curriculum specialists—from the means to the ends. When many individuals grow and prosper, then that society flourishes since it is comprised of many individuals. The original question set forth by Goodlad can be answered now. Education is growth and the meaning that the growth has for the individual and society; it is a never ending process (so long as life exists), and the richer the meaning the better the quality of the educational process.

MAJOR PHILOSOPHIES

In any consideration of the influence of philosophical thought on curriculum, several classification schemes are possible; no superiority is thus claimed for the categories used in the following discussion. The ideas as organized here are those that often evolve during curriculum development.

Four major philosophies have influenced education in the United States: idealism, realism, pragmatism, and existentialism. Here, we present short overviews to define and identify each philosophy. The first two philosophies are traditional, and the latter two are contemporary.

Idealism

Plato is often identified as giving classic formulation to idealist philosophy, one of the oldest that exists. The German philosopher Hegel created a comprehensive view of the historical world based on idealism. In the United States, transcendentalist philosophers Ralph Waldo Emerson and Henry Thoreau outlined an idealist conception of reality. In education, Fredrich Froebel, the founder of kindergarten, was a proponent of idealist pedagogy. William Harris, who popularized the kindergarten movement when he was superintendent of schools in St. Louis, Missouri, and who became U.S. Commissioner of Education at the turn of the twentieth century, used idealism as a source for this administrative philosophy. The leading contemporary proponent of idealism is J. Donald Butler.[9]

Idealism emphasizes moral and spiritual reality as the chief explanation of the world. Truth and values are seen as absolute, timeless, and universal. The world of mind and ideas is permanent, regular, and orderly; it represents a perfect order. Eternal ideas are unalterable and timeless. To know is to rethink the latent ideas that are already present in the mind. The teacher's task is to bring this latent knowledge to consciousness. As a primarily intellectual process, learning involves recalling and working with ideas; education is properly concerned with conceptual matters.[10]

The idealist educator prefers the order and pattern of a subject matter curriculum that relates ideas and concepts to each other. The most important subjects and highest form of knowledge recognize relationships and integrate concepts to each other. In this vein, the curriculum is hierarchical, and it constitutes the cultural heritage of humankind; it is based on learned disciplines, illustrated by the liberal arts curriculum.

At the top of this hierarchy are the most general or abstract subjects: philosophy and theology; they cut across time, place, and circumstances, and they apply to a wide range of situations and experiences. Mathematics is important because it cultivates the power to deal with abstract thinking. History and literature also rank high because they are sources of moral and cultural models. Lower in the curricular ladder are the natural and physical sciences, which deal with particular cause and effect relationships. Language is also an important subject, because it is necessary for communication and facilitates conception of thought.

Realism

Aristotle is often linked to the development of realism, another traditional school of thought. Thomas Aquinas's philosophy, which combined realism with Christian doctrine, developed an offshoot of realism, called Thomism, on which much of Catholic education and religious studies today are rooted. Pestalozzian instructional principles, which began with concrete objects and ended with abstract concepts, were based on realism. Such modern educators as Harry Broudy and John Wild are leading realists.[11]

The realist views the world in terms of objects and matter. People can come to know the world through their senses and their reason. Everything is derived from nature and is subject to its laws. Human behavior is rational when it conforms to the laws of nature and when it is governed by physical and social laws.

Like the idealist, the realist stresses a curriculum consisting of organized, separate subject matter, content, and knowledge that classifies objects. For example, the experiences of humankind comprise history. Animals can be studied as zoology. Like the idealist, the realist locates the most general and abstract subjects at the top of the curricular hierarchy and gives particular and transitory subjects a lower order of priority. Logic and lessons that exercise the mind and that cultivate rational thought are stressed. Concepts and systems that can be organized into subjects—such as

ethical, political, and economic thought—are also included in the curriculum. The three R's (reading, writing, and arithmetic) are also necessary in a person's basic education.[12]

Whereas the idealist considers the classics to be the ideal subject matter, because the curriculum can be fixed and will not vary with time, the realist views subject matter experts as the source of authority. For the idealist, knowledge comes from studying the external ideas and universal truths found in the arts, but for the realist reality and truth emanate from both science and art.

Pragmatism

In contrast to the traditional philosophies, pragmatism, also referred to as experimentalism, is based on change, process, and relativity. Whereas idealism and realism emphasize subject matter, disciplines, and content or ideas, pragmatism construes knowledge as a process in which reality is constantly changing. Learning occurs as the person engages in problem solving; problem solving is, moreover, transferable to a wide variety of subjects and situations. Knowing is considered a transaction between learner and environment. Basic to this interaction is the notion of change. Both the learner and environment are constantly changing, as are the transactions or experiences. To disregard social change and to consider only what is changeless, as the idealists do, or only our heritage, as the realists do, is unrealistic and unwise. Concepts of unchanging or universal truths, such as the traditional philosophies advocate, are based on faith. The only guides that people have in their interaction with the social world or environment are established generalizations or tentative assertions that are subject to further research and verification.

To a pragmatist, nothing can be viewed intelligently except in relation to a pattern. The whole affects the parts, and the parts and the whole are all relative. The ideal teaching method is concerned not so much with teaching the learner what to think as with teaching him or her to critically think. Teaching is more exploratory than explanatory. The method is more important than the subject matter. What is needed is a method for dealing with change and scientific investigation in an intelligent manner.

Scientific developments at the turn of the twentieth century accelerated the pragmatic philosophy. Society's accepting scientific explanations for phenomena and its recognizing the forces of change challenged the long-standing traditional views of idealism and realism. In 1859, Charles Darwin's *Origin of the Species* shook the foundations of the classic view of humans' notion of the universe. Charles Peirce, a mathematician, and William James, a psychologist, developed the principles of pragmatism, which (1) rejected the dogmas of preconceived truths and eternal values, and (2) promoted the method of testing and verifying ideas. The truth was no longer absolute or universal, but rather it had to be proven in relation to facts, experience, and/or behaviors.[13]

The great educational pragmatist was John Dewey, who viewed education as a process for improving (not accepting) the human condition. The school was seen as a specialized environment that coincided with the social environment. No demarcation exists between school and society. The curriculum, ideally, is based on the child's experiences and interests, and prepares him or her for life's affairs and for the future.[14] The subject matter is interdisciplinary, rather than located within a single or group of disciplines. The stress is on problem solving, not mastering organized subject matter, and using the scientific method, not a bunch of facts or a point of view.

The pragmatists consider teaching and learning to be a process of reconstructing experience according to the scientific method. Learning takes place in an active way as learners, either individually or in groups, solve problems. These problems, as well as the subject matter, will vary in response to the changing world. For the learner, it is most important to acquire the method or process of solving problems in an intelligent manner.

Existentialism

Whereas pragmatism is mainly an American philosophy that evolved just prior to the turn of the twentieth century, existentialism is mainly a European philosophy that originated years before the turn of the century but became popular after World War II. In American education, such people as Maxine Greene, George Kneller, and Van Cleve Morris are well-known existentialists who stress individualism and personal self-fulfillment.[15]

According to existentialist philosophy, people are thrust into a number of choice-making situations. Some choices are minor and others are significant, but the choice is the individual's, and the decisions lead to personal self-definition. A person creates his or her own definition and in doing so makes his or her own essence. We are what we choose to be. The essence we create is a product of our choices; this varies, of course, among individuals.

Existentialists prefer to free learners to choose what to study and also to determine what is true and by what criteria to determine these truths. The curriculum would avoid systematic knowledge or structured disciplines, and the students would be free to select from many available learning situations. The learners would choose the knowledge they wish to possess. On both of these curricular points, some educators would criticize the philosophy as too unsystematic or laissez-faire to be included at the elementary school level.

Existentialists believe that the most important kind of knowledge is about the human condition and the choices that each person has to make, and that education is a process of developing consciousness about the freedom to choose and the meaning of and responsibility for one's choices.[16] Hence, the notion of group norms, authority, and established order—social, political, philosophical, religious, and so on—is rejected. The existentialists recognize few standards, customs or traditions, or eternal truths; in this respect, existentialism is at odds with the ideas of idealism and realism.

Some critics (mainly traditionalists or conservatives) claim that existentialism as a philosophy for the schools has limited application because education in our society, and in most other modern societies, involves institutionalized learning and socialization, which require group instruction, restrictions on individuals' behavior, and bureaucratic organization. Schooling is a process that limits students' freedom and that is based on adult authority and on the norms and beliefs of the mass or common culture. The individual existentialist, exerting his or her will and choice, will encounter difficulty in school—and in other large, formal organizations.

An existentialist curriculum would consist of experiences and subjects that lend themselves to philosophical dialogue and acts of choice making. Because the choice is personal and subjective, subjects that are emotional, aesthetic, and philosophical are appropriate. Literature, drama, film making, art, and so on, are important, because they portray the human condition and choice-making conditions. The curriculum would stress self-expressive activities, experimentation, and methods and media that illustrate emotions, feelings, and insights. The classroom would be rich in materials that lend themselves to self-expression, and the school would be a place in which the teacher and students could pursue dialogue and discussion about their lives and choices.[17] See Table 2-1.

TABLE 2-1   Overview of Major Philosophies

PHILOSOPHY	REALITY	KNOWLEDGE	VALUES	TEACHER'S ROLE	EMPHASIS ON LEARNING	EMPHASIS ON CURRICULUM
Idealism	Spiritual, moral, or mental; unchanging	Rethinking latent ideas	Absolute and eternal	To bring latent knowledge and ideas to consciousness; to be a moral and spiritual leader	Recalling knowledge and ideas; abstract thinking as the highest form	Knowledge based; subject based; classics or liberal arts; hierarchy of subjects: philosophy, theology, and mathematics are most important
Realism	Based on natural laws; objective and composed of matter	Consisting of sensation and abstraction	Absolute and eternal; based on nature's laws	To cultivate rational thought; to be a moral and spiritual leader; to be a source of authority	Exercising the mind; logical and abstract thinking are highest form	Knowledge based; subject based; arts and sciences; hierarchy of subjects: humanistic and scientific subjects
Pragmatism	Interaction of individual with environment; always changing	Based on experience; use of scientific method	Situational and relative; subject to change and verification	To cultivate critical thinking and scientific processes	Methods for dealing with changing environment and scientific explanations	No permanent knowledge or subjects; appropriate experiences that transmit culture and prepare individual for change; problem-solving topics
Existentialism	Subjective	Knowledge for personal choice	Freely chosen; based on individuals' perception	To cultivate personal choice and individual self-definition	Knowledge and principles of the human condition; acts of choice making	Choices in subject matter, electives; emotional, aesthetic, and philosophical subjects

EDUCATIONAL PHILOSOPHIES

Although aspects of educational philosophy can be derived from the roots of idealism, realism, pragmatism, and existentialism, a common approach is to provide a pattern of educational philosophies. Four agreed-upon philosophies of education have emerged: perennialism, essentialism, progressivism, and reconstructionism. Each of these four philosophies of education has roots in one or more of the four major philosophical traditions. For example, perennialism draws heavily on the principles of realism, essentialism is rooted in idealism and realism, and progressivism and reconstructionism stem from pragmatism. Some reconstructionism has linkages to existentialist knowing and teaching. See Curriculum Tips 2-1.

Perennialism

Perennialism, the oldest and most conservative educational philosophy, is rooted in realism. Much of colonial and postcolonial American education, up to the late nineteenth century, was dominated by perennialist thinking. At the elementary school level, the curriculum stressed the three Rs, as well as moral and religious training; at the secondary level, it emphasized such subjects as Latin, Greek, grammar, rhetoric, logic, and geometry.

As a philosophy of education, perennialism relies on the past, especially the past asserted by agreed-upon, universal knowledge and cherished values of society. It is a plea for the permanency of knowledge that has stood the test of time and for values that have moral, spiritual, and/or physical constancies of existence. It is a view of the unchanging nature of the universe, human nature, truth, knowledge, virtue, beauty, and so on. As Robert Hutchins, a long-time advocate of perennialism, noted: "The function of man as man is the same in every society.... The aim of the educational system is the same in every age and in every society where such a system can exist; it is to improve a man as man."[18] With this interpretation, education becomes constant, absolute, and universal.

For perennialists, the answers to all educational questions derive from the answer to one question: What is human nature? The perennialists contend that human nature is constant. Humans have the ability to reason and to understand the universal truths of nature. The goal of education is to develop the rational person and to uncover universal truths by carefully training the intellect. Character training is also important as a means of developing one's moral and spiritual being.

The curriculum of the perennialist is subject centered; it draws heavily on defined disciplines or logically organized bodies of content—what proponents call "liberal" education—with emphasis on language, literature, and mathematics, on the arts and sciences. The teacher is viewed as an authority in the field whose knowledge and expertise are unquestionable. The teacher, accordingly, must be a master of the subject or discipline and must be able to guide discussion. Teaching is, in fact, the art of stimulating discussion and the inherent rational powers of the students. Teaching is primarily based on the Socratic method: oral exposition, lecture, and explication.

Students' interests are irrelevant for curriculum development because students are immature and lack the judgment to determine what are the best knowledge and values to learn. Whether the students dislike the subject matter is secondary.[19] There is only one common curriculum for all students, with little room for elective subjects, vocational, or technical subject matter.

Permanent Studies. The notion of permanent or essential studies addresses knowledge and truths today. According to perennialists, it is permanent studies that comprise our intellectual heritage. This content is based on what is commonly called the liberal arts, or, according to Robert Hutchins the "Great Books" of the Western world that cover the foundations of Western thought and its scientific and cultural knowledge. The approach is to read and discuss the great works of great thinkers, which, in turn, should discipline the mind and cultivate the intellect. Among the great books are the works of Plato, Aristotle, St. Augustine, St. Thomas Aquinas, Erasmus, and Shakespeare.

The idea is to read these writers in their original language, which is why students must learn Latin and Greek. In addition to the classics, and the study of language, Hutchins urges the study of the three Rs, as well as grammar, rhetoric, logic, advanced mathematics, and philosophy.[20] This is basically the curriculum of the past; it treats

---

Curriculum Tips 2-1

Testing Philosophy

Since philosophy reflects values and beliefs, some people might argue there is no right or wrong philosophy. Values and beliefs are not amenable as correct or incorrect answers to math problems. Philosophies can be judged by the actions to which they lead and/or by standards which suggest the quality of thinking. It is this second method that was outlined by L. Thomas Hopkins in his classic curriculum text more than 50 years ago. (To be sure, his criterion for a philosophy is tied to beliefs based on what is "good.")

1. *Clarity.* A good belief is unambiguous. The meaning of it is clear. Those who use it can agree upon some acceptable working interpretation.
2. *Consistency with the facts.* A good belief is founded on extensive and accurate search for the facts. It is not founded on snap judgments, suppressed information, and deliberate or unrecognized propaganda.
3. *Consistency with experience.* A good belief must square with experience. It must seem reasonable by working out satisfactorily in the life of the individual. It must be tested by the consequences in improving experience.
4. *Consistency with other beliefs.* A good belief must be consistent with other beliefs and *well verified by experience.* It should be inconsistent with accepted beliefs *not verified by experience.* Unverified beliefs need the revision that new beliefs furnish.
5. *Utility.* A good belief is distinguished by its usefulness in suggesting other good beliefs. It must be fruitful. It must lead to new suggestions, new hypotheses, more accurate observations, better discrimination between facts and propaganda, more reliable forecasts of probabilities for the future.
6. *Simplicity.* Other things being equal, that belief is best which makes the fewest assumptions and which is based on the most obvious hypotheses.

Source: L. Thomas Hopkins, *Interaction: The Democratic Process* (Boston: D.C. Heath, 1941), p. 191.

---

human nature as rational and knowledge as absolute and unchanging. For Hutchins, this type of education "develops intellectual power . . . it is not a specialized education or a pre-professional education; it is not a utilitarian education. It is an education calculated to develop the mind."[21] It is a universal, broad education that prepares the individual to think, to prepare for many possible jobs, and to deal with life and the real world. By studying the great ideas of the past, one can better cope with the future.

Paideia Proposal. A somewhat recent revival of perennialism appeared with the publication *Paideia Proposal* by Mortimer Adler. Adler de-

veloped three types of curriculum and instruction to improve the intellect: acquisition of *organized knowledge* to be taught by didactic instruction, development of *basic learning skills* by coaching and understanding of *ideas,* and *values* to be taught by the Socratic method.[22] Further outlined in Table 2-2, the three areas of concentration are the same as outlined by John Dewey in *Democracy and Education* and later by Ralph Tyler in *Basic Principles of Curriculum and Instruction.*

A broad liberal education is considered the best and only type of education for *all* students; in short, the same curriculum and quality of teaching and learning should be provided to all students. An academic or broad curriculum is considered to

TABLE 2-2 The Paideia Course of Study

CURRICULUM/INSTRUCTIONAL CONCENTRATION	METHOD	CONTENT
Acquisition of knowledge	Didactic instruction, teaching by telling Lectures, explanations Standard questions Laboratory demonstrations Use of textbooks	Language[a] Literature Math Science History, geography Fine arts
Learning (intellectual) skills	Coaching Exercises, problems Supervised practice Use of computers and other instructional tools	Reading, writing[b], speaking, listening Observing, measuring, estimating Critical judgment
Ideas and values	Socratic questioning Active participation Philosophical essays and debates Creative products[c]	Discussion of major books, not texts Interdisciplinary subject matter (literature, history, science, philosophy, etc.) Involvement in linguistic and artistic activities

Source: Adapted from Mortimer J. Adler, *The Paideia Proposal: An Educational Manifesto* (New York: Macmillan, 1982), pp. 23–32.
[a]Traditional academic subject matter.
[b]Linguistic, math, and science skills.
[c]Highly creative and individualized projects.

have the most practical value, as compared to vocational or specialized training for future employment. Anyone trained for a particular job will have to be retrained when he or she starts the job. Among the subjects identified as indispensable for all students are language, literature, fine arts, mathematics, natural sciences, history, and geography. Although it emphasized fundamental subjects, the Paideia group did not consider subject matter as an end in itself but rather as the context for developing intellectual skills. Among the sought-after intellectual skills were the three Rs, speaking, listening, observing, measuring, estimating, and problem solving. Together, the fundamental subjects and intellectual skills lead to a still higher level of learning, reflection, and awareness. For Adler, like Hutchins, the purpose of education is to cultivate significant knowledge

and thinking skills; the "best books"—great books, as they were called by Hutchins—are recommended by the Paideia program.

The education advocated by perennialists appeals to a small group of educators who tend to stress intellectual meritocracy. Such educators emphasize testing students, enforcing tougher academic standards and programs, and identifying gifted and talented students. Their education fosters a common curriculum, usually liberal arts, and offers little or no opportunity for students to choose electives related to their interests or goals. For the perennialists, genuine equality of education is maintained by providing quality of education for all—of high intellectual fiber. To track some students into a vocational curriculum is to deny the latter genuine equality of educational opportunity. True equity can be satisfied only by access to quality education: a *common, perennial* curriculum.

Returning to the Liberal Arts.   A few years ago, Allan Bloom, in *The Closing of the American Mind,* voiced concern about education being relative to particular times and places, instead of being consistent with universal standards and subjects.[23] Like other perennialists, Bloom asserts that cultural relativism—with its emphasis on trivial pursuits, quick fixes, relevancy and self-esteem—has eroded the quality of American education. Our media and educational institutions are marked by an easy-going, flippant, indifference to critical thought. Deprived of a serious liberal arts and science education, avoiding an engagement with the great works and great ideas of the past, our youth lack educational depth.

On a national level, Bloom contends we are heading for educational nihilism—a disrespect for tough academics and critical thought. Our schools, and especially universities, are not places where serious thought occurs. Our educational institutions fail in their fundamental task of educating people and providing a place for serious learning and scholarship. We have welcomed the false doctrine of equality and have rejected universal standards of excellence. We refuse to take a position on what is right and wrong, based on standards of truth (of course, we can argue whose truth); rather, we welcome no-fault choices.

Indeed, if we want to ask ourselves how and where we went wrong, why we are in social and economic decline, Bloom offers a conservative analysis and sense of fundamental reform. To remedy American education and to neutralize the problems caused by cultural relativism, Bloom, as did Hutchins over 25 years ago, seeks to reestablish the idea of an educated person along the great books and great thinkers line and to reestablish the virtues of a liberal education.

Bloom, in a more recent book,[24] essentially reiterates his call for an education that is more challenging and prizes that which is crucial to the well-being of the national culture.

Essentialism

Another traditional and conservative philosophy is essentialism. This philosophy is rooted in both idealism and realism and surfaced in the 1930s as a reaction to progressivism and developed into a major position during the Cold War and the Sputnik era of the 1950s and early 1960s. The ideas of essentialism were formulated by William Bagley of Teachers College, Columbia University, and were later developed by Arthur Bestor of the University of Illinois and Admiral Hyman Rickover.[25]

According to essentialists, the school curriculum should be geared to the fundamentals or essentials: the three Rs at the elementary school level and five academic or essential subjects—that is, English, mathematics, science, history, and foreign language—at the secondary school level. Although subject centered like perennialism, essentialism is not rooted in the past but is more concerned with the contemporary scene. Both perennialism and essentialism reject such subjects as art, music, physical education, homemaking, and vocational education as fads and frills, and thus appeal to those who favor limiting educational expenses (because these subjects are more expensive in terms of facilities, materials, and student-teacher ratios than academic subjects). Perennialists, however, totally reject these subjects as wasteful and senseless, whereas essentialists grudgingly award half-credit for these so-called minor subjects, although they do limit the number and hours that students can take them. This latter requirement tends to parallel the present secondary school curriculum.

Perennialists tend to regard the student's mind as a sponge for absorbing knowledge; essentialists, too, are concerned with facts and knowledge, but they are also interested in conceptual thought and principles and theories of subject matter. Both groups feel that all students, regardless of abilities and interests, are to be offered the same common curriculum—intellectual in content—but with the quantity and rate adjusted to the capacity of the individual learner.[26] Just how far each student should go is related to his or her specific abilities.

Many essentialists, like the perennialists, embrace an approach to education that emphasizes the mastery of the essential skills, facts, and concepts that form the basis of the subject matter. Wrote Admiral Rickover, "For all children, the educational process must be one of collecting factual knowledge to the limit of their absorptive capacity."[27] A curriculum that takes into account student interests or social issues is wasteful, as are teaching methods that rely on psychological theories. As Bestor declared, "Concern with the personal problems of adolescents has grown so excessive as to push into the background what should be the schools' central concern, the intellectual development of its students."[28] The school is viewed as being sidetracked, from its original mission when it deemphasizes cognitive needs, and attends to the social and psychological problems of students. (Most current task force reports on academic excellence, incidentally, agree with this assessment.) Tough discipline and training, and a good deal of homework and serious studies, permeate the curriculum. As Rickover asserted: "The student must be made to work hard" at his or her studies, and "nothing can really make it fun."[29]

The role of the essentialist teacher follows the perennialist philosophy. The teacher is considered a master of a particular subject or discipline and a model worthy of emulation. A teacher is to be respected as an authority because of the knowledge and high standards he or she holds. The teacher is very much in control of the classroom and decides on the classroom curriculum with minimal student input.

Essentialism today is reflected in the public demand to raise academic standards and to improve the students' work and minds. It is evidenced in such reports as *A Nation at Risk* (and other reports on excellence discussed in Chapter 5) and in the current proposals outlined in Ernest Boyer's *High School* and Theodore Sizer's *Horace's Compromise* (also about high school). Although current essentialist philosophy is more moderate than it was during the Sputnik era—it provides, for example, for less able students—it still emphasizes academics (not play) and cognitive thinking (not the whole child). It is reflected in the two movements below that emerged in response to the general relaxation of academic standards during the late 1960s and 1970s. These movements, while currently challenged by some, seem to have enough support from both educators and the general public to last well into the next century.

Back-to-Basics Curriculum. Automatic promotion of marginal students, the dizzy array of

elective courses, and textbooks designed more to entertain than to educate are frequently cited as sources of the decline in students' basic skills. Today's concerns parallel, to some extent, those voiced immediately after the Sputnik era. The call is less for academic excellence and rigor, however, than for a return to basics. Annual Gallup polls have asked the public to suggest ways to improve education; since 1976 "devoting more attention to teaching the basics" and improving curriculum standards" have ranked no lower than fifth in the list of responses; in the 1980s these suggestions surfaced as the number one, two, or three concern each year.[30]

By 1988, all the states had implemented statewide testing programs for various grade levels; the tests were, in fact, mandated in twenty-seven states. As an offshoot of this movement, as many as thirty-six states required beginning teachers to evidence minimum competencies in basic skills (spelling, grammar, mathematics), academic knowledge (English, social studies, science, mathematics, arts, etc.) and/or pedagogical practices for the purpose of certification.[31]

Although the back-to-basics movement means different things to different people, it usually connotes an essentialist curriculum with heavy emphasis on reading, writing, and mathematics. "Solid" subjects—English, history, science, and mathematics—are taught in all grades. English means traditional grammar, not linguistics or nonstandard English; it means Shakespeare and not *Lolita*. History means U.S. and European history, and perhaps Asian and African history, but not African-American history or ethnic studies. Science means biology, chemistry, and physics, not ecology. Math means old math, not new math. Furthermore, these subjects are required for everyone. Elective courses, mini-courses, even the integrated social science and general science courses are considered too "soft."

Proponents of the movement are concerned that too many illiterate students are passed from grade to grade and eventually graduate, that high school and college diplomas are meaningless as measures of academic performance, that minimum standards must be established, and that the basic skills and subjects are essential for employment and self-survival in modern society. Some of these advocates are college educators who would do away with open admissions, credit for life experiences or for remedial courses, and grade inflation. They would simply insist on reasonable high school and college standards, and they would use tests to monitor educational standards over time and to pressure students, teachers, and parents to perform their responsibilities.[32]

Although the movement is spreading, and state legislators and the public seem convinced of the need for minimum standards, some unanswered questions remain: What standards should be considered minimum? What do we do with students who fail to meet these standards? Are we punishing the victims for the schools' inability to educate them? How will the courts and then the school districts deal with the fact that proportionately more minority than white students fail the competency tests in nearly every case? Is the issue minimum competency or equal educational opportunity? And, when all is said and done, are we not, educationally speaking, reinventing the academic wheel?

Worried reformers also point out that parental involvement in education has been victimized by a change in family structure: rising divorce rates, percentages of children in single-family homes, numbers of married mothers of young children working outside the home, and a corresponding number of latchkey children which has tripled in the last 25 years.[33] The result is that parents have less time and energy to devote to their children's basic education or to supervise them.

Emphasizing Content, De-emphasizing Process.
E. D. Hirsch's *Cultural Literacy,* a national bestseller, focuses on the background *knowledge* necessary for cultural (Hirsch calls it "functional") literacy and effective communication for our nation's populace. Complementing his narrative is a compilation of some 5,000 "essential" items from history, geography, literature, science, and technology.[34] Table 2-3 lists a sample of 50 names, phrases, and concepts (dates are not listed) from the text to test your own literacy.

Although the items are supposedly a mix of historical and current names, people, places, and terms—national and international in scope—most of the items reflect a conservative interpretation of literacy: More than 80 percent of the total items refer to events, people, or places from previous

TABLE 2-3   Fifty Names, Phrases, and Concepts Essential for Literate Americans

Absolute monarchy	Centigrade
Acculturation	Chamberlain
Acid rain	Chekhov, Anton
Aeneas	Chernobyl
Aesop's fables	Cholesterol
Alien and Sedition Acts	Chutzpah
Apollo program	*Cid* (title)
Auxiliary verb	Clemens, Samuel
Babylon	Cobb, Ty
Bacillus	Cohan, George M.
Bangkok	Cologne
Bard of Avon	Colon
Bay of Biscay	Common Market
Becket, Saint Thomas á	Communist Manifesto
Berlin, Irving	Congressional Record
Big Ben	Congress of Vienna
Black, Hugo	Cyclops
Brussels	Czar
Brutus	Damascus
Calvin, John	Dante
Candide (title)	Darrow, Clarence
Canterbury Tales	D-Day
Cape Hatteras	Degas, Edgar
Capital expenditure	Detente
Catch-22 (title)	Dien Bien Phu

Source: E. D. Hirsch, *Cultural Literacy: What Every American Needs to Know,* rev. ed. (Boston: Houghton Mifflin, 1987), Appendix.

centuries, and about 25 percent deal with the classics.

Instead of placing emphasis on process or teaching students how to think, Hirsch stresses the importance of specific information in all levels of schooling. Knowing the facts, for him and a growing number of other essentialists (William Bennett, Chester Finn, Diane Ravitch, and others), increases the students' capacity to comprehend what they read, see, and hear. The need for background knowledge or a core of essential knowledge is judged important for future communication and specialization. In recent years these people argue we have overlooked content and have stressed process—or thinking skills—without regard to subject matter. The outcome has been a decline in national literacy.

For Hirsch and other essentialists, the notion that learning to think, even learning to read, involves a process of acquiring a certain set of skills—without regard to content—is wrong. The idea breaks down very quickly as soon as students advance beyond simple subject matter and/or begin to read for information. Processes or skills are only part of the picture. An educated person has command of knowledge. For traditional educators, the goal of education is not to prepare youth for the future, but rather to enculturate the young. The need is to transmit the shared knowledge and values of adult society to youth. Without the transmission of a shared cultural core to the young, traditionalists argue that our society will become fragmented and our ability to accumulate and communicate information to various segments of the populace will become limited.

Excellence in Education. A spin-off to the back-to-basics movement was the demand in the 1980s for educational excellence and tougher academics. This trend was also in tune with the post Cold War-Sputnik era, when essentialists exerted a considerable influence on the school curriculum; today, it coincides with a broader theme of not only military defense but also technology and economic competition. The dimensions of the problem of academic quality were amply documented in several policy reports on academic excellence—the best known being *A Nation at Risk,* released in the mid-1980s, and the *National Goals for Education,* published in 1990—all calling for reform to improve the quality of education in the United States and emphasizing international "competition" and "survival"—themes reminiscent of the post-Sputnik era as well.[35]

Overall, the trend is for higher achievement (not just minimum competency) for all children (not just college-bound students) in the academic areas, which means that we need to stress cognitive achievement (not the whole child) and rigorous grading, testing, and discipline (not relaxed standards). The emphasis is on higher standards for passing courses and meeting graduation requirements.

For some this approach means more than emphasizing the basic ability to think, reason, and problem solve. It means promoting such serious subjects such as calculus, physics, and advanced foreign languages at the high school level; it means upgrading our definition of basic skills to include advanced skills and knowledge, including computer skills as the fourth R—which are required for tomorrow's technological world. Stress is on increasing and improving the quality of instruction, upgrading our teachers and schools, and making the most of our human capital so we can compete on an economic basis. Unquestionably, the emphasis is on productivity. Moreover, the health and vitality of our country's economy and political position are linked to strengthening our educational institutions.

Others allow wider latitude in defining excellence and permit various models or criteria of excellence. Some still criticize the overemphasis on mathematical and scientific excellence in the schools, and the consequent underemphasis or ignoring of other conceptions of excellence—linguistic, humanistic, musical, spatial, bodily kinesthetic, moral, interpersonal, intrapersonal, and information processing areas.[36] Some are also concerned that equity and equality will be shoved under the rug, with too much stress on cognitive excellence—a return to a post-Sputnik-type emphasis on academically talented students but not high school dropouts.[37] Some fear that this emphasis on excellence will lead to disappointment; they say it is wrong to assume that increased testing and more course requirements will automatically raise the level of student performance. Students, teachers, and parents must also be motivated, and technical and financial support at the school and school district level must be evidenced. See Curriculum Tips 2-2.

In any event, the general theme of this movement is excellence, not adequacy, and many forms of it. The focus is on productivity, increased testing, more homework, better selection of textbooks, and more competent personnel. Both educators and the public agree that students must not only master basic or prerequisite skills, but they must also excel, think creatively, solve problems, and develop their fullest human potential. Finally, the public even seems willing to spend increased monies for real school reform and for upgraded curricula.

Progressivism

Progressivism developed from pragmatic philosophy and as a protest against perennialist thinking

=== *Curriculum Tips 2-2* ===

Recognizing and Rewarding Academic Excellence

Along with higher academic standards, schools are introducing academic incentives for increasing student achievement. Some suggestions for motivating and rewarding high-achieving students follow.

1. Involve parents in their children's learning, especially in early grades. Provide classes for parents in how to help children learn, to motivate them, and to encourage academic initiative and independence.
2. Display past and current "Academic Scholars," such as straight A students, merit finalists, and valedictorians on an Academic Honors Wall. Display photographs permanently.
3. Recognize improvement and achievement by expanding honor rolls, sending personalized letters to parents, and printing names in school newsletters.
4. Each quarter or semester, teachers select top scholars from their respective grade levels. Certificates, plaques, medals, trophies, savings bonds, or classic books can be awarded.
5. Conduct a special academic assembly each semester; recognize high-achieving students in local newspapers and magazines. Honor students (and their parents) with a special luncheon or dinner.
6. Develop special enrichment classes (at the elementary level) and special advanced-level and honor programs for the academically gifted and talented (at the secondary level).
7. Develop homework and tutoring programs for both at-risk students and latchkey and average students who may need assistance in one or two subjects. Use high-achieving students as peer tutors.
8. Recognize academic students to the same extent as or even more than the athletes of the school. Form academic clubs that provide status and publicity for the participants.
9. Cooperate with local business and industry to publicize and/or award high-achieving students.
10. Make school videos of student leaders, including past and present high achievers, and associate academic excellence with successful alumni.
11. Be sensitive about too much academic competition among students. Try to maintain a balance between cognitive and social goals and to recognize deserving (not necessarily only A) students, too.
12. Implement study clubs, reading clubs, or special skills clubs on Saturdays or during the summer for students who need extra help in selected areas or who are studying for the NAEP, ACT, or SAT tests.

in education. The progressive movement in education was also part of the largest social and political movement of reform that characterized much of American society at the turn of the twentieth century. It grew out of the political thought of such progressives as Robert LaFollette, Theodore Roosevelt, and Woodrow Wilson, as well as from the muckraker movement of the 1920s. Progressivism is considered a contemporary reform movement in educational, social, and political affairs.

The educational roots of progressivism can be traced to the reform writings of Horace Mann and Henry Barnard of the nineteenth century, and later to the work of John Dewey in the early twentieth century.[38] In his most comprehensive work, *Democracy and Education,* Dewey claimed that democracy and education went hand in hand;

democratic society and democratic education are participatory and emergent, not preparatory and absolute. Dewey viewed the school as a miniature democratic society in which students could learn and practice the skills and tools necessary for democratic living.[39]

According to progressivist thought, the skills and tools of learning include problem-solving methods and scientific inquiry; in addition, learning experiences should include cooperative behaviors and self-discipline, both of which are important for democratic living. Through these skills and experiences the school can transmit the culture of society while it prepares the students for a changing world. Because reality is constantly changing, Dewey saw little need to focus upon a fixed body of knowledge, as did the perennialists and essentialists. Progressivism, instead, placed heavy emphasis on *how* to think, not *what* to think. Traditional education, with its "method of imposition from the side of the teacher and reception, [and] absorption from the side of the pupil," wrote Dewey, "may be compared to inscribing records upon a passive phonographic disc to result in giving back what has been inscribed when the proper button is pressed in recitation or examination."[40]

For Dewey and other progressivist thinkers, the curriculum was interdisciplinary in nature, and books and subject matter were part of the learning process rather than sources of ultimate knowledge. The role of the teacher was unique when operating under progressive thinking. The teacher served as a guide for students in their problem-solving and scientific projects. Dewey and William Kilpatrick both referred to this role as the "leader of group activities." The teacher and students planned activities together (although Dewey later affirmed that the final authority rested with the teacher), but the teacher was to help students locate, analyze, interpret, and evaluate data—to formulate their own conclusions.[41]

The progressive movement became splintered into several different wings, including the child-centered, activity-centered, creative, and neo-Freudian groups. Dewey criticized these groups for misinterpreting and misusing his ideas. Just as he condemned the old philosophies that pursued knowledge for its own sake, he attacked those who thought knowledge had little or no value. Not only did he attack "traditional ideas as erecting silence as a virtue," he also criticized those who sought to liberate the child from adult authority and social controls. He declared "progressive extremists" and "laissez-faire" philosophies to be destructive to the ideas of progressivism, and he warned that "any movement that thinks and acts in terms of an ism becomes so involved in reaction against other isms that it is unwittingly controlled by them."[42]

Dewey was not alone in his criticism of progressive educators. As criticisms mounted, Boyd Bode, another leading proponent of progressivism, warned his associates of the impending crisis in a book entitled *Progressive Education at the Crossroads.*[43] He cautioned that "progressive education stands at the parting of the ways." The movement "nurtured the pathetic hope that it could find out how to educate by relying on such notions as interests, needs, growth and freedom." In its social and psychological approach to learning, in its "one-sided devotion to the child, it betrayed the child," and deprived him or her of appropriate subject matter. If progressivism continued its present course without changing its focus, "it would be circumvented and left behind."[44] Bode's words proved prophetic. More and more progressivists responded to the growing criticism and self-justifying theories and educational ideas that involved trivialities and errors.

Although the progressive movement in education encompassed many different theories and practices, it was united in its opposition to certain traditional school practices: (1) the authoritarian teacher; (2) excessive reliance on textbook methods; (3) memorization of factual data and techniques by drill; (4) static aims and materials that reject the notion of a changing world; (5) use of fear or corporal punishment as a form of discipline; and (6) attempts to isolate education from individual experiences and social reality. However, the movement's inability to outline a uniform theory of the purpose of schooling, or even to establish a set of principles, contributed to its downfall.[45]

Progressive education was both a movement within the broad framework of American education and a theory that urged the liberation of the child from the traditional emphasis on rote learning, lesson recitations, and textbook authority. In opposition to the conventional subject matter of the traditional curriculum, progressives experimented with alternative modes of curricular organization—utilizing activities, experiences, problem solving, and the project method. Progressive education focused on the child as the learner rather than on the subject, emphasized activities and experiences rather than verbal and literary skills, and encouraged cooperative group-learning activities rather than competitive individualized lesson learning. The use of democratic school procedures was considered a prelude to community and social reform. Progressivism also cultivated a cultural relativism that critically appraised and often rejected traditional value commitments.

Although the major thrust of progressive education waned in the 1940s and 1950s, with the advent of essentialism, the philosophy did leave its imprint on education and the schools of today. Contemporary progressivism is expressed in several movements, including those for a relevant curriculum, humanistic education, and radical school reform.

Relevant Curriculum. As the 1960s unfolded, students took a more active role in their education, as a spin off to the student movement, and perceived the subject-centered curriculum as irrelevant to the social times and demanded a more progressive and student-centered curriculum. It was now argued that learners must be motivated and interested in the learning task, and the classroom should build on real-life experiences.

The call for relevance came, in fact, from both students and educators. Advocates of this approach saw as needs (1) the individualization of instruction through such teaching methods as independent study and special projects; (2) revised and new courses on such topics of student concern as sex education, drug addiction, race relations, urban problems, and so on; (3) educational alternatives, as well as electives, minicourses, and open classrooms; (4) the extension of the curriculum beyond the school's walls through such innovations as work-study programs, credit for life experiences, off-campus courses, and external degree programs; and (5) the relaxation of academic standards and admission standards to schools and colleges.[46]

Humanistic Curriculum. The humanistic curriculum also began as a reaction to what was viewed as an overemphasis on subject matter and cognitive learning in the 1960s and 1970s. In his best-selling book, *Crisis in the Classroom,* Charles Silberman advocated humanizing American schools.[47] He charged that schools are repressive, and that they teach students docility and conformity. He believed that schools must be reformed, even at the price of de-emphasizing cognitive learning and student discipline. He suggested that elementary schools adopt the methods of the British infant schools. At the secondary level, he suggested independent study, peer tutoring, and community and work experiences.

The humanistic model of education stems from the human potential movement in psychology. Within education it is rooted in the work of Arthur Jersild, who linked good teaching with knowledge of self and students, and in the work of Arthur Combs and Donald Snygg, who explored the impact of self-concept and motivation on achievement.[48] Combs and Snygg considered self-concept the most important determinant of behavior.

A humanistic curriculum emphasizes affective rather than cognitive outcomes. Such a curriculum draws heavily on the works of Abraham Maslow and Carl Rogers.[49] Its goal is to produce "self-actualizing people," in Maslow's words, or "total human beings," in Rogers's. The works of both psychologists are laced with such terms as maintaining, striving, enhancing, and experiencing—as well as independence, self-determination, integration, and self-actualization.

Advocates of humanistic education contend that the present school curriculum has failed miserably by humanistic standards, that teachers and schools are determined to stress cognitive behaviors and to control students *not* for their own good but for the good of adults. Humanists emphasize more than affective processes; they seek higher domains of consciousness. But they see the schools as unconcerned about higher planes of understanding, enhancement of the mind, or self-knowledge.

Humanists would attempt to form more meaningful relationships between students and teachers; they would foster student independence and self-direction, and they would promote greater acceptance of self and others. The teacher's role would be to help learners cope with their psychological needs and problems, to facilitate self-understanding among students, and to help them develop fully.

A drawback to humanist theory is its lack of attention to cognitive learning and intellectual development. When asked to judge the effectiveness of their curriculum, humanists generally rely on testimonials and subjective assessments by students and teachers. They may also present such materials as students' paintings and poems or talk about "marked improvement" in student behavior and attitudes. They present very little empirical evidence, however, to support their stance. See Curriculum Tips 2-3.

Radical School Reform.   During the late 1960s and 1970s, intense attacks were leveled on teachers and schools by radical critics of education, sometimes called "radical romanticists" or "neo-progressives." The criticisms were widely published in the mass media, especially in magazines like *The Atlantic Monthly, Harper's,* the *New Republic,* the *New York Times Magazine,* and the *Saturday Review)*. These radicals also published many popular books on their views.

Prominent radicals like Edgar Friedenberg, John Holt, Paul Goodman, A. S. Neill, and Ivan Illich expressed considerable disdain toward established methods of schooling, compulsory schooling, adult authority, and school rules. Radical critics like Henry Giroux and Peter McLaren went even further in expressing contempt for the very society within which schools exist. All these critics have essentially referred to students as prisoners, to teachers as prison guards or dupes of the system, and to schools as essentially prisons where students are locked up intellectually and emotionally, thus restricting their free expression and democratic actions. Schools are considered to be highly discriminatory places that sort and track students for various jobs that extend class differences in society. Schools participate in perpetuating the social logic of production and consumption, which benefits the few and marginalizes the many.[50]

Friedenberg has argued that teachers "dislike and distrust" the students they teach, and that they "fear being involved with young people in any situation that is not under their complete control." Teachers have a "repressed hostility toward their students" and "resentment," a kind of ill temper, suppressed anger, and jealousy because of students' youthful energy and freedom.[51]

John Holt's book, *How Children Fail,* is his most influential text.[52] There is nothing positive in it about teachers or the school processes; it deals instead with how teachers and schools turn off students. Holt describes the conventions of the classroom: teachers' enforcing rigid rules and children's focusing on right answers, learning to be stupid, and learning not to learn. He goes into great detail about how children adopt strategies of fear and failure to please their teachers. The successful students become cunning strategists in a game of beating the system—figuring out how to outsmart the teacher, how to get the answer out of the teacher, or how to fake the answer.

Paul Goodman's thesis is that our society is sick and full of spurious and false values that have produced sick schools. He contends that schools have little to do with education; they provide jobs for millions of people and a market for textbook companies, building contractors, and graduates of schools of education. In the early grades, the schools provide "a baby-sitting service" for the parents and keep kids off the street. In the middle and senior years, "they are the arm of the police, providing cops and concentration camps paid for in the budget under the heading of 'Board of Education.' " From kindergarten to college, schools teach youth to adjust to a sick society and provide "a universal trap [in which] democracy begins to look like regimentation."[53] Goodman's solution is to do away with compulsory education, to which he refers as "miseducation" and to "drastically cut back formal schooling because the present extended tutelage is against nature and arrests growth."[54]

A. S. Neill, a romantic progressivist, recounts the way he operated his school, Summerhill, in Suffolk, England. He wrote about the innate goodness of the child, and about the replacement of authority for freedom against which Dewey warned:

> . . . *we set out to make a school in which we should allow children to be themselves. In order to do this, we had to renounce all discipline, all direction, all suggestion, all moral training. . . . All it required was what we had—a complete belief in the child as a good, not an evil being. For almost forty years, this belief in the goodness of the child*

================== *Curriculum Tips 2-3* ==================

Affective Methods to Enhance Learning

Progressive philosophy and humanistic education increase the student's self-understanding and self-awareness, allow students to personalize and individualize learning, and match (at least consider) their personal needs and interests with academic experiences. The classroom is characterized by activity, not passivity; cooperation, not competition; and many learning opportunities other than textbooks and teacher-dominated situations. To help the teacher and curriculum worker provide a leadership role in progressive and humanistic approaches, we provide the following guidelines.

1. Demonstrate real interest and concern for each student.
2. Challenge students to become personally and actively involved in their own learning; encourage them to grow toward self-direction and self-control over learning.
3. Help students define personal goals; recognize their efforts in pursuit of a chosen goal.
4. Structure learning activities so that each student can accomplish his or her own personal goals and experience success.
5. Relate content to students' personal goals, needs, and interests.
6. Match task requirements to students' age, development, and abilities.
7. Offer constructive and corrective feedback, but put the emphasis on being constructive.
8. Test students if necessary, but delay grading their performance (say until the fourth or fifth grade).
9. Use local resources to obtain information and solve problems; actively involve students in learning that involves different materials, people, and places.
10. Provide alternative ways for learning; minimize memory, rote, and drill activities.
11. Help students achieve their own competence and mastery; let them know that their learning is the result of their own efforts, for which they are responsible.
12. Recognize students' improvement and achievement.
13. Encourage students to share materials and resources and to work in groups.
14. Encourage students to contribute their ideas and feelings, to accept and support each other—not to criticize or ridicule one another—and to be considerate of others who need help or are slow to learn.

---

has never wavered; it rather has become a final faith.[55]

Neill claimed that the "child is innately wise and realistic. If left to himself without adult suggestions of any kind," he will develop on his own. Those "who are to become scholars will be scholars," and those "who are only fit to sweep the streets will sweep streets."[56] Neill is not concerned with formal teaching or instruction; he does not believe in examinations or in homework. Those who want to study will study, and those who prefer not to study will not—regardless of how teachers teach or what they say. If a child wants to go to class, great; if not, so what? Neill's criteria for success have nothing to do with school or economic outcomes; rather they relate to the ability to "work joyfully" and "live positively." Following these guidelines, most of the students who attend Summerhill allegedly turn out to be successful in life.

Ivan Illich, another radical critic, went beyond his contemporaries in his plans for remaking schools. He argued for a new society that required the prior deschooling of society.[57] Illich completely rejected school as a viable agency. If schools were eliminated, education could be open to all and could become a genuine instrument of human liberation: Learners would no longer have an obligatory curriculum imposed upon them; they would be liberated from institutional and capitalistic indoctrination. There would no longer be discrimination and a class society based on possession of a certificate.

In lieu of school, Illich recommended small learning networks characterized by the following: *educational objects,* that is, shops, libraries, museums, art galleries, and so on that are open to learners; *peer matching,* that is, identifying and bringing together students who wish to engage in a particular learning activity; *skill exchanges,* that is, exchanges between those who are competent in a particular skill, and who wish to teach it, and those who wish to learn it; and *educators-at-large,* that is, counselors who serve as advisors to students and parents and intellectual initiators and administrators who operate the networks.

Henry Giroux posits that public education is in a dire state of crisis. He states that it is not an isolated crisis solely affecting a certain aspect of our society. This crisis negatively influences our very concept of democracy. Interestingly, he notes that the crisis that schools confront is implicated in and actually produced by a transformation in the very nature of democracy itself.[58] Giroux interprets democracy from a Marxist orientation. Essentially, he views the current practice of democracy as exclusive, rather than inclusive in that many are left out of the promises to which our system subscribes. To Giroux, what is at stake is the "refusal to grant public schooling a significant role in the ongoing process of educating people to be active and critical citizens capable of fighting for and reconstructing democratic public life."[59]

Peter McLaren is even more extreme in his views. He goes so far as to state that capitalist schooling is generally perverse, in that it strives through its curriculum to create a culture of desire—not to nurture a communal consensus but rather to hide from students and the general public the gaps in our society, the contradictions of our stances, and our intolerance of difference. Schooling in its solicitation of desire hides from its citizens the realms of difference. He argues, "perverts cannot tolerate difference, so they 'invent in its place a quasi-delirious image of a non-

lack.'"[60] Schools run by such people present to their students an illusion of harmony. McLaren admits that contemporary schooling dares students to become productive, loyal citizens. However, this exhortation to students to "be all that they can be" is "always already situated within a total obedience to normative codes of conduct and standardized regimes of valuing."[61]

This McLaren states "is not empowering education but a perverse form of prohibition in which desire as human agency is not permitted to explore its own constitutive possibilities. Students are treated as objects of consumption as they are simultaneously taught the value of becoming consuming subjects."[62] Thus, schools are engaged in a perverse ritual in which they are actually molding students to be compatible with the dominant view of society. Students are denied access to forming their own destinies.

Reconstructionism

The reconstructionist philosophy itself is based on early socialistic and utopian ideas of the nineteenth century; nonetheless, it was the Economic Depression that gave it rebirth and new life. The progressive educational movement was at its height in popularity then, but a small yet significant group of progressive educators still became disillusioned with American society and impatient for reform. This group argued that progressivism put too much emphasis on child-centered education that mainly served the individual child and the middle class, with its play theories and private schools. What was needed was more emphasis on society-centered education that took into consideration the needs of society (not the individual) and all classes (not only the middle class).

At the 1932 annual meeting of the Progressive Education Association, George Counts urged progressive educators to consider the social and economic problems of the era and to use the schools to help reform society. In his speech, "Dare the School Build a New Social Order?" (which was later published as a book), Counts suggested that the schools become the agent of social change and institution for social reform. In a rhetorical and highly charged statement, Counts stunned his progressive colleagues with the following statement:

. . . If Progressive Education is to be genuinely progressive, it must . . . face squarely and courageously every social issue, come to grips with life in all its stark reality, establish an organic relation with the community, develop a realistic and comprehensive theory of welfare, fashion a compelling and challenging vision of human destiny, and become less frightened than it is today at the bogeys of imposition and indoctrination.[63]

The social issues of the 1930s, according to Counts, involved racial and class discrimination, poverty, and unemployment—and progressive education had ignored these issues. The social issues today are similar, although the list is larger: racial, ethnic, and sexual inequality; poverty, unemployment, and welfare; computers and technology; political oppression and war; environmental pollution; disease; hunger; AIDS; and depletion of the earth's resources.

Theodore Brameld, who is often considered the originator of the term reconstructionism in 1950 (actually Dewey coined the term),[64] has asserted that reconstructionism is a crisis philosophy, appropriate for a society in crisis, which is the essence of our society and international society today.[65] According to Brameld, students and teachers must not only take positions, they must also become change agents to improve society. Neutrality in the classrooms or schools, that in which we often engage under the guise of objective and scientific inquiry, is not appropriate for the democratic process. Writes Brameld, "Teachers and students have a right to take sides, to stand up for the best reasoned and informed partialities they can reach as a result of free, meticulous examination and communication of all relevant evidence." In particular, teachers must measure up to their social responsibilities. Brameld goes on: "The immediate task before the [teaching] profession is to draw upon this strength and thus to strengthen control of the schools by and for the goal-seeking interests of the overwhelming majority of mankind."[66]

As for the curriculum, it had to be transformed to coincide with a new social-economic-political education; it had, in other words, to incorporate realistic reform strategies. For reconstructionists, analysis, interpretation, and evaluation of problems are insufficient; commitment and action by students and teachers are needed. Society is always changing, and the curriculum has to change; students and teachers must be change agents. A curriculum based on social issues and social services is ideal.

The reconstructionists, including such recent proponents as Mario Fantini, Harold Shane, and Alvin Toffler, seek a curriculum that emphasizes cultural pluralism, equality, and futurism.[67] Students are taught to appreciate life in a world of many nations. A reconstructionist program of education (1) critically examines the cultural heritage of a society as well as the entire civilization, (2) is not afraid to examine controversial issues, (3) is deliberately committed to bring about social and constructive change, (4) cultivates a future planning attitude that considers the realities of the world, and (5) enlists students and teachers in a definite program to enhance cultural renewal and interculturalism. In such a program, teachers are considered the prime agents of social change, cultural renewal, and internationalism. Teachers are organized not to strengthen their own professional security, but rather to encourage widespread experimentation in the schools and to challenge the outdated structures of society. They are considered to be the vanguard for a new social order—somewhat utopian in nature.

Internationalists. A reconstructionist educator tends to be very sensitive to global issues and analyzes them as part of the larger social order. Although, historically, the United States has taken a relatively isolationist position, interdependence among nations no longer allows Americans to remain ignorant of developments in distant countries. Educators now feel the need to place a greater emphasis on understanding other nations and cultures than they have in the past.

Such terms as "global village," "global interdependence," "shrinking world," and "greenhouse effect" reflect our new concerns that the oceans no longer protect us and we are forced to reflect on the international tendencies of the times. Increasingly, one group of curriculum experts is seeking an *international component* in national curricula. This does not suggest a common curriculum, but rather that the goals, content, and experiences of each nation's school curricula enhance its mutual understanding about international society and global cooperation. Sometimes called a world curriculum, or universal core, each nation would continue to promote its own culture, values, and political/economic systems, but students would learn a common core of knowledge and skills essential for global peace and cooperation.[68]

One advocate of this international curriculum is Kenneth Boulding; he maintains that students need to acquire an awareness of global events and tools for understanding "worldwide systems." These systems are social, political, economic, physical, biological, communicative, and evaluative.[69] This new curriculum would focus on understanding the earth's ecosystem and world problems. Some might argue that the idea is unrealistic, too encompassing, or not possible to implement as schools are presently organized. Indeed, there are some 15,000 school districts, each with their own curricula, multiple textbooks, and ideal teaching methods. Perhaps all these global concepts cannot be fully implemented, but the idea of a new core or world-wide curriculum for all students is certainly intriguing and worth considering.

As technology increasingly links members of the world community, it is likely that this focus to curriculum will increase. Indeed, people are saying that there is no "there," there is only "here." America is in the world; Americans cannot be ignorant of the world and their place within it. Our gross national product and standard of living are connected with the world community and influenced by global activities.

Reconceptualists.   Currently, reconceptualists are the most vocal within the curricular community. They do not all speak with one voice, but they do seem to be bound together in their shared view of the narrowness of the technical or Tylerian approach to curriculum development and their view that curriculum is much more than an educational concern. The reconceptualists seem bound more by a way of thinking, an orientation to the field, than a dogma or philosophy.[70]

The reconceptualists have criticized the majority of curricularists as exemplifying a lockstep, means–ends approach based on technocratic and bureaucratic school models that are not sensitive to people's inner feelings and experiences. Furthermore, the reconceptualists have found fault with more mainstream curricularists for not

viewing society in a broad context. Actually, we would argue that it is not that the more traditional curricularists do not take society into consideration when theorizing about or planning curricula, but that traditionalists do not see society from the viewpoints of the reconceptualists.

The reconceptualists have expanded the field of curriculum to shape their viewpoints. They have included in curricular conversation the intuitive, personal, mystical, linguistic, political, social, and spiritual. Such orientations, they argue, are necessary to address the broad problems and issues of society. They purport that the current society exhibits high levels of alienation, an ignoring of many groups, and a personal indifference to the very human needs of citizens of the schools and the society in general.[71] They state that more traditional and technical means of curricular activity perpetuate the inequities both within and outside the school. The more traditional approaches to curriculum assume a simplicity to living that just does not exist.

According to Pinar, the field of curriculum has already been reconceptualized. The well-established movement has moved us from a preoccupation with creating curricula to striving to understand curricula.[72] Certainly, the curriculum field and curricularists within it reflect a very broadly conceived curriculum; however, it is not really accurate to state that the field has been reconceptualized. Those who subscribe to postmodern views would argue that the field can never really attain a fixed state; the field is essentially an open system and always in a state of development, conceptualizing and reconceptualizing itself. And one can accept the dynamism of the field of curriculum without subscribing to the social and political agenda of many of the reconceptualists.

Certainly, the reconceptualists have brought into curricular conversation aesthetic and existentialist views, discussions, and procedures. They have stressed broad problems and issues. With some degree of success, they have attempted, at least among themselves, to reflect, refine, rethink, reinterpret, and to them reconceptualize the field of curriculum. When reading the reconceptualists, one realizes that these are socially sensitive and politically concerned intellectuals who reflect and refine important issues that have philosophical, psychological, political, and economic implications. However, they are not the only intellectuals in the field who are so concerned.

Reconceptualists accept many aspects of progressive philosophy, including learner-centered, relevant, humanistic, and radical school-reform models. However, they reiterate and detail a bit more of the dynamic, holistic, transcendental, linguistic, and artistic meaning of teaching learning. They are more concerned with personal self-knowledge, inner self, personal reflection, psychologies of consciousness, and spiritual and moral introspection. They contend there is more to knowledge and knowing than empirical or even logical, verifiable data. Expanded ideas of inner consciousness, "third force," or humanistic psychology, and existentialist ideas serve as the foundations for their views.

Content and experiences that emphasize language and communication skills, personal biographies, art, poetry, dance, drama, literature, psychology, ethics, religion, and other aesthetic, humanistic, and spiritual subject matter comprise a good part of the reconstructionist curriculum—subjects not part of the normal curriculum or certainly not the major foci. Maxine Greene advocates this curriculum, which she calls "personal expression," "intellectual consciousness," and "reflective self-consciousness.[73] Paulo Freire refers to this as a curriculum of "human phenomenon," "problematic situations," and "background awareness" that has the potential "to transform the world."[74] According to William Pinar, this subject matter deals with "personal becoming," "autonomy," the "soul" and "heart," "affiliative needs," "mature personality," "trust" and "love," "self-direction," "sensitivity," and "enjoyment"[75]—that is, psychological, philosophical, spiritual, and existentialist attitudes and behaviors.

Reconceputualists are also concerned with social, political, and economic ideas and ideology, and in this context reflect reconstructionist philosophy. Many of their ideas, rooted in the school of Dewey, Counts, and Rugg, deal with inequities and/or conflict concerned with socioeconomic relationships, sexual and racial roles and attitudes, the relationship between labor and capital, and the consequences of political power. Reconceptualists are also concerned with current technocratic and bureaucratic systems that dominate the individual and that reduce the person to a powerless

and manipulated cog. Many envision schools as an oppressive instrument of society that controls and coerces, even oppresses, students through various customs and mores and teaching-learning practices.

Some reconceptualists have been labeled neo-Marxists. Michael Apple, for one, has tried to highlight the relationship between what he perceives to be political, economic, and cultural domination of the individual in relation to schools and society. Such domination "is vested in the constitutive principles, codes, and especially the common sense consciousness and practices underlying our lives, as well as by overt division and manipulation."[76] In other words, the everyday structures and institutions of our society, including schools, convey meaning and conditions that shape our lives and that take control over us; the dominant social, political, and economic system pervades in all critical aspects of the curriculum.

Elsewhere, Apple points out that just as there is "unequal distribution of economic capital in society, so, too is there a similar system of distribution surrounding cultural capital." In technological societies, schools become "distributors of this cultural capital."[77] They play a major role in distributing various forms of knowledge, which in turn leads to power and control over others.

Both Illich and Freire contend that the larger system is oppressive and in need of major overhaul. Illich, who is also considered to be a radical critic, outlines a curriculum that is less institutionalized, formal, and discriminatory for purposes of "emancipation." He relies on a "grass-roots" curriculum that seeks to engage students, teachers, and community members.[78] Freire develops a "pedagogy for the oppressed" for students and the poor and describes how people can move through different stages to ultimately be able to take action and overcome oppression. To effect major change, at what Freire calls the "critical transforming stage," people must become active participants in changing their own status through social action that aims at changing the larger social order. Freire calls for a dialogue or match between students and adults who are sensitive to change. The curriculum is to focus on community, national, and world problems—and is to be based on a core or interdisciplinary approach.[79]

In general, the curriculum advocated by in this wing of reconceptualists emphasizes the social sciences—history, political science, economics, sociology, and some psychology and philosophy—and not the hard sciences. The thrust is to develop individual self-realization and freedom through cognitive and intellectual activities and then to liberate people from the restrictions, limitations, and controls of society. The idea is to move from knowledge to activity, from reflections to action. The curriculum attempts to create new conditions and environments that improve the human condition and the institutions of society. It is, according to James Macdonald, "a form of 'utopianism,' a form of political and social philosophizing."[80] All the oppressed—youth, poor, minorities, women, and so on—are considered agents for change. The model, in essence, is an updated version of old reconstructionism, which viewed students and teachers as agents of change. In the new version, reconceptualism, the teacher is often construed as an agent of oppression, representative of the larger and coercive society.

Equality of Educational Opportunity. No country has taken the idea of equality more seriously than ours. Politically, the idea is rooted in our Constitution, written more than 150 years prior to the emergence of reconstructionism as a philosophy. The origins of American public schools are also dominated by the concept of equal opportunity and the notion of universal, free education. The rise of the "common school" was spearheaded by Horace Mann who asserted, "Education beyond all other devices of human origin is the greatest equalizer of the condition of men— the balance-wheel of the social machinery."[81]

Equality of opportunity in this context would not lead to equality of outcomes; this concept did not attempt a classless society. As David Tyack wrote, "For the most part, working men did not seek to pull down the rich; rather they sought equality of opportunity for their children, an equal chance at the main chance."[82] Equality of opportunity in the nineteenth and early twentieth centuries meant an equal start for all children, but the assumption was that some would go farther than others. Differences in backgrounds and abilities, as well as motivation and luck, would create differences in outcomes among individuals, but the

school would assure that children born into any class would have the opportunity to achieve status as persons born into other classes. Implicit in this view was that the "schools represented the means of achieving the goal . . . of equal chances of success" relative to all children in all stratum.[83]

In retrospect, the schools did not fully achieve this goal, according to some observers, because school achievement and economic outcomes are highly related to social class and family background.[84] Had the schools not existed, however, social mobility would have been further reduced. The failure of the common school to provide social mobility raises the question of the role of school in achieving equality—and the question of just what the school can and cannot do to affect cognitive and economic outcomes.

The modern view of educational equality, which emerged in the 1950s through the 1970s, goes much further than the old view. In light of this, James Coleman has outlined five views of inequality of educational opportunity, the latter four of which parallel reconstructionist philosophy: (1) inequality defined by the same curriculum for all children, with the intent that school facilities be equal; (2) inequality defined in terms of the racial composition of the schools; (3) inequality defined in terms of such intangible characteristic as teacher morale and teacher expectations of students; (4) inequality based on school consequences or outcomes for students with equal backgrounds and abilities; and (5) inequality based on school consequences for students with unequal backgrounds and abilities.[85]

The first two definitions deal with race and social class; the next definition deals with concepts that are hard to define; the fourth definition deals with school expenditures and school finances. The fifth definition is an extreme interpretation: Equality is reached only when the outcomes of schooling are similar for all students—those in minority as well as dominant student groups.

When inequality is defined, in terms of equal outcomes (both cognitive and economic), we start comparing racial, ethnic, and religious groups. In a heterogeneous society like ours, this results in some hot issues, including how much to invest in human capital, how to determine the cost-effectiveness of social and educational programs, who should be taxed and how much, to what extent are we to handicap our brightest and most talented minds (the swift racers) to enable those who are slow to finish at the same time, and whether affirmative action policies lead to reverse discrimination.[86] Indeed, we cannot treat these issues lightly, because they affect most of us in one way or another and lead to questions over which wars have been fought.

In his classic text on excellence and equality, John Gardner points out that in a democracy the differences among groups cannot be dwelled on and we go out of the way to ignore them. He describes the dilemma.

> *Extreme equalitarianism—or what I would prefer to say equalitaranism wrongly conceived—which ignores differences in native capacity and achievement, has not served democracy well. Carried far enough, it means . . . the end of that striving for excellence which has produced mankind's greatest achievements.*
>
> *. . . no democracy can give itself over to extreme emphasis on individual performance and still remain a democracy—or to extreme equalitarianism and retain its vitality. A society such as ours has no choice but to seek the development of human potentialities at all levels. It takes more than educated elite to run a complex, technological society. Every modern industrialized society is learning that hard lesson.*[87]

The issues that Gardner raised directly affected the social fabric of the country and have echoed loudly in the past twenty-five years. They have given rise to educational equality and equal opportunity legislation that has permeated many aspects of school and society. The reconstructionists, among other educators, have raised many of the same issues, including school desegregation, compensatory education, multicultural education, handicapped education, more effective schooling, and affirmative action (who goes to college, who gets what jobs, and who manages society). These issues have no easy answers, and they will continue to plague us. See Table 2-4.

CONCLUSION

Philosophy gives meaning to our decisions and actions. In the absence of a philosophy, the educator is vulnerable to externally imposed pre-scriptions, to fads and frills, to authoritarian schemes, and to other "isms." Dewey was so convinced of the importance of philosophy that he viewed it as the all-encompassing aspect of the educational process—as necessary for "forming fundamental dispositions, intellectual and emotional, toward nature and fellow man." If one accepts this conclusion, it becomes evident that many aspects of curriculum, if not most of the educational process in school, are developed around philosophy. Even if we believe that Dewey's point is an overstatement, we should still recognize the pervasiveness of philosophy in determining our views of reality, what values and knowledge are worthwhile, and decisions in education in general and curriculum making in particular.

Major philosophical viewpoints that have emerged within the curriculum field may be viewed along a continuum—traditional and conservative versus contemporary and liberal—idealism, realism, pragmatism, and existentialism. These general or world philosophies have influenced educational philosophies, sometimes called educational theories or views, along the same continuum: perennialism and essentialism as traditional and conservative, and progressivism and reconstructionism as contemporary and liberal. (See Table 2-5.) Very few schools adopt a single philosophy; in practice, most schools combine various philosophies. Moreover, our position is that no single philosophy, old or new, should serve as the exclusive guide for making decisions about schools or about the curriculum. All philosophical groups (outlined in this chapter) want the same thing of education, that is, they wish to improve the educational process, to enhance the achievement of the learner, to produce better and more productive citizens, and to improve society. Because of their different views of reality, values, and knowledge, however, they find it difficult to agree on how to achieve these ends.

What we need to do, as curricularists, is to search for the middle road, a highly elusive and abstract concept, where there is no extreme emphasis on subject matter or student; cognitive development or sociopsychological development; excellence or equality. What we need is a prudent school philosophy, one that is politically and economically feasible and that serves the needs of

TABLE 2-4 Overview of Educational Philosophies

EDUCATIONAL PHILOSOPHY	PHILOSOPHICAL BASE	AIM OF EDUCATION	KNOWLEDGE	ROLE OF EDUCATION	CURRICULUM FOCUS	RELATED CURRICULUM TRENDS
Perennialism	Realism	To educate the rational person; to cultivate the intellect	Focus on past and permanent studies; mastery of facts and timeless knowledge	Teacher helps students think rationally; based on Socratic method, oral exposition; explicit teaching of traditional values	Classical subjects; literary analysis; constant curriculum	Great books; Paideia proposal; returning to the liberal arts
Essentialism	Idealism, realism	To promote the intellectual growth of the individual; to educate the competent person	Essential skills and academic subjects; mastery of concepts and principles of subject matter	Teacher is authority in his or her subject field; explicit teaching of traditional values	Essential skills (three Rs) and essential subjects (English, science, history, math, and foreign language)	Back to basics; cultural literacy; excellence in education
Progressivism	Pragmatism	To promote democratic, social living	Knowledge leads to growth and development; a living-learning process; focus on active and relevant learning	Teacher is guide for problem solving and scientific inquiry	Based on student's interests; involves the application of human problems and affairs; interdisciplinary subject matter; activities and projects	Relevant curriculum; humanistic education; radical school reform
Reconstructionism	Pragmatism	To improve and reconstruct society; education for change and social reform	Skills and subjects needed to identify and ameliorate problems of society; learning is active and concerned with contemporary and future society	Teacher serves as an agent of change and reform; acts as a project director and research leader; helps students become aware of problems confronting humankind	Emphasis on social sciences and social research methods; examination of social, economic, and political problems; focus on present and future trends as well as on national and international issues	International education; reconceptualism; equality of educational opportunity

TABLE 2-5 Traditional and Contemporary Education Philosophies

TRADITIONAL PHILOSOPHY (PERENNIALISM, ESSENTIALISM)	CONTEMPORARY PHILOSOPHY (PROGRESSIVISM, RECONSTRUCTIONISM)

Society and Education

1. Formal education begins with the school; schools are considered the major institution of the child's education.	1. Formal education begins with the family; the parents are considered the most important influence in the child's education.
2. School transmits the common culture; individual's major responsibility is to society, performing societal roles; conformity and cooperation are important.	2. School improves society; individual's fulfillment and development can benefit society; independence and creativity are important.
3. Education is for the aims of society; it involves authority and moral restraint.	3. Education involves varied opportunities to develop one's potential and engage in personal choices.
4. Certain subjects and knowledge prepare students for democracy and freedom.	4. Democratic experiences in school help prepare students for democracy and freedom.
5. Education formulated mainly in cognitive terms; focus on academic subjects.	5. Education concerned with social, moral, and cognitive terms; focus on the whole child.
6. Values and beliefs tend to be objective and, if not absolute, then based on agreed standards or truths.	6. Values and beliefs are subjective, based on the individual's view of the world.

Knowledge and Learning

7. Emphasis on knowledge and information.	7. Emphasis on resolving problems and functioning in one's social environment.
8. Emphasis on subjects (content).	8. Emphasis on students (learners).
9. Subject matter selected and organized by teacher.	9. Subject matter planned by teacher and students.
10. Subject matter organized in terms of simple to complex, centered on the past.	10. Subject matter organized in terms of understanding relationships, centered on present or future.
11. Unit/lesson plans organized according to topics or concepts.	11. Unit/lesson plans organized according to problems or student interests.
12. Subject matter is compartmentalized according to distinct fields, disciplines, or study areas.	12. Subject matter is integrated; includes more than one related subject.

Instruction

13. Textbooks and workbooks dominate; teaching and learning largely contained to classroom.	13. Varied instructional materials; teaching and learning include community resources.
14. Whole-group learning, fixed schedules, and uniform time periods.	14. Whole, small, and individualized groups, flexible schedules, and adjustable time periods.
15. Homogeneous grouping; tracking of students into special programs.	15. Heterogeneous grouping; some tracking of students but widely differentiated programs.
16. Passive involvement of students in assimilating what teacher or textbook says.	16. Active involvement of students in seeking information that can be used or applied.
17. Emphasis on uniformity of classroom experiences and instructional situations.	17. Emphasis on variability of classroom experiences and instructional situations.

Purpose and Programs

18. Emphasis is on liberal arts and science.	18. Mix of liberal arts, practical, and vocational subjects.
19. Emphasis is on specialization or scholarship.	19. Emphasis is general and for the layperson.
20. Curriculum is prescribed; little room for electives.	20. Curriculum based on student needs or interests; room for electives.
21. Excellence and high standards; special consideration for high achievers.	21. Equality and flexible standards; special consideration for low achievers.

Source: Adapted from Allan C. Ornstein, "Philosophy as a Basis for Curriculum Decisions," *High School Journal* (December–January 1991), pp. 106–107.

students and society. Implicit in this view of education is that too much emphasis on any one philosophy, sometimes at the expense of another, may do harm and cause conflict. How much we emphasize one philosophy, under the guise of reform or for whatever reason, is critical because no one society can give itself over to extreme "isms" or political views and still remain a democracy. The kind of society into which we evolve is in part reflected in our educational system, which is influenced by the philosophy that we eventually define and develop.

In the final analysis, curriculum workers must understand that they are continuously faced with curriculum decisions and that philosophy is important in determining these decisions. Indeed,

few school people scrutinize their curriculum with regard to the school's philosophy or mission statements. Often teachers and administrators plan and implement long reams of behavioral objectives with minimal regard to the overall philosophy of the school. Curriculum workers need to provide assistance in developing and designing school practices that coincide with the philosophy of the school and community. Teaching, learning, and curriculum are all interwoven in our school practices and should reflect a school philosophy. It is important, then, for school people, especially curricularists, to make decisions and take action in relation to the philosophy of their school and community.

ENDNOTES

1. William Van Til, "In a Climate of Change," in R. R. Leeper, ed., *Role of Supervisor and Curriculum Director in a Climate of Change* (Washington, D.C.: Association for Supervision and Curriculum Development, 1965), p. 18.

2. L. Thomas Hopkins, *Interaction: The Democratic Process* (Boston: D. C. Heath, 1941), pp. 198–200.

3. John I. Goodlad et al., *Curriculum Inquiry* (New York: McGraw-Hill, 1979).

4. Ronald C. Doll, *Curriculum Improvement: Decision Making and Process,* 8th ed. (Boston: Allyn and Bacon, 1992), p. 27.

5. John Dewey, *Democracy and Education* (New York: Macmillan, 1916), pp. 186, 383–384.

6. Ibid., p. 384.

7. Ralph W. Tyler, *Basic Principles of Curriculum and Instruction* (Chicago: University of Chicago Press, 1949), pp. 33–34.

8. John I. Goodlad, *What Schools Are For* (Bloomington, Ind.: Phi Delta Kappan Educational Foundation, 1979). See also Goodlad, *A Place Called School* (New York: McGraw-Hill, 1984).

9. J. Donald Butler, *Idealism in Education* (New York: Harper & Row, 1966).

10. Morris L. Bigge, *Educational Philosophies for Teachers* (Columbus, Ohio: Merrill, 1982); Howard Ozman and Sam Craver, *Philosophical Foundations of Education,* 3rd ed. (Columbus, Ohio: Merrill, 1986).

11. Harry S. Broudy, *Building a Philosophy of Education* (Englewood Cliffs, N.J.: Prentice Hall, 1961); John Wild, *Introduction to a Realist Philosophy* (New York: Harper & Row, 1948).

12. Broudy, *Building a Philosophy of Education;* William O. Martin, *Realism in Education* (New York: Harper & Row, 1969).

13. Ernest E. Bayles, *Pragmatism in Education* (New York: Harper & Row, 1966); John L. Childs, *Pragmatism and Education* (New York: Holt, Rinehart and Winston, 1956).

14. John Dewey, *Experience and Education* (New York: Macmillan, 1938).

15. Maxine Greene, *Existential Encounters for Teachers* (New York: Random House, 1967); George F. Kneller, *Existentialism in Education* (New York: Wiley, 1958); and Van Cleve Morris, *Existentialism and Education* (New York: Harper & Row, 1966).

16. Harold Soderquist, *The Person and Education* (Columbus, Ohio: Merrill, 1966); Donald Vandenberg, *Human Rights in Education* (New York: Philosophical Library, 1983). See also Israel Scheffler, *Of Human Potential: An Essay in the Philosophy of Education* (Boston: Routledge & Kegan Paul, 1986).

17. Maxine Greene, *Landscapes of Learning* (New York: Teachers College Press, Columbia University, 1978); Donald Vandenberg, "Human Dignity, Three Human Rights, and Pedagogy," *Educational Theory* (Winter 1986), pp. 33–44.

18. Robert M. Hutchins, *The Conflict in Education* (New York: Harper & Row, 1953), p. 68.

19. Bigge, *Educational Philosophies for Teachers*; Daniel Tanner and Laurel N. Tanner, *Curriculum Development: Theory into Practice* (New York: Macmillan, 1980).

20. Robert M. Hutchins, *The Higher Learning in America* (New Haven, Conn: Yale University Press, 1936).

21. Robert M. Hutchins, *A Conversation on Education* (Santa Barbara, Calif.: The Fund for the Republic, 1963), p. 1.

22. Mortimer J. Adler, *The Paideia Proposal: An Educational Manifesto* (New York: Macmillan, 1982); Adler, *Paideia Problems and Possibilities* (New York: Macmillan, 1983); and Adler, *The Paideia Program: An Educational Syllabus* (New York: Macmillan, 1984).

23. Allan Bloom, *The Closing of the American Mind* (New York: Simon & Schuster, 1987).

24. Allan Bloom, in Brad Miner, ed., *Good Order: Right Answers to Contemporary Questions* (New York: Simon & Schuster, 1995).

25. See William Bagley, "Just What Is the Crux and the Conflict between the Progressives and the Essentialists?" *Educational Administration and Supervision* (September 1940), pp. 508–511; Arthur Bestor, *Educational Wastelands* (Urbana, Ill.: University of Illinois Press, 1953); and Hyman Rickover, *Education and Freedom* (New York: E. P. Dutton, 1959).

26. See Daniel Tanner, "Curriculum History," in H. E. Mitzel, ed., *Encyclopedia of Educational Research,* 5th ed. (New York: Macmillan, 1982), pp. 412–420.

27. Hyman G. Rickover, "European vs. American Secondary Schools," *Phi Delta Kappan* (November 1958), p. 61.

28. Arthur Bestor, *The Restoration of Learning* (New York: Knopf, 1955), p. 120.

29. Rickover, "European vs. American Secondary Schools," p. 61.

30. Stanley M. Elam, "The Gallup Education Surveys," *Phi Delta Kappan* (September 1983), p. 26. See also Gallup polls published in the September or October issues of *Phi Delta Kappan,* 1984 to 1990.

31. *The Condition of Education 1989* (Washington, D.C., U.S. Government Printing Office, 1989), Table 1.30–1, p. 127; Allan C. Ornstein, "National Reform and Instructional Accountability," *High School Journal* (October–November 1990), pp. 51–56.

32. Gregory R. Anig, "Educational Standards, Testing, and Equity," *Phi Delta Kappan* (May 1985), pp. 623–625; David Hill, "What Has the 1980s Reform Movement Accomplished?" *Education Digest* (February 1990), pp. 3–6; and Daniel U. Levine and Allan C. Ornstein, "Research on Classroom and School Effectiveness," *Urban Review* (July 1989), pp. 81–95.

33. Kenneth H. Bacon, "Many Educators View Involved Parents as Key to Children's Success in School," *Wall Street Journal,* July 31, 1990, pp. 1B, 4B. Lynette Long and Thomas L. Long, "Latchkey Adolescents: How Administrators Can Respond to Their Needs," *NASSP Bulletin* (February 1989), pp. 102–108.

34. E. D. Hirsh, *Cultural Literacy: What Every American Needs to Know,* rev. ed. (Boston: Houghton Mifflin, 1987).

35. Larry Cuban, "Four Stories About National Goals for American Education," *Phi Delta Kappan* (December 1990), pp. 264–271; Bill Honig, "Target Areas for Reaching National Goals," *Education Digest* (October 1990), pp. 18–22; and Allan C. Ornstein, "The National Reform of Education," *NASSP Bulletin* (May 1992).

36. Howard Gardner, "National Education Goals and the Academic Community," *Education Digest* (February 1990), pp. 41–43; Elliot W. Eisner, "What Really Counts in School," *Educational Leadership* (February 1991), pp. 10–17.

37. Harold Howe II, "American 2000: A Bumpy Ride on Four Trains," *Phi Delta Kappan* (November 1991), pp. 192–203; David S. Seeley, "Carrying School Reform into the 1990s," *Future Choices* (Fall 1989), pp. 53–57; and Grant Wiggins, "Standards, Not Standardization, " *Educational Leadership* (February 1991). pp. 18–25.

38. R. Freeman Butts, *Public Education in the United States* (New York: Holt, Rinehart and Winston, 1978); Lawrence A. Cremin, *The Transformation of the School* (New York: Knopf, 1961).

39. John Dewey, *Democracy and Education* (New York: Macmillan, 1916).

40. John Dewey, "Need for a Philosophy of Education," *New Era in Home and School* (November 1934), p. 212.

41. John Dewey, *How We Think,* rev. ed. (Lexington, Mass.: D.C. Heath, 1933); William Kilpatrick, *Foundations of Method* (New York: Macmillan, 1925).

42. John Dewey, *The Child and the Curriculum* (Chicago: University of Chicago Press, 1902), pp. 30–31.

43. Boyd H. Bode, *Progressive Education at the Crossroads* (New York: Newson, 1938).

44. Ibid., p. 44.

45. Cremin, *The Transformation of the School*; Joel Spring, *The American School: 1642–1990* (New York: Longman, 1990).

46. Herbert Kohl, *The Open Classroom* (New York: Random House, 1969); Jonathan Kozol, *Free Schools* (Boston: Houghton Mifflin, 1972). See C. M. Bowers and David J. Flinders, *Responsive Teaching* (New York: Teachers College Press, Columbia University, 1990).

47. Charles A. Silberman, *Crisis in the Classroom* (New York: Random House, 1971).

48. Arthur T. Jersild, *In Search of Self* (New York: Teachers College Press, 1952); Jersild, *When Teachers Face Themselves* (New York: Teachers College Press, 1955); and Arthur Combs and Donald Snygg, *Individual Behavior,* 2nd ed. (New York: Harper & Row, 1959). See also Arthur Combs, ed., *Perceiving, Behavioring, Becoming* (Washington, D.C.: Association for Supervision and Curriculum Development, 1962); Combs, *A Personal Approach to Teaching* (Boston: Allyn and Bacon, 1982).

49. Abraham H. Maslow, *Toward a Psychology of Being* (New York: Van Nostrand Reinhold, 1962); Maslow, *Motivation and Personality,* 2nd ed. (New York: Harper & Row, 1970); Carl R. Rogers, *Client-Centered Therapy* (Boston: Houghton Mifflin, 1951); Rogers, *On Becoming a Person* (Boston: Houghton Mifflin, 1961); and, Rogers, *Freedom to Learn for the 1980s,* 2nd ed. (Columbus, Ohio: Merrill, 1983).

50. Michael W. Apple, "The Politics of Official Knowledge in the United States," *Journal of Curriculum Studies* (July–August 1990), pp. 377–383; Eisner, "What Really Counts in Schools"; and Herbert Kohl, "Toward Educational Change and Economic Justice," *Phi Delta Kappan* (May 1991), pp. 678–681.

51. Edgar Z. Friedenberg, *The Vanishing Adolescent* (Boston: Beacon Press, 1959), pp. 26, 91, 110. See also Edgar Z. Friedenberg, *Coming of Age in America* (New York: Random House, 1967); see also Peter McLaren, "Education as a Political Issue: What's Missing in the Public Conversation," in Joel L. Kincheloe and Shirley R. Steinberg, eds., *Thirteen Questions,* 2nd ed. (New York: Peter Lang, 1995), pp. 265–280.

52. John Holt, *How Children Fail* (New York: Pitman, 1964).

53. Paul Goodman, *Compulsory Mis-education* (New York: Horizon Press, 1964), pp. 20–22.

54. Paul Goodman, *New Reformation* (New York: Random House, 1970), p. 86.

55. A. S. Neill, *Summerhill: A Radical Approach to Child Rearing* (New York: Hart, 1960), p. 4.

56. Ibid., pp. 4, 14.

57. Ivan Illich, *Deschooling Society* (New York: Harper & Row, 1971).

58. Henry A. Giroux, "Educational Visions: What Are Schools for and What Should We Be Doing in the Name of Education?" in Joel L. Kincheloe and Shirley R. Steinberg, eds. *Thirteen Questions,* 2nd ed., pp. 295–303.

59. Ibid., p. 296.

60. Peter McLaren, "Critical Pedagogy and the Pragmatics of Justice," in Michael Peters, ed., *Education and the Postmodern Condition* (Westport, Conn: Bergin & Garvey, 1995), p. 91.

61. Ibid, p. 92.

62. Ibid., p. 92.

63. George S. Counts, *Dare the School Build a New Social Order?* (New York: Day, 1932), pp. 7–8. See also Robert R. Sherman, "Dare the School Build a New Social Order—Again?" *Educational Theory* (Winter 1986), pp. 87–92.

64. See John Dewey, *Reconstruction in Philosophy* (New York: Holt, 1920).

65. Theodore Brameld, *Ends and Means in Education* (New York: Harper & Row, 1950); Brameld, *Patterns of Educational Philosophy* (New York: World, 1950).

66. Theodore Brameld, "Reconstructionism as Radical Philosophy of Education," *Educational Forum* (November 1977), p. 70.

67. Mario D. Fantini, *Regaining Excellence in Education* (Columbus, Ohio: Merrill, 1986); Harold Shane, *Educating for a New Millennium* (Bloomington, Ind.: *Phi Delta Kappan,* 1981); and Alvin Toffler, *Previews and Premises* (New York: Morrow, 1983).

68. Ruud J. Garter, "International Collaboration in Curriculum Development," *Educational Leadership* (December–January 1987), pp. 4–7; David Hill, "Rediscovering Geography: It's Five Fundamental Themes," *NASSP Bulletin* (December 1989), pp. 1–7; and Jon Nixon, "Reclaiming Coherence: Cross-Curriculum Provision and the National Curriculum," *Journal of Curriculum Studies* (March–April 1991), pp. 187–192.

69. Kenneth B. Boulding, *The World as a Total System* (Beverly Hills, Calif.: Sage, 1985).

70. Elliot W. Eisner, "Curriculum Ideologies," in Philip W. Jackson, ed., *Handbook of Research on Curriculum* (New York: Macmillan Publishing Company, 1992), pp. 302–326.

71. Ibid.

72. Referenced in Patrick Slattery, *Curriculum Development in the Postmodern Era* (New York: Garland Publishing, Inc., 1995).

73. Maxine Greene, "Interpretation and Re-Vision: Toward Another Story," in J. T. Sears and J. D. Marshall, eds., *Teaching and Thinking About Curriculum* (New York: Teachers College Press, Columbia University, 1990), pp. 75–78; Greene, *Landscapes of Learning,* p. 163.

74. Paulo Freire, *Pedagogy of the Oppressed* (New York: Herder & Herder, 1970), pp. 75, 100, 108; *The Politics of Education: Culture, Power and Liberation* (Westport, Conn.: Bergin & Garvey, 1985).

75. William Pinar, "Sanity, Madness, and the School," in W. Pinar, ed., *Curriculum Theorizing: The Reconceptualists* (Berkeley, Calif.: McCutchan, 1974), pp. 364–366; 369–373, 381.

76. Michael W. Apple, *Ideology and Curriculum* (Boston: Routledge & Kegan Paul, 1979), p. 4. See also Apple, *Teachers and Texts* (Boston: Routledge & Kegan Paul, 1986).

77. Michael Apple and Nancy R. King, "What Do Schools Teach?" in R. H. Weller, ed., *Humanistic Education* (Berkeley, Calif.: McCutchan, 1977), p. 30.

78. Illich, *Deschooling Society.*

79. Paulo Freire and Donaldo Macedo, *Literacy: Reading the Word and the World* (Westport, Conn.: Bergin & Garvey, 1989); Freire, *Pedagogy of the Oppressed.*

80. Macdonald, "Curriculum and Human Interests," p. 293.

81. Horace Mann, *The Republic and the School,* rev. ed. (New York: Teachers College Press, Columbia University, 1957), p. 39.

82. David B. Tyack, *Turning Points in American Educational History* (Waltham, Mass.: Blaisdell, 1967), p. 114.

83. Henry M. Levin, "Equal Educational Opportunity and the Distribution of Educational Expenditures," in A. Kopan and H. J. Walberg, eds., *Rethinking Educational Equality* (Berkeley, Calif.: McCutchan, 1974), p. 30.

84. See James S. Coleman et al., *Equality of Educational Opportunity* (Washington, D.C.: U.S. Government Printing Office, 1966); Christopher Jencks et al., *Inequality: A Reassessment of the Effect of Family and Schools in America* (New York: Basic Books, 1972). Also see Kathleen Bennett and Margarett D. LeCompte, *How Schools Work: A Sociological Analysis of Education* (New York, Longman, 1990).

85. James S. Coleman, "The Concept of Equality of Educational Opportunity," *Harvard Educational Review* (Winter 1968), pp. 7–22.

86. Nathan Glazer, "The Affirmative Action Stalemate," *Public Interest* (Winter 1988), pp. 99–114; Also see Herman Belz, *Equality Transformed* (New Brunswick, N.J.: Transaction, 1992).

87. John W. Gardner, *Excellence: Can We Be Equal and Excellent Too?* (New York: Harper & Row, 1961), pp. 17–18, 83, 90

3

HISTORICAL FOUNDATIONS OF CURRICULUM

Focusing Questions

1. Why is it important to know the historical foundations of curriculum?
2. How were European educational ideas modified by American schools?
3. How did American democratic ideas contribute to the rise of public schooling in the United States?
4. In what ways did American nationalism during the first half of the nineteenth century influence the curriculum?
5. How did nineteenth-century European pioneers of pedagogy influence the American school curriculum?
6. What unique problems were evidenced in the nineteenth century as the elementary (secondary) school curriculum developed?
7. How did the Committee of Fifteen and Committee of Ten influence curriculum for the twentieth century?
8. How did scientism in education influence curriculum making?
9. What roles can historians of curriculum play within the field of curriculum?
10. What value do you give to having a historical sense of curriculum?

All human activities, including those that take place within the field of curriculum, occur within time, within context. Although few people would challenge this statement, many scholars, and especially practitioners in the field of curriculum, either do not remember the historical foundations of curricular activity or do not think such knowledge essential. Perhaps a few feel that looking at history is looking backward. Curricular activities are engaged to actualize future possibilities.

Increasing numbers within the curriculum field recognize that we do, in fact, need a historical sense regarding our field. Curriculum is not an old field. A majority of scholars would place its birth in 1918 with the publication of Franklin

Bobbitt's book *The Curriculum.* Certainly, curriculum became a focus of scholarship with that publication. However, curriculum has always been a concern, even if we did not specify the concept curriculum. Today, curriculum history is a well-respected field of scholarship. This scholarly focus will add to our understanding of curriculum, both past and present. The historical foundations of curriculum are melded into the history of American education and, for this reason, we will present a review of this history.

By analyzing the history of American education and therefore the history of curriculum, we can view curriculum primarily in terms of evolving subject matter or content and the dominant philosophy of perennialism. However, it may be more productive for our understanding of the field, both past and present, to think of curriculum as less concerned with epistemological questions and more with a sociology of knowledge. During the first 200 years (or more) of curriculum, educators were increasingly concerned with the social and economic significance of the school content to be taught.[1] This sociology of knowledge became firmly established with the rise of progressivism, which followed the early period of behaviorism and scientism in education.

In considering the historical foundations of curriculum, we might think that a clear view of curriculum history will be achieved. However, as we engage in historical analyses, we will find that we gain a multiplicity of views and a realization of and an appreciation for the complexity of interpretations. In studying this foundation of curriculum, we will come to appreciate that it is under constant revision. New knowledge of the foundation requires such action.[2] One thing that is certain, however, is the significance of context. Curricula are created by real people within temporal, political, social, economic, and cultural contexts. These people act out of beliefs in appropriate social action, views of knowledge, acceptance of political ideologies, allegiances to class value systems, incorporation of economic motives, and even adherence to religious convictions. As we shall see, deciding on what curriculum to teach has always been contested.[3]

We begin our discussion with the colonial period and proceed through the eighteenth, nineteenth, and twentieth centuries. Most of our discussion focuses on the last 100 years. In the interest of brevity, we examine only the broad sweep of curriculum and how the curriculum evolved.

THE COLONIAL PERIOD: 1642–1776

The historical foundations of curriculum are largely rooted in the educational experiences of colonial Massachusetts. Massachusetts was settled mainly by Puritans who adhered to strict principles of theology. Unlike contemporary schools, the first schools in New England were closely related to the Puritan church. The major purpose of school, according to educational historians, was to

teach children to read the Scriptures and notices of civil affairs.[4]

Reading, therefore, was the most important subject, followed by writing and spelling, for purposes of understanding the catechism and common law. Since colonial days, then, reading and related language skills have been basic to American education and basic to the elementary school curriculum.

Three Colonial Regions

Colonial schools established in Massachusetts were derived from two sources: legislation of 1642, which required parents and guardians of children to make certain that their charges could read and understand the principles of religion and the laws of the Commonwealth; and the "Old Deluder Satan" Act of 1647, which required every town of fifty or more families to appoint a reading and writing teacher. Towns of 100 or more families were to employ a teacher of Latin so that students could be prepared for entry to Harvard College.[5] The other New England colonies, except Rhode Island, followed the Massachusetts example.

These early laws reveal how important education was to the Puritan settlers. Some historians have regarded these laws as the roots of American school law and the public school movement. It is obvious that the Puritans did not want an illiterate class to grow in colonial America. They feared that such a class might comprise a group of dependent poor, an underclass, which would be reminiscent of that in England and other parts of Europe, and which they wanted to avoid. They also wanted to ensure that their children would grow up being committed to the religious doctrines.

In the middle colonies, unlike New England, no common language or religion existed. Writes George Beauchamp, "Competition among political and religious groups retarded willingness to expend the public funds for educational purposes."[6] No single system of schools could be established. What evolved instead were parochial and independent schools, related to different ethnic and religious groups, and the idea of community or local control of schools (as opposed to New England's concept of central or district-wide schools). The current notion of cultural pluralism thus took shape and form some 200 years ago.

Until the end of the eighteenth century educational decisions in the Southern colonies were generally left to the family. Legislative action was taken, however, in behalf of poor children, orphans and illegitimate children—to ensure that their guardians provided private educational or vocational skills. Nevertheless, the plantation system of landholding, slavery, and gentry created a small privileged class of white children (children of plantation owners) who had the benefit of private tutors. For most poor whites who tilled the soil, formal education was nonexistent. Unable to read and write, many of them grew up to be subsistence farmers like their parents before them. Black slaves' children were forbidden to learn to read or write and were relegated as the underclass of the plantation system. In short, the economic and political system of the early South "tended to retard the development of a large-scale system of schools. This education [handicap] was felt long after the Civil War period."[7]

Despite the regional variations between the schools of New England, the middle Atlantic colonies, and the South, all three areas were influenced by English political ideas. And, despite differences in language, religion, and economic systems, religious commitment had a high priority throughout all schools and society; the family, too, played a major role in the socialization and education of all children. What was later to become the three Rs evolved from these schools as well.

"The curriculum of the colonial schools consisted of reading, writing, and [some] arithmetic along with the rudiments of religious faith and lessons designed to develop manners and morals."[8] It was a traditional curriculum, stressing basic-skill acquisition, timeless and absolute values, social and religious conformity, faith in authority, knowledge for the sake of knowledge, rote learning, and memorization. It was based on the notion of child depravity (children were born in sin, play was idleness, and child's talk gibberish), and thus the teacher needed to apply constant discipline. This approach to the curriculum dominated American education until the rise of progressivism.

Colonial Schools

The schools were important institutions for colonial society, as they are for today's. One difference is that a smaller percentage of the school-aged children attended elementary school on a regular basis compared to today, and a much smaller percentage of youth attended secondary school, much less graduated.

The Town School. In the New England colonies, the town school was a locally controlled and popular elementary school. Often it was a crude, one-room structure, dominated by the teacher's pulpit at the front of the room and attended by both boys and girls of the community. Students sat on benches and studied their assignments until called on to recite by the schoolmaster. The children ranged in age from 5 or 6 to 13 and 14. Attendance was not always regular; it depended on weather conditions and on individual families' needs for their children to work on their farms.[9]

Parochial and Private Schools. In the middle colonies, parochial schools and private schools predominated; the elementary schools were established by missionary societies and various religious and ethnic groups to educate their own children. Like the New England town schools, these schools focused on reading and writing and religious sermons. In the South, upper-class children attended private schools oriented to reading, writing, arithmetic, and studying the primer and Bible; less fortunate children attended charity schools (if they were lucky) to be trained in the three Rs, to recite religious hymns (which was less demanding than reading the Bible), and to learn vocational skills.

Latin Grammar Schools. At the secondary level, the sons of the upper class attended Latin grammar schools, first established in Boston in 1635, to be prepared for entry into college. These schools catered to those who planned to enter the professions (medicine, law, teaching, and the ministry) or to spend their lives as business owners or merchants.[10]

A boy would enter a Latin grammar school at the age of 8 or 9 and remain for eight years. His curriculum consisted of studying the classics. "There were some courses in Greek, rhetoric . . . and logic, but Latin was apparently three-quarters of the curriculum in most of the grammar schools, or more. . . ."[11] Little or no attention was given to the other arts and sciences. "The religious atmosphere was quite as evident . . . as it was in the elementary school" with the "master praying regularly with his pupils" and quizzing them "thoroughly on the sermons. . . ."[12] The regimen of study was exhausting and unexciting, and the school's role that of handmaiden of the church. As Samuel Morrison reminds us, the Latin grammar school was one of colonial America's closest links to European schools, and its curriculum resembled the classical humanist curriculum of the Renaissance (when schools were primarily intended for children of the upper classes and their role was to support the religious and social institutions of that era).[13]

The Academy.   The academy, established in 1751, was the second American institution to provide education at the secondary level. Based on the ideas of Benjamin Franklin, and intended to offer a practical curriculum for those not going to college, it had a diversified curriculum of English grammar, classics, composition, rhetoric, and public speaking.[14] Latin was no longer considered a crucial subject. Students could choose a foreign language based on their vocational needs—for example, a prospective clergyman could study Latin or Greek, and a future businessman could learn French, German, or Spanish. Mathematics was to be taught for its practical application to a job rather than as an abstract intellectual exercise. History was the chief ethical study, not religion. The academy also introduced many practical and manual skills into the formal curriculum; these formed the basis of vocational curriculum in the twentieth century: carpentry, engraving, printing, painting, cabinet making, farming, bookkeeping, and so on.

College.   Most students went to Harvard or Yale after they graduated from Latin grammar schools. College was based on the Puritan conception that those called to the ministry needed to be soundly educated in the classics and scriptures. The students had to demonstrate their competency in Latin and Greek and the classics.

Latin grammar schools prepared students for Harvard or Yale college—much like high school academic programs prepare students for college today. The current relationship between the course offerings of secondary school and college admission requirements was, in fact, set in motion more than 200 years ago. Writes Ellwood Cubberley, "The student would be admitted into college 'upon Examination' whereby he could show competency 'to Read, Construe, Parce Tully, Vergil and the Greek Testament; and to write Latin in Prose and to understand the Rules of Prosodia and Common Arithmetic' as well as to bring 'testimony of his blameless and inoffensive life.' "[15]

The Harvard/Yale curriculum consisted of courses in Latin, grammar, logic, rhetoric, arithmetic, astronomy, ethics, metaphysics, and natural sciences. The curriculum for the ministry or other professions also included Greek, Hebrew, and ancient history.

Old Textbooks, Old Readers

Because the hornbook, primer, Psalter, Testament, and Bible were considered textbooks, they were widely read (depending on the reading ability of the students). By and large, most elementary textbooks, until the time of the American Revolution, were of English origin or were direct imitations of English texts.[16] Children learned the alphabet, Lord's Prayer, some syllables, words, and sentences by memorizing the *hornbook*—a paddle-shaped board to which was attached a single sheet of parchment covered by a transparent sheath made by flattening cattle horns.

When the *New England Primer* was published in the last decade of the seventeenth century, it replaced the English primer. It was not only the first American basal reader, it was also the most widely used textbook in the colonies for over 100 years; more than 3 million copies were sold. The *New England Primer* was permeated with religious and moral doctrines. The somber caste of the Puritan religion and morals was evident as students memorized sermons and learned their ABCs through rote and drill:

A—In Adam's Fall
   We sinned all
B—Thy Life to mend
   This book attend
C—The Cat doth play
   And after slay . . .
Z—Zacheus he
   Did climb the tree
   His Lord to see.[17]

In 1740 Thomas Dilworth published a *New Guide to the English Tongue,* which contained a mixture of grammar, spelling, and religious material. It was followed a few years later by the *School Master's Assistant,* a widely used mathematics text.

The narrowness of the elementary curriculum and the limited use of textbooks were illustrated by Noah Webster, an ardent cultural nationalist, years later in a letter to Henry Barnard, then Commissioner of Education of Connecticut:

> before the Revolution . . . the books used were chiefly or wholly Dilworth's Spelling Books, the Psalter, Testament, and Bible. No geography was studied before the publication of Dr. Morse's small books on that subject, about the year 1786 or 1787. No history was read, as far as my knowledge extends, for there was no abridged history of the United States. Except the books above mentioned, no book for reading was used before the publication of the Third Part of my Institute, in 1785. . . . The Introduction of my Spelling Book, first published in 1783, produced a great change in the department of spelling. . . . No English grammar was generally taught in common schools when I was young, except that in Dilworth, and that to no good purpose.[18]

THE NATIONAL PERIOD: 1776–1850

A new mission for education, which began to emerge during the Revolutionary period, continued through the early national period. Many leaders began to link free public schooling with the ideas of popular government and political freedom. Wrote President Madison, "A popular government without popular information, or the means of acquiring it, is but a prologue to a farce or a tragedy or perhaps both." Jefferson expressed a similar belief when he asserted: "If a nation expects to be ignorant and free in a state of civilization, it expects what never was and never will be."

The emphasis on life, liberty, and equality was highlighted in the great documents of the era: the Declaration of Independence, the Bill of Rights, and the Northwest Ordinances. In 1785 these ordinances divided the Northwest Territory into townships and reserved the sixteenth section of "every township for the maintenance of public schools." In 1787, they reaffirmed that "schools and the means of education shall forever be encouraged" by the states. The federal government thus recognized its commitment to education and exhibited its willingness to advance its cause, while assuring the autonomy of state and local schools, guaranteed by the U.S. Constitution. As a result of these Ordinances, thirty-nine states received over 154 million acres of land for schools from the federal government.[19]

By the turn of the nineteenth century, secular forces had developed sufficiently to challenge and ultimately cause the decline of religious influence over elementary and secondary schools. Among these secular forces were the development of democracy, the development of a strong federal government, an emerging cultural nationalism, the idea of religious freedom, and new discoveries in natural sciences.

Rush: Science, Progress, and Free Education

Dr. Benjamin Rush (1745–1813) represented this new era. In 1791, he wrote that the emphasis on the classics led to the prejudice the masses felt for institutions of learning. As long as Latin and Greek dominated the curriculum, universal education beyond the rudiments was wishful thinking. In a new country, in which the chief task was to explore and develop natural resources, as well as to promote democracy, education should be functional to these concerns. "Under these circumstances, to spend four or five years in learning two dead languages, is to turn our backs upon a gold mine, in order to amuse ourselves catching butterflies." If the time spent on Latin and Greek were devoted to science, continued this champion pragmatist, "the human condition would be much improved."[20]

Rush went on to outline a plan of education for Pennsylvania and the new Republic: free elementary schools in every township consisting of 100 families or more, a free academy at the county level, and free colleges and universities at the state level for the future leaders of society. The public would pay for the expenses, but, in the end, Rush argued, the educational system would reduce our taxes because a productive and well-managed workforce and entrepreneur force would result. (It was the same argument among other points that Horace Mann was to make 30 years later when he spearheaded the common school movement.) Rush's curriculum emphasized reading, writing, and arithmetic at the elementary school level; English, German, the arts, and especially the sciences at the secondary and college level; and good manners and moral principles from the beginning to the end of the educational sequence.

Jefferson: Education for Citizenship

Faith in the agrarian society and distrust toward the proletariat of the cities were basic in Thomas Jefferson's (1743–1826) idea of democracy. A man of wide-ranging interests that embraced politics, agriculture, science, and education, Jefferson assumed the state had the responsibility to cultivate an educated and liberated citizenry to ensure a democratic society. In "A Bill for the More General Diffusion of Knowledge," introduced in the Virginia legislature in 1779, Jefferson advocated a plan that provided educational opportunities for both common people and landed gentry "at the expense of all."[21] To Jefferson, formal education was largely a state or civic concern, rather than a matter reserved to religious or upper-class groups. Schools should be financed through public taxes.

Jefferson's plan subdivided the counties of Virginia into wards, each of which would have a free elementary school to teach reading, writing, arithmetic, and history. His proposal also provided for the establishment of twenty grammar schools at the secondary level, for which gifted students who could not afford to pay tuition would be provided scholarships. There, the students would study Latin, Greek, English, geography, and higher mathematics. Upon completing grammar school, half the scholarship students would be assigned positions as elementary or ward school teachers. The ten scholarship students of highest achievement would attend William and Mary College. Jefferson's plan promoted the idea of school as a selective agency to identify bright students for

continuing education, as well as the traditional idea of equality of opportunity for economically less fortunate students.

Neither Jefferson's proposal for Virginia nor Rush's proposal for Pennsylvania was enacted. Nonetheless, the bills indicate the type of educational theorizing characteristic of the young nation. Coupled with Franklin's academy, and its practical curriculum based on business and commercial principles of education rather than classical and religious principles, these bills demonstrated the purpose of education to be to promote good citizenship, social progress, and utilitarianism. The classical curriculum and religious influence were, in effect, beginning to decline. Rush and Jefferson (and to a lesser extent Franklin) were all concerned with equality of educational opportunity—that is, they proposed universal education for the masses of children and youth, and methods for identifying students of superior ability, who were to receive free secondary and college educations at public expense.

Webster: Schoolmaster and Cultural Nationalism

The United States differed from most new countries struggling for identity in that it lacked a shared cultural identity and national literature. In its struggle against the "older" cultures and "older" ideas, the new nation went to great lengths to differentiate itself from England.[22] Noah Webster (1758–1843) called passionately upon his fellow Americans to "unshackle [their] minds and act like independent beings. You have been children long enough, subject to the control and subservient to the interests of a haughty parent. . . . You have an empire to raise . . . and a national character to establish and extend by your wisdom and judgment."[23]

In 1789, when the Constitution went into effect as the law of the land, Webster argued that the United States should have its own system of "language as well as government." The language of Great Britain, he reasoned, "should no longer be our standard; for the taste of her writers is already completed, and her language on the decline."[24] By the act of revolution, the American people had declared their political independence from England, and now they needed to declare their cultural independence as well.

Realizing that a sense of national identity was conveyed through a distinctive national language and literature, Webster set out to reshape the English language used in the United States. He believed that a uniquely American language would (1) eliminate the remains of European usage, (2) create a uniform American speech that would be free of localism and provincialism, and (3) promote self-conscious American cultural nationalism.[25] The creation of an American language would become the linguistic mortar of national union; it would, however, have to be phonetically simple to render it more suitable to the common people.

Webster directly related the learning of language to organized education. As they learned the American language, children also would learn to think and act as Americans. The American language that Webster proposed would have to be taught deliberately and systematically to the young in the nation's schools. Because the curriculum of these Americanized schools would be shaped by the books that the students read, Webster spent much of his life writing spelling and reading books. His *Grammatical Institute of the English Language* was published in 1783. The first part of the *Institute* was later printed as *The American Spelling Book,* which was widely used throughout the United States in the first half of the nineteenth century.[26] Webster's *Spelling Book* went through many editions; it is estimated that 15 million copies had been sold by 1837. Webster's great work was *The American Dictionary,* which was completed in 1825 after twenty-five years of laborious research.[27] Often termed the "schoolmaster of the Republic," Noah Webster was an educational statesman of the early national period whose work helped to create a sense of American language, identity, and nationality.

McGuffey: The Reader and American Virtues

William Holmes McGuffey (1800–1873), who taught most of his life in Ohio colleges, also entered the debate on American cultural nationalism. The author of America's most popular textbooks of the period, called the *Readers,* McGuffey acknowledged with respect and gratitude America's "obligations to Europe and the descendants of the English stock" in science, art,

law, literature, and manners. America had made its own contributions to humankind, however; they "were not literary or cultural, but moral and political." The seeds of popular liberty "first germinated from our English ancestors, but it shot up to its fullest heights in our land."[28] America had furnished to Europe proof that "popular institutions, founded on equality and the principle of representation, are capable of maintaining governments," that it was practical to elevate the masses, what Europe called the laboring and lower class, "to the great right and great duty of self-government."[29] Thus, McGuffey balanced the cultural indebtedness of the country with its political and social promise, the full realization of liberalism and traditions of the American common folk.

It is estimated that over 120 million copies of McGuffey's five *Readers* were sold between 1836 and 1920.[30] What McGuffey did was to combine the virtues of the Protestant faith with those of rural America—patriotism, heroism, hard work, diligence, and virtuous living. The tone was moral, religious, capitalistic, and pro-American; the selections of American literature included orations by George Washington, Patrick Henry, Benjamin Franklin, and Daniel Webster. Through his *Readers,* McGuffey taught several generations of Americans. He also provided the first graded *Readers* for our schools and paved the way for a graded system, which had its beginnings in 1840. So popular were his *Readers,* and so vivid and timeless his patriotism and faith in American institutions—home, work, church, and nationhood—that many of his *Readers* (also his *Pictorial Primer*) have been reintroduced today in some rural, conservative, and/or fundamentalist schools. See Curriculum Tips 3-1.

NINETEENTH-CENTURY EUROPEAN EDUCATORS

Even though much criticism was leveled against European thought, American education was greatly influenced by it. At the college level, German educators influenced the fields of natural science, psychology, and sociology; many of our research-oriented universities were based on the German model. At the public school level, K–12, German (and Swiss) thought introduced romantic and pro-

---

Curriculum Tips 3-1

The Need for Historical Perspective

All professional educators, including curriculum specialists, need a historical perspective to integrate the past with the present. Not only does an understanding of history help us not repeat the mistakes of the past, but it also better prepares us for the present, both in terms of the abstract and real world.

There are many other reasons to have an understanding of history and the history of education:

1. The development of ideas in education is part of our intellectual and cultural heritage.
2. Our notion of an educated person (or professionally literate person) is too narrow and technical; we need to expand the idea that an educated person (or professional person) is one who is steeped in an understanding in the humanities and social sciences, which stems from history.
3. A discussion of various theories and practices in education requires an understanding of historical (as well as philosophical, psychological, and social) foundations.
4. An understanding of historical foundations in education helps us integrate curriculum, instruction, and teaching.
5. History can be studied for the purpose of understanding current pedagogical practices.
6. In developing a common or core curriculum, a historical perspective is essential.
7. With a historical perspective, curriculum specialists can better understand the relationship between content and process in subject areas.
8. Through the use of history, especially case examples, we have more opportunity to add a moral dimension to our academic education.
9. The history of education permits practitioners to understand relationships between what students have learned (past) and what they are learning (in the present).
10. The study of education history is important for its own theoretical and research purposes.

---

gressive ideas—and a curriculum and instructional method that were psychologically oriented and considered the needs and interests of the students. The English also affected American education by providing models of schooling that ranged from efficient to romantic.

However strongly American patriots may have desired a distinctive cultural life, they could not, as men and women of common sense and learning, turn their backs on the wealth and wisdom of European ideas. Moreover, the rising current of educational thought in the Old World was not all steeped in old-fashioned and classical ideas, because progressive and scientific principles were beginning to evolve.

The theme of reform characterized much of the educational discussions of the time. The limitations of the "traditional curriculum and typical school of this era were recognized by educational

leaders in Europe and America, and many of the features that were now firmly established in [curriculum] theory and practice can be traced to the ideas of the men and women who were ahead of their time."[31] The traditional curriculum, which emphasized Latin, Greek, and the classics, was de-emphasized. New pedagogical practices were developed that ran contrary to the methods of rote learning, memorization, and corporal punishment.

Pestalozzi: General and Special Methods

During the early American period of education, educational reformers were influenced by Johann Heinrich Pestalozzi (1746–1827), a Swiss educator. According to one educational historian, "Pestalozzi, probably more than any other educational reformer, laid the basis for the modern elementary school and helped to reform elementary-school practice."[32] Pestalozzi maintained that the educational process should be based on the natural development of the child and his or her sensory influences—similar thinking to that of current progressives and environmentalists. Pestalozzi's basic pedagogical innovation was his insistence that children learn through the senses rather than with words. He labeled rote learning as mindless, and he emphasized instead linking the curriculum to children's experiences in their homes and family lives.

Education, according to Pestalozzi, was to develop by considering the "general" method and "special" method. The general method called for educators, who were loving persons, to provide emotional security, trust, and affection for the children. The special method considered the auditory and visual senses of the children in the teaching process. To this end, Pestalozzi devised the "object" lesson, in which children studied common objects that they saw and experienced in their daily environments—plants, rocks, artifacts, and so on. The object lesson enhanced three types of learning—form, number, and sound. Children would first determine the form of the object, then draw it, then name it. From the lessons in form, number, and sound came more formal instruction in the three Rs.

Pestalozzi's ideas had great impact on early nineteenth-century American education. William McClure and Joseph Neef, and later Horace Mann and Henry Barnard, when the latter was U.S. Commissioner of Education, all worked to introduce his ideas into American schools.[33] His basic concepts of education became part of progressive schooling and later appeared in the move for curriculum relevancy and humanistic curriculum.

Froebel: The Kindergarten Movement

Friedrich Froebel (1782–1852), a German educator, is known for his development of the kindergarten, what he called the "child's garden." Froebel formulated his educational principles around 3- and 4-year-old children; he believed that their schooling should be organized around play and individual and group interests and activities. This suggested a less formal and lock-step curriculum—one based on love, trust, and freedom, as well as the child's self-development.

Froebel's kindergarten was a prepared environment in which learning was based on the children's self-activities and self-development and on the children's trust and affection along the lines of Pestalozzi. Songs, stories, colorful materials, and games—what classical curriculum advocates would criticize as wasteful—were part of the formal curriculum. The children could manipulate objects (spheres, cubes, and circles), shape and construct materials (clay, sand, cardboard), and engage in playful activities (build castles and mountains, run and exercise).[34] Together these activities were to comprise the learning environment and provide a secure and pleasant place where children could grow naturally.

The kindergarten concept was brought to America by German immigrants, and the first American kindergarten was established in Watertown, Wisconsin, in 1855 by Margaret Schurz. William Harris, Superintendent of Schools in St. Louis, Missouri, and later U.S. Commissioner of Education, was instrumental in implementing the idea on a broader scale. The kindergarten is now an established part of American education, and many of Froebel's ideas of childhood experiences and methods of play are incorporated into current theories of early childhood education and progressive schooling.

Herbart: Moral and Intellectual Development

A famous German philosopher, Johann Freidrich Herbart (1776–1841), maintained that the chief aim of education was moral education, and that the traditional curriculum was too rigid and limited for this purpose. The need was to expand curriculum offerings and educate the good person who had diversified interests and a balanced perspective on life. Herbart specified two major bodies of subject matter: knowledge interests and ethical interests. Knowledge interests involved empirical data, factual data, and theoretical ideas; ethical interests involved personal convictions, benevolence, and regard for the social welfare of others, justice, and equity. Herbart wanted history, English, mathematics, and science integrated into all stages and grade levels of the curriculum. He also introduced the idea of *correlation* of all subjects to integrate the curriculum, an idea that influenced curriculum specialists who favored a core curriculum in the 1940s and 1950s.

Herbart was influential in integrating the techniques of instruction with learning, whereby the teacher would address the needs and interests of the students. It was a psychological process and involved the following:

1. *Preparation:* The teacher considers previous learning experiences and stimulates readiness of the learner.
2. *Presentation:* The new lesson is introduced.
3. *Association:* The new lesson is related to ideas or materials previously studied.
4. *Systemization:* Rules, principles, or generalizations of the new ideas are mastered by the learner.
5. *Application:* The new lesson is given meaning by testing and applying the new ideas to pertinent problems or activities.[35]

Speaking of Herbart's contribution to the instruction of teaching, John Dewey said: "Few attempts have been made to formulate a method, resting on general principles, of conducting a recitation. One of these is of great importance, and has probably had more influence upon the learning of lessons than all others put together; namely, the analysis by Herbart of a recitation into five successive steps."[36]

Herbart's formal steps of instruction were not only adopted by classroom teachers, they were applied to teacher training as well. In theory, teachers were asked to prepare their lessons by thinking of five steps and asking: What do my students know? What questions should I ask? What events should I relate? What conclusions should be reached? How can students apply what they have learned? To a large extent, these instructional principles influenced the teaching-learning principles Dewey expressed in *How We Think;* they still serve as guidelines for teachers who use the developmental lesson approach.

Spencer: Utilitarian and Scientific Education

Herbert Spencer (1820–1903) was an English social scientist who based his ideas of education on Charles Darwin's theories of biological evolution and survival of the fittest. Spencer maintained that social development takes place according to the evolutionary process by which simple societies had evolved to more complex social systems, characterized by an increased variety of specialized professions and occupations.[37] Because of the laws of nature, only intelligent and productive populations would adapt to environmental changes. Less intelligent, weak, or lazy people would slowly disappear. The doctrine had immense implications for education based on excellence, the notion of social-economic progress, and the idea of intellectual development based on heredity.

Spencer also criticized religious doctrines and classical subject matter in education as nonscientific and unrelated to contemporary society. Rather, he advocated a curriculum fit for industrialized society—one that was scientific and practical (utilitarian). He believed that traditional schools were impractical and ornamental, a luxury for the upper class that failed to meet the needs of the people living in modern society.

For Spencer, the major purpose of education was to "prepare for complete living." Curriculum needed to be arranged according to this purpose. Spencer constructed a curriculum by prioritizing human activities so as to advance human survival and progress. His curriculum included the following activities, in order of importance: activities that (1) sustain life, (2) enhance life, (3) aid in rearing children, (4) maintain one's social and political relations, and (5) enhance leisure, tasks, and feelings.[38]

In his famous essay, "What Knowledge Is Most Worth?," Spencer argued that science was the most practical subject for the survival of the individual and society, yet it occupied minimal space in the curriculum because impractical and ornamental traditions prevailed. Spencer also maintained that students should be taught how to think (or problem solve) and not what to think.[39]

Although many of Spencer's ideas about religion, evolution, and social progress created a furor—and they still do among religious and political observers today—the ideas fitted well with those of thinkers in the second half of the nineteenth century, which was characterized by industrial growth, colonial expansion, and manifest destiny among European countries and the United States. Spencer's notion of discovery learning also influenced twentieth-century curricularists, both Deweyite progressive educators and later academic disciplinary educators.

THE RISE OF UNIVERSAL EDUCATION: 1820–1920

During the early nineteenth century America expanded westward. Life on the new frontier deepened America's faith in the common or average person, who built the new nation. Equality and rugged individualism were important concepts, expressed in the Declaration of Independence and reaffirmed by Westerners, who believed that all people were important and that in order to survive each had a job to do—despite different backgrounds. The common person, whether educated or not, was elected to various political offices; faith abounded in the capacity of humans to improve their lives. This kind of faith in the common people and in American civilization underscored to the frontier people the necessity of school.[40]

In the cities of the East, especially among the immigrant populations, there was also faith in the common person, in social mobility, and in the American dream of life, liberty, and equality. The upper class may not have had the same faith; nonetheless, the traditional argument (since Franklin, Rush, and Jefferson)—that mass education was necessary for intelligent participation in political democracy and that it must extend beyond the common school to high schools and colleges—helped convert the American populace to supporting free schooling.

Monitorial Schools

The monitorial school was a European invention, based on Joseph Lancaster's model of education. It spread quickly to the large American urban centers, where the immigrant population was increasing, and to the frontier, where there was need for a system of schools. Its attraction, in the 1820s and the following decades, was its economy and efficiency: Bright student monitors served as instructors. The teacher taught the lesson to the monitors (high-achieving students) and they in turn presented the materials to their classmates—what some observers today might call "cooperative

learning." The instruction was highly structured, and it was based on rote learning and drilling the three Rs.

Proponents of such teaching stressed that besides its economy, it kept potentially idle students busy while the teacher was occupied with other students. The class was divided into smaller groups, with a monitor in charge of each group. The students were kept actively involved in practice and drill activities and moved along at their own pace. Teachers were freed from some of their instructional chores and permitted to adopt new instructional roles—but mostly as inspectors and supervisors. The monitorial system was thus also considered "efficient" education.[41]

The monitorial system deemphasized classical education for the three Rs and religious theory for moral doctrines and citizenship, demonstrated the need for and possibility of systematic instruction, acquainted many people with formal education, and made educational opportunities more widely available. Most important, it promoted mass education and tax-supported elementary schools.[42] At the peak of its popularity, in the 1840s, it was organized in some high schools and suggested for the colleges.

But the monitorial system was considered too mechanical, and it was criticized for using students who knew little to teach those who knew even less. By the middle of the nineteenth century, its popularity waned.

Common Schools

The common school was established in 1826 in Massachusetts, when the state passed a law requiring every town to choose a school board to be responsible for all the schools in the local area. Eleven years later, the Massachusetts legislature created the first state board of education, and Massachusetts organized the public common schools under a single authority. Connecticut quickly followed the example of its neighbor.[43] These common schools were devoted to elementary education with emphasis on the three Rs. The movement was spearheaded by Horace Mann and rooted in the ideas of progressive thought.

As a member of the Massachusetts legislature and later as the first Massachusetts Commissioner of Education, Horace Mann skillfully rallied public support for the common school by appealing to various segments of the population. To enlist the business community, Mann sought to demonstrate that "education has a market value" with a yield similar to "common bullion." The "aim of industry . . . and wealth of the country" would be augmented "in proportion to the diffusion of knowledge."[44] Workers would be more diligent and more productive. Mann also established a stewardship theory, aimed at the upper class, that the public good would be enhanced by public education. Schools for all children would create a stable society in which people would obey the laws and add to the nation's political and economic well-being. To the workers and farmers, Mann asserted that the common school would be a great equalizer, a means of social mobility for their children. To the Protestant community, he argued that the common school would assimilate ethnic and religious groups, promote a common culture, and help immigrant children learn English and the customs and laws of the land.[45] He was convinced that the common school was crucial for the American system of equality and opportunity, for a sense of community to be shared by all Americans, and for the promotion of a national identity.

Although the pattern for establishing common schools varied among the states, and the quality of education varied as well, the foundation of the American public school was being forged through this system. The schools were common in the sense that they housed youngsters of all socioeconomic and religious backgrounds, from age 6 to 14 or 15, and were jointly owned, cared for, and used by the local community. Because a variety of subjects was taught to children of all ages, teachers had to plan as many as ten to twenty different lessons a day.[46] Teachers also had to try to keep their schoolrooms warm in the winter—a responsibility shared by the older boys, who cut and fetched wood—and cool in the summer. Schoolhouses were often in need of considerable repair, and teachers were paid miserably low salaries.

In New England, the state legislatures encouraged the establishment of school districts and elected school boards and state laws to govern the schools. But it was on the frontier where the common school flourished, where there was faith in the common person and a common destiny. The common one-room schoolhouse "eventually led to one of America's most lasting, sentimentalized pictures—the 'Little Red Schoolhouse' . . . in almost every community." It had problems and critics, but it symbolized the pioneers' spirit and desire to provide free education for their children. "It was a manifestation of the belief held by most of the frontier leaders that a school was necessary to raise the level of American civilization."[47]

This small school, meager in outlook and thwarted by inadequate funding and insufficient teachers, nevertheless fit with the conditions of the American frontier—of expansion and equality. It was a "blab school," according to Abe Lincoln, but it was the kind of school in which the common person's children—even those born in log cabins—could begin their "readin," "writin," and "cipherin,"[48] and could advance to limitless achievements. It was a school local citizens could use as a polling place, a center for Grange activities, a site for dances, and a location for community activities; it was a school controlled and supported by the local community.

The traditions built around the common school—the idea of neighborhood schools, local control of schools, and government support of schools—took a firm hold on the hearts and minds of Americans. America's confidence in the common school helped fashion the public schools later in the nineteenth century; it also influenced our present system of universal education.

The Elementary School Curriculum Evolves. There was no agreement on an appropriate or common curriculum for the elementary school. The trend, throughout the nineteenth century, was to add courses to the essential or basic subjects of reading, spelling, grammar, and arithmetic. Religious doctrine changed to "manners" and "moral" instruction by 1825; the subject matter of textbooks was heavily moralistic (one reason for the popularity of McGuffey), and teachers provided extensive training in character building. By 1875 lessons in morality were replaced by courses in "conduct," which remained part of the twentieth-century curriculum. The traditional emphasis on curriculum was slowly altered, as more and more subjects were added—including geography and history by 1850; science, art (or drawing), and physical education by 1875; and nature study (or biology and zoology), music, and home and manual training by 1900. Table 3–1 shows this evolution of the elementary school curriculum.

Secondary Schools

The common school created the basis for a tax-supported and locally controlled elementary school education. The American high school was established on this base. By 1900 the majority of children aged 6 to 13 were enrolled in public elementary school, but only 11.5 percent of those aged 14 to 17 were enrolled in public secondary schools (and only 6.5 percent of the 17-year olds graduated). As shown in Table 3–2, not until 1930 did the secondary school enrollment figure exceed

50 percent. By 1970, the percentage of elementary aged children attending school was 98 percent, and the percentage of secondary aged children was 94 percent (and 75 percent were graduating). The great enrollment revolution for elementary schools took place between 1850 and 1900; for high schools it evolved between 1900 and 1970. From the 1980s to the early 1990s, enrollment percentages leveled off. From the mid-1990s to the present, percentages are increasing slightly at the elementary level.

The Academy

In the early nineteenth century, the academy began to replace the Latin grammar school; by the

TABLE 3-1   Evolution of the Elementary School Curriculum, 1800–1900

1800	1825	1850	1875	1900
Reading	*Reading*	*Reading*	*Reading*	*Reading*
	Declamation	Declamation	Literary selections	*Literature*
Spelling	*Spelling*	Spelling	*Spelling*	Spelling
Writing	Writing	*Writing*	Penmanship	Writing
Catechism	Good behavior	Conduct	Conduct	Conduct
Bible	Manners and morals	Manners		
Arithmetic	*Arithmetic*	*Mental arithmetic*	*Primary arithmetic*	*Arithmetic*
		Ciphering	Advanced arithmetic	
	Bookkeeping	Bookkeeping		
	Grammar	*Grammar*	*Grammar*	Grammar
		Elementary language	Oral language	*Oral language*
	Geography	Geography	Home geography	Home geography
			Text geography	*Text geography*
		U.S. history	U.S. history	History studies
			Constitution	
		Object lessons	Object lessons	Nature study
			Elementary science	Elementary science
			Drawing	Drawing
				Music
			Physical exercises	Physical training
				Play
	Sewing			Sewing
				Cooking
				Manual training

Source: From E. P. Cubberley, *The History of Education* (Boston: Houghton Mifflin, 1920), p. 756.
Note: Italics indicate the most important subjects.

TABLE 3-2 Percentage of Students Enrolled in Secondary School and College, 1900–1980

	14- TO 17-YEAR-OLDS ENROLLED IN SECONDARY SCHOOL	17-YEAR-OLDS GRADUATING HIGH SCHOOL	18- TO 21-YEAR-OLDS ENROLLED IN COLLEGE
1900	11.5	6.5	3.9
1910	15.4	8.8	5.0
1920	32.3	16.8	7.9
1930	51.4	29.0	11.9
1940	73.3	50.8	14.5
1950	76.8	59.0	26.9
1960	86.1	65.1	31.3
1970	93.4	76.5	45.2
1980	93.7	74.4	46.3
1990[a]	92.8	72.6	47.1

Source: From *Digest of Educational Statistics, 1982, 1985–1986, 1989* (Washington, D.C.: U.S. Government Printing Office, 1982, 1986, 1989), Table 35, p. 44; Table 9, p. 11. Tables 6, 49, pp. 13, 62; *Projections of Education Statistics 1992–1993* (Washington, D.C.: U.S. Government Printing Office, 1988), Table 15, p. 19.
[a]Projections based on governmental sources.

middle of the century, it was dominant. It offered a wide range of curricula, and it was designed to provide a practical program (for terminal students) as well as a college preparatory course of study. By 1855 more than 6,000 academies had an enrollment totaling 263,000 students[49] (more than two-thirds of the total secondary school enrollment of that period).

"One of the main purposes" of the academy, according to Ellwood Cubberley, "was the establishment of . . . subjects having value aside from mere preparation for college, particularly subjects of modern nature, useful in preparing youth for the changed conditions of society. The study of real things rather than words about things, and useful things rather than subjects merely preparatory to college became prominent features of the new course of study."[50]

By 1828 as many as fifty different subjects were offered by the academies of the state of New York. The top fifteen, in rank order, were: (1) Latin, (2) Greek, (3) English grammar, (4) geography, (5) arithmetic, (6) algebra, (7) composition and declamation, (8) natural philosophy, (9) rhetoric, (10) philosophy, (11) U.S. history, (12) French, (13) chemistry, (14) logic, and (15) astronomy. By 1837, the state Board of Regents reported seventy-two different subjects.[51]

Although no typical academy existed, with so many different course offerings, the academy inadvertently served the major function of preparing students for college. The traditional curriculum, or the classical side of the academy, continued in the new setting. Writes Elmer Brown, "The college preparatory course was the backbone of the whole system of instruction" in the better academies. Although practical courses were offered, "it was the admission requirements of the colleges, more than anything else, that determined their standards of scholarship."[52] And, writes Paul Monroe, "The core of academy education yet remained the old classical curriculum . . . just as the core of the student body in the more flourishing academies remained the group preparing for college."[53]

The era of the academies extended to the 1870s, when academies were replaced by public high schools. The academies, nevertheless, served as finishing schools for young ladies—with courses in classical and modern language, science, mathematics, art, music, and homemaking. Also, they offered the "normal" program for prospective common school teachers by combining courses in the classics with principles of pedagogy. A few private military and elite academic academies still exist today.

The High School

Although a few high schools existed in the early half of the nineteenth century (the first one was founded in 1821 in Boston), the high school did not become a major American institution until after 1874, when the Michigan court ruled, in the Kalamazoo decision, that the people could establish and support high schools with tax funds if they consented. There was some initial resistance—the fear that the taxes for the high schools would only benefit a small portion of the youth population—but after the court decision, the high school spread rapidly and compulsory attendance laws were established on a state-by-state basis. The idea of high school attendance for all youth, based on the notion of equality of educational opportunity, was a major educational reform.

Students were permitted to attend private schools, but the states had the right to establish minimum standards for all. By 1890, the 2,525 public high schools in the United States enrolled more than 200,000 students, compared to 1,600 private secondary schools, which had fewer than 95,000 students. By 1900 the number of high schools had soared to 6,000, while the number of academies had declined to 1,200.[54] The public high school system, contiguous with common schools, had evolved. Although as late as 1900 the high schools were still attended by only a small percentage of the total youth population, the inclusion of terminal and college preparatory students as well as rich and poor students under one roof was evidence that the American people had rejected the European dual system of secondary education. Fifty years later, when the American high school had fully evolved, James Conant was to present his argument for the comprehensive high school on the basis that it integrated all types of learners and helped eliminate class distinctions. The comprehensive high school provided curriculum options for all students.

The high schools stressed the college preparatory program, but they also served to complete the formal education of terminal students. They offered, in addition, a more diversified curriculum than the academies. At the turn of the century, high schools began to offer vocational and industrial courses as well as commercial and clerical training courses. Despite all their problems and criticisms, the public high schools evolved into democratic and comprehensive institutions for social and political reform. They produced a skilled workforce in an expanding industrial economy, and they assimilated and Americanized millions of immigrant children in our cities.

The Secondary School Curriculum Evolves.

The curriculum of the Latin grammar school was virtually the same at the beginning and end of the colonial period. Table 3–3 lists the most popular courses. As indicated, Latin, Greek, arithmetic, and the classics were stressed. The academy introduced greater variation—courses for practical studies, for example—in the curriculum. By 1800, the academy offered about twenty-five different subjects (the table lists the seventeen most popular courses). Between 1850 and 1875, the peak period of the academy, estimates are that some 150 courses were offered.[55] The fifteen most popular ones in rank order were as follows: (1) algebra; (2) higher arithmetic; (3) English grammar; (4) Latin: (5) geometry; (6) U.S. history; (7) physiology; (8) natural philosophy; (9) physical geography; (10) German; (11) general history; (12) rhetoric; (13) bookkeeping; (14) French; and (15) zoology.[56]

There was no real philosophy or aim to these courses, except that most were college preparatory in nature, even though the original aim of the academy was to offer a practical program. It was believed then that a broad program with several course offerings was the hallmark of a better academy. The curriculum just expanded.[57]

After 1875, the high school rapidly grew and the academy rapidly declined. The secondary courses listed in Table 3–3 between 1875 and 1900 were high school courses. The curriculum continued to expand. The great variety in course offerings would allegedly allow the students to find where their interests and capabilities might be.[58] See Curriculum Tips 3-2.

TABLE 3-3   Evolution of Secondary School Curriculum, 1800–1900

1800–1825	1825–1850	1850–1875	1875–1900
Latin Grammar School			
Latin	Latin		
Greek	Greek		
Arithmetic	Arithmetic		
Classical literature	Classical literature		
	Ancient history		
Academy and High School			
Latin	Latin	Latin	Latin
Greek	Greek	Greek	Greek†
Classical literature	Classical literature	English literature	English literature
Writing*	Writing*	Composition*	Composition*
Arithmetic*	Arithmetic*	Arithmetic*	Arithmetic*
		Higher arithmetic	
Geometry	Geometry	Geometry	Geometry
Trigonometry	Trigonometry	Trigonometry	Trigonometry
	Algebra	Algebra	Algebra
Bookkeeping*	Bookkeeping*	Bookkeeping*	Bookkeeping*†
English grammar	English grammar	English grammar	English
Rhetoric	Rhetoric	Rhetoric	Rhetoric*
Oratory	Oratory†		
	Debating	Debating†	
Surveying*	Surveying*		
Astronomy*	Astronomy*	Astronomy	Astronomy*†
Navigation*	Navigation*†		
Geography	Geography	Physical geography	Physical geography†
	Natural philosophy	Natural philosophy†	
		Meteorology	Meteorology†
		Chemistry	Chemistry
		Physiology	Physiology
			Health education
		Botany	Botany†
		Zoology	Zoology†
			Biology
			Physics
Foreign language*	Foreign language*	Foreign language	Foreign language
(French, Spanish,	(French, Spanish,	(French, Spanish,	(French, Spanish,
German)	German)	German)	German, Italian)
Philosophy	Philosophy	Mental philosophy	
		Moral philosophy†	
	History	General history†	World history
	Greek history	Greek history†	Ancient history

(continued)

TABLE 3-3   Continued

1800–1825	1825–1850	1850–1875	1875–1900
	U.S. history	U.S. history	U.S. history Civil government Political economy Manual training* Home economics* Agriculture* Music Art Physical education

Source: Adapted from Calvin Davis, *Our Evolving High School Curriculum* (New York: World Book, 1927), p. 38; Committee of Ten, *Report of the Committee on Secondary Studies* (Washington, D.C.: National Education Association, 1893), p. 4; Newton Edwards and Herman G. Richey, *The School in the American Social Order,* 2nd ed. (Boston: Houghton Mifflin, 1963), p. 250; and Gerald R. Firth and Richard D. Kimpston, *The Curricular Continuum in Perspective* (Itasca, Ill.: Peacock, 1973), pp. 102–104.
*Considered as part of practical studies.
†All but disappeared; limited enrollments.

THE TRANSITIONAL PERIOD: 1893–1918

From the colonial period until the turn of the twentieth century, the traditional curriculum, which emphasized classical studies for college-bound students, dominated at the elementary and secondary levels. The rationale for this emphasis was that the classics were difficult, and were thus the best source for intellectualizing and for developing mental abilities (a view later supported by the mental discipline approach to learning). The more difficult the subject and the more the students had to exercise their minds, the greater the subject's value. Such ideas of knowledge and subject matter, as well as mental rigor, were rooted in the philosophy of perennialism.

Along with the classics, more and more subjects were added to the curriculum. As a result the need was growing to bring some unity or a pattern for curriculum organization out of the chaotic and confused situation, especially at the secondary level, where subject matter was expanding the most. According to two educators, "subjects taught varied from school to school. There was no uniformity as to time allotments, and grade placements of topics or subjects pursued" differed from school to school.[59]

A companion problem existed. Most children, even as late as the turn of the century, completed their formal education at the elementary school level, and those students who did go to secondary schools usually ended their formal education upon graduation. As late as 1890, only 14.5 percent of the students enrolled in high school were preparing for college, and less than 3 percent went on to college.[60] Hence, the needs of more than 85 percent of these students were still being overlooked for only the top 15 percent; the discrepancy was more lopsided if the college track was considered. Reformers began to question the need for two curriculum tracks at the elementary level—one for high school-bound and the other for nonhigh school-bound children—the dominance of college over the high school, and the emphasis on mental discipline and the classics.

Reaffirming the Traditional Curriculum: Three Committees

With these unsettled questions as background, the National Education Association (NEA) organized three major committees between 1893 and 1895: the Committee of Fifteen on Elementary Educa-

---

=== *Curriculum Tips 3-2* ===

Process of Historical Research

How does one go about conducting historical research? For students, teachers, and historians alike, the six suggestions below should have meaning and value regarding how to go about doing historical research.

1. Define a problem or an issue that has roots in the past or attempt to recreate a historical event and give it meaning.
2. Use primary sources (documents and other printed or written evidence) that relate to the event or problem and that were part of the context in which it occurred.
3. Use secondary sources (literature after the event occurred) that historians have developed to interpret it.
4. Based on the examination of authentic primary and secondary sources, recreate an event, a life, or a situation from the past; interpret that event to give it meaning for people in the present.
5. Use history, especially case examples or case studies, to add a moral dimension to our teaching.
6. Do not try to rewrite history; it is to be explained or reinterpreted to add meaning.

Source: Adapted from Gerald Gutek, unpublished materials, January 1992.

---

tion, the Committee of Ten on Secondary School Studies, and the Committee on College Entrance Requirements. These committees were to determine the specifics of the curricula for these schools. Their reports "standardized" the curriculum for much of this century. In the words of Ellwood Cubberley, "The committees were dominated by subject-matter specialists, possessed of a profound faith in mental discipline." No concern for student "abilities, social needs, interest, or capabilities . . . found a place in their . . . deliberations."[61]

The Committee of Fifteen. The Committee of Fifteen was heavily influenced by Charles Eliot, president of Harvard University, who had initiated vigorous discussion on the need for school reform in the years preceding, and by William Harris, then the U.S. Commissioner of Education, a staunch perennialist, who believed in strict teacher authority and discipline. Both Eliot and Harris wanted the traditional curriculum to remain intact. Eliot's plan, which was adapted by the Committee, was to reduce the elementary grades from ten to eight. The Committee stressed the

three Rs, as well as English grammar, literature, geography, and history. Hygiene, culture, vocal music, and drawing were given 60 minutes, or one lesson, per week. Manual training, sewing, and/or cooking, as well as algebra and Latin, were introduced in the seventh and eighth grades.

In general, the Committee resisted the idea of newer subjects and the principles of pedagogy or teaching that had characterized the reform movement of the European pioneers since the early 1800s. The Committee also rejected the idea of kindergarten and the idea that the children's needs or interests should be considered when planning the curriculum.[62] Any idea of interdisciplinary subjects or curriculum synthesis was rejected. Isolation of each branch of knowledge, or what John Dewey, in *Democracy and Education,* and Ralph Tyler, in *Basic Principles of Curriculum and Instruction,* later referred to as "compartmentalization" of subject matter, was considered the norm; it still is today in most schools.

The Committee of Ten. The Committee of Ten was the most influential of the three committees. Its recommendations best illustrate the tough-minded, mental discipline approach supported by Eliot, who was the chair. The Committee identified nine academic subjects as central to the high school curriculum. As shown in Table 3-4, they were: (1) Latin; (2) Greek; (3) English; (4) other modern languages; (5) mathematics (algebra, geometry, trigonometry, and higher or advanced algebra); (6) physical sciences (physics, astronomy, and chemistry); (7) natural history or biological sciences (biology, botany, zoology, and physiology); (8) social sciences (history, civil government, and political economy); and (9) geography, geology, and meteorology.

The Committee recommended four different programs or tracks: (1) classical; (2) Latin scientific; (3) modern languages; and (4) English. The first two required four years of Latin; the first program emphasized English (mostly classical) literature and math, and the second program, math and science. The modern language program required four years of French or German (Spanish was considered not only too easy, but also not as important a culture or language as French or German). The English program permitted four years of either Latin, German, or French. Both of these programs also included literature, composition, and history.

The Committee of Ten took a position and claimed that the latter two programs, which did not require Latin or emphasize literature, science, or mathematics, were "in practice distinctly inferior to the other two."[63] In taking this position, the Committee indirectly tracked college-bound students into the first two or superior programs and noncollege-bound students into the latter two or inferior programs. To some extent, this bias reflected the Committee's composition—eight of the ten members represented college and private preparatory school interests.

The Committee ignored art, music, physical education, and vocational education, maintaining that these subjects contributed little to mental discipline. In analyzing the effects of the Committee's action, two curricularists wrote: "The choice of these subjects and the omission of others from consideration was enough to set the course for secondary education" for many years and to indirectly set the tone at the elementary level, too. As "might be expected," the Committee suggested that "the nine subjects be taught sooner" and that all subjects except Latin and Greek be taught at the elementary school level.[64]

Even though very few students at that time went to college, this college preparatory program established a curriculum hierarchy, from elementary school to college, that promoted academics and ignored the majority of students, who were noncollege bound. Today, even though we offer vocational, industrial, and/or technical programs, the academic program is still considered superior to and of more status than the other programs.

The Committee on College Entrance Requirements. When this Committee met in 1895, it reaffirmed college dominance over the high school, in terms of admission requirements and classical subjects for mental training at the high school and college levels. Consisting mainly of college and university presidents, including Eliot, the Committee recommended to strengthen the college preparatory aspect of the high school curriculum, believing that it best served all students. It also made recommendations regarding the number of credits required in different subjects for college admission; it served as a model for the Carnegie Unit, a means for evaluating credits for college admission, imposed on the high schools in 1909 and still in existence today in most high schools.

Pressure for a Modern Curriculum

Gradually, demands were made for various changes to be made in the schools to meet the needs of a changing society. The pace of immigration and industrial development led a growing number of educators to question the classical curriculum and the constant emphasis on mental discipline and incessant drill. This shift in curriculum was influenced by the scientific movement in psychology and education in the late nineteenth and early twentieth centuries, particularly the pragmatic theories of Charles Peirce and William James; the social theories of Darwin, Herbart, and Spencer; and the impact of Pestalozzi, Froebel, Montessori, and others on pedagogy. The movement rejected the mental discipline approach and classic curriculum (both of which stressed that certain traditional and "cultural" subjects were best for disciplining the mind), as well as faculty

TABLE 3-4 Secondary School Programs and Subjects Proposed by Committee of Ten, 1893

FIRST YEAR	SECOND YEAR	THIRD YEAR	FOURTH YEAR
Latin — 5 p.*	Latin — 4 p.	Latin — 4 p.	Latin — 4 p.
English Literature 2 p. } 4 p.	Greek — 5 p.	Greek — 4 p.	Greek — 4 p.
English Composition 2 p. }	English Literature 2 p. } 4 p.	English Literature 2 p. } 4 p.	English Literature 2 p. } 4 p.
German [or French] — 5 p.	English Composition 2 p. }	English Composition 1 p. }	English Composition 1 p. }
Algebra — 4 p.	German continued — 4 p.	Rhetoric 1 p. }	Grammar 1 p. }
History of Italy, Spain, and France — 3 p.	French, begun — 5 p.	German — 4 p.	German — 4 p.
Applied Geography (European political-continental and oceanic flora and fauna) — 4 p.	Algebra 2 p. } 4 p.	French — 4 p.	French — 4 p.
	Geometry 2 p. }	Algebra 2 p. } 4 p.	Trigonometry } 2 p.
	Botany or Zoology — 4 p.	Geometry 2 p. }	Higher Algebra }
	English History to 1688 — 3 p.	Physics — 4 p.	Chemistry — 4 p.
		History, English and U.S. — 3 p.	History (intensive) and Civil Government — 3 p.
		Astronomy, 3 p 1st 1/2 yr. }	Geology or Physiography, 4 p. 1st 1/2 yr. } 4 p.
		Meteorology, 3 p. 2nd 1/2 yr. }	Anatomy, Physiology, and Hygiene, 4 p. 2nd 1/2 yr. }
25 p.	33 p.	34 p.	33 p.

Source: From Committee of Ten, *Report of the Committee of Ten on Secondary School Studies* (Washington, D.C.: National Educational Association, 1893), p. 4.

*p. = periods.

psychology (that is, enhancing the "faculties" or mind of the child through stimulation of the senses). Instead, the new scientism put emphasis on vocational, technical, and scientific subjects—fitting into the concurrent age of industrialism, colonialism, and materialism.

Increased pressure against the traditional curriculum was evident at the turn of the century—with the educational ideas of John Dewey and Francis Parker, the Gestalt psychology and child psychology movements (which focused on the whole child), the learning theories of behaviorism and transfer learning (which involved connections between stimuli and responses), and the progressive movement in schools and society.

The argument eventually appeared that the classics had no greater disciplinary or mental value than other subjects, and that mental discipline (which emphasized rote, drill, and memorization) was not conducive to the inductive method of science or compatible with contemporary educational theory. Wrote Edward Thorndike, the most influential learning psychologist of the era:

> The expectation of any large difference in general improvement of the mind from one study rather than another seems doomed to disappointment. The chief reason why good thinkers seem superficially to have been made such by having taken certain school studies is that good thinkers have taken such studies. . . .Now that good thinkers study Physics and Trigonometry, these seem to make good thinkers. If abler pupils should all study Physical Education and Dramatic Art, these subjects would seem to make good thinkers.[65]

Even Latin came under attack, by none other than old-time perennialists. In 1917, for example, Charles Eliot, a former advocate of Latin, was saying Latin should no longer be compulsory for high school or college students.[66] Abraham Flexner, a former teacher of the classics who had become a celebrity with his exposé of the American medical schools, claimed that Latin had "no purpose" in the curriculum and that the classics were out of step with scientific developments.[67] Flexner, who had become a strong advocate of utilitarianism, argued that tradition was an inadequate criterion for justifying subject matter. In short, society was changing and people could alter the conditions around them; the stress on psychology and science and the concern for social

and educational reform made evident the need for a new curriculum.

Flexner: A Modern Curriculum. In a famous paper, "A Modern School," published in 1916, Abraham Flexner (1866–1959) rejected the traditional curriculum of the secondary school and proposed a "modern" curriculum for contemporary society. Flexner's curriculum consisted of four basic areas: (1) science (the major emphasis of the curriculum); (2) industry (occupations and trades of the industrial world); (3) civics (history, economics, and government); and (4) aesthetics (literature, languages, art, and music).[68] Modern languages would replace Latin and Greek. Flexner concluded that, unless a utilitarian argument could be made for a subject, it had little value in the curriculum, regardless of traditional value.

Flexner's concepts of utility and modern subject matter tend to resemble Spencer's views on science and subject matter. The difference is that Flexner's timing was on the mark, and Spencer was ahead of his time. Flexner was tuned to the changing social and political times during which many educators were willing to listen to his proposals. In 1917, for example, Flexner's "Modern School" was established at the Lincoln School of Teachers College, Columbia University. The school combined the four core areas of study, with emphasis on scientific inquiry; it represented Dewey's type of progressivism and science of education, and it also reflected the fact that Dewey was now teaching at Columbia University.

Dewey: Pragmatic and Scientific Principles of Education. The same year Flexner published his modern school report, John Dewey (1859–1952) published *Democracy and Education,* in which can be found all elements of his philosophy as well as their implications for the educational process.[69] In the book, Dewey showed the relationship between education and democracy and set forth the notion that democracy itself was a social process that could be enhanced through the school. Dewey considered schools as neutral institutions that could serve the ends of either freedom or repression and authority. Dewey envisioned school in America as an instrument of democracy.

Thus, the aims of education went hand in hand with the particular type of society involved;

conversely, the society that evolved influenced the aims of education.

Dewey argued that subjects could not be placed in a value hierarchy and that attempts to do so were misguided. Any study or body of knowledge was capable of expanding the child's experience, and "experiencing"—that is, being stimulated to develop and internalize intellectual capabilities—was the process of educating the child. Traditional subjects such as Latin or Greek were no more valuable than music or art.

One subject that may be more important to Dewey is science. Science, for Dewey, was another name for knowledge, and it represented "the perfected outcome of learning—its consummation. . . . What is known, certain, settled" and what "we think with rather than that which we think about" is science or rationalized knowledge. Dewey considered scientific inquiry to be the best form of knowledge for a society, because it consisted of the "special . . . methods which the race has slowly worked out in order to conduct reflection under conditions whereby its procedures and results are tested."[70] He thus elevated the place of science in education.

What is relevant to educating an individual to function well as a free person in a free society remained constant for Dewey. His emphasis on the "method of inquiry," which is really synonymous with "intelligent behavior," is as valued today as it was seventy-five years ago.

Judd: Systematic Studies and Social Sciences.
Charles Judd (1873–1946) was the colleague of John Dewey; in fact, he was the head of the Department of Education at the University of Chicago when Dewey directed the lab school. Along with Dewey and others, he constructed a science of education based on the methods of finding facts and then applying them as a basis for reasoning out solutions to problems and for making decisions. Whereas Charles Peirce and William James referred to this method as pragmatism, Judd referred to it as "scientism in education."

Judd was an evolutionist and felt the laws of nature could be used to educate the young. He used statistical research (which was then in its infancy stage) to determine the worth of curriculum content, that is, which subjects would best promote thinking and dealing with the problems of contemporary life. By preparing students to deal with problems, not acquire endless knowledge, he argued students would be prepared to deal with the changing world and the problems they would encounter as adults.

The justification for the method of determining subject matter was outlined in Judd's book *The Scientific Study of Education,* which was concerned with what he called "systematic studies . . . of the curriculum."[71] His emphasis was on reading, writing, and spelling based on words shown statistically to be used by successful adults, as well as on math problems applied to practical problems of everyday life. Utilitarian and pragmatic in philosophy, he urged that elementary students be exposed to "career education" to help them formulate ideas about the world of work and thus prepare them for the evolving social order. At the secondary level, Judd sought practical subjects that had a vocational or technical orientation, not a "cultural" or elitist one. For slower students, he advocated English, business math, mechanics or stenography, and office management—what later was to become part of the commercial and vocational tracks in high school. For average and talented students, he urged a curriculum consisting of science, mathematics, modern language, and the social sciences—what later was to be labeled the academic track.

Judd influenced the next generation of theorists, who sought to systematize curriculum making by applying scientific methods to curriculum development. These new theorists, sometimes called *technicians,* starting with Bobbitt and Charters in the 1920s and ending with Tyler in the 1950s, evoked his educational utility and social science/research methods.

Commission on the Reorganization of Secondary Education.
In 1918 the NEA Commission on the Reorganization of Secondary Education published the famous *Cardinal Principles of Secondary Education,*[72] a highly progressive document. Influenced by Flexner's "A Modern School" and Dewey's *Democracy and Education,* the Commission stressed the whole child (not just the cognitive area of study), education for all youth (not just college-bound youth), diversified areas of study (not classical or traditional studies), common culture, ideas, and ideals for a democratic society (not religious, elitist, or mental, discipline learning).

The Commission noted the following:

1. *Seven major aims or "Cardinal Principles" should comprise education: health, command of the fundamentals, worthy home membership, vocation, citizenship, leisure, and ethical character.*
2. *High school should be a comprehensive institution based on the various social and economic groups that populate the nation.*
3. *The high school curriculum should offer various programs to meet various student needs—agricultural, business and commercial, vocational, and college preparatory.*
4. *The current ideas of psychology of education, principles of pedagogy, measurement, and evaluation should be applied to the curriculum and instruction of the high school.*
5. *American education comprises a set of defined institutions that should function in conjunction with, rather than in isolation from, each other.*

Indeed, the high school was assuming its modern curricular patterns—combining academic programs with several nonacademic programs. The choice of subject matter was being fine-tuned to emphasize five basic or essential subjects such as English, math, science, social science, and modern language. Classical languages and classical literature took a back seat to modern languages and English literature. Aims and subjects were related, not separated or compartmentalized. The idea of mental discipline was replaced by utilitarian modes of thought and scientific inquiry. There was a growing recognition that curriculum, too, should not be compartmentalized but interdisciplinary, and that it should not be static, but change as society changed. The needs and interests of the students were now considered. Most important, there was recognition of the responsibility of schools (including the high school) to serve all children and youth, not just college-bound youth. The era of progressive education was about to begin impacting the schools—and traditional education (which had dominated American education for so long) was vanishing.

CURRICULUM AS A FIELD IS BORN: 1918–1949

The early twentieth century was a period of educational ferment. Scientific methods of research, the influence of psychology, the child study movement, the idea of efficiency in industry, and the muckracker-progressive movement in society all influenced education. Many of the resulting ideas were applied to curriculum. From them evolved the process and how-to-do aspects of curriculum. Curriculum was now viewed as a science, with principles and methodology, not just as content or subject matter. The ideas of planning and describing a curriculum, as opposed to describing curriculum in terms of subjects and the amount of time needed to study each subject, appeared in the literature.

Bobbitt and Charters: Behaviorism and Scientific Principles

Franklin Bobbitt (1876–1956) and Werrett Charters (1875–1952) were influenced by the idea of efficiency, promoted by business and industry, and the scientific management theories of Frederick Taylor, who analyzed factory efficiency in terms of time and motion studies and concluded that each worker should be paid on the basis of his or her individual output (as measured by the number of units produced in a specified period of time).[73] Efficient operation of the schools, sometimes called "machine" theory by sociologists and economists, became a major goal in the 1920s. Often ensuring efficiency meant eliminating small classes, increasing the student-teacher ratio, cutting costs in teacher salaries, and so on, and then preparing charts and graphs to show the resultant lower costs. Raymond Callahan later branded this idea the "cult of efficiency."[74] The effects were to make curriculum making more scientific and to reduce teaching and learning to precise behaviors with corresponding activities and learning experiences that could be measured. These ideas were cultivated by Taylor's faithful followers: Bobbitt and Charters.

Bobbitt's book, *The Curriculum,* published in 1918, is considered by some observers as the first book devoted solely to curriculum as a science and to curriculum in all its phases. Bobbitt outlined the principles of curriculum planning by focusing on an activities approach, which he defined as "a series of things which children and youth must do and experience by way of developing abilities to do things well and make up the affairs of adult life."[75] To Bobbitt the purpose of curriculum was to outline what knowledge was important for each subject, and then to develop various activities to train the learner and enhance his or her performance.

Bobbitt understood the importance of analyzing the process of curriculum making, especially the need for specifications, tasks, and detail to what one wanted to accomplish and then measure—all part of machine theory and the cult of efficiency, as well as the behaviorist movement of the era. Adherence to the traditional curriculum, which emphasized subject matter, did not provide educators with methods for developing curricula. Bobbitt described the problems as he set out to organize a course of studies for the elementary grades:

> We need principles of curriculum making. We did not know that we should first determine objectives from a study of social needs. We supposed education consisted only of teaching the familiar subjects. We had not come to see that it is essentially a process of unfolding the potential abilities of [students]. . . .We had not learned that studies are means, not ends."[76]

Bobbitt further developed his objectives and activities approach in the early 1920s in *How to Make a Curriculum.* Here he outlined more than 800 objectives and related activities to coincide with student needs. These activities ranged from the "ability to care for [one's] teeth, . . . eyes, . . . nose, and throat, . . . ability to keep the heart and blood vessels in normal working condition, . . . to keep home appliances in good working condition . . . to spelling and grammar."[77]

Bobbitt's methods were quite sophisticated for the period. Moreover, his guidelines for selecting objectives can be applied today: (1) *eliminate* objectives that are impractical or cannot be accomplished through normal living; (2) *emphasize* objectives that are important for success and adult living; (3) *avoid* objectives opposed by the community; (4) *involve* the community in selecting objectives; (5) *differentiate* between objectives that are for all students and those that are for only a portion of the student population; and (6) *sequence* the objectives in such a way as to establish how far students should go each year in attaining them—that is, establish criteria for achievement.

Taken out of context, however, Bobbitt's list of hundreds of objectives and activities, along with the machine or factory analogy that he advocated, was easy to criticize.[78] Nevertheless, Bobbitt's insistence that curriculum making was a specialty based on scientific methods and procedures was important for elevating curriculum to a field of study, or what he called a "new specialization." His offer was that educators try his method with the intention of improving it or suggesting a better one. He was one of the first to propose the idea of a curriculum specialist, with special training.

Charters advocated the same behaviorist, precise approach, which he termed a "scientific" approach. He viewed the curriculum as a series of objectives that students must attain by way of a series of learning experiences. In his book on *Curriculum Construction,* Charters, who was influenced by the machine theory of business, envisioned curriculum as the analysis of definite operations—a process he termed *job analysis*—such as those involved in running a machine.[79]

Charters's statement about the weakness of curriculum is still relevant today: that even though curriculum writers often begin "with the statement of aim, none has been able to derive a curriculum logically from his statement of aim." In almost every case, a "mental leap [is made] from the aim to the subject matter, without providing adequate principles such as would bridge the gap . . . and lead us from aim to selection of materials."[80] Charters attempted to bridge the gap by proposing a curriculum derived from specific objectives and precise activities. He considered objectives to be observable and measurable, an outlook that is similar to today's notion that behavioral objectives can be sound and definable. He felt the state of knowledge at that time did not permit scientific measurement that would specifically identify the outcomes of the objectives, but he set out to develop a method for selecting objectives, based on social consensus, and for applying subject matter and student activities to analysis and verification. Although Charters did not use the term *evaluation* during this period, he was laying the groundwork for curriculum evaluation, which surfaced twenty years later.

As prime initiators of the behavioral and scientific movements in curriculum, Bobbitt and

Charters had a profound impact on curriculum. They (1) developed principles for curriculum making, involving aims, objectives, needs, and learning experiences (which they called activities); (2) highlighted the use of behavioral objectives, which has a legacy in various contemporary educational ideas, such as the use of instructional objectives and curriculum evaluation; (3) introduced the ideas that objectives are derived from the study of needs (later called needs assessment) and that objectives and activities are subject to analysis and verification (later called evaluation); and (4) emphasized that curriculum making cuts across subject matter, and that a curriculum specialist need not necessarily be a specialist in any *subject,* rather a professional in *method* or *process.*

Finally, Bobbitt and Charters taught at the University of Chicago when Tyler was a graduate student in the department of education (in fact, Tyler was Charters's graduate assistant). Tyler was highly influenced by their behaviorist ideas, particularly that (1) objectives derive from student needs and society, (2) learning experiences relate to objectives, (3) activities organized by the teacher should be integrated into the subject matter, and (4) instructional outcomes should be evaluated. Tyler's stress on evaluation as a component of curriculum is rooted in the research background of Charters, who helped his graduate student get appointed to his first teaching and evaluation position in 1929 as Head of Testing and Evaluation for the Ohio State Bureau of Educational Research (Charters had assumed the directorship of the bureau the previous year). Tyler's principles of curriculum and instruction, especially his four major components (objectives, learning experiences, methods of organization, and evaluation), are rooted in Bobbitt's and especially Charters's ideas.

Kilpatrick: The Progressive Influence

The increasing rise of progressive education and universal education, that is, education for the masses, led to an attack against the rigidity and rote memorization of the classical curriculum, the emphasis on tough subject matter, and the high school curriculum standardized on the basis of preparation for college. The progressive move-

ment consisted of many wings, and among the most influential were the child-centered and activity-centered curricularists. Subject matter emphasis was replaced by emphasis on the student or learner; the needs and interests of the child dominated the new thinking; and cognitive processes were replaced by social processes. The curriculum was organized around classroom and school social activities, group enterprises, and group projects. See Curriculum Tips 3-3.

Creative self-expression and freedom were the major goals of the child-centered movement, and this was a reaction against the rigid and domineering influence of the traditional curriculum. While the method relied on Dewey's progressivism, it was Dewey who made several criticisms in the 1920s and 1930s about this new education, which he felt to be a distortion of his original ideas and to lack purpose and method as well as teacher direction. According to Dewey, the method of surrounding students with materials but not suggesting a purpose or a plan, but rather allowing students to respond according to their interests, "is really stupid [and] attempts the impossible which is always stupid."[81]

William Kilpatrick, a colleague of Dewey when he moved to Teachers College, Columbia University, attempted to merge the current behaviorist psychology of the day, particularly Thorndike's (connectionism) and Watson's (conditioning) theories with Dewey's and Judd's progressive philosophy, which became known as the "Project Method,"[82] or what was later called *purposeful activity.* Kilpatrick combined four steps in methodology, which were actually more behaviorist than progressive: purposing, planning, executing, and judging, with his projects (ranging from classroom projects to school and community projects).

Two of his doctoral students applied many of his ideas in the Missouri schools. One was Junius Merian, who called Kilpatrick's projects "subjects of study" and organized them into four areas: observation, play, stories, and hard work.[83] The second student, Ellsworth Collings, developed a curriculum around the real-life experiences of children. He had both teachers and students present several guided experiences or activities that were related and developmental in nature; one activity led to another. "The curriculum was contin-

=== *Curriculum Tips 3-3* ===

Enriching the Curriculum

The following suggestions combine Kilpatrick's activities curriculum and Rugg's child-centered curriculum. In general, the suggestions integrate elementary's schooling with the philosophy of progressivism, which evolved during the first half of the twentieth century. The specific suggestions are still viable today for those schools and teachers who stress a student-centered curriculum.

1. Study the cumulative record of each child.
2. Compare the achievement score with ability indices.
3. Examine a pupil's creative production for words, symbols, and topics that are used frequently.
4. Listen to pupils talk about themselves.
5. Provide opportunity for a choice of activities.
6. Visit each pupil's home, if possible.
7. Help each pupil learn as much as possible about his or her values, attitudes, purposes, skills, interests, and abilities.
8. Be willing to allow pupils to say what they think.
9. Encourage students to reflect on their beliefs and values.
10. Analyze with pupils their interpretations of their in-class and out-of-class experiences.
11. Organize class activities around individual or group study of problems important to the individuals involved.
12. Help each pupil to state his or her purposes, both immediate and long term. Share with pupils the information available about their present status.
13. Clarify with pupils the limitations (in time, materials, and resources) of the situation.
14. Ask each pupil to formulate a plan of work.
15. Encourage each pupil to collect and share materials.
16. Make possible the collection of information in out-of-class situations.
17. Use record-keeping as a way of helping the individual student to organize his or her learning.

Source: Kimball Wiles, *Teaching for Better Schools* (Englewood Cliffs, N.J.: Prentice Hall, 1952), p. 286.

uously made 'on the spot' by the joint action of pupils and teachers." The idea was that such a joint endeavor "would mean most for the children."[84] His projects were similar to Merian's four study areas but included more field trips and community activities.

Although advocates such as Boyd Bode and John Childs treated these ideas as "innovative" and "new,"[85] there was almost nothing new with the idea of purposeful activity. The idea was rooted in the curriculum ideas of Bobbitt and Charters, as expressed by their stress on objectives and related activities, and the philosophy of Dewey, particularly his doctrine of growth, which was derived from "purposeful activity," and "modes of action" to meet the needs and interests of students.

Kilpatrick's project method was mainly implemented at the elementary schools, like the activity movement, because both were child centered. His method was fully developed in his text, *Foundations of Method,* and became part of the activity movement. Nonetheless, he argued that the difference was that his doctrine had "social purpose," whereas the activity-centered curriculum had only "child purpose." When forced to decide who should plan the curriculum, the child or teacher, Kilpatrick opted for the child, arguing that "if you want to educate the boy to think and plan for himself, then let him make his own plan."[86] In this respect, he differed from Dewey, who put more emphasis on the role of the teacher.

For Kilpatrick, the child had to learn to "search . . . compare . . . think why . . . and in the end . . . make his own decision."[87] The teacher could serve as a guide, but not as the source of information or dispenser of knowledge. When Kilpatrick's project method was eventually introduced in the high school curriculum, it became fused with social studies and the core curriculum. All these curriculum experiences meshed subject matter, social issues, and social problems important to students involved.[88]

Kilpatrick was also part of the wing of the radical progressive movement, later called reconstructionism, which was concerned with social issues and saw traditional education (expressed in perennialist terms) as reactionary. Bode, Caswell, Counts, and Rugg were part of this new social movement. Although these radicals criticized the Committee of Ten and felt its members had legitimized traditional systems of education, Kilpatrick (like members of the Committee) was concerned about "a curriculum containing a bewildering variety of more or less unrelated subjects." New subjects were being added "as occasion arose," lacking in philosophy or related goals.[89] But whereas the traditional curricularists of the Committee of Ten urged a curriculum based on perennialist philosophy, clearly compartmentalized and tough academics, with emphasis on Latin, language, and science, Kilpatrick argued for progressive philosophy, integrated subject matter, and a general education with emphasis on values and social issues. Whereas the Committee of Ten saw school as a place where students go to primarily acquire knowledge, Kilpatrick and his progressive colleagues saw school as a "way of life" and "ideal community" where students practiced "cooperation, self-government . . . and application of intelligence . . . to problems as they may arise."[90]

The traditional practice of education focused on certain subjects, usually the three Rs at the elementary level and basic academic subjects at the secondary level. These were considered as logically organized bodies of subject matter. The basic method for teaching these subjects was through rote practices. Kilpatrick and his followers challenged both of these positions regarding method and the assumption about logically organized subject matter. As Collings asserted, the activities movement made the individual child the focus of thinking in a social context. The child's growth along social lines, not the mastery of content, was the purpose of education.[91] School was preparation for life; it had social purpose.

In the end, the emphasis in education was the student—interested, active, and interacting with peers in school and adults in the community. Students had needs, interests, and problems growing out of their experiences with each other, their family, and community. Hence, the curriculum had to be derived not from organized bodies of subject matter, but from real-life experiences and expressed in terms of purposeful activities.

The Twenty-Sixth Yearbook

In 1930, the National Society for the Study of Education (NSSE), an honor society with headquarters at the University of Chicago, published its twenty-sixth yearbook in two parts, *Curriculum-Making: Past and Present* and *The Foundations of Curriculum Making*.[92]

The committee that developed the two volumes consisted of twelve members, including Harold Rugg (the chairperson) and William Bagley, Franklin Bobbitt, Werrett Charters, George Counts, Charles Judd, and William Kilpatrick, among others. Leaders of curriculum development during that period were mainly scientific-oriented (including Bobbitt and Charters) and progressive (including Counts, Judd, and Kilpatrick), and many were affiliated with the University of Chicago, which emphasized this science of education.

The Yearbook comprised two parts. The first part began as a harsh criticism of traditional education and its emphasis on subject matter, rote learning, drill, and mental discipline. It then became a synthesis of progressive practices and programs—the best and most innovative since the turn of the century—in public and private schools across the country. Part II has become a landmark text. It described the state of the art in curriculum making up to that period of time, and it included a consensual statement by the group on the nature of curriculum making. It is still relevant today.

The committee recognized the need for curriculum reform and the need for "those who are constructing our school curriculum" to determine "an overview . . . [and] orientation . . . to curriculum making."[93] With this idea in mind, the Yearbook outlined characteristics of the ideal curriculum—a curriculum that:

1. *Focuses on the affairs of human life.*
2. *Deals with the facts and problems of the local, national, and international community.*
3. *Enables students to think critically about various forms of government.*
4. *Informs and develops an attitude of open mindedness.*
5. *Considers student interests and needs as well as opportunities for debate, discussion, and exchange of ideas.*
6. *Deals with the issues of modern life and the cultural and historical aspects of society.*
7. *Considers problem-solving activities and practice in choosing alternatives.*
8. *Consists of carefully graded organization of problems and exercises.*
9. *Deals with humanitarian themes, and purposeful and constructive attitudes and insights.*[94]

This description of the ideal curriculum is basically one that might be developed today.

In the same vein, Harold Rugg maintained that the people should formulate the aims and purposes of education through committees or legislative groups; the appropriate materials and methods of instruction "through which to achieve those aims and purposes [were] . . . technical . . . demanding special professional preparation." The role of trained curriculum specialists was to plan the curriculum in advance and to include four tasks (which were later to become the basis of Tyler's four principles): (1) "a statement of objectives, (2) a sequence of experiences [to achieve] the objectives, (3) subject matter found to be . . . the best means of engaging in the experiences, and (4) statements of immediate outcomes of achievements to be derived from the experiences." Rugg concluded that curriculum was adapting scientific methods and that there was

need "for specialization and for professional . . . training."[95] Experienced teachers and specialists in curriculum making should work together to organize the content and materials within the various fields of subject matter—what many schools do today.

The Yearbook represented a tremendous advance in clarifying problems curriculum workers were encountering and in proposing procedures for the future in curriculum making. It had major influence in many school districts (both large and small, as well as city, suburban, and rural), as illustrated by the plan that was later called "The Eight-Year Study," and by the ideas that Ralph Tyler and Hilda Taba expressed in their classic texts 20 and 30 years later.

Rugg and Caswell: The Development Period

During the late 1920s, the 1930s, and the early 1940s, a number of important books were published on curriculum principles and processes and on techniques for helping the teacher in curriculum making. Harold Rugg (1886–1960), the chairperson of the NSSE Yearbook, shared the faith of Bobbitt and Charters in a "science of curriculum." By training Rugg was an engineer, but, like Dewey, he had a broad view of curriculum that focused on the whole child and the way the child would grapple with the changing society. In this respect, Rugg was a progressive thinker as well as a forerunner of reconstructionism.

In 1928, Rugg and Shumaker coauthored their controversial text, *The Child-centered School*. In an era which stressed student input in planning the curriculum, the authors stressed the need for curriculum specialists to construct the curriculum.[96] They also stressed the role of the teacher in implementing the curriculum at the classroom and instructional level. Hence, the teacher needed to preplan; the idea of student input was rejected by Rugg, as was the idea of a curriculum based on the needs and interests of students. Such a curriculum would lack direction and logic. But the idea of a preplanned, fixed curriculum was antithetical to the progressive doctrine that was becoming more influential during this period. More in line with progressivism, however, Rugg advocated cooperation among educational professionals from different areas, including teachers, administrators, test experts, and curriculum specialists from various fields.

Rugg's attention in the 1930s and the 1940s shifted almost entirely to the integration of history, geography, civics, and economics—commonly called social studies. Some of his ideas about labor history and collectivism and his criticisms of American life, compounded by his activities with the teachers' union, resulted in a great deal of criticism from Establishment groups. Like Counts and Dewey, Rugg, too, had the distinction of having an FBI file.[97]

During the mid-1920s and 1930s, most school districts and state education departments were developing curriculum guides. However, the selection of methods and activities was left to the teachers. Hollis Caswell (1901–1989), was concerned that this practice was limited; he wanted to shift emphasis from formulating a course of study to improving instruction. He envisioned curriculum making as a means of helping teachers coordinate their instructional activities with subject matter and students' needs and interests. He considered courses of study as guides or sources that teachers could use to plan their daily work, but not as plans they should follow in detail. He sought to combine three major curriculum components: content, teacher's instruction, and student's learning.

Caswell attempted to assist teachers by providing a step-by-step procedure for curriculum making. He and his colleagues outlined seven points, in question form, that still have relevancy today:

1. *What is a curriculum?*
2. *Why is there need for curriculum revision?*
3. *What is the function of subject matter?*
4. *How do we determine educational objectives?*
5. *How do we organize curriculum?*
6. *How do we select subject matter?*
7. *How do we measure the outcomes of instruction?*[98]

Influenced by Bobbitt's definition of curriculum as "that series of things which children and youth must do and experience," Caswell and Campbell, in their classic text *Curriculum Development,* maintained that the curriculum must consider "all elements in the experience of the learner."[99] They thought curriculum should synthesize the fields of philosophy, psychology, and sociology—what other curricularists would later refer to as the foundations of curriculum. To a large extent, Caswell envisioned curriculum as a field with few limitations on content; rather, he thought curriculum represented a procedure or process that incorporated scientific steps of development, organization, instruction, and evaluation.

Caswell and Campbell believed that the curriculum must address three basic elements: children's interests, social functions, and organized knowledge. The curriculum was to provide the proper scope and sequence of subject matter at every grade level. The *scope* was to represent broad themes based on social functions (similar to educational aims), such as conservation of natural resources, worthy home membership, democratic living, and so on. The *sequence* was based on experiences according to the children's interests. *Subject matter* was suggested to match the social functions and the learner's interests; the knowledge that was taught was to be measured as outcomes of instruction.

Eight Year Study.   Although traditional subject matter and methods dominated the school curriculum, the progressive movement was still influential in certain parts of the country, particularly in Denver, St. Louis, and Winnetka. While most high schools implemented the mainstream curriculum, there were sharp criticism and outspoken differences among elementary school progressive educators. Most high school teachers and principals were reluctant to implement progressive changes because the curriculum was (as it is today) test driven and dominated by college admission requirements.[100]

The Progressive Education Association launched the "Eight Year Study," from 1932 to 1940, to show that a new curriculum designed to meet the needs and interests of students was just as effective as one designed around traditional tests and admission requirements to college. As many as 30 progressive or experimental high schools and 1,475 graduates were matched with corresponding schools and students from traditional college preparatory tracks. It was found that the experimental or progressive group did just as well as or better than the control or traditional group on cognitive, social, and psychological bases.

Despite the evidence suggesting that the progressive curriculum was as good or better for college preparation, the traditional academic program prevailed. Nevertheless, the study demonstrated the essential principles of curriculum making as purported by the Twenth-sixth Yearbook of the National Society for the Study of Education (NSSE). The study established a curriculum commission largely around the ideas of Rugg (and the Yearbook), and it led to several books; among the best known are those by Wilford Aiken and Harry Giles.[101] One major participant in the project was Giles's colleague Ralph Tyler. Many of Tyler's ideas, later to be published in *Basic Principles of Curriculum and Instruction,* stemmed from the principles and ideas generated by the Study (as well as the NSSE Yearbook).

Although the idea of stating objectives in behavioral terms had been introduced 20 years prior to the Study, it was this group of curriculum specialists that first introduced it on a national level; and, because of the visibility of the Study, it has remained a standard approach since. The Study group insisted on classifying or grouping objectives into homogeneous types or related categories. Tyler and Taba were both later to use this idea as a basis for classifying objectives into the (1) acquisition of knowledge, (2) intellectual skills, (3) attitudes and feelings, and (4) academic skills or study habits.[102] See Curriculum Tips 3-4.

Members of the Eight Year Study understood that education was designed to change people (an idea rooted in Dewey and Thorndike) and that objectives would classify the desired behavioral changes. It was further understood that the nature of objectives required an evaluation to determine whether the objectives had been achieved or to what extent. The Study confirmed the need for comprehensive evaluation, as part of curriculum making, including data on (1) *student achievement,* such as initial levels of mastery, standardized tests, social and psychological skills, and creativity; (2) *social factors,* such as social class, peer group, community patterns, and motivational abilities; (3) *teaching-learning processes,* such as classroom management, homework assignments, and student-teacher interaction; and (4) *instructional methods,* such as discussions, demonstrations, problem solving, and discovery.

Taba worked on the evaluation team of the Study, along with Tyler, and later developed the idea of comprehensive evaluation in her work as chair of the ASCD's Commission on Evaluation in the 1940s and 1950s and in her classic text, *Curriculum Development: Theory and Practice,* in 1962. Tyler also played a key role in the evaluation of the Study, and some of his ideas were the basis of the evaluation component of the Study; they were further elaborated in his classic text, *Basic Principles of Curriculum and Instruction,* in 1949.

It later became apparent that the ideas of curriculum making developed by the Study did not filter down to the schools because teachers were not deeply involved in the curriculum. Most curriculum committees failed to include teachers, and restricted them to examining classroom textbooks and materials or modifying curriculum guides developed by central district offices. The exclusion of teachers from clarifying school goals and program objectives, organizing subject matter and learning activities, and participating in the evaluation process confirmed the traditional top-down practice of curriculum making of the period.

Tyler: Basic Principles

An account of curriculum as a field is not complete without discussion of Ralph Tyler, (1902-1994). Although Tyler published more than 700 articles and sixteen books on the subjects of curriculum, instruction, and evaluation, he is best known for his small book, *Basic Principles of Curriculum and Instruction.*[103] Originally written as a course syllabus for his students at the University of Chicago, the book was published in 1949; it has already gone through over thirty-five printings.

In 128 pages, Tyler covers the basic questions that he believes should be answered by anyone involved in planning or writing a curriculum for any subject or grade level:

1. *What educational purposes should the school seek to attain?*
2. *What educational experiences can be provided that are likely to attain these purposes?*
3. *How can these educational experiences be effectively organized?*

Curriculum Tips 3-4

Classifying Objectives

Those in charge of formulating objectives should pay close attention in translating school goals into objectives. The process is twofold: (1) formulating objectives into subject areas and/or grade levels, often called program objectives, and (2) categorizing objectives into related categories or clusters. The example below, derived from the South Bend school district, involves elementary social studies and was developed during the era of the Eight Year Study. It includes three of four categories later advocated by Tyler and Taba as a method for grouping objectives. Most interesting, the objectives are still relevant today.

1. Children need to understand (knowledge):
   a. That all peoples of the world are in some way dependent on each other and must get along with each other.
   b. That our world is constantly changing.
   c. That events, discoveries, and inventions may improve some ways of living but create problems in others.
   d. That people have established communities and governments to meet their needs.
   e. That groups develop traditions, values, and ways of doing things, and new generations learn these from their elders.
   f. That the physical geography of a place affects way people live.
2. Children need to learn how (skills):
   a. To seek information from many sources and to judge its validity.
   b. To organize facts and form generalizations based on facts.
   c. To carry on a discussion based on facts and to make generalizations or conclusions.
   d. To plan, to carry out plans. and to evaluate the work and the planning.
   e. To accept responsibility as part of living.
   f. To develop a set of values for judging right and wrong actions.
3. Children need to become (attitudes):
   a. Willing to undertake and carry through a job to completion.
   b. Anxious to help others and to work with others for desirable group goals.
   c. Appreciative of others like and unlike themselves.

Source: For Our Time: A Handbook for Elementary Social Studies Teachers (South Bend, Ind.: School City of South Bend, 1949). pp. 229–230.

---

4. *How can we determine whether these purposes are being attained?*[104]

Tyler was highly influenced by the progressive social theories of Judd and Dewey, as well as the learning theories of Thorndike and Piaget. He drew from the behaviorists, too, including Bobbitt and Charters. His philosophy and principles of curriculum were influenced by older contemporaries, such as George Counts (while Tyler was at the University of Chicago) and Boyd Bode (while he was at Ohio State University).

We might consider Tyler's model an elaboration of Rugg's four major tasks in curriculum and also a condensed version of the NSSE's Twenty-Sixth Yearbook. The Tyler model depicts a rational, logical, and systematic approach to curriculum making. Although it embraces no philosophical or political bias in the sense that any subject can be organized around the model, its ideas are rooted in progressivism (it emphasizes the needs of the learner), scientific procedures (its principles are applicable in varying situations), and behaviorism (its objectives are the most important consideration, in Tyler's own words).

Tyler's book, nevertheless, has been highly influential, because of its rational, no-nonsense, and sequential approach. In just over 100 pages, Tyler laid out a basic procedure to follow with easy-to-understand examples. Tyler gives students a manageable description, a series of concise steps, through which to plan curriculum.

Although critics have judged Tyler's model to be inadequate, naive, overly lockstep, and technocratic, and have censured it for its oversimplifying view of curriculum making as the collection of small bits of behavior,[105] it still works for many. Because it is simple to grasp, it serves as a starting point for curriculum students (which was its original intention).

Perhaps the most important reason Tyler is so influential is that he worked closely with a number of influential colleagues, besides Taba, such as Paul Diederich, Harold Dunkel, Maurice Hartung, Virgil Herrick, and Joseph Schwab, who accepted many of his ideas and who also influenced curriculum. In addition, many of Tyler's students at Ohio State University, such as Edgar Dale, Louis Heil, Louis Raths, and Harold Shane, and at the University of Chicago, such as Elliot Eisner, Ned Flanders, Thomas Hastings, David Krathwohl, Malcolm Provus, and Louise Tyler were influenced by Tyler and also became prominent in the field. Most important, a number of Tyler's other students, including Ben Bloom, Lee Cronbach, John Goodlad, Ken Rehage, Ole Sand, and Herbert Thelen, were also his colleagues for many years.[106] With the exception of Eisner, these colleagues continuously praised Tyler's work in the professional literature. See Table 3-5 for an overview of theorists up to and including Tyler.

CURRENT FOCUS

The Tyler model summed up the best principles of curriculum making for the first half of the twentieth century. This model has been utilized and adapted by many curricularists. In fact, many practitioners in schools consider the Tyler model as a metanarrative of the way to create curricula. However, at this time, all metanarratives, whether curricular, social, economic, or political, are being challenged. Both practitioners and curriculum scholars realize that the study of curriculum and its enactment within current times is at times confusing and at all times complex.[107] To some, we are in a time of kaleidoscopic postmodern visions, and we cannot reduce the curriculum to a particular focus or a single definition or a sole perception of a new master narrative.[108] Whether one accepts that we are indeed in a postmodern time, we are certainly in a time unprecedented in its complexity.

Analyses of the current and emerging times suggest that curriculum decision makers will have to maintain closer union with curriculum historians, especially with curriculum historians who focus on recent history. As Goodson points out, the need will continue to increase for curricularists to engage in dialogue with curriculum historians as we realize that such scholarly work will afford all educators with a more complete understanding of the total context within which curricula have been and are created and delivered.[109] Curricular historians will reveal for our consideration the various subtexts that have existed and continue to exist within human action placed in a time frame.

The time is past when we can accept unequivocally the "kind of science that has dominated educational research, including (curriculum) development, that has nurtured a belief in decontextualized precision for the sole purpose of management and control."[110] This had led to prescriptive models of curriculum and instruction, uniform methods of teaching and testing, and outcomes of learning that can be standardized and measured. This tendency toward scientific principles, the acceptance of a metanarrative regarding curriculum making, and educational research, in general, has resulted in nonexpressive and nonemotional forms of education—education that is value neutral and technical and that neglects the human spirit.[111]

Several curricularists today—like Mike Apple, Maxine Greene, Herb Kliebard, Gail McCutcheon, William Pinar, and William Doll—have lost faith in the ability of scientific principles and technical models to solve curriculum problems.

TABLE 3-5 Overview of Curriculum Theorists 1918–1949

THEORIST	PURPOSE	PRINCIPLES	CONTENT	MAJOR BOOK
Franklin Bobbitt (1876–1956)	Curriculum as a science Emphasis on student needs Prepare students for adult life Clarify objectives Cost-effective education	Grouping and sequencing objectives with corresponding activities Clarifying instructional specifications and tasks	Basic three Rs in elementary schools Academic subjects in high school Subject matter and related activities planned by teacher	*The Curriculum,* 1918 *How to Make a Curriculum,* 1924
Werrett Charters (1875–1952)	Curriculum as a science Emphasis on student needs (and needs assessment) Bridging theory and practice in curriculum	Curriculum process, described as job analysis Listing of objectives and corresponding activities Verification of objectives through evaluation	Subject matter related to objectives Subject matter and corresponding activities planned by teacher	*Curriculum Construction,* 1923
William Kilpatrick (1871–1965)	School as a social and community experience Curriculum identified as purposeful activities Child-centered curriculum Child development and growth	Project method, a blend of behaviorism and progressivism Teacher and student planning, emphasis on the student Emphasis on pedagogy or instructional activities: creative projects, social relationships, and small-group instruction	Educating a generalist, not a specialist Integrated subject matter Problem solving	*Foundations of Method,* 1926

THEORIST	PURPOSE	PRINCIPLES	CONTENT	MAJOR BOOK
Harold Rugg (1886–1960)	Education in context with society Child-centered curriculum Whole child Curriculum specialist as an engineer	Statement of objectives, related learning experiences, and outcomes Teacher plans curriculum in advance	Emphasis on social studies	*The Child Centered Curriculum* (with Ann Shumaker), 1928
Hollis Caswell (1901–1989)	Foundations of education (history, philosophy, etc.) influence curriculum development Relationship of three major components: curriculum, instruction, and learning Student needs and interests Curriculum organized around social functions (themes), organized knowledge, and learners' interests	Curriculum as a set of experiences Curriculum guides as a source of teacher planning Teachers coordinate instructional activities to implement curriculum	Subject matter organized in relation to student needs and interests Subject matter developed around social functions and learners' interests	*Curriculum Development* (with Doak Campbell), 1935
Ralph W. Tyler (1902–1994)	Curriculum as a science and extension of school's philosophy Clarify purposes (objectives) by studies of learners and contemporary life, suggestions from subject specialists, and use of philosophy and psychology Student needs and interests Relationship between curriculum and instruction	Curriculum as a rational process Using objectives to select and organize learning experiences Using evaluation to determine outcomes (whether objectives have been achieved) Vertical and horizontal relationship of curriculum	Subject matter organized in terms of knowledge, skills, and values Emphasis on problem solving Educating a generalist, not a specialist	*Basic Principles of Curriculum and Instruction*, 1949

Like Eisner, they have turned to various personal, aesthetic, and linguistic concepts to formulate—or better yet, to reformulate—curriculum.

If you believe that the study of historical foundations will furnish a clearer understanding of the field of curriculum both past and present, and will provide some insight into the future, you may be disappointed. Certainly, such study will allow us to create programs, but we must realize that our creations are not permanent scientific procedures on which we can depend, regardless of the times. Rather, our procedures are very much influenced by the times, by our levels of knowledge of the concepts and principles of curriculum creation and delivery, and by the fact we are changing, growing persons.

In accepting curriculum history as an essential foundation for all engaged in curricular activity, we must link our actions regarding curriculum to the numerous realms of human activity. Possessing a historical sense, we will realize that dialogue and collaboration are necessary. We will comprehend that curricular activity exists within various "configurations of factors that are time bound and context-specific" and out of such dynamics emerge appropriate actions for particular times, rather than one best system.[112]

Possessing a historical sense of curriculum allows us to realize and relish the fact that the field of curriculum is dynamic and continuing to mature. The field is moving beyond schools to include programs in business, industry, military, government, and health fields and to incorporate content and knowledge from many other disciplines, such as philosophy, psychology, sociology, and political science. The field also draws on knowledge that extends beyond the cognitive and physical. The spiritual dimensions of human beings are being considered as appropriate curricular content.

These new foci will generate diverse questions and stimulate new methods of inquiry, new procedures for research. Curriculum specialists are adapting the tools of both quantitative and qualitative research methodologies; drawing on the fields of computer science and cybernetics; drawing on new approaches to instructional technology; and incorporating new procedures of system analysis. In short, curriculum is an increasingly dynamic and diverse field of study and is becoming more interdisciplinary, scientific, and qualitative in both a modern and postmodern manner.

Conclusion

From the colonial period to around World War I, curriculum was a matter of evolving subject matter. Some reform ideas concerned pedagogical principles, mainly as a result of European influence and the emerging progressive reform movement of the mid and late nineteenth century. But these ideas were limited to theoretical discussions and a few isolated and innovative schools. The perennialist curriculum, which emphasized the classics and timeless and absolute values based around religious and then moral doctrines, remained dominant for the first 150 years of our nation's history.

The idea of principles and processes of curriculum began to take shape after the turn of the twentieth century, along with emphasis on scientific principles and progressive philosophy. Curriculum as a field of study, with its own methods and theories and ways of solving problems, has made real advances ever since the 1920s. Most of the advances have actually taken place since Tyler wrote his basic text on curriculum. Many of these advances are discussed elsewhere in this text.

Endnotes

1. Herbert M. Kliebard, "Constructing a History of the American Curriculum," in Philip W. Jackson, ed., *Handbook of Research on Curriculum* (Macmillan Publishing Co., 1992), pp. 157–184.
2. William F. Pinar, William M. Reynolds, Patrick Slattery, and Peter M. Taubman, *Understanding Curriculum* (New York: Peter Lang, 1995).

3. Kliebard, "Constructing a History of the American Curriculum."
4. John S. Brubacher, *A History of the Problems of Education* (New York: McGraw-Hill, 1947); R. Freeman Butts and Lawrence A. Cremin, *A History of Education in American Culture* (New York: Holt, Rinehart and Winston, 1953).

5. Warren H. Button and Eugene Provenzo, *History of Education and Culture in America*, 2nd ed. (Englewood Cliffs, N.J.: Prentice Hall, 1989); Butts and Cremin, *A History of Education in American Culture.*

6. George A. Beauchamp, *The Curriculum of the Elementary School* (Boston: Allyn and Bacon, 1964), p. 34.

7. Allan C. Ornstein and Daniel U. Levine, *An Introduction to the Foundations of Education*, 5th ed. (Boston: Houghton Mifflin, 1993), p. 161. See also S. Alexander Rippa, *Education in a Free Society,* 7th ed. (New York: Longman, 1992).

8. Beauchamp, *The Curriculum of the Elementary School,* p. 36.

9. Paul Monroe, *Founding of the American Public School System* (New York: Macmillan, 1940); Samuel E. Morrison, *The Intellectual Life of Colonial New England* (New York: New York University Press, 1956).

10. Robert Middlekauff, *Ancients and Axioms: Secondary Education in the Eighteenth-Century New England* (New Haven, Conn.: Yale University Press, 1963).

11. Elmer E. Brown, *The Making of Our Middle School* (New York: Longman, 1926), p. 133.

12. Newton Edwards and Herman G. Richey, *The School in the American Social Order,* 2nd ed. (Boston: Houghton Mifflin, 1963), p. 102.

13. Morrison, *The Intellectual Life of Colonial New England.* Joel Spring, *The American School: 1642–1990* (New York: Longman, 1990).

14. John H. Best, *Benjamin Franklin on Education* (New York: Teachers College Press, Columbia University, 1962).

15. Ellwood P. Cubberley, *Public Education in the United States,* rev. ed. (Boston: Houghton Mifflin, 1947), p. 30.

16. R. Freeman Butts, *The American Tradition in Religion and Education* (Boston: Beacon Press, 1950); Gerald R. Firth and Richard D. Kimpston, *The Curricular Continuum in Perspective* (Itasca, Ill.: Peacock, 1973).

17. Paul L. Ford, *The New England Primer: A History of Its Origins and Development,* rev. ed. (New York: Dodd, Mead, 1897), pp. 329–330.

18. Henry Barnard, *Educational Developments in the United States* (Hartford, Conn.: Connecticut Department of Education, 1867), p. 367.

19. Cubberley, *Public Education in the United States;* Merle Curti, *The Social Ideas of American Educators* (New York: Littlefield, Adams, 1959).

20. Benjamin Rush, *A Plan for the Establishment of Public Schools* (Philadelphia: Thomas Dobson, 1786), pp. 29–30.

21. Thomas Jefferson, "A Bill for the More General Diffusion of Knowledge," in P. L. Ford, ed., *The Writings of Thomas Jefferson* (New York: Putnam, 1893), p. 221.

22. Merle Curti, *The Growth of American Thought,* rev. ed. (New York: Harper & Row, 1951).

23. Hans Kohn, *American Nationalism: An Interpretive Essay* (New York: Macmillan, 1957), p. 47.

24. Noah Webster, *Dissertations on the English Language* (Boston: Isaiah Thomas, 1789), p. 27.

25. Harvey R. Warfel, *Noah Webster: Schoolmaster to America* (New York: Macmillan, 1936).

26. Henry Steele Commager, ed., *Noah Webster's American Spelling Book* (New York: Teachers College Press, Columbia University, 1962).

27. Robert K. Leavitt, *Noah's Ark, New England Yankees and the Endless Quest* (Springfield, Mass.: Merriam, 1947); Richard M. Rollins, "Words as Social Control: Noah Webster and the Creation of the American Dictionary," *American Quarterly* (Fall 1976), pp. 415–430.

28. William H. McGuffey, *New Fifth Eclectic Reader* (Cincinnati: Winthrop Smith, 1857), p. 271.

29. William H. McGuffey, *Newly Revised Eclectic Fourth Reader* (Cincinnati: Winthrop Smith, 1853), p. 313.

30. John H. Westerhoff, *McGuffey and His Readers: Piety, Morality, and Education in Nineteenth Century America* (Nashville, Tenn.: Abingdon, 1978).

31. William B. Ragan and Gene D. Shepherd, *Modern Elementary Curriculum,* 7th ed. (New York: Holt, Rinehart and Winston, 1992), p. 23.

32. Edgar W. Knight, *Education in the United States,* 3rd ed. (Boston: Ginn, 1951), p. 512.

33. See Henry Barnard, *Pestalozzi and Pestalozzianism* (New York: Brownell, 1862).

34. Friedrich Froebel, *The Education of Man,* trans. W. Hailman (New York: Appleton, 1889).

35. Johann F. Herbart, *Textbook of Psychology* (New York: Appleton, 1894).

36. John Dewey, *How We Think* (Boston: D. C. Heath, 1910), p. 202.

37. Andreas Kazamias, *Herbert Spencer on Education* (New York: Teachers College Press, Columbia University, 1966).

38. Herbert Spencer, *Education: Intellectual, Moral and Physical* (New York: Appleton, 1860).

39. Michael W. Apple, "The Politics of Official Knowledge in the United States," *Journal of Curriculum Studies* (July–August 1990), pp. 377–383.

40. See Everett Dick, *Vanguards of the Frontier* (New York: Appleton-Century, 1940); William W. Folwell, *The Autobiography and Letters of a Pioneer Culture* (Minneapolis: University of Minnesota Press, 1923).

41. Joel Spring, *The Storting Machine Revisited* (New York: Longman, 1989).

42. Button and Provenzo, *History of Education and Culture in America;* Monroe, *Founding of the American Public School System.*

43. Frederick M. Binder, *The Age of the Common School: 1830–1865* (New York: Wiley, 1974).

44. V. T. Thayer and Martin Levit, *The Role of the School in American Society,* 2nd ed. (New York: Dodd, Mead, 1966), p. 6.

45. Lawrence A. Cremin, *The Republic and the School: Horace Mann on the Education of Free Man* (New York: Teachers College Press, Columbia University Press, 1957); Jonathan Messerlie, *Horace Mann: A Biography* (New York: Knopf, 1972).

46. Andrew Gulliford, *America's Country Schools* (Washington, D.C.: National Trust for Historic Preservation, 1985).

47. James H. Hughes, *Education in America,* 3rd ed. (New York: Harper & Row, 1970), p. 233.

48. Carl Sandburg, *Abraham Lincoln: The Prairie Years* (New York: Harcourt, Brace, 1926), p. 19.

49. Theodore R. Sizer, *The Age of Academies* (New York: Teachers College Press, Columbia University, 1964).

50. E. P. Cubberley, *The History of Education* (Boston: Houghton Mifflin, 1920), p. 697.

51. Edwards and Richey, *The School in the American Social Order;* Firth and Kimpston, *The Curricular Continuum in Perspective.*

52. Brown, *The Making of Our Middle Schools,* p. 230.

53. Monroe, *Founding of the American Public School System,* p. 404.

54. Edward A. Krug, *The Shaping of the American High School: 1880–1920* (New York: Harper & Row, 1964); Daniel Tanner, *Secondary Education: Perspectives and Prospects* (New York: Macmillan, 1972).

55. Cubberley, *Public Education in the United States;* Edwards and Richey, *The School in the American Social Order;* and Monroe, *Founding of the American Public School System.*

56. Davis, *Our Evolving High School Curriculum;* David H. Kamens and Yun-Kyung Cha, "The Legitimation of New Subjects in Mass Schooling," *Journal of Curriculum Studies* (January–February 1992), pp. 43–60.

57. Krug, *The Shaping of the American High School.*

58. John H. Bishop, "The Productivity Consequences of What Is Learned in High School," *Journal of Curriculum Studies* (March–April 1990), pp. 101–126; Kamens and Cha, "The Legitimation of New Subjects in Mass Schooling."

59. Thayer and Levit, *The Role of the School in American Society,* p. 382.

60. *Report of the Year 1889–90* (Washington, D.C.: U.S. Bureau of Education, 1893), pp. 1388–1389. See also Table 3–2.

61. Cubberley, *Public Education in the United States,* p. 543.

62. Paul Gagnon, *Historical Literacy: The Case of History in American Education;* Robert S. Zais, *Curriculum: Principles and Foundations* (New York: Harper & Row, 1976).

63. *Report of the Committee of Ten on Secondary School Studies,* book ed. (New York: American Book, 1894), p. 48.

64. Daniel Tanner and Laurel Tanner, *Curriculum Development: Theory into Practice,* 2nd ed. (New York: Macmillan, 1980), p. 233. See also Richard Pratte, *The Civic Imperative* (New York: Teachers College Press, Columbia University, 1988).

65. Edward L. Thorndike, "Mental Discipline in High School Studies," *Journal of Educational Psychology* (February 1924), p. 98.

66. Charles W. Eliot, "The Case against Compulsory Latin," *Atlantic* (March 1917), pp. 356–359.

67. Abraham Flexner, "Parents and School," *Atlantic* (July 1916), p. 30.

68. Abraham Flexner, "A Modern School," *Occasional Papers,* No. 3 (New York: General Education Board, 1916); Flexner, *A Modern College and a Modern School* (New York: Doubleday, 1923).

69. John Dewey, *Democracy and Education* (New York: Macmillan, 1916).

70. Ibid., p. 190.

71. Charles H. Judd, *Introduction to the Scientific Study of Education* (Boston: Ginn, 1918).

72. Commission on the Reorganization of Secondary Education, *Cardinal Principles of Secondary Education,* Bulletin No. 35 (Washington, D.C.: U.S. Government Printing Office, 1918).

73. Frederick W. Taylor, *The Principles of Scientific Management* (New York: Harper & Row, 1911).

74. Raymond E. Callahan, *Education and the Cult of Efficiency* (Chicago: University of Chicago Press, 1962).

75. Franklin Bobbitt, *The Curriculum* (Boston: Houghton Mifflin, 1918), p. 42.

76. Ibid., p. 283.

77. Franklin Bobbitt, *How to Make a Curriculum* (Boston: Houghton Mifflin, 1924), pp. 14, 28.

78. Elliot W. Eisner, *The Educational Imagination,* 3rd ed. (New York: Macmillan, 1993); Herbert Kliebard, *The Struggle for the American Curriculum: 1893–1951* (Boston: Routledge, 1986).

79. W. W. Charters, *Curriculum Construction* (New York: Macmillan, 1923).

80. Ibid., pp. 6–7. See also W. W. Charters, "Idea Men and Engineers in Education," *Educational Forum* (Spring 1986), pp. 263–272. Originally published in *Educational Forum* (May 1948), pp. 399–406.

81. John Dewey, "Individuality and Experience," in J. Dewey, ed., *Art and Education* (Marion, Pa.: Barnes Foundation, 1929), p. 180.

82. William H. Kilpatrick, "The Project Method," *Teachers College Record* (September 1918), pp. 319–335.

83. Junius L. Merian, *Child Life and the School Curriculum* (New York: World Book, 1920).

84. Ellsworth Collings, *An Experiment with a Project Curriculum* (New York: Macmillan, 1923).

85. Boyd Bode, *Modern Educational Theories* (New York: Macmillan, 1927); John L. Childs, *Education and the Philosophy of Experimentalism* (New York: Appleton, 1931).

86. William H. Kilpatrick, *Foundations of Education* (New York: Macmillan, 1926), p. 212.

87. Ibid., p. 213.

88. John McNeil, *Curriculum: A Comprehensive Introduction* (Glenview, Ill.: Scott, Foresman, 1990); Tanner and Tanner, *Curriculum Development*.

89. William H. Kilpatrick, ed., *The Educational Frontier* (New York: Century, 1933), pp. 4–5.

90. Ibid., p. 19

91. Ellsworth Collings, *Project Teaching in Elementary Schools* (New York: Century, 1928).

92. Guy M. Whipple, ed., *Curriculum-Making: Past and Present,* Twenty-Sixth Yearbook of the National Society for the Study of Education, Part I (Bloomington, Ill.: Public School Publishing Co., 1930; Whipple, ed., *The Foundations of Curriculum-Making,* Twenty-Sixth Yearbook of the National Society for the Study of Education, Part II (Bloomington, Ill.: Public School Publishing Co., 1930).

93. Harold Rugg, "Forward," in Whipple, ed., *Curriculum-Making: Past and Present,* p. 1.

94. Harold Rugg, "The School Curriculum and the Drama of American Life," in Whipple, ed., *Curriculum-Making: Past and Present,* pp. 3–16.

95. Harold Rugg, "Three Decades of Mental Discipline: Curriculum-Making via National Committees," in Whipple, ed., *Curriculum-Making: Past and Present,* pp. 52–53.

96. Harold Rugg and Ann Shumaker, *The Child-Centered School* (New York: World Book, 1928), p. 118.

97. David Pratt, *Curriculum: Design and Development* (New York: Harcourt, Brace, 1980). Also see Henry J. Perkinson, *The Imperfect Panacea: American Faith in Education, 1865–1990,* 3rd ed. (New York: McGraw-Hill, 1991).

98. Sidney B. Hall, D. W. Peters, and Hollis L. Caswell, *Study Course for Virginia State Curriculum* (Richmond: Virginia State Board of Education, 1932), p. 363.

99. Hollis L. Caswell and Doak S. Campbell, *Curriculum Development* (New York: American Book, 1935), p. 69.

100. Ralph W. Tyler, "Curriculum Development in the Twenties and Thirties," in R. M. McClure, ed., *The Curriculum: Retrospect and Prospect,* Seventeenth Yearbook of the National Society for the Study of Education, Part I (Chicago: University of Chicago Press, 1971), pp. 26–44; Tyler, "The Five Most Significant Curriculum Events in the Twentieth Century," *Educational Leadership* (December–January 1987), pp. 36–38. Also see Louis Rubin, "Educational Evaluation: Classic Works of Ralph W. Tyler," *Journal of Curriculum Studies* (March–April 1991). pp. 193–198.

101. Wilford Aiken, *The Story of the Eight Year Study* (New York: Harper & Row, 1942); H. H. Giles, S. P. McCutchen, and A. N. Zechiel, *Exploring the Curriculum* (New York: Harper & Row, 1942).

102. Hilda Taba, "Evaluation in High Schools and Junior Colleges," in W. S. Gray, ed., *Reading in Relation to Experience and Language* (Chicago: University of Chicago Press, 1944), pp. 199–204; Taba, *Curriculum Development: Theory and Practice* (New York: Harcourt, Brace, 1962); Ralph W. Tyler, *Basic Principles of Curriculum and Instruction* (Chicago: University of Chicago Press, 1949); and E. R. Smith and Ralph W. Tyler, eds., *Appraising and Recording Student Progress* (New York: Harper & Row, 1942).

103. Ralph W. Tyler, *Basic Principles of Curriculum and Instruction* (Chicago: University of Chicago Press, 1949).

104. Ibid., p. 1.

105. Henry Giroux, *Teachers as Intellectuals* (Westport, Conn.: Bergin & Garvey, 1988); Herbert M. Kliebard, "Reappraisal: The Tyler Rationale," in A. A. Bellack and H. M. Kliebard, eds., *Curriculum and Evaluation* (Berkeley, Calif.: McCutchen, 1977), pp. 34–69; and James T. Sears and J. Dan Marshall, eds., *Teaching and Thinking About Curriculum* (New York: Teachers College Press, Columbia University, 1990).

106. Marie K. Stone, *Principles of Curriculum, Instruction, and Evaluation: Past Influence and Present Effects.* Ph.D. dissertation, Loyola University of Chicago, January 1985. Also from conversations by one of the authors with John Beck, April 12, 1991.

107. Henry A. Giroux, "Educational Visions: What Are Schools for and What Should We Be Doing in the Name of Education?" in Joe L. Kincheloe and Shirley R. Steinberg, eds. *Thirteen Questions,* 2nd ed. (New York: Peter Lang, 1995), pp. 295–303.

108. Patrick Slattery, *Curriculum Development in the Postmodern Era* (New York: Garland Publishing, Inc., 1995).

109. Ivor F. Goodson, *Studying Curriculum* (New York: Teachers College Press, 1994).

110. Robert V. Carlson and Gary Akerman, eds., *Educational Planning* (New York: Longman, 1991), p. 102.

111. Elliot W. Eisner, *The Enlightened Eye* (New York: Macmillan Publishing Co., 1991).

112. Kliebard, "Constructing a History of the American Curriculum."

4

PSYCHOLOGICAL FOUNDATIONS
OF CURRICULUM

Focusing Questions

1. In what ways do psychological foundations enable curriculum workers (teachers and curriculum developers) to perform their educational responsibilities?
2. How would you compare the three major theoretical schools of learning?
3. How has the view of multiple intelligences influenced the field of curriculum? How might this concept of intelligence influence the field in the future?
4. How does constructivism incorporate the most recent views of learning?
5. How should the concept of learning styles influence the thinking of those responsible for curriculum development and delivery?
6. How should an educator utilize the information about various types of thinking?
7. How would you define humanistic learning in schools?
8. In what ways can addressing emotional intelligence be justified in the curriculum?

Psychology is concerned with the question of how people learn. And curriculum specialists ask how psychology can contribute to the design and delivery of curriculum. Or, put another way, how can curriculum specialists incorporate psychological knowledge to increase the probability that students will learn? Psychology provides a basis for understanding the teaching and learning process. Both processes are essential to curricularists, for it is only when students learn and understand the curriculum and gain knowledge and power to use it that the curriculum has actual worth. Other questions of mutual interest to psychologists and curriculum specialists are the following: Why do learners respond as they do to the efforts of the teachers? What are the impacts of cultural experiences on students' learning? How should curriculum be organized to enhance learning? What impact does the school culture have on students' learning? What is the optimal level of student participation in learning the various contents of the curriculum?

No curriculum scholar or practitioner would deny the criticalness of this psychological foundation. All agree that teaching the curriculum and learning the curriculum are interrelated, and psychology cements the relationship. This disciplined field of inquiry furnishes theories and principles of learning that influence teacher–student behavior within the context of the curriculum. However, those involved in both the development and teaching of curriculum are well advised to remember that there are competing theories and principles within this foundation. We have not arrived at certainty as to how people learn. Indeed, much current activity within this foundational field is calling into question "sacred" views on how people learn and how people should teach. A revolution is occurring in the study of the mind, involving not only psychologists but individuals from a wide range of sciences and disciplines. It is likely that medical researchers studying the brain may uncover information that will cause upheavals in curricularists' thinking about the psychological foundations. However, one thing is certain; psychological foundations will continue to be a key basis for curricular thought and action. Such thinking is not new.

For John Dewey, psychology was the basis for understanding how the individual learner interacts with objects and persons in the environment. The process goes on for life, and the quality of interaction determines the amount and type of learning. Ralph Tyler considered psychology to be a "screen" for helping determine what our objectives are and how our learning takes place.[1] More recently, Jerome Bruner linked psychology with modes of thinking that underlie the methods employed in various bodies of knowledge comprising specific disciplines. The goal of utilizing these methods is to formulate concepts, principles, and generalizations that form the structure of the disciplines.[2] In short, psychology is the unifying element of the learning process; it forms the basis for the methods, materials, and activities of learning, and it subsequently serves as the impetus for many curriculum decisions.

Historically, the major theories of learning have been classified into three groups: (1) behaviorist or association theories, the oldest one of which deals with various aspects of stimulus-response and reinforcers; (2) cognitive-information processing theories, which view the learner in relationship to the total environment and consider the way the learner applies information; and (3) phenomenological and humanistic theories, which consider the whole child, including his or her social, psychological and cognitive development. When behaviorist theories are discussed separately, learning tends to focus on conditioning, modifying, or shaping behavior through reinforcement and rewards. When cognitive information processing theories are stressed, the learning process focuses on the student's developmental stages and multiple forms of intelligence, as well as problem solving, critical thinking, and creativity. The phenomenological aspects of learning deal with needs, attitudes, and feelings of the learner and entail more alternatives in learning.

BEHAVIORISM

The behaviorists, who represent traditional psychology, are rooted in philosophical speculation about the nature of learning—the ideas of Aristotle, Descartes, Locke, and Rousseau. They emphasize conditioning behavior and altering the environment to elicit selected responses from the learner. This theory has dominated much of twentieth-century psychology.

Connectionism

One of the first Americans to conduct experimental testing of the learning process was Edward Thorndike, and he is considered the founder of behavioral psychology. At Harvard, Thorndike began his work with animals, a course of experimentation other behaviorists adopted as well.[3] Thorndike focused his work on testing the relationship between a stimulus and a response (classical conditioning) He defined learning as habit formation—as connecting more and more habits into a complex structure. He defined teaching, then, as arranging the classroom so as to enhance desirable connections as bonds.

Thorndike developed three major laws of learning: (1) the *Law of Readiness*—when a "conduction" unit is ready to conduct, to do so is satisfying and not to do so is annoying; (2) the *Law of Exercise*—a connection is strengthened in proportion to the number of times it occurs, and in proportion to average intensity and duration; and (3) the *Law of Effect*—responses accompanied by satisfaction are important for strengthening the connection; conversely, responses accompanied by discomfort weaken the connection.[4]

The Law of Readiness suggests that, when the nervous system is ready to conduct, it leads to a satisfying state of affairs; this has been misinterpreted by some educators as referring to educational readiness, such as readiness to read. The Law of Exercise provides justification for drill, repetition, and review and is best illustrated today by behavior modification and basic-skill instructional approaches. Although rewards and punishments were used in schools for centuries prior to Thorndike's formulation of the Law of Effect, his theory did make more explicit and furnished justification for what was already being done. B. F. Skinner's operant model of behavior, programmed instruction, and many current ideas based on providing satisfying experiences to the learner, as well as reinforcement in the form of feedback, are rooted in this law.

Thorndike maintained that (1) behavior was influenced more likely by conditions of learning; (2) attitudes and abilities of learners could change (and improve) over time through proper stimuli; (3) instructional experiences could be designed and controlled; and (4) it was important to select appropriate stimuli or learning experiences that were integrated and consistent—and that reinforced each other. For Thorndike, no one subject was more likely than another to improve the mind; rather, learning was a matter of relating new learning to previous learning. Thus, the "psychology" of mental discipline was attacked, and this attack meant that there was no hierarchy of subject matter.

Thorndike's Influence: Tyler, Taba, and Bruner

Coinciding with Thorndike's (1874–1949) theories, both Tyler and Taba maintained that learning had application and thus could be transferred to other situations.[5] This meant that rote learning and memorization of knowledge were unnecessary. The student could organize and classify information into existing mental schemata or patterns and use it in different situations. Much of Thorndike's theories of learning impacted on the behaviorist and logical approach outlined by Tyler and Taba. However, both Tyler and Taba disagreed with Thorndike's view of connections between specific stimuli and specific responses. Rather, they outlined a more generalized view of learning, one that more closely corresponds with a cognitive approach. Whereas Bobbitt and Charters opted for

the more precise behavioral approach to learning, along Thorndike's lines, which viewed objectives in context with highly specific habits to be acquired, Tyler and Taba were inclined to take Dewey's and Judd's approach: That learning was based on *generalizations* and the teaching of important *principles* (terms used by the latter four educators) to explain concrete phenomena.[6]

Note that both Tyler and Taba gave credit to Thorndike in their classic texts. Tyler's recognition of Thorndike was minimal; nevertheless, he spent considerable space discussing connectionism and organizing learning principles along Thorndike's transfer theories. Taba devoted an entire chapter to "the transfer of learning," as well as the influence that Thorndike and others had on this learning theory. Like Thorndike, Taba argued that practice alone does not necessarily strengthen memory or the transfer of learning, which served to free the curriculum from the rigid roteness and drill of the past. "Since no program, no matter how thorough, can teach everything, the task of all education is to cause a maximum amount of transfer."[7] The idea was to develop content or methods that led to generalizations and that had wide transfer value; this led to Taba's advocating problem-solving and inquiry-discovery techniques.

The notions of "learning how to learn" and "inquiry discovery," although popularized by Bruner, are rooted in Thorndike. Thorndike, and later Bruner, assumed that learning that involves meaningful organization of experiences can be transferred more readily than learning acquired by rote.[8] The more abstract the principles and generalizations, the greater the possibility of transfer. (This also corresponds with Dewey's idea of reflective thinking and the steps that he outlined for problem solving.)

For Bruner, learning the structure of a discipline provided the basis for the specific transfer of learning. The abilities to learn and to recall and use some information later are directly related to the learner's having a structural pattern by which information can be transferred to new situations. Transfer of learning is much more frequent when learning is of a basic, general nature. One difference between Thorndike and Bruner should be noted, however. Whereas Thorndike found that no one subject was more important than another subject for meaningful learning, Bruner gave great emphasis to science and mathematics as the major disciplines for teaching structure.

Classical Conditioning

The classical conditioning theory of learning emphasizes that learning consists of eliciting a response by means of previously neutral or inadequate stimuli; some neutral stimulus associated with an unconditioned stimulus at the time of response gradually acquires the ability to elicit the response. The classical conditioning experiment by Ivan Pavlov is widely known. In this experiment, a dog learned to salivate at the sound of a bell. The bell, a biologically neutral or inadequate stimulus, was being presented simultaneously with food, a biologically nonneutral or adequate stimulus. So closely were the two stimuli associated by the dog that the bell came to be substituted for the food, and the dog reacted to the bell as he originally had to the food.[9]

The implications for human learning were important. Some neutral stimulus (bell) associated with an unconditioned stimulus (food) at the time of the response gradually acquired the association to elicit the response (salivation). The theory has led to a wealth of laboratory investigations about learning and has become a focal point in social and political discussions—for example, Aldous Huxley's futuristic novel *Brave New World* and the movies *The Deer Hunter, Jacob's Ladder,* and *Silence of the Lambs.*

On the American scene, James Watson used Pavlov's research as a foundation for building a new science of psychology based on *behaviorism.* The new science emphasized that learning was based on the science of behavior, what was observable or measurable, and not on cognitive processes. The laws of behavior were derived from animal and then human studies and were expected to have all the objectivity of the laws of science.[10]

For Watson and others, the key to learning was to condition the child in the early years of life, based on the method Pavlov had demonstrated for animals. Thus, Watson once boasted:

> Give me a dozen healthy infants, well-informed, and my own specified world to bring them up and I'll guarantee to take anyone at random and train him to be any type of specialist I might select—a doctor, lawyer, artist . . . and yes, even into beg-

garman and thief, regardless of his talents, . . . abilities, vocations, and race.[11]

Operant Conditioning

Perhaps more than any other recent behaviorist, B. Frederick Skinner attempted to apply his theories to the classroom situation. Basing a major part of his theories on experiments with mice and pigeons, Skinner distinguishes two kinds of responses: *elicited,* a response identified with a definite stimulus, and *emitted,* a response that is apparently unrelated to an identifiable stimulus. When a response is elicited, the behavior is termed *respondent.* When it is emitted, the behavior is *operant*—that is, no observable or measurable stimuli explain the appearance of the response.[12] In operant conditioning, the role of stimuli is less definite; often, the emitted behavior cannot be connected to a specific stimulus.

Reinforcers can be classified, also, as primary, secondary, or generalized. A *primary* reinforcer applies to any stimulus that helps satisfy a basic drive, such as for food, water, or sex. (This reinforcer is also paramount in classical conditioning.) A *secondary* reinforcer is important for people, such as getting approval from friends or teachers, receiving money, or winning school awards. Although secondary reinforcers do not satisfy primary drives, they can be converted into primary reinforcers. Because of the choice and range of secondary reinforcers, Skinner refers to them as *generalized* reinforcers. Classroom teachers have a variety of secondary reinforcers at their disposal, ranging from words of praise or smiles to words of admonishment or punishment.

Operant behavior will discontinue when it is not followed by reinforcement. Skinner classifies reinforcers as positive or negative. A *positive* reinforcer is simply the presentation of a reinforcing stimulus. A student receives positive reinforcement when a test paper is returned with a grade of A or a note that says "Keep up the good work." A *negative* reinforcement is the removal or withdrawal of a stimulus. When the teacher shouts to the class, "Keep quiet," and the students quiet down, the students' silence reinforces the teacher's shouting. Punishment, on the other hand, calls for the presentation of unpleasant or harmful stimuli or the withdrawal of a (positive) reinforcer, but it is not always a negative reinforcer.[13] Although Skinner believes in both positive and negative reinforcement, he rejects punishment because he feels it inhibits learning.[14]

Acquiring New Operants

Skinner's approach of selective reinforcement, whereby only desired responses are reinforced, has wide appeal to educators because he has demonstrated its application to the instructional and learning process. An essential principle in the reinforcement interpretation of learning is the variability of human behavior, which makes change possible. Individuals can acquire *new operants*—that is, behavior can be shaped or modified and complex concepts can be taught to students. The individual's capability for the desired response is what makes the shaping of behavior or the learning possible. Behavior and learning can be shaped through a series of successive approximations or a sequence of responses that increasingly approximate the desired one. Thus, through a combination of reinforcing and sequencing desired responses, new behavior is shaped; this is what some people today refer to as *behavior modification.*

Although behavior modification approaches vary according to the student and the behavior being sought, they are widely used in conjunction with individualized-instructional techniques, programmed learning, and classroom management techniques. Student activities are specified, structured, paced, reinforced, rewarded, and frequently assessed in terms of learning outcomes or behaviors desired. With this approach, curriculum may be defined by Popham and Baker's definition: "all planned outcomes for which the school is responsible" and "the desired consequences of instruction."[15]

Observational Learning and Modeling. Albert Bandura has contributed extensively to what we know today about how students learn through observation and modeling. In a classic study, he showed how aggressive behavior can be learned from viewing human adults acting aggressively in real situations as well as in films and cartoons. The same children also learned nonaggressive behavior by observing humans of subdued temperaments.[16]

The repeated demonstration that people can learn and have their behavior shaped by observing another person or even film (obviously, the influence of TV is immense) has tremendous implications for modifying tastes and attitudes, how we learn and perform, or whether we want to develop soldiers or artists. For behaviorists, the idea suggests that cognitive factors are unnecessary in explaining learning; through modeling, students can learn how to perform at sophisticated levels of performance. While recognizing the value of reinforcement and reward, the learner needs mainly to attend and acquire the necessary responses through observation and then to model the behavior later. See Curriculum Tips 4-1.

Hierarchical Learning. Robert Gagné has presented a hierarchical arrangement of eight types of learning sets or behaviors that has become a classic model. The first five may be defined as behavioral operations, the next two as both behavioral and cognitive, and the last (and highest form of thinking) as cognitive in nature. The behaviors are based on prerequisite conditions, resulting in a cumulative process of learning. The eight types of learning and examples of each follow:

1. *Signal learning.* (classical conditioning, a response to a given signal). Example: Fear response to a rat.
2. *Stimulus response.* (operant conditioning [S-R], a response to a given stimulus). Example: Student's response to the command, "Please sit."
3. *Motor chains.* (linking together two or more S-R connections to form a more complex skill). Example: Dotting the i and crossing the t to write a word with an i and t.
4. *Verbal association.* (linking together two or more words or ideas). Example: Translating a foreign word.
5. *Multiple discriminations.* (responding in different ways to different items of a particular set). Example: Discriminating between grass and trees.
6. *Concepts.* (reacting to stimuli in an abstract way). Examples: animals, grammar, and so on.
7. *Rules.* (chaining two or more stimulus situations or concepts). Examples: Animals have offspring. An adjective modifies a noun.

Curriculum Tips 4-1

Behaviorism in Classroom Learning Situations

A wide range of behaviors can be used when applying behavioral theories in the classroom. These suggestions have meaning for behaviorist teaching and learning situations.

1. Consider that behavior is the result of particular conditions; alter conditions to achieve desired behaviors.
2. Use reinforcement and rewards to strengthen the behavior you wish to encourage.
3. Consider extinction or forgetting by reducing the frequency of undesirable behaviors.
4. Reduce undesirable behaviors as follows:
   a. Withhold reinforcement or ignore the behavior.
   b. Call attention to rewards that will follow the desired behavior.
   c. Take away a privilege or resort to punishment.
5. When students are learning factual material, provide frequent feedback; for abstract or complex material, provide delayed feedback.
6. Provide practice, drill, and review exercises; monitor learners' progress.
7. Consider workbooks, programmed materials, and computer programs that rely on sequenced approaches.
8. When students struggle with uninteresting material, use special reinforcers and rewards to motivate them.
   a. Select a variety of reinforcers students enjoy (candy bars, bubble gum, baseball cards).
   b. Establish a contract for work to be performed to earn a particular reward or grade.
   c. Provide frequent, immediate rewards.
9. Make use of observational learning.
   a. Select the most appropriate model.
   b. Model the behavior clearly and accurately.
   c. Insist that learners attend to what is being modeled.
   d. Provide praise when the desired behavior is exhibited.
   e. Have the learner practice the observed behavior.
   f. Provide corrective feedback during practice.
   g. Repeat demonstrations when necessary.
   h. Reinforce desired behaviors.
   i. Model behavior in similar settings in which learners will use the new skills.
10. Assess changes in learning and behavior.
    a. Diagnose learning problems.
    b. Establish levels of competency or mastery.
    c. Provide feedback.
    d. Integrate old tasks or skills with new ones.
    e. Reteach, when necessary.
    f. Take other actions.

---

8. *Problem solving.* (combining known rules or principles into new elements to solve a problem). Example: Finding the area of a triangle given the dimensions of two sides.[17]

Gagné also describes five learning outcomes that can be observed and measured and for him encompass all the domains of learning: (1) *intellectual skills,* "knowing how" to categorize and use verbal and mathematical symbols, forming concepts through rules, and problem solving; (2) *information,* which can be described as "knowing what," knowledge about facts, names, and dates; (3) *cognitive strategies,* skills needed to process and organize information, what today is called "learning strategies" or "learning skills"; (4) *motor skills,* the ability to coordinate movements, including simple muscle movements and complex movements, which comes with practice and coaching; and (5) *attitudes,* feelings and emotions learned through positive and negative experiences.[18]

The five outcomes overlap with the three domains (cognitive, psychomotor, and affective) of the taxonomy of educational objectives (see Chapter 9). The first three capabilities mainly fall within the cognitive domain, motor skills correspond with the psychomotor domain, and attitudes correspond with the affective domain. The mental operations and conditions involved in each of the five outcomes are different. Writes Gagné, "Learning intellectual skills requires a different design of instructional events from those required for learning verbal information or from those required for learning motor skills, and so on."[19]

As part of the instructional process, Gagné introduced the idea of *task analysis,* which is a common procedure used in business, industry, and the military. A task is broken down into the small and sequenced steps necessary to achieve an intended outcome. By breaking down a learning task into skills required, a teacher can pinpoint problem areas, make appropriate corrections, and make sure students have the necessary skills and subskills to complete the task. Following are some examples of task analysis:

1. To solve subtraction problems:
   a. To arrange sets of numbers to be subtracted
   b. To add numbers
   c. To identify plus and minus signs
   d. To recognize the meaning of numbers
   e. To write numbers
2. To evaluate statements made by government officials concerning the economy:
   a. To know economic principles and relationships
   b. To comprehend national and international events

c. To distinguish between evidence and opinion
d. To identify limitations of evidence
e. To draw conclusions from evidence

Behaviorism and Curriculum. Behaviorism still exerts a major impact on education. Educators who are behaviorists and who are in charge of curricula use many principles of behaviorism to guide the creation of new programs. Although what influences learning differs for different students, curriculum specialists can adopt procedures to increase the likelihood that each student will find learning relevant and enjoyable. When new topics or activities are introduced, connections should be built on positive experiences each student has had. Things about which each student is likely to have negative feelings should be identified and modified, if possible, to produce positive results.

The behaviorists believe that the curriculum should be organized so students experience success in mastering the subject matter. Of course, all curriculum persons, regardless of their psychological camps, have this view. The difference is that the behaviorists are highly prescriptive and diagnostic in their approach, and they rely on step-by-step, structured methods for learning. For students who have difficulty learning, curriculum and instruction can be broken down into small units with appropriate sequencing of tasks and reinforcement of desired behavior.

Behaviorist theories, it should be noted, have been criticized as describing learning too simply and mechanically—and as perhaps reflecting overreliance on classical animal experimentation. Human learning involves complex thinking processes beyond respondent conditioning (or recall and habit) and operant conditioning (or emitted and reinforced behavior). According to Robert Travers, a further concern is that there is little justification to define learning in terms of a "collection of small bits of behavior each of which has to be learned separately." Although behavior consists of organized sequences, it is not a collection of tiny bits of behavior. The stress of prescribed, lock-step procedures and tasks—and a "belief that a behavioral science should be definable in terms of observable events—[are] hardly justifiable today."[20]

The latter criticism may be an overstatement, because many behaviorists today recognize cognitive processes much more than classical or S-R theorists, and they are flexible enough to hold that learning can occur without the individual's having to act on the environment or exhibit overt behavior. To the extent that traditional behavioral theory can be faulted for having to rely on identifying all behavior, many behaviorists today are willing to consider that cognitive processes partially explain aspects of learning.

But behaviorism is alive and well; it is linked to many current educational practices impacting on classrooms and schools. Writes Robert Glaser:

> *Much of the application of psychological theory currently going on in schools represents the earlier behavioristic approach. The concepts of behavioral objectives, and behavior modification, for example, now pervade all levels of education, including special education, elementary school instruction in basic literary skills, and personalized systems of instruction . . .* [21]

In general, combining behaviorism with learning includes careful analyzing and sequencing of the learners' needs and behaviors. Principles of testing, monitoring, drilling, and feedback are characteristic. The learning conditions needed for successful outcomes are carefully planned through small instructional steps and sequences of responses that increasingly approximate the desired behavior or learning. These basic principles tend to coincide with today's basic skill training programs in reading and language development (such as DISTAR, SQ3R, and Continuous Progress), as well as methods of individualized instruction, direct instruction, mastery learning, instructional training (design), and competency-based education. These steps and sequences are shown in Table 4-1. Although these procedures are predetermined and planned in advance, some observers might claim they have a cognitive flavor, too.

The contributions of behaviorists to both psychology and curriculum have been great during this century, and it is likely that behaviorism will continue to influence the curriculum field. However, most behaviorists are aware that, as we learn more about humans and their learning, we cannot adhere to rigid doctrines. Perspectives that allow for investigations of the mind and psyche have been incorporated into behaviorism.[22] Cognitive developmental theories are being integrated into some behaviorists' approaches to human learning.

DEVELOPMENTAL PSYCHOLOGY

Any time we categorize any phenomena we run the risk of misinterpretation. Today, most psychologists classify human growth and development as cognitive, social, psychological, and physical. And while an individual grows and develops along all these fronts, most psychologists agree that learning in school is mainly cognitive in nature. Despite this acknowledgment, some psychologists, known as developmentalists, are more concerned with the developmental aspect of human learning; others, known as cognitive structuralists, focus more on the way in which content is structured for learning; and a third major group, the cognitive scientists, investigates the various cognitive structures that individuals create in order to generate meaning and ultimately knowledge.

Most, if not all, psychologists would agree that humans and their learning are the sum total of the results of their interactions with their worlds. However, there is no agreed upon way to determine exactly to what extent the characteristics (cognitive, social, psychological, and physical) of an individual are the result of inherited limitations or potential or the harmful or favorable circumstances in a person's environment. Considerable controversy continues about the extent or role of heredity versus environment in determining cognitive outcomes (that is, IQ scores and achievement scores) in school. As increasing numbers of educators view the results of schooling as more than just achievement scores, these debates are likely to intensify. It is essential that curriculum specialists be aware of these debates because the issue affects education and teaching theories in general.

Cognitive Development

Most cognitive theory is developmental; that is, it supposes that growth and development occur in progressive stages. Jean Piaget presents the most comprehensive view of this theory.[23] The Swiss psychologist's work came to the attention of American educators during the 1950s and

TABLE 4-1 Instructional Components by Current Authorities: A Behaviorist Approach to Teaching and Learning

DIRECT INSTRUCTION: ROSENSHINE MODEL	MASTERY LEARNING: BLOCK AND ANDERSON MODEL
1. *State learning objectives.* Begin lesson with a short statement of objectives.	1. *Clarify.* Explain to students what they are expected to learn.
2. *Review.* Introduce short review of previous or prerequisite learning.	2. *Inform.* Teach the lesson, relying on whole-group instruction.
3. *Present new materials.* Present new materials in small, sequenced steps.	3. *Pretest.* Give a *formative* quiz on a no-fault basis; students can check their own papers.
4. *Explain.* Give clear and detailed instructions and explanations.	4. *Group.* Based on results, divide the class into mastery and nonmastery groups (80 percent is considered mastery).
5. *Practice.* Provide active practice for all students.	5. *Enrich and correct.* Give enrichment instruction to mastery group; give corrective (practice/drill) to nonmastery group.
6. *Guide.* Guide students during initial practice; provide seatwork activities.	6. *Monitor.* Monitor student progress; vary amount of teacher time and support for each group based on group size and performance.
7. *Check for understanding.* Ask several questions; assess student comprehension.	7. *Post test.* Give a *summative* quiz to nonmastery group.
8. *Provide feedback.* Provide systematic feedback and corrections.	8. *Assess performance.* At least 75 percent of students should achieve mastery by the summative test.
9. *Assess performance.* Obtain student success rate of 80 percent or more during practice session.	9. *Reteach.* If not, repeat procedures starting with corrective instruction (small study groups, individual tutoring, alternative instructional materials, extra homework, reading materials, practice and drill).
10. *Review and test.* Provide for spaced review and testing.	

GUIDED INSTRUCTION: HUNTER MODEL	SYSTEMATIC INSTRUCTION:[a] GOOD AND BROPHY MODEL
1. *Review.* Focus on previous lesson; ask students to summarize main points.	1. *Review.* Review concepts and skills related to homework; provide review exercises.
2. *Anticipatory set.* Focus students' attention on new lesson; stimulate interest in new materials.	2. *Development.* Promote student understanding; provide examples, explanations, demonstrations.
3. *Objective.* State explicitly what is to be learned; state rationale or how it will be useful.	3. *Assess comprehension.* Ask questions; provide controlled practice.
4. *Input.* Identify needed knowledge and skills for learning new lesson; present material in sequenced steps.	4. *Seatwork.* Provide uninterrupted-seatwork; get everyone involved; sustain momentum.
5. *Modeling.* Provide several examples or demonstrations throughout the lesson.	5. *Accountability.* Check the students' work.
6. *Check for understanding.* Monitor students' work before they become involved in lesson activities; check to see they understand directions or tasks.	6. *Homework.* Assign homework regularly; provide review problems.
7. *Guided practice.* Periodically ask students questions or problems and check their answers. Again monitor for understanding.	7. *Special reviews.* Provide weekly reviews to check and enhance learning; provide monthly reviews to further maintain and enhance learning.
8. *Independent practice.* Assign independent work or practice when it is reasonably sure that students can work on their own with minimal frustration and understanding.	

[a]Originally developed for math instruction.

1960s—coinciding with the rising influence of cognitive developmental psychology, the environmentalist theories, and the compensatory education movement.

Like many other investigators today, Piaget describes cognitive development in terms of stages from birth to maturity. The overall stages can be summarized as follows:[24]

1. *Sensorimotor stage* (birth to age 2). The child progresses from reflex operations and undifferentiated surroundings to complex sensorimotor actions in relation to environmental patterns. The child comes to realize that objects have permanence; they can be found again. The child begins to establish simple relations between similar objects.

2. *Preoperational stage* (ages 2 to 7). In this stage objects and events begin to take on symbolic meaning. For example, a chair is for sitting; clothing is what we wear. The child shows an increased ability to learn more complex concepts from experience as long as familiar examples are provided from which to extract criteria that define the concept. (For example, oranges, apples, and bananas are fruit; the child must have the chance to touch and eat them.)

3. *Concrete operations stage* (ages 7 to 11). The child begins to organize data into logical relationships and gains facility in manipulating data in problem-solving situations. This learning situation occurs, however, only if concrete objects are available or if actual past experiences can be drawn upon. This child is able to make judgments in terms of reversibility and reciprocal relations (for example, that the left and right are relative to spatial relations) and conservation (that is, a long, narrow glass may hold the same amount of water as a short, wide one).

4. *Formal operations stage* (age 11 onward). This stage is characterized by the development of formal and abstract operations. The adolescent is able to analyze ideas and comprehend spatial and temporal relationships. The young person can think logically about abstract data, evaluate data according to acceptable criteria, formulate hypotheses, and deduce possible consequences from them. He or she can construct theories and reach conclusions without having had direct experience in the subject. At this stage there are few or no limitations on what the adolescent can learn;

learning depends on his or her intellectual potential and environmental experiences.

Piaget's cognitive stages presuppose a *maturation process* in the sense that development is a continuation and is based on previous growth. The mental operations are sequential and successive. The stages are hierarchical, and they form an order of increasingly sophisticated and integrated mental operations. Although the succession of stages is constant, stages of attainment vary within certain limits that are a function of heredity and environment. Although hereditary or environmental factors may speed up or slow down cognitive development, they do not change the stages or the sequence.

Environmental experience is the key to Piaget's cognitive theories, as it was also the crux of Dewey's learning principles. The educator's role involves "the shaping of actual experience by environing conditions" and knowing "what surroundings are conducive to having experiences that lead to growth."[25] Three basic cognitive processes form the basis of the environmental and experiential theories of both Piaget and Dewey.

For Piaget, *assimilation* is the incorporation of new experiences into existing experiences; it represents a coordination of the child's experiences into his or her environment. But assimilation, alone, does not have the capacity to handle new situations and new problems in context with present cognitive structures. The child must organize and develop new cognitive structures in context with existing structures—that is, how he or she thinks. This is *accommodation,* whereby the child's existing cognitive structures are modified and adapted in response to his or her environment. *Equilibration* is the process of achieving balance between those things that were previously understood and those yet to be understood; it refers to the dual process of assimilation and accommodation of one's environment.[26]

This coincides with Dewey's "conceptions of situation and interaction [which] are inseparable from each other" and which form the basis of continuity.[27] For Dewey, a *situation* represents the experiences of the environment affecting the child, similar to assimilation. *Interaction* is concerned with current or latitudinal transactions taking place between the child and his or her environment, including his or her capacities to establish meaning, similar to accommodation. *Continuity* refers to longitudinal learning or to situations and interactions that follow, similar to equilibration.

Piaget's Influence: Tyler, Taba, Bruner, and Kohlberg

Piaget's (1896–1980) three cognitive processes (and Dewey's educational experiences) also serve as a basis for Tyler's three methods of organizing learning experiences: (1) *continuity* suggests that the curriculum should possess vertical reiteration; that is, the skills and concepts should be "recurring" and there should be "continuing opportunity for these skills to be practiced"; (2) *sequence* suggests that the curriculum should include progressive development of understanding and that "each successive experience builds upon the preceding one [and] go more broadly and deeply into matters involved"; (3) *integration* "refers to the horizontal relationships of curriculum experiences" and means that the organization of experiences should be "unified . . . in relation to other elements" of the curriculum being taught and that subjects "should not be isolated . . . or taught as a single course" from the rest of the subjects.[28]

Taba not only spends considerable time reviewing Piaget's four stages of cognitive development and the implications they have for intelligence and mental development; she also concludes that learning experiences must be "designed to match assessment of age levels at which certain processes of thought can occur." The idea is to transform complex concepts and subject matter into mental operations appropriate to the learner and to develop a curriculum that provides for "increasing deeper and more formal levels" of thinking. "Building such a curriculum would naturally also involve a better understanding of the hierarchies [Piaget's stages] of concept formation and mental operations [and] a better understanding of the sequences in the development of thought."[29]

Similarly, Taba notes Piaget's cognitive processes—assimilation, accommodation, and equilibration—in her discussion of generalizations and abstract thinking. She is concerned with organizing curricula and teaching new experiences so

they are compatible with existing experiences (assimilation), moving from concrete experiences to concepts and principles (accommodation), and classifying and understanding new relationships (equilibration). The basis of what Taba calls "curriculum strategies for productive learning" are rooted in Piaget's synthesis of experiences into more complex forms and levels.

For Bruner, learning how things are related means learning the structure of knowledge. Such learning is based on Piaget's ideas of assimilation and accommodation.[30] The student who comes to grasp how bits of information within a subject area are related is able to continually and independently relate additional information to a field of study. Learning some "thing" should not be an end of learning, but, as Piaget and Dewey suggest, should be related to other aspects of subject matter and should be general enough to apply in other problems or situations. The structure of knowledge provides the basis for this kind of specific transfer of learning.

Piaget's equilibration forms the basis of Bruner's notion of a "spiral curriculum": previous learning is the basis of subsequent learning, that learning should be continuous, and that subject matter is related to and built on a foundation (from grade to grade). Bruner is also influenced by Dewey, who uses the term *continuity* in learning to explain that what a person has already learned "becomes an instrument of understanding and dealing effectively with the situations that follow."[31] Bruner also uses the term continuity, in the same way as Piaget and Dewey, to describe the spiral curriculum: how subject matter and mental operations can be "continually deepened by using them in a progressively more complex form."[32]

Bruner considers that the act of learning consists of three related processes, similar to Piaget's cognitive processes:

1. *Acquisition* is the grasping of new information; it mainly corresponds to assimilation. Such information may be "new" to one's store of data; it may also replace previously acquired information, or it may merely refine or further qualify previous information.
2. *Transformation* is the individual's capacity to process new information so as to transcend or go beyond it. Means for processing such information

are extrapolation, interpolation, or translation into another form. This process mainly overlaps with accommodation.

3. *Evaluation* is the determination of whether or not information has been processed in a way that renders it appropriate for dealing with a particular task or problem. It closely corresponds with equilibration.

Piaget was also concerned with the moral development of children, an interest that was investigated in some detail by Lawrence Kohlberg. Kohlberg studied the development of children's moral standards and concluded that the way we think about moral issues is not simply a reflection of our society, but is also based on stages of growth or age. Kohlberg outlined six developmental types of moral judgements grouped into three moral levels or stages, corresponding to Piaget's cognitive stages of development.

1. *Preconventional level.* Children at this level have not yet developed a sense of right or wrong. The level is comprised of two types of children: (1) children who do as they are told because they fear punishment, and (2) children who realize that certain actions bring rewards.

2. *Conventional level.* At this level, children are concerned about what other people think of them. As a result, their behavior becomes largely other directed. There are two types in this level: (3) children who seek their parents' approval by being "nice," and (4) children who begin thinking in terms of rules.

3. *Postconventional level.* Children's morality is based on what other people feel or on their precepts of authority. This level also includes two types: (5) children who are able to view morality in terms of contractual obligations and democratically accepted laws, and (6) children who view morality in terms of individual principles of conscience.

Kohlberg and Piaget support the cognitive developmental view of morality, that is , there is a considerable amount of reasoning in moral judgements and behavior, although they differ on specifics. Whereas Piaget stresses that there are very real differences in the way children think about morality at different ages, Kohlberg found considerable overlap at the various ages. Both also

believe that social arrangements and society play a major role; however, Piaget gives maturation more emphasis. Kohlberg says:

> As opposed to Piaget's view, the data suggest that the "natural" aspects of moral development are continuous and a reaction to the whole social world rather than a product of a certain stage, a certain concept... or a certain type of social regulations.[33]

What is educationally critical is that the teacher (in conjunction with learning psychologists and curriculum specialists) should determine the appropriate emphasis to be given to each of Piaget's stages of cognitive development and processes of thinking. Educators should be mindful that Piaget's cognitive processes overlap with Tyler's methods, Taba's strategies, Bruner's processes, and Kohlberg's moral stages. Additionally, educators should realize that Piaget's work should still be considered theoretical, still open to question, and not fact to be followed blindly in developing and teaching the curriculum.

Focus on Thinking and Learning

Presently, many if not most psychologists are concerned with the cognitive structures that individuals invent and utilize to make sense, to think about knowledge. These persons, identified as cognitive scientists, essentially focus their energies on the processes of thinking, that is, on what is happening inside a person's head.[34] These scholars are concerned with the functioning of mind. Just what does go on in a person's mind when that individual engages in various types of thinking? This is no small query. The brain is complex, as is the process of thinking. We have developed various ways to classify thinking and the structure of human intellect.

Structure of Intellect. J. P. Guilford generated a model that visually presents the complexity of the intellect and human thinking. In this model, Guilford classifies mental abilities three dimensionally.[35] The model comprises:

1. *Operations:* mental operations dealing with the processing of certain content.
  a. Evaluation (making assessments or decisions)

  b. Convergent thinking (generating relationships and analogies)
  c. Divergent thinking (creative thinking and production)
  d. Memory (remembering of knowledge)
  e. Cognition (knowledge)
2. *Products:* mental operations related to the application of operations to content.
  a. Units (comprehending figural, symbolic, and semantic data)
  b. Classes (classifying units)
  c. Relations (perceiving connections between items)
  d. Systems (a coherent body of knowledge)
  e. Transformations (changes in preexisting data)
  f. Implications (association of previously unrelated items)
3. *Contents:* mental operations confined to information and comprehension.
  a. Figural (material perceived by the senses)
  b. Symbolic (letters and digits organized in a general system—that is, an alphabet or number system)
  c. Semantic (a form of ideas or verbal meanings)
  d. Behavioral content (social intelligence or understanding of oneself and others)

These three dimensions, represented graphically in Figure 4-1 by a $5 \times 6 \times 4$ geometric model of five operations, six products, and four contents, yield 120 cells or distinct mental abilities. By 1985, more than 100 abilities had been recognized and separated by factor analysis. Guilford concluded that the vacant cells indicate uncovered mental abilities. It is possible, however, that our cognitive tests do not measure the other mental operations or that such abilities do not exist. The Guilford model is highly abstract and theoretical and involves administering and grading many extra tests. Rather than a single index of IQ (or of aptitude), we are required to report several scores. Thus, the theoretical issues surrounding intelligence and cognitive operations take on added complexity. Although some critics might argue that the model is dated because it lacks information-processing concepts, the theory and operations behind the model are still very relevant. The model of 120 specific abilities requires cur-

riculum specialists, test specialists, and learning theorists to consider multiple thinking processes, as well as a three-dimensional model for learning with several categories under each dimension.

Multiple Intelligences. Howard Gardner also argues for a theory of multiple intelligences and, like Guilford, he contends that there are different mental operations associated with intelligence. But Gardner feels the search for empirically grounded structures or components of intelligence may be misleading, since it avoids many roles and skills valued by human cultures. However, Guilford maintains that the criteria for intelligence and the related mental operations and a priori schemes can be quantified. Gardner maintains that there are many different types of intelligence and that too often (at least in a technological society) we emphasize only verbal or linguistic factors. He outlines six types of intelligence: (1) linguistic, (2) musical, (3) logical-mathematical, (4) spatial, (5) bodily kinesthetic, and (6) personal/social.[36]

In connection with Gardner's ideas, we might conclude that there is a place in school not only for the 3 R's, or core academic subjects, but also for music, art, speech, and even people skills (winning friends, influencing people, negotiating, and the like). These bodies of knowledge and processes can be considered part of multiple intelligence. They have a place in our "other-directed" society and help people interpret and deal with social situations that can foster economic achievement and success in adulthood.

Subscribing to Gardner's ideas means not only being a cognitivist but also a "positive cognitivist," if we can coin a new term. It means there are many opportunities and chances in life. Someone who can dance, sing, act, or hit a baseball or golf ball can rise to the ranks of the masters. If encouraged and given a chance, many of our school dropouts would not be wasted. Therefore, those in charge of planning and implementing the curriculum must expand their vision beyond intellectual and academic pursuits, without creating "soft" subjects or a "watered down curriculum." We must nurture all types of intelligence and all types of excellence that contribute to the worth of the individual and society. We must be guided by reason and balance and consider the versatility of children and youth. We need to be aware of their

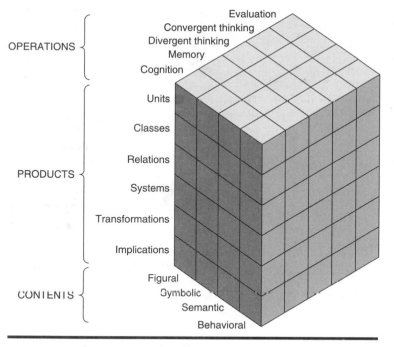

OPERATIONS
- Evaluation
- Convergent thinking
- Divergent thinking
- Memory
- Cognition

PRODUCTS
- Units
- Classes
- Relations
- Systems
- Transformations
- Implications

CONTENTS
- Figural
- Symbolic
- Semantic
- Behavioral

FIGURE 4-1   The Structure of Intellect

Source: From J. P. Guilford, *The Nature of Human Intelligence* (New York: McGraw-Hill, 1967), p. 1.

multiple strengths and abilities and the multiple ways of thinking and learning—and that there are multiple ways of reaching Rome or finding the end of the rainbow.

Learning Styles. If we assume, and we would argue that it is safe to do so, that people possess multiple intelligences and have at their disposal various ways of thinking, it is also appropriate to consider that people have various preferences for ways of thinking and approaches to learning. It seems common sense to state that people have preferences for certain methods of learning and find such methods effective.[37] Some people learn better from reading than from hearing about the material, while others prefer just the opposite. We know that many students learn more effectively from physical activities than from a verbal explanation. There is much discussion about the value of hands-on activities.

Learning styles have received attention for almost three decades, although the research has not generated any conclusive evidence.[38] There has

been wide support of learning styles from educators specializing in learning disabilities.[39]

Recent attention to learning styles has been presented under learning modalities. Some researchers have investigated the topic as right–left hemispheric brain processing or right–left brain preference. Early research by Witkin[40] on field dependence and field independence may have triggered this attention.

While we should not overinterpret various conclusions about learning styles, we can obtain insight into the variability of how individuals think and learn. However, learning styles or preferences are not innate characteristics. People do have preferences, but they learn them both consciously and unconsciously.[41] Also, we should not just cater to a preferred style of thinking or learning. Individuals should have full complements of ways of learning, or strategies of thinking. If we only teach to students' strengths, we may limit their functioning within the learning realm.

R. M. Felder and L. K. Silverman[42] developed a set of categories by which one can get a sense of learning styles. It deals with (1) how information is best perceived (visually or auditorially); (2) the type of information preferentially perceived (sensory, intuitive); (3) how one prefers information to be organized (inductively, deductively); (4) how information is processed (actively, reflectively); and (5) how one progresses to understanding (sequentially, globally). Persons who visually deal with information prefer pictures, diagrams, and demonstrations, while those who favor an auditory mode enjoy receiving and interacting with information via words and sounds. Persons with a sensory preference for information attend to sights, sounds, and physical sensations. Intuitive persons process information via insights and hunches, what Bruner might call intuitive leaps in the learning. Inductive and deductive approaches are well enough known; they need no explanation. Active learners like physical activity in their learning. They want to engage people in discussion. Reflective persons prefer introspection. Those who are advocates of sequentially arriving at their understandings see learning and thinking as occurring in a sequence of steps. Their global counterparts process information in leaps and bounds, engaging information more holistically. We might call such persons synthesizers.

No student should approach learning as a "Johnny one-note," and neither should a teacher have only a "one-note" instructional strategy. Humans are complex, as are their styles of learning. Psychologists are concerned, or should be, with the total orchestration of approaches, styles, preferences, processes, and modes that individuals employ in discovering and inventing meaning and generating knowledge.

Emotional Intelligence.   For most people, psychologists included, *Homo sapiens* is viewed and celebrated as the thinking species.[43] For most educators, attention to student learning has centered on the rational mind. Indeed, even in this chapter, we focus on the various ways of thinking. When we think of intelligence, we think of intellectual intelligence, the IQ. However, as Daniel Goleman posits, a view of human nature that ignores the emotional aspect of humans is shortsighted.[44] Indeed, some argue that if we neglect the emotional "mind" of individuals we may do them a greater

disservice than if we shortchange the development of their rational mind. Certainly, both the rational and emotional aspects of individuals are crucial to complete living. Individuals employ their emotions in regulating how they act, just as they draw on their intellect or their cognitive knowledge.

Emotions in our modern world have been shortchanged. Educators have urged students when making arguments to "stick to the facts." "Be logical" often is a clarion call inside and outside classrooms. However, it really is not possible to be devoid of emotions or feelings. We cannot make an argument using logic without some sense of feeling about the argument. We cannot be emotionally neutral in our relation to a lesson or a topic of inquiry. We know this. We have all heard students say, "I like this topic," or "That makes me sick." We all know that students will discount facts about which they do not feel good. Emotions strongly influence how we relate to people or treat certain information, or even construct meaning.

Goleman states that the root of the word emotion is *motere,* Latin for "to move." The prefix "e" suggests away, thus emotion suggests "move away." Emotions contain the power to affect action. Children, especially when they first come to school, clearly exhibit how emotions lead their actions. It seems that as we become more adult we tend to divorce or at least conceal our emotions from our actions.

Implicit in the bifurcation of emotional action from rational action is our prizing of rational action over emotional action; we tend to think of the latter as essentially negative or at least dysfunctional. Anger, fear, or sadness may be viewed unfavorably. Love, which we accept as positive, seems out of place when speaking of rational thought. However, with many individuals shifting to postmodern thought and recognizing the impossibility of separating ourselves from our knowledge worlds, there is increasing focus on emotions, or on what some are calling emotional intelligence.

With the publication of his 1985 book, *Frames of Mind,* Gardner is credited with getting us not to view intelligence as a monolithic concept. He suggested that people possess a wide spectrum of intelligence. His noting that people possessed a personal–social intelligence opened the way for people to begin to think of emotional intelligence and to validate the inner life of persons. Gardner spoke of both interpersonal and intrapersonal intelligence. *Interpersonal intelligence* refers to the ability of an individual to understand other people—what makes them tick and how they work and how one can work with them. *Intrapersonal intelligence,* Gardner asserts, is a correlative ability. Individuals with this ability can look inwardly, can develop or possess the capacity to form an accurate inner sense of one's self, and can use such understanding to operate effectively in life.[45]

Perhaps the most well-known person to take Gardner's work into the emotional realm is Peter Salovey, a Yale psychologist. Salovey has outlined the ways in which an individual can bring intelligence to his or her emotions.[46] Salovey has taken Gardner's personal intelligences and generated five main domains that expand these abilities. The first domain is *self-awareness*. Here the focus is on a person's recognizing an emotional response as it happens and realizing how it affects his or her functioning. "Know thyself" in the emotional realm is the keystone to activating emotional intelligence. The second domain is *managing emotions*. This relates to learning strategies by which one can handle one's emotions so as to bring benefit to one's self. People skilled in this domain experience less stress and can process life's ups and downs with skill. The third domain is *motivating oneself.* Recognizing that one has emotions and that one can manage them will be of little worth without realizing that one must put forth energy to motivate oneself to action. Emotional self-control is essential to effective living. The fourth domain is *recognizing emotions in others*. This seems obvious, yet many people seem to think that they are the only person with feelings. People need to possess empathy, to be attuned to the emotions and emotional needs of others. This is essential for effective social relations. The fifth domain is *handling relationships.* This domain relates to those understandings and skills that affect responding to and managing emotions in others. Those skilled in this domain possess interpersonal effectiveness.

Certainly, these five domains are not absolute; neither are they really separate from ratio-

nal abilities. However, we can be certain that all people have these or similar domains and recognize that people will differ in their emotional domain abilities. Educators, especially, must recognize that people's abilities in these domains are plastic. We can educate people and people can educate themselves in ways that address their emotional intelligence. The development of this intelligence is essential in that the challenges to our society seem to be in the social interactions realm rather than in the technological realm of society.[47]

Constructivism. A central theme in developmental psychology and its focus on thinking and learning has been the individual as the active person in the process. The central question has been how the individual engages himself or herself in the cognitive process. This differs from the driving question of the behaviorists: What can an external force, that is, a teacher, do to enact or elicit a response from an individual? This central question of developmental psychologists is very evident in the current discussion of constructivist theory.

Actually, the focus of constructivism is not unique to psychology. Indeed, it has roots in several areas, such as linguistics, sociology, and philosophy.[48] What these various scholars share is the view that individuals actively construct knowledge within social realms that serve to shape the very knowledge constructed. Essentially, individuals participate in the creation of their meaning via various cognitive processes, or means of thinking, and the reality that they create is subjective rather than objective. Much of this thinking is part of the subtext of postmodernism, which is discussed in Chapter 7.

Getting the student to be active in learning the curriculum is part of the constructivism emphasis. To constructivists, each learner must participate in generating meaning. Such learning can only exist in situations in which the new learning is constantly being connected with already existing knowledge, that is, prior experiences.[49] This learning is optimized if the student is aware of the processes that he or she is employing. Such awareness of one's cognitive processes and the products or anything related to them is defined as *metacognition*. Metacognition of the constructivist processes means that an individual student is cognizant of the procedural knowledge being employed in order to create knowledge, regulate it, and utilize it.[50]

Constructivists believe that the task for learners is not to passively accept information by mimicking the wording or conclusions of others, but rather to engage themselves in internalizing and reshaping or transforming information via active consideration.[51] While there may exist a real world out there about which we wish to learn, the meaning of the world does not exist independently of us.[52] Meaning is imposed on the world by those who reflect, those who think about the world. It is we who structure the world, as we construct reality so as to comprehend it. However, there is no ultimate shared reality. Reality is the result of an individual's constructivism. But since no two people actually view reality from the same vantage point or bring identical personal histories to the process of learning and thinking, there can never be total agreement as to the outcome of constructivism. There is always uncertainty regarding conclusions. While individuals can and will note agreement as to a conclusion to an inquiry, their understanding cannot be identical. Each person has followed a different path, even if employing the "same" cognitive processes. Each person's cognitive processes have been situationally determined. Each individual's interpretation of information has been influenced by the person's entire history of interaction.[53]

It is likely that constructivism will continue to be a focus of psychologists as well as other scholars. Certainly, philosophers will persist in reflecting and debating the nature of the reality in which learners situate their construction of meaning. Those educators concerned with delivering the curriculum will definitely challenge the notion that a curriculum can be constructed by students. Even students may get into the discussion as to the value of this focus to the psychological foundations of curriculum. Many students may feel that to "construct" their own meaning negates the vast wealth of accumulated knowledge. "Why not just learn it? Why must one make every conclusion so complicated by putting one's own 'spin' on meaning?" And, certainly, curricularists and other educational scholars will deliberate as to what specific types of thinking are most essential to the construction of meaning. And do all people employ similar types of thinking? As the next section demonstrates, there are many conceptions of thinking that need to enter our deliberations.

Problem Solving and Creative Thinking

Since the Sputnik era, many curriculum theorists have renewed their examination of various aspects of problem solving and creative thinking. The common belief is that these methods of thinking constitute a highly sophisticated form of processing information. Some curricularists, especially those who talk about the structure of disciplines, feel they are complementary: students must be given supportive conditions in which they can develop different forms of creativity, but at the same time they must be held responsible for confirming or disproving the value or correctness of their assumptions. Problem-solving procedures are their means of doing so, for they do not lead to creative discovery, but rather they establish the validity of the discoveries. In this context, problem solving and creative thinking are considered methods of inquiry conducive of scholars and scientists.[54]

An opposing view is that problem solving (in the past referred to as reflective thinking and today called critical thinking) is based on inductive thinking, analytical procedures, and *convergent* processes. Creative thinking, which includes intuitiveness and discovery, is based on deductive thinking, originality, and *divergent* processes. Problem solving, in this second view, is conducive to rational and scientific thinking and is the *method* of arriving at a solution to a task or to a correct answer, whereas creativity is conducive to artistic and literary thinking and is a *quality* of thought. There is no right solution or answer when creativity is the goal.

Actually, problem solving and creativity may or may not go hand in hand. Some people perform well on problems without being creative, and others can be highly creative but do poorly in problem-solving tasks. But the fact that we can distinguish between both thinking processes does not necessarily suggest that they are mutually independent of each other; research does suggest that a creative individual is just as likely or unlikely to be a good problem solver, and, in reverse, that a good problem solver may or may not be creative.[55]

Perhaps the most important thing to note is that these complex cognitive tasks should be taught as generic skills and principles—relevant for all subject matter. The idea is to develop metacognitive strategies that students can transfer to many curriculum areas and content materials, as opposed to repeating the mistakes of an earlier period whereby experts claimed that each discipline had its own structure and thinking manner. The need is to develop reflective-thinking, critical-thinking, intuitive-thinking, and discovery-thinking strategies that fit a wide variety of course and content situations, not for mathematicians or historians to claim their own metacognitive strategies.

Reflective Thinking. Problem solving played a major role in Dewey's overall concept of education. Dewey not only believed that problem-solving activities in school developed intelligence and social growth, but also that the skills developed in problem solving could be transferred to resolving everyday problems of society. Dewey's concept of problem solving is rooted in his idea of the scientific method and has become a classic model:

1. Becoming aware of a difficulty (or a felt difficulty).
2. Identifying the problem.
3. Assembling and classifying data and formulating hypotheses.
4. Accepting or rejecting the tentative hypotheses.
5. Formulating conclusions and evaluating them.[56]

Dewey's problem-solving method encourages systemic interpretation of everyday experiences through the reasoning process. This method coincides with his strong belief in a science of education (see Chapter 2). Because Dewey considers that the chief function of the school is to improve the reasoning process, he recommends adapting this problem-solving method to other subjects at all levels. Problems selected for study should be derived from student interests, for a student who is not motivated will not really perceive a problem.

Others, however, criticize the problem-solving method as producing the misconception that scientists have a be-all and end-all formula for finding answers to practical problems. James Conant, for example, defines the problem-solving approach as a series of six steps that can be used both by experimental scientists in the laboratory and by laypersons confronted with everyday situations that need to be solved:

1. Recognizing a problem and formulating objectives.
2. Collecting relevant information.
3. Formulating an hypothesis.
4. Deducing from the hypothesis.
5. Using tests by actual trial.
6. Depending on the outcome, accepting, modifying, or discarding the hypothesis.[57]

Conant believes that problem solving is not enhanced by science. The scientific method is not readily applied to everyday problems, he claims; rather, science has simply borrowed the method of testing hypotheses from the practical person. Whereas Dewey's model, developed for all disciplines, involved social problem solving, Conant's model was used by the advocates of science and math (not social thinking) during the Sputnik era. The predominant notion then was that each discipline had its own method of problem solving.

Both models and their derivatives are considered by some researchers to be incomplete. First, the analysis occurs after the person has solved the problem. Second, the models ignore intuition, insight, and ideas that are nonlogical and perhaps even personal—in short, procedures that cannot be easily observed or tested but that are sometimes used successfully in problem solving. Present theories of cognitive processes suggest that logical and observable steps are not always used in problem solving, nor are the steps always related. Finally, different problem-solving techniques are used for different subjects or disciplines and different grade levels. Presumably, they have common features, but they also involve specific variance.

Critical Thinking. Critical thinking and thinking skills are the terms used today to connote problem solving and related behaviors. This old idea under a new label is endorsed by the outpouring of articles in the professional literature, by a host of conferences and reports on the subject, and by the majority of states taking steps to bolster critical thinking for all students.

Although several teaching procedures, teacher-training programs, and taxonomies of critical thinking have surfaced in recent years, the latest opinion is that critical thinking is a form of intelligence that can be taught (it is not a fixed entity). The leading proponents of this school are Robert Ennis, Matthew Lipman, and Robert Sternberg.

Ennis identifies 13 attributes of critical thinkers. They tend to (1) be open minded, (2) take a position (or change a position) when the evidence calls for it, (3) take into account the entire situation, (4) seek information, (5) seek precision in information, (6) deal in an orderly manner with parts of a complex whole, (7) look for options, (8) search for reasons, (9) seek a clear statement of the issue. (10) keep the original problem in mind, (11) use credible sources, (12) remain relevant to the point, and (13) exhibit sensitivity to the feelings and knowledge level of others.[58]

Lipman distinguishes between *ordinary thinking* and *critical thinking.* Ordinary thinking is simple and lacks standards; critical thinking is more complex and is based on standards of objectivity, utility, or consistency. He wants teachers to help students change (1) from guessing to estimating, (2) from preferring to evaluating, (3) from grouping to classifying, (4) from believing to assuming, (5) from inferring to inferring logically, (6) from associating concepts to grasping principles, (7) from noting relationships to noting relationships among relationships, (8) from supposing to hypothesizing, (9) from offering opinions without reasons to offering opinions with reasons, and (10) from making judgments without criteria to making judgments with criteria.[59]

In a series of texts, called *Philosophy for Children,* Lipman outlines a strategy for teaching critical thinking. Children spend a considerable portion of their time thinking about thinking, and about ways in which effective thinking is distinguished from ineffective thinking. After reading the stories in the text, children engage in classroom discussions and exercises that encourage them to adapt the thinking process depicted in the stories.[60] The assumption behind Lipman's program is that children are by nature interested in such philosophical issues as truth, fairness, and personal identity. Children can and should learn to think for themselves, to explore alternatives to their own viewpoints, to consider evidence, and to make distinctions and draw conclusions. (See Curriculum Tips 4-2.)

Sternberg seeks to foster many of the same intellectual skills, listed in Table 4-2, albeit in a very different way. He points out three mental processes that enhance critical thinking: (1) *meta components*—high-order mental processes used to plan what we are going to do, monitor what we are doing, and evaluate what we are doing; (2) *performance components*—the actual steps or strategies we take; and (3) *knowledge-acquisition components*—processes used to relate old material to new material and to apply and use new material.[61] Sternberg does not outline a "how" approach like Lipman; rather, he outlines general guidelines for developing and/or selecting a program. See Table 4-2.

Note that some educators, including most phenomenologists and humanistic theorists, contend that teaching a person to think is like teaching someone to swing a golf club or tennis racket; it involves a holistic approach, not a piecemeal effort, as implied by Ennis, Lipman, and Sternberg. "Trying to break thinking skills into discrete units may be helpful for diagnostic proposals," according to two critics, "but it does not seem to be the right way to move in the teaching of such skills." Critical thinking is too complex of a mental operation to divide into small processes; the approach depends on "a student's total intellectual functioning, not on a set of narrowly defined skills."[62]

Perhaps the major criticism has been raised by the method's own proponent. Sternberg cautions that the kinds of critical thinking skills we stress in school and the way we teach them "inadequately prepares students for the kinds of problems they will face in everyday life."[63] We believe that because our critical skill programs stress "right" answers and "objectively scorable" test items, they are removed from real-world relevance. Most problems in real life have social, economic, and psychological implications. They involve interpersonal relations and judgments about people, personal stress and crisis, and dilemmas involving choice, responsibility, and survival.

===== *Curriculum Tips 4-2* =====

Teaching Critical Thinking

Teachers must understand the cognitive processes that constitute critical thinking, be familiar with the tasks, skills, and situations to which these processes can be applied, and employ varied classroom activities that develop these processes. Robert Ennis provides a framework for such instruction. He divides critical thinking into four components, each consisting of several specific skills that can be taught to students.

1. Defining and clarifying:
    a. Identifying conclusions
    b. Identifying stated reasons
    c. Identifying unstated reasons
    d. Seeing similarities and differences
    e. Identifying and handling irrelevance
    f. Summarizing
2. Asking appropriate questions to clarify or challenge:
    a. Why?
    b. What is the main point?
    c. What does this mean?
    d. What is an example?
    e. What is not an example?
    f. How does this apply to the case?
    g. What difference does it make?
    h. What are the facts?
    i. Is this what is being said?
    j. What more is to be said?
3. Judging the credibility of a source:
    a. Expertise
    b. Lack of conflict of interest
    c. Agreement among sources
    d. Reputation
    e. Use of established procedures
    f. Known risk to reputation
    g. Ability to give reasons
    h. Careful habits
4. Solving problems and drawing conclusions:
    a. Deducing and judging validity
    b. Inducing and judging conclusions
    c. Predicting probable consequences

Source: Robert H. Ennis, "A Logical Basis for Measuring Critical Thinking," *Educational Leadership* (October 1985), p. 46.

TABLE 4-2   Principal Thinking Skills Underlying Intelligent Behavior

Recognizing and defining the nature of a problem

Deciding on the processes needed to solve the problem

Sequencing the processes into an optimal strategy

Deciding on how to represent problem information

Allocating mental and physical resources to the problem

Monitoring and evaluating one's solution processing

Responding adequately to external feedback

Encoding stimulus elements effectively

Inferring relations between stimulus elements

Mapping relations between relations

Applying old relations to new situations

Comparing stimulus elements

Responding effectively to novel kinds of tasks and situations

Effectively automatizing information processing

Adapting effectively to the environment in which one resides

Selecting environments as needed to achieve a better fit of one's abilities and interests to the environment

Shaping environments so as to increase one's effective utilization of one's abilities and interests

Source: From Robert J. Sternberg, "How Can We Teach Intelligence?" *Educational Leadership* (September 1984), p. 40. Reprinted with permission of the Association for Supervision and Curriculum Development. Copyright © 1984 by the Association for Supervision and Curriculum Development. All rights reserved.

How we deal with illness, aging, or death (someone else's or even our own eventual demise), or with simple things like starting new jobs or meeting new people, has little to do with the way we think in class or on critical thinking tests. But they are important matters. By stressing cognitive skills in classrooms and schools, we ignore the realities and milieu of life.

Creative Thinking.   Standardized tests do not always accurately measure creativity; in fact, we have difficulty agreeing on what creativity is and who is creative. There are many types of creativity—artistic, musical, scientific, manual, and so on—yet we tend to talk about creativity as an all-encompassing term. Creative students are often puzzling to teachers. They are difficult to characterize; their novel answers frequently seem threatening to teachers, and their behavior often deviates from what is considered "normal." Sometimes, teachers discourage creativity and punish creative students. Curriculum specialists also tend to ignore them in their curriculum plans (subject matter or course descriptions, subject guides, and subject materials and activities), because they represent only a small proportion (about 2 to 5 percent, depending on the definition) of the student population. Also, curriculum specialists have little money earmarked to support special programs and personnel for these students. Frequently, educators lump creative children in with highly intelligent or gifted children, even though high intelligence and high creativity are not necessarily related; and there are many types of creative children.

In a classic, cross-cultural study, E. P. Torrance used sixty-two statements to investigate elementary and secondary teachers' ratings of the "ideal" creative personality. From 95 to 375 teachers in each of the following countries were sampled: United States, Germany, India, Greece, and the Philippines.[64]

For example, the United States and Germany (technologically developed countries) both encourage independent thinking, industriousness, and curiosity; these traits do not appear important in the less developed countries. Greece and the Philippines reward remembering, which connotes convergent thinking, but many American researchers consider this type of thinking anticreative. Teachers in all the countries, especially the less developed ones, stress that being well-liked, considerate of others, and obedient are important ideals.

There is little agreement on a definition of creativity except that all believe it represents a quality of mind: It comprises both a cognitive and humanistic component in learning; although no one agrees upon an exact mix, it is probably more cognitive than humanistic. According to Carl Rogers, the essence of creativity is its novelty, and, hence, we have no standard by which to judge it. In fact, the more original the product, the more likely it is to be judged by contemporaries as foolish or evil.[65] The individual creates primarily because creating is self-satisfying and because the behavior or product is self-actualizing. (This is the humanistic side of creativity, even though the process and intellect involved in creating are cognitive in nature.) Eric Fromm defines the creative attitude as (1) the willingness to be puzzled—to orient oneself to something new without frustration; (2) the ability to concentrate; (3) the ability to experience oneself as a true originator of one's acts; and (4) the willingness to accept conflict and tension caused by the climate of opinion or lack of tolerance for creative ideas.[66]

Robert Sternberg identified six attributes associated with creativity from a list of 131 mentioned by American laypeople and professors in the arts, science, and business: (1) lack of conventionality, (2) integration of ideas or things, (3) aesthetic taste and imagination, (4) decision-making skills and flexibility, (5) perspicacity (in questioning social norms), and (6) drive for accomplishment and recognition.[67] He also makes important distinctions among creativity, intelligence, and wisdom. Creativity overlaps more with intelligence ($r = 0.55$) than it does with wisdom ($r = 0.27$), but there is more emphasis on imagination and unconventional methods with creativity, as opposed to intelligence, which deals with logical and analytical absolutes. Wisdom and intelligence are most closely related ($r = 0.68$), but differ in emphasis on mature judgment and use of experience with different situations.

All three types of people, creative, intelligent, and wise, can solve problems, but they do so in different ways. Creative people tend to be divergent thinkers, and teachers must understand that creative students go beyond ordinary limitations of classrooms and schools and think and act in unconventional and even imaginary ways. Intelligent people rely on logic, have a good vocabulary, and store of information. Such students tend to be convergent thinkers, score high on conventional tests, and probably perform well on Hirsch's cultural literary test (see Chapter 2). Few students exhibit wisdom, since this comes with age and experience. Nonetheless, there are sufficiently mature students who show good judgment, make

expedient use of information, and profit from the advice of others and their own experiences. They "read between the lines" and have a good understanding of peers and adults (including their teachers). They usually exhibit cognitive intelligence, what we would label as traditional intelligence, and also social intelligence, what we might label as "people" skills.

For teachers, the definition of creativity comes down to how new ideas have their origin. We are dealing with both logical and observable processes and unconscious and unrecognizable processes. The latter processes give teachers trouble in the classroom and sometimes lead to misunderstanding between teachers and creative students. For some students the methods of Edison and Einstein seem appropriate—theoretical, deductive, and developmental. For others, creativity may correspond more closely to the insights and originality of Kafka, Picasso, Bob Dylan, or Michael Jackson. See Table 4-3.

Intuitive Thinking. Intuitive thinking is not new. But this thinking process was either overlooked because teaching practices have relied instead on facts and rote, or ignored, because it was difficult to define and measure. Bruner popularized the idea in his book about the *Process of Education.* The good thinker not only has knowledge, but also an intuitive grasp of the subject. Intuitive thinking is part of a process of discovery that is similar to the scholar-specialist's engaging in hunches, playing with ideas, and understanding relationships so that he or she can make discoveries or add to the storehouse of new knowledge.

The following explanation by Bruner is a good description of how some people work with intuitive thinking:

> *Intuitive thinking characteristically does not advance in careful, well-defined steps. Indeed, it tends to involve maneuvers based seemingly on implicit perception of the total problem. The thinker arrives at an answer, which may be right or wrong, with little, if any, awareness of the process by which he reached it. He rarely can provide an adequate account of how he obtained his answer, and he may be unaware of just what aspects of the problem situation he was responding to. Usually intuitive thinking rests on familiarity with the domain of knowledge involved and with*

TABLE 4-3 Appropriate Curriculum and Instruction for Gifted Students

CHARACTERISTICS	LEARNING NEEDS	CURRICULUM IMPLICATIONS	INSTRUCTIONAL IMPLICATIONS
Ability to handle abstractions	Presentation of symbol systems at higher levels of abstraction	• Reduce basic skills curriculum • Introduction of new symbol systems at earlier stages of development (computers, foreign language, statistics, and so on)	• Develop advanced materials and products related to content • Integration of content by key ideas, issues, and themes • Include high-level and divergent questioning strategies
Power of concentration	Longer time frame that allows focused, in-depth work in an area of interest and challenge	• Diversified scheduling of curriculum work • Chunks of time for special project work and small-group efforts	• Advanced reading materials • Faster-paced instruction • Problem solving and special projects
Ability to make connections and establish relationships among disparate data	Exposure to multiple perspectives and domains of inquiry	• Interdisciplinary curriculum opportunities such as special concept units, humanities, and the interrelated arts • Use of multiple text materials and resources	• Reorganize content according to concepts and high-level skills • Integrate ideas across related content • More frequent discussions
Ability to memorize well and learn rapidly	Rapid movement through basic skills and concepts in traditional areas; economical organization of new areas of learning	• Restructured learning frames (that is, speed up and reduce reinforcement activities) • New curriculum organized according to its underlying structure	• Special programs organized around global and technological issues • Accelerate instruction
Multiple interests; wide information base	Opportunity to choose area(s) of interest and to study a chosen area in greater depth	• Learning center areas in the school for extended time use • Self-directed learning packets • Individual learning contracts	• Small-group and independent study • Extension, enrichment, and in-depth study • Connect multiple areas of curriculum • Cluster by abilities and interests

Source: Adapted from Joyce Van Tassel-Baska, "Appropriate Curriculum for Gifted Learners," *Educational Leadership* (March 1989), Tables 1–2, pp. 13–14.

its structure, which makes it possible for the thinker to leap about skipping steps and employing shortcuts in a manner that requires later rechecking of conclusions by more analytical means.[68]

This has very little to do with a convergent or step-by-step approach. It speaks of the revelation of discovery—the sheer knowing the stuff— but coupled with the ability to put knowledge to use and to find new ways in which to fit things together. According to this interpretation, problem solving and free discovery come together; knowledge is dynamic, built around the process of discovery, without precise steps or rules to follow.

Discovery Learning.   Since the Sputnik era, the inquiry-discovery method has been examined in conjunction with the discipline-centered curriculum—as a unifying element related to the knowledge and methodology of a domain of study. Taba, Bruner, Phenix, and Inlow were products of this era.[69] Taba was influenced by Bruner, Phenix was to a lesser extent influenced by both of them, and Inlow was influenced by all three. All four educators were more concerned about *how* we think than with *what* we think or what knowledge we possess.

Although Bruner went to great lengths to fuse the inquiry-discovery methods in the sciences and mathematics, Phenix, Taba, and Inlow claimed that the discovery method was separate from inquiry and that both methods of thinking cut across all subjects (not just science and math). Phenix, for example, proposed that discovery was a form of inquiry that dealt with new knowledge, hypotheses, and hunches. Most of his efforts were spent defining inquiry, which he claimed was the method of deriving, organizing, analyzing, and evaluating knowledge (like problem solving). Inquiry was considered to bind together all the separate aspects of knowledge into a coherent discipline; it was viewed as more important than discovery.

Taba and Inlow contrasted discovery learning with verbal and concrete learning. Most of traditional learning was described as a process of *transmitting* verbal and concrete information to the learner; it was authority centered, subject centered, highly organized, also flexible and open. Discovery, on the other hand, involved extensive exploration of the concrete at the elementary level. For older students, according to Inlow, it involved "problem identification, data organization and application, postulation, . . . evaluation and generalization."[70] For Taba, it meant "abstracting, deducing, comparing, contrasting, inferring, and contemplating."[71] All these discovery processes are rational and logical, and thus infer a problem-solving or convergent component. Inlow and Taba, however, were quick to point out that discovery also included divergent thinking and intuitiveness; Taba also added creativity and limitless learning to help define discovery.

Bruner, who is well known for elaborating the idea of discovery, defined it as the learning that takes place when students are not presented with subject matter in its final form, when subject matter is not organized by the teacher but by the students themselves. Discovery is the formation of coding systems, whereby students discover relationships that exist among the data presented.

Successful discovery experiences make the learner more capable of discovering new experiences and more willing to learn for the sake of learning.

Cognition and Curriculum

Most curriculum specialists, and learning theorists and teachers, tend to be cognitive oriented, because (1) the cognitive approach constitutes a logical method for organizing and interpreting learning, (2) the approach is rooted in the tradition of subject matter, and (3) educators have been trained in cognitive approaches and better understand them. Even many contemporary behaviorists, as previously mentioned, incorporate cognitive processes in their theories of learning. Because learning in school involves cognitive processes, and because schools emphasize the cognitive domain of learning, it follows that most educators feel that learning is synonymous with cognitive developmental theory.

The teacher who has a structured style of teaching would prefer the problem-solving method, based on reflective thinking and/or the scientific method. Most curricularists tend to be cognitive oriented in their approach to learning, but we feel that this learning model is incomplete and that something gets lost in its translation to the classroom. For example, we feel that many schools are not pleasant places for learners and that the "quality of life" in classrooms can be improved.

We are reminded of John Goodlad's description of schools. After visiting more than 1000 elementary and secondary schools, Goodlad concluded that most students are not engaged in problem-solving tasks, but passive-rote tasks, and that they are rarely asked to "initiate anything . . . or create their own products."[72] In short, real and meaningful learning rarely takes place in schools. Although Goodlad is a cognitive curricularist, he finds that the teaching-learning process boils down to teachers predominantly talking and students mostly responding to the teachers. The workbook and textbook are the main sources of instruction; rarely are students permitted to talk to each other, and rarely do they become involved in problem-solving or creative activities. According to Goodlad, much of the so-called learning theories and educational reforms have been blunted at the classroom door.

Curriculum specialists must understand that school should be a place where students are not afraid of asking questions, not afraid of being wrong, not afraid of not pleasing their teachers, and not afraid of taking cognitive risks and playing with ideas. With all our cognitive theory, we would expect students to want to learn and know how to learn, but we observe, both in the literature and in the real world of schools, that after a few years of school most students have to be cajoled to learn and have learned how not to learn. So-called "successful" students become cunning strategists in a game of beating the system and figuring out the teacher. To be sure, schools should be more humane places where students can fulfill their human potential. With this in mind, we turn to humanistic learning.

PHENOMENOLOGY AND HUMANISTIC PSYCHOLOGY

Traditional psychologists do not recognize phenomenology or humanistic psychology as a school of psychology, much less a wing or form of psychology. Their contention is that most psychologists are humanistic, because they are concerned with people and with bettering society. Moreover, they claim that the label *humanism* should not be used as a mask for generalizations based on little knowledge and "soft" research. Nonetheless, a number of observers have viewed phenomenology, sometimes called humanistic psychology, as a "third force" learning theory—after behaviorism and cognitive development. Phenomenology is sometimes considered a cognitive theory because it emphasizes the total organism or person. The distinct difference between the cognitive and affective aspects of learning, however, have led us to separate these domains.

The most obvious contrast with the mechanistic and deterministic view of behaviorism is the phenomenological version of learning, illustrated by the individual's awareness that he or she is an "I" who has feelings and attitudes, who experiences stimuli, and who acts on the environment. We carry some sense of control and freedom to produce certain conditions in our environment. When we speak of this awareness, we are speaking of the self. The study of immediate experiences as one's reality is called *phenomenology* and is influenced by, and perhaps even based on, an existentialist philosophy. Most phenomenological ideas are derived from and for clinical settings; nevertheless, educators are becoming aware that they have implications for the classroom as well.

Phenomenologists point out that the way we look at ourselves is basic for understanding our behavior. What we do, even to what extent we learn, is determined by our concepts of ourselves.[73] If someone thinks he or she is Napoleon, he or she will act like Napoleon, or at least convey his or her concept of Napoleon. If someone thinks he or she is dull or stupid, his or her cognitive performance will be influenced by that self-concept.

Gestalt Theory

Phenomenologist ideas are rooted in early field theories and field-ground ideas, which view the total organism in relationship to the environment, or what is called the "field," and the learner's perception of this environment and the personal meaning in a given situation. Learning must be explained in terms of the *wholeness* of the problem. Human beings do not respond to isolated stimuli, but to an organization or pattern of stimuli.

Field theories are derived from Gestalt psychology of the 1930s and 1940s. The German word *Gestalt* connotes shape, form, and configuration. In this context, various stimuli are perceived in relation to others within a field. What one perceives will determine the meaning he or she gives to the field; likewise, one's solutions to other problems will depend on his or her recognition of relationships between individual stimuli and the whole.[74] This is considered the *field-ground* relationship, and how the individual perceives this relationship determines behavior. Perception alone is not a crucial factor in learning; rather, the crucial factor is structuring and restructuring the field relationships to form evolving patterns.

On this basis, learning is complex and abstract. When confronted with a learning situation, the learner analyzes the problem, discriminates between essential and nonessential data, and perceives relationships. The environment is continuously changing, and thus the learner is continuously reorganizing his or her perceptions. In terms of teaching, learning is conceived as a selective process by the student. Curriculum specialists must understand that learners will perceive something in relation to the whole; what they perceive and how they perceive it is related to their previous experiences.

Maslow: Self-actualizing Persons

Abraham Maslow, a well-known phenomenologist, has set forth a classic theory of human needs. Based on a hierarchy, and in order of importance, the needs are:

1. *Survival needs.* Those necessary to maintain life: needs for food, water, oxygen, and rest.
2. *Safety needs.* Those necessary for routine and the avoidance of danger.
3. *Love and belonging needs.* Those related to affectionate relations with people in general and to a place in the group.
4. *Esteem needs.* Those related to receiving recognition as a worthwhile person.
5. *Knowing and understanding needs.* Those more evident in persons of high intelligence than those of limited intelligence, a wanting to learn and organize intellectual relationships.
6. *Self-actualization needs.* Those related to becoming the best person one can be, to develop one's fullest potential.[75]

These needs have obvious implications for teaching and learning. A child whose basic needs—say, love or esteem—are not filled will not be interested in acquiring knowledge of the world. The child's goal to satisfy the need for love or esteem takes precedence over learning and directing his or her behavior. To some extent, Maslow's ideas that have classroom implications are based on Pestalozzi and Froebel, who believed

in the importance of human emotions and a methodology based on love and trust.

Maslow coined the term *humanistic psychology,* which stresses three major principles: (1) centering attention on the experiencing person, and thus focusing on experience as the primary phenomenon in learning; (2) emphasizing such human qualities as choice, creativity, values, and self-realization, as opposed to thinking about people in mechanistic (or behaviorist) terms and learning in cognitive terms; and (3) showing ultimate concern for the dignity and worth of people and an interest in the psychological development and human potential of learners as individuals.[76]

The teacher's and curriculum maker's role in this scheme is to view the student as a whole person. The student is to be positive, purposeful, active, and involved in life experiences (not S-R or only cognitive experiences). Learning is to be a lifelong educational process. Learning is experimental, its essence being freedom and its outcome full human potential and reform of society.

The goal of education, for Maslow, is to produce a healthy and happy learner who can accomplish, grow, and actualize his or her human self. Self-actualization and its attendant sense of fulfillment are what the learner should strive for and what teachers should stress in the classroom situation. Self-actualizing people are psychologically healthy and mature. Maslow characterized them as (1) having an efficient perception of reality; (2) being at ease and comfortable with themselves and with others; (3) not overwhelmed with guilt, shame, or anxiety; (4) relatively spontaneous and natural; and (5) problem centered rather than ego centered.[77]

Rogers: Nondirective and Therapeutic Learning

Carl Rogers, perhaps the most noted phenomenologist, has established counseling procedures and methods for facilitating learning. His ideas are based on those of early field theorists and field-ground theories; reality is based on what the individual learner perceives: "Man lives by a perceptual 'map' which is not reality itself."[78]

This concept of reality should make the teacher aware that the level and kind of response to a particular experience will differ among children. Children's perceptions, which are highly individualistic, influence their learning and behavior in class, for example, whether they will see meaning or confusion in what is being taught.

Rogers views therapy as a method of learning to be utilized by the curriculum worker and teacher. He believes that positive human relationships enable people to grow; therefore, interpersonal relations among learners are just as important as cognitive scores.[79] The teacher's role in nondirective teaching is that of a facilitator, very much like the existentialist teacher, who has close professional relationships with students and guides their human growth and development. In this role, the teacher helps students explore new ideas about their lives, their school work, their relations with others, and their interaction with society. The counseling method assumes that students are willing to be responsible for their own behavior and learning, that they can make intelligent choices, and that they can share ideas with the teacher and communicate honestly as people who are confronted with decisions about themselves and about life in general.

The curriculum is concerned with process, not products, personal needs, not subject matter; psychological meaning, not cognitive scores; and changing environmental situations (in terms of space and time), not predetermined environments. Indeed, there must be freedom to learn, not restrictions or preplanned activities. The psychological and social conditions of the environment limit or enhance a person's field or life space. A psychological field or life space is a necessary consideration in the curriculum, and everything that is taking place in relation to a specific learner at a given time gives meaning to the field and eventually to learning.

Value Clarification

Value clarification, sometimes called value building, is part of the teacher-learning process. Value clarificationists have a high regard for creativity, freedom, and self-realization. They prefer that learners explore their own preferences and make their own choices.

The values a person holds depend on many factors, including environment, education, and personality. People often suffer from value confusion, whose symptoms are apathy, uncertainty, in-

consistency, overconforming, or overdissenting.[80] Value clarification is designed to help persons overcome value confusion and become more positive, purposeful, and productive, as well as to have better interpersonal relations.

In a popular text, Louis Raths and his colleagues outlined the process of valuing: "(1) choosing freely . . . ; (2) choosing from alternatives . . . ; (3) choosing thoughtfully . . . ; (4) prizing and cherishing . . . ; (5) affirming . . . ; (6) acting upon choices . . . ; [and] (7) repeating . . . as a pattern of life."[81] They developed various dialogue strategies, writing strategies, discussion strategies, and activity strategies for teaching valuing on a how-to-do basis. Table 4-4 illustrates some dialogue strategies for the seven valuing processes. These are actually instructional strategies to be recommended by the curriculum specialist and used by the teacher.

It is possible to identify other ways of teaching valuing. The first is *inculcation,* teaching accepted values with the support of common law. Next is *moral development,* highlighting moral and ethical principles of application. Third is *analysis of issues* and situations involving values. Fourth is *clarification,* the method Raths emphasizes. Finally is *action learning,* trying and testing values in real-life situations.[82] In addition, the approaches used by Abraham Maslow and Carl Rogers may be described as *evocation,* calling forth from the learner personal values and the ability to make choices and become self-actualizing.

Although the stress is on attitudes and feelings, and on human processes, there is a cognitive component in value clarification, just as in the *Taxonomy of Educational Objectives* there are corresponding cognitive components within the affective domain of learning.[83] One must think and engage in various cognitive forms of analysis, synthesis, evaluation, and even problem solving to engage in value clarification. The strategies for value clarification also involve what Raths calls "choosing" and "prizing," or what we see as a stress on attitudes, feelings, aspirations, self-concept, interests—and these are not easy to quantify or measure.

Phenomenology and Curriculum

Phenomenologists view the individual in relation to the field in which he or she operates. In this,

TABLE 4-4 Clarifying Questions Suggested by the Seven Valuing Processes

1. Choosing freely
   a. Where do you suppose you first got the idea?
   b. How long have you felt that way?
   c. What would people say if you weren't to do what you say you must do? . . .
2. Choosing from alternatives
   a. What else did you consider before you picked this? . . .
   b. Are there reasons behind your choice?
   c. What choices did you reject before you settled on your present idea or action? . . .
3. Choosing thoughtfully
   a. What would be the consequences of each alternative available? . . .
   b. What assumptions are involved in your choice? . . .
   c. Now if you do this, what will happen to that? . . .
4. Prizing and cherishing
   a. Are you glad you feel that way? [Why?] . . .
   b. What purpose does it serve? . . .
   c. In what way would life be different without it?
5. Affirming
   a. Would you tell the class the way you feel some time?
   b. Would you be willing to sign a petition supporting that idea? . . .
   c. Should a person who believes the way you do speak out? . . .
6. Acting upon choices
   a. Have you examined the consequences of your act? . . .
   b. Where will this lead you? How far are you willing to go?
   c. How has it already affected your life?
7. Repeating
   a. What are your plans for doing more of it?
   b. Should you get other people interested and involved? . . .
   c. How long do you think you will continue?

Source: From Louis E. Raths, Merrill Harmin, and Sidney B. Simon. *Values and Teaching,* 2nd ed. (Columbus, Ohio: Merrill, 1978), pp. 64–65.

phenomenologists have much in common with constructivists. But what determines behavior and learning is mainly psychological. The personal experiences of the individual are accessible to others only through inferences; thus, such data are questionable in terms of scientific evidence. But to the phenomenologist, the raw data of personal experiences are vital to understand learning. Perhaps the data cannot be measured accurately and perhaps they are vague, but they are "out there." The definitions and the processes are also subjective and evaluative, rather than precise and substantive. Besides the concept of humanistic psychology, the scope and subject matter are used synonymously with many other concepts, in-cluding existentialist psychology, neoprogressivism, creativity, love, higher consciousness, valuing, transcendentalism, psychological health, ego identity, psychoanalysis[84]—almost anything that suggests maximum "self-fulfillment," "self-actualization," and "self-realization."

Although this umbrella aspect of phenomenology makes it difficult to provide a clear, agreed-upon definition of the term, the same broadness makes the concept acceptable to educational reformers of various psychological orientations. The fact that phenomenology means different things to different people is one reason for its easy acceptance, but it is also a basis for criticism. Nonetheless, phenomenologists attempt to rescue learning theory from the narrow and rigid behaviorists and from overstress on cognitive processes.

Motivation and Achievement. Phenomenologists seek to understand what goes on inside us— our wants, desires, and feelings, and ways of perceiving and understanding. While cognitive functions are recognized, teachers and schools must first make a commitment to deal with the social and psychological factors of learning. A student who is frustrated, distraught, or emotionally upset will learn very little; rather, he or she will resist, withdraw, or act out his or her problems. Student needs must be satisfied. Similarly, their self-esteem and self-concept must be recognized as essential factors related to learning. Without good feelings about oneself, and without a sense of curiosity or motivation, there is little chance for continual cognitive (or even psychomotor) learning. A learner must feel confident about performing the skill or task required, be eager to learn, and feel that what she or he is being asked to perform is psychologically satisfying. This applies to learning the ABCs, how to hit a baseball or dance the two step, or how to socially interact with others.

Today, many schools are employing organized approaches to try to ensure that learners feel good about themselves and about learning. William Glasser, for example, envisions schools without failure. Students understand and are involved in rules of behavior, teachers are supportive, and classrooms are characterized by openness and positive student interaction. Schools must be a friendly place, not coercive, to maximize the learning potential of students, especially those students who have experienced failure[85] (or who are unsure about themselves).

We have to reform schools not by changing the length of the school day or year or the amount of homework or by beefing up the curriculum, but by first making school more satisfying to students and more consistent with their interests, so that they gain a sense of power, fulfillment, and importance in the classroom. When we learn to deal with the psychological requirements of learners, when we become sensitive to what makes them want to learn, we can then focus on what they need to learn. *Affective needs are more important than cognitive needs.* Similarly, solutions to the problems of discipline and achievement are related to and based primarily on making students feel someone listens to them, thinks about them, cares for them, and feels that they are important.

The humanistic approach to learning involves a certain amount of warmth, genuineness, maturity, and concern for people, in our case children and youth. The focus is not on academic achievement, rather on the whole child—on his or her social, psychological, physical, and cognitive needs. For this reason, progressive educators are more likely to adopt many of the phenomenologists' theories, without even knowing that they are, since many of these ideas coincide with classic progressive thinkers from Pestalozzi and Froebel to Parker and Washburne.[86]

In the final analysis, learning in school occurs in groups with a formalized curriculum (although some might argue that there is also an informal or hidden curriculum). The child is but one learner among as many as thirty students, all needing some attention and following a text that usually promotes passivity, not activity. Everything in and around us competes for our attention or motivation. When we pay attention to something, it usually means we are not paying attention to something else. All of us, including our students, must make choices on how we dispense our attention and time. When attention wanders, or when students cannot focus on their tasks, this means that the tasks are too complex or signals are being sent which connote some kind of sociopsychological problem, often which needs our intervention.

The question that arises, then, is how can curriculum workers, especially teachers, motivate students to pay attention to long division problems or Shakespearean sonnets when youngsters are being bombarded by a host of needs, interests, and feelings that often compete for their attention and time? How can we better incorporate their needs, interests, and feelings into the teaching-learning process?

As educators, we need to support and nurture various learning opportunities for our students, we need to recognize several different domains of learning, not only cognitive domains, and we need to provide rewards, at least recognition, for various forms and levels of achievement, including effort, improvement, imagination, intuition, individuality, vitality, enthusiasm and maturity—all those shades of gray that have little to do with standard achievement scores but are still important for enhancing personal wholeness and modern society and in the end make the real difference in life.

The Concept of Freedom.   The idea of personal freedom is another important issue in phenomenology or humanistic psychology. We may not always use the freedom we have, or we may misuse it, but it is there. One of the early humanistic psychologists put it this way: "I think people have a great deal more freedom than they ever use, simply because they operate out of habits, prejudices, and stereotypes. . . .[T]hey have a lot more self-determinism than is reflected in the traditional . . . view of humans as reactive beings. . . .[W]e have more freedom than most of today's psychology admits."[87]

The idea of freedom is the essence of Roger's thesis for learning. The more children and youth are aware of their freedom, the more opportunity they have to discover themselves and develop fully as people.[88] Freedom permits the learners to probe, explore, and deepen their understanding of what they are studying. It permits them latitude to accomplish goals and find the fit between goals and achievements and past learning and new learning—and the direction these new meanings have for additional learning. Freedom broadens the learners' knowledge of alternative ways of perceiving themselves and the environment.

Freedom was the watchword of the radical school, free school, and alternative school movements of the 1960s and 1970s, and it was part of the educational choice and private school movements of the 1980s and 1990s. These movements increase various possibilities for learning and schooling and for enhancing diverse school environments that match the diversity of the needs, feelings, attitudes, and abilities of learners. The free school, alternative school, and radical school movements basically overlap; they were fueled by child-centered education and humanistic psychology. Even though they protested against established teaching and school practices and knew they were against traditional education, they were never able to develop a detailed plan for reform.

Unquestionably, curricularists must enhance students' opportunities and alternatives for learning without lessening the teachers' authority. They need to find the "golden mean": student freedom without license and teacher authority without control—a very elusive ideal. The idea is to design a curriculum that helps learners realize their fullest potential in a behavioral, cognitive, and humanistic sphere of learning.

In Search of a Curriculum.   Because each individual has specific needs and interests related to his or her self-fulfillment and self-realization, there is no generally prescribed humanistic curriculum. Rather, the learners draw on those experiences, subject matter, and intellectual skills necessary to attain full potential. The humanities and arts, especially philosophy, psychology, and aesthetics, would be appropriate content because they further introspection, reflection, and creativity. A curriculum of affect, one that stresses attitudes and feelings, would also be acceptable. Math and science would be considered unnecessary. Appropriate labels might be "relevant curriculum," "humanistic curriculum," "value-laden curriculum," or "existentialist curriculum."

Should the student reject the teacher's interpretation of subject matter, it is the student's right to do so. It is more important that the student-teacher relationship be based on trust and honesty so that the student knows when the teacher's ideas of a subject are wise and deserve respect. Student choice would be crucial—the power to decide what to do and how to do it, a sense of control over one's ideas and work. School routine and rules would be minimal; learners would be left alone to do what they want to do, as long as it does not harm anyone or present a potential danger. Frequent evaluation, criticism, and competition would not be considered conducive to learning. The essence of many recent instructional trends, such as academic time, direct instruction, and mastery learning (which stress prescribed behaviors and tasks, well-defined procedures and outcomes, constant drill and testing), would be rejected as narrow, rigid, and high pressured.

Most reconceptualists would accept the phenomenologist-humanistic interpretation of learning because both these curricularists and learning theorists value the uniqueness of human personality.

Both groups prefer classrooms characterized by freedom, an existential educational experience, and subjects in the humanities and arts, not the hard sciences. Reconceptualists tend to approve this learning theory because it rejects the rational means-ends approach, the same processes that the traditional or hard curricularists follow.[89] Instead of presenting empirical data to justify the means, phenomenologists and reconceptualists rely on psychological and philosophical positions for validating ends proposed.

When asked to judge the effectiveness of their curriculum, both phenomenologists and humanists (like reconceptualists) rely on testimonials and subjective assessments by students and teachers. They may also present such materials as students' paintings, poems, interviews, reports, biographies, and projects or talk about improvement in student behavior and attitudes.[90] They present very little empirical evidence or student achievement scores, however, to support their stance. Moreover, phenomenologists are not in agreement about how to teach self-actualization, self-determination, human striving, and so on, or about how to determine what subject matter is worthwhile, how to mesh the paintings, poems, and personal biographies with learning outcomes, and how to test or confirm many of their ideas.

There is great need to examine and construct a relevant, humanistic curriculum and to enhance the self-actualizing, self-determining learning processes. However, until the just described issues are resolved we shall continue to flounder in the phenomenologist area of learning. Those who trust the behavioral or cognitive-developmental process in teaching and learning, or the traditional or scientific spirit in curriculum making, will continue to distrust the "third force" in psychology and the "soft" approach to curriculum.

CONCLUSION

Psychology has had significant impact on curriculum throughout this century. Such impact is likely to increase. It appears that there is an increasing revolution occurring within this foundation. The core beliefs as to the nature of learning and the nature of the learner are being challenged. We are positing various theories of the mind that add complexity to our discussions about this curriculum foundation.

We believe that this revolution is occurring within the three major camps in psychology. Behaviorism is being transformed into a more sophisticated form of connectionism. However, there is no direct link to early behaviorists theories and contemporary connectionism. Certainly, within the cognitive science camp there is much revolutionary thought. Scholars are working with an expanded notion of cognition that places the mind within the context of an external world. Many submovements are part of what some are calling ecological cognitive science. Scholars within the phenomenological–humanistic psychology camp are challenging each other to actually redefine or reconceptualize human nature. Our biology is being emphasized; our biological nature is increasingly being appreciated as to how such nature enables us to learn and interact.

We are not machines, and the mind is not a computer. Accepting these statements means that we must use with caution those references to computers and less technical machines to explain human thinking and learning. Humans are biological beings influenced by their biology and their cultures and influencing their biology and cultures. Our intellect is an ever changing dynamic complex. The psychological foundation of curriculum will assist us in learning more about this complex so that we, as curricularists, can create educational programs that will nurture more advanced, more total, more complete human learning.

ENDNOTES

1. Ralph W. Tyler, *Basic Principles of Curriculum and Instruction* (Chicago: University of Chicago Press, 1949).

2. Jerome S. Bruner, *The Process of Education* (Cambridge, Mass.: Harvard University Press, 1959).

TABLE 4-5 Overview of Learning Theories and Principles

PSYCHOLOGIST	MAJOR THEORY OR PRINCIPLE	DEFINITION OR EXPLANATION
Behaviorist		
Thorndike	Law of effect	When a connection between a situation and response is made, and it is accompanied by a satisfying state of affairs, that connection is strengthened; when accompanied by an annoying state of affairs, the connection is weakened.
Pavlov-Watson	Classical conditioning	Whenever a response is closely followed by the reduction of a drive, a tendency will result for the stimulus to evoke that reaction on subsequent occasions; association strength of the S-R bond depends on the conditioning of the response and stimulus.
Skinner	Operant conditioning	In contrast to classical conditioning, no specific or identifiable stimulus consistently elicits operant behavior. Based on Thorndike's law of effect, operant conditioning means that if an operant response is followed by a reinforcing stimulus, the strength of the response is increased.
Bandura	Observational learning	Behavior is best learned through observing and modeling. Emphasis is placed on vicarious, symbolic, and self-regulatory processes.
Gagné	Levels of learning	Eight types of learning are identified, from simple to complex, mostly behavioral and a few cognitive; they are based on orderly, prerequisite, and cumulative processes of learning.
Cognitive		
Piaget	Cognitive stages of development	Four cognitive stages form a sequence of progressive mental operations; the stages are hierarchical and increasingly more complex.
	Assimilation, accommodation, and equilibration	The incorporation of new experiences, the method of modifying new experiences to derive meaning, and the process of blending new experiences into a systematic whole.
Guilford	Structure of intellect	Three major dimensions of thought—contents, operations, and products—each subdivided into several factors combine and interact to form 120 possible factors.

(continued)

TABLE 4-5 Continued

PSYCHOLOGIST	MAJOR THEORY OR PRINCIPLE	DEFINITION OR EXPLANATION
	Cognitive	
Guilford	Convergent-divergent thinking	A qualitative method of thinking; the first corresponds with problem solving, reflective thinking, and the scientific method; the second corresponds with creative thinking, intuitive thinking, and the artistic method.
Gardner	Multiple intelligences	A cross-cultural, expanded concept of what is intelligence—such areas as linguistics, music, logical-mathematical, spatial, body-kinesthetic, and personal.
Dewey	Reflective thinking	Being in a situation, sensing a problem, clarifying it with information, working out suggested solutions, and testing the ideas by application.
Ennis-Lipman-Sternberg	Critical thinking	Teaching students how to think, including forming concepts, generalizations, cause-effect relationships, inferences, consistencies and contradictions, assumptions, analogies, and the like.
Bruner-Phenix	Structure of a subject	The knowledge, concepts, and principles of a subject; learning how things are related is learning the structure of a subject.
	Inquiry-discovery method	A method or quality of thinking that uses a body of organized knowledge; the first method tends to be convergent and the second tends to be divergent.
	Humanistic	
Maslow	Human needs	Six human needs related to survival and psychological well-being; the needs are hierarchical and serve to direct behavior.
Rogers	Becoming a person	Becoming a person means being open to experience, developing trust, and accepting oneself.
	Freedom to learn	Becoming a full person requires freedom to learn; the learner is encouraged to be open, self-trusting, and self-accepting.
Raths	Value clarification	Analysis of personal preferences and moral issues to reveal or clarify one's values—that is, beliefs, attitudes, and opinions.

TABLE 4-6 Overview of Major Learning Theories

BEHAVIORAL LEARNING

We learn by doing and observing others.

Reinforcement is essential for learning to occur.

Practice (with feedback) improves learning and retention.

Spaced recalls are essential for remembering information.

Learning through rewards is preferable than under the conditions of punishment.

Learning proceeds from simple to complex and part to whole behavior.

Learning should proceed in small, step-by-step, simple units.

Learning is hierarchical, based on sequential readiness.

Desired performance or learning outcomes should be stated in advance (and by objectives).

Learning is observable and/or measurable.

COGNITIVE-DEVELOPMENTAL LEARNING

Cognitive stages of development are related to age.

Cognitive development is sequential and based on previous growth.

The capacities of students are important; bright students are capable of learning more and at a more rapid rate than other students.

Learning can be modified as a result of the interaction of the self with the environment.

Learning involves the assimilation of new experiences with prior experiences.

Learning is best achieved through active participation in the environment; the teacher can improve the environment to stimulate learning.

There are several components and types of intelligence; there is no one single indicator or type of behavior that connotes intelligent behavior.

Students learn best when they can generalize information, that is, whole to part learning.

Students who learn how to learn will learn more in school than those who are dependent on the teacher to learn.

Transfer of learning increases when students have the opportunity to solve problems.

HUMANISTIC LEARNING

Teachers are sensitive to the students' world, not just the adult world.

Learners are viewed as individuals, with diverse needs. abilities, and aptitudes.

The learners' self-concept and self-esteem are considered as essential factors in learning.

Learning is considered holistic, not just cognitive; the act of learning involves emotions, feelings, and motor-dependent skills.

Learning is based on warm, friendly, and democratic student-teacher interactions; coercive and strict disciplinary measures are minimized.

The quality (or processes) of learning is considered as important (in some cases more important) than the quantity (or products) of learning; teachers nurture learners.

Students share ideas, work together, and tutor and help each other; homogeneous grouping, academic tracking, and competitive testing or programs are minimized.

Students and teachers plan together the experiences or activities of the curriculum.

Students are given choices (with limitations) and freedom (with responsibilities); the extent of choices and freedom is related to the maturity level and age of the students.

Learning is based on life experiences, discovery, exploring, and experimenting.

3. Edward L. Thorndike, *Animal Intelligence* (New York: Macmillan, 1911).

4. Edward L. Thorndike, *Psychology of Learning,* 3 vols. (New York: Teachers College Press, Columbia University, 1913); *The Fundamentals of Learning* (New York: Teachers College Press, Columbia University, 1932).

5. Tyler, *Basic Principles of Curriculum and Instruction;* Hilda Taba, *Curriculum Development: Theory and Practice* (New York: Harcourt, Brace, 1962).

6. John Dewey, *How We Think* (Boston: D. C. Heath, 1910); Dewey, *My Pedalogic Creed* (Washington, D.C.: National Education Association, 1929); and Charles H. Judd, *Education and Social Progress* (New York: Harcourt, Brace, 1934).

7. Taba, *Curriculum Development: Theory and Practice,* p. 121.

8. Bruner, *The Process of Education.*

9. Ivan P. Pavlov, *Conditioned Reflexes,* trans. G. V. Anrep (London: Oxford University Press, 1927). The experiment was conducted in 1903 and 1904.

10. John B. Watson, *Behaviorism* (New York: Norton, 1939).

11. John B. Watson, "What the Nursery Has to Say about Instincts," in C. A. Murchison, ed., *Psychologies of 1925* (Worcester, Mass.: Clark University Press: 1926), p. 10.

12. B. F. Skinner, *Science and Human Behavior* (New York: Macmillan, 1953).

13. Ibid.; B. F. Skinner, *Reflections on Behaviorism and Society* (Englewood Cliffs, N.J.: Prentice Hall, 1978).

14. B. F. Skinner, "The Science of Learning and the Art of Teaching," *Harvard Educational Review* (Spring 1954), pp. 86–97.

15. W. James Popham and Eva I. Baker, *Systematic Instruction* (Englewood Cliffs, N.J.: Prentice Hall, 1970), p. 48.

16. Albert Bandura, *Social Learning Theory* (Englewood Cliffs, N.J.: Prentice Hall, 1977).

17. Robert M. Gagné, *The Conditions of Learning,* 4th ed. (New York: Holt, Rinehart and Winston, 1987).

18. Robert M. Gagné, Leslie J. Briggs, and Walter W. Wager, *Principles of Instructional Design,* 3rd ed. (New York: Holt, Rinehart and Winston, 1988).

19. Gagné, *The Conditions of Education,* p. 245.

20. Robert M. Travers, *Essentials of Learning,* 5th ed. (New York: Macmillan, 1982), p. 505.

21. Robert Glaser, "Trends and Research Questions in Psychological Research on Learning and Schooling," *Educational Researcher* (November 1979), p. 12. See also Glaser, "Education and Thinking: The Role of Knowledge," *American Psychologists* (February 1984), pp. 93–104.

22. Linda Darling-Hammond and Jon Snyder, "Curriculum Studies and the Traditions of Inquiry: The Scientific Tradition," in Philip W. Jackson, ed. *Handbook of Research on Curriculum* (New York: Macmillan Publishing Co., 1992), pp. 41–78.

23. Jean Piaget, *Judgment and Reasoning in the Child* (New York: Harcourt, Brace, 1948).

24. Jean Piaget, *The Psychology of Intelligence,* rev. ed. (London: Broadway, 1950). See also Hans Furth and Harry Wachs, *Thinking Goes to School: Piaget's Theory in Practice* (New York: Oxford University Press, 1974).

25. John Dewey, *Experience and Education* (New York: Macmillan, 1938), p. 40.

26. Jean Piaget, *The Child's Conception of Physical Causality* (New York: Harcourt, 1932). See also Piaget, *The Equilibrium of Cognitive Structures,* trans. T. Brown and K. J. Thampy (Chicago: University of Chicago Press, 1985).

27. Dewey, *Experience and Education,* p. 43.

28. Tyler, *Basic Principles of Curriculum and Instruction,* pp. 84–86.

29. Taba, *Curriculum Development: Theory and Practice,* pp. 118–119.

30. Bruner, *The Process of Education.*

31. Dewey, *Experience and Education,* p. 44.

32. Bruner, *The Process of Education,* p. 13.

33. Lawrence Kohlberg, "Moral Development and Identification," in N. B. Henry and H. G. Richey, eds., *Child Psychology,* Sixty-second Yearbook of the National Society for the Study of Education, Part 1 (Chicago: University of Chicago Press, 1963), pp. 322–323.

34. Carl Bereiter and Marlene Scardamalia, "Cognition and Curriculum," in Philip W. Jackson, ed., *Handbook of Research on Curriculum,"* pp. 517–542.

35. J. P. Guilford, *The Nature of Human Intelligence* (New York: McGraw-Hill, 1967).

36. Howard Gardner, *Frames of Mind,* rev. ed. (New York: Basic Books, 1985); Gardner, *The Unschooled Mind: How Children Think and How Schools Should Teach* (New York: Basic Books, 1991).

37. Jerrold E. Kemp, Gary R. Morrison, and Steven M. Ross, *Designing Effective Instruction* (New York: Merrill, an imprint of Macmillan College Publishing Co., 1994).

38. Ibid.

39. Linda Crafton, *Challenges of Holistic Teaching: Answering the Tough Questions* (Norwood, Mass: Christopher–Gordon Publishers, Inc., 1994).

40. H. A. Witkin, *Personality Through Perception* (New York: Harper, 1954).

41. Crafton, *Challenges of Holistic Teaching.*

42. R. M. Felder and L. K. Silverman in Kemp, et. al. *Designing Effective Instruction.*

43. Daniel Goleman, *Emotional Intelligence* (New York, Bantam Books, 1995).

44. Ibid.

45. Howard Gardner, as referenced in Goleman, *Emotional Intelligence.*

46. Peter Salovey, as referred to in Goleman, *Emotional Intelligence.*

47. Daniel Goleman, *Emotional Intelligence.*

48. Arthur N. Applebee and Alan C. Purves, "Literature and the English Language Arts," in Philip W. Jackson, ed., *Handbook of Research on Curriculum,* pp. 726–748.

49. David J. Martin, *Elementary Science Methods, A Constructivist Approach* (Albany, N.Y.: Delmar Publishers, 1997).

50. Francis P. Hunkins, *Teaching Thinking Through Effective Questioning,* 2nd ed. (Norwood, Mass: Christopher-Gordon Publishers, Inc., 1995).

51. Jacqueline G. Brooks and Martin G. Brooks, *The Case for Constructivist Classrooms* (Alexandria, Va: Association for Supervision and Curriculum Development, 1993).

52. Ibid.

53. Ibid.

54. Bruner, *The Process of Education;* Philip H. Phenix, *Realms of Meaning* (New York: McGraw-Hill, 1964); and Joseph J. Schwab, "The Concept of the Structure of a Discipline," *Educational Record* (July 1962), pp. 197–205.

55. See Jacob W. Getzels and Philip D. Jackson, *Creativity and Intelligence: Explorations with Gifted Students* (New York: Wiley, 1962); Robert J. Sternberg, ed., *Handbook for Human Intelligence* (New York: Cambridge University Press, 1982); and Michael A. Wallach and Nathan Kogan, *Modes of Thinking in Young Children: A Study of the Creativity-Intelligence Distinction* (New York: Holt, Rinehart, 1965).

56. Dewey, *How We Think.*

57. James B. Conant, *Science and Common Sense* (New Haven: Yale University Press, 1951).

58. Robert H. Ennis, "Logical Basis for Measuring Critical Thinking Skills," *Educational Leadership* (October 1985), pp. 44–48; Ennis, "Critical Thinking and Subject Specificity," *Educational Researcher* (April 1989), pp. 4–10.

59. Matthew Lipman, "Critical Thinking—What Can It Be?" *Educational Leadership* (September 1988), pp. 38–43.

60. Matthew Lipman et al., *Philosophy for Children,* 2nd ed. (Philadelphia: Temple University Press, 1980). Also see Lipman, *Philosophy Goes to School* (Philadelphia: Temple University Press, 1988).

61. Robert J. Sternberg, "How Can We Teach Intelligence?" *Educational Leadership* (September 1984), pp. 38–48; Sternberg, "Thinking Styles: Keys to Understanding Performance," *Phi Delta Kappan* (January 1990), pp. 366–371.

62. William A. Sadler and Arthur Whimbey, "A Holistic Approach to Improving Thinking Skills," *Phi Delta Kappan* (November 1985), p. 200. Also see John Barell, *Teaching for Thoughtfulness* (New York: Longman, 1991).

63. Robert J. Sternberg, "Teaching Critical Thinking: Possible Solutions," *Phi Delta Kappan* (December 1985), p. 277.

64. E. Paul Torrance. *Rewarding Creative Behavior* (Englewood Cliffs, N.J.: Prentice Hall, 1965).

65. Carl Rogers, "Toward a Theory of Creativity," in M. Barkan and R. L. Mooney, eds., *Conference on Creativity: A Report to the Rockefeller Foundation* (Columbus: Ohio State University Press, 1953), pp. 73–82.

66. Eric Fromm, "The Creative Attitude," in H. H. Anderson, ed., *Creativity and Its Cultivation* (New York: Harper & Row, 1959), pp. 44–54.

67. Robert J. Sternberg, "Intelligence, Wisdom, and Creativity: Three Is Better than One," *Educational Psychologist* (Summer 1986), pp. 175–190; Sternberg, "Practical Intelligence for Success in School," *Educational Leadership* (September 1990), pp. 35–39.

68. Bruner, *The Process of Education,* pp. 56–57.

69. Bruner, *The Process of Education;* Gall M. Inlow, *Maturity in High School Teaching* (Englewood Cliffs, N.J.: Prentice Hall, 1964); Philip H. Phenix, *Realms of Meaning* (New York: McGraw-Hill, 1964); and Taba, *Curriculum Development: Theory and Practice.*

70. Inlow, *Maturity in High School,* p. 78.

71. Taba, *Curriculum Development: Theory and Practice,* p. 156.

72. John I. Goodlad, "A Study of Schooling: Some Findings and Hypotheses," *Phi Delta Kappan* (March 1983), p. 468.

73. Arthur W. Combs and Donald Snygg, *Individual Behavior,* 2nd ed. (New York: Harper & Row, 1959); Combs, *A Personal Approach to Teaching* (Boston: Allyn and Bacon, 1982).

74. Kurt Koffka, *Principles of Gestalt Psychology* (New York: Harcourt, 1935); Wolfgang Kohler, *Gestalt Psychology,* 2nd ed. (New York: Liveright, 1947); and Max Wertheimer, *Productive Thinking* (New York: Harper & Row, 1945).

75. Abraham H. Maslow, *Toward a Psychology of Being,* 2nd ed. (New York: Van Nostrand Reinhold, 1968); Maslow, *Motivation and Personality,* 2nd ed. (New York: Harper & Row, 1970).

76. Ibid.

77. Abraham Maslow, *The Farther Reaches of Human Nature* (New York: Viking Press, 1971); Maslow, *Motivation and Personality.*

78. Carl Rogers, *Client-Centered Therapy* (Boston: Houghton Mifflin, 1951), p. 485.

79. Carl Rogers, *A Way of Being* (Boston: Houghton Mifflin, 1981); Rogers, *Freedom to Learn for the 1980s,* 2nd ed. (Columbus, Ohio: Merrill, 1983).

80. Louise M. Berman and Jessie A. Roderick, eds., *Feeling, Valuing, and the Art of Growing* (Washington, D.C.: Association for Supervision and Curriculum Development, 1977); Maxine Greene, *The Dialectic of Freedom* (New York: Teachers College Press, Columbia University, 1988).

81. Louis E. Raths, Merrill Harmin, and Sidney B. Simon, *Values and Teaching,* 2nd ed. (Columbus, Ohio: Merrill, 1978), pp. 27–28.

82. Ronald C. Doll, *Curriculum Improvement: Decision Making and Process,* 8th ed. (Boston, Mass.: Allyn and Bacon, 1992).

83. David R. Krathwohl, Benjamin S. Bloom, and Betram Maisa, *Taxonomy of Educational Objectives, Handbook II: Affective Domain* (New York: McKay, 1964).

84. Charlotte Buhler, "Basic Theoretical Concepts of Humanistic Psychology," *American Psychologist* (April 1971), pp. 378–386; Arthur W. Combs et al., *Perceptual Psychology: A Humanistic Approach to the Study of Persons* (New York: Harper & Row, 1976); and Edmund V. Sullivan, *Critical Psychology and Pedagogy: Interpretation of the Personal World* (Westport, Conn.: Bergin & Garvey, 1990).

85. William R. Glasser, *Schools Without Failure* (New York: Harper & Row, 1969); Glasser, *Control Theory in the Classroom* (New York: Harper & Row, 1986).

86. Allan C. Ornstein, "Components of Curriculum Development," *Illinois School Research and Development Journal* (Spring 1990), pp. 204–212.

87. Gordon Allport, "A Conversation," *Psychology Today* (April 1971), p. 59.

88. Rogers, *Freedom to Learn.*

89. Michael Apple, *Teachers and Texts* (New York: Routledge & Kegan Paul, 1986); Henry A. Giroux, *Teachers as Intellectuals: Toward a Critical Pedagogy of Learning* (Westport, Conn.: Bergin & Garvey, 1988). Also see John McNeil, *Curriculum: A Comprehensive Introduction,* 4th ed. (Glenview, Ill.: Scott, Foresman, 1990).

90. William H. Schubert, "Reconceptualizing and the Matter of Paradigms," *Journal of Teacher Education* (January–February 1989), pp. 27–32; J. Smyth, "A Critical Pedagogy of Classroom Practice," *Journal of Curriculum Studies* (November–December 1989), pp. 483–502; and Sean A. Walmsley and Trudy P. Walp, "Integrating Literature and Composing into the Language Arts," *Elementary School Journal* (January 1990), pp. 251–274.

5

SOCIAL FOUNDATIONS OF CURRICULUM

Focusing Questions

1. Why is it important for persons with curricular responsibilities to understand that schools exist within social contexts?
2. What are some major views as to the social purposes of schools? Which do you support? Why?
3. What are some curricular implications of accepting that Americans share common core values and beliefs?
4. What major changes have occurred in this century that influence society and thus the schools? What changes might you anticipate in the future?
5. What are the major challenges educators confront in dealing with diversity?
6. Why are the concepts of race, class, and gender so essential to consider within the field of curriculum?
7. What social priorities need to be addressed by educators? By the general public?

Schools exist within, not apart from, social contexts. Through their curricula, schools influence the cultures of the people that the schools serve. Likewise, the cultures affect and shape the schools and their curricula. Schools, through their teaching of the curriculum, can alter society, and society can mold the school and its curriculum. We cannot meaningfully consider the development or delivery of curriculum without reflecting on the relationship of schools and society.

Schools today exist at a time when the many voices representing the different views of what it means to be a social being are gaining audience. Adding to the complexity of the social scene is the fact that technology is allowing people representing various cultures and societies around the world to also affect the social dynamic. These people are conversing, sharing views, considering different values, and acquainting themselves with each other's practices and customs.

Never has there been a time when knowing the social foundations of curriculum been as important as now; they are crucial to our making decisions that enable meaningful curricula to be created and offered. Never has there been a period in our history when the people within our borders have reflected such a diversity of customs, beliefs, values, languages, religions, and social institutions. The current and emerging times require curricularists at all levels of activity in the field to understand the social foundations and to grasp the social implications of the nature and purposes of education.

Society, Education, and Schooling

Some curricularists state that education is neutral. It can be used for constructive or destructive ends, to promote one type of political institution or "ism" or another. However, taking such a stance is misleading. Education is a value-based activity, engaging individuals in experiencing or accepting what is valued by society. If some content is included in the curriculum rather than other content, it is because it has worth, or value, in the eyes of those who selected the content. It also has a particular utility. Few would argue with the notion that the transmission of culture is the primary task of a society's educational system. The values, beliefs, and norms of a society are maintained and passed to the next generation not merely by teaching about them, but also by embodying them in the very operation of the educational system. The way we structure our school buildings and classrooms and organize students and teachers reflects our cultural views and values. To those who challenge the validity of the transmission of culture and urge instead a prime purpose of transforming the culture, we would reply that in a dynamic, open society the very action of transmission is essentially one of transforming. Social knowledge and custom are not inert; there are constantly being reshaped as more information is encountered and as people engage in cultural–social interaction.

The inclusion of transformation within the actions of transmission seems evident in Dewey's thinking. For Dewey, education was the means of both perpetuating (transmitting) and improving (transforming) society. To perpetuate and improve society, educators had to be very selective in determining and organizing the experiences of the learners. It is "a primary responsibility of educators . . . (to) be aware of the general principle of the shaping of actual experiences by environing conditions" and to understand "what surroundings are conducive to having experiences that lead to growth." For Dewey, experience must be channeled properly, "for it influences the formation of attitudes of desire and purpose."[1] Thus educators have an awesome responsibility to reflect and then determine, with the help of others in society, what content and activities (or what Dewey calls "experiences") enhance individual personal and social growth and lead to the improvement of society.

In reflecting on the social foundations of curriculum, we must recognize that schools are only one institution, albeit the primary one, in technological societies for educating and, in turn, socializing citizens. In societies where formal schools are not well established, individuals are still educated via institutions such as the family and community or tribal groups. However, as the world becomes more complex and interrelated, even these societies will have to create more formal schooling to address the social and cultural needs of their people. Certainly, schools will continue to play significant roles in modern technological, industrial, and information societies. As information explodes in both quantity and complexity, schools and other formal educational institutions will find it necessary to give even greater thought to varied curricula. We must never forget that the curriculum worker, in determining the content, experiences, and environments of education, plays a key role in shaping and indirectly socializing students.

Society and American Modal Personality

Diversity and cultural pluralism are hallmarks of current American society. Yet there are things about those who live in the United States that define them as Americans, and not, say, Canadians or Mexicans. There are certain behaviors, attitudes, and outlooks that define a modal personality. Certainly, Americans, as products of American schools, are distinguishable from Europeans and other nationals. Curricularists must recognize that, despite our differences, we Americans do share some common dimensions; a national civic social culture is shaping us. This national civic social culture even contours how we go about forming and transforming our social scene. A prime purpose of public schools is to nurture an understanding of and participation in this macro civic culture, while recognizing the diversity of the microcultures that influence the civic culture.

American schools are designed to foster the health and well-being of American culture. But, as Conrad Arensberg and Arthur Niehoff put forth, "What is meant by American culture?"[2] A related question is whether there is a modal American personality? Ruth Benedict wrote, "No culture yet observed has been able to eradicate the differences in temperament of the persons who compose it.[3] Yet members of a society do have much in common: they are nursed or fed on schedule, educated in similar fashion, marry one or several spouses, live by labor or perform common economic tasks, profess spiritual beliefs. These shared beliefs and practices temper individual differences so that individuals behave in similar, but not identical, ways. According to Benedict, the norms of society govern interpersonal relations and produce a modal personality, that is, the attitudes, feelings, and behavior patterns that most members of a society share.

Despite the current talk about cultural pluralism, there still exists in the United States a modal personality. Even recent arrivals to our shores are striving, usually through schools, to gain this personality. We have a core around which we construct our social reality. All people who live in this country, especially those born and raised here, have been influenced by a national civic culture in both recognized and unrecognized ways. Even our social critics are American social critics, much more like their fellow citizens than different from them. Affirming a modal American personality does not deny that various subcultures are woven into our social fabric. What it does mean is that "irrespective of religion, national origin, race, class, and sex, there are points of likeness that will occur more frequently" among Americans and persons living in America than among peoples living in other countries.[4]

Points of Likeness. Arensberg and Niehoff do an effective job in defining the American modal personality. These authors do not reject that Americans exhibit a great diversity in their wealth, education, manners, and tastes. What they do point out is that, despite diversities of ethnic group, origin, tradition, and economic level, Americans possess a "surprising conformity in language, diet, hygiene, dress, basic skills, land use, community settlement, recreation."[5]

Americans are closer together in their moral outlooks, political beliefs, and social attitudes than one would find in the tribal or ethnic plu-

ralisms extant in the new nations of Africa and South Asia. Certainly, we are not of one mind with regard to the particulars of a situation or issue, but in this country we share a common conceptual understanding regarding what it means to be a member of society. We share ideals, even though we frequently fall short of attaining them.

Belief in the Possible. Perhaps one characteristic of most Americans is their belief that anything is possible. "Work hard and you will succeed"; this is still the subtext of the American dream. Even slogans such as "Just do it" suggest this. Most of us have heard that anyone can grow up to be president. And although some would say that this is "pie in the sky" talk, President Clinton did not come from a privileged class. In fact, very few of our presidents have come from the privileged classes.

Schools, in how they present the curriculum, are selling this message. Work hard, make the effort. Even social critics who challenge schools to liberate students from oppression demonstrate their belief that it is possible to rise above one's circumstances. One can leave the inner city and succeed. One can even succeed in the inner city with the right attitudes regarding effort. One can be optimistic knowing that humans exhibit tremendous plasticity.

Part of our modal personality is a firm belief that what counts in America is not where you came from but what you do. The measure of a person is his or her achievements. Certainly, we do have status differences among the population. People vary as to occupation, wealth, and education. However, most of us believe that people gain success in life through achievement rather than inheritance. This is not to discount that persons have been marginalized because of their ethnicity or gender. Nevertheless, even these individuals believe that they should be judged by what they can do, achieve, or contribute, rather than being categorized by their inherited backgrounds.

There is a saying that "the person with the most toys wins." There is much truth to this in that many people judge a person as having achieved, as having arrived, if that person has a lot of material goods, especially material goods of high quality. This belief in material goods defining success is embedded in our national psyche. The American dream is often equated with owning one's own house in the suburbs. And so many persons have gone after this dream in this century that we are now a nation of cities and suburbs. We are no longer a rural country; few rural schools exist, and our way of thinking is not rural.

Presently, there is a challenge to counting successful achievement by the number of consumer goods. Social critics have said that the worth of education needs to be judged on some other basis than economic. Getting an education should be sold on a more solid base than its economic clout. Yet, this argument is ingrained in us.

We hear that we need to achieve by attaining the human values of concern for others, an appreciation for diversity, and by attaining higher levels of spirituality. We need to direct our attention away from self-gratification and more to the welfare of others. Economics should no longer constitute the driving force of public education.[6] In all the dialogue about achievement, whether it be about acquiring material goods, driven by an out-of-control consumerism, or about attaining human attributes that benefit humankind, there is that foundational belief that "we can do it." It is possible. We can be in command of ourselves, and we can attain community.

Social critics note that educators need to grasp the meaning of "a sovereign of possibility."[7] People arguing for this as a totalizing vision posit that this vision is more than having the good life; it is being the good person in this life. This vision of possibility is connected to the spiritual nature of humans. In a real sense, the argument for celebrating possibility is giving new testimony to the belief that people can live full lives that are not measured by material objects, but rather are judged by their inner selves. People are coming to accept more completely that we should be judged by the quality of our character. This view is shared by the majority of people. Curricularists should remember this.

A Preference for Duality. Some of us call it either–or thinking, a preference for putting concepts into pairs, often with the first concept the preferred. Arensberg and Niehoff call this aspect of our modal personality a preference for making twofold judgments based on principle.[8] We may well be captives of our Indo-European language heritage in preferring this kind of thinking and resultant action.

We feel comfortable in assigning a situation or action to a category to which we have indicated preference and contrasting it to a situation or action that we hold up for rejection or avoidance. We view education as it currently exists as either liberating or oppressive and educators as either sensitive to students or insensitive. We view behaviors as either right or wrong. One attains either success or experiences failure. One is either moral or immoral. Schools are either public or private. One is either modern or postmodern. One is either religious or nonreligious. In following this preference for duality, there is a tendency for us to think in terms of absolutes. With regard to education, one either knows the material or not; one either masters the curriculum or does not. This perhaps is one modal trait that we need to challenge. We need to think in terms of degrees of difference rather than absolutes.

A Belief in Moral Bases for Right Action. Those who live in the United States possess a morality that in many ways sets them apart from others in the world community. This is not to say that others are not moral individuals. Rather, we maintain that the moralism that shapes the American psyche is unique. Americans, especially today, frequently deliberate about appropriate action from a basis of morality. When American educators discuss the rights of individuals to an education that empowers, they are speaking quite often from the belief that people have a moral right to that which furthers their humanness. And people who oppress, while perhaps not engaged in outright illegal action, are nevertheless behaving immorally. It is morally wrong to discriminate. It is morally wrong to deny people choice. Americans seem to believe that they possess an intuitive sense of the right.[9] Recognizing and accepting this sense of the right can guide our individual and collective conduct.

While, currently, many challenge the behaviors and views of various groups, we still bring a moral tone to the discussion. There seems to be a moral dimension to the discussion about drugs, sex, crime. There is also evidence of our characteristic of viewing behavior in terms of absolutes. "Just say no" to either sex or drugs shows this.

A Belief in the Work Ethic.　　It is often heard that Americans are the hardest working people on the earth. As a nation, we have the least amount of time for vacations from our work, usually just two weeks compared to six weeks of paid vacation time in Germany. We instill in our youth the importance of work, saying that school will prepare you for the world of work. Get a good education and get a good job. We even attempt to motivate our students in their dealings with the curriculum by stating that learning is their work. Work hard in school; give it your all.[10]

Work hard now, and you can play later. As a people, we do tend to separate work and play. Work is necessary and purpose driven; it need not be enjoyable, although we do seem to be changing on this point. Work is so integral to the American culture that frequently we classify ourselves and others by the work done. And we assign status to various types of work. She is a doctor; he is a lawyer; he is a beautician; she is a bus driver. We come to think that work that pays well has more value than work that does not. We tend to judge people by their work. Often peoples' roles are determined by their work.

Work is essential to the well-being of the individual and the general society. Put simply, work is that which we do to obtain money for ourselves and our families. It is necessary. No work, no paycheck at the end of the week. We are very task oriented as a people, and we believe that if you work hard you will attain success. Of course, some people will say that the general society is prejudiced toward some individuals so that even their hard work is not rewarded. But the truthfulness of this claim shows that there is still a belief in the work ethic.

That work is so essential to our cultural fabric is further revealed by how we look at time. Time is money. Don't waste time. In education we have such concepts as academic time, time on task, and total allowable time to educate students to the importance of time. We run our nation on an industrial time. We regulate our work weeks by time. When we work overtime, we expect more pay. Even teachers, who think themselves professionals, balk at attending school meetings scheduled after hours.

Much of our thinking about time is the result of the development of the industrial nation. As we further enter the information age, we may well challenge our concepts of time. Already, we can access the Internet not in real time, but in available time. The World Wide Web can be experienced in personal time. Messages may be put into the system while we sleep for us to read when we awake. However, we still think of time in much the same way as we did at the beginning of this century. There is a time for work and a time for play. There is a time for vacation and a time for school. People are even suggesting that there should be more time for schools, more academic learning time. Some schools are extending the school years; some districts are going to all-year schools, although such schools are not really increasing the academic time of students, but rather changing the placement of academic time and spacing it over the entire year.

That schools are changing their academic year relates to our viewing time as a resource, as money. Currently, the public demands that schools be accountable. Much of this is because the public wants schools to use time more efficiently. The public wants more bang for its educational dollar. Even legislators are demanding that university professors document how they are using their time. College students are being urged to use their study time more efficiently so that they can complete their degrees more quickly. The faster they go through college, the more efficient the use of time, that is, of educational dollars.

Those who have lived in the United Stated for some time are firm believers in the work ethic and in the precise management of time. We like planes that depart and arrive on time. We like people who are punctual in keeping their appointments. We expect students and teachers to arrive on time for their day's work. We even regulate our leisure with an eye toward precise time. Monday-night football is an American institution. It would not feel right to have Thursday-night football. Most people would feel naked without their wristwatches. The tick of the watch is almost the pulse of America.

A Belief in Equity.　　Americans as a whole believe in the equal rights of individuals to attain all that they can according to their talents and energies. Some social critics claim this is false. And certainly, in our history, there have been times and there continue to be instances where some people have not been afforded equal opportunities to attain the American dream. But critics believe that there should be such equality of opportunity. Critics' complaints do not challenge this American belief, but rather urge us to live up to our ideals.

Perhaps our belief in equality, that no one is better than anyone else or should be given special privileges, comes in part from our Declaration of Independence, which is the only government document in the world that "promises" life, liberty, and the pursuit of happiness. The Declaration states that people have an inalienable right to have life, to attain liberty, and to seek happiness.

Equity does not mean that all will be the same or attain the same. People can have equal chances to be successful and should have the freedom to pursue success, but success will depend largely on the energies of the individual. Often success is equated with achievement.

Connected to this belief in equity is a belief in the individual and the benefits of allowing individuals to have personal freedom and individual expression.[11] Related to giving individuals equal opportunities to develop their freedom and expression is the need to nurture individual responsibility, not only to self but to community. Equal rights, most Americans believe, require equal responsibilities for right action.

The challenges of equity for educators is not to assume that equity means sameness. Equal educational opportunity does not mean having all students experience the same curriculum or learn via the same pedagogical methods. Equal means that individuals have the right and chance to experience that which is necessary and meaningful to them for their benefit and for the good of the nation at large. Equity as a concept will continue to be in tension with the concept of freedom— freedom to be different, to achieve above others, or to separate oneself from others. Equity for most Americans refers to the right to be able to participate in the American dream, not to live out the dream in a limited conformity.

Some reading this book will take exception to the belief that those within the United States exhibit some common points of likeness. Some will challenge the notion of an American modal personality. We are just too diverse as a nation. There is no civic macro culture. However, we would argue that, while we are indeed a diverse and varied mix of peoples, we do have some shared views and beliefs that define us. And these views and beliefs find their way into our curriculum and influence the ways in which we deal with others and with students inside and outside schools. American schools are conceived as serving the children of America so that they can develop understandings, beliefs, and actions that deepen their participation in their local, national, and world communities in ways that exhibit a commitment to certain intellectual, civic, and moral understandings and behaviors.[12]

A DYNAMIC, CHANGING SOCIETY

One reason that it is so essential to consider the social foundations in curriculum work is that never before has there been such a rapid rate of change in all aspects of society as presently. The appropriate curricula for various groups cannot be determined with certainty, for groups are changing, ethnic demands are emerging, information is exploding, behaviors are being modified, and values are being altered. Having modal beliefs does not erase the fact that the particulars of society are changing.

Educators put themselves and their programs at peril if they ignore the social dynamics of the society in which they are living. Certainly in the past, educators in general, and teachers and curriculum workers in particular, found that it was sufficient to uncritically accept the tendencies of the times in which they found themselves and to develop school programs that mirrored contemporary social and political forces. However, the demands today are not to create programs that mirror society solely, but rather to generate programs that allow individuals to participate in the continual shaping of society. Hedrick Smith urges us to rethink America. Americans need new ways of thinking about themselves as a people, about how they are educated and how they engage in social, political, and economic activities.[13] While we may not agree with his recommendations, they do show that people are demanding from both conservative and radical quarters that we redefine ourselves as a national and world people. This urge to continually redefine ourselves is actually a modal characteristic of Americans. While we honor tradition to some degree, we are always challenging it and thinking of ways to "bring it forward."

Today, the words of William Van Til are more important than ever. He noted

> There is a danger to individuals and to society in an education which accepts uncritically and reflects unthinkingly. . . . The danger is that some forces which mutually reinforce each other may take us down roads contrary to the American (ideal)—the ideal of the individual who is free, morally responsible, and important. Some tendencies of the times, if uncritically accepted and implemented by education, could lead to the powerless man in the powerful society.[14]

Society as a Source of Change

Contemporary society is changing so swiftly that we have difficulty coping with it and adjusting ourselves to the present and preparing for the future. We are forced to look to the schools for help in understanding and living with social change, but schools are conservative institutions that usually lag behind change.

The differential rates of change in different parts of society give rise to the phenomenon known as *cultural lag*. Usually, changes in the scientific, commercial, and industrial aspects of culture come first, followed by lags in the institutions of society. People seem to accept material changes more readily than institutional changes, and they seem to resist changes in fundamental ideological ideas.

The amount of cultural lag within a society varies with the amount of social change. If there is little or no social change, obviously the lag, if it exists, is small. In Western society, especially in the United States, consistent and fundamental change is occurring in many aspects of society. As our society has entered a period of rapid change (which has accelerated since World War II) and as each new change has set off a whole chain of other events, this lag has become acute.

Rate and Direction of Change. There are two basic ways to conceive change—rate and direc-

tion. The rate of change has implications that are quite apart from, and sometimes more important than, the direction of change.

One way to illustrate the *rate of change* is to divide the last 100,000 years of human existence into lifetimes of approximately 75 years each (equivalent to an average lifespan in our society), or a total of 1,333 lifetimes. Only during the last sixty lifetimes has it been possible to communicate effectively from one lifetime to another through writing. Only in the last six lifetimes did humankind see a printed word. Only in the last two has anyone anywhere used a motor, and only in the last one have we used electricity.

In this connection, Alvin Toffler noted over 25 years ago that we were entering a period of *future shock:* We have too many goods and services from which to choose, and our ability to choose wisely from all these options was becoming increasingly limited because of human overload (for example, try choosing the best long-distance phone company).[15]

Another way of appreciating the rate of change is to consider that to a person born in 1940, who was 50 years old in 1990, the following occurred:

1. Telecommunications became, for practical purposes, instantaneous.
2. The speed of information processing increased a millionfold.
3. The rate of population increase went up more than a millionfold.
4. Jet aircraft, radar, space missiles, and space satellites became commonplace.
5. Major organs, such as the human heart, kidneys, and liver, were transplanted.
6. Moon and Martian landings were successfully completed.[16]

To this list, add the following:

1. Genetic engineering, test-tube babies, and sex selection became realities (and the slowing of the aging process is at our fingertips).
2. With a portable remote system (weighing less than one pound) a TV viewer can instantly (at the speed of light) tune into one or more of 100 channels and connect live to any part of the world through a satellite communication system.

3. More than 75 percent of the items on super-market shelves today did not exist in 1940. Plastic money has since replaced paper money as the major medium of exchange.

4. Computers are common in everyday life, including in schools; robots are commonplace in commerce and industry, and they will soon be in homes as well.

5. Whereas three-fourths of Americans employed by industry in 1940 were manufacturing goods, today more than 60/75 percent are providing services; we have changed from an industrial society to a "postindustrial society" or what some people call the third technological revolution" or "third wave."

6. The median age of the U.S. population rose from 26 in 1940 to 30 in 1980 to 34.5 in 1990 and is likely to rise to 37 by 2000. The proportion of people 65 and over increased from 7% in 1940 to 11.3% in 1980 and is expected to increase to 18% by 2000.

7. The number of working mothers increased from 18% in 1950; by 1990 two-thirds were working and the trend toward greater female participation in the labor force is expected to continue. The increase in working mothers is in part related to the general decline in the American standard of living, which started in the 1960s, and has created a new phenomenon of latchkey children. By 1990, there were some 8 million latchkey children between ages 6 and 13.

One way to illustrate the *direction of change* is to consider world population growth. Philip Hauser estimated that for 600,000 years the world population expanded by 0.02 per thousand per year. On a two-dimensional graph such as Figure 5-1, this growth appears as a straight horizontal line. During the past 500 years, however, the growth line has shifted essentially from a horizontal position to a vertical one. At the present time, population growth has expanded from 2 percent per millennium to more than 2 percent per year—a thousandfold increase per year.[17]

This shift in direction constitutes a fundamental change that simply cannot be comprehended as a mere quantitative change. (The quantitative shift represents only one dimension of change in population growth.) Other equally important directional changes in society involve advances in science, communication, transportation—all of which affect the quality of life and which have global impact.

Educators, especially curriculum specialists, need to reduce educational lag and to avoid plan-

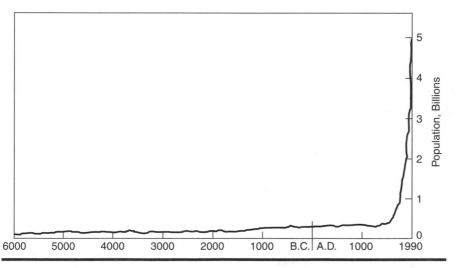

FIGURE 5-1 World Population Growth, 6000 B.C. to 2000 A.D.

ning schools for the next century that are suited for the 1980s—a typical 20-year lag period that often exists between schools and society. The fact of rapid change and the need to plan schools today for tomorrow bring to mind serious questions: What policies govern our society? At a global level, what should be our educational aims? How do we identify the "good" life and what role do the schools play? How do schools reduce the gap between the "haves" and "have nots"? How do the schools prepare students for the world of tomorrow, when teachers who are trusted to do the job mainly rely on a knowledge base that is quickly becoming, if it is not already, dated?

Schools as an Agent of Change

If we take a broad, long view of schools, that is, a *macro* view, we can observe noticeable changes in schools over time. Historically, according to Philip Jackson, "one has only to think of the wooden benches and planked floors of the early American classroom as compared with the plastic chairs and tile flooring in today's suburban schools to note changes."[18] We can strengthen the contrast by looking back to the one-room schoolhouse: Students of many ages were crowded in one room; the teacher stood behind the pulpit (like the church minister) preaching the daily lessons; no blackboards or chalk were used; the desks and chairs were bolted down; the sun was the major source of light; and firewood was the main source of heat. Schools, today, are dramatically different.

If we look at the school during our lifetime— that is, a *micro* view—say, when we were attending elementary school, we note that the changes have been minimal. Unruh and Alexander have summarized the milieu of change since the 1950s: "Surface changes, small and isolated innovations and lack of comprehensive approaches to changes" have prevailed in the schools. The underlying assumption, or the reason for the lack of change, has been that "the school as an institution was headed in the right direction except that it needed to exert more effort toward its previous goals and make content and instruction more palatable to students. It was taken for granted that there was nothing wrong in the schools [and] . . . it was the student" and not the schools "that needed to be changed."[19]

Although the research in education may be impressive in quantity, very few noticeable changes have resulted in schooling since our days as students. We are basically using the same instructional methods in the classroom that we were using 50 years ago, according to one observer. On the other hand, the changes and improvements in science, technology, and medicine within the last 5 years have been impressive, and they have affected almost all of our lives in some way.

We might expect educational aims and subject matter to change as society imposes new social and political demands on the schools, and as new knowledge is created. And they do! However, we should not expect the structure and organization of schools to change dramatically.

We must understand that schools are highly bureaucratic and conservative (or traditional) institutions that operate with standardized norms of behavior, written rules and regulations, and well-defined tasks dispersed among administrators, teachers, and students. As parents and/or teachers who were once students, we can return to school and readily cope and function almost immediately because the behaviors and tasks, the rituals, rules, and regulations, have not changed much since we were children.

As teachers, curriculum specialists, administrators, and students interact on a daily basis in the operation of a school, a social order develops: A set of routines and rules surfaces and group norms and organizational values become pervasive and shape individual personalities and behavior. Hoy and Miskel describe this process: "The school is a system of social interaction; it is an organized whole comprised of interacting personalities bound together in an organic relationship." The school is "characterized by an interdependence of parts, a clearly defined population, differentiation from its environment, a complex network of social relationships, and its own unique culture."[20] The outcome is a host of institutional norms and patterns of behaviors that govern the interaction between teachers and students and between curriculum specialists and other support staff. Observers use terms like *intrinsic character, institutional realities,* or *cultural patterns* to describe these social characteristics and interactions. When taken together, they tend to result in a persuasive method of socializing and controlling the people who attend and/or work in schools, and they tend to inhibit change.

As schools plan for change, education can no longer be reserved for the traditional age cohort, or early years of life, 5 to 16. Schooling must be expanded both downward (to cope with problems of working mothers and to better prepare at-risk students for school) and upward (to provide greater variety of educational resources at different stages of people's lives and to prepare them for second or third careers).[21] The idea of a "step-in, step-out" approach to educational systems for life-long education is gaining in popularity. Both Combs and Illich point out that education must be expanded to include "learning networks" that combine informal and formal models of schooling.[22]

Furthermore, the idea of literacy must also be expanded to include not only basic or functional literacy, but also cultural literacy, scientific literacy, computer literacy, technological literacy, television (or electronic) literacy, and research literacy.

Dealing with Diversity.   As a nation, we have always had a plurality of cultures. True, we started out as an English colony, and this history has influenced our evolution. However, we have been successful since gaining our independence in enabling the diverse cultural groups that have come to our shores to mold themselves to such a degree that most of these minorities are now classified as white. To be sure, the Africans brought originally as slaves and the indigenous peoples of the land have experienced different histories.

However, never in our history have we had such a culturally diverse student population in our schools as now. Never have we as educators been more challenged to rid ourselves of those school practices that try to organize and homogenize students into one standard or average group. Never have we been made more aware of the need to discard whole-class grouping, tracking, and common pedagogies. Literally, the complexion of our students is changing from white to various shades of color.

This adding of color and cultural diversity will continue into the foreseeable future. Most of the peoples coming to our shores will not share a European culture. In the period 1981–1990, the percentage of Asian immigrants went from 13 percent to a high of 38 percent (U.S. Bureau of the Census, 1993). These people are bringing in new values, new mores, and new languages. Already in California, people of color are the majority. In the Seattle schools, over 34 languages are spoken. English as a second language is an essential part of the curriculum for speakers of these diverse tongues.

The challenges confronting educators are varied and numerous. Curricularists must generate curricula that are both responsive to students' diversity, while at the same time transferring and transforming the civic culture that serves as the binding for the American nation. We need to have curricula that enable students to incorporate those values and behaviors that are of benefit to the body politic and general society. The curriculum must allow a weaving of diverse social and cultural threads into a national fabric that is inclusive.

Educators need different learning goals, different school programs, and different pedagogical approaches; flexible curricula; and even varied educational environments to address the needs of all students. We cannot afford to socially or economically marginalize any students. The curriculum must promote in students a knowing-in-action as recommended by Schon.[23] The curriculum must nurture in students those perspectives that enlighten and empower students to be active participants in a dynamic, emerging society.

Race, Class, and Gender.   When dealing with diversity, certain curriculum scholars frequently chastise the schools for creating curricula that reproduce the inequities in the general society. Schools have served to marginalize the less fortunate: those who have membership in races different from white, those who are members of the lower classes, and those who are females. While there is some truth to these arguments, when dealing with race, class, and gender, it is important to realize that race and class are primarily political concepts. With gender we are dealing with a social construct. Race as a concept is essentially used in political terms to identify primarily persons of color. The term race is not acknowledged by cultural anthropologists or biologists. "Race as a meaningful criterion within the biological sciences has long been recognized to be a fiction.[24]

But, currently, we use race to define political social groups that can be recognized by the color of their skin.

Ethnic groups, of which we are all members, are collectivities of people who on the basis of selected differences, such as language, religion, beliefs, and mores, consider themselves as distinct from other groups. Ethnic groups come in all colors, white included. And there are numerous ethnic groups within a particular racial group as we employ the term. There is as much diversity among Asian groups immigrating into this country as there is among European or African groups coming to this country. Educators will make a serious error in addressing diversity if they think that all groups of color are the same.

The issue of how to address diversity in the curriculum will continue to be tension producing, since within our schools some educators accept the concept of *assimilation* of various ethnic groups and some the concept of *plurality*. Some assimilationists argue that nurturing ethnic plurality, a social heterogeneity, would in fact balkanize our nation.[25] Others argue that the assimilationists' concept of a melting pot is myth. We are more like a "salad bowl"—all in the same salad but maintaining our unique features. We would argue that there is truth to both group's assertions. The melting pot is not myth to the extent that in our ethnic classifications we currently have the category of white. There is tremendous diversity of ethnic heritage among whites, yet for most people they are blended in and even defined as white, Anglo-Saxon, and Protestant. The majority of whites in this country fail to meet all three of these characteristics.

Those who accept the salad bowl concept recognize that our nation is composed of many voices and many ethnic groups. These individuals, sometimes identified as pluralists, say that in focusing on the melding of a major unitary culture assimilationists have neglected to consider that such a stance suggests domination by one group and subordination of other groups.[26] It is true, as argued by the pluralists, that we in the United States are not all of one mind. And the diversity of the mind-sets in the country will continue as we accept to our shores varied immigrants from around the world. Pluralists argue that we can both honor our diversity, celebrate it in our curriculum, and still cooperate and collaborate in a single society. This view suggests that we acknowledge the diversity of our students in the school curriculum, but also that students should experience curricula such that they become committed to the core values and practices that make us an American society. We are both a single society and a clustering of diverse societies.

The issue of class is also of concern to curricularists. The American school is conceptualized from a middle-class orientation, but increasing numbers of students coming to our schools are not currently members of this class. They have values different from middle-class individuals. They have language patterns and social conventions that are not middle class. Some hold that, while these students are certainly different, their class-influenced behaviors are of equal value to those held by middle-class persons. The debate as to the legitimacy and value of Black English or Ebonics was an issue in California in 1997. Many members of a particular school community argued that Ebonics was equal to standard English and should be taught in the schools. Ways of dealing with other people, views of the future, perceptions of success, and ideas as to what it means to be educated all differ among the classes.

The issue of class in curricular conversation has been much influenced by Marxist theory. Marxist and neo-Marxist educators have argued about the rights of the proletariat and their challenges to the bourgeoisie. Much talk today is about how to rescue the "underclass" from the perils of poverty, poor education, and discrimination. Certainly, we have poor children. And we must have a curriculum that gives them the tools and attitudes to succeed and escape the cycle of poverty and the often accompanying violence.

But, despite all the talk about the haves and the have nots, most people, even people of color, are in the haves category. As of 1997, a majority of African Americans were in the middle class.[27] However, since many individuals were not, we are still challenged to reduce the numbers of students in poverty and to provide them with appropriate curricula.

In the United States, we view class lines as permeable. With education and effort, people can succeed. Even critics of our social and educational system must admit that there are far too many examples of successful people to give credence to the belief that schools consciously or unconsciously plan via their curriculum to keep students down, to marginalize them, or to assure that they are deprived of their rights as citizens.

If schools are to nurture educational experiences that are inclusive, then we need to recognize that this has to do with our values, language, beliefs, and economic standing. It is impossible for schools to include all students into one ethnic group. Ethnicity cannot be changed. But it is very much possible for schools to bring people into a common social class in which people share core values, common language, and similar beliefs with regard to the human family and share in the economic well-being of the country. This does not mean that we will be identical in our class level, but we can have enough similarities to be recognized as members of this class, whether we call it middle class or something else.

Gender is the last term of the radical battle cry. As previously mentioned, gender is not a biological given; Sari Knopp Biklen and Diane Pollard note that "Gender is a category of analysis that refers to the social construction of sex. What we have come to identify as belonging to men's or women's behaviors, attitudes, presentation of self, and so on is produced by social relationships and continually negotiated and maintained within cultures."[28] However, what seems to confuse our discussion of gender issues and how they can or should influence curricular deliberation is the practice of using the words "sex" and "gender" as synonyms.[29] Sex refers to a biological given. Gender is not; it is created by social or cultural factors. For the most part, male and female will remain constant in the future. However, what is considered masculine and feminine is open to modification.

A key issue for curricularists is how the curriculum affects gender. In our creation and presentation of curriculum, do we privilege one gender and devalue another? Educators throughout history have created educational programs that in fact have elevated the masculine gender while shackling the feminine gender. We have even developed values and manners of dealing with information that favor men over women. History is overflowing with examples in which boys and men have been nurtured to gain high levels of achievement and success, while girls and women have had their options limited and their growth curtailed. Of course, we realize that this is a particular construction of history. Some would dispute this interpretation. They would argue that men and women by their biological natures are designed for different purposes, each equally central to the well-being of society. Thus education had the responsibility to prepare boys and girls for those duties necessary for the overall society. Men had to be hunters, providers outside the home. Women had to be the guardians of the hearth and raise and nurture children. This debate has gone on since the beginning of time. It is still current, although many are challenging such a segregation of roles.

Sexually, we know that boys and men are biologically different from girls and women. But are the genders different? And, if different, should the curricula experienced be different? We do not plan in this book to solve this argument. We only wish to point out that the gender factor must be considered when engaging in curriculum deliberation and delivery. However, we are of the mindset that education should be for the benefit of all; no person should be privileged or marginalized because of gender. Many feminists who are engaged in scholarship for the advancement of girls and women's rights want the curricula offered to be redesigned and reconceptualized so that significant aspects of the female experience and female ways of knowing are included in the curriculum for all to experience. These feminists, sometimes identified as *cultural feminists*, wish this new content to serve as transformational fodder for the reconstruction of the overall society.[30] They believe that schools and the curricula must be redesigned so that feminine values are given equal honor with masculine values. Others known as *liberal feminists* do not call for a total reconceptualization of the curriculum. Rather they argue that the curriculum as it now exists can be presented in a way so that students are not taught to behave in sex-stereotyped ways. With such instruction, society would deal equitably with both sexes.[31]

It appears that underlying the gender issue is the issue of equity. Equity can suggest fairness, but being fair does not mean doing identical things, or having identical curricula. However, many view our current curricula as not being fair, or equitable, for girls and women. The subtext of the hidden curriculum sends powerful messages to girls that certain subjects, primarily mathematics and science, are not for them. Indeed, some radical feminists have postulated that even when these subjects are presented, they are taught as knowledge that men have generated. Women had no role in the development of these disciplines. Furthermore, the disciplines are presented as having been developed through certain ways of thinking that can be considered masculine: being objective, devoid of emotion, uninfluenced by values. Entire areas of inquiry by women are unacknowledged. Even conclusions about the world and the people within it are based primarily on studies of men only, yet the results are applied to women. For many feminists, and even others not in this camp, the curriculum is patriarchal and does not serve girls and women well.[32]

Not only is the curriculum patriarchal, it is sexist and delivered in a sexist manner. There is an inherent bias in the curriculum content that portrays women and girls in unfavorable lights or ignores them altogether as contributing members of society. Women and girls are members of a lesser sex, and the boundaries of their gender have constrained their progress. Social meanings and histories of masculinity have devalued all that is deemed feminine. Not only do many teachers, so critics claim, not include the study of women and their contributions, but teachers deal inequitably with girls in their classrooms. Many teachers, even women teachers, favor boys, actually giving them more time in classroom interaction. Other researchers have found that standardized tests favor boys over girls.[33]

Certainly, we believe that the curriculum of schools should not be sexist. However, whether one considers the curriculum to be sexist is shaped by how one interprets gender and how schools respond to it. We should have curricula that enable individuals to soar, to reach and maximize their potential. If gender is a social construct, it should be constructed for the benefit of all. And we have argued that gender is socially defined, albeit it does derive from our recognition of biological differences between males and females.

Some hold that gender, while socially defined, actually does exist prior to the social meanings it is given.[34] Gender is a function of our biological nature, and individuals of each gender possess certain innate dispositions to act and think in particular ways. For instance, the inherent condition of caring is considered to be female. Likewise, aggression is inherently male. We take the caring condition of females and socialize females to serve in capacities that require caring. Likewise, we take aggression and shape males to exhibit socially appropriate outlets for aggression, such as certain sports or in protecting the nation state. Carol Gilligan, at least in her early work, seems to say certain ways of thinking or of relating to the world are innate to women.[35] To say this is not to be sexist; it is to recognize a fact of nature. What curricularists must do is to equally privilege women's ways of knowing with men's ways of knowing. Difference is not the problem. The problem lies in the ways gender differences are valued and stigmatized. However, difference is not totally determined by biological dispositions. Differences are created and values are assigned to differences by society.

The issue of dealing with gender in appropriate ways is going to continue. And it should. Being equitable in dealing with gender means that both genders should have access to knowledge, should have their dealing with knowledge legitimated, and should have their contributions to the advancement of knowledge recognized and celebrated. As knowledge in the information age is being constructed, deconstructed, and reconstructed, we need to realize that the concept of gender is also undergoing modification. Some might say that gender cannot be altered. However, we point out that we live in times in which we can change physically the sex of individuals, so altering gender is certainly possible. Poststructuralist thinkers are already challenging the postulate of a stable gender identity created by the general society. In its stead, they propose the concept of varied genders, fluid genders, a notion of multiple selves.[36] There is ample evidence of fluid gender identities and outward signs of gender. In our society, men and boys with earrings are no longer uncommon. Even skirts and fingernail polish for men have been introduced. Women now smoke cigars.

In this information age, we are experiencing new knowledge, hybrid fields of scholarly work, and new technologies that facilitate our creating, processing, accessing, and distribution of information. It is essential for curricularists to realize that new information and new technology are introduced into a preexisting social, political, and economic order. We cannot escape the fact of our being in a present and emerging time in which current and past practices and notions color our views and behaviors, in this case about the issue of gender.

There is no denying that certain knowledge and curricular content, both in the past and present, are largely viewed as more appealing to men than to women. Mathematics, science, and engineering are still viewed by many as men's fields. The same is true for computer science. We need to be careful that we do not send girls and women messages that the content of the information age and its technologies are the domains of men and boys. Girls and women must be allowed to find these subjects, disciplines, and technologies appealing. And they do when given the chance. This does not mean that they will deal with the information age in a gender-neutral way, nor should it. But if knowledge is power, and it is, and if knowledge will be the coin of the realm in the future, and it is already, then educators must make sure that all students, both male and female, have access to gaining this power and the skills to utilize it wisely for the benefit of themselves and the general society.

The challenges for dealing with diversity, with race, class, and gender, are extremely complex, in large part because race, class, and gender are not entities that one can keep separate. Rather race, class, and gender intermix and interact. In our classrooms, we have students who are female, of color, and underclass. We also have females who are of color but of upper class. We have males who are of color and upper class. As we can see, there are various permutations. Perhaps the key for educators is the realization that we are all members of particular ethnic, if not racial, groups; we all are members of various class or social groups, and we all have gender as well as sexual identity. These attributes make us diverse and unique, but they also bespeak of a commonness. The commonness is that we all have these attributes. Regardless of the specific differences we have, we are members of the human family. Remembering this may assist educators in dealing

with the diversity issue. This never was a small task, nor is it ever likely to become easy.

Knowledge as an Agent of Change

The accumulated body of organized knowledge about people and the world may be viewed as an extension of and interaction process with contemporary society. As society changes, so does our knowledge; in reverse, as our knowledge base increases, additional changes take place in society as well. The changes in Western society and growth in knowledge result from our striving to understand, control, and change the physical and social environment around us. (Changes take place in other societies, too, although today their growth in knowledge tends to be slower.) The schools should also be considered as a major data source for knowledge, especially for children and youth, in terms of (1) screening knowledge against aims society sets for education, (2) identifying important kinds of knowledge, and (3) determining what can and should be taught.

Explosion of Knowledge. Since the 1950s, many educators have continued to call attention to the explosion of knowledge. Every 15 years or so, our significant knowledge doubles, and this trend makes it important to continuously reappraise and revise existing curricula. "It can be affirmed unequivocally," says Bentley Glass, "that the amount of scientific knowledge available at the end of one's life will be almost one hundred times what it was when he was born." Moreover, 95 percent of all the scientists who ever lived are alive today.[37]

Similarly, Warren Ziegler maintains that (1) more mathematics has been created since 1900 than during the entire period of history, (2) half of what a graduate engineer studies today will be obsolete in 10 years, and (3) half of what a person learns is no longer valid by the time he or she reaches middle age.[38] We add to this list that nearly half of what we will need to know to function in scientific or technical jobs by the year 2200 is not even known today, by anyone.

The idea that knowledge is increasing exponentially or geometrically obscures the fact that the development of knowledge in many fields, especially science and technology, is more typically related to "branching": that is, the creation of several subdivisions or specialties within fields, not just simple growth. Each advance in a particular field has the potential for creating another branch. (In education, one can find some indicators of proliferation of several fields of study or branches, including curriculum and instruction, and within each field or branch several specializations of knowledge and job titles. With this increase of knowledge, there are several new curriculum journals, papers, and speeches, all adding to the proliferation of knowledge.) The almost incredible explosion of knowledge threatens to overwhelm us unless we can find ways to deal with this new and growing wealth of information; new knowledge must be constantly introduced into the curriculum while less important material is pruned away. In assessing the ongoing rush of knowledge, Alvin Toffler asserts that knowledge taught should be related to the future. "Nothing should be included in the required curriculum unless it can be strongly justified in terms of the future. If this means scrapping a substantial part of the formal curriculum, so be it."[39] To deal with this knowledge explosion, as it shapes the future, curriculum specialists have two major problems that require continuous attention: (1) what knowledge to select and (2) how to organize it.

What Knowledge Is of Most Worth? This question, which was raised by Spencer more than 100 years ago, has social implications; it is certainly more relevant today, because of the complexity of and changes in society, than it was during Spencer's time. In recent years, the question has, in fact, been repeated by many different curricularists.[40] Actually, the question dates back to ancient Greece, when Plato and Aristotle questioned the value of knowledge in relation to society and governmental affairs, and to ancient Rome, when Quintilian set forth the original seven liberal arts—grammar, rhetoric, logic, arithmetic, geometry, astronomy, and music—as the ideal curriculum for educated citizens of public life: senators, lawyers, teachers, civil servants, and politicians. During the modern school period, these seven liberal arts have expanded to include many other subjects.

Table 5-1 shows a survey of coursework in five basic subject areas (plus computer science)

TABLE 5-1 Average Years of Coursework Completed by Graduating High School Seniors, 1982 and 1987

	1982	1987
English	3.80	4.00
Mathematics	2.54	2.97
Science	2.19	2.59
Social studies (and history)	3.10	3.33
Foreign languages	1.05	1.46
Computer science	0.11	0.43

Source: The Condition of Education, 1990, Vol. 1 (Washington, D.C.: U.S. Government Printing Office, 1990). Table 1.13, p. 48.

for 1982 and 1987. In all subject areas, coursework among graduating high school seniors has increased, especially in mathematics and science. The percent for each subject area suggests what school officials, adult society, and students consider to be most worthwhile knowledge.

Considering that we live in a highly technocratic and scientific society, one in which knowledge has great impact on our standard of living and in a world in which the push of a button can have enormous impact on our lives, the enrollments in science and mathematics have serious implications for the future of our country. A similar concern was voiced over 30 years ago, when our standard of living was increasing more rapidly and when we were more influential as a superpower. Then, James Conant stressed that students needed to enroll in more courses in science, mathematics, and foreign language.[41] The concerns of the Sputnik era first resurfaced in the 1980s, and have continued in the 1990s, under the theme of excellence in education, and there is the same feeling of urgency. Our failure to heed Conant's warning continues and is viewed by some as one reason for our decline as the leading political and economic giant of the world, and for the general decline of our manufacturing capability and standard of living.

As a point of comparison, consider that Japanese students are required to take 23 percent of their total junior high school curricula in science and mathematics. In high school, they are required to take 1 1/4 science courses per year and 1 1/2 math courses per year (including calculus and statistics). Japanese students outperform American students in science and mathematics on the International Association for the Evaluation of Educational Achievement (IEA) study.[42]

Because our knowledge is changing so rapidly, we must continuously ask ourselves what is the most worthwhile knowledge, and we must continuously reappraise what we mean by worthwhile. A number of paradigms have been developed along these lines. Schwab, for example, takes an eclectic approach to organizing curriculum in context with change. He is willing to accept various curriculum modes, and he points out that there are limitations to almost any approach. We need to organize a curriculum that is conducive to change and that enables scholars and practitioners to work together and test their ideas in the context of changing problems and issues of society.[43]

Organizing Knowledge.   The way we organize knowledge refers to a body of knowledge, a discipline, a field of study, or the curriculum content. These are basically synonymous terms that suggest a subject-centered approach (as opposed to a student-centered approach) to curriculum and a cognitive approach (as opposed to a behaviorist or humanistic one) to teaching and learning. This approach, according to Ruggiero and Zais, relies on logic and rational thinking to organize information, concepts, generations, and principles of school subjects, or what others call the "structure" of the subject.[44] The assumption is that the interconnection of information, concepts, and the like, constitutes bodies of information that have been validated and are the result of seeking practical, social, and educational ends; however, the result is compartmentalization of subjects.

Harry Broudy outlines four criteria for classifying knowledge: (1) agreed upon terms and concepts used for representing abstract ideas, (2) a network of related facts, generalizations, and rules or principles that are accepted as valid, (3) a method of investigation specific to itself, and (4) rules of evaluating evidence.[45] According to Phenix and Schwab, knowledge is organized into disciplines that possess their own methods of inquiry for generating new knowledge. Thus new

knowledge is never ending as long as prior knowledge is organized into a true discipline or subject. For these two curricularists, disciplines prove their worth by their own ability to generate new knowledge by adhering to methods of inquiry and rules of evidence and evaluation.[46]

Knowledge classifications are not be-end, end-all categories. With time and in various social settings, they change; thus subject matter in school should also be modified on a regular basis. Indeed, old knowledge must be pruned away, while new knowledge should be assimilated and integrated into specific knowledge areas and new contexts. Ideally, new knowledge should be integrated into a moral legal context. Whose morality? The standards of that society which is governed by a constitutional process (that protects people from other people and provides people basic rights) and promotes worthwhile and just consequences.

Areas of Knowledge.   The organization of knowledge into areas, bodies of information, or classifications has occupied world thinkers for centuries, from Plato and Aristotle to Whitehead and Russell. For example, Aristotle organized knowledge into three classes: (1) *theoretical,* such as science and math; (2) *practical,* such as politics and ethics; and (3) *productive,* such as music and architecture. This classification scheme served well for his historical period; it was direct, simple, and easy to understand and lacked a hierarchical belief or position that one area or domain of knowledge was more important than the other.

Phenix organizes knowledge into six patterns or "realms of meaning": (1) *symbolics,* consisting of ordinary language, mathematics, and nondiscursive symbols (expression of feelings, values, and insights); (2) *empirics,* comprising physical science, biology, psychology, and social science; (3) *aesthetics,* including music, visual arts, movement arts, and literature; (4) *synnoetics,* consisting of personal knowledge; (5) *ethics,* referring to moral knowledge and law; and (6) *synoptics,* that is, history, religion, and philosophy.[47]

The ideal curriculum, according to Phenix, consists of *depth* of understanding and *mastery* in one realm, contending that "a person has to choose the one channel [or realm] into which he can pour his energies with maximum effect." He argues against an "all-around knowledgeable person . . . [for] people who scatter themselves in many directions dissipate their powers and never transcend superficiality." Thus Phenix urges that we educate the "specialist" or "scholar" and views the "generalist" as quaint and impractical. Today, Phenix would most likely resist the idea of a "common" or "core" curriculum as too general and superficial, evidenced by his "ideal curriculum," which focuses on "narrow rather than broad . . . scope." For him, "depth of knowledge and skills should be the goal," rather than what he calls "superficial acquaintance with a variety of fields."[48]

Finally, Weinstein and Fantini attempt to integrate a cognitive and humanistic view toward knowledge and learning. Referring to knowledge as "content vehicles," they contend that content should "include not only conventional subject areas (English, social studies, mathematics, science, and so on)," but also foundation disciplines such as "psychology, sociology, anthropology, philosophy," and so on, as well as "classroom situations, . . . out of school experiences, [and] the children themselves."[49] Fantini considers people more important than subject matter, but subject matter is still important for the self-actualization of people. They write, "Unless knowledge relates to feeling, it is unlikely to affect behavior appreciably."[50]

Knowledge and Future Learning. To cope with the vast array of change in society, Ornstein furnishes ten guiding principles:

1. *Knowledge should comprise the basic tools.* This includes reading, writing, arithmetic, and oral communication, as well as computer literacy. The basic tools are means to an outcome, not an end in themselves. Students need to learn more than the basics, but without the basics they cannot move beyond simple knowledge or think critically in the subject fields.

2. *Knowledge should facilitate learning how to learn.* The school should help the learners acquire the skills, tools, and processes necessary to become more adept at learning and to use existing knowledge to learn new knowledge. Teachers must limit the temptation to teach a host of facts and right answers; they must encourage learners to assume responsibility for their own learning.

3. *Knowledge should be applicable to the real world.* Book knowledge that cannot be applied to everyday life is easily forgotten. It does not help the learners participate productively in society. The schools must resist teaching theory that cannot be applied to practice.

4. *Knowledge should improve the learners' self-concepts, awareness skills, and senses of personal integrity.* Stressing cognitive learning, or facts and figures, without considering the personal, emotional, and even spiritual state of the individual, is only considering half of learning. Knowledge should be used to develop the learners' feelings and personal integrity. It should enable them to get along with themselves and others, and to be relatively content with themselves and others. Unhappy or anxiety-laden individuals cannot make the best use of their cognitive skills.

5. *Knowledge should consist of many forms and methods.* There are many roads to learning and many avenues of inquiry. What works for one learner does not always work as well as for another, because there are many different styles of learning and patterns of thinking (in part related to sex, class, culture, and intelligence). Schools need to provide various options and alternatives for acquiring knowledge and learning. Schools must also recognize they are only one of many sources of learning and intellectual authority; they compete with the home, community, peer group, and mass media.

6. *Knowledge should prepare the individual for the world of technology.* The individual, in modern society, must learn to live with computers, robots, lasers, telecommunications, and space exploration. A truly educated, productive, and well-rounded individual will be able to function in an accelerating world of science and technology (that is, individuals should be scientifically and technologically literate).

7. *Knowledge should prepare individuals for the world of bureaucracy.* Bureaucracy is a growing social phenomenon that also characterizes modern society. The school system is one of many formal institutions that is run by the complicated machinery of social organization; actually, it is the first of many bureaucratic organizations that the child will encounter in life. The individual in school, in church, in the military, in the hospital, on the job and in dealing with government must learn to cope with the enormous size of bureaucracy.

8. *Knowledge should permit the individual to retrieve old information.* No individual can accumulate all the knowledge necessary to fully develop his or her human potential. The individual must understand how to retrieve old knowledge and then to modify or transform it to gain new knowledge. Knowledge is a powerful tool, and in an age of information processing, those able to retrieve and then apply information intelligently will be most productive and powerful and best able to compete in contemporary society.

9. *Knowledge acquisition should be a lifelong process.* It must be recognized that schools play a diminishing role as the learners grow and develop. Schools provide only a preliminary and temporary base of knowledge that is eventually superseded by other institutions and different forms of education. Other educational tools, such as books, newspapers, television, videos, and computers, assume greater importance and more influence than textbooks or other school materials for continuing the educations of both youngsters and adults. As adolescents develop into adults, their experiences extend beyond schools. They acquire most new learning, in fact, outside of schools.

10. *Knowledge should be taught in context with values.* Knowledge learned is processed through the social and philosophical lens of the individual; it therefore becomes value laden. In a very real sense, what we learn, and what we do not learn, are based on a process of choosing, a filtering process, that is itself based on values. How we interpret knowledge, how we build and use it, partially reflect the act of valuing and the value structure we emphasize. The greatest danger in teaching knowledge is to ignore the values that shape the individual and society; this is teaching in a vacuum and without vision.[51]

PROCESSING SOCIAL–EDUCATIONAL PRIORITIES

The twentieth century has been one of increasingly rapid change, unprecedented in rate and range. The new century fast approaching is likely to generate even more speed to these changes. All aspects of society will be affected. Technology will enable us to process change and may well alter the very nature of change. The issues we have faced in this century will be with us in the next. The issue of assuring that all students are educated, the issue of increased politicizing of the curriculum, the increasingly diverse voices of our population, the issue of how to most appropriately use technology so that knowledge and social community are advanced, and the issue of how to make schools not only reformed, but actually reconceptualized so that they are responsive to local, national, and international communities will remain.

As the social, political, and economic contexts have changed in this century, we have looked to our schools to assist us both to cope with the changes and to participate in varying degrees in the management of the changes. As a society, we have reacted to change and social pressures by revisioning the aims or priorities of education. In turn, the schools have responded to our demands by changing their programs. They have opened their doors to external groups, both private and public, who seek to further their interests and promote their causes, often pressuring schools to teach or not to teach certain subjects. At times, there has been consensus, at other times not. It is not likely that we will attain complete agreement on curricula, much less agreement for any length of time on the aims or priorities of education. The challenge confronting educators is how to process the pressure, the popular rhetoric, the slogans of the day, as well as the concerns and demands of various public groups, and balance them with regard to what is good for the general public and the nation at large.

Education for All Students

It has taken over two centuries to arrive at the belief that all students should be educated. As a society, we are now of the mind-set that all students *must* be educated in order to deal with and participate in the information century. Elliot Eisner states that we currently have two primary aims that we consider important in education:

> *We would like our children to be well informed— that is, to understand ideas that are important, useful, beautiful, and powerful. And we also want them to have the appetite and ability to think ana-*

lytically and critically, to be able to speculate and imagine, to see connections among ideas, and to be able to use what they know to enhance their own lives and to contribute to their culture.[52]

We have not always held to these two aims. Indeed, prior to the turn of the twentieth century, education addressed different aims. Education emphasized a perennialist outlook and stressed traditional subject matter, mental discipline, and school for academically able students. However, in this century, some of us have moved from the perennialist outlook to one that now seems to capture the aims Eisner has stated. The move has had its ups and down. Indeed, the period between World War I and World War II, punctuated by calls for social and economic reform, may be characterized by the rise and fall of progressive education.

The educational aims of the progressive era and the curriculum reflected the growing child psychology movement and endorsed meeting the diverse needs of all students, providing a common ground for teaching, enhancing American ideas and educating all citizens to function in a democratic society.

During this period, the *Cardinal Principles of Secondary Education* were formulated.[53] Only one of the seven principles or aims of secondary education was concerned with the fundamentals of cognitive learning. The aims cited in 1918 are still, in one form or another, the major aims and goals of contemporary education. The most important aspect of the document is that it emphasized that secondary schools should aim to educate all youth for "complete living," not just one segment of the student population, such as academically able students. Also, it did not emphasize subject matter or mental vigor. The Commission noted that more than two-thirds of entering high school students dropped out prior to graduation, and that an increasing number of immigrant children had to be educated, socialized, and provided with appropriate economic and civic skills.[54]

Twenty years later, the Educational Policies Commission of the NEA, which included the presidents of Harvard and Cornell Universities, the Commissioner of Education, and a number of progressive educators issued a report entitled *The Purpose of Education in American Democracy.*[55]

Concerned with the problems of out-of-school youth and unemployment resulting from the Great Depression, these educators issued a comprehensive set of four goals: self-realization, human relations, economic efficiency, and civic responsibility. Each goal had several subcategories.

During the mid 1940s, the Educational Policies Commission continued to modify the aims of education. Influenced by World War II, it stressed aims related to democracy and world citizenship, as well as those related to the general needs of children and youth. According to another influential report, *Education for All American Youth,* youth must develop "Ten Imperative Needs":[56] (1) economic and vocational skills; (2) good health and physical fitness; (3) community and citizenship duties; (4) family duties; (5) consumer skills; (6) scientific skills; (7) literature, art, and music skills; (8) leisure activities; (9) ethical values; and (10) rational abilities. These needs were mostly sociopsychological and physical in nature; only two were concerned with subject matter, and a third focused on cognitive learning in general.

Recapping from the 1918 Seven Cardinal Principles to the 1944 Ten Imperative Needs, the aims are representative of an era dominated by progressivism and by an offshoot science of child psychology. During this period, emphasis was placed on the "whole child" and "life adjustment." Subject matter was de-emphasized, while social, psychological, vocational, moral, and civic responsibilities were stressed. In general, the traditional concept of curriculum as a body of subjects came under attack by progressive educators; the major emphasis focused on the "child-centered," "experience-centered," and "activity-centered" curriculum.[57]

Focus on Academically Talented Students

After World War II, during the era of the Cold War and the Soviet Sputnik flight, the aforementioned aims and curriculum focus became targets for criticism. Americans were appalled that our country was losing the space race to the Soviet Union and that our skies were no longer impregnable.

Even though the influential Harvard Report, published at the end of World War II, looked optimistically to educating the whole person and providing a general education as means of developing the common understanding important to all citizens in a free society, powerful forces called for a return to academic essentials and old-fashioned mental discipline. Historian Arthur Bestor stated that the main subjects in elementary school should be reading, writing, and arithmetic, with some emphasis on science and history. At the high school level, the curriculum should stress math, science, history, English, and a foreign language.[58] Admiral Hyman Rickover questioned why Johnny could not read while Ivan could and did. He demanded that, in the national interest, there be a return to the basics, a beefing up of our science and mathematics courses, and "a deemphasis on life-adjustment schools and progressive educational lists."[59]

Werner von Braun, a German-educated missile expert, testified before a U.S. Senate Committee in 1958 to urge ending "family life" and "human relations" subjects and adopting the European system of education, which emphasized "technical and scientific subjects" and academic excellence.[60] As for the nonacademic or less able student, little recognition or interest seemed to exist with von Braun, or for that matter with the educational establishment.

In 1952, as Chair of the Educational Policies Commission, James Conant had endorsed a progressive policy document that urged a student-centered, whole-child approach to schooling. By 1959, Conant's vision was still "to provide a good general education for *all* the pupils," but he now emphasized "educating those with a talent for handling advanced subjects." After visiting fifty-five high schools across the country that had "a good reputation," Conant concluded that "the academically talented student, as a rule, is not being sufficiently challenged, does not work hard enough, and his program of academic subjects is not of sufficient range."[61]

In the midst of intense criticism toward schools and school people, Conant came to the defense of the educational establishment and saw little need for radically changing schools. Conant's influential book, *The American High School Today,* was a blueprint for moderate reform: for upgrading the curriculum, especially mathematics, science, and foreign language; requiring more academic subjects; tightening standards and grades; pushing students to their maximum cognitive

potentials; and grouping students according to their abilities. Although Conant gave some consideration to slow and average learners, his major emphasis for reform was related to serving the needs of the highly gifted (the intellectually highest 3 percent of the student population on a national basis) and the academically talented (the top 20 percent in terms of scholastic aptitude).[62] Indeed, many of Conant's ideas could be considered a return to the mental discipline approach under the modern version of essentialist philosophy.

Many policy statements issued during this period focused on academically bright students, the three Rs at the elementary school level, and traditional academic subjects at the high school level. For example, the White House Conference on Education in 1955 stressed quality and proposed that "educational programs [must] fully exercise and develop the abilities of especially bright students."[63] Five years later the President's Commission on National Goals gave top priority to science, mathematics, and foreign languages and called for "a testing program beginning in grade one if not before . . . and ability grouping from the earliest years of school. Every effort [was to be] made in and out of school to provide enrichment for the gifted student.[64]

Focus on Subject Matter. Hard on the heels of Sputnik and these national policy reports came federal legislation supporting training, equipment, and programs in subject fields deemed vital to defense. The major legislation, called the National Defense Act (1958), singled out science, mathematics, modern languages, and guidance (often construed as a way of steering youth into the three academic fields and into college if they had the ability). The focus on certain subjects and academically talented youth was often couched in terms of a free people's surviving in a world in which Communism was spreading and in which the American sky was at risk.

Most important, large sums of money for beefing up the curriculum were readily available for the first time from both government and foundation sources. During the aftermath of Sputnik, William Van Til wrote, "The end result was that both national interest and available funds [in education] coincided. The scholars had a genuine opportunity to reconstruct the content of their separate subjects."[65] This was particularly true at the secondary level. To many leaders of this period, it was clear that the way to proceed to reconstruct subject matter was to call together the scientific community and university scholars, who most intimately knew the particular subject, along with some curriculum specialists, who might help with regards to methodology.

From this dialogue among scientists and scholars came a host of national curriculum projects that centered on science and math. These included the Biological Sciences Curriculum Study (BSCS), Chemical Education Material Study (CEMS), Physical Science Study Committee (PSSC), and the School Mathematics Study Group (SMSG). The new wave of curriculum reform emphasized the subject matter rather than students' needs or interests or societal problems. Most of the leaders of this movement made sweeping claims for the superiority of the new curriculum, what they often called the "new science" and the "new math."

The subject matter was reconstructed around disciplines with special methods of inquiry (that is, around major concepts and principles) and science and mathematics came to represent the highest disciplinary value as evidenced by Bruner and the Woodshole conference.[66] Proliferation of special projects in these subjects was followed by other projects in the social sciences and humanities intended to beef up the curriculum, especially the academic subjects of secondary schools, and to embrace the discipline approach for the science and math projects. But the search for structure in English, history, foreign language, and so on, proved unattainable. Even in science and mathematics, the idea of a disciplinary structure eventually declined.

Focus on Disadvantaged Students

The 1960s and early 1970s ushered in a period in which the social conscience of America burst forth, coinciding with our concern over poverty, racial discrimination, and equal educational opportunity. New aims and educational priorities surfaced to meet the climate of change. With the majority of students not going on to college and with a large percentage of students dropping out

of school or graduating as functional illiterates, serious problems could be anticipated if our aims and priorities continued to be narrowly directed at our most able students. The shift to the problems of disadvantaged students gradually accelerated until this population became the number one concern in education. Exemplifying the change, James Conant, an early proponent of challenging the gifted students, gradually shifted his views.

In 1961, Conant wrote *Slums and Suburbs.* Only two years before, Conant had advocated academic rigor and upgraded academic subjects, as well as greater attention to the top 20 percent of high school students. Now he urged educators and policy makers to pay closer attention to the inner-city and disadvantaged children. He proposed that slum schools be upgraded and greater attention be paid to the less able students. Conant wrote:

> I am concerned we are allowing social dynamite to accumulate in our large cities. . . . Leaving aside human tragedies, I submit that a continuation of this situation [youth out of school and out of work] is a menace to the social and political health of the large cities.
>
> The improvement of slum conditions is only in part a question of improving education. But the role of the schools is of utmost importance. . . . Added responsibility, however, requires additional funds. Indeed the whole question of financing public education in the large cities is a major national concern.[67]

Given the student unrest and urban riots of the 1960s, it was easy to accept the arguments of an impacted crisis in schools and society. The government reports that were published in the 1960s strongly suggested an impending social upheaval. The needs of disadvantaged groups were stressed, both in schools and society, and these needs were reflected in such reports as the National Advisory Commission on Civil Disorders in 1967 and the HEW Urban Task Force Report in 1970.

The outcome was a host of compensatory programs funded by the federal government, although state and local money as well as foundation money was also available. The Elementary and Secondary Education Act (ESEA), passed in 1965, immediately provided $1 billion in Title I funds (sometimes called compensatory funding) to supplement and improve the education of poor and minority group children. Ten years later, Title I money totaled $2 billion per year, or about $200 extra per disadvantaged child. By 1980, Title I expenditures were more than $3 billion per year, and other federal compensatory expenditures totaled another $2 billion or more, a total of about $500 extra per disadvantaged child. During this 15-year period, over $35 billion had been appropriated by the federal government.[68] Today, Chapter I funds have replaced most of the early ESEA money, and the amount of federal funding for the disadvantaged continues to increase: $5.3 billion in 1990, plus another $6 billion earmarked for vocational and postsecondary disadvantaged students.[69]

Expanded Priorities: New Disadvantaged Groups

The focus on the disadvantaged extended into the 1970s; in fact, the definition of the disadvantaged was enlarged to include multicultural, bilingual, and handicapped students and, to a lesser extent, women. Our multicultural and bilingual efforts were characterized by increased federal funding for Hispanic, Asian American, and Native American students; by the Bilingual Act in 1968, which expanded bilingual programs in American schools; and by the 1974 U.S. Supreme Court ruling in *Lau* v. *Nicholas,* which stated that schools must take steps to help students who "are certain to find their classroom experiences wholly incomprehensible" because they do not understand English. The courts, as well as policymakers and educators, took an active role in providing educational opportunities for limited-English speaking (LES) and non-English speaking (NES) students.[70] Despite controversies that surfaced concerning specific approaches and programs and recruitment of personnel, bilingual and multicultural education grew in importance during the 1970s. Congressional appropriations for bilingual education increased from $6.1 million in 1970 to $169 million in 1980. In 1990, appropriations were $203 million, illustrating that these funds have now leveled off.[71]

During the 1970s, much activity and concern also surfaced over special education, especially for the handicapped and for students with learning disabilities. New pressure groups, new courses,

advanced degrees, new certification requirements, and new teachers and faculty at colleges and universities stimulated recognition of special education, as have new policies and programs. The Education for all Handicapped Children Act (PL 94-142) of 1975 is the cornerstone of these policies and programs, and it has been expanded by Amendment PL 99-457, passed in 1986, which extends the full rights and protection of the law to handicapped children ages 3 to 5 and was implemented in the 1990–1991 school year.[72]

Handicapped students are defined by this act as those who are mentally retarded, hard of hearing, deaf, orthopedically impaired, other health impaired, speech impaired, visually handicapped, emotionally disturbed, or learning disabled and, by reason thereof, require special education and related services. The legislation mandates a free and appropriate education for all handicapped children and youth. Handicapped students must be provided with special education and related services at public expense under public supervision and direction. Schools must not only adopt policies that serve all handicapped students, but they must conduct searches to locate such students as well.

Today, concern for the handicapped is very much alive, and the courts continue to take an active role in protecting the rights of and improving educational opportunities for the handicapped. Approximately 11 percent of the public school enrollments are considered handicapped, compared to 5 percent in 1975 (the year handicapped legislation went into effect).[73] This increase indicates that educators and policymakers recognize that many students who did not receive help in the past in fact need special help—not that contemporary students have more problems than students of earlier generations.

Concern for the gifted and talented students reached a low point during the 1960s and 1970s. The commitment to educating the gifted and talented was slight compared to efforts directed at the disadvantaged and at other special populations, such as bilingual, handicapped, or learning-disabled students. As two authorities stated, only "a very small percentage of the gifted and talented population [was] being serviced by existing programs, [about] 4 percent of the 1.5 to 2.5 million children."[74] A low funding priority and lack of trained personnel, coupled with few pressure groups for the gifted and talented, resulted in a scarcity of programs for these children.

Reform at the School Level

Much of what needs to be done to reform schools needs to be done at the local level; that is where the problems must be resolved, although the problems are large and multidimensional and require action at many governmental levels, as well as by businesses. Promulgating, legislating, and even packaging change are not the same as actually changing. Analysis of past efforts to improve schools has resulted in a much better understanding of the steps that must be taken to ensure that reform efforts have a significant and lasting impact. Among the lessons that can be deduced from past reform efforts at the school level are the following developed by Ornstein and Levine.

1. *Adaptive problem solving.* Reform or innovation frequently has little or no effect on students because numerous problems arise to stifle practical application. For example, experts may devise a wonderful new science curriculum for fourth graders and school districts may purchase large quantities of the new curriculum materials, but teachers may choose not to use the materials or may not know how to use them. Innovations are not likely to be implemented successfully unless the organization introducing them is *adaptive* in the sense that it can identify and solve day-by-day implementation problems.

2. *School-level focus.* Because the innovating organization must identify and solve day-to-day problems, the focus in bringing about change must be at the level of the individual school building where many of the problems occur.

3. *Implementability.* Successful school reform also depends on whether changes introduced are implementable in the sense that teachers perceive that they can adopt and utilize these reforms effectively. Among the most important aspects of implementability are *compatibility* with the social context of potential users and *accessibility* to those who do not already understand or share the underlying ideas.

4. *Principal's leadership.* Implementation of a significant innovation requires change in many

institutional arrangements, including scheduling of staff and student time, selection and utilization of instructional methods and materials, and mechanisms for making decisions. The building principal usually is the key person in successfully implementing change. In addition, the faculty must have a shared vision of the kinds of changes that are possible and necessary to improve their instructional program.

5. *Teacher involvement.* Because people who are expected to alter their working patterns will not cooperate fully unless they have a voice in designing and implementing change, teachers must have an opportunity to select and evaluate innovations. Teachers must also be given the time, resources, and opportunity to collaborate and make decisions.

6. *Staff development.* Staff development is a core activity in the school improvement process. Staff development to support improvement should be centered on the school as the basic unit, not on the individual teacher. In the case of an elementary school, the entire staff should participate; in secondary schools, departments may be the appropriate unit for some activities. Staff development should be an interactive process in which teachers and administrators work together at every stage. Collaborative planning develops collegial responsibility for improvement.

7. *School–business cooperation.* Many schools and school districts are attempting to improve the quality of education by cooperating with other institutions, particularly business and industry. Some of the most promising programs include "partnership" or "adopt-a-school" programs in which a business or another community institution works closely with an individual school and provides assistance such as tutors or lecturers, funds, equipment or materials, and even personnel on loan (such as a computer specialist). To some extent, the old stewardship concept of business has resurfaced, reminiscent of Horace Mann's call for the private sector to become involved in the business of education for the good of business.[75] See Curriculum Tips 5-1.

Charter School Movement. "The time has come to close down some of our largest urban districts and start all over."[76] Some people have stated that reforming schools and their curricula

---

======================= *Curriculum Tips 5-1* =======================

Principles for Improving Schools

A number of important principles result in school effectiveness and excellence. Based on recent efforts to improve schools and the school reform literature in general, many principles that school leaders can adapt for improving their own schools are listed here.

1. The school has a clearly stated mission or set of goals.
2. School achievement is closely monitored.
3. Provisions are made for *all* students, including tutoring for low achievers and enrichment programs for the gifted.
4. Teachers and administrators agree on what is good teaching and learning; a general philosophy and psychology of learning prevail.
5. Emphasis on cognition is balanced with concerns for students' personal, social, and moral growth; students are taught to be responsible for their behavior.
6. Teachers and administrators expect students to learn and convey these expectations to students and parents.
7. Teachers are expected to make significant contributions to school improvement.
8. Administrators provide ample support, information, and time for teacher enrichment.
9. A sense of teamwork prevails; there is interdisciplinary and interdepartmental communication.
10. Incentives, recognition, and rewards are conveyed to teachers and administrators for their efforts on behalf of the team and school mission.
11. The interests and needs of the individual staff members are matched with the expectations of the institution.
12. The staff has the opportunity to be challenged and creative; there is a sense of professional enrichment and renewal.
13. Staff development is planned by teachers and administrators to provide opportunities for continuous professional growth.
14. The school environment is safe and healthy; there is a sense of order (not control) in classrooms and hallways.
15. Parents and community members are supportive of the school and are involved in school activities.
16. The school is a learning center for the larger community; it reflects the norms and values of the community, and the community sees the school as an extension of the community.

Source: Adapted from Allan C. Ornstein "Reforming American Schools: The Role of the States," *NASSP Bulletin* (October 1991), Table 2, p. 52.

---

requires not just tinkering, but actually starting all over. One movement in the reforming of schools has been the charter school movement. This movement, which essentially started in Minnesota with one school, has spread to twenty-five states and hundreds of schools.[77] The central concept of a charter school is that individuals who wish to do something different apply for a contract or "charter" that would officially and legally allow them to carry out their innovation. No longer would the public school district have the exclusive franchise to educate. Other groups, such as the state board of education, public universities, or even a city council could sponsor public schools. The organizers of such charter schools usually do apply to the public school district to sponsor the establishment of such a school, but organizers can seek such support from some other public group today.

The charter school movement has caught the attention of many parents and even citizens without children in school, for it is seen as providing choice and also allowing parental voices to be heard in the education process. The chartering process also involves community leaders, along with business people and professional educators. Each charter school has a board of directors with members drawn from the parents and community members who would be served by the particular charter school.

A selling point for charter schools is that they allow individuals to develop curricula that reflect diverse philosophies and serve diverse student populations. There is no one curricular focus for all students. Programs are individualized as are pedagogical approaches. In Michigan, where the movement is strong, charter schools are relatively small, with the majority of the schools having fewer than 200 students.

Charter schools are usually established to have a particular curricular focus or to serve a particular student population. For instance, some charter schools have programs that emphasize interdisciplinary instruction with a math–science–computer focus. Other schools may have an arts focus. In some schools the curriculum emphasizes technical training and a school-to-work program. Some schools are designed to emphasize a particular ethnic focus, such as African American or Native American. However, all charter schools in the various states must meet state curricular guidelines. In Michigan, all charter schools must follow the recommended core curriculum which emphasizes mathematics, science, social studies, and language arts.[78]

The concept of charter schools is that schools would be freed from unnecessary rules, regulations, and red tape that keep innovation from happening and hinder true reform. However, in some cases principals of charter schools find that they have just as much red tape, often without the assistance of a central office to process such tape. Charter schools receive funding for each student from either the state or the school district. Those managing the school must document that they are using the funds to deliver an effective curriculum. If parents are not satisfied with the curriculum, they can take their children out of the school, and with the children go the funds "attached" to the children. Thus, unlike the traditional school, charter schools must attract students to keep their programs alive.

Paul Hill states that charter schools just do not go far enough. He suggests contract schools as a means of reforming education. Essentially, the idea is to contract out the control of individual schools to independent contractors, who would be legally bound to deliver curricula that produce desired results. Having an independent contractor manage a public school would supposedly get rid of the red tape, the bureaucracy that many claim stifles being creative with the school curriculum.[79]

The contractors would have to market their services, noting mission, curriculum, financial plan, assessment procedures, and hiring practices. Thus an outside firm would create and manage a public school. The outside firm could be just that, a business created to run schools, just as we have firms that purchase franchises to run hotels. But it need not be a business running the school. A teacher–parent group could bid for a contract for a school. Such cases are really not much different from the charter school. A professional association might put in a bid. Even a religious organization might seek a contract, although that would raise interesting issues regarding separation of church and state. But that is not the only issue that could be raised from contract schools. If a company were to make a bid, might it not use the school as a means of advertising its product? If a political group were to secure a contract, what is to prevent it from engaging in indoctrination of students? Hill's idea adds to the social complexity of school reform. His views may be a first step in privatizing public education in the next century, although that does not seem likely to happen on a large scale.

NATIONAL TASK FORCE REPORTS ON EDUCATION

In the mid-1980s, national attention turned to the need for educational excellence and higher academic standards for all students. The educational dimensions of these needs were amply documented in several policy reports between 1983 and 1991, all calling for reforms to improve the quality of education in the United States. See Table 5-2.

To support their alarming statements about the decline of American education and the need for academic reform, the policy reports detailed a host of gloomy trends and statistics.

1. Schools and colleges had shifted away from requiring students to take what had 20 years ago been the standard academic core curriculum for graduation: foreign language, mathematics. science, English, and history. Elective courses and remedial courses had replaced many standard academic courses.

2. Grade inflation was on the rise, and students were required to complete less homework (75 percent of high school students completed less than one hour of homework a night).

3. Average achievement scores on the Scholastic Aptitude Test (SAT) demonstrated a virtually unbroken decline from 1963 to 1988. Average verbal scores fell some 40 points (466 to 428), and mathematics scores dropped nearly 20 points (492 to 471).[80]

4. International comparisons of student achievement, completed in the 1970s, revealed that on nineteen academic tests American students were never first or second and, in comparison with other industrialized nations, were last seven times. In 1988, they scored last in math (averaging 94 points below first-ranked Korea) and second to the bottom in science (averaging 71 points below first-ranked Korea). U.S. students also scored last in geographical knowledge, more than one-third lower than their first-ranked counterparts in Sweden.[81]

5. Some 23 to 25 million American adults were functionally illiterate by the simplest tests of everyday reading and writing.

6. About 13 percent of all 17-year-old youths in the United States were considered functionally illiterate, and this illiteracy rate jumped to 40 percent among minority youth.

7. Business and military leaders complained that they were required to spend millions of dollars annually on costly remedial education and training programs in the basic skills or three Rs.

Between 1975 and 1985, remedial mathematics courses in four-year colleges increased by 72 percent and by 1985 constituted one-fourth of all mathematics courses taught in these institutions. As many as 25 percent of the recruits in the Armed Forces could not read at the ninth-grade level.

8. All these sordid figures pile up and stare at us, despite the facts that our student/teacher ratios were 17:1 in 1988, which put us seventh lowest in the world (whereas such countries as Japan and Korea have over 30 students per teacher) and that our pupil expenditures for education were the second highest in the world (about $300 less than first-ranked Switzerland).[82]

These deficiencies came to light at a time when the demand for highly skilled military personnel and workers in labor and industry was accelerating rapidly and amid growing concern that the United States was being overtaken by other industrialized nations in commerce, science, and technology.

The major policy reports and their sponsoring agencies are summarized in Table 5-2. Nine of the thirteen reports emphasized the need to strengthen the curriculum in the core subjects of English, math, science, foreign language, and social studies. The focus was thus on a *common curriculum.* Technology and computer courses were mentioned often, either as components of science or math or as separate subject areas (sometimes referred to as the fourth R). High-level cognitive and thinking skills were also stressed. Most of the reports concerned all students: providing various programs and personnel for disadvantaged and learning disabled students, as well as for average and above average students. The notion of *equity* was paramount, although not always loud and clear. Nevertheless, the theme of *excellence* still seemed to stress academic, college-bound, and even gifted students; emphasis was still on core academic subjects and advanced science and mathematics.

All the reports emphasized tougher standards and tougher courses, and eight out of the thirteen proposed that colleges raise their admission requirements. Most of the reports also talked about increasing homework, time for learning, and time in school, as well as instituting more rigorous

TABLE 5-2 Overview of Selected Recommendations of Thirteen Reports on Education, 1983–1991

REPORT AND SPONSOR	CURRICULUM OBJECTIVES	CONTENT EMPHASIS	SCHOOL ORGANIZATION	GOVERNMENT-BUSINESS ROLE
Academic Preparation for College, The College Board	Improve student competencies in reading, writing, speaking, listening, reasoning, math, and study skills Raise college entrance standards	English, math, science, computers, foreign language	Stress study and independent learning Incentives to students	Develop a national standard for academic achievement in secondary education
Action for Excellence, Education Commission of the States	Establish minimum competencies in reading, writing, speaking, listening, reasoning, and economics Strengthen programs for gifted students Raise college entrance standards	English, math, science, foreign language, history, computer literacy	Consider longer school day Emphasize order and discipline More homework More rigorous grading with periodic testing Independent learning	Foster partnerships between private sector and education Increase federal funds for education
Educating Americans for the 21st Century, National Science Foundation	Devote more time to math and science in elementary school and secondary schools Provide more advanced courses in science and math Raise college entrance standards	Math, science, technology, computers	Consider longer school day, week, and/or year Twelve-year plan for math and science	Federal input in establishing national goals for education Increase NSF role in curriculum development and teacher training
High School, Carnegie Foundation for Achievement in Teaching	Mastery of language, including reading, writing, speaking, and listening Expand basic academic curriculum Student transition to work and further education Strengthen graduation requirements	Core of common learning, including English, history, civics, math, science, technology Computer literacy	Improve working conditions for teachers Utilize technology to enrich curriculum Flexible schedules and time allotments One track for students School-community learning activities Greater leadership role for principal	More connections between school and community, business, and universities Increase parent and community coalitions with and service to schools Utilize retired personnel from business and colleges Federal scholarships for science and math teachers

(continued)

TABLE 5-2   Continued

REPORT AND SPONSOR	CURRICULUM OBJECTIVES	CONTENT EMPHASIS	SCHOOL ORGANIZATION	GOVERNMENT-BUSINESS ROLE
Making the Grade, Twentieth-Century Fund	Improve basic-skill programs Improve learning in English, math, and science Initiate general programs for students with learning problems and a voucher program for the disadvantaged	Basic skills English, math, and science Computer literacy	Reward teacher performance Special programs for poor, minority, handicapped, bilingual, and immigrant students	Increase federal aid for special programs for disadvantaged student populations Increase federal aid for programs to develop scientific literacy among all students and advanced math and science for academically able secondary students
A Study of High Schools, National Association of Secondary School Principals	Reduce traditional subject matter Emphasize higher-order thinking skills	Interdisciplinary curriculum Problem-solving activities and learning experiences	Eliminate age grouping Eliminate teacher specializations Incentives to students Out-of-school learning activities	Federal support for special students, including learning disabled and gifted
A Nation at Risk, National Commission on Excellence in Education	Improve textbooks and other instructional materials Provide more rigorous courses in vocational education, arts, and science Strengthen graduation requirements Raise college entrance requirements	Five new basics: English, math, science, social studies, and computer science	Consider seven-hour school day Tighten attendance and discipline More homework More rigorous grading and periodic testing Group students by performance rather than age	Federal cooperation with states and localities Meet needs of disadvantaged student populations as well as gifted and talented National standardized tests in context with national interest in education
The First Lesson: A Report on Elementary Education in America, The Secretary of Education	Improve basic skills for young children Improve complex learning tasks and abilities for higher-grade children Increase knowledge base essential for democratic society and national identity Improve textbook and workbook writing and selection Raise academic standards	Basic skills, especially reading through phonics Problem-solving skills in mathematics and hands-on learning and discovery in science Unified sequence stressing history, geography, and civics Computer literacy and cultural literacy	Lengthen school day More homework More rigorous testing Parental choice in children's schools Reward teacher performance	Community-wide and parental responsibility in education Teacher and school accountability Improve training programs for elementary teachers; emphasis on arts and science rather than methods courses

(continued)

TABLE 5-2   Continued

REPORT AND SPONSOR	CURRICULUM OBJECTIVES	CONTENT EMPHASIS	SCHOOL ORGANIZATION	GOVERNMENT-BUSINESS ROLE
The Early Years, Carnegie Foundation for the Advancement of Teaching	Focus on plight of at-risk children, the nation's underclass Emphasis on basic skills Priority on childhood education	Language-development, including reading, writing, and listening skills	Flexible school schedules reflecting changing family and work patterns Longer school day and school year Reward teacher performance; attract better teachers Parental choice for after school and summer programs; end of traditional summer vacation	Increased federal aid for education of at-risk children Increased role of business and industry Greater involvement of teachers in decision-making, increased pay
Time for Results: The Governors' 1991 Report on Education, National Governors' Association	Focus on teenage pregnancy, school dropouts, adult illiteracy, and drug abuse Improve school leadership and management Better use of technology in the classroom Increase state role and responsibility in education Higher academic standards at all grade levels	Basic skills, math, science, and technology Research and development in education	Kindergarten for all children; early childhood programs for all at-risk children Parental education programs Parental choice in selecting children's school Reliable and valid assessment of student performance Year-round schooling Reorganize and regulate schools and school districts that are "academically bankrupt"	National school board to certify teachers Increased pay and accountability for teachers and principals Improved teacher training and educational leadership programs Greater involvement in education of local leaders, teachers, parents, citizens, and business people Greater state role, regulation, and spending in education Annual progress reports on what each state is doing to carry out educational reform
The Disappearing Quality of the Workforce: What Can We Do to Save It? National Alliance of Business	Educate all youth in basic skills Provide students with high-level skills required for our information and service economy Face our education problems Restructure education; provide financial support Increase the quality of the nation's workforce	Basic skills Critical thinking skills Tutoring programs Raise academic standards and high school graduation requirements	Reduce school dropout rates Increase attendance rates Improve national test scores and achievement levels Increase adopt-a-school programs Teacher/administrative accountability Staff development/ mentor programs	Business leaders must take an active role in implementing education reform Collaborative efforts between business and education groups Reshape education at state and local levels Involve citizen, parent, political and business groups

(continued)

TABLE 5-2 Continued

REPORT AND SPONSOR	CURRICULUM OBJECTIVES	CONTENT EMPHASIS	SCHOOL ORGANIZATION	GOVERNMENT-BUSINESS ROLE
Investing in People: A Strategy to Address America's Workforce Crisis U.S. Department of Labor	Commitment to basic skills and literacy Invest in human capital Increase federal and business support in education and human resource programs Upgrade workforce quality Upgrade high school graduation, college entry, and labor market standards Develop national goals and timetables to improve education and training	Basic skill programs for dropouts Literacy programs for illiterate adults Lifetime education and training Combine vocational and technical education	Reduce dropout rates Increase attendance rates Increase parent participation Increase business-community presence in schools Reduce competitive learning; increase cooperative learning More rigorous teacher training and testing of new teachers	Partnerships between business, labor, and government at all levels Business to fund incentive programs to improve teacher/school performance Increase government and training programs to address needs of private sector and labor Tax credits for education and training programs for private sector
National Goals for Education, U.S. Department of Education	Focus on all students, with emphasis on at-risk students Equip students with knowledge and skills necessary for responsible citizenship and world of work Ensure readiness for school; upgrade school standards and student achievement Improve adult literacy and life-long education Provide a safe and drug-free school environment	Basic knowledge and skills Reasoning and problem-solving skills Math, science, English, history, and geography Drug and alcohol prevention programs Citizenship, community service, cultural literacy, and knowledge of the international community	Preschool programs for all disadvantaged learners Parental training for child's early learning; parental choice in children's schools Up-to-date instructional technology Multilayer system of vocational, technical, and community colleges More student loans, scholarships, and work study programs in higher education Upgrade teacher preparation; reward teachers but hold them accountable	Inspire reform at the federal, state, and local levels Enlist assistance of parents, community, business, and civic groups; all parts of society must be involved Create effective apprenticeships, job training, teacher–employee exchanges, and adopt-a-school programs Increase flexibility, innovation, accountability, and results Targets established for the year 2000

Source: Revised from first edition of book; also see Allan C. Ornstein, "The National Reform of Education," *NASSP Bulletin* (May 1992).

grading, testing, homework, and discipline. They mentioned, too, upgrading teacher certification, increasing teacher salaries, increasing the number of and rewarding science and math teachers, and providing merit pay for outstanding teachers. Overall, they stressed excellence (not equity), academic achievement (not the whole child), and increased productivity (not relevancy or humanism).

Many of the reports expressed concern that the schools are pressed to play too many social roles, that the schools cannot meet all these expectations, and that the schools are in danger of losing sight of their key role—teaching the basic skills and the core academic subjects, new skills for computer use, and higher-level cognitive skills for the world of work, technology, and even military defense.

PLANNING FOR EDUCATIONAL CHANGE

As long as society is dynamic and composed of a conglomeration of cultural and social groups, the debate over the aims of education will stir up controversy and change. Perhaps this is good; perhaps this is what makes a society viable and able to resist decay.

In examining the aims, priorities, or reforms of education from the turn of the century until today, we see considerable reiteration, but we also note considerable evolution linked to sweeping social change. For example, the early twentieth-century adherents of mental discipline advocated rigorous intellectual training, as did the essentialist critics and conservative thinkers of the 1950s and mid-1980s and early 1990s. At the turn of the century, public schools stressed an academic curriculum, and this priority reasserted itself during the era of the Cold War and the space race; it reappeared, too, in the 1980s and 1990s as a result of concern over economic competition with foreign countries and foreign relations with the former USSR. In the early 1900s, progressive educators sought to broaden the aims of school to serve all children and youth, especially nonacademic and vocationally oriented students; beginning in the early 1960s and continuing into the 1970s, this priority reappeared with emphasis on poor and minority students, and later bilingual and handicapped students. Although concern for disadvan-

taged groups remains, the pendulum has now moved to the center. Our priorities are more diffuse, and we are concerned about various other students as well.

Appraising and Reflecting

Educational aims should be as changeable as the changing social and political conditions and the groups of people that formulate them. Panels and commissions are often organized to formulate aims. They may operate at various government and educational levels—federal, state, regional, and local—but those at the national level have the most influence and those at the local level have the least (in terms of overall impact).

Aims are modified by the need for reform, or what is considered relevant and necessary to meet a crisis or problem. When it comes to reform, however, Americans tend to delineate a variety of proposals, often conflicting notions of where the problem is and what solutions are feasible. As Boyer notes, Americans seem addicted to school reform and become propelled by "a kind of erratic lunging from one extreme to another."[83]

Unquestionably, educational aims, and especially school reform, must be relevant or meaningful to the times. If the schools are not adaptable to changing conditions and social forces, how can they expect to produce people who are? This issue is pointedly illustrated in a satire on education entitled *The Saber Tooth Curriculum*, which describes a society whose major tasks for survival were catching fish to eat, clubbing horses, and frightening away saber tooth tigers.[84] The school in this society set up a curriculum to meet its needs—teaching courses in these three areas of survival. Eventually conditions changed; the streams dried up, and the horses and tigers disappeared. Social change necessitated learning new tasks for survival, but the school curriculum continued to feature courses in catching fish, clubbing horses, and frightening saber tooth tigers.

Today we live in a highly technical, automated, and bureaucratic society; we are faced with pressing social and economic problems—an increasingly diverse ethnic population, aging cities, the effects of centuries of racial and sexual discrimination, an aging population, unemployment and a displaced workforce, exhaustion of our natural resources, and the pollution of the physical environment. These forces and trends are highly interrelated; they mutually reinforce each other, and they are accelerating. In an era of space technology, telecommunications, computers, and robots, schools cannot continue to teach the skills that were appropriate for the Industrial Revolution. We must have schools that teach the kinds of skills and information and develop the kinds of attitudes requisite for success in a knowledge society. We need curricula that go beyond just having us well informed; we need education that contributes to the further evolution of our consciousness, a consciousness that will enable us to speculate, imagine, appreciate, emphasize.[85] We need dispositions developed in school and in general society that allow us successful participation with our diverse fellow citizens. Future successes with our newly evolving political, social, and economic environments will depend to a large extent on how well curricularists draw from the social foundations to create curricula of relevance and educational aims of significance.

CONCLUSION

Social forces have always had a major influence on schools and in turn on curriculum decisions. Some of these forces originate from society at large and others from the local community. In either case, educators are faced with a choice: To accept and mirror the tendencies of the times or to appraise and improve the times. One view represents a perennialist notion of education, the other a reconstructionist notion; however, we would like to view the choice in terms of a traditional versus futuristic way of looking at schools. The latter approach suggests that educators can analyze and evaluate the trends taking shape in society. In doing so, they can decide on appropriate aims and curricula, and they can thus prepare students for the world of tomorrow by providing them with the knowledge and values they need to make wise decisions. Curriculum workers—indeed, all participants in curriculum decisions—play a major role in accomplishing these goals.

ENDNOTES

1. John Dewey, *Experience and Education* (New York: Macmillan, 1938), pp. 39–40.
2. Conrad M. Arensberg and Arthur H. Niehoff, "American Cultural Values," in Joan H. Strouse, ed., *Exploring Themes of Social Justice in Education* (Upper Saddle River, N.J.: Merrill, an imprint of Prentice Hall, 1996), pp. 32–45.
3. Ruth Benedict, *Patterns of Culture* (Boston: Houghton Mifflin, 1934), p. 253.
4. Arensberg and Niehoff, "American Cultural Values."
5. Ibid.
6. James Moffett, *The Universal Schoolhouse* (San Francisco: Jossey–Bass Publishers, 1994).
7. Barry Kanpol, "Is Education at the End of a Sovereign Story or at the Beginning of Another? Cultural–Political Possibilities," and Lyotard, in Michael Peter, ed., *Education and the Postmodern Condition* (Westport, Conn.: Bergin & Garvey, 1995), pp. 147–165.
8. Arensburg and Niehoff, "American Cultural Values."
9. Philip Selznick, *The Moral Commonwealth* (Berkeley: University of California Press, 1992).
10. Arensberg and Niehoff, "American Cultural Values."
11. Moffett, *The Universal Schoolhouse.*
12. Henry A. Giroux, "Educational Visions: What Are Schools for and What Should We Be Doing in the Name of Education?" in Joe L. Kincheloe and Shirley R. Steinberg, eds., *Thirteen Questions,* 2nd ed. (New York: Peter Lang, 1995), pp. 295–303. See also Arensberg and Niehoff, "American Cultural Values."
13. Hendrick Smith, *Rethinking America* (New York: Avon Books, 1995.)
14. William Van Til, "In a Climate of Change," in R. R. Leeper, ed., *Role of Supervisor and Curriculum Director in a Climate of Change* (Washington, D.C.: Association for Supervision and Curriculum Development, 1965), p. 16. See also John O'Neil, "Preparing for the Changing Workplace," *Educational Leadership* (March 1992), pp. 6–9.
15. Alvin Toffler, *Future Shock* (New York: Random House, 1970).
16. *Curriculum Change toward the 21st Century,* an NEA Bicentennial Committee Report (Washington, D.C.: National Education Association, 1977), pp. 89–90; Thomas J. Sergiovanni and John H. Moore, *Schooling for Tomorrow* (Boston: Allyn and Bacon, 1989. Also see Daniel Bell, *The Third Technological Revolution* (New York: Basic Books, 1984); and Alvin Toffler, *The Third Wave* (New York: Morrow, 1980).
17. Philip M. Hauser, "Urbanization: An Overview," in J. K. Hadden, L. H. Masotti, and C. J. Larson, eds., *Metropolis in Crisis* (Itasca, Ill.: Peacock, 1971), pp. 51–74.

18. Philip W. Jackson, *Life in Classrooms* (New York: Holt, Rinehart and Winston, 1968), p. 6.
19. Glenys G. Unruh and William M. Alexander, *Innovations in Secondary Education,* 2nd ed. (New York: Holt, Rhinehart and Winston, 1974), p. 2. Ornstein, *Urban Education* (Columbus, Ohio: Merrill, 1972), p. 50.
20. Wayne K. Hoy and Cecil G. Miskel, *Educational Administration: Theory, Research, and Practice,* 3rd ed. (New York: Random House, 1987), p. 51.
21. Allan C. Ornstein, "Emerging Curriculum Trends: An Agenda for the Future," *NASSP Bulletin* (February 1989), pp. 37–48; Albert Shanker, "The End of the Traditional Model of Schooling," *Phi Delta Kappan* (January 1988), pp. 334–357.
22. Arthur Combs, *A Personal Approach to Teaching* (Boston: Allyn and Bacon, 1982); Ivan Illich, *Deschooling Society,* 2nd ed. (New York: World, 1983).
23. Donald A. Schon, *Educating the Reflective Practioner* (San Francisco: Jossey–Bass, 1990).
24. William F. Pinar, William M. Reynolds, Patrick Slattery, Peter M. Taubman, *Understanding Curriculum* (New York: Peter Lang, 1995). Quote from H. Gates, Jr., "Introduction to Race, Writing, and Difference," *Critical Inquiry,* 12(1), 1985, pp. 10–20.
25. A. M. Schlesinger, *The Disuniting of America* (Knoxville, Tenn.: Whittle Books, 1991).
26. Richard Pratte, "Social Heterogeneity, Democracy, and Democratic Pluralism," in Kenneth D. Benne and Steven Tozer, *Society as Educator in an Age of Transition,* Eighty-sixth Yearbook of the National Society for the Study of Education, Part II (Chicago: University of Chicago Press, 1987), pp. 148–185.
27. Joel Spring, "Equality of Educational Opportunity," in Joan H. Strouse, ed., *Exploring Themes of Social Justice in Education* (Upper Saddle River, N.J.: Merrill, an imprint of Prentice Hall, 1996), pp. 224–256.
28. Sari Knopp Biklen and Diane Pollard, "Sex, Gender, Feminism, and Education," in Sari Knopp Biklen and Diane Pollard, eds., *Gender and Education,* Ninety-Second Yearbook of the National Society for the Study of Education, Part 1 (Chicago: University of Chicago Press, 1993), pp. 1–11.
29. Nel Noddings, "Gender and the Curriculum," in Philip W. Jackson, ed., *Handbook of Research on Curriculum* (New York: Macmillan Publishing Co., 1992), pp. 659–684.
30. Ibid.
31. Elsabeth Hansot, "Historical and Contemporary Views of Gender and Education," in Sari Knopp Biklen and Diane Pollard, *Gender and Education,* pp. 12–24.
32. Pinar et al., *Understanding Curriculum.*
33. Joel Spring, "Equality of Educational Opportunity."
34. Deborah P. Britzman, "Beyond Rolling Models: Gender and Multicultural Education," in Biklen and Pollard, *Gender and Education,* pp. 25–42.
35. Carol Gilligan, *In a Different Voice* (Cambridge, Mass.: Harvard University Press, 1982).
36. Elsabeth Hansot, "Historical and Contemporary Views."
37. Bentley Glass, *The Timely and the Timeless* (New York: Basic Books, 1980), p. 39.
38. Warren L. Ziegler, *Social and Technological Developments,* rev. ed. (Syracuse, N.Y.: Syracuse University Press, 1981).
39. Toffler, *Future Shock,* p. 132.
40. Arno Bellack, "What Knowledge Is of Most Worth?" *High School Journal* (February 1965), pp. 318–332; Donald E. Orlosky and B. Othanel Smith, *Curriculum Development: Issues and Insights* (Chicago: Rand McNally, 1978); and Decker F. Walker and Jonas F. Soltis, *Curriculum and Aims* (New York: Teachers College Press, Columbia University, 1986).
41. James B. Conant, *The American High School* (New York: McGraw-Hill, 1959).
42. Kay M. Troost, "What Accounts for Japan's Success in Science Education?" *Educational Leadership* (December–January 1984), pp. 26–29; Herbert J. Walberg, "Improving School Science in Advanced and Developing Countries," Review of Educational Research (Spring 1991), pp. 25–70.
43. Joseph L. Schwab, *The Practical: A Language for Curriculum* (Washington, D.C.: National Education Association, 1970).
44. Vincent R. Ruggiero, *The Art of Thinking,* 2nd ed. (New York: Harper & Row, 1988); Robert S. Zais, *Curriculum: Principles and Foundations* (New York: Harper & Row, 1976). See Jerome S. Bruner, *The Process of Education* (Cambridge, Mass.: Harvard University Press, 1960).
45. Harry S. Broudy, *Building a Philosophy of Education,* 2nd ed. (Englewood Cliffs, N.J.: Prentice Hall, 1961).
46. Phenix, *Realms of Meaning;* Joseph J. Schwab, "Problems, Topics, and Issues," in S. E. Elam, ed., *Education and the Structure of Knowledge* (Chicago: Rand McNally, 1964), pp. 4–43.
47. Phenix, *Realms of Meaning.*
48. Ibid., p. 268.
49. Gerald Weinstein and Mario D. Fantini, *Toward Humanistic Education: A Curriculum of Affect* (New York: Praeger, 1970), p. 50.
50. Mario D. Fantini, "Reducing the Behavior Gap," *NEA Journal* (January 1968), pp. 23–24.
51. Allan C. Ornstein, "Knowledge as a Source of Change" *NASSP Bulletin* (April 1988), pp. 72–75.
52. Elliot W. Eisner, "Cognition and Representation," *Phi Delta Kappan* (January 1997), pp. 348–353.
53. Commission on the Reorganization of Secondary Education, *Cardinal Principles of Secondary Education,* Bulletin No. 35 (Washington, D.C.: U.S. Government Printing Office, 1918).

54. Allan C. Ornstein, "Aims of Education for Today and Tomorrow," *Educational Horizons* (Fall 1982), pp. 41–49.

55. Educational Policies Commission, *The Purpose of Education in American Democracy* (Washington, D.C.: National Education Association, 1938).

56. Educational Policies Commission, *Education for All American Youth* (Washington, D.C.: National Education Association, 1944).

57. Decker Walker, *Fundamentals of Curriculum* (San Diego: Harcourt, Brace, 1990). See also Allan C. Ornstein, "Curriculum Contrasts: A Historical View," *Phi Delta Kappan* (February 1982), pp. 404–408.

58. Arthur Bestor, *The Restoration of Learning* (New York: Knopf, 1956).

59. Hyman G. Rickover, *Education and Freedom* (New York: Dutton, 1959), p. 190.

60. *Science and Education for National Defense,* Hearings before the Committee of Labor and Public Welfare, U.S. Senate, Eighty-Eighth Congress (Washington, D.C.: U.S. Government Printing Office, 1958), p. 65.

61. Conant, *The American High School Today,* p. 15.

62. Ibid.

63. *Proceedings, White House Conference on Education* (Washington, D.C.: U.S. Government Printing Office, 1955), p. 12.

64. *Goals for Americans: The President's Commission on National Goals* (Englewood Cliffs, N.J.: Prentice Hall, 1960), p. 85.

65. Van Til, "In a Climate of Change," p. 21.

66. Jerome S. Bruner, *The Process of Education* (Cambridge, Mass.: Harvard University Press, 1959).

67. James B. Conant, *Slums and Suburbs* (New York: McGraw-Hill, 1961), p. 2.

68. Allan C. Ornstein and Daniel U. Levine, "Compensatory Education: Can It Be Successful? What Are the Issues?" *NASSP Bulletin* (May 1981), pp. 1–15; A. Harry Passow, "Urban Education in the 1970s," in A. H. Passow, ed., *Urban Education in the 1970s* (New York: Teachers College Press, Columbia University, 1971), pp. 1–45.

69. *Digest of Educational Statistics, 1990* (Washington, D.C.: U.S. Government Printing Office, 1990), Table 327, p. 343.

70. Carol D. Lee, "Literacy, Cultural Diversity, and Instruction," *Education and Urban Society* (February 1992), pp. 279–291; Diane Ravitch, "A Culture in Common," *Educational Leadership* (January 1992), pp. 8–11.

71. *Digest of Educational Statistics, 1990,* Table 326, p. 337.

72. Allan C. Ornstein, Daniel U. Levine, and Janet W. Lerner, "Education of Young Handicapped and At-Risk Children," *Illinois School Research and Development Journal* (Fall 1989), pp. 24–32.

73. *The Condition of Education,* 1990, Vol. 1 (Washington, D.C.: U.S. Government Printing Office, 1990), Table 1.12, p. 47; *The School-Age Handicapped* (Washington, D.C.: U.S. Government Printing Office, 1990), Table 1, p. 30.

74. A. Harry Passow and Abraham J. Tannebaum, "Education of the Gifted and Talented," *NASSP Bulletin* (March 1976), pp. 4–5; Donovan R. Walling, "Gifted Children: A Neglected Minority," *Curriculum Review* (September–October 1986), pp. 11–13.

75. Allan C. Ornstein and Daniel M. Levine, "School Effectiveness in Reform," *Clearing House* (November–December 1990), pp. 115–118.

76. Anne C. Lewis, "A Modest Proposal for Urban Schools," *Phi Delta Kappan* (September 1996), pp. 5–6.

77. Larry Myatt and Linda Nathan, "One School's Journey in the Age of Reform," *Phi Delta Kappan* (September 1996), pp. 24–25.

78. James N. Goenner, "Charter Schools: The Revitalization of Public Education," *Phi Delta Kappan* (September 1996), pp. 32–36.

79. Lynnell Hancock, "Bureaucracy Is Choking Public Education to Death," *U.S. News and World Report* (December 1996–January 1997), pp. 40–42.

80. *Digest of Education Statistics 1989,* Table 108, p. 120.

81. *The Condition of Education 1989,* Vol. 1, Charts 1.3, 1.5, pp. 13, 17; *Digest of Education Statistics 1989,* Tables 347, 349, pp. 390–391.

82. *The Condition of Education 1989,* Chart 1.18, p. 107; *Digest of Education Statistics 1989,* Table 340, p. 385. Also see John Hood, "Education: Money Isn't Everything," *Wall Street Journal,* February 9, 1990, p. 14.

83. Ernest Boyer, "The Future Is Now," *Newsweek* (Fall–Winter 1990), p. 73. Special report.

84. Harold Benjamin, *The Saber Tooth Curriculum* (New York: McGraw-Hill, 1939).

85. Stephen L. Talbott, *The Future Does Not Compute* (Sebastopol, Calif.: O'Reilly & Associates, Inc., 1995).

6

CURRICULUM THEORY

Focusing Questions

1. Explain the tension between theory and practice.
2. In what ways is theory central to curricular action?
3. What is the meaning of theory?
4. What are the key functions of theory?
5. How have the theoretical positions of reconceptualists and postmodernists influenced curricularists' thinking?
6. What are some benefits of thinking of curriculum as various types of text?
7. Explain the differences among the major theoretical camps.

The foundation of curriculum that is least appreciated is curriculum theory. Many in education and the general public feel that curriculum theory or theoretical propositions have little to do with the practical world of curriculum development and delivery. Indeed, you the reader may be thinking that this is a chapter that can be skipped; this is a chapter that will have nothing practical to say.

This alienation, which Ivor Goodson says is profound, has a long-standing history. Perhaps the negative reaction of many educators, especially practitioners in the field, to theoretical positions is due to the fact that many curriculum theories do not relate to the real world of the schools. As Goodson posits, many current curriculum theories are utopian, not realistic. They are only concerned with what ought to be or might be, not "with the art of the possible."[1] In short, teachers look at such theories as "pie-in-the-sky," without any chance of actually being used to guide the creation of an educational program for the "now." Many of these theories, Goodson argues, do not make any attempt to explain, one of the key functions of theory. Rather, they exhort people to "right action,"

but the right action is often determined by a particular ideology or "ism."

Certainly, curriculum theory can exhort, can serve as a prescription. The prescriptive function of theory is often drawn from the various philosophical orientations that one brings to the curriculum arena. Often the "isms" and ideologies are distilled from one's philosophical "read" of the world. Underlying each of the educational philosophies discussed in Chapter 2 are various implied prescriptions as to how to select the content of the curriculum, organize the content, design the instructional aspect of the educational program, and make value judgments as to whether individuals have learned. Theory is a part of our thinking whether we educators are aware of it or not. We would argue that awareness of theory as an essential curriculum foundation is requisite to effective curriculum action in the schools.

If educators and the general public continue to be alienated from theory, considering it as something impractical, we are not likely to fully comprehend the dynamics of curriculum; we are not likely to succeed in creating, delivering, and assessing curricula that address the needs of current and anticipated times. A. Wise, several years ago stated, "Inevitably, it (educational policy) must be based upon some theories or hypotheses about educational practice. If these assumptions are correct, the policy will have its intended consequences."[2]

Not only are the various educational philosophies influential in theoretical thinking, but the various approaches to curriculum development mentioned in Chapter 1 also draw their orientations from theoretical stances. The behaviorist approach to curriculum is based largely on psychological theories of learning. The systems approach and managerial approach to curriculum development also have theoretical bases. Likewise, the humanistic approach draws from both philosophy and various political theories. Much dialogue emanating from the social foundations is based on various theoretical postures. Talk about postmodernism can be understood more clearly by understanding the movements' theoretical bases.

Theory really cannot be absent from our deliberations. Some have proclaimed that the age of curriculum development is past, and we have entered into an age of seeking understanding. We agree that today there is an emphasis on understanding what we are seeking in terms of education and its prime vehicle, the curriculum. But this shift is not, as Pinar suggests, one from development to understanding.[3] Certainly we are focusing on understanding curriculum "writ large"; however, we also are seeking to apprehend how curricula are created and developed and why certain groups should be involved and the manner of their involvement. We are no longer satisfied with merely being technicians following curriculum development recipes in blind adherence to past models of previous thinking. Contrary to what some theorists say, those concerned with generating ways to create dynamic curricula are not an "intellectually inactive and inert group" of curriculum specialists.[4] Indeed, some are very active at the cutting edges of postmodernism, feminism, and phenomenology. They are very much immersed in investigating how current curricula are created and maintained and how particular programs evolve and emerge in response to dynamic times. They wish to produce theoretical knowl-edge that can serve the practical purposes of explaining, prescribing, guiding, and describing what people involved in education do within the curriculum arena and within the general social context.[5]

With theory, curriculum decision makers can draw on the most advanced and valid knowledge available and apply it to many situations. We can provide ourselves with ways of viewing the world and how it works so that education will be "real," will relate to the world, and will have applicability to real issues and challenges. Having a grasp of theoretical knowledge allows us within the field to be more skilled in analyzing and synthesizing data, organizing concepts and principles, and suggesting new ideas and relations. It even allows us to bring into focus visions of the future that are within the possible.

THEORETICAL PERSPECTIVES

The challenge of bringing into focus visions of the future and then skillfully initiating actions that assure attainment of these visions is not small. Curriculum is a complex phenomenon existing within ever expanding social and political dynamics. Both theoreticians and practitioners would agree that this is a valid "read" of curriculum. And they both would concur that as we question how to create valued curricula we actually generate more questions.[6] Many of these questions guide curriculum theorizing as part of an ever renewing attempt to interpret curricular reality.[7] Such questions comprise an attempt to create a system of meaning, a creation of vehicles for understanding all aspects of curricular activity and how individuals relate and react to the curriculum created.

Practitioners might better accept curriculum theory and theorizing if they were just of one type, just one way of viewing the world and of interpreting its meaning. If theory were simple, perhaps fewer people would cry "don't give me that theory, I want something practical I can use." However, theory cannot be simple, for it attempts to make meaning, to be a way of seeing phenomena that are not in themselves simple. A complex phenomenon like curriculum cannot be explained by a simple or simplistic theory.

Perhaps we can be more receptive to theory if we realize that theorizing is a process that engages us in imagining the how and why of certain phenomena. It challenges us to analyze why we think a curriculum should be developed in a certain way for particular students and focused on certain content. Theory can also suggest ways in which we can teach what we think is important. It does not specifically state "do this, and this will happen." This may be one reason that practitioners in the past developed a distaste for theory. Theory produced a body of data that was valid in abstract generalizations, but rarely could be applied in a specific situation. But practitioners and theoreticians alike will do well to remember that it is through theory that we see, think, and know.[8]

In many ways, theory is an expression of belief.[9] Thinking of theory in this way connects theoretical thinking to philosophical thinking and to ways of looking at the world, seen and imagined.

The complexity of curriculum and the complexity surrounding curriculum can only be processed by having some theoretical understanding. Many years ago, Hilda Taba noted that "any enterprise as complex as curriculum requires some kind of theoretical or conceptual framework of thinking to guide it."[10] George Posner argues that theoretical perspectives allow us to contemplate and "see" educational landscapes in particular ways.[11] Curricularists must advance their understanding of the theoretical aspects of the field if they are to conceptualize and develop curricula of value for students.

George Beauchamp has asserted that all theories are derived from three broad categories of knowledge: (1) the humanities; (2) the natural sciences; and (3) the social sciences.[12] These *divisions of knowledge* are well established as the basic realms of knowledge. For example, under the humanities are the disciplines of philosophy, music, art, and literature. Under the social sciences are the disciplines of history, sociology, psychology, and anthropology, among others. Under the natural sciences are the disciplines of chemistry, physics, botany, geology, and so on.

Beauchamp argues that from these basic knowledge divisions come areas of *applied knowledge*—architecture, medicine, engineering, education, and law, to name a few. What distinguishes applied realms of knowledge from disciplines is that applied realms draw their content and indeed their authority from theory in the disciplines. Education, for example, draws from psychology, sociology, and history and uses information from biology when referring to human growth and development. It takes much of its emphasis from philosophy. What makes education a field of knowledge is the manner in which it combines knowledge from various disciplines and formulates rules and procedures for using the knowledge.

Beauchamp has identified a series of subtheories in education: administrative theories, counseling theories, instructional theories, evaluation theories, and curriculum theories. There are two major categories of curriculum theories—design theories and engineering theories. *Design theories* address the basic organization of the curriculum plan. For this, curricularists draw on philosophy as well as on social and psychology theory.

Engineering theories explain, describe, predict, or even guide curriculum-development activities. They involve specific plans, principles, and/or methods or procedures. Engineering theories of curriculum are also partially based on principles of measurement and statistics.

The Meaning of Theory

Despite the myriad works on the nature and function of theory, curriculum specialists have not produced a universal definition of theory. This is not too surprising because the three basic realms of knowledge—humanities, social sciences, and natural sciences—all look at reality differently and generate definitions of theory that reflect their interests.

Although differences exist among the major types of theory, some commonalities are evident as well. Most definitions of theory deal with sets of events or phenomena and the relationships among these events. Abraham Kaplan provides a useful general statement defining theory: "A theory is a way of making sense of a disturbing situation so as to allow us most effectively to bring to bear our repertoire of habits, and even more important, to modify habits or discard them altogether, replacing new ones as the situation demands. . . ."[13] Theory will appear as the device for interpreting, criticizing, and unifying established laws, modifying them to fit data unanticipated in their formation, and guiding the enterprise of discovering new and more powerful generalizations.

Richard Snow states that "a theory is essentially a symbolic construction that is designed to bring generalizable facts or laws into systematic connection." The theory itself consists of a set of units that can be "facts, concepts, or some variables, and a noting of relationships among the units identified."[14]

Sources of Curriculum Theory

Joseph Schwab in his landmark paper on curriculum stated that we had no curriculum theory, and perhaps were not spending our time wisely in trying to develop one.[15] Notwithstanding Schwab's conclusion, there are numerous theories and theoretical orientations employed in contemplating, creating, and managing curriculum. However, many of these theories are drawn from various fields of study rather than from the curriculum field itself. A challenge for curricularists is to determine just what aspect of the field of curriculum we are processing. Our assumption is that the field of curriculum should involve curricularists in theorizing about curriculum design and curriculum development.

Reflecting on the nature of curriculum design draws heavily from the philosophical foundations. Often the statements we make about the nature of knowledge and the nature of reality are influenced by our philosophical views. Also, individuals concerned about creating curricula that will enhance the quality of students' lives draw from philosophical dispositions. Critical theory, which will be discussed in more detail later, certainly addresses the quality of students' lives. It is essentially a social–political theory that draws on a certain interpretation of reality and urges people to engage in self-reflection so that they can alter their perspectives of the social–political world. This theory not only relates to interpreting the social world, but also fosters an understanding of curriculum and pedagogy in ways that serve to "emancipate" students.

Critical theory is value oriented and heavily influenced by philosophical underpinnings. Allan Glatthorn notes that many of the value-oriented theorists strive to raise our consciousness regarding educational issues.[16] They urge us to consider and to reflect on those value issues that form the bases of our educational programs. In many ways, these theorists draw from both the philosophical camps and from political theory.

Persons reflecting on curriculum development also have many theories outside of curriculum proper to guide their action or to employ in explaining particular phenomena. Many theories of change can be used when contemplating and engaging in curriculum development. Numerous theories of organizational development also influence curriculum development activity. Theories of group behavior also affect curriculum development. All the theories that we can consider when contemplating curriculum development tend to be based on logic and the arrangements of sequences or steps.

Most theories are still rather traditional in the sense that they draw from well-recognized areas of research and knowledge. Frances Klein points out, however, that there are some new entries into the field of curriculum theorizing. Still, even with these new entries, most curricularists do seem to agree on two points. First, curricularists agree that curriculum is of fundamental importance to our teachers and students, and to the nature of teaching and learning. Second, curriculum development is greatly influenced by the values we bring to the process.[17]

What seems to be common among persons using alternative bases for curriculum theorizing is that they share a dissatisfaction with the traditional ways in which we either think about or create a curriculum. Many of these curriculum theorists start with essentially different beliefs and values about the curriculum. Frequently, they envision the future of the school and its curriculum in ways that greatly diverge from mainstream curricularists. Many draw their arguments from fields that until recently were never considered relevant to educational thinking, fields such as art, phenomenology, psychoanalysis, literature, critical theory, and neo-Marxist philosophy.[18]

THE CLASSIC BASES OF CURRICULUM THEORIZING

While much activity within the alternative modes of theorizing exists, there are curricularists who still divide theory either into scientific theory or humanistic theory. It is important that we not accept the posture of either-or thinking regarding scientific theory or humanistic theory. Both have value in assisting us in working within the field of curriculum.

Scientific Theory

Natural scientists in this century have made great advances in their realm of knowledge, largely because of their extensive utilization of what is called scientific theory. In many instances, scientific theory has been given the status of exemplar for theory formation and statement.

Within the natural sciences, the term *theory* sometimes refers to a set of propositions inductively derived from empirical findings. These generalizations refer to various facts, laws, or hypotheses that are related to each other in a systematic way and that form a type of whole—an entity. Scientific theory, then, is comprised of general facts, laws, or hypotheses related to each other.

Perhaps the most widely accepted definition of scientific theory is delineated by Herbert Feigl and includes a "set of assumptions from which can be derived by purely logicomathematical procedures, a larger set of empirical laws. The theory furnishes an explanation of these empirical laws and unifies the subject matter."[19]

According to this definition, theory is a cluster of logically connected statements that generalize to and offer explanations of particular cases. In its explanations of the various cases to which it refers, theory unifies myriad data and the propositions relevant to those data.

Fred Kerlinger asserts that the basic aim of science is theory, that is, the aim of science is to identify basic statements that explain natural events. He notes that theories are general explanations that enable scientists to understand the phenomena studied.[20] Instead of attempting to explain every separate event, for example, the behavior of students in one activity, scientists formulate general statements about similar events or behavior so that they can link many events or behaviors. Instead of describing how different children each solved a particular science problem, the theorist would derive from his or her observations a general explanation of most, if not all, kinds of problem solving. The investigator would then present the general statement as a theory of problem solving.

Philosophical and Humanistic Theory

Scholars in the humanities use theory to formulate consistent and logical explanations of humans' place in the world. Such theories produce a set of assumptions or beliefs that *explain what ought to be*. These assumptions, derived inductively from the scholars' professional experiences and knowledge of the world, contrast their thinking with that of colleagues in specific disciplines. Philosophers' theories describe their outlooks—their views of reality and their place within it.

Much of the theory that relates to education, and specifically to curriculum, stems from the philosophical and/or humanistic orientation.[21] A tenet of existentialism is that to become fully human, or at least more human, people must be engaged actively in their world; without engagement, individuals become detached and isolated. This "theory of engagement" is based on philosophical matters rather than scientific validation.

Philosophical and humanistic theory fits into the category Herbert Kliebard has identified as a concern for systematic analysis of a set of related concepts or problems.[22] Theory at this level is essentially the result of an attempt to clarify the nature of concepts and problems, and their understanding rarely depends on empirical support. Empirical considerations play only a minor role. Rather, validation of the theory relies on the logic of various positions and the articulation of values.

Philosophical and humanistic theory is largely normative (based on values). It essentially indicates what should or should not be included or done in some action. Humanistic theory emphasizes the melding of the emotional and physical with the intellectual. It addresses coherence and a way of knowing, that is, the meshing of ideas and actions together.[23] Using such theory, curricularists should have guidelines about what to do or not do in creating the curriculum, that is, about what they should include in and perhaps what they should exclude from the curriculum.

THE FUNCTIONS OF THEORY

Educators may ask, "Why do we need theory at all?" Often, they do not wait for a reply and state, "I do not need your damn theory." However, we really cannot escape theory. Whether we recognize theory or not, our very actions are informed by theory or theoretical and philosophical stances. To think that theory is irrelevant to our actions is to apply a theoretical–philosophical stance to the argument against theory. Curriculum theorizing is an expression of humans' visioning life.[24] All people want to know; they desire to have a basis for explaining their world or justification for arguing their position. All people, scientists and philosophers included, by their nature are "programmed" to seek understanding, to make meaning. The aim of science is to understand the phenomena studied. Philosophers also seek answers to their questions: What is knowledge, what is reality, what is of value?

Theory comes from the Greek word *theoria* connoting "wakefulness of mind." It is a type of "pure viewing" of truth. Theory explains reality; it makes people aware of their world and its interactions. Many writers have ascribed four functions to theory: (1) description; (2) prediction; (3) explanation; and (4) guidance.[25] Although some writers disagree about which function is paramount, most view all as important and as closely related.

Description. Description provides a narrative classification of knowledge in a particular theoretical field. It furnishes a structure through which individuals' interpretations of complex activities can be verified. It organizes and summarizes knowledge. A theory "tells" us that there are certain variables and that they interact in particular ways or have certain relationships to other variables; it does not indicate why certain variables are important nor why they are interrelated. Theory presents an account of events. It unifies phenomena and arranges the information so that the scope and internal relationships, though not explained, are at least discernible.[26]

Prediction. The second function of theory is rather obvious. A theory can predict the occurrence of as yet unobserved events on the basis of explanatory principles embedded in it. Perhaps this is the ultimate function of theory. Of course, cautious people always regard a theory with some degree of tentativeness; for a theory, regardless of the accumulated data to support it, cannot account for all situations. If it did, it would not be a theory but a law. Nonetheless, the more diverse observa-

tions a theory can explain, the greater should be people's confidence in using it to predict the phenomena in question.

Explanation. Explanation addresses "why." It not only points out the relationships between phenomena, but suggests either explicitly or implicitly the reasons for the relationships. The best explanations relate to what people know as opposed to what they may mistakenly believe. For example, an explanation of students' learning difficulties in terms of "evil spirits" would be less believable than an explanation stressing students' motivation and interests.

Guidance. Theory also acts as a guide. It helps researchers choose data for analysis and make economical summaries of the data. The theory generated promotes further investigation. In essence, it serves a directive function. Many scientists assert that this is the true or primary responsibility of scientific theory—to serve as the guide for further study. "What is important is that laws propagate when they are united in a theory; theory serves as matchmaker, midwife, and godfather all in one."[27]

Theorists cannot divorce themselves from their values and knowledge when addressing the directive functions of theory. Values will influence, suggest, even prescribe what their behavior should be. Collecting the facts is a necessary first step in theory building—but what facts, whose rendition of the facts? Without theoretical orientations, people cannot decide what facts to gather or what issues to address. Their values influence what facts and relationships are relevant to them. Their values, in other words, guide their theorizing.

When serving as a guiding function, theory works whether one is a scientist or a humanistic existentialist. All people's thinking about reality is influenced by theoretical–philosophical posturing. Theory, as van Manen says, is an act of imagining. We employ theory to shape our imagining, indeed to define whether something is fact or nonfact. "It is through theory that we may hope to reach what theory points to."[28] Theory is an expression of belief; belief in our theory stance influences what we deem important and thus our actions in interpreting and developing curriculum. The purposes of education to which we subscribe are influenced by our theoretical postures and belief systems. How we view the various foundations of curriculum and their relationships to our thinking is shaped by our beliefs, our theoretical stances.

Accepting the guidance function of theory enables us to employ theory as a vehicle that contributes to our resourcefulness. Such resourcefulness should generate questions that have worth in guiding our actions as we engage in curriculum development, delivery, and analysis.[29] Every time we state that we need to have a certain curriculum or that we need to organize the curriculum in a certain way we are engaged in theoretical talk. Such talk is central to our educational dialogue. And we all engage in such talk; we all have beliefs; and we all express them.

THEORY BUILDING

Essentially, the process of theory development is tied to inductive and deductive thinking. Sometimes, these are considered to be two different approaches to theory generation, but typically both are employed together to create theory.

Induction means building a theory by accumulating and summarizing a variety of inquiries. People using induction rely rather heavily on empirical data. They form propositions on the basis of research that began as tentative hypotheses they tested and validated.[30]

Deduction, in contrast to induction, is the process of inferring necessary conclusions from a combination of premises whose truth has either been accepted as given or assumed to be true. People employing deduction develop theory by constructing logical sequences.[31] They proceed from the general to the specific.

Steps in Theory Building

To engage in theory is to deal with symbols, facts, or words that can be classified into large concepts and generalizations. The ability to see and describe relationships among symbols or facts and then put these ideas into words is also part of theory building. The problem with theory is when it must be applied in the real world. To be sure, there is danger in abstracting ideas that make sense on paper and then testing or using them in specific

situations. Because people are not easy to control or manipulate, our theories often faulter in real-life situations. See Curriculum Tips 6-1.

Defining Terms. One of the basic rules in theory building is to be clear about terms. According to Beauchamp, agreement on terms is an essential ingredient in the work of a theorist. The terms theorists employ and the concepts implied by those terms are the building blocks of the theory. Selecting terms is governed by two rules: (1) The wording must be clear, and (2) the terms, once defined, must be used consistently.[32]

Terms define what is to be observed. They refer to concepts, and they are the variables between which empirical relationships are to be sought. Concepts are either nominal or operational.[33] *Nominal* definitions present the attributes of a term or concept. In contrast, *operational* definitions indicate the context in which the concept is employed.

Some terms really cannot be defined either by referring to nominal attributes or by referring to other operationally defined terms. Yet they are a critical, basic part of theory. These *primitive* terms are accepted by those who use them in their theoretical work. In mathematics, for example, the terms "point" or "straight line" are primitive terms. They really cannot be nominally or operationally defined; all we can say is that a "point" is a point. In education, such terms as "felt needs" and "experience" are primitive terms.[34] Although theorists may not always be able to refrain from using primitive terms, they should try to use them as infrequently as possible.

Another category of terms used in theory is *theoretical* terms or operational constructs; theories with any degree of sophistication contain such terms. A construct is a concept that represents relationships among things and/or events and their properties.[35] Theoretical terms cannot be defined directly by observing particular events. Rather they can be defined by their relationships to other terms that are operationally defined. Educators use a large number of such terms—motivation, cognitive dissonance, attitude, perceptual structuring, set, and social need.

Classifying. The second activity in theory building is classification. At this stage, theorists

---

Curriculum Tips 6-1

Contemplating Theory Building

Theory building is not an exact science, and many of us can engage in theorizing just by contemplating about theory. The following points can help us in such "theorizing."

1. Set aside time to reflect on what you are doing. You need to schedule such time; otherwise, everyday concerns will dominate your actions.
2. Record what you have been doing; make note of patterns and deviations from actions.
3. Focus on one important aspect of curriculum or instruction. Describe this focus. Be conscious of the words (concepts, terms) you are using to describe this focus.
4. Note the general questions that seem to arise from writing your description.
5. Note the relationships that appear among the various aspects of your focus.
6. Record your conclusions. Reflect and modify your conclusions. Be willing to admit to the dangers of abstract relationships—or making conclusions.

---

attempt to organize and integrate what they know about the areas being theorized. They begin summarizing discovered uniformities of relationships between two or more variables or concepts.[36] Their classifications or statements of classifications can have varying degrees of precision, but this does not diminish their place in theory building. Classification allows theorists to discover gaps in their knowledge that must be filled through research activities if they are to give meaning to their theorizing.

When classifying information, theorists group facts and generalizations into homogeneous groups. However, even if categories seem to be taking shape, explanations of the interrelationships among the categories or of the relationships among the facts and generalizations within any single information cluster may still be lacking.

The steps in theory generation are all influenced by our philosophical views. How we define terms is influenced by our "read" on reality. Do we perceive reality as something out there that can be manipulated? Or do we contemplate reality as "invented" by the person or constructed by the theorist? Additionally, our views of the various political, social, and psychological foundations affect how we engage in the steps of theory building or making sense of educational phenomena. Much educational political talk addresses race, class, and gender. The concept of race, as

educators use the term, is influenced by an understanding of political reality. It is different from the way biologists use the term. In fact, biologists do not even recognize the concept of race as valid. When educators assume a particular relationship among race and learning, they are employing these terms greatly influenced by political and social theory. How we interpret our contexts is very much colored by our philosophical–theoretical postures. We really cannot get outside ourselves. Persons who consider themselves modern in their outlook will process theory-building tasks differently from those who adhere to a postmodern posture. When engaged in theorizing, and we all engage in such intellectual activity, we are attempting to ground our actions within the dynamics of education.

CURRICULUM THEORY

Theory as we have defined it is a set of statements so worded that it can be used as a means of communication among people and as a directive to those who wish to study the field of curriculum.

The challenge to curricularists is to make sense out of the complexity of the field of curriculum and to determine whether they should create their own curriculum theory or theories, borrow theories from other disciplines—such as psychology, sociology, anthropology, and philosophy—or do both. To create a single curriculum theory that would describe, and more importantly explain, curriculum is perhaps an unrealistic goal; curriculum covers too many aspects of education.

Curriculum theory has been the subject of conversation and the focus of reflection by many concerned with curriculum. Even in the early years when the field of curriculum was gaining identity and stature, curricularists were concerned with defining a theoretical basis.

Early Theory in Curriculum

The publication of Franklin Bobbitt's *The Curriculum* can probably be cited as the starting point of theorizing in curriculum. It also represented one of the early books in scientific theorizing. Bobbitt urged his fellow educators to borrow from the new technology to guide educational functioning. He believed strongly that the principles of management and the application of theory could help educators be more precise and efficient in creating and implementing their programs.[37]

Scientific theory was viewed by many to have the quality of objectivity. Theory could serve to describe and explain what is. Theory of phenomena would allow educators to predict the consequences of putting certain phenomena into action.

Many new discoveries in testing and statistics furnished those who wished to engage in theory building with tools that enabled them to manage more carefully investigations and process more precisely data gathered. Persons in curriculum theory drew guidance from the context of the times. This was especially true of Bobbitt and Charters, both of whom were expert in the field of research and evaluation. Both theorists linked the idea of activity analysis with formulating curriculum decisions. The idea was to correlate the objectives of the subject with specific activities—those tasks and skills that students had to learn to prepare for productive living. However numerous these activities were, educators had to make decisions about which activities were to be stressed in school.[38]

During the last years of the nineteenth century and the early years of this century, Dewey was engaged in creating a curriculum theory. Even though Dewey may not have considered his work to be a curriculum theory, but rather a science in education, it still holds value for curriculum theorists.[39] Dewey's theory draws on the notion that the development of the individual and the development of the human race are similar in their overall stages. His theory attempts to show the relationship between schools and society and the various aspects of experience and education as they relate to the learner.[40]

Dewey urged educators to tie knowledge in the curriculum to human experiences relevant to children; moreover, he urged that children experience knowledge through various activities. The experience-centered curriculum, which we discuss in Chapter 8, drew much of its theoretical support from this "theory" advanced by Dewey. It also gave rise to the curriculum activity movement. Dewey actually attempted to reproduce in his experimental elementary school at the University of Chicago the actual conditions of social life. Children would learn about how humans processed their environment by being involved in similar actions in school.

Educators might well ask, then, if persons such as Bobbitt or Charters approached curriculum from various theoretical stances, and Dewey attempted to test out theory in his school, why did curriculum theorizing remain undeveloped?[41] Perhaps because educators have talked a "better game" of theory than they have "played."

Theory at Mid-century

Much of the early talk about curriculum did not consider theory per se. However, in the 1940s, curriculum writings begin to discuss actual theory. The first major discussion on the topic took place at the University of Chicago in 1947. The various participants at this conference produced a paper addressing curriculum theory, but no curriculum theory emerged from the meeting. The papers, which appeared as a monograph three years later, did conclude with a challenge: "As a further effort in hastening the communications between groups of interested people and in the development of more adequate theory, someone might spend some time trying to describe the nature of such theory, its tasks, its subject matter, its tests, and its uses."[42]

Tyler, some might argue, took up the challenge in his book's presentation of the basic principles of curriculum and instruction. But Tyler's approach, if it can even be considered theoretical, was more attuned to curriculum development than to an overall theory of curriculum.[43] Beauchamp, however, was instrumental in adding to the field of curriculum theory. His 1950 book, *Curriculum Theory,* addressed the topic.[44] Even so, although the book has gone through four editions, it still leaves us without an agreed upon curriculum theory. Some of the major theories that have evolved are as follows:

Maccias' Theory.   During the last 30 years, the formative years of curriculum theory, a more diversified view of curriculum theory has evolved. Elizabeth and George Maccia, for example, presented four different kinds of curriculum theory. They noted that curriculum specialists speculate about forms, events, values, and practices. Consequently, they organized theory as formal theory, event theory, valuational theory, and praxiological theory.[45]

1. *Formal theory.*   This theory deals with speculation about the structure of the disciplines that comprise the curriculum. Curricularists usually draw their understanding of such theory from philosophers and members of the particular disciplines in question. Such theory is nonvaluational; it deals with what is and what exists, rather than what ought to be.
2. *Event theory.*   This theory, very similar to what we have been discussing as scientific theory, refers to speculation about occurrences. It attempts to predict what will occur given certain circumstances.
3. *Valuational theory.*   This theory involves speculation about the appropriate means to attain the objectives most desired and to include the content judged to be the best. In contrast to event theory, valuation theory does involve values or norms. It deals with "ought-ness."
4. *Praxiological theory.*   Such theory refers to speculation about appropriate means to attain what is considered valuable. It is about practices. It can support the creation of curriculum policy, the means we employ to adopt particular objectives and specific practices in schools.

The Maccias asserted that curricularists could use theory to guide their building of a definition of curriculum, as well as in the planning and development of curriculum.

Johnson's Theory.   In contrast to the Maccias, Mauritz Johnson stated that curriculum specialists should first define curriculum making and then direct their energies at theory building. He argued that most past efforts to build curriculum theory had centered on programs, with the result that attention was really on curriculum development.[46] As shown in Figure 6-1, Johnson distinguished between the curriculum plan and the process of curriculum development by defining the former as an output of the latter; he also revealed the differences among curriculum, instruction, and teacher behavior. His attention to objectives puts him in the behavioral camp. Although curricularists may not agree with Johnson's definition of curriculum—an intended series of learning outcomes—they should realize the usefulness of distinguishing between theorizing about curriculum as a plan and theorizing about the means by which such plans are generated.

Macdonald's Theory.   Macdonald presented a model of the major systems in schooling: curriculum, instruction, teaching, and learning.[47] The model, not actually a theory, points out possible key components involved in the dynamics of curriculum and instruction. It presents a map indicating the key features of the educational landscape.

Though curriculum is quite large in the drawing, Macdonald's model shows it as one of four interacting systems. Macdonald defines *curriculum* as the social system that actually produces a plan for *instruction,* which he in turn defines as another social system within which formal teaching and learning take place. *Teaching* is different from instruction and is defined as a personality system—the teacher—acting in a particular manner to facilitate learning. *Learning* is defined as a personality system, too; the student becomes involved in specialized task-related behaviors. All these systems come together in the center, depicted in Figure 6-2 by a shadowed spot. At this juncture, the curriculum goals become operative in the instructional encounter because of the efforts of the teacher and the behavior of the students.

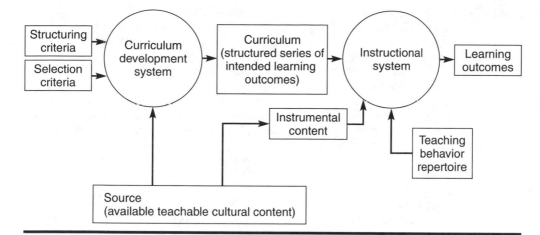

FIGURE 6-1   Curriculum as an Output-Input of One System.

Source: From Mauritz Johnson, "Definitions and Models in Curriculum Theory," *Educational Theory* (April 1967), p. 23.

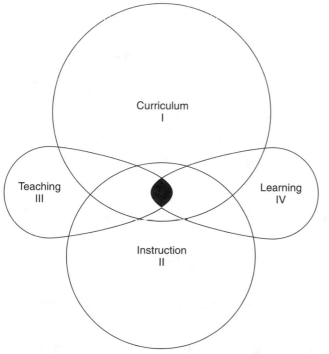

FIGURE 6-2   The Interaction of Four Systems.

Source: From James B. Macdonald, "Educational Models for Instruction," in J. B. Macdonald and R. R. Leeper, eds., *Theories of Instruction* (Washington, D.C.: Association for Supervision and Curriculum Development, 1965), p. 95.

Macdonald's model clarifies the interrelationships between teaching, learning, instruction, and curriculum. It points out that each can be considered a system in its own right, but that in the reality of the school, the systems interface with each other so as to produce some specialized subsystems. Still, the model leaves theorists without answers about how they would determine the nature and scope of the curriculum. The reality of the curriculum in action is certainly more complex than depicted by this model.

Educators continue to believe that theory can produce hypotheses that can be tested in the world of concrete experience. They believe still that theory can enable them to describe reality and, more importantly, to begin to explain it. It also can serve as a policy map suggesting what they should do.

But the challenge is immense. Gail McCutcheon states that few examples of curriculum theories really integrate data resulting from analyses, interpretations, and understandings of curriculum phenomena.[48] She has argued that curriculum persons need more examples that have a clear value for them and that draw from multiple disciplines. Other curricularists have also addressed this issue, focusing on how the various psychological theories can contribute to curriculum thinking and action.[49]

Some curriculum theorists state that educators must derive curriculum theory from their analyses of curricula-in-use. Decker Walker has faulted many in the curriculum field for being so concerned with prescribing procedures for creating curricula that they have not paid sufficient attention to how curricula are created or to the nature of the programs generated.[50] He argues that curriculum theories can help curricularists view curriculum in a different light and thus generate novel interpretations of curriculum. He suggests that theories can be conceived as clustered in families, each having a different purpose and perhaps a different form. But all theories focus on rationalizing, conceptualizing, and explaining practice. Walker notes that some theories being advanced fit into the current society without question, whereas others are being presented within a context of a new hypothetical, as yet unformed, society.

Elizabeth Vallance notes that curriculum theory is practical and based on real situations; such theorizing in curriculum occurs in every school.[51] Taking this stance, curricularists are encouraged to survey, analyze, synthesize, and test the knowledge available about curriculum problems. They should look at the data available and attempt to make practical application. Vallance notes that the data observed may be part of a new curriculum package, or the textbooks just purchased by a district, or the political climate of the school. Even though the data that theorists might view could be different data than classroom teachers might value, the process of theorizing is similar. See Curriculum Tips 6-2. See also Table 6-1 for an overview of major curriculum theories.

METAPHORS AND THEORETICAL CAMPS

Some curriculum theorists have argued that theoretical problems stem from faulty or nonproductive conceptions of curriculum. Dwayne Huebner has urged that educators discontinue their use of logical-rational language that stresses effectiveness, objectiveness, and behavioristic principles of learning and instead employ a language that centers on the economic and political policies that impact on education.[52] He wants educators also to use language that will direct their attention to how learners are provided with choices in subject matter—for example, how can a teacher best involve a student with the myriad cultures of the world so as to enhance the student's global awareness? Huebner has argued that educators have used a language that encourages control over the students, rather than liberation.

More recently, Henry Giroux has urged educators to employ pedagogic language that engages students in finding their own voices and experiencing other voices of diverse cultures. He also advocates a discontinuance of the logical rational language, a belief in one master narrative, substituting instead a language that recognizes the personal, the emotional, the ethical, the uncertain.[53]

Kliebard suggests that a way in which educators can perhaps cure their myopia is to use different metaphors from those that currently influence their thinking.[54] Because a technological orientation to curriculum essentially dominates the field, the metaphors of factory and production are common. Kliebard would propose substituting a metaphor that would enable curricularists to reconceptualize their view of the school and its curriculum. He notes that some social reconstructionists employ the metaphor of culture as a form of capital.

====== *Curriculum Tips 6-2* ======

Translating Theory into Practice

Blending theory with practice is an old ideal. If we are to make serious progress toward this goal in curriculum, as in other fields, we need to recognize certain basic steps.

1. *Read the literature.* Any attempt to relate theory and practice must be based on knowledge of the professional literature.
2. *Identify the major terms.* The need is for curriculum theorists and practitioners to identify and agree on the major constructs, concepts, and questions for discussion.
3. *Check the soundness of existing theories.* Existing theories need to be analyzed in terms of validity, evidence, accuracy, underlying assumptions, logic of argument, coherence, generalizability, values, and biases.
4. *Avoid fads.* New fads and hot topics must not be introduced to practitioners under the guise of a new theory—or even as reform or innovation. When a new program or method is introduced into the professional literature or at some professional conference, this is not the time to jump on the bandwagon, much less to call it theory; it is the time to pull back and wait for evaluations or complaints to surface.
5. *Align theory with practice.* Theory must be considered in context with the real world of classrooms and schools; it must be plausible, applicable, and realistic in terms of practice.
6. *Test theory.* If the theory is credible and makes common sense, then it must be empirically tested by trying it in practice and measuring the results. It should be introduced first on a small scale, comparing experimental and control schools.
7. *Interpret theory.* The results must be tested and interpreted in terms of realistic conditions over realistic time periods. The theory must be evaluated in schools for a minimum of one year and ideally over a three-year period to test for "fading out."
8. *Modify theory and reduce its complexity.* A theory is a generalizable construct supported by language or quantitative data. Nonetheless, theory must be modified from paper to practice, from the abstract to the concrete world, from complex concepts to lay terms. When we move theory to practice, we include many people (and resources) to make it work. Theory must fit with people (not mold people to theory) to move it from an idea to action.

Paulo Freire has critiqued the metaphor of education as banking. Education in this metaphor would be an action of deposition. The students are the depositories and the teacher is the depositor.[55] Note, however, that following a metaphor too closely can be dangerous. According to a banking metaphor, for instance, the student is considered a passive receiver of the deposit; he or she is only to receive, memorize, and repeat. Moreover, this metaphor also brings into focus that educators should ensure that "cultural capital" is deposited equally into each student's account.

People do not usually think consciously about the conceptual systems by which they organize their world. In most of the things they do, they just act and think more or less automatically along pathways that have become comfortable to them. But, if they think about their language, they find themselves in conceptual (and metaphorical) camps that organize their realities. Both William Pinar[56] and John McNeil have presented conceptual organizers that group curriculum persons into three camps.[57]

Traditionalists

Traditionalists value service to practitioners. They view curricula as plans and stress those procedures requisite for creating such plans. Traditionalists are concerned with the essential roles of the

TABLE 6-1 Overview of Theories Affecting Curriculum Field

THEORY	AUTHOR(S)	TYPE OF THEORY	CLASSIC BASE	FUNCTION
Curriculum as systematic activity, as management	Bobbitt, Charters	Curriculum theory	Scientific	To explain, describe
Curriculum as reflecting the stages of human development	Dewey	Curriculum theory	Scientific	To explain, prescribe
Curriculum as praxis	Maccia	Curriculum theory	Scientific	To guide, prescribe
Curriculum as intended series of learning outcomes	Johnson	Curriculum theory	Scientific	To describe
Curriculum as interacting systems	Macdonald	Curriculum theory	Scientific	To describe, explain
Curriculum as metaphor	Kliebard, Freire	Curriculum theory	Humanistic	To prescribe
Curriculum as experience for social purpose	Pinar	Curriculum theory	Humanistic	To prescribe
Education as process, as structuring knowledge	Bruner	Instructional theory	Scientific	To explain, prescribe
Education as implementing the curriculum	Oliva	Instructional theory	Scientific	To explain
Teaching as transformation	Giroux	Instructional theory	Humanistic (critical theory)	To prescribe, describe

key curriculum players and the bases for the selecting, organizing, and sequencing of curriculum content.

A close relationship exists between traditionalists and school personnel. But this closeness has prevented them from creating new ways of talking about curriculum that could result in more productive educational programs.[58] While this orientation to curriculum emphasizes the role of organized subject matter, there is among these traditionalists and school practitioners some contemplation of new ways of organizing curricula. The discussion on integrated curricula, core curricula, and Science/Technology/Society (the STS curricula) exemplify this new conceptualizing and theorizing about curriculum. Such curriculum scholars as John Dewey, Franklin Bobbitt, Ralph Tyler, Hilda Taba, George Beauchamp, Ronald Doll, and John Goodlad are in this camp.

Traditionalists tend to be involved in *structural theorizing* that focuses on identifying elements in the curriculum and determining their relationships. Such theorizing centers on the decisions and decision makers (sometimes called players or engineers) involved in curriculum planning. Those who focus on curriculum development and curriculum planning emphasize rationality and logic.[59]

Structural theorists contend that educational practice is not an art but rather, extensively, a science, or at least a scientific approach. They assume that the key events occurring in the educational process can be identified, described, and to some extent controlled. Frances Klein states that these traditionalists, when contemplating curricula, believe in a scientific, technological, and rational process. They presume that curricula can be created by taking a behavioristic reductionistic process. They also maintain that it is possible to create curricula prior to its employment within the classroom. Goals, content, and instructional experiences can be preplanned; moreover, teachers can be trained to present such curricula efficiently and effectively.[60]

Conceptual Empiricists

These persons are often researchers and/or measurement oriented and view their primary mission as engaging in research that will be theory producing. They argue that scientific knowledge of human behavior, including the curriculum, is possible. They claim that the research and the resulting theory are of practical value because they enable school practitioners to articulate the reasons for their actions. This, in turn, increases the likelihood that they will realize the traditional goals of the school.

People in this camp are Benjamin Bloom, Jerome Bruner, David Berliner, George Posner, Robert Stake, and Herb Walberg. All these people are actively exploring the application of cognitive science to curriculum and instructional research as well as to cognition and learning to guide the arrangement of curriculum content and its delivery in the classroom.

Dorothy Huenecke asserts that people who are in the conceptual empiricist camp engage in *substantive theorizing*.[61] The theory activity is designed to highlight appropriate content for the curriculum. Conceptual empiricists, engaged in substantive theorizing, analyze current situations and suggest alternatives to current patterns of content and experiences that comprise most curricula. They question what teachers are teaching, why they have arranged the school content in the ways they have, and what influence they have on learners.

Most conceptual empiricists emphasize content-based theories, in part because many are also cognition-oriented psychologists. Perhaps the best known content-based theory is the structure of disciplines which is discussed in Chapter 8. This theoretical orientation explains that knowledge can be structured according to its key concepts and that these concepts can be organized to reveal major relationships. In a curriculum so organized, students could easily grasp the concep-

tual basis of knowledge resulting in a more detailed understanding.

Reconceptualists, Critical Theorists

Curricularists who are in this camp maintain the view that intellectual and scientific distance from curriculum practice are required if those in charge of education are to effectively critique and theorize existing programs. Engaging in reconceptualizing theory, one attempts to actually drive a wedge between theory and practice. In theorizing, the intent is not to actually improve a particular practice at one particular juncture, but rather to gain a "wisdom" about the nature of the phenomena about which one is raising questions.

People in this camp urge educators to shift their attention from curriculum development to curriculum understanding.[62] While we agree that we now know much about curriculum development, we would argue that we cannot categorically state that we know all that there is to know about development. However, the field of curriculum is centering much of its activity on trying to comprehend curriculum, and rightly so. Even authors of synoptic texts like ours realize that we need to understand both what we do and the context within which we function.

Presently, the reconceptualists are focusing on a critique of the field, which they believe is too immersed in practical and technologically oriented approaches to curriculum. They feel that true understanding will come from aesthetic, humanistic, and existential postures. Focusing on understanding oneself will lead to truly heightened consciousness.

Pinar seems to be the most visible of the reconceptualists, but James Macdonald has been credited with coining the term *reconceptualist*. Macdonald had argued that curricularists were far too concerned with logic and rationality in approaching their work, and so they often totally ignored the aesthetics of the curriculum.[63] They needed to reconceptualize—to take a new focus— to furnish new direction and to de-emphasize providing practitioners with prescriptive formulas for efficiently delivering the curricula.

A theme common to much of the work and writings of reconceptualists is liberation. Some people, who draw heavily from existentialism and phenomenology, propose that liberation comes from within the person. Pinar has given prominence to this stance in what he calls autobiographical theory.[64] This theory is incorporated in *currere*. Currere "refers to an existential experience within institutional structures. Currere is a strategy devised to disclose experiences, so that we may see more of it and see more clearly." The method employs self-analysis. Through such a method, learners investigate their own response to life—and therefore to educational situations.[65]

The method involves (1) recalling and describing the past and then analyzing its psychic relation to the present, *the regressive step;* (2) describing one's imagined future and determining its relation to the present, *the progressive step;* and (3) placing this analytic understanding of one's education in its cultural and political context, *the analytical step.* From engaging in these three steps, one generates a learning that is highly personal and unique. Pinar states that this is the fourth step, *the synthetical.* Individuals require a method for processing their experiences such that they derive meaning from them and control over their lives.[66] Autobiographical theory is really *guidance,* not for the creation of curricula, but rather a *map* suggesting how one might or, rather, should experience curricula.

The theme of liberation takes much of curriculum theorizing away from curriculum per se and focuses instead on the social and political realms within which persons will experience specific curricula. This theorizing about social and political realms connects curriculum theorizing to the social foundations of curriculum. Indeed, the concerns of people such as Michael Apple, Paulo Freire, and Henry Giroux, which focus on the dynamics of power, control, and influence, are very much in the political social camp. Their questioning as to who is in charge of the educational system and for what purpose is very much a political question. Their questions are all political questions: "Who controls the type of knowledge that is to be experienced in the school? Who controls the amount of knowledge that will be presented to various groups of students? Who creates the criteria that will determine success? These theorists want to liberate schools and society from the political and economic establishment. They consider current schools as repressive and not responsive to the evolving times.

Many of these reconceptualists draw on critical theory. The main thrust of critical theory is to enable people to reflect and critique the dominant socioeconomic class structure and the ways in which the curriculum serves to perpetuate such structure. The theory draws from Marxism and neo-Marxist theories. Robert Young notes that the early critical theorists urged us to see schooling as part of the larger social order. For example, Marx viewed the social order as being oppressive to the workers, and as maintaining an underclass—or what he called the proletariat. It was the purpose of education to enable these workers to recognize their oppression and to use education to overcome such oppression.[67] Many of the early reconstructionists, such as George Counts and Harold Rugg, also envisioned the social order as discriminatory and oppressive toward the masses of the poor and working class. This emphasis on overcoming oppression, on liberation or emancipation, continues with current critical theorists.

To the critical theorist, liberation or emancipation means freeing oneself from the accepted ideology of current social conventions, beliefs, and modes of operation. It uses theory to get individuals to reflect on the current scene and to realize that it needs modification. People need to organize socially so that they will have the power to create new worlds and new societies. Students must be empowered by the curriculum to question the values of the current social and political scene. They are to analyze the current reality and then reflect on those beliefs and ideas that contribute to their lives.

Critical theorists contend that individuals' places in society result not from their free choices, but rather from the actions performed by the economically elite who control our competitive economy. Critical theorists argue that individuals are enslaved in our highly capitalist system. People strive to obtain meaningless certificates to the point that they are more interested in the document than in intelligence. Students, for instance, are more interested in passing tests than in gaining knowledge. The system forces us all to be passive recipients of the rewards. Critical theorists wish to use theory to enable curriculum developers to create programs that will free students of this form of existence. The main aim is to make students fully aware of themselves and of the fact that society must be altered to allow both self-freedom and collective freedom.[68]

Critical theorists counsel individuals to be aware of more than their economic shackles. Curricular experiences should promote in students an awareness of themselves as social beings. With such recognition, students will realize that their political views, religious beliefs, and understandings of gender role, even their views of the nature of meaning, are shaped by dominant perspectives.[69] Awareness of how these dominant perspectives influence them will nurture desires to change, to take charge of themselves, to alter their perspectives of what it means to be a person living in communion with others. Cognizant of how the dominant group limits their potential, students will be able to mount strategies to liberate themselves.

Critical theorists do not claim objectivity or espouse a neutrality. Indeed, their "take on the current world" is very negative. Critical theorists "shout" about their values and aims. They work toward and write about ways to attain an education that will erase social inequality, the marginalization of groups, and the suffering of the oppressed.[70] Their rallying cry seems to be "race, class, and gender." Critical theorists use theory as prescription and guidance. Frequently, they employ their theoretical stances to delegitimize any opposing views. In a sense, they have become entrapped in their own metanarrative by only looking at the world from a particular political bias.

Closely aligned with critical theory, if not just an aspect of it, is feminist theory. Feminist theoreticians reflect and hypothesize on the imbalances and inequities experienced by women in our society and the world. They contemplate the reasons for this and ways in which to liberate women from patterns of oppression. Feminist theory aims to make the world better for women. Theories are required to guide an emancipatory politics for women and others.[71]

Emancipatory politics certainly directs our attention to the social–political foundation. Answers to the questions raised by feminists require going outside what is curriculum and how to organize it. The questions relate to who is controlling the content of the curriculum and for what purpose. How are women depicted in the curriculum? Who has access to the privileged subjects of the curriculum?

Some feminists hold that, if feminist theory is a systematic synthesis of various feminist studies that clearly reveal gender inequality and other forms of discrimination, the purpose of feminist theory is to lay the foundations for creating theories or a theory of justice.[72] This focus on justice will require all of us in education, and in curriculum specifically, to reflect on our philosophical foundations, as well as the social–political foundations.

Feminists, like critical theorists, are concerned with emancipation from a society and its schools, which are basically viewed from a negative stance. This is emancipation not given, but rather taken. Marilyn Frye posits that the first and most fundamental act of feminist emancipation was for feminists to grant themselves authority as perceivers of their own situations in a world that both included and excluded them. In recognizing this authority, feminists discovered agreement in the experiences and perceptions of women. Feminists celebrated women's experience–voice and perceptual–knowledge as a means of both rewriting and re-creating the world. Analyzing and thus drawing from this accumulation of women's experiences, feminist theorists are striving and succeeding in creating theories that will address perceived inequities. As Frye notes, "what we are about is remetaphoring the world."[73]

The idea of creating new metaphors of the world also applies to the realms of curriculum. Different ways of viewing the curriculum influence how people theorize about it. Pinar continues to be a leader in suggesting different metaphors to influence our thinking. But he is not the only one. The authors of this text often think of curriculum as literary theater that brings to life meaningful scripts that engage the student audience in learning. However, Pinar has suggested that, besides thinking of curriculum as autobiographical–biographical text, as already briefly discussed, it is also productive for us to consider curriculum as political text, racial text, gender text, postmodern text, aesthetic text, theological text, and institutional text. Certainly, advocates of critical theory and feminist theory are very much believers in curriculum as political and gender texts. Our view of curriculum as theater reveals curriculum as aesthetic text. While there are not theories for each of these metaphoric considerations, there is at least the activity of theoretical talk.

Postmodernists

Theorizing about curriculum as if it were various texts fits well into postmodernism. In postmodernism, which can be interpreted to be an era or an attitude, or an attitude within an era, there is a reluctance to accept any one way of viewing the world. Postmodernists posit that there is not one way to interpret or theorize about the curriculum. No one master or grand narrative exists. No one paradigm is dominant. No one way of thinking of the curriculum reigns supreme. Curriculum is not just one thing. Our theorizing about curriculum cannot be viewed as precise, systematic hypothesizing and testing of hypotheses.

A difficulty in putting in print a definition of postmodernism is that print solidifies definition. There is and should be much argument as to what postmodernism is and even if it actually exists. It is useful for curricularists to conceptualize postmodernism as an attempt to accept and then to understand the fluid, emergent, and complex natures of reality, in our case the curriculum and its contexts. Modernism, which sprang forth in the Enlightenment period, accepts the world as a knowable mechanical machine. Postmodernism defines the world as emergent, fluid, chaotic, open, and interactive. It is an ongoing world. For us, the curriculum emerges, but never can be pinned down.

New terms, new concepts, and new paradigms attract followers. While discussion about postmodernism is really not common conversation among most practitioners, numerous curricularists have identified themselves, by their writing or conversations, as being postmodern. We find hybrid types or theorists identifying themselves as postmodern-feminists or postmodern-critical theorists. Such hybridizing is productive, for its challenges our ways of thinking and opens us to the excitement of pursuing new ideas, ways of thinking, and ways of doing. Postmodernism is an era of continual births, of new orders emerging our of the "soup" of chaos.

The term postmodern is increasingly included in the titles of curriculum books. William Doll has writing about a postmodern perspective on curriculum.[74] Patrick Slattery has written about curriculum development in the postmodern[75] era. Michael Peters has edited a text dealing with education and the postmodern condition.[76] One

might take some of these theorists to be in opposition to modernism. However, those involved in curricular reflection and activity might be better served to consider postmodernism as a movement to encourage and expand pluralism and to avoid the orthodoxy that some have defined as the hallmark of modernism. Charles Jencks states that postmodernism is not in opposition to modernism; rather, it is a continuation of modernism and its transcendence.[77]

Postmodernism centers on pluralism by stressing the mixing of genres, creating hybrid subject matter, celebrating differences of purpose, and applauding divergences of audiences. And all this variety is made even more exciting, complex, and dynamic in that everything is to be contested, nothing is sacred, no idea is exempt from challenge, and no curriculum is perennial.[78]

Postmodernism has a hybridizing intent, tearing out the threads of knowing and its cultural contexts and continually reweaving the threads—a garment being woven, constructed, and "dewoven," deconstructed, and rewoven and reconstructed.[79] David Harvey notes that most startling to most of us is postmodernism's "total acceptance of the ephemerality, the discontinuous, the fragmentation, and the chaotic.[80] Chaos rules! Harvey notes that Foucault instructs us to "develop action, thought, and desires by proliferation, juxtaposition, and disjunction . . . to prefer what is positive and multiple, difference over uniformity, flows over unities, mobile arrangements over systems."[81] Ideally, all educators should reflect on how to construct "glimpses," glimmers, of understanding, that will direct curricular actions.

Postmodernism is essentially a refusal to accept any unified representation of the world. There is no grand narrative or structure that explains all of life and the world that supports it. Realities are not well-established connections, but rather perpetually shifting fragments.[82] No system stands by itself to be discovered and then understood. To believe so is to accept the view of modernism and the connected view of structuralism. No underlying structures are invariant.[83] With regard to curriculum design, this means that there is no basic, unchanging structure of disciplines. Disciplines of knowledge, from which much of curriculum comes, are essentially fluid. Postmodernists also ascribe to poststructuralism, the view that no underlying structure exists and that there is a continual breaking apart and reattaching in new combinations of the "stuff" of reality.[84] Much theoretical discussion about poststructuralism deals with language and how we come to create and understand it. While many educational practitioners might consider language remote from classroom concerns, it is important to reflect on just what language is, since the curriculum is recorded and arranged in symbolic form, for example, language, and we teach the curriculum via the vehicle of language.

Modernists believe that there is a tight and identifiable relation between what is said (the signified or message) and how it is being said (the signifier or medium). In a sense, the teacher discussing a mountain is talking about something real. Once connections are made, they stand. Poststructuralists and postmodernists (perhaps we can consider them the same) believe that these relations between reality and language and the manner in which speech occurs are in continual flux; new combinations of meaning are occurring. Concepts discussed are constantly being reshaped by the very act of discussion. No meaning is fixed. We construct meaning; we create text. Readers deconstruct text in order to reconstruct their personal meaning of text.[85]

Theorizing about poststructuralism within postmodernism is important if we consider curricula as types of text and pedagogy as types of language. Certainly, we need not accept the results of such theorizing as definite. Indeed, a postmodernist would insist that we remain open to challenging our own "favored" positions and actually "walking away" from those arguments and positions that we hold most dear. If we are unwilling to do this, then we have accepted a meta or grand narrative. We have become a victim of our own ideology. We have sabotaged our continual search for meaning and the usefulness of meaning.

We need to engage in continual deconstruction of our world, and of our curriculum world. This does not mean destruction. Rather it means engaging in a manner of thinking, more so than accepting a particular philosophy, that allows us to look inside one text for another, to meld one text into another, and/or to create an entirely new text from the texts encountered.[86]

Much of the current theoretical "talk" can be understood more completely if we think of curricula as various texts, and culture as a series of texts affecting each other and generating additional texts, and politics as varied texts competing for our attention. Some posit that not only do people holding and creating various texts interact and challenge each other, but the very texts being interwoven have lives of their own.[87]

Much of the theoretical talk within the postmodernist camp causes us to look at curricular foundations with different eyes. The foundations are not static; neither are they separate. Our reflection on curricular matters must draw on the weaving and reweaving of our understandings of these foundations. As Slattery notes,

> curriculum ... in the postmodern era emphasizes discourses that promote understanding of the cultural, historical, political, ecological, aesthetic, theological, and autobiographical impact of the curriculum on the human conditions, social structures, and ecosphere rather than the planning, design, implementation, and evaluation of context-free and value-neutral schooling events and trivial information.[88]

What should I teach on Monday? This question has never been more challenging. And the answer to our query at any one time is likely to, actually must, change as the total dynamics of life continues. Never has there been a time when the theoretical and philosophical understandings of the myriad realms of life been more central to curricular work.

DIRECTIONS FOR THE FUTURE

Theorizers focusing on curriculum, regardless of their particular philosophical camp, do share a common concern: to make sense of human experience and human knowledge in order to promote in people (teachers and students) those competencies, skills, understandings, and values requisite for growth and prosperity. This is no small task—to account for and to affect the quality of human experiences. It is this very complexity of human experience that makes theorizers recognize the extraordinarily difficult thing that they are attempting to do—to generate theories of curriculum so as to guide, explain, describe, and in some cases predict action.

Curriculum Inquiry

Curricularists are confronted with making sense of the world, not only to describe it but to manage it in the present and to entertain and initiate ways of modifying it in the future. The reconceptualists have suggested that curricularists take on a psychoanalytic posture in order to discover their inner worlds before describing and guiding their outer worlds. Decker Walker, who is classified by some as a conceptual curricularist, has outlined five questions:

1. What are the major features of a given curriculum?
2. What are the personal and social consequences that a given curriculum feature elicits?
3. What accounts for the stability and change in curriculum features?
4. What accounts for people's judgments of the merit or worth of various curriculum features?
5. What sorts of curriculum features should be part of a curriculum designed for a particular purpose?[89]

Walker apparently views curriculum as a practical field of study that is to create some product that, when experienced by students, will make a difference in their learning. However, Walker's concept of a "curriculum feature" is vague. Perhaps, however, a precise conception is not possible because there are so many definitions and conceptions of the curriculum.

To make sense out of the dynamics of the curriculum field, curricularists need to analyze the total educational environment in which experience occurs. This includes the school and the outside community. A "good" theory of curriculum cannot ignore the influence of the surrounding environment or the meaning generated by the theory will be incomplete. Even when approaching curriculum from a global or macroanalytic stance, however, curricularists will not be able to manage the total picture or use such theory to manage the total educational drama. At best, they will be able to plan or modify portions of the curriculum and the environment affecting them.

Conceptualizing the Task

There is much diversity of thought about what curriculum is, what it should be, and how it should be theorized. Debate exists, too, about the units of analysis in theorizing about and conducting research in this field. Is the unit of analysis the school district, the school, the classroom, or the student? Is the unit of analysis the interacting network extant between the school and the local community? Is the unit the content, the experiences, the skills, or the values we are attempting to convey?

The task for theorizers of curriculum is to reflect about the many dimensions of this field. Curriculum types can theorize about the total curriculum field, where the field is going and why—its overall dynamics. Or they can theorize on a micro level—about the various elements or aspects of curriculum, say curriculum development, curriculum implementation, or curriculum evaluation. Whether theorists approach the field of curriculum globally or break it into micro elements, we must realize that a diversity of approaches exists influenced by the "mind sets" these theorists bring to their inquiries.

A BALANCED APPROACH TO THEORIZING

For most of this century, the traditional school of theorizing has been dominant. Especially in research, this school has relied primarily on quantitative inquiry. Empirical investigation has been the norm, and the classroom has been viewed as a laboratory in which variables are to be manipulated in a controlled atmosphere.

This type of research is valid and will continue to be employed. However, curricularists who wish to understand curriculum as a phenomenon that is much more than just a subject in school are realizing that much information can be gained from qualitative inquiry in the schools and the general society. Indeed, many curricularists recognize that we need to draw our theorizing approaches and investigative methods from fields formerly thought to be outside education, fields such as sociology, linguistics, political science, anthropology, phenomenology, psychiatry, and theology.

Those who urge us to consider curricula as various types of texts are drawing from many of these new fields. And those who advocate poststructuralism and postmodernism are not only drawing from these new fields, but also are giving new interpretations to the more traditional fields of inquiry. Scientific theorizing and the research supporting such have changed much from the "postures" of scientists at the beginning of the twentieth century. A crucial point is that all involved are theorizing about the nature and purpose of the curriculum, approaching their realities through their own perspectives, and being influenced by their own ideologies.

Those involved in the field of curriculum, and this includes practitioners, seek understanding of the curriculum phenomenon. It is essential that we all accept that our actions toward understanding require "a many-pronged inquiry that uses any means that might have bearing" on our search.[90] We can approach our inquiries from a particular ideology, but we must recognize that other ideologies of merit exist or may come into being. We need to possess a willingness to function within various ideological camps in our engagements with the field of curriculum.

Balance does not require a midpoint. Balance depends on the weight one gives to various positions, questions, theories, dispositions, values, and views. It is likely that curriculum theorizing will become even more complex. We are far beyond the times of either–or, modern or postmodern. We are both–and in our views. We are modern and postmodern. We are both liberal and conservative, both structuralists and poststructuralists, both static and emergent.

In discussing postmodern times, David Harvey has noted that our times must be considered "fragmentary and ephemeral by the sheer plurality and elusiveness of cultural forms wrapped in the mysteries of rapid flux and change."[91] However one names the times, Harvey's comments are "right on." In our seeking to understand curriculum, we need to realize that we only have partial pictures, only fragments of life's puzzles. We need to be wary of confining ourselves within our terminology and trapping ourselves in particular approaches. Curriculum as a field is fluid, with strong currents and countercurrents exerting forces and counterforces. Whatever our theorizing is about and whatever our methods of theoretical inquiry, we are very much immersed within a chaotic field of curriculum extant within chaotic social and natural worlds. Curriculum theory "writ large" is even more important for all educators, given the dynamics of present and emerging times.

CONCLUSION

In this chapter we primarily discussed the state of curriculum theory. We presented the nature of theory by outlining the various types of theory possible and the different functions that theory could serve. It is not likely that total agreement about the nature and purpose of theory will be forthcoming in the near future. Hopefully, there is some level of agreement about the steps necessary for theorizing. The first step is conceivably the greatest challenge: to come to some kind of agreement about what terms to use. Until theorists have some consensus on the meaning of major terms in curriculum, they are going to be hard pressed to produce many theories of high utility.

Although the "slipperiness" of terms has perhaps prevented a dominant curriculum theory from arising from the field, models depicting the curriculum and its various components are certainly not lacking. We presented several in this chapter to give readers a feel for the diversity of opinion, as well as to note the common elements that draw the attention of curricularists.

Where do we go from here? What is the future of theory? Some theorists will likely continue to study curriculum from a macro perspective and others from a micro perspective. Regardless of approach, a balance will be needed; not only a balance of approach, but also a balance among the types of professionals involved in theorizing and a balance among curricularists in schools, colleges, universities, and even in state, regional, and federal agencies.

ENDNOTES

1. Ivor F. Goodson, *Studying Curriculum* (New York: Teachers College Press, 1994).

2. A. Wise, *Legislated Learning: The Bureaucratization of the American Classroom* (Berkeley: University

of California Press, 1979), as quoted in Ivor F. Goodson, *Studying Curriculum*, p. 26.

3. William F. Pinar, William M. Reynolds, Patrick Slattery, and Peter M. Taubman, *Understanding Curriculum* (New York: Peter Lang, 1995).

4. Ibid.

5. Goodson, *Studying Curriculum*.

6. Joe L. Kincheloe and Shirley Steinberg, "The More Questions We Ask, The More Questions We Ask," in Joe L. Kincheloe and Shirley R. Steinberg, eds., *Thirteen Questions* (New York: Peter Lang, 1995), pp. 1–11.

7. Bradley J. Macdonald, ed., *Theory as a Prayerful Act* (New York: Peter Lang, 1995).

8. Max van Manen, "Pedagogical Theorizing." Paper presented at the annual AERA conference, April 1980, referenced in Macdonald, ed., *Theory as a Prayerful Act*, p. 181.

9. Macdonald, ed., *Theory as a Prayerful Act*.

10. Hilda Taba, *Curriculum Development: Theory and Practice* (New York: Harcourt Brace, 1962).

11. George J. Posner, *Analyzing the Curriculum* (New York: McGraw-Hill, 1992).

12. George A. Beauchamp, *Curriculum Theory,* 4th ed. (Itasca, Ill.: Peacock, 1981).

13. Abraham Kaplan, *The Conduct of Inquiry* (San Francisco: Chandler, 1964), p. 295.

14. Richard E. Snow, "Theory Construction for Research on Teaching," in R. M. Travers, ed., *Second Handbook of Research on Teaching* (Chicago: Rand McNally, 1973), p. 78.

15. Joseph Schwab, *The Practical: A Language for Curriculum* (Washington, D.C.: National Education Association, 1970).

16. Allan A. Glatthorn, *Curriculum Leadership* (Glenview, Ill.: Scott, Foresman, 1987).

17. M. Frances Klein, "Approaches to Curriculum Theory and Practice," in J. T. Sears and J. D. Marshall, eds., *Teaching and Thinking about Curriculum* (New York: Teachers College Press, Columbia University, 1990), pp. 3–14.

18. Ibid.

19. Herbert Feigl, "Principles and Problems of Theory Construction in Psychology," in W. Dennis, ed., *Current Trends of Psychological Theory* (Pittsburgh: University of Pittsburgh Press, 1951), pp. 182–195.

20. Fred N. Kerlinger, *Foundations of Behavioral Research,* 2nd ed. (New York: Holt, Rinehart, 1976), p. 10.

21. Ira J. Gordon, ed., *Criteria for Theories of Instruction* (Washington, D.C.: Association for Supervision and Curriculum Development, 1968).

22. Herbert M. Kliebard, "Curriculum Theory: Give Me a 'For Instance,' " *Curriculum Inquiry* (Summer 1977), pp. 257–268.

23. Richard D. Kimpston, Howard Y. Williams, and William S. Stockton, "Ways of Knowing and the Curriculum," *Educational Forum* (Winter 1992), pp. 153–172.

24. Macdonald, ed., *Theory as a Prayerful Act.*

25. Max van Manen, "Edifying Theory: Serving the Good," *Theory into Practice* (Winter 1982), pp. 44–49.

26. May Brodbeck, "Logic and Scientific Method in Research on Teaching," in N. L. Gage, ed., *Handbook of Research on Teaching* (Chicago: Rand McNally, 1963), pp. 44–93.

27. Kaplan, *The Conduct of Inquiry,* p. 20.

28. van Manen, "Pedagogical Theorizing," referenced in Macdonald, ed., *Theory as a Prayerful Act.*

29. Ibid.

30. Kenneth R. Hoover, *The Elements of Social Scientific Thinking* (New York: St. Martin's Press, 1984).

31. C. E. Noble, "Induction, Deduction, Abduction," in M. H. Marx and F. E. Goodson, eds., *Theories in Contemporary Psychology,* 2nd ed. (New York: Macmillan, 1976), pp. 300–308.

32. Beauchamp, *Curriculum Theory.*

33. Brodbeck, "Logic and Scientific Method in Research on Teaching."

34. Gordon, *Criteria for Theories of Instruction.*

35. M. H. Marx, "Theorizing," in Marx and Goodson, eds., *Theories in Contemporary Psychology,* pp. 261–285.

36. Francis P. Hunkins, "How We Frame Our Questions," unpublished paper, 1997.

37. Franklin Bobbitt, *The Curriculum* (Boston: Houghton Mifflin, 1918).

38. Bobbitt, *The Curriculum;* W. W. Charters, *Curriculum Construction* (New York: Macmillan, 1923).

39. Kliebard, "Curriculum Theory: Give Me a 'For Instance.' "

40. John Dewey, *The School and Society* (Chicago: University of Chicago Press, 1900).

41. Kliebard, "Curriculum Theory: Give Me a 'For Instance.' "

42. Beauchamp, *Curriculum Theory,* p. 35.

43. Ralph W. Tyler, *Basic Principles of Curriculum and Instruction* (Chicago: University of Chicago Press, 1949).

44. Beauchamp, *Curriculum Theory.*

45. Occasional papers by Elizabeth Maccia and George Maccia (Columbus, Ohio: Bureau of Educational Research and Service, Ohio State University, 1963–1965).

46. Mauritz Johnson, "Definitions and Models in Curriculum Theory," *Educational Theory* (April 1967), pp. 17–32.

47. James B. Macdonald, "Educational Models for Instruction," in J. B. Macdonald and R. R. Leeper, eds., *Theories of Instruction* (Washington, D.C.: Association for Supervision and Curriculum Development, 1965), pp. 93–98.

48. Gail McCutcheon, "What in the World Is Curriculum Theory?" *Theory into Practice* (Winter 1982), pp. 18–23.

49. Bernice J. Wolfson, "Psychological Theory and Curricular Thinking," in A. Molnar, ed., *Current Thought on Curriculum* (Alexandria, Va.: Association for Supervision and Curriculum Development, 1985), pp. 53–72.

50. Decker F. Walker, "Curriculum Theory Is Many Things to Many People," *Theory into Practice* (Winter 1982), pp. 62–65.

51. Elizabeth Vallance, "The Practical Uses of Curriculum Theory," *Theory into Practice* (Winter 1982), pp. 4–10.

52. Dwayne Huebner, "Toward a Remaking of Curricular Language," in W. Pinar, ed., *Heightened Consciousness, Cultural Revolution, and Curriculum Theory* (Berkeley, Calif.: McCutchan, 1974), pp. 36–37.

53. Henry A. Giroux, *Postmodernism, Feminism, and Cultural Politics* (Albany, N.Y.: State University of New York Press, 1991).

54. Kliebard, "Curriculum Theory as Metaphor."

55. Paulo Freire, *The Politics of Education, Culture, Power, and Liberation* (South Hadley, Mass.: Bergin & Garvey, 1985).

56. William Pinar, "Notes on the Curriculum Field 1978," *Educational Researcher* (September 1978), pp. 5–12.

57. John McNeil, *Curriculum: A Comprehensive Introduction,* 4th ed. (Glenview, Ill.: Scott Foresman, 1990).

58. William Pinar, "Heightened Consciousness, Cultural Revolution and Curriculum Theory: An Introduction," in W. Pinar, ed., *Heightened Consciousness, Cultural Revolution, and Curriculum Theory,* pp. 1–15.

59. Dorothy Huenecke, "What Is Curriculum Theory? What Are Its Implications for Practice?" *Educational Leadership* (January 1982), pp. 290–294.

60. Klein, "Approaches to Curriculum Theory and Practice."

61. Huenecke, "What Is Curriculum Theory? What Are Its Implications for Practice?"

62. Pinar et. al., *Understanding Curriculum.*

63. James Macdonald, "Curriculum Theory," in J. R. Gress and D. E. Purpel, eds., *Curriculum: An Introduction to the Field* (Berkeley, Calif.: McCutchan, 1978), pp. 44–56.

64. Pinar et al., *Understanding Curriculum.*

65. W. Pinar, ed., *Curriculum Theorizing: The Reconceptualists,* pp. 283–298; William Pinar and Madeline Grumet, *Toward a Poor Curriculum* (Dubuque, Ia.: Kendell-Hunt, 1976); and Pinar, *Contemporary Curriculum Discourse* (Scottsdale, Ariz.: Gorsuch Scarisbrick, 1988).

66. Pinar et al., *Understanding Curriculum.*

67. Robert Young, *A Critical Theory of Education* (New York: Teachers College Press, Columbia University, 1990).

68. Klein, "Approaches to Curriculum Theory and Practice"; Schubert, *Curriculum: Perspective, Paradigm, and Possibility.*

69. Kincheloe and Steinberg, "The More Questions We Ask, The More Questions We Ask."

70. Ibid.

71. Regenia Gagnier, "Feminist Postmodernism: The End of Feminism or the End of Theory?" in Deborah L. Rhode, ed. *Theoretical Perspectives on Sexual Difference* (New Haven, Conn.: Yale University Press, 1990), p. 21–30.

72. Ibid.

73. Marilyn Frye, "The Possibility of Feminist Theory," in Deborah L. Rhode, ed., *Theoretical Perspectives on Theoretical Difference* (New Haven, Conn.: Yale University Press, 1990), p. 183.

74. William E. Doll, Jr., *A Post Modern Perspective on Curriculum* (New York: Teachers College Press, 1993).

75. Patrick Slattery, *Curriculum Development in the Postmodern Era* (New York: Garland Publishing, Inc., 1995).

76. Michael Peters, ed., *Education and the Postmodern Condition* (Westport, Conn.: Bergin and Garvey, 1995).

77. Charles Jencks, ed., *The Post-Modern Reader* (New York: St. Martin's Press, 1992).

78. Ibid.

79. Ibid.

80. David Harvey, "The Condition of Postmodernity," in Jencks, ed., *The Post-Modern Reader,* p. 302.

81. Foucault, cited in Harvey, "The Condition of Postmodernity."

82. Harvey, "The Condition of Postmodernity."

83. Pinar et al., *Understanding Curriculum.*

84. Harvey, "The Condition of Postmodernity."

85. Ibid.

86. Ibid.

87. Ibid.

88. Slattery, *Curriculum Development in the Postmodern Era,* p. 152.

89. Decker Walker, "What Are the Problems Curricularists Ought to Study?" *Curriculum Theory Network* (Vol. 4, 1974), pp. 217–218.

90. Robert Cummings Neville, *The Highroad around Modernism* (Albany, N.Y.: State University of New York Press, 1992).

91. Harvey, "The Condition of Postmodernity," p. 315.

7

CURRICULUM DEVELOPMENT

Focusing Questions

1. How would you describe the technical-scientific approach to curriculum development?
2. What roles did Bobbitt and Charters play within the field of curriculum development?
3. In what ways are the various models of the technical-scientific approach alike?
4. Define the nontechnical approach to curriculum development.
5. Explain how the deliberation model of curriculum development connects the technical and the nontechnical approaches to curriculum development.
6. How can curriculum development be approached as conversation?
7. How does the postpositivist model of curriculum enhance the idea of intuition and/or imagination in education?
8. Which components are central to the curriculum development process?
9. Who are the key participants in developing a curriculum? Should the roles of students, parents, and community residents be increased?

A select group of curriculum scholars has announced that the "era of curriculum development is past."[1] The field of curriculum is no longer preoccupied with development. Rather, those tilling the fertile soil of curriculum are now solely driven to understand curriculum. Granted, curricularists are concerned with broad issues such as social policy, cultural mores, and political power struggles, but educators in schools confronted with engaging students in learning and empowering them to construct their own meanings and to comprehend the meanings of scholars still wish to know how to take curriculum as vision to actual program. Even scholars who claim that the era of curriculum development is past contradict themselves, to some degree, when they note that to understand curriculum does not reduce the desire of educators to change the curriculum at both theoretical and actual levels.

Certainly, scholars as well as practitioners of curriculum are concerned with more than just creating and implementing courses of study. Both wish to comprehend the processes by which curricula are conceived, created, implemented, and evaluated. But an expanded range of concerns among curricularists does not mean that there is nothing more to know about curriculum development or that we need not consider alternative ways of creating curriculum.

The domain of curriculum development is not static. New procedures are being suggested for changing existing curricula that draw on postmodern ways of thinking and employ new paradigms of curricular thought. We in the field of curriculum have not murdered curriculum development either as an area of thought or as a means of making real educational programs appropriate for existing and evolving times. It is surely not in the spirit of deliberation within the curriculum community to classify as "intellectually inactive" those who wish to include procedures of curriculum development in curriculum talk. Indeed, many persons who classify themselves as avantgarde curriculum postmodernists are suggesting ways of engaging individuals in creating curricula. We still have much to learn about curriculum development.

It is the belief of the authors of this text that successful education, however it is defined, requires careful planning. Without planning, confusion and conflict are likely to characterize curriculum activity. Educators originate curriculum development strategies. They formulate master plans prior to creating or implementing a program for students. How they conceptualize the plan will be influenced by their awareness of and sensitivity to issues—both present and anticipated. Certainly, few people can construct a curriculum without giving some thought to goals; to content; to learning experiences, methods, and materials; and to evaluation.

The need to plan effective curricula is obvious; the difficulty, however, is that there are various ways to define curriculum development. Also, several curriculum designs dictate what factors should receive attention: subject matter, students, or society. Also, it is difficult to be precise or to plan what is not defined with any universality. Not everyone agrees what curriculum is or what is involved in curriculum development. We present here a broad definition to allow the different views and interpretations to coexist with ours—which posits that curriculum development draws on visions of what curriculum is and what curriculum is for, as well as on principles from both our technical and scientific past and our emerging nontechnical postmodern stances. Curriculum development consists of various processes (technical, humanistic, and artistic) that allow schools and schoolpeople to realize certain educational goals.

Ideally, all those affected by a curriculum should be involved in the process of development.

Although numerous models exist from which to choose, most models can be classified as either technical or nontechnical, or holistic. Perhaps this type of classification represents our current stage of curriculum knowledge development. Many social and educational critics indicate that we are leaving or have left the modern period, which stressed the technical, the precise, the certain and have entered into the postmodern period, which emphasizes the nontechnical, the emergent, the uncertain. However, our history in the modern or technical period is much longer than our time in this new age, the postmodern. Thus we have more technical models upon which to draw guidance in curriculum development. The newness of this emergent time that we are experiencing is suggested by the fact that we really do not know what to call it, so we call it the postmodern. Likewise, we are stymied in our attempts to be original in naming our emerging processes of curriculum development. We just classify them as nontechnical.

The authors are cognizant that there is a danger in creating a dualism in curriculum development approaches. Dualisms, such as technical–nontechnical, imply that the first term or concept presented is the preferred. For example, high is contrasted with low, up with down, education with training, and big with small, all suggesting that high is better than low, up better than down, education better than training, and so on. Those who argue that the time of curriculum development is past place understanding with development in a dualism that suggests that it is better to understand than to develop.

By classifying an approach as nontechnical or technical, we do not mean to present either approach as positive or negative. Rather, we wish to contrast two basic postures. Persons who believe in a curriculum design that stresses subject matter usually favor technical approaches to curriculum development. Individuals who celebrate the learner as key to curriculum focus frequently advocate employing a nontechnical or holistic approach. Persons who consider the curriculum a vehicle for addressing social problems can favor either approach.

The authors are also aware of the danger of suggesting that contrasting categories are exclusive. In real curriculum work, people are messy in creating educational programs, in formulating units and lessons for their classes. While one needs to separate and contrast in order to discuss approaches in a text such as this, in actuality there is a fuzziness in boundaries, a permeability between the boundaries of the approaches.

TECHNICAL-SCIENTIFIC APPROACH

The technical-scientific approach to education and to curriculum is a way of thinking. To those who believe in the approach, it is not a vehicle for dehumanizing education, but rather a way of planning curricula to optimize students' learning and to allow them to increase their output. According to this point of view, curriculum development is a plan or blueprint for structuring the learning environment and coordinating the elements of personnel, materials, and equipment.

A technical-scientific view can enable us to comprehend curriculum from a macro or broad view and to understand it as a complex unity of parts organized to serve a common function—the education of individuals. It also allows us to have a plan in mind.

The technical-scientific approach requires that educators use a rational approach to accomplish their tasks and that they believe that it is possible to outline systematically those procedures that will facilitate the creation of curricula. The various models employ a means-end paradigm that suggests that the more rigorous the means, the more likely the desired ends will be attained. Followers of this approach indicate that such a systematically designed program can be evaluated. However, others question just how precise the evaluation can be.

The various technical-scientific models exhibit what James Macdonald would call a "technological" rationality as opposed to an "aesthetic rationality." Macdonald notes that there is a press for this rationality in the way schools are organized.[2] Persons who have this orientation tend to believe that there is a large body of educational knowledge and that efforts should be made to ensure that students are presented with opportunities to gain such knowledge. Macdonald wrote that those with a technological consciousness prize optimum growth, maximum efficiency, and effectiveness of the system in delivering education.

History of Technical-Scientific Approach

Students of the history of curriculum development have located the origin and substance of the technical-scientific model in the schools' attempt, at the turn of the century, to adapt the principles of bureaucracy to methods that could be considered scientific. Early educators reasoned that using empirical methods (surveys and analysis of human conduct) would answer the curriculum question: What shall be taught? The push for a science of curriculum making paralleled the rise of science— biology, physics, and chemistry—during the nineteenth and twentieth centuries and also the notion of "machine theory"—time and motion studies— evolving in the world of business and industry. In education, especially in curriculum, these models evolved with the work of Bobbitt and Charters.

Bobbitt and Charters. Bobbitt compared creating a curriculum to the task of constructing a railroad. Once the general route is planned, the railroad builder then gets into the particulars of engaging in surveying and eventually laying of track. Developing a curriculum is essentially like planning the route that a person must travel from infancy "to the goals of his growth, his culture, and his special abilities."[3] The educator must, like the railroad engineer, "take a broad over-view of the entire field . . . [see] the major factors in perspective and in relation." In doing this, a general plan for the educational program can be formulated. To this general plan could be added specific "surveying actions [for] determining content and experiences necessary for the [learner]."[4]

For Bobbitt the first task of curriculum development was to "discover the activities which ought to make up the lives of students and along with these, the abilities and personal qualities necessary for proper performance."[5] From this activity analysis, educational objectives were derived. Bobbitt was insistent that the analysis address the actual activities of humans being sure to consider the broad range of human experiences. Bobbitt's contemporary, Werrett Charters, was also a believer in activity analysis. However, Charters noted that "changes in the curriculum are always preceded by modifications in our conception of the aim of education."[6] The selection of school content and experiences was influenced by our aims, the ideals, we wish to address.

Charters wanted educators to connect aims or ideals with activities that individuals performed. Charters suggested a sequence of steps for curriculum construction that is still rather timely, showing the foundational impact he had on the thinking of his contemporaries and subsequent generations of curriculum decision makers. He noted that curriculum construction had four steps: "(1) selecting objectives, (2) dividing them into ideals and activities, (3) analyzing them to the limits of working units, and (4) collecting methods of achievement."[7]

For Charters, philosophy supplied the ideals that were to serve as objectives and standards. He noted that the curriculum could contain both primary and derived subjects. *Primary subjects* were those found directly within the items of a job analysis, derived from other subjects. Thus educators looking at the task of being a weather reporter would note that the activity required one to fill out various types of reports, indicating that report writing would be included under the subject of English. The job activity of weather reporting, while showing a need for report writing, also required a knowledge of physics and mathematics. Charters defined such information as comprising *derived subjects,* noting that "these are service subjects which are important not because they are directly useful in the performance of activities, but because they are derived from material which has practical service value."[8]

These two men firmly established the scientific movement in curriculum making. They pointed out that curriculum development is a process that will, if followed, result in a meaningful program for pupils. They initiated a concern for the relation of goals, objectives, and activities, pointing out that the selection of goals is a normative process, whereas the selection of objectives and activities is empirical and scientific. They indicated that curricular activity can be planned and systematically studied and evaluated.

Through the efforts of men like Bobbitt and Charters, concern grew for curriculum as a field of study. The field achieved independent status upon the establishment of the Society for Curriculum Study in 1932. In 1938, Teachers College at Columbia University established a department of curriculum and teaching. For the next 20 years, Teachers College dominated the field of curriculum, even surpassing the earlier influence of the University of Chicago.

The Tyler Model: Four Basic Principles. Without doubt, Tyler's is one of the best known, technical-scientific models. In 1949, Tyler published *Basic Principles of Curriculum and Instruction,* in which he outlined a rationale for examining the problems of curriculum and instruction.[9] He mentioned that those involved in curriculum inquiry must try to define the (1) purposes of the school, (2) educational experiences related to the purposes, (3) organization of these experiences, and (4) evaluation of the purposes.

By "purposes," Tyler was referring to objectives. He indicated that curriculum planners should identify these general objectives by gathering data from three sources: the subject matter, the learners, and the society. After identifying numerous general objectives, the curriculum planners were to refine them by filtering them through two screens, the philosophy of the school and the psychology of learning. What resulted from such screening were specific instructional objectives. Note, however, that even though Tyler used the term *instructional objectives* he was not advocating the narrow behavioral objectives that have been advocated in recent years.

Tyler then discussed how to select educational experiences that would allow the attainment of objectives. Learning experiences had to take into account both the previous experience and the perceptions that the learner brings to a situation. Also, the experiences were to be selected in light of what educators know about learning and human development.

Tyler next talked about the organization and sequencing of these experiences. He purported that the ordering of the experiences had to be somewhat systematic so as to produce a maximum cumulative effect. He thought that organizing elements, such as ideas, concepts, values, and skills, should be woven as threads into the curriculum fabric. These key elements could serve as organizers and means and methods of instruction, and they could relate different learning experiences among different subjects. The ideas, concepts, values, and skills could also link content within particular subjects.

Tyler's last principle deals with evaluating the effectiveness of planning and actions. Tyler considered evaluation to be important in curriculum development. He realized that it was necessary if educators were to find out whether the learning experiences actually produced the intended results. Also, it was important to determine whether the program was effective or ineffective. An evaluation should relate to all the objectives.

Although Tyler did not display his model of curriculum development graphically, several other people have. The authors' diagram of this procedure follows in Figure 7-1.

There is no denying that Tyler's thinking has greatly influenced the field of curriculum, especially curriculum development. The four questions that Tyler raised had and still have great appeal because they appear so reasonable. Despite much current criticism of Tyler's work as being too linear, that is, cause to effect, there is no denying that his thinking continues to be popular with school district personnel.[10] Even on university campuses, despite all the rhetoric at national curriculum conferences and the proclamations by some curricularists, Tyler's thinking is still evident. Individuals continue to be guided by his rationale due to its very reasonableness and workability. It works despite one's context or one's philosophical orientation.[11]

Tyler was asked in 1977 if he would change the "rationale" that he formulated in the 1940s. He indicated that in reviewing the initial syllabus from which came his four essential questions he found no reason to alter his rationale. However, he did note that he would put more emphasis on the active role of the student in the learning process. He also would attend to the nonschool areas of student learning in developing curriculum.[12] This advice continues to be timely. Today, there are more players in curriculum decision making, and the curriculum functions within the general society as well as in the school.

The Taba Model: Grass-roots Rationale.
Tyler's message certainly would have died out if he had been a voice crying in the wilderness. However, he was not; he had company, and still has. Among his colleagues was Hilda Taba, who was very influential in giving his approach to curriculum an added boost. In her book on curriculum development, *Curriculum Development: Theory and Practice* (1962), she argued that there was a definite order to creating the curriculum. Pursuing such order would facilitate attaining a more thoughtful and dynamically conceived curriculum.[13] Where Taba differed from Tyler was that she believed that those who teach the curriculum, the teachers, should participate in developing it. She advocated what has been called the grass-roots approach,[14] a model whose steps or stages

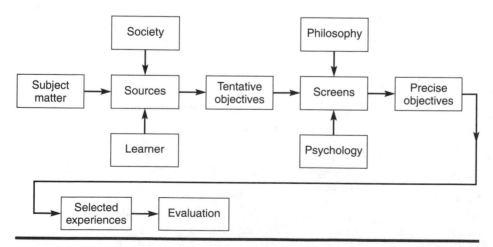

FIGURE 7-1   Tyler's Curriculum Development Model

are similar to Tyler's. Although Tyler did not advocate that his model only be employed by persons in the central office, educators during the early days of curriculum making thought that the central authorities really had the knowledge for creating curricula. This was the top-down or what some have called the administrative or line-staff model. Ideas from curriculum experts were frequently given to teachers to develop, and then administrators supervised the teachers to ensure that the ideas were implemented.

Taba felt that the administrative model was really in the wrong order. The curriculum should be designed by the users of the program. Teachers should begin the process by creating specific teaching-learning units for their students. She advocated that teachers take an inductive approach to curriculum development—starting with specifics and building to a general design— as opposed to the more traditional deductive approach—starting with the general design and working toward the specifics.

Taba noted seven major steps to her grass-roots model in which teachers would have major input:

1. *Diagnosis of needs.* The teacher (curriculum designer) starts the process by identifying the needs of the students for whom the curriculum is to be planned.

2. *Formulation of objectives.* After the teacher has identified needs that require attention, he or she specifies objectives to be accomplished.

3. *Selection of content.* The objectives selected or created suggest the subject matter or content of the curriculum. Not only should objectives and content match, but also the validity and significance of the content chosen needs to be determined.

4. *Organization of content.* A teacher cannot just select content, but must organize it in some type of sequence, taking into consideration the maturity of the learners, their academic achievement, and their interests.

5. *Selection of learning experiences.* Content must be presented to pupils and pupils must engage the content. At this point, the teacher selects instructional methods that will involve the students with the content.

6. *Organization of learning activities.* Just as content must be sequenced and organized, so must

the learning activities. Often the sequence of the learning activities is determined by the content. But the teacher needs to keep in mind the particular students whom he or she will be teaching.

7. *Evaluation and means of evaluation.* The curriculum planner must determine just what objectives have been accomplished. Evaluation procedures need to be considered by the students and teachers.

Taba's model has much merit. Nonetheless, according to some educators, putting such an effort into a grass-roots framework weakens it. Robert Zais maintains that the primary weakness is that it applies the concept of participatory democracy to a highly technical, complex, and specialized process. This does not mean that teachers cannot be involved—indeed, they must if curricula are to be actually used in the classroom. It does mean, however, that a "one person-one vote" rationale will not guarantee effective curricula.[15] Also, the grass-roots design assumes that teachers have the expertise and, perhaps more importantly, the time to engage in such extensive curricular activity. However, we do need to recognize that the grass-roots approach has made it abundantly clear that a broad base of involvement is essential for curriculum decision making.

Curriculum making requires compromise among administrators from the central office, supervisors from the local school, and teachers, students, and community members. Traditionally, the central office staff is charged with directing those actions that enable the various participators to engage in curriculum development. In a nontraditional approach, members of the community and teaching profession are given primary responsibility for developing the curriculum. See Curriculum Tips 7-1.

Hunkins's Decision-making Model. Hunkins presented another model of curriculum development that at first glance appears to be another technical–scientific example. It has seven major stages: curriculum conceptualization and legitimization; diagnosis; content selection; experience selection; implementation; evaluation; and maintenance. A scheme of the model is illustrated in Figure 7-2

What sets this model apart is its recommended first stage of curricular decision making:

===== *Curriculum Tips 7-1* =====

Steps Used in Planning Curricula

There is a commonness to most technical-scientific and top-down approaches to curriculum development. The sameness results from a certain logic implicit in thinking through curriculum planning. Ronald Doll lists a compendium of suggestions for planning programs that reveals this "sameness" in the scientific-technical approach.

1. *Surveying the scene.* It is logical to identify the context within which we are going to create a program. This surveying action is what allows district personnel to ascertain what makes their school system the same as or different from other systems.
2. *Assessing needs.* Needs most often focus on individuals, usually on students and occasionally on teachers. Rarely are the needs of the organization of the school considered in a needs assessment.
3. *Identifying and defining problems.* Once needs are identified, we require some demarkation of the nature of the problem. Not all needs are identified at the outset of the planning process; many emerge as the stages are activated.
4. *Recalling accepted aims and goals.* Needs and problems are shaped in part by the aims and goals of those involved in the planning and those present in the community in which the school is located. From the analysis of aims and goals, curriculum planners are able to generate program objectives or instructional objectives for the curricula.
5. *Marking proposals—and evaluating them.* At this step, we consider essential problems and the means of addressing them. Proposals are considered in light of the general aims and goals previously deemed appropriate for the school.
6. *Preparing designs.* Here, the shaping of the components of design and the selecting of the particular design for the program occur. Instructional materials and methods are reviewed and recommended.
7. *Organizing the work force.* This step seems a bit out of sequence. The school district in its adoption process looks at the work force in their attempt to establish and implement the curriculum.
8. *Supervising the planning process.* For planning to proceed smoothly, the process must not only be administered, but also supervised to determine if all is going as intended. Supervision may be directed by central/district policy, but usually it will be done at the school level by those directly involved in planning and developing the curriculum.
9. *Utilizing the products of planning.* This step is essentially performed by the classroom teacher. The degree of acceptance of the new program/material depends on whether teachers have been involved in the planning process and whether necessary inservice has been provided so that teachers feel comfortable with the new material and/or program.
10. *Applying evaluation means.* This refers to raising questions as to whether the actions of planning and implementation have actually produced some program that effectively addresses the aims, goals, and objectives of the curriculum. The key questions are "Does the program work? To what extent? How can it be improved?"

Source: Adapted from Ronald C. Doll, *Curriculum Improvement: Decision Making and Process,* 9th ed. (Boston: Allyn and Bacon, 1996).

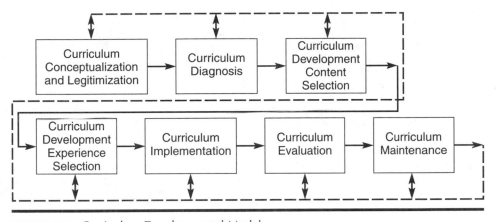

FIGURE 7-2 Curriculum Developmental Model.

Source: Francis P. Hunkins, *Curriculum Development Program Improvement* (Columbus, Ohio: Merrill, 1980), p. 17.

curriculum conceptualization and legitimization. This first stage demands that participants engage in deliberation regarding the nature of curriculum and also its educational and social–political value. This first stage requires curriculum decision makers, whoever they may be, to engage in a search for an understanding of curriculum, as well as just creating educational programs. It addresses the concerns of reconceptualists, of putting stress on understanding the nature and power of curriculum.

In this first stage one confronts the various conceptions of curriculum and recognizes that the field of curriculum is complicated, that making decisions about what ought to be taught and experienced by students is no simple decision. Such decisions are fraught with subtexts and power politics, as well as the social and cultural views that demand understanding and sophisticated thinking.[16] Those involved in the process of development realize that they must engage in deliberation in order to agree on what the curriculum is to mean in their school or school system. They must have a sense of the current discourses on curriculum. They must realize that curricular decision making and actions related to implementing programs are done in a social context. The field of curriculum is filled with various voices. Some are in harmony and others are engaged in separate and even divisive dialogue. In this first stage, one converses with the players to interpret the dis-

courses generated in the field by both scholars and practitioners.[17]

Also at this juncture we must legitimize our views of curriculum and its purposes. What should be known should certainly have value. But value is negotiated. Why is what we want to include in the curriculum legitimate activity? On what do we base our decisions? Ideally, those engaged in respectful deliberation will understand both the nature of curriculum and the assumptions and rationales that support the content suggested and actions recommended. No other model of curriculum development stresses as clearly the need for such essential curricular thinking and deliberation.

The second stage of the model, *curriculum diagnosis,* involves two major tasks: translating needs into causes and generating goals and objectives from the needs. In some instances, an identified need is caused not by the curriculum void, but by the nonteaching of that curriculum by teachers. Rather than generate a new program, what might be required is an in-service program for teachers to make them committed to and comfortable with the program already in place. When a new curriculum is judged as appropriate for addressing the needs of students, then goals and objectives are generated to serve as guidelines, and sometimes as statements of expected learning outcomes. Such goals and objectives serve as frameworks for determining content, the next stage in the model.

Content selection deals with the "what" of the curriculum. Content is the "stuff" of the curriculum. It is the "what" that is to be taught, the "what" that students are to learn. Content is the foundation of the curriculum. Content refers to facts, concepts, principles, theories, and generalizations. Content also refers to cognitive processes that learners employ when thinking about or studying the content. Also, content as process refers to the procedures students learn to use to apply their knowledge and skills and to communicate what they know to others.

The next step in the model is *experience selection.* This stage deals primarily with instruction. The key questions relate to how the content is to be delivered to students or experienced by them. What teaching methods will be employed? What educational activities will be designed to make learning effective and enjoyable? How will the content, the what, of the curriculum be experienced so that the goals and objectives selected for the schools' program are attained? At this stage the teacher decides what instructional materials will be employed: textbooks, software programs, films, reference books, primary materials, maps, pictures, and so on.

After experiences have been selected, organized, and matched with the content of the program, the curriculum is essentially ready for *implementation.* Curriculum implementation has two stages, an initial piloting of the curriculum to work out any minor problems in the program and the final diffusion of the tested program. To assure that the curriculum as designed will be delivered to and experienced by students, a management system needs to be set up by which the new program is introduced to the staff to develop a commitment to and comfort with the new program.

Once the program is implemented, we then engage in *evaluation.* This stage is usually conducted through the life of the curriculum: to furnish data so that decisions can be made to continue, modify, or discontinue the program. Often, schools only plan a series of student achievement tests to assess the effectiveness of a curriculum. A greater variety of means of gaining information should be considered.

The final stage of this model is *maintenance.* Curriculum maintenance encompasses the methods and means by which an implemented program is managed to assure its continued effective functioning. It deals with issues such as making sure that the new staff is educated into the ongoing system. It makes sure that budgets are sufficient to resupply necessary materials. It means that supervisors are available to assist teachers when a new strategy or content organization is to be tried. It infers communicating with the community, continuing a dialogue, so that parents feel a sense of ownership with the ongoing program. Often, once a curriculum has been implemented, schools forget that there needs to be some management design for continuing the program, for keeping it focused on the goals and objectives of the new program. Curricula not followed by a maintenance plan tend to disappear into the daily routine of the classroom, with teachers sometimes personalizing the programs to the point where they have little resemblance to the original curriculum.

A unique feature of this technical model is the feedback and adjustment loop depicted by the dashed lines. This loop allows decision makers as they proceed through the model to refer back to previous stages and to make necessary modifications.

This loop is an important feature of the model. It makes the model a systems view of curriculum decision making. This feedback loop denotes dynamism. It draws on the principle that a system is integrated into its environment.[18] Curriculum development employing this feedback and adjustment loop acts on the environment in which it finds itself and is also acted on by it. This aspect of the model contextualizes the process of curriculum making. One cannot ignore the space in which one's actions occur. One must be conscious of the space, the environment within which curricular decisions are and have been made. Past decisions and actions are open to analysis and change.[19] From the author's view, this stage in the model addresses many of the concerns of the critics of technical models, who say such models are not related to the times or to the context in which decisions are made.

Other technical-scientific models exist. Even though these model types tend to be used by advocates of subject-centered designs, who are perhaps more in the traditional philosophical and technological camps, the models really can be employed to develop a curriculum for any and all of the curriculum design orientations. Curricularists can be systematic in creating subject-centered, child-centered, or problem-centered curricula.

NONTECHNICAL-NONSCIENTIFIC APPROACH

The danger in noting that one set of approaches is systematic or rational is the implication that the other camp is nonsystematic or nonrational. Advocates of methods of curriculum development not in the technical-scientific camp, however, are not suggesting disorder. Rather, they are taking issue with some of the key assumptions underlying the technical-scientific approach and questioning some of the consequences that result from utilizing this approach to curriculum development.

The technical-scientific approach to curriculum suggests that the process of curriculum development has a high degree of objectivity, universality, and logic. It works on an assumption that reality can be defined and represented in symbolic form. Knowledge, as it were, can exist as a matter of fact, unaffected by the very process of creating and learning it. It states that the aims of education can be made known, can be stated precisely, and can be addressed in a linear fashion. The technical-scientific approach to curriculum exemplifies the belief in modernism, a view that praises rationality, objectivity, and certainty. In a sense, this approach views the world as a complex machine, but a machine that can be observed and manipulated.

In contrast, those in the nontechnical camp stress the subjective, personal, aesthetic, heuristic, and transactional. They stress not the outputs of production but rather the learner, especially through activity-oriented approaches to teaching and learning. Those favoring this approach note that not all ends of education can be known nor, indeed, do they need to be known in all cases. This approach considers that the curriculum evolves rather than being planned precisely.[20]

Advocates of this approach might well identify themselves as postmodern. Here the world is viewed not as a machine but as a living organism.

Individuals cannot objectively view this organism from outside. Rather, individuals are intimately involved in the very phenomena in which they are participating. Individuals who consider themselves postmodern realize that one cannot separate curriculum development from the people involved in the process or from those who will experience the curriculum. One cannot decontexualize the process.

Common among advocates of this approach is that the key focus of curriculum activity is not the content, the subject matter per se, but rather the individual. Subject matter tentatively selected in the development process has importance only to the degree that a student can find meaning in it for himself or herself. Subject matter should provide opportunities for a reflection on and the grist for a critique of knowledge, for engaging the student dynamically in the creation of meaning.[21]

Persons with this orientation toward the curriculum and its development view learning as holistic compared to a compendium of discrete parts arranged in some artificial sequence. We cannot really departmentalize learning into precise steps or specific domains such as the cognitive, affective, and psychomotor. Rather than developing curricula prior to students coming to school, teachers actually become co-learners with the students, engaging each other in an educational conversation about topics of mutual interest and concern. Thus, in many of these nontechnical models, the curriculum, rather than being developed, actually evolves from joint teacher-pupil interaction. Part of the students' challenge is to create and interact with that which they will learn.

Essentially, the technical-scientific view toward curriculum development relies heavily on rationalism (thinking) and empiricism (sensing). The nontechnical-nonscientific orientation relies heavily on intuitionism (feeling) and on what Macdonald has called an "aesthetic rationality" in contrast to a "technological rationality."[22]

Advocates of the nontechnical-nonscientific approach to designing curricula are likely to support child-centered and to a lesser extent problem-centered designs. But as some examples of nontechnical-nonscientific designs will hopefully show, these are still purposeful approaches that can be employed systematically.

Nontechnical-nonscientific approach advocates challenge assumptions about whether all aims and goals of education can be known. They do not accept the position of the logical positivists—that if something exists it can be perceived and measured. This also applies to formulating conclusions about school and society: All of the concerns and subjects nontechnical curricularists examine do not have a means-ends logic as defined by technocratic or behaviorist educators.

Taking the Middle Ground

The middle ground regarding approaches to curriculum development may well be the wisest tack to take at a time when much debate exists as to whether we are really in a postmodern period in which reason and certainty are out and intuition and uncertainty are in. Perhaps we are just in a phase of late modernism.[23] Some argue that "town criers" of the postmodern phase of cultural and intellectual development are perpetrators of myth, purveyors of superstition.[24]

We suggest that this is a time in which we are questioning our engagements in various activities. For those responsible for curriculum decision making, we are indeed challenging our past ways of developing curriculum—querying our roles and trying to discover means of engaging affected parties in the processes of deciding what students ought to learn. Many of the nontechnical curriculum development models reported in this section seem to reflect the uncertainty of the times. Thus our models should allow for this uncertainty. The models presented in this section show the human side of curriculum development. Curriculum development appears to be a living, breathing organism, rather than a cold, precise, exact, and certain machine that dehumanizes those involved in its development and those who experience the products of such development.

Glatthorn: Naturalistic Model. Allan Glatthorn's naturalistic model seems to take a middle-ground approach. It is neither modern, although it does advocate following a sequence of specific stages, nor postmodern, although it can be argued that it promises a great deal of uncertainty and surprises. Glatthorn posits that the technical model, the one that accepts the assumptions of modernity, is limited by its insensitivity to the politics of curriculum making and that curriculum cannot be generated in a manner that is neat, systematic, or ends oriented.

Glatthorn's model contains the following eight steps:

1. *Assess the alternatives.*   Persons involved in planning should commence the process by systematically examining alternatives to the current curriculum. Those employing the technological approach might also begin at this stage, but such persons seem to advance too hastily to developing the course, not spending time reflecting on and critiquing current practice. While not taking the posture of a critical theorist, he encourages serious reflection on what the school is offering and advocates that people contemplate alternatives.

2. *Stake out the territory.*   Here individuals define the course parameters, the learning audience, and learning activities. At the conclusion of this stage, we have in place a tentative course prospectus that addresses for whom the course is designed, whether it will be elective or required, its basic information and knowledge, and how it relates to existing courses in the school.

3. *Develop a constituency.*   This step attends to the humanness of curriculum development and to its innately political character. Thus, before proceeding too far along the development process, those charged with program creation should realize their own personal convictions and biases. Likewise, developers should realize that there will be those in the system who oppose the new program because of their personal and professional beliefs. Thus, to advance the course development, participating parties must convince others to join forces. They must communicate with various groups and convince them of the soundness of the program being created.

4. *Build the knowledge base.*   Once the curriculum development team has sufficient support among colleagues, it is necessary to create a knowledge base required for program creation. This knowledge base is about content or subject matter, but it also relates to gathering data on the students, on faculty skill and receptivity to the suggested program, community willingness to support the innovation, and what research information might lend credence to the new program.

5. *Block in the unit.*   At this step, developers determine the nature and number of the units or parts, attending to the general objectives for the unit as well as how unit topics might be sequenced. Attention is given again to the question of what students are to learn from engaging with these units. In contrast to the technological approach, rather than one particular sequence defined for all students to follow, there are several avenues, all sensitive to students' interests, learning styles, and other differences.

6. *Plan quality learning experiences.*   After blocking in the units, developers engage in designing particular sets of learning experiences that will address the general objectives. This stress on learning experiences, rather than on subject matter, distinguishes this approach and qualifies it as nontechnical. We admit the reader may have some difficulty in accepting that this student-centered focus is sufficient to classify this as truly a nontechnical process. But the planning of learning experiences suggests that there is no clear-cut technical delineation of what will transpire in the curriculum unit. The developers are creating possible options that will address numerous curriculum objectives and that will trigger numerous divergent outcomes.

7. *Develop the course examination.*   In this naturalistic process, there is more emphasis on divergent means of assessment. Tests (and grades) do not drive the curriculum. Both teacher and student participate in determining the means of documenting whether learning has occurred and the quality of such learning. Student portfolios, biographies, and other alternative forms of assessment are acceptable procedures, as opposed to only standardized forms.

8. *Develop the learning scenarios.*   The final step of the process is creating learning scenarios rather than the standard curriculum guide. These scenarios denote a detailed statement of the unit objectives, a suggested number of lessons, and a recommended list of learning experiences, with suggestions as to how to personalize them in the classroom. The scenarios also contain reprints of materials necessary to support the learning experiences.[25]

The Deliberation Model

In the technical models previously discussed, people followed a rather precise type of thinking and action. However, even these models left it up to the participants to determine the specifics of the thinking and acting. If the stage indicated content selection, there was no actual guidance as to how one would select the content, what procedures and what questions one would employ. The deliberation model addresses this gap in curriculum development. Indeed, McCutcheon notes that deliberation is the essential process engaged in curriculum development.[26] Through deliberation, individuals engage in curriculum decision making. In this process, educators make known their ideas and values as to what is essential for learning and necessary to be taught—what content is to be praised—and the very functions of education itself.

The deliberation model represents a means of reasoning about the practical problems of what to include in the curriculum. The process is nontechnical primarily because it does not accept a linearity of action. That is, it is not necessary to blindly follow steps 1, 2, and 3. As Senge notes, reality exists in circles and is constructed of overlapping and interacting systems.[27] Deliberation acknowledges this circularity of reality. It allows people to consider the interrelatedness of decisions and actions. It enables individuals to realize that means and ends affect each other, constantly modifying the very reality about which one is deliberating. It is this rejection of linearity, of precise cause–effect, means–ends thinking, that places this approach in the nontechnical camp. But it is still a mid approach. It can be included in late modern thinking. Indeed, one of the key advocates of this approach to curriculum decision making was Schwab.[28] Reid has noted that deliberation is the most appropriate way to deal with the uncertain practical problems that are the "stuff" of curriculum development activities. Deliberation draws on systems thinking, on feedback and adjustments, or the cybernetic principle, which is certainly not postmodern, but a sophisticated recognition of the uncertainty of dealing with reality.[29]

Dillon reveals the basis of deliberation in systems thinking by noting that the activity of deliberation proceeds essentially from problem to proposals to solution.[30] This process occurs within a recognized socially constructed context. People are cognizant of the players in the process and aware of their views, ideas, and agendas.

Curriculum development through deliberation occurs within cultural contexts. Currently, this is one of the challenges confronting curriculum creators. How can one generate solid curricula taking into account the complex of cultural mores, myths, rituals, values, and symbols that shape the construction of meaning and influence its application in the world.[31] In a dynamic and diverse society, how can we deliberate so that right action (enabling appropriate curriculum) is accomplished.

Curricular deliberation must be sensitive to the players' social structures. It must recognize individuals' political agendas. It must address the psychological states of all engaged parties. What type of knowledge and what view of knowledge does the person involved in deliberation bring to the process? What are the bases on which we trust others' agendas, ideas, and values? How do the views of others square with our views?

Effective deliberation is not a mindless activity that "just evolves." There are suggested stages to consider. However, these stages must not be considered a linear series of actions or decision points. Each stage is processed bearing in mind the context of the stage and the mutual interaction among all the other stages in the deliberation process. The procedure does not assume precision in the process of deciding what ought to be included in the curriculum. In deliberation, there will be surprises. Indeed, surprises are welcomed. Individuals are encouraged to keep an open eye for the unexpected. There is no agreement as to the exact number of stages. Reid suggests four: searching for the problem, searching for data, searching for solutions, and searching for resolution.[32] The model presented in this chapter has six stages as suggested by Noye.[33]

Six-phase Deliberation Model. The six phase model of deliberation is comprised of (1) public sharing, (2) highlighting agreement and disagreement, (3) explaining positions; (4) highlighting changes in position; (5) negotiating points of agreement, and (6) adopting a decision.

Public Sharing. To create a curriculum, a group must come together. This seems obvious, but often when groups gather to create curricula they do not come to share but to convince. Granted that deliberation is part of the rhetoric of persuasion, but there must be sharing prior to arguing for what the curriculum ought to be.

The characteristics of *simultaneity* and *social dimension* occur in this public sharing and actually in all the stages. *Simultaneity* refers to the existence of diverse matters that have to be considered all at the same time. *Simultaneity* deals with the myriad agendas of the individuals involved. In public sharing, one recognizes the competing demands of the group. The *social dimension* refers to the fact that, as it interacts over time, the group actually moves from a cluster of individuals to a community. As the group evolves, members establish how they will discuss issues and desires and how they will privilege and praise various views. Specifically, the group defines appropriate and inappropriate behaviors.

At this juncture, the group makes evident the various assumptions regarding the nature and purpose of the curriculum. Perceived needs are presented. Possible contents and potential pedagogies are introduced. Individuals identify information that they think has potential relevance to the task of creating a curriculum or curricula. People are encouraged to communicate their beliefs regarding the nature of content. What is a student, what are optimal learning environments, what are teachers' functions? Theories are made known, dreams divulged, concerns introduced, and hidden agendas revealed.

At the conclusion of this phase, to which the group can return at any time, the group's thinking should be recorded about the commonplaces of content, student, teacher, and school and the challenges confronting the curriculum group. The group is now ready for phase 2, the highlighting of agreements and disagreements.

Highlighting Agreements and Disagreements. In public sharing, the group has already laid the foundation for this second phase. Individuals identify agreements and common interests, beliefs, and understandings regarding the nature of school and the curriculum, what they think should be taught, and the approach to instruction that is most valuable to the roles of teacher and the student. Mindful of the public sharing, individuals determine where their core beliefs harmonize with others in the deliberative team.[34]

Individuals engaged in this second phase soon realize that agreements are not complete. Disagreements exist as to the commonplaces of school, curriculum, school environments, teacher, and students. Not all will concur that a particular problem exists. In recognizing disagreements, the deliberative group acknowledges the possibility of conflict. Some people think conflict is negative, that it works to dismantle the group. If one holds this view, then he or she wishes to avoid or reduce conflict. However, individuals must separate conflicting positions from the persons who hold the positions. The challenge is to legitimize opposing views regarding curriculum and the other commonplaces, without feeling compelled to accept them. Once the group has highlighted common and alternative views of educational problems and curricular options, the members are poised for phase 3, explaining positions.

Explaining Positions. It is one thing to have individuals' agreements and disagreements noted; it is quite another to explain positions. Yet explanation is essential. In explaining positions, the complexity of the process of curriculum creation becomes evident. Here all involved in curriculum development are searching for and organizing data to make clear various positions.[35] This searching is part of the practical aspect of creating curricula. Why do I think this is a problem? What data support a proclaimed shortcoming as in fact real? Is a particular group of students failing, and do they really need this type of curricular solution?

Elucidating positions is more than just data gathering. It is detailing the assumptions or philosophical orientations that individuals bring to curricular deliberation. Realists have a particular read on the purpose of school, on just what the curriculum should be. Likewise, existentialists interpret data from their particular orientations. Radical theorists, with their assumptions about the current society, justify their positions by drawing on their reading of current happenings.

In explaining positions, members of the curriculum deliberative team realize that, while it is essential to share and explain divergent viewpoints, there is still the shared group purpose of creating a curriculum. To create such a curriculum takes individuals who appreciate each other as professionals and do not consider their colleagues to be adversaries.[36] This is no small feat. To do this, curriculum developers must view themselves as members of a community of scholars, and the group leader needs to have considerable skill in guiding groups. After explaining positions, the group is ready for phase 4, highlighting changes in position.

Highlighting Changes in Position. This phase of deliberation naturally evolves from the activity of explaining positions. As people listen to their colleagues explain their views, the new data furnished often are enough to trigger a reconsideration of some point or points regarding the curriculum. People find themselves convinced by an argument given. There is no shame in changing one's mind. In deliberation, all involved are engaged in a mutual give and take so as to synthesize best decisions as to what the curriculum should be. When people change their minds, they should make such changes known. Such highlighting of changes in positions actually cements the group's collaboration. And this sharing sets the stage for phase 5, negotiating points of agreement.

Negotiating Points of Agreement. This fifth phase of the deliberative process engages participants in searching for solutions. Here participants seek closure, however tentative, about what the curriculum will be, what topics students will experience, what instructional approaches will be employed, and what educational intents will be satisfied. While deliberation is not totally negotiation, it does contain some. As Reid notes, deliberation is rhetorical in that its ultimate objective is persuasion.[37] People use the deliberative process to persuade others, and perhaps even themselves, that they are pursuing right action regarding the creation and suggested delivery of a curriculum. In the sharing, highlighting, and explaining of positions, people believe that the power of arguments and the soundness and reliability of data will facilitate making proper choices regarding the curriculum.

At this phase, individuals are challenged to identify possible curricular solutions to educational needs. Here curriculum decision makers must realize the need to come together with selected curricula that are innovative, creative, and responsive to students' diverse needs. The actual coming together is the sixth phase of deliberative curriculum making.

Adopting a Decision.   At this final phase, individuals achieve consensus as to the nature and purpose of the curriculum by denoting specific curricular topics, pedagogy, educational material, school environment, ways of implementation, and ways of assessment. The group resolves what ought to be done to address the educational needs identified in the earlier phases of deliberation. What the curriculum as plan looks like depends greatly on the social, political, and philosophical composition of the curriculum deliberation team.

A key feature of deliberation and one that places it within the nontechnical category of curriculum approaches is its feature of incompleteness. Individuals creating curricula through deliberation recognize that the deliberations, discussions, and sharing and challenging of ideas and views always remain unfinished or incomplete. The environment within which curriculum deliberation occurs is dynamic. One cannot comprehend the totality of the situation. There are always parts of the situation that will remain unrecognized and unknowable at any particular point.[38]

Uncertainty exists in the process. At phase 1, individuals are not sure of the problem or focus. As Reid, referring to Schwab, commented, the method of the practical deliberation, "begins not with some prespecified statement of the problem to be addressed, . . . but from the feeling that some state of affairs is unsatisfactory."[39] The problem or the issue actually is socially constructed as the group deliberates. This is counter to a technical model of curriculum development. The process is also socially constructed. The group realizes that the process possesses uncertainty, surprises, and instabilities. Rather than being upset at this "messiness" of process, individuals are enlivened by it and alert to recognize novel ideas and approaches to addressing the "oughtness" of what the curriculum should be.

Conversational Approach.   How educators at various levels of schooling perceive curriculum influences how they create curricula. Individuals who consider the curriculum as a product or a plan frequently view curriculum creation or development as a rational series of steps to be followed somewhat independently of context. Persons in the nontechnical camp often view curriculum more as drama or conversation. People do not develop a conversation; they create opportunities for talk. As Applebee indicates, the challenge for curriculum planning (development or creation) is that of creating a conversational domain and suggesting ways in which relevant conversations can occur within it.[40]

If we accept that curriculum represents a particular type of conversation, it makes sense to employ conversation, somewhat stylized yet flexible, for creating "knowledge talk." Looking at curriculum creation as conversational activity enables those involved to appreciate that curriculum development is essentially a social activity with moral political aspects.[41] Such consideration brings into focus concepts that appear ignored in technical approaches. Significant concepts in the conversational model are ideology, beliefs, values, empowerment, power, and consensus. Participants realize that numerous conversations are necessary to create the arenas in which education will occur. There exist new ways of knowing, doing, relating, and conversing. Creating curricula through conversation relies less on procedure or on the employment of particularistic tools or stages than on generating themes from the "ebb and flow of authentic dialogue and debate."[42] Still, such discourse has guidelines. The conversation has focuses that evolve from the initiating dialogue. These guidelines are just that; they are not steps to be followed religiously but stages, phases, or junctures at which people engage in curricular talk. This approach to curriculum creation is conversation, not speech making. Speech making is much more formal; there are rules, and often these rules are laid on the speech maker from outside. Conversation is more under the control of the conversants; no rules come from external sources that must be followed to legitimate the talk.

The following phrases of the conversational approach are adapted from a questioning strategy developed by Hunkins. This makes sense in that questions are integral to conversation. The phases adapted to curriculum creation are (1) free association, (2) clustering interests, (3) formulating questions or curricular focuses, (4) sequencing questions or curricular focuses, and (5) constructing contexts for the focuses.[43]

Free Association. Too often people come to curricular conversation with their minds made up as to what should be taught. They accept the knowledge traditions of science, mathematics, and the humanities. While one can draw from the traditional divisions of knowledge, one needs to remain somewhat open as to the particulars that need to be taught or learned. Individuals responsible for curriculum gather to let their minds wander over whatever information is at hand. This is a type of cognitive browsing, touching on various topics and ideas that come to mind, allowing oneself the luxury of reflecting on possible connections and the potential networking of various knowledge domains.[44] In this stage, no firm judgment is made about these ideas or topics. Ideally, individuals allow their wanderings to pass through the various social contexts at local, state, and national levels. One can wander worldwide as well.

Clustering Interests. People conversing together soon realize that as they talk certain interests, concerns, wishes, desires, and preferences seem to jump out. These interests indicate what the conversants consider potentially important, who then share why they believe this topic of interest is valuable to the education process. People listening to their own and others' talk soon realize emergent patterns. One can link these points in the conversation. These interests can be then collapsed into one large interest.

Formulating Questions or Curricular Focuses. At this third phase, participants reflect on named interests and clusters of interests and interrogate themselves and their colleagues. What do I or others want to know about these interests? What *ought* we to know about this interest or topic? What questions are essential for individuals to raise to gain command of implied information? What questions are essential to consider to engage individuals in culturally significant conversation? What conversations matter in the engagement and betterment of contemporary civilization?[45]

Sequencing Questions or Curricular Focuses. After determining significant curricular focuses

and answering related questions, one determines how to orchestrate these topics in ways that will engage students in these conversations. Are there suggested avenues that one might travel when dealing with curricular focuses? Do some questions require attention prior to other questions? At this stage participants consider how they can arrange curricula so that when students become engaged their conversations will be carried forward.[46]

Constructing Contexts for the Focuses. Conversation does not occur within a vacuum. Neither should the curriculum created by this approach be considered separate from social and educational contexts. Here the conversationalists add flesh to the curriculum. Participants consider the types of environments necessary for engaging students in conversation about the material. Pedagogic approaches and the educational material requisite for making the curriculum come alive are considered. The players, or "talkers," are brought into the educational space. Now those who have been engaged in this curricular conversation have notions about what students ought to learn and ought to know and how they ought to behave; they even have some sense as to how and about what they ought to think.

Ideally, in following the conversational approach to curriculum creation, students will have curriculum that will nurture their functioning with their knowledge. Students will be able to *do* science, history, and mathematics, rather than just knowing about science, history, and mathematics. This approach to creating educational programs presents curricula that should encourage the players to apply their knowledge in action, that is, in context. Curricula so designed celebrate the social dimension of engaging in curriculum. Curricula thus created are not conceived as plans but rather as narratives about which people can converse and to which they can contribute.

Postpositivist–Postmodern Models

Presently, some curricularists' thinking directly challenges a paradigm of thought that has been accepted since the time of Isaac Newton. This new thinking demands more than transferring our actions from a technical to a nontechnical approach to curriculum construction. These curricularists advocate that those charged with curricular responsibilities go further than what is suggested in the deliberative and conversational approaches to curriculum creation. In a very real sense, these persons advocate that we detach ourselves completely from the following of "good forms," of accepted procedures that follow preestablished rules. They suggest that our actions in creating curricula cannot be judged according to a determining judgment.[47] Old criteria cannot be employed to critique new curricula.

Since the time of Newton, scholars have perceived their world as a finely running mechanical machine. They believed, at least theoretically, that at some level the world is governed by certain fundamental laws. From the study of the world, we could discover order and certainty. Donald Schon argues that this technological rationality, this viewing of the world as a machine that we could study and manipulate objectively as a bystander, means that it is possible to determine with a great deal of certainty exactly what is happening in any given situation. The second assumption indicates that, given the fact of certainty, individuals can understand the phenomena under question on the basis of cause and effect. Third, it is possible to generate the means of obtaining data that will test out the certainty of reality. Finally, the results of such experiments or investigations are amiable to evaluation such that the results can be generalized to other situations.[48]

These assumptions support the technological-scientific approach to curriculum development. However, in the past decade and a half, these assumptions have been challenged by an increasing number of social scientists. Some of these people are called postpositivists in that they are challenging the positivistic thinking that Newton introduced. Others are identified as postmodern thinkers, attributing again to Newton the beginning of modern thought. Regardless of the labels, many persons arguing for a more dynamic curriculum and a more dynamic means of creating it are coming from a multitude of academic positions.

As educators, we need to commence questioning that all meaning is knowable and that all knowledge can be represented by finitary propositions.[49] Curriculum and curriculum making represent an uncertain system and an uncertain set of

procedures for dealing with these systems. People such as James Macdonald were fond of arguing about the need for an aesthetic rationality to at least complement our technological rationality.[50] Similarly, Elliott Eisner has suggested that curriculum development is a process of transforming images and aspirations about education into programs. He intentionally uses the terms images and aspirations, believing that the conditions of curriculum development are rarely clear in all dimensions to those who would create educational programs.[51] Eisner does not believe it possible for an educator, or anyone for that matter, to prescribe formulas for another to follow.

The postmodern view causes curriculum makers to assume an openness to process, an eye for the unexpected, and a willingness to let individuals interact with systems as they evolve. This view allows chaos to occur so that order may result. In the same vein, artistry is considered a special way of knowing or perceiving, of constructing reality. Artistry fills in those spaces left vacant by the application of a technical rationality.[52] Ends are not perceived so much as ends but as beginnings, a view advocated by Dewey, although William Doll points out that postmodernism did not develop until after Dewey's death. Perceiving ends not as ends but as evolving beginnings is essential for examining the relation between being and becoming and between permanence and change.[53]

Traditionalists in the application of the technical approach to curriculum and its development argue for being and permanence. Proponents of the postmodern approach to curriculum believe that the actual planning process assumes its own ethos. Ends are transformed into new beginnings; people in the process are altered; students, teachers, and even course materials are changed as the dynamics and chaos unfold. The end of learning in such a curriculum is not consensus or agreement; rather, it is the students' search for "instabilities." Students are not presented with ideas or information with which they will agree, but with encounters with content arranged such that students will see that they have to seek more to find frameworks and generate fresh understandings. Essentially, the aim of curricula designed from this viewpoint is not to have students arrive at understandings, but essentially to realize that they have more work to do, to continually make their understandings new.[54] The energy driving such actions comes in part from the actions themselves, rather than being applied to the process from outside sources. Curriculum becomes a process of development to be experienced in unique and at first unimagined ways, rather than a static body of knowledge to be presented within a strict time table.

For the postmodernists or postpositivists, curriculum participants are engaged in a critical dialogue with themselves and others in the planning process and interact with an evolving content of the curriculum. The exact nature of the interactions is uncertain. Indeed, as Slattery comments, postmodernism exhorts educators to view curricular activity as exercises in aesthetics, intuition, eclecticism, and mystery.[55] Viewing curricular activity through such a lens means that the postmodern approach to curriculum creation, as well as a postmodern curriculum, can never be articulated with a universal precision.

Realizing this uncertainty, planners are open to new ideas, to surprise, to content taking off in new directions in consequence of some unanticipated event. Even when things appear calm, at equilibrium, they will at times behave in disorganized or chaotic ways.[56] Accepting this mode of thought, planners realize that curriculum is not something that is "boxed" or preplanned and given to individuals. Rather, as Young notes, meaning in curriculum results from the interactions of individuals. Meaning does not exist in separate compartments. Meaning results from a person's becoming aware of the interconnections between and among the various realms of knowledge, people, and social/political reality.[57]

In short, the curriculum developer or planner looks at the dynamics of the education situation. The individual realizes that the situation at hand is unstable and dynamic. The players in the system, including teachers, students, and parents, are not static types. The society in which the school finds itself is evolving. The levels of pedagogic knowledge are changing. This knowledge influences teaching, as well as our understanding about the nature of individuals and their learning, and is in a state of flux. As an overview, we come to realize that many of the systems do not evolve in any set pattern. Also, we realize that, with the diversity of individuals and situations, there is no one set pattern for arranging the content and experiences of the curriculum. Indeed, the plans allow for things to be random, to evolve as the situation develops. However, once plans are put into place, there is a certain irreversibility. Students will never go back to a prior time of not knowing something once that something has been taught. They will never be younger. But the outcomes to be anticipated are not prescriptive or convergent, are essentially not ends, but new and evolving beginnings, resulting in what we could call "dissipative structures."[58]

In concluding this section on postpositivist or postmodernist models, we are challenged to put to paper any model. The postmodernists reject any metanarrative or meta approach to any activity. Everything is emergent. Thus, if we depict on paper a model of curriculum development, it only exists for an instant and is soon to be changed by the dynamics of emergent situations. In a way it is like the quark, a subatomic particle, which only exists for a tiny fraction of an instant.

Even those who claim adherence to the postmodern seem hard pressed to note how one actually creates such a curriculum. Rather, they emphasize what postmodern curriculum development focuses on or what it supports. Few specifics exist as to how to do it. And if specifics are denoted, one is essentially urged to deconstruct the specifics and reconstruct them to meet the changes resulting from the emergent in the social contexts.

Certainly, this approach to curriculum development requires players to approach the process as community action. Curriculum development is social. However, all human action is social, even actions performed by modernists. Postmodern action also is mutually corrective, requiring a recursive interpretation. That also can be said of the "feedback and adjustment" aspect of the systems approach or the deliberative approach, which we label modern. Postmodern curriculum development also respects the interplay of individuals and groups.[59] This also is relevant to deliberative approaches, and even to technical approaches, which are sensitive to group dynamics.

Perhaps the way out of this dilemma of putting something on paper that will only exist for an instant is to note that there are as many models and variations of models of postmodern curriculum development as there are individuals engaged in the process. Rather than have a model, this approach to curriculum creation is an attitude or a series of attitudes that invites participants into dynamic reflection. It is an approach, if such a claim can be made, to believe in *paralogy,* the practice of searching for instabilities so as to seek out underlying emerging frameworks from which we can construct meaning, ever realizing that such meaning is essentially not reality, but an allusion to what we conceive to be true.[60]

A voice in the movie *Field of Dreams* kept informing the main character that "if you build it, he will come." The statement referred to the building of a baseball field in the middle of a cornfield. Perhaps a paraphrase of this statement can serve to guide persons wishing to follow a postmodern approach to curriculum creation. "If you gather together to create a curriculum, it will emerge." If you gather like-minded people sensitive to the dynamic contexts within which curricula will emerge and exist, you will discover that a pattern, however temporary, will evolve that will suggest curricula responsive to students and the general public.

Certainly, there are patterns that groups of individuals will employ to create curricula. But the patterns will not be standardized. However, over time, some patterns may emerge as dominant, but only to change at some unpredicted time interval.

Perhaps the best advice that can be offered to readers is to suspend their disbelief that such a nonmodel can work and to try it. Gather together with fellow teachers and curriculum persons and commence talking. See what happens. Allow yourself to mull around in uncertainty for awhile. You will begin to see certain views emerging; there will be a public sharing as in the deliberation process. There will be a suggestion that certain needs exist and that certain knowledge ought to be learned. Humans by nature organize their environment, set priorities, and map out topics and approaches to topics. The postmodern is really an approach that allows us to be creative and emergent regarding curriculum development. There is no solace of good forms.[61] There are no preestablished procedures to direct action. Nevertheless, we can take comfort in realizing that, when human beings are allowed to be creative, they are.

Table 7-1 gives an overview of the technical approaches to curriculum development discussed in the previous section. Also included in the table is an overview of the nontechnical approaches discussed in this section.

COMPONENTS TO CONSIDER IN DEVELOPING A CURRICULUM

Curricularists deal with the question, "*What* shall be included for purposes of learning?" After that they deal with *how* to present or arrange the *what* that is selected for learning, so that students can learn or experience it. In other words, first they deal with knowledge and content specifically, and then they deal with teaching and learning experiences. Regardless of their philosophical orientation, they should not ignore these two elements.

Curriculum Content

All curricula have content, regardless of their design or developmental models. How individuals view the content is affected by their view of knowledge and reality—their philosophical postures. Those who believe in the traditional philosophies "discover" knowledge by using their senses. Also, to them knowledge is "objective"; it can be measured and therefore tested.

Those who view the world from a progressive posture "invent" knowledge according to their relationships with others and the environment. People accepting this philosophical orientation today are advocates of constructivism. They realize that learners need to be seriously engaged in constructing meaning. Knowledge is not just something told to them. They must personally construct their sense of something. The meaning and truth of students' experiences depend on their relationships to the situation in which they are acting.

Those who are part of the romantic position view knowledge and likewise content from an existential or phenomenological epistemology. To these individuals, knowledge and reality refer to the immediate inner experience of the self. Knowledge and truth in this view are self-awareness or self-insight. This form of truth is extended beyond the self as a person attempts to understand other human beings.[62]

TABLE 7-1 Overview of Curriculum Development Approaches

APPROACH	MAJOR ASSUMPTIONS	VIEW OF CURRICULUM	MAJOR MODELS
Technical scientific	Major steps can be identified, managed	Knowable components that can be selected and organized	Bobbitt, Charters: Curriculum activities Tyler: Four basic principles
	Curriculum development has high degree of objectivity, logic,	A compendium of parts	Taba: Grass-roots rationale
	Curriculum development involves key decision points, is rational	Curriculum is the organization and delivery of contents and experiences	Hunkins: Decision-making model
Nontechnical	Curriculum development is subjective, personal, aesthetic, transactional	Curriculum viewed as quality activities	Glatthorn: Naturalistic model
	Curriculum development is "specialized talk"	Curriculum viewed as conversation	The Deliberation model: Conversational approaches
	Curriculum development is a dynamic process fraught with much uncertainty	Curriculum is an emerging phenomenon with which humans interact; it is a dynamic and uncertain system	Post-positivist models

Individuals within the rather open boundaries of postmodernism view knowledge as dynamic and evolutionary. It is not static, not something that can be observed and manipulated from clinical or detached settings. An individual is part of the very knowledge structure being investigated. We do not observe knowledge, we actually participate in its making. Knowledge is a process that influences the learner and is thereby also influenced by the learner. Knowledge results from a structuring and a reconstructing of perceived and also invented realities. Knowledge is that which results from the environment within which humans find themselves.[63]

Conceptions of Content. Groups charged with curriculum planning have options in content selection that are influenced by their philosophical outlooks. Actually, they have the problem of overchoice. There is too much content to include, and they must somehow make sense of what is available and select that which will enable students to learn the most—whatever curriculum design or developmental model they implement. This task can perhaps be made a bit easier if curricularists think of just how they define curriculum content and what it comprises.

Some educators argue that it is more important to learn process than content. Such a statement dichotomizes content and process, when in reality they should receive equal emphasis in the school's curriculum. Process is a type of specialized content, related to methodology and procedures. It is called procedural knowledge as opposed to declarative knowledge, which relates to facts, concepts, and generalizations. Parker and

Rubin indicate that process suggests "random or ordered operations which can be associated with knowledge and with human activities." Varied processes can help create knowledge, as well as "communicate and utilize knowledge."[64]

Emphasis on process does not reduce the value of students' gaining knowledge, but rather affirms that students need to be active in their learning. Furthermore, such underscoring of process indicates that students must progress beyond the simple acquisition of knowledge; they must use the knowledge if they are to gain appreciation and understanding of it.

Content is more than just information to be learned for school purposes. It must be information that relates to learners' concerns and be organized so that the learner finds the information useful and possessing deep meaning. When selecting content the curriculum planner must take into account the potential of the content to address all the cognitive, social, and psychological dimensions of the individual student.

Some curricularists might conclude that content is really another term for knowledge. Content (subject matter) is a compendium of facts, concepts, generalizations, principles, and theories similar to disciplined knowledge. Additionally, school content does incorporate methods of processing information. But, knowledge, whether disciplined, like chemistry, or nondisciplined, like environmental education, is concerned with the advancement of understanding and the exploration of unknown areas. In contrast, content and processes arranged in school subjects do not provide students with opportunities for advancing the realm of knowledge, but rather opportunities for discovering knowledge that is new to them but known by scholars and practitioners outside the school. School content, then, is distinguished from knowledge by its purpose. Figure 7-3 might make these distinctions clearer.

Organization of Content. The capitalized version of knowledge in the diagram is all information that has been organized by scholars for the advancement of understanding. Such knowledge is organized according to various knowledge theories. Paul Hirst has advanced a "forms of knowledge" theory that organizes knowledge into distinct domains with unique types of concepts in specialized relationships. For instance, he observes that mathematics has unique categorical concepts of number, integer, and matrix. Physics has unique concepts of matter and energy. These concepts are organized into specialized networks whose relationships influence the particular types of meanings that can be derived from them. These specialized organizations of knowledge can be distinguished by the different types of tests, or processes, used by learners in these respective domains as subjects.[65]

How knowledge is organized in "reality" depends on the philosophical views of the scholar. Curriculum planners who favor subject-centered designs would accept most, if not all, of what Hirst discusses. However, those who accept learner-centered curriculum designs might consider that the school curriculum organizes personal knowledge rather than what some would call objective knowledge. Persons like Hirst (and other subject-centered advocates) in many cases view knowledge as things and relationships that are real and awaiting discovery in the outer world. To the learner-centered design champion, however, knowledge relates to the individual's personal and social world and how he or she defines reality.

Perhaps the best posture for curriculum designers is to recognize the many variations among interpretations of knowledge and its organization. They would be wise to remember what Bruner was quick to point out, that the knowledge they identify and create cannot be conceived of in

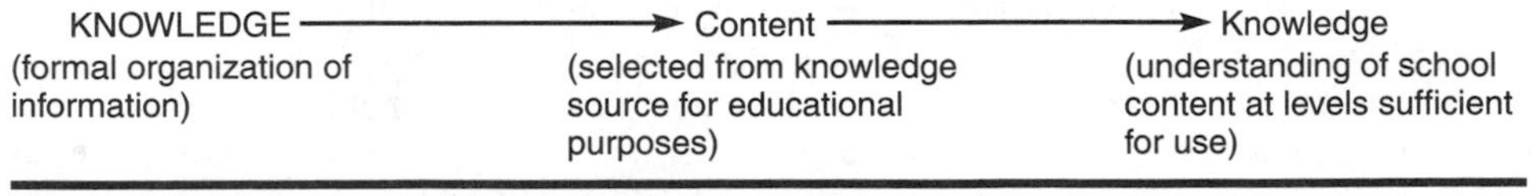

KNOWLEDGE ⟶ Content ⟶ Knowledge
(formal organization of information)　(selected from knowledge source for educational purposes)　(understanding of school content at levels sufficient for use)

FIGURE 7-3　World Knowledge to School Knowledge

terms of absolute truth: "Knowledge is a model we construct to give meaning and structure to regularities in experience." The way we organize knowledge is an invention for "referring experiences economical and connected. We invent concepts such as force in physics, ... motive in psychology, style in literature as a means [for] comprehension."[66]

Faced with organizing content for the curriculum, program planners usually use two organizers: logical and psychological. In following the *logical* organization, they organize content according to certain rules and concepts. In economics, for example, the concepts of supply and demand are major organizers. Without these concepts, the idea of capital and labor or the marketplace cannot be grouped. Arranging economics content in this manner makes sense, but it really does not denote the way an individual might actually learn economics.

To detail this process, curricularists consider a *psychological* organization: How do students learn or process information? Most educators assume that content should be organized by going from the students' immediate environment to a more distant environment. Content, in other words, should be organized so that the concrete is experienced first, then the more abstract. This psychological factor is a key principle of sequencing content.

Criteria for Selecting Content. Regardless of their curriculum design preferences or their philosophical orientations, curriculum planners have to apply criteria in choosing curriculum content. Although the criteria are common to most curricular orientations, educators in the various philosophical camps might place greater emphasis on particular criteria.

Self-sufficiency. Israel Scheffler argues that the prime guiding principle for content selection is helping the learners to attain maximum self-sufficiency in the most economical manner. He elaborates three types of economy: economy of teaching effort and educational resources, economy of students' efforts, and economy of subject matter's extent of generalizability.[67] This criterion—helping learners to attain maximum self-sufficiency—is also supported by many hu-

manists, radicals, and reconceptualists as a means by which learners can actualize their potential and crystallize their identities.

Significance. Content to be learned is significant only to the degree to which it contributes to the basic ideas, concepts, principles, generalizations, and so on, of the overall aims of the curriculum. Content should also consider the development of particular learning abilities, skills, processes, and attitude formation.

Taba noted that we should not just select content based on the cognitive aspects of learners, but also on their affective dimensions.[68] Even though most curriculum planners note that significance is central, they often disagree as to what is significant. Those who favor subject matter designs think of significance in terms of what knowledge needs to be transmitted to students. Those who favor learner-centered designs think of significance in terms of how it contributes to the meaningful experiences of the pupils. Those who advocate problem-centered designs would consider significance in terms of particular social, political, and economic issues.[69]

William Reid noted that content should be selected with an eye to its cultural significance. Does the content to be learned or constructed add to the overall culture of the nation or group? This criterion is somewhat controversial, for it assumes that there is agreement as to the civic culture. Just how do we define culture? Does the content selected contribute to students' senses of being part of the culture? Closely related to this criterion is that content should be selected that serves local, regional, and national interests. The challenge is to come to a consensus as to what such interests are.[70]

Validity. Validity is the authenticity of the content selected. In this time of information explosion, knowledge selected for school content can quickly become obsolete and even incorrect. As new knowledge is discovered, content assumed valid may become misleading or even false. Validity must be verified at the initial selection of curriculum content, but it also needs to be checked at regular intervals through the duration of the curricular program to determine if content originally valid continues to be so.

Validity would seem to be a rather straight-forward criterion. Something is either accurate or inaccurate; something either happened or it did not. Nevertheless, the ideological stance that any individual brings to a situation vastly influences what he or she perceives as valid. This is why some can state that certain information in school content is valid or truthful, while others can consider the same information invalid. Revisionists, radical school critics, reconstructionists, and post-positivists would state that much of the curriculum offered to students is invalid.[71]

Interest. Another criterion is interest. To those who favor the learner-centered design, this is a key criterion. These persons note that knowledge exists in the learner when it is meaningful to his or her life. When it fails to be meaningful, it dehumanizes education.[72] The interest criterion has been with us since the times of the child-centered school in the 1920s. Advocates of this movement urged that the child should be the source of the curriculum; in other words, the children's interest should determine the curriculum.

Those currently advocating a learner-centered curriculum point out that the content of the curriculum must be selected with students' interests in mind. But the school experience should create and broaden interests as well as address them. A key question is: "Are students' current interests of long-lasting educational value for both the students and society?" Dealing with this question is difficult because it assumes educators possess some degree of perception regarding future society and students' places in that future.

The criterion of students' interests should be weighted and adjusted to allow for students' maturity, their prior experiences, the educational and social value of their interests, and the way they are expected to interact within society. Attending to this criterion of interest means that, in selecting content or arranging for content to be experienced or constructed, the educator must be sure that the content does engage the individual. The content must contribute to the welfare of the student.[73] The unique nature of the student, the client, must be recognized and given privilege.

Utility. Utility concerns the usefulness of the content. Again, how a person defines usefulness is influenced by his or her philosophical view and favored curriculum design. Usefulness to those favoring the subject-centered design is often judged in terms of how the content learned will enable students to use that knowledge in job situations and other adult activities. Usefulness to those in the learner-centered camp is related to how the content enables the individual to gain an accurate perception of his or her self-identity and to attain meaning in his or her life. Is the content useful for the learner developing his or her human potential? Proponents of the problem-centered mode would think of content as having utility if it has direct application to ongoing life and to social and political issues.

Learnability. Could anyone select content without considering this obvious criterion? Some critics of the schools say yes. Certain contents are selected that are out of the range of experiences of particular students and are thus difficult, if not impossible, to learn. Furthermore, selected contents are sometimes arranged and presented in ways that make their learning difficult for some students. Critics often say that content selected reflects a middle-class bias and that it is organized to favor those who have convergent (and right-answer) learning styles. The learnability criterion relates to the optimal placement and appropriate organization and sequencing of content. Furthermore, it addresses the issue of appropriateness for the intended student audience.

Feasibility. Feasibility, the last criterion, forces curriculum planners to consider content in light of the time allowed, the resources available, the expertise of current staff, the nature of the political climate, the existing legislation, and the amount of public monies available. Although educators may think that they have an entire world of content from which to choose, they do have limitations on their actions. Even the number of days in the school calendar, for example, limits what can be taught. So do the size of the classroom and the personnel of the school. Content selection has to be considered within the context of the existing reality, which usually boils down to economics and politics.

In this connection, David Pratt analyzes economic and political feasibility in terms of "constraints." The curriculum, he argues, is "largely governed by [such] constraints, [and] unfeasibility is commonly due to the magnitude of the constraints." It may be necessary to "ask whether any of the constraints can be changed."[74] Here we allude to economic compromises, shifting funds, altering public opinion, compromising or negotiating with pressure groups, and/or becoming involved in school-community politics.

Curriculum Experiences

Curriculum content is the "meat" of the curriculum plan, but we can consider the experiences planned for the students as the "heart." Experiences are the key factors that shape the learners' orientations to the content and, ultimately, their understanding of it. Taba noted that "perhaps the first important consideration in achieving a wider range of objectives is the fact that the learning experiences, and not the content as such, are the means for achieving all objectives besides those of knowledge and understanding."[75]

In focusing on curriculum experiences, we are stressing curriculum as a verb, or something to be lived, not as a noun, or something to be possessed.[76] In curriculum experiences, many educators center on engaging students in their own learning, inviting them to construct their own meanings and to make their own sense of the curriculum, not just to receive the sense of others.

Curriculum experience involves the instructional component of the curriculum. Instruction refers primarily to the human interaction between teacher and student in ways that are designed to achieve the goals of the school. It is specialized behavior planned in light of particular objectives. It consists of teaching methods and activities that take place in the classroom for the purpose of attaining the schools' goals. There are multitudes of both teaching methods and educational activities. Examples of teaching methods are inquiry strategies, lecture, discussion, and demonstration. Examples of educational activities are viewing films, conducting experiments, viewing videos, interacting with computer programs, taking field trips, and listening to speakers. Both are integral parts of the curriculum and must be carefully considered in light of the content selected.

At a theoretical level, instruction includes all the actions of teachers necessary to influence the students' behavior and, ultimately, their learning. The particular actions of a teacher may vary according to the teaching method and/or educational activities, but they all have the purpose of influencing students' behavior and learning.

Experiences versus Activities. When discussing curriculum, we do not make a fine distinction between teaching methods and educational activities. Rather, we group all the actions of both teachers and students under the title learning experiences. But this was not always the case. At the turn of this century, the terms *learning activities* and *learning experiences* were absent in the educational literature. We read instead about *recitations, exercises,* and *projects.* But with the evolution of the field of psychology, and also the work of progressivism led by Kilpatrick and Ellsworth Collings (a doctoral student of Kilpatrick's), the activities of the learners received more attention in the educational equation."[77]

Educators began to realize that the term *learning activities* did not describe adequately the dynamics of the teaching-learning situation. Many children could be engaged in the same learning activities, but the experiences each pupil derived might be quite different. By 1935, the term *learning activities* was being replaced with the term *learning experiences.* Most writers of curriculum today talk of learning experiences, especially since Tyler used the term in his classic text, *Basic Principles of Curriculum and Instruction.*

Wholeness and Continuity. Students' curriculum experiences should be such that they see life's wholeness and continuity in activity. Students should see that every concrete entity is experienced within a context of wider relationships and possibilities. Conscious life is always open to a never-ending web of entailments and unfoldings. No content of experience is just what it appears to be here and now without any further prospects or associations.[78]

All content can be considered as being at the edge of chaos. All content has the potential to explode into an infinity of new knowledge and new patterns. In experiencing the curriculum, one should appreciate that one really never knows what is going to happen next.[79] Knowledge invites those who seek it to be creative, to be open to new forms.

Means and Ends. Persons who favor learner-centered designs and problem-centered designs tend to view learning experiences as means—as valuable in themselves. Means-oriented curricularists seem to be looking at effects that are more personal and individual and that perhaps address human needs. They are looking at the effects of the experiences to determine whether or not students gain a sense of personal fulfillment and power over their own lives and a commitment to responsible action.

But many in the curriculum field, though they do not necessarily ignore completely the process aspect of the educational experience, place major emphasis on the ends of education. These individuals favor subject-centered curriculum designs. Curriculum development activities and implementation strategies are performed with the intention of achieving the aims and goals of the school. Instruction is the means for attaining the content that has been selected and the overall goals of the program. Ends-oriented curricularists view learning opportunities not as valuable in themselves but as instrumental in attaining specified consequences. These persons are product-oriented. They look at the outcomes resulting from the interface of students, teachers, and the curriculum. They are interested in results, not just inherent attributes of experiences. See Curriculum Tips 7-2.

Criteria for Selecting Experiences. Some criteria are useful for considering potential content and experiences. Validity, especially congruence of objectives and goals, is an appropriate example. Other criteria are expressed by the question: "Will the experience do what we wish it to do in light of the overall aims and goals of the program and specific objectives of the curriculum?" Following are specific extensions of this question. Are the experiences

1. Valid in light of the ways in which knowledge and skills will be applied in out-of-school situations?
2. Feasible in terms of time, staff expertise, facilities available within and outside of the school, community expectations?
3. Optimal in terms of students' learning the content?
4. Capable of allowing students to develop their thinking skills and rational powers?

5. Capable of stimulating in students greater understanding of their own existence as individuals and as members of groups?
6. Capable of fostering in students an openness to new experiences and a tolerance for diversity?
7. Such that they will facilitate learning and motivate students to continue learning?
8. Capable of allowing students to address their needs?
9. Such that students can broaden their interests?
10. Such that they will foster the total development of students in cognitive, affective, psychomotor, social, and spiritual domains?[80]

Relationship of Content and Experiences. No curriculum, regardless of its design, can ignore content and experiences. Although subject-centered designs stress content, they also consider its delivery. Learner-centered designs focus on the students and their experiences, but they, too, consider the experiences in relation to what is learned.

What educators need to remember is that, in reality, content and experiences do not exist apart. If students are reading a book, they are combining both an experience and content. Content and learning experiences always comprise curriculum unity. Students cannot just engage in learning or in studying without experiencing some activity and some content. Likewise, teachers cannot deal with content without being engaged in some experience or some activity.

Curriculum planners sometimes separate content from experience. However, they realize that in the actual delivery of educational programs both elements coexist. Taba noted, "One can speak of effective learning only if both content and process are fruitful and significant."[81]

Educational Environments

As we cannot separate content from experiences in the actual delivery of a curriculum, neither can we divorce the experiencing of content from the space within which experience occurs. As Patrick Slattery comments, education is a human activity that is greatly affected by environment.[82] The space in which individuals place themselves or are placed affects their inner experiences. Slattery

════ *Curriculum Tips 7-2* ════

Desirable Features for Intended Curricula

Content selection is a crucial stage in the curriculum development process. Besides attending to this selection criteria, thought must be given to the experiences suggested to accompany the content chosen. The following points should assist in organizing curriculum that will contribute to the attainment of worthy content and experiences.

1. The activities suggested by the materials should nurture the development of ideas, skills, and ways of perceiving and thinking that have educational value for the student and society.
2. The content and related experiences should challenge students on an intellectual, social, and perhaps even spiritual basis.
3. The content and experiences should allow for varied modes of presentation to move students away from an overreliance on the textbook as the source of school knowledge.
4. The content should be selected so as to allow students to make connections with content learned in other aspects of the curriculum and from their community at large.
5. The content and experiences should be selected so that they suggest further avenues for inquiry and affect the emotional levels of students to motivate them to engage in such inquiry.

Source: Adapted from Elliot W. Eisner, "Creative Curriculum Development and Practice," *Journal of Curriculum and Supervision* (Fall 1990), pp. 62–73.

notes that Orr argues that landscape shapes mindscape.[83]

Until recently, educators have not given much attention to the environment of the school other than to make sure that the children had adequate light, places to sit, desks upon which to write, and places to hang their clothes. As John Holt pointed out, "We would have to worry a lot less in our schools about 'motivating' children, about finding ways to make good things happen, if we would just provide more spaces in which good things *could* happen." Space, Holt noted, creates activity; it allows students "to generate places and moods."[84]

Educational space is crucial to meaningful educational experiences. Children who experience a creative environment are much more likely to be stimulated, to realize their potential, and to be excited about learning. The environments educators design should facilitate students' attending to the experiences and content that they have selected and organized. The environments should stimulate purposeful student activity. They should allow for a depth and range of content and experiences that facilitate learning.[85]

Educational environments should engage, challenge, and arouse students regarding their learning.[86] There continues to be much talk currently about educational reform. While much of this talk relates to new ways to organize the curriculum content, there is some concern about the space in which the curriculum is to be experienced. Postmodern education has discussed how educational experiences are connected to the classroom or educational environment. For instance, Goodlad talks about the ecology of classrooms.[87]

Persons who favor subject-centered designs might give only scant consideration to the educational environment. They might feel that it matters little where learning is to occur. But even these persons would have to admit that if, for example, a teacher were presenting science information the laboratory environment would, at times, be more appropriate than the lecture hall. Persons who favor learner-centered designs, on the other hand, might be more inclined to take seriously the planning of meaningful environments. Spaces are needed to allow individuals to grow; they are part of the quality of experience for students. Ideally, persons creating programs, regardless of their design preference, will take into consideration the nature of the space in which the curriculum is to be realized by both teachers and students. See Curriculum Tips 7-3.

Criteria for Environment.   Educational environments should address social needs, security needs, and belongingness needs, as well as the development of inner awareness, appreciation, and empathy for others. In addition, they should enable students to master intended learnings. The environments should stimulate purposeful student activity, and they should allow for a depth and range of activities that facilitate learning.

Indeed, educational environments should contribute to the development of learning cultures that foster authentic activities. Authentic activities of knowledge production and knowledge work resemble those of persons outside schools engaged in scholarly or other work. For instance, students studying history in a school culture would be doing history that reflects authenticity in action compared to a historian.[88] Students engaged in mathematics would be dealing with concepts, heuristics, algorisms in ways resembling mathematicians.

In some cases, the educational environment has to be outside the classroom. Hawkings and Vinton stated long ago that classrooms can no longer be the sole learning environment.[89] Lang notes that "occupants of classrooms must 'peek' out with windows, to the world beyond for illumination and views."[90] Educators charged with curriculum design and implementation have yet to really take this suggestion seriously.

Brian Castaldi has suggested that, when contemplating and designing educational environments, planners keep in mind four criteria: adequacy, suitability, efficiency, and economy.[91] *Adequacy* refers to the space planned: Is it of sufficient size to accommodate the students for whom the space is intended? Adequacy also refers to environmental controls: Is the light sufficient so that students can read with ease? Are the visual displays big enough so that students can see them? Are the materials serviceable for the learning

styles of the students? Are the acoustics appropriate so that students can hear?

When dealing with the criterion of adequacy, we also consider the relationships between the various spaces within a school. How do spaces designed for individual investigation relate to spaces planned for storage and retrieval of educational materials? How do spaces created for small-group investigation relate to spaces designed for small-group viewing of educational media? Will students be able to move around the room without disrupting other students?

Closely related to adequacy is *suitability*. Is the shape of the environment suitable for the type of activity planned? If some information is going to be demonstrated, is the environment such that all students can see with ease? If students are to engage in discovery, does the environment help or hinder such activity?

Ensuring *efficiency* involves attending to those characteristics of educational space that are likely to improve its instructional effectiveness or operational characteristics: Does the environment allow the educational activity to be carried out with a minimum of effort? Will the environment facilitate the greatest amount of learning with the least amount of effort by students and teachers? If students are to listen to audio tapes at their desks, can they be placed where they will not be disturbed by unnecessary noise or by students engaged in other activities?

The final criterion, *economy,* relates to actual savings, in terms of capital outlay, that can be achieved by the initial architectural design or by a modification of an existing environment for a particular aspect of the curriculum. Economy deals with the cost of teaching some part of the curriculum in the environment provided. It also relates to economy of students' and teachers' efforts. Time is a resource, and curricula are designed to make maximum use of time to achieve basic program goals and objectives. Sometimes, for example, students spend a major part of their day just waiting for the teacher to get to them. Sometimes, teachers spend too much time going from one part of the school to another to engage in a different school activity. It could be that planners can design educational environments so that students and teachers are very near to the appropriate spaces for their different activities.

Curriculum Tips 7-3

Dealing with the Physical and Health Factors
of the Environment

Until recently curriculum leaders did not give much attention to the curriculum environment. One way of viewing this environment is to look at the physical and health factors that impact on student learning. The factors considered below represent a "nuts and bolts" view, typical of a supervisor or practitioner who deals in the real world of classrooms and schools as opposed to the theoretical world.

1. **Arrangements.** Identify the activities that will take place and the best way to combine or arrange the physical layout or setting. Different configurations must be evaluated on the basis of how they will accommodate lectures, demonstrations, experiments, etc. Other factors include storage space, electrical/telephone outlets, teacher work space, student learning space (open/closed) and grouping patterns (whole group, small group, and independent learning) or spaces.
2. **Floors, Ceilings, Windows.** There is a need to consider carpeting vs. tile in terms of cost, durability, and aesthetics. Electro-static charges are important, too, in terms of human sensitivity and technical equipment (especially computers). Ceiling materials and window treatments affect acoustics and lighting.
3. **Temperature.** The research data suggest that students learn best when the temperature is 70 to 74 degrees Fahrenheit, since they are seated and somewhat inactive in most classroom situations. They also learn best when the relative humidity is between 40 to 60 percent.
4. **Electrical.** Electrical wires should run parallel to the walls, and when they run across floors they should be taped down to prevent accidents. Equipment and adapter plugs should be stored when not in use, and in no one's way when in use. There should be more than one circuit in a classroom to guard against possible line failure, and surge suppressors need to be installed in schools/classrooms that cannot risk data loss in the event of a power surge.
5. **Lighting.** In most cases windows are suitable for providing adequate light, coupled with the standard fluorescent lighting to save money. In small learning areas, recessed lighting is more effective than fluorescent light.
6. **Acoustics.** Room noise can be a problem, especially when students are active or involved in an open classroom setting and are permitted to talk or engage in multiple activities at the same time. Neutralizing noise with appropriate floor, ceiling, and window treatments are basic considerations; some schools are experimenting with soft background music, and in other schools special window panes have been installed to reduce outside noise.
7. **Security.** Physical security is a consideration in entryways, hallways, and schoolyards, especially in terms of unwarranted intruders. It is also a factor when storing office and instructional equipment, as well as with student lockers and teacher closets. Schools are increasingly installing special locks and bolts, steel plates with locking cables, electronic trackers, closed circuit television, and alarm systems connected to police departments.
8. **Dust.** Elimination of dust has always been a concern. When remodeling or designing a new school, all chalkboards should be replaced with dry marker boards. Special consideration should also be given to paper and disk storage.
9. **Safety.** To protect students (or teachers) from injury and school and liability, the smart administrator learns to identify and eliminate as many hazards as possible. Science labs, gyms, cafeterias, and schoolyards are major places where accidents take place, but also injuries do occur in classrooms, hallways, and auditoriums.

Source: Allan C. Ornstein, "Components of Curriculum Development," *Illinois School Research and Development* (Spring 1990), pp. 208–209.

Lang has furnished another list of essential criteria for optimal educational space: volume, acoustical qualities, illumination, temperature, communication, and material finishes.[92] Under *volume,* the educator must consider the scale and shape of the space for the educational activity. As human beings we have attitudes and feelings that influence how we perceive space. If we want children to enjoy silent reading, we may wish to have a space so organized that it is cozy. Sometimes students may wish to be in a confined space for the activity; at other times, they may desire open space.

"Let's quiet down and think for a moment." Such a statement occurs numerous times each day. An educator wants meaningful sound and instances of quietness in a classroom. Often teachers find that their lesson is interrupted because of noise coming from either within the classroom or outside it. How can one make the *acoustics* of the classroom or some other environment such that noise is not a distracter? Much cooperative work these days might be less stressful for all involved if the acoustics of the space were appropriate for the educational activity.

Illumination refers to the light present in the educational environment. When making curriculum decisions, most of us do not consider illumination, other than the fact that we might have to turn on the lights on a dreary day. However, people react differently to different levels and kinds of light. Also, students in particular need to have some views in the classroom. Perhaps a lesson on poetry writing requires students to gaze out a window. We need to reflect on classroom views when creating learning opportunities.

Temperature is rarely considered in lesson planning. Yet we can become irritated if the classroom is too hot or too cold. Different children have different preferences for temperature. Schools are a long way from providing uniquely personal control over classroom temperature, but at least educators need to be aware of this criterion.

The criterion of *communication* refers to the ways that classroom spaces can be arranged within the classroom and connected to areas outside the classroom. Many lessons in the future will be geared to the Internet. Does the educational environment facilitate such connection? Lang notes that classroom spaces must allow for the linkage of data and voice among learning modules within individual spaces in the school and connections to the community and the world.

The last criterion Lang discusses is *material finishes.* "Human beings react emotionally to color, texture, and shape."[93] When planning educational environments, teachers and other educational decision makers must realize that children are sensitive to the colors, textures, and even smells around them. Students' personal histories and cultural backgrounds influence how they perceive types of educational space. In planning curricula, teachers should reflect on how to make the learning atmosphere welcoming, one that states "stay awhile, enjoy the learning."

While most educators will have to do much guessing on how to deal with these criteria, we need to be aware of them. We must be willing to keep an alert eye to the educational environment and make adjustments to the space in ways that contribute to students' productive learning.

PARTICIPANTS IN DEVELOPING THE CURRICULUM

Developing or designing a curriculum involves a large number of persons, both school based and community based. It also involves different levels of planning: the classroom level, the school level, the national level, and even the international level. Sometimes the designers work in harmony, and sometimes they are at odds with each other. In fact, concern among people or groups for certain types of curricula makes curriculum development largely a political activity in which there is competition for authority and control, for scarce resources, and for primacy of certain values.

Political Arena Participants

Most educators work to have their particular views or purposes of education become dominant. The politics of education is concerned with who benefits and how those benefits are determined. Curriculum is concerned with providing programs for learners. Curriculum participants, both educators and noneducators, have to determine what types of curricula will benefit what students, how to select those curricula, who will receive the benefits of particular curricula, and how to deliver those benefits.[94]

School Arena Participants

Macdonald advocated that all parties affected by the curriculum should be involved in deciding its nature and purpose. He presented a model that showed several groups, all directing their thinking, feelings, and knowledge to curriculum activity. The model, shown in Figure 7-4, depicts the major players in continuous interactions.

Teachers. The teacher occupies a central position in curriculum decision making. The teacher decides what aspects of the curriculum, newly developed or ongoing, to implement or stress in a particular class. The teacher also determines whether to spend time, and how much of it, on developing basic skills or critical thinking skills. Observers point out that when teachers shut the classroom door they determine the details of the curriculum regardless of the curriculum plans of others. Teachers are clearly the most powerful implementers regarding curriculum.[95]

In addition to being curriculum participants at the classroom level, teachers are also involved with curriculum committees. Some of these committees are organized by grade level, for example, a fifth-grade curriculum committee; others are organized by subject area. Some might be organized according to the type of student under consideration; for example, a committee for the gifted or a committee for the learning disabled. The committee format is the standard way of involving teachers in curriculum activity outside the classroom level.[96]

Actually, teachers should be involved with every phase of curriculum development. Although not all teachers wish to be involved in all stages of curriculum development, all teachers, by the nature of their role, are involved in the implementation of the curriculum: Teaching is implementing the curriculum. Teachers need to be part of the total curriculum-development activity, from the formation of aims and goals to the evaluation and maintenance of the curriculum.[97]

Teachers should by their very roles be practicing intellectuals. Indeed, Henry Giroux argues that the teacher should be viewed as an intellectual engaged in some form of thinking. Teachers should be viewed not as "performers professionally equipped to realize effectively any goals set for them. Rather [teachers] should be viewed as [professionals] with a special dedication to the values of the intellect and the enhancement of the critical powers of the young."[98] Schon advances that teachers should be reflective practitioners

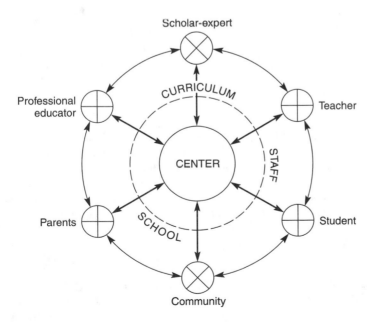

FIGURE 7-4 Continuous Interaction Model for Curriculum Activity.

Source: Adapted from James B. Macdonald, "Responsible Curriculum Development," in E. W. Eisner, ed., Confronting Curriculum Reform (Boston: Little, Brown, 1971), p. 71.

engaged in actions resulting from careful considerations of the nature of the task.[99] Going one step further, teachers need to work in school-university and school-community partnerships to improve curriculum and teaching, to build the knowledge base in curriculum and teaching, and to professionalize teaching and the teachers' role in curriculum development.

Students.   If we accept that all who are affected by the curriculum need to be involved in its planning, we cannot ignore the students. Students seldom have formal influence on what they will learn or even on the manner of their experiencing the content. This is, however, changing in some schools. Students, especially at the secondary level, are sometimes involved in curriculum committees. Many schools are also involving secondary students in conducting surveys and needs assessments. As Ronald Doll notes, students are the "consumers" of education and they deserve to supply input to educators regarding curricular matters.[100]

Educators are ill advised to ignore what learners think and feel. Also, we would advance that, if we are attempting to empower teachers in the curriculum process, we also need to empower students to assume some control, to a degree appropriate for their ages, over their learning. If the curriculum is to truly evolve from the conversations of involved parties, we cannot keep students out of the conversation in which we plan what they are to learn.

Principals.   Principals long have been considered to be the curriculum leaders in the school setting. However, this still may be more the ideal than absolute fact, since many principals are still go-betweens from the central office to parents and the school staff. Currently, it appears that the roles of principals, along with the roles of teachers, regarding curriculum activity are changing. Part of this is due to the effort to restructure the schools. As Mary Raywid notes, those who consider themselves restructuralists have proposed two broad strategies for attaining their goals regarding changes in authority and governance. The first is to return authority for decision making to the school site and to democratize the process of decision making. The other is to extend to teachers

the right to choose or develop the program for which they are responsible.[101]

There seems to be growing support for school-site management. John Goodlad in his major study of schools recommended that the school be recognized as the primary unit of education. If the school site is to be the "place of action" with regard to curriculum decision making, then the principal must be a visionary leader possessing a clear view of the mission of the school and a strong belief in his or her professional values.[102] The principal must be able to communicate the sense of mission to teachers and others affected by the curriculum and to engage teachers and others in the actual refinement of the mission of the school. Principals must exert care to be the curriculum and instructional leader in the school and not just the person in charge of the managerial functions of the school.

Principals realize, especially those involved in school-site management schemes, that effective functioning and managing change results when those at the school recognize themselves as a community with shared values and ideology. Ideally, principals acknowledge that with school site-based management there will be many committees, and these committees will involve community members and even students in decision making. While such committees are a part of "restructured" schools, there is still some debate as to whether community members will have advisory roles or decision-making authority to set policy for the school. In either case, it is the principal's responsibility to guarantee that the actions of the players in the school, in the curriculum arena, are not counterproductive.

In large schools, we envision the principal as a facilitator of curriculum: furnishing time for curricular activities, arranging for in-service training, sitting on curriculum advisory committees as a resource agent, and refining the mission of the school. In small schools, we would expect principals to serve more actively as curriculum initiators, developers, and implementers. Regardless of the specific roles that principals will play, the shift to site-based management can make the principal a much more powerful figure, since he or she is now the visible person to both teachers and community members; or the principal can share responsibilities in curriculum planning with other participants.

Curriculum Specialists. Curriculum specialists play a major role in curriculum development and implementation activities. They are known by many titles: chairpersons, supervisors, coordinators, or directors. An individual's title usually gives some idea of his or her responsibilities. Persons called curriculum coordinators or directors are usually educators who are known as curriculum generalists.[103] They have a broad knowledge of the nature of curriculum and are experts in creating and implementing curricula. They usually do not have a content major. Other generalists in a school district are known as directors of elementary or secondary education. Usually, these persons have expertise in administration as well as curriculum, but their focus is either elementary or secondary.

Persons with specific content specialties are often titled as supervisors, chairs, or heads of a particular subject area, for example, supervisor (chair, head) of science. These persons have some background in curriculum, but they have a content major and are often more concerned with supervising instruction.[104]

Curriculum specialists are responsible for ensuring that programs are conceptualized, designed, and implemented. This requires a high level of understanding of curriculum and skill in managing people. Curriculum specialists need knowledge of curriculum design and development, in translating curriculum theory into practice, and in supervising and evaluating instruction. Unruh and Unruh have noted that curriculum specialists must be sensitive, patient, and skilled in human relations. Additionally, they need competence in decision making and leadership. The authors identified ten tasks of the curriculum specialist: (1) defining goals and objectives; (2) developing needs and problems; (3) creating conceptual models of curriculum development; (4) developing plans, strategies, and procedures that encourage people to work together; (5) fostering interrelationships and comprehensiveness in curriculum development; (6) involving people in curriculum development; (7) communicating within and outside of the schools; (8) increasing professionalism regarding curriculum; (9) planning implementation; and (10) evaluating the curriculum.[105]

Assistant (Associate) Superintendent. In many school districts, the person with the primary responsibility for curriculum activity is the assistant or associate superintendent. This person, a line administrator, reports directly to the superintendent, who is in the forefront. In large school districts curriculum directors or coordinators report to the assistant or associate superintendent. Ideally, this assistant or associate superintendent (1) chairs or serves as advisor to the general curriculum advisory committee; (2) is responsible for informing the superintendent of the major trends occurring in the field of curriculum and how these trends are being translated in the school system; (3) works with elementary and secondary directors or coordinators regarding curricular activity; (4) is in charge of the budget for curricular activity; (5) provides input in the statement of philosophy, aims, and goals; (6) guides evaluation relevant to aims and goals; and (7) manages long-term and short-term activities designed to strengthen programs.[106] This educator also helps formulate policies concerning curriculum innovation.

Superintendent. The chief administrator of the school system is the superintendent, who is charged with keeping the system running. The superintendent responds to matters before the school board, initiates curriculum activity, starts programs for the in-service training of teachers, informs all district personnel of changes occurring in other schools, and processes demands coming from outside the system for change or maintenance of educational offerings.

Good superintendents also inspire change and enable curricula to be responsive to changing demands. They are directly responsible to the school board for the total educational action in the district. They must establish the means for curricular action, interpret all aspects of the school's program to the board, and set up communication networks to inform the public of and involve the public in the curriculum process.

Boards of Education. Boards of education are the legal agents for the schools. Comprised of laypersons usually elected as representatives of the general public, these boards are spokespersons for the community who are responsible for the overall management of the schools. They are also responsible for being informed about the realm of curriculum and for relating the existing curriculum to the goals of the school system. School boards, in fact, have the final say about whether a new program is funded or implemented districtwide. They enact district policies that facilitate the development and implementation of new curricula. They vote the funds that enable curricula to go from an idea to reality.

School boards, along with the central administrative staffs, seem to be losing some control in running school districts. In some cases, control has been taken away by the actions of state legislatures defining just what basic education is. In other cases, special-interest groups have gone to court to alter board policies if such policies are found unacceptable. In some communities, board members have been recalled by angry community members. In many school districts the school board, rather than being the leader in determining curriculum and policy, plays a secondary role. Federal, state, and local professionals carry the charge for creating new curricula.

Lay Citizens. Few people would contest that the schools belong to the public. But, although laypeople have been assuming increasing roles in curriculum activity, the role of the lay community in curriculum matters is still minimal. Most of the public, though perhaps concerned in general terms with the schools, are really not interested in becoming actively engaged in curriculum development. Most possess little knowledge about course content, course designs, or models of curriculum development. In general, parent involvement in school affairs drops off considerably as students grow older and enter middle level and high school; also, the secondary schools often neglect the importance of parental involvement in their students' education, much less school affairs.[107]

Research indicates that citizen participation in curriculum policy making tends to be superficial and reactive. Citizens sometimes participate, however, when goals are being determined and often when the changes have been completed. This may be because considering and implementing new programs involve needs analysis, and so receive media coverage. Most authorities maintain that the community should be involved in curriculum activity. However, there is still some discussion as to the extent and manner of its participation. Ideally, citizens should be involved in

real problems and should be members of formal committees or groups established by the school district. They can, for example, be members of school-sponsored committees. Parents and citizens should play greater roles in curriculum matters if site-based management becomes fully implemented.

Participants Outside the School District

Many participants outside the school district affect the nature and scope of the curriculum and influence who will plan the curriculum. These participants exist at various levels.

The Federal Government. For much of this century, the federal government was content to allow the states and the local districts to deal with curricular matters. But beginning in the 1960s the federal government became a powerful force in determining the kinds of educational materials and their uses in the schools. This corresponded with the post-Sputnik era, followed by the War on Poverty. Federal dollars established and maintained regional laboratories and centers, first for science and math and then later for disadvantaged and minority groups.

Today, controversy exists over the role and extent of involvement by the federal government in curriculum matters. It has been suggested, for example, that the federal government might well assume five specific roles. The federal government

1. Could identify critical educational issues, many of which are related to curriculum, such as the demand for back to the basics or a common curriculum for all students.
2. Could synthesize the vast amount of knowledge regarding education, specifically curriculum.
3. Could promote research regarding curriculum materials.
4. Could support the application and dissemination of knowledge about curriculum.
5. Could encourage the preparation of persons interested in the field of education, including curriculum.[108]

Currently, the federal government, despite fostering the creation of national goals for education, appears to be withdrawing from playing a major role in education, leaving the key responsibilities with the states.

State Agencies.   States have increased their role in educational policymaking. Much of this growth has been at the expense of the local school district. In many states, the state board of education has made formal recommendations and issued guidelines as to what the curriculum should contain and how it should be organized. The growing involvement of the states is based in part on the position that the management of education is truly a state function, a posture that is augmented by the decrease in federal funds.[109]

States affect the curriculum in many ways. State legislatures frequently publish guidelines on what shall be taught. They also mandate such courses as driver education and drug education to deal with perceived social problems. Pressure groups operating on a state basis frequently push their interests upon the curriculum. Often these associations or groups lobby in the legislatures to treat particular content and/or address certain students. With the publication of the numerous reports on the reform of education, state agencies throughout the nation have initiated minimum competency testing and gate-keep tests aimed at upgrading academic content and standards.

State boards of education seem to be taking a more active role in determining competencies and certification requirements of teachers, supervisors, and administrators. In some states, a special certificate, with specific curriculum courses is needed to become a supervisor or administrator. State legislators are taking a more active role in financing education, and thus indirectly affect new programs and funding of old programs. Then there are the state governors who have assumed the recent role of educational innovators—in context with the national reform movement in education.

Regional Organizations.   States often participate voluntarily in curriculum matters. Two regional organizations have become formalized to ensure such participation: regional educational laboratories and research and development (R and D) centers. Regional educational laboratories influence school curricula by providing guidance in

the production of materials and by furnishing consultants who serve on planning teams. R and D centers investigate specific curricular problems, among other problems, whose results can be of value to curriculum planners. R and D centers also aid curriculum specialists by documenting the effectiveness of particular programs or approaches.

Another type of regional organization is the intermediate school district. The term "intermediate district," "educational service district," or "educational service agency" refers to an office or agency in a middle position between the state department of education and local school districts. About 40 states have some form of intermediate school district. The average intermediate district comprises twenty to thirty school districts in about fifty square miles.[110]

In recent years, intermediate districts have provided school districts with resource personnel in such general areas of education as curriculum, instruction, and evaluation; in specialized areas, such as education of the handicapped, gifted and talented, and bilingual students; and in more specific areas, such as prekindergarten education, vocational education, data processing, and computer education.

Other Participants

1. *Educational publishers.*   In large part, publishers have given the country an unofficial national curriculum. In most schools, the textbooks used frequently determine the curriculum. The power of the textbook is particularly evident when we realize that nearly 75 percent of the students' total classroom time is spent engaged with instructional materials. An even greater percentage of time, 90 percent, is spent with instructional materials when students are doing homework. What students "know" usually reflects their textbooks' content.[111]

2. *Testing organizations.*   Along with educational publishers, testing organizations, such as the Educational Testing Service or Psychological Corporation, have also contributed to the making of a "national" curriculum. By standardizing the content tested, these organizations have affected what content the curriculum will cover and how much emphasis will be given to particular topics.

3. *Professional organizations.* Organizations such as the Association for Supervision and Curriculum Development, the National Council of Teachers of English, the National Council for the Social Studies, and the American Educational Research Association have indirectly influenced the curriculum. Their members bring messages and goals set forth at state and national conferences back home to be tried out in the local schools. Increasingly, such professional organizations are formalizing networks of schools (and school districts) to communicate curricular concerns and to mount studies whose published reports set guidelines and standards for the creation of curricula.

Other Groups. Many other people and groups outside of the schools also influence the curriculum one way or another. Colleges and universities directly and indirectly influence curriculum development. Many educational consultants to the schools come from the colleges. Business and private industry are building closer connections to schools by providing special personnel, donating equipment and materials, and funding programs of special interest. Groups who define themselves as minorities, entitled to special treatment in content areas and special programs, often organize to affect the curriculum. Sometimes, individual educators and lay critics assume the role of educational reformers, and they attempt, mostly through their writings, to give direction to curriculum development. Various foundations have also influenced curriculum formation, largely by supplying funds. The Ford, Rockefeller, Carnegie, and Kettering foundations have made the most active efforts to modify the curriculum through pilot and experimental programs.

CONCLUSION

Curriculum planners really have an overchoice of curriculum development models from which to choose. Which models they select are influenced by their philosophical orientations and approaches to curriculum. Several subject-centered models emphasize a technical-scientific approach to curriculum development, the major approach to curriculum creation today.

Likewise, several models of a nontechnical-nonscientific approach to curriculum exist; these consider curriculum from a more "evolutionary" viewpoint. Educators who accept learner-centered designs tend to favor these models.

Diversity of approach characterizes curriculum creation; however, certain curriculum elements are universal and require attention from all curricularists. Content, experiences, and environments, for instance, are constants regardless of design or development, that is, whether a particular curriculum is being systematically planned or evolving naturalistically. A curriculum without content is no curriculum. A curriculum without experiences cannot be delivered or encountered by students. And a curriculum without a planned environment cannot be implemented by teachers.

The various models available and the numerous elements of curriculum present challenges to a vast array of participants, who exist at many levels—from the local to the national. People will no doubt continue to argue about who should have the major part in curriculum decision making.

ENDNOTES

1. William F. Pinar, William M. Reynolds, Patrick Slattery, and Peter M. Taubman, *Understanding Curriculum* (New York: Peter Lang, 1995).
2. James B. Macdonald, "The Quality of Everyday Life in School," in J. B. Macdonald and E. Zaret, eds., *Schools in Search of Meaning* (Washington, D.C.: Association for Supervision and Curriculum Development, 1975), pp. 76–94.
3. Franklin Bobbitt, *How to Make a Curriculum* (Boston: Houghton Mifflin, 1924), p. 2.
4. Ibid., p. 9.
5. Franklin Bobbitt, *The Supervision of City Schools: Some General Principles of Management Applied to the Problems of City School Systems,* Twelfth Yearbook of the National Society for the Study of Education, Part I (Bloomington, Ill.: 1913), p. 11.
6. W. W. Charters, *Curriculum Construction* (New York: Macmillan, 1923), p. 5.
7. Ibid., p. 101.
8. Ibid., p. 105.

9. Ralph Tyler, *Basic Principles of Curriculum and Instruction* (Chicago: University of Chicago Press, 1949).

10. William E. Doll, Jr., *A Post Modern Perspective on Curriculum* (New York: Teachers College Press, Columbia University, 1993).

11. Francis P. Hunkins and Patricia A. Hammill, "Beyond Tyler and Taba: Reconceptualizing the Curriculum Process," *Peabody Journal of Education* (Spring 1994), pp. 4–18.

12. Ralph W. Tyler, "The Tyler Rationale Reconsidered, 1977," in George Willis, William H. Schubert, Robert V. Bullough, Jr., Craig Kridel, and John T. Holton, *The American Curriculum: A Documentary History* (Westport, Conn.: Praeger, 1994), pp. 393–400.

13. Hunkins and Hammill, "Beyond Tyler and Taba."

14. Hilda Taba, *Curriculum Development: Theory and Practice* (New York: Harcourt Brace, 1962).

15. Robert S. Zais, *Curriculum: Principles and Foundations* (New York: Harper and Row, 1976); Posner, *Analyzing the Curriculum* (New York: McGraw-Hill, 1992).

16. Pinar et al., *Understanding Curriculum.*

17. Ibid.

18. Dominique Genelot, "The Complex World of Deliberation," in J. T. Dillon, ed., *Deliberation in Education and Society* (Norwood N.J.: Ablex Publishing Corp., 1994), pp. 81–98.

19. Arthur N. Applebee, *Curriculum as Conversation* (Chicago: University of Chicago Press, 1996).

20. Catherine Cornbleth, *Curriculum in Context* (New York: Falmer Press, 1990); George O. Posner, *Analyzing the Curriculum.*

21. M. Frances Klein, "Approaches to Curriculum Theory and Practice," in J. T. Sears and J. D. Marshall, eds., *Teaching and Thinking about the Curriculum* (New York: Teachers College Press, Columbia University, 1990), pp. 3–14; Robert Young, *A Critical Theory of Education* (New York: Teachers College Press, Columbia University, 1990).

22. James B. Macdonald, "Curriculum Theory," in W. Pinar, ed., *Curriculum Theorizing: The Reconceptualists* (Berkeley, Calif.: McCutchan, 1975), pp. 5–13; Macdonald, "Theory, Practice and the Hermeneutic Circle," in W. Pinar, ed., *Contemporary Curriculum Discourses* (Scottsdale, Ariz.: Gorsuch, Scarisbrick, 1988), pp. 101–113.

23. Robert Cummings Neville, *The Highroad Around Modernism* (Albany, N.Y.: State University of New York Press, 1992).

24. Paul R. Gross and Norman Levitt, *Higher Superstition: The Academic Left and Its Quarrels with Science* (Baltimore: The Johns Hopkins University Press, 1994).

25. Allan A. Glatthorn, *Curriculum Leadership* (Glenview, Ill.: Scott, Foresman, 1987).

26. Gail McCutcheon, *Developing the Curriculum: Solo and Group Deliberation* (New York: Longman Publishers, 1995).

27. P. Senge, *The Fifth Discipline* (New York: Doubleday, 1990) cited in McCutcheon, *Developing the Curriculum.*

28. Joseph Schawb, *Science, Curriculum and Liberal Education: Selected Essays,* I. Westbury and N. D. Willikof, eds. (Chicago: University of Chicago Press, 1978), cited in McCutcheon, *Developing the Curriculum.*

29. McCutcheon, *Developing the Curriculum.*

30. J. T. Dillon, "The Questions of Deliberation," in J. T. Dillon, ed., *Deliberation in Education and Society* (Norwood, N.J.: Ablex Publishing Corp., 1994), pp. 3–24.

31. Genelot, "The Complex World of Deliberation."

32. William A. Reid, *The Pursuit of Curriculum* (Norwood, N.J.: Ablex Publishing Corp., 1992).

33. Didier Noye, "Guidelines for Conducting Deliberations," in Dillon, ed., *Deliberations in Education and Society,* pp. 239–248.

34. McCutcheon, *Developing the Curriculum.*

35. Reid, *The Pursuit of Curriculum.*

36. Noye, "Guidelines for Conducting Deliberations."

37. Reid, *The Pursuit of Curriculum.*

38. Genelot, "The Complex World of Deliberation."

39. Reid, *The Pursuit of Curriculum.*

40. Applebee, *Curriculum as Conversation.*

41. Robert V. Carlson and Gary Akerman, eds., *Educational Planning* (New York: Longman, 1991).

42. Applebee, *Curriculum as Conversation,* p. 41.

43. Francis P. Hunkins, *Teaching Thinking Through Effective Questioning* (Norwood, Mass.: Christopher–Gordon Publishers, Inc., 1995).

44. Ibid.

45. Applebee, *Curriculum as Conversation.*

46. Ibid.

47. Jean-Francois Lyotard, "What Is Postmodernsim?" in Charles Jencks, ed., *The Post-Modern Reader* (New York: St. Martin's Press, 1992), pp. 138–150.

48. Donald A. Schon, *Educating the Reflective Practitioner* (San Francisco: Jossey-Bass, 1990).

49. Mark Johnson, *The Body in the Mind* (Chicago: University of Chicago Press, 1984).

50. J. Macdonald, "The Quality of Everyday Life in School."

51. Elliott W. Eisner, *The Educational Imagination,* 3rd ed. (New York: Macmillan, 1993).

52. Mark Johnson, *The Body in the Mind* (Chicago: University of Chicago Press, 1984); Schon, *Educating the Reflective Practitioner.*

53. William E. Doll, "Teaching a Post-Modern Curriculum," in James T. Sears and J. Dan Marshall, eds., *Teaching and Thinking about Curriculum* (New York: Teachers College Press, Columbia University, 1990), pp. 39–47.

54. Michael Peters, "Legitimation Problems: Knowledge and Education in the Postmodern Condition," in

Michael Peters, ed., *Education and the Postmodern Condition* (Westport, Conn.: Bergin & Garvey, 1995), pp. 21–39.

55. Patrick Slattery, *Curriculum Development in the Postmodern Era* (New York: Garland Publishing, Inc., 1995).

56. William E. Doll, "Teaching a Postmodern Curriculum."

57. Young, *A Critical Theory of Education.*

58. Ilya Prigogine and Isabelle Stengers, *Order Out of Chaos* (New York: Bantam Books, 1984).

59. Slattery, *Curriculum Development in the Postmodern Era.*

60. Lyotard, "What Is Postmodernism?"

61. Ibid.

62. Richard D. Kimpston, Howard Y. Williams, and William S. Stockton, "Ways of Knowing and the Curriculum," *Educational Forum* (Winter 1992), pp. 153–172.

63. Young, *A Critical Theory of Education.*

64. J. C. Parker and Louis J. Rubin, *Process as Content: Curriculum Design and the Application of Knowledge* (Chicago: Rand McNally, 1966), p. 2.

65. Paul Hirst, *Knowledge and the Curriculum* (Boston: Routledge & Kegan Paul, 1974).

66. Jerome S. Bruner, *On Knowing: Essays for the Left Hand* (Cambridge, Mass.: Harvard University Press, 1963), p. 120.

67. Israel Scheffler, "Justifying Curriculum Divisions," in J. Martin, ed., *Readings in the Philosophy of Education: A Study of Curriculum* (Boston: Allyn and Bacon, 1970), pp. 27–31.

68. Taba, *Curriculum Development: Theory and Practice.*

69. Asa G. Hilliard, "Why We Must Pluralize the Curriculum," *Educational Leadership* (December-January 1992), pp. 12–15; John O'Neil, "Preparing for the Changing Workplace," *Educational Leadership* (March 1992), pp. 6–9.

70. Reid, *The Pursuit of Curriculum.*

71. Henry A. Giroux, *Postmodernism, Feminism and Cultural Politics* (Albany, N.Y.: State University of New York Press, 1991).

72. James A. Beane, *Affect in the Curriculum* (New York: Teachers College Press, Columbia University, 1990).

73. Reid, *The Pursuit of Curriculum.*

74. David Pratt, *Curriculum: Design and Development* (New York: Macmillan, 1980), p. 116.

75. Taba, *Curriculum Development: Theory and Practice,* p. 278.

76. Slattery, *Curriculum Development in the Postmodern Era.*

77. Allan C. Ornstein, "Curriculum Contrasts: A Historical View," *Phi Delta Kappan* (February 1982),

pp. 404–408; Ornstein, "Components of Curriculum Development," *Illinois School Research and Development* (Spring 1990), pp. 204–212.

78. Maxine Greene, *The Dialectic of Freedom* (Teachers College Press, Columbia University, 1988); Philip H. Phenix, "Transcendence and the Curriculum," in E. W. Eisner and E. Vallance, eds., *Conflicting Conceptions of Curriculum* (Berkeley, Calif.: McCutchan, 1974), pp. 117–135.

79. Roger Lewin, *Complexity: Life at the Edge of Chaos* (New York: Macmillan Publishing Company, 1992).

80. Ronald C. Doll, *Curriculum Improvement: Decision Making and Process,* 9th ed. (Boston: Allyn and Bacon, 1996); Ornstein, "Components of Curriculum Development," p. 206.

81. Taba, *Curriculum Development: Theory and Practice,* p. 290.

82. Slattery, *Curriculum Development in the Postmodern Era.*

83. David W. Orr, *Ecological Literacy: Education and the Transition to a Postmodern World* (Albany: State University of New York Press, 1992), cited in Patrick Slattery, *Curriculum Development in the Postmodern Era.*

84. John Holt, "Children Are Sensitive to Space," in T. G. David and B. D. Wright, eds., *Learning Environments* (Chicago: University of Chicago Press, 1975), p. 83.

85. Francis P. Hunkins and Patricia A. Hammill, "Quality Curriculum: Determining the Urban Vision," *Education and Urban Society* (May 1991), pp. 292–301.

86. Francis P. Hunkins, "Creating Outrageous Educational Spaces," speech given at University of Washington, 1995.

87. Author's conversations with John Goodlad at the University of Washington.

88. Hunkins, "Creating Outrageous Educational Spaces."

89. Donald Hawkins and Dennis Vinton, *The Environmental Classroom* (Upper Saddle River, N.J.: Prentice Hall, 1973).

90. Dale Lang, *Essential Criteria for the American School Classroom* (Seattle: University of Washington, Masters Thesis, School of Architecture, 1995), p. 42.

91. Brian Castaldi, *Educational Facilities: Planning, Modernization, and Management,* 3rd ed. (Boston: Allyn and Bacon, 1987).

92. Lang, *Essential Criteria for the American School Classroom.*

93. Ibid.

94. Ann Lieberman, *Rethinking School Improvement: Research, Craft, and Concept* (New York: Teachers College Press, Columbia University, 1986).

95. M. Frances Klein, "A Conceptual Framework for Curriculum Decision Making," in M. Frances Klein, ed., *The Politics of Curriculum Decision Making* (Al-

bany, N.Y.: State University of New York Press, 1991), pp. 24–41.

96. Richard D. Kimpston and Douglas H. Anderson, "The Locus of Curriculum Decision Making and Teachers' Perceptions of Their Own Attitudes and Behaviors toward Curriculum Planning," *Journal of Curriculum and Supervision* (Winter 1986), pp. 100–110.

97. Anne Reynolds, "What Is Competent Beginning Teaching? A Review of the Literature," *Review of Educational Research* (Spring 1992), pp. 1–35.

98. Henry A. Giroux, *Teachers as Intellectuals* (Granby, Mass.: Bergin & Garvey, 1988), p. 125.

99. Schon, *Educating the Reflective Practitioner.*

100. Doll, *Curriculum Improvement, Decision Making and Process.*

101. Mary Anne Raywid, "Rethinking School Governance," in R. F. Elmore, *Restructuring Schools: The Next Generation of Educational Reform* (San Francisco: Jossey-Bass, 1990), pp. 152–206.

102. John Goodlad, *A Place Called School* (New York: McGraw-Hill, 1984).

103. James A. Beane, Conrad E. Toepfer, and Samuel J. Alessi, *Curriculum Planning and Development* (Boston: Allyn and Bacon, 1986).

104. Carl D. Glickman, ed., *Supervision in Transition* (Alexandria, Va.: Association for Supervision and Curriculum Development, 1992).

105. Glenys G. Unruh and Adolph Unruh, *Responsive Curriculum Development,* 2nd ed. (Berkeley, Calif: McCutchan, 1984).

106. Roald F. Campbell et al., *The Organization and Control of American Schools,* 6th ed. (Columbus, Ohio: Merrill, 1990); Thomas J. Sergiovanni et al., *Educational Governance and Administration,* 3rd ed. (Boston: Allyn and Bacon, 1992).

107. Joyce L. Epstein, "Parent Reactions to Teacher Practices of Parent Involvement," *Elementary School Journal* (January 1986), pp. 277–294; Bob Stouffer, "We Can Increase Parent Involvement in Secondary Schools," *NASSP Bulletin* (April 1992), pp. 5–8.

108. Keith Goldhammer, "The Proper Federal Role in Education Today," *Educational Leadership* (February 1989), pp. 350–353.

109. Michael Fullan, *The New Meaning of Educational Change,* 2nd ed. (New York: Teachers College Press, Columbia University, 1991).

110. Allan C. Ornstein and Daniel L. Levine, *Foundations of Education,* 5th ed. (Boston: Houghton Mifflin, 1993).

111. David L. Elliott and Arthur Woodward, eds. *Textbooks and Schooling in the United States.* Eighty-ninth Yearbook of the National Society for the Study of Education, Part I (Chicago: The University of Chicago Press, 1990).

8

CURRICULUM DESIGN

Focusing Questions

1. What are some sources of curriculum design?
2. How can curriculum design be defined?
3. When contemplating the design of curriculum, what key dimensions need to be considered?
4. Why is the design dimension of integration currently receiving so much attention?
5. Which design stresses the unity of knowledge?
6. What are the major representative curriculum designs?
7. Which curriculum design is the most commonplace in American schools?
8. Which design might become the most compatible with postmodern thinking? Why do you think so?

Anyone charged with the development and delivery of curriculum has a conception of what a curriculum is and what parts comprise it. Additionally, one has some notion or notions of how the parts are arranged and how they interrelate. Thinking about the "shape" or "gestalt" of a curriculum plan, or, more specifically, the actual arrangement of the parts of the curriculum plan, is thinking about curriculum design. Sometimes called curriculum organization, design refers to the arrangement of the elements of a curriculum into a substantive entity. In this chapter, curriculum design is used as a noun. That is, it refers to the naming of the arrangement of certain curriculum components. Some curricularists use design as a verb for the actual process of creating a curriculum or instructional plan with a particular organization of elements. Design used as a verb is a synonym for curriculum development. Designs

are developed or selected. The design that someone actually selects is influenced by his or her curricular approach and philosophical orientation.

The parts, sometimes called components or elements, that are arranged in a curriculum design are (1) aims, goals, and objectives; (2) subject matter; (3) learning experiences; and (4) evaluation approaches. The nature of these components and the manner in which they are organized in the curriculum plan comprise what we mean by curriculum design. Although most curriculum plans have within their design these four essential elements, often they are not given equal weight. Frequently, content or subject matter receives the primary emphasis. But, sometimes, schools do create designs that stress primarily objectives and evaluation approaches. Other designs give primary emphasis to learning experiences or activities.

COMPONENTS OF DESIGN

When considering curriculum design, the curriculum decision maker confronts the question: What general structure of the curriculum can I develop so that the parts promote and/or provide insight to the whole?

Thinking about the design, the arrangement of the parts of the curriculum, causes us to reflect on the approaches to curriculum we are contemplating or accepting. Attending to design questions allows us to consider the philosophical and learning theories to determine if we are basing our arrangements of the curriculum components on something that has a rational basis. Posner and Rudnitsky point out that any systematic approach to creating curricula must also be processed within the context of a theoretical framework.[1] The need is to base our design decisions so that they are consonant with our basic beliefs concerning people, what they should learn and how they should learn.

Curriculum design is concerned with the nature and arrangement of four basic curricular parts. These parts are rooted in the classic work of Harry Giles in his report on "The Eight-Year Study." He used the term "components" to show the relationship and included learning experiences under "method and organization."[2] The relationship is shown in Figure 8-1.

The design's four components suggest to the curriculum maker four questions: What is to be done? What subject matter is to be included? What instructional strategies, resources, and activities will be employed? And what methods and instruments will be used to appraise the results of the curriculum? According to Giles, the four components interact with each other; decisions made about one component are dependent on decisions made about the others. While Giles presented the paradigm, it is very similar to a model that Tyler developed several years later. Tyler's model, however, denotes a linear attention to the key elements of the curriculum, while Giles's paradigm shows ongoing interaction among the components.[3]

Curriculum design involves various philosophical or theoretical issues, as well as practical issues. A person's philosophical stance will affect his or her interpretation and selection of objectives, influence the content selected and how it will be organized, affect decisions about how to teach or deliver the curriculum content, and guide judgments about how to evaluate the success of the curriculum developed.

Indeed, individuals may not even be willing to employ the same names for the components. Many argue that identifying objectives as one component indicates allegiance to modernity and rejection of postmodernity, a more productive stance. Objectives suggest a certainty of outcome and a willingness to control individuals so as to achieve that outcome. Many say that education should be an invitation for individuals to participate in emerging uncertainties. Objectives are just too precise. Regardless of position, creating a curriculum is done with some purpose in mind. It has some intent. Even open exploration is an intention that serves a function similar to that of stating objectives. It guides the "why" of having individuals engaged.

Persons aligned with postmodernism still need to reflect on content or knowledge, the substance of the curriculum. Whether we view this content or knowledge as certain fact or emergent understanding, it still is a component, a commonplace if you will, of the curriculum design. There is always going to be a "what" of the curriculum.

Much current talk centers on engaging students in the construction, deconstruction, and reconstruction of knowledge. This refers to the components of method and organization. When

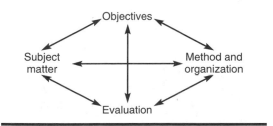

FIGURE 8-1 The Components of Design.

Source: From H. Giles, S. P. McCutchen, and A. N. Zechiel, *Exploring the Curriculum* (New York: Harper, 1942), p. 2.

Pinar suggests that we consider curriculum a verb, he is still indicating that we should attend to this component. Curriculum as journey deals with this component of method, however much the rhetoric about this component might camouflage it.[4]

Contained within current discussion is concern with the component of evaluation or assessment. Whether knowledge is static or dynamic and emergent, one still wants to determine if students react with understanding. Even if one argues that final measurement is impossible, one is still dealing with this component.[5] The very making of meaning requires some type of assessment. The very notion of deconstruction, the taking apart of information, to gain a better understanding of it, however temporary, still comprises evaluation.

While not all curriculum designs will neatly have the exact four components noted by Giles, all designs do have components that demand attention. A curriculum design provides a framework or frameworks implying values and priorities.

Ronald Doll points out that there is confusion when people think about curriculum design and instruction. He denotes that curriculum design is the parent of instructional design.[6] That is, curriculum is the total plan that arranges the four components of the curriculum (objectives, content, experiences, and evaluation means). Instructional design refers specifically to one component, the potential experiences for students. Instruction does not address objectives, or content; rather, it "maps" out pedagogically and technologically defensible teaching methods and educational activities that engage students in learning the content of the curriculum. In instructional design, individuals raise questions as to what teaching methods and materials can be employed that will facilitate learning. What resources will be appropriate for the particular lesson indicated in the curriculum plan? How should we arrange our students, and which students should be involved in particular activities? Ideally, when curriculum workers contemplate a particular curriculum, they should also make instructional design decisions within the context of curriculum.

Sources for Curriculum Design

Those charged with curriculum design must clarify their philosophical and social views of society and the individual learner—or what are commonly called the sources of curriculum. To determine the influences of curriculum design, attention must be given to how such sources will influence education. How the curriculum planner responds to the question of the sources of ideas for education will affect his or her views of curriculum design. For this reason, it is essential for curriculum designers to identify their philosophical and social orientations. If they ignore philosophical and social questions, their curriculum designs will have limited or confused rationales. Taba notes that "much of the distance between theory and practice may be caused by just such lack of rationale."[7]

Ronald Doll describes four sources of ideas that undergird curriculum designs: science, society, eternal verities, and Divine Will.[8] These sources are somewhat similar to those sources of curriculum identified by Dewey and Bode and popularized by Tyler: knowledge, society, and the learner.[9]

Science as a Source.   Curriculum workers who rely on science as a source usually maintain that the scientific method provides meaning for the curriculum design. The design would contain only those elements that can be observed and quantified. In a design based on this stance, problem solving would have a prime position. However, it may be misleading to cite science as a source of ideas for curriculum design; the real emphasis of this design is not just on scientific procedure, but also on procedural knowledge (or knowledge of process). Those designs that stress learning how to learn or "thinking" curricula would emphasize scientific procedures, and the various means by which we process knowledge. But Elliot Eisner has argued that teachers need to understand, besides scientific ways of knowing, aesthetic modes of knowing, interpersonal modes, practical modes, and even spiritual ideas.[10]

Much of what is stated about thinking processes comes from a knowledge of cognitive psychology. What is advocated in terms of problem-solving procedures is derived from our understanding of science and other organizations of knowledge, such as psychology. Some educators would have these ideas regarding procedural knowledge and thinking strategies stand alone as a prime source of the curriculum. Given the times, when the knowledge realm is exploding so rapidly, the only constant seems to be the procedures by which we process knowledge.

To be sure, this view of curriculum design coincides with the scientific and rational world of Western culture. But we also live in a pluralistic world with many different cultures. This latter view accepts the universe not as static, but as self-generating, complex, and evolving. It is a universe that *is becoming* rather than just existing for our detached scientific viewing.[11] This new view of the reality goes by many different names, postmodernism, postpositivism, and third-wave thinking, in contrast to the mainstream view, called positivism or modernism that we have been operating under for several centuries.

Society as a Source. Curriculum designers favoring society as a source for the curriculum believe that school is an agent of society, and thus the school should draw its ideas for the curriculum from the analysis of the social situation. This social foundation has been a most important curriculum foundation. John Dewey certainly realized that educators needed to be in touch with needs of society. It was from a careful study of society that we could determine that which was meaningful and most likely to last. Viewing society as a source would give educators indications of where to modify the curriculum.

While it perhaps has never been easy to get an accurate "reading" of how society is evolving, it is perhaps even more problematic today given an information-based society with large numbers of diverse and well-informed people. The schools must realize that they are not separate from the larger culture and local community in which they are located. Schools are designed to serve the broad social interests of society, as well as the local community. We also know that we cannot ignore in our curriculum design the diversity of our citizens, especially our multiple cultures, ethnic groups, and social classes. Curriculum design can only be completely understood if it is contextualized socially, economically, and politically.[12] The challenge is how to address the unique needs of students and particular demands of diverse social groups and still allow students to gain understanding of the common culture, as well as common, agreed on competencies to engage pro-

ductively in society. Indeed, the search for a common curriculum presupposes that there is something general and universal for all to know. It assumes that there is a public interest that needs to be addressed. This public interest is not the interest of a specific group. Rather, it is a composite of interests that meets the needs of all.[13]

It would seem that if educators are to create curricula with effective designs, they will have to realize the need for collaboration among people and groups. As John Naisbitt has reported, we are at a time of increasing participatory democracy in which the individuals affected by decisions are demanding a role in making those decisions. Perhaps never before in the history of our nation has society as a source influencing curriculum design been more pronounced. It is quite probable that the curricular designs coming from collaborative dialogue will produce some designs currently not even imagined.[14]

Eternal and Divine Sources. Some people consider that designers should simply draw on the past for guidance as to what is appropriate content. These persons believe that the curricular design should be intended to perpetuate society. This traditional view, which reflects a perennialist philosophy, proposes selecting those eternal truths advanced by the great persons of the past. Such designs stress the content element and that certain content (subjects) is more important than other content.

Divine will as an undergirding factor of curriculum design is related to eternal truth and notes that the elements of the curriculum are revealed to humans through the Bible or other religious documents. While this "source" of curriculum design played a significant role in our nation's early colonial schools, for the last century it really has had little influence in public schools primarily due to the mandated separation of church and state.[15] But, to many private and parochial schools, this source of the curriculum is still valid and a major influence.

An interesting development in recent times is the issue of spirituality and its relationship to knowing. When we hear the word spiritual, we usually think religion. However, while we have believed in separation of church and state, and thus tended to downplay divine sources as influencing curriculum design, we have come to realize the significance of people's values and personal morality. To be sure, one of the criticisms of Western society is its emphasis on science and rationality, its stress on material wealth, at the expense of spiritual and/or moral values.

Dwayne Huebner has argued that talk of the spirit "and spiritual" in education need not refer to a divinity. "The talk is about lived reality, about experience and the possibility of experiencing. . . . The 'spiritual' is of this world, not of another world; of this life, not of another life." For Huebner, to have spirit is to be in touch with the forces or energies of life.[16] Being in touch with spirit allows one to see the essences of reality and to generate new ways of looking at knowledge, new relationships among people, and even new ways of perceiving one's existence.

More recently, Moffett noted that being spiritual is most practical. It allows for mindfulness, attention, and total awareness of what is going on around you and within you at all times.[17] Individuals who are spiritual develop empathy; they produce illuminated thought. Drawing on this source for design allows one to achieve a fuller knowing than just relying on science as the source of design. Drawing on this source enables the curriculum to be undergirded by questions about the nature of the world, the purpose of life, and what it means to be human and to be knowledgeable.

This source of curriculum design may well become even more prominent in the future. Pinar has introduced the concept of curriculum as theological text.[18] Looking at curriculum and its design from such a view integrates a new sense of spirituality. Indeed, compatible with Moffett's point on achieving a fuller knowing, Pinar comments that looking at curriculum as religious text may indeed allow for a blending of truth and faith, knowledge and ethics, and thought and action. No longer will these be considered polar opposites, with the suggestion that the former of a pair is the better of the two.[19] Certainly, some will take issue with this source of curriculum design. Indeed, they may actively work against its gaining any significance in curricularists' thinking. However, it does seem that curriculum types will need to be a little more cosmopolitan and tolerant in their thinking when contemplating eternal and divine sources as influencing the curriculum.

Knowledge as a Source. As already indicated, some might interpret science as the source of the curriculum design as too limiting because it ignores content from other fields of study. If we consider knowledge itself as one of the prime sources of curriculum, we certainly will not leave out any particular content. Hunkins has gone so far as to suggest that knowledge is perhaps the only source of curriculum, and that society and what we know about learners really serve as filters in the selection of content.[20]

However, Hunkins is quick to point out that making knowledge the sole source of curriculum is not to say that knowledge is some static phenomenon there for the taking. Indeed, he realizes that there is much to discuss about the nature, conditions, and social construction and reconstruction of knowledge, the purposes of such activities, and the very rules by which knowledge comes into being and is utilized. To say that knowledge is the sole or primary source of curriculum design is not to say that knowledge is a metadiscourse to be accepted uncritically. One can accept the centrality of knowledge to the curriculum and also embrace the postmodern stance of "incredulity toward metanarratives."[21]

Certainly, knowledge cannot be ignored. Herbert Spencer placed knowledge within the framework of curriculum when he asked, "What knowledge is of most worth?" It is the same question that Arno Bellack raised 80 years later when he examined knowledge in relationship to the various disciplines and structure of a curriculum.[22]

Those who place knowledge at the center, or as a key source, realize that it is organized in specialized ways. Disciplined knowledge has a particular structure and a particular method or methods by which its scholars extend its boundaries. Undisciplined knowledge does not have unique content, but has content that is clustered according to the focus of the investigation. Physics has a unique conceptual structure and a unique process. But home economics is undisciplined in that its content is not unique to itself but is drawn from various other disciplines and adapted to a special focus.

The Learner as a Source. Some believe that the curriculum should be derived from what we know about the learner: how he or she learns, forms attitudes, generates interests, and develops values. Some might find it strange that we all would not realize that the learner should be the key in guiding our thinking about curriculum design. Certainly, we have not ignored the learner. As Pinar posits, "students have occupied important 'places' in curriculum discourses from the beginning."[23] It seems to be rather a matter of focus. For progressive curricularists, humanistic educators, and many curricularists engaged in postmodern dialogue, the learner is considered the primary source.

Stressing the learner as the key influencing factor in designing the curriculum causes us to draw heavily on the psychological foundations. Today, much scholarly activity deals with the ways that minds work to create meaning. Much cognitive research has provided curriculum designers with ways to develop educational activities in the curriculum plan to facilitate perceiving, thinking, and learning. A key feature of curricular designs that draw on the learner as source emphasized learning by doing.[24] This, of course, dates back to Dewey who asserted that learning requires students to apply knowledge and solve problems.

Another key feature of this design is the emphasis on the social construction and reconstruction of knowledge and the empowerment of individuals to be engaged in these processes. This feature actually serves to connect this source to knowledge as a source. There also seems to be some overlap between science as a source, where the emphasis is on strategies for processing knowledge, and the learner as source where we draw our design from what we know about how individuals process information in order to learn. Of course, we could argue that all sources of curriculum design do overlap. We do not just draw from one source and consciously exclude the others. In developing a theory of imagination, educators deal with content that can be placed either under science as a source or learner as a source. We might even argue that imagination draws from the eternal truths.[25]

Using the learner as source for curriculum design means that we take those hallmarks of what makes a person a learner and try to emphasize them in the curriculum organization. We attempt to customize education so as to nurture the unique in students. We accept as a purpose of the cur-

riculum the emancipation of the individual. We realize that students must be nurtured to explore and manipulate their inner and outer worlds, their intellect, and their spirits.[26] As we discover more about the complexities of learning and reacting and imagining, we will bring more precision to this design. We are just beginning to recognize that imaginative activity is a factor in thinking and learning—and has been largely ignored in the past. It is perhaps in this realm where much creative thinking regarding curriculum design will occur. See Curriculum Tips 8-1.

Conceptual Framework: Horizontal and Vertical Organization

Curriculum design, the organization of the components or elements of curriculum, exists along two basic organizational dimensions: horizontal and vertical. *Horizontal* organization engages the curriculum worker with the concepts of scope and integration, that is, the side-by-side arrangement of curriculum elements. For instance, arranging content from the separate subjects of history, anthropology, and sociology into a course dealing with contemporary studies involves horizontal organization. Taking content from one subject, such as mathematics, and relating it to content in another, such as science, is another example of horizontal design.

Vertical organization, which centers on the concepts of sequence and continuity, is concerned with the longitudinal placement of curriculum elements. Placing "the family" in first-grade social studies and "the community" in second-grade social studies is an example of vertical organization. Frequently, curricula are organized so that the same topics are introduced and treated in different grades, but at more detailed and difficult levels. This also is vertical organization. For instance, in mathematics the concept of set is introduced in first grade and reintroduced or mentioned at each succeeding year in the elementary curriculum. This corresponds with Bruner's idea of the "spiral curriculum."[27]

Even though design decisions are essential, it appears that curricula in schools are not the result of careful design deliberations. In most school districts, overall curricular designs receive little attention. Curriculum often exists as disjointed

---

Curriculum Tips 8-1

Establishing a Broad Curriculum Design

Curriculum design refers to the placement of the key elements of curriculum and the relationships of these elements to one another, a type of mapping of the curriculum course of study. Here are a few helpful recommendations for developing a broad curriculum view, which one author calls a "map."

1. Be sure you comprehend the rationale for the course in context with the goals of the school (or the school district).
2. Be sure you understand the objectives of the course according to state or school district guidelines.
3. Clarify the focus of the course: Should it be designed to stress subject matter, learner needs, societal needs, or all three in some particular balance or weighting?
4. Determine if there is a special need, audience, or program for the course.
5. Identify the important components: content, skills, attitudes, and values.
6. Examine the components of the curriculum map to see if they (a) meet the objectives of the course, (b) address all the key thinking processes, (c) match student abilities according to the data obtained from needs assessment, (d) stimulate student interest, (e) are feasible in terms of school time allotted and school resources, and (f) are balanced in terms of content, skills, and attitudes.
7. Decide on the components so that they can be used as a framework for your unit planning.
8. Show the map to an experienced colleague or supervisor, and revise as necessary.

Source: Allan C. Ornstein, *Institutionalized Learning in America* (New Brunswick, N.J.: Transaction, 1990), p. 132.

---

clusters of content organized as particular items that frequently duplicate and/or conflict with other items. Robert Zais has noted that many courses in the schools' curricula are really the result of current "educational" fashion and not careful deliberations about design.[28]

DESIGN DIMENSION CONSIDERATIONS

Curriculum design is a statement noting the relationships that exist among the components or elements of a curriculum. Curricularists must, when considering design, view it on several dimensions: scope, sequence, continuity, integration, articulation, and balance.

Scope. When considering the design of a curriculum, educators need to address the breadth and depth of its content, that is, its scope. Tyler, in his classic book, referred to scope as consisting of all the content, topics, learning experiences, and organizing threads comprising the educational plan.[29] John Goodlad and Zhixin Su reiterated this definition of scope more recently, pointing out that it refers to the horizontal organization of the substance of the curriculum.[30]

By scope, we mean not only the depth and range of content to be provided students, but also all the varieties and types of educational experiences that are created to engage students in their learning. Scope not only refers to cognitive learning but also to affective learning, and some would argue to spiritual learning.[31] Sometimes the scope of the curriculum is less broad, representing just a simple listing of key topics and activities.

When teachers and other educators are deciding what content to include in the curriculum and the amount of detail to the content, they are engaged in considering the scope of the curriculum. In many ways, the current knowledge explosion has made dealing with scope almost overwhelming. Also, the recognized diversity among students puts increasing demands on teachers as to the scope of the content to include and activities to organize. Many teachers realize that the scope of possible topics and content areas to cover is just too broad. Some teachers respond to the overload of content by ignoring certain content areas or not including new content topics into the curriculum. Others attempt to relate certain topics to each other to create curriculum themes or threads.

Doll suggests that the scope of the curriculum can perhaps be kept at manageable levels by only addressing a limited number of objectives. These objectives would refer to general clusters of content that would be kept from expanding to a number beyond control.[32] The challenge is to achieve consensus with others that the chosen content categories are indeed of greater educational significance than those not selected. The challenge of determining scope goes back to the basic question posed by Herbert Spencer, "What knowledge is of most worth?"

When considering scope, we need to attend to the cognitive, affective, and psychomotor domains of learning. (We might add the moral or spiritual domain.) This further complicates scope, for decisions must be made that determine what will be covered and what will be the detail not only within each domain, but also which domain will receive the most emphasis. Tradition shows that the cognitive domain has received the greatest emphasis, drawing on the realm of knowledge. Frequently, at the secondary level of schooling, we draw upon disciplines of knowledge and their main concepts to determine the scope of the curriculum. However, there has recently been attention to assure that the affective domain, dealing with values and attitudes, and the psychomotor domain, dealing with motor skills and coordination, are addressed.

Sequence. When considering sequence, curricularists are challenged to deal effectively with the curricular elements so that the curriculum fosters cumulative and continuous learning, or what is referred to as the *vertical* relationship among curricular areas. Specifically, curricularists must de-

cide how content and experiences will occur and reoccur so that students have opportunities to connect and enrich their understanding of the curriculum presented or experienced.[33]

Taba has noted that people dealing with sequence have addressed content but have given little or no attention to the sequences of processes—those skills requisite for dealing with the content. She argued that this failure to pay serious attention to sequence in terms of the cumulative development of intellectual and affective processes has resulted in less-than-optimal curricula, as well as problems articulating among the levels of schooling.[34]

Persons addressing sequence have been aware of the longstanding controversy over whether the sequence of content and experiences should be based on the logic of the subject matter or on the way in which individuals process knowledge. Those arguing for sequence based on psychological principles draw on an understanding of and research on human growth, development, and learning. Piaget's research has provided a framework for sequencing content and experiences (or activities) and relating expectations to what we know about how individuals function at various cognitive levels.[35] Most school districts, when they formulate curriculum objectives, content, and experiences by grade levels, consider the students' stages of thinking. The curriculum is thus sequenced according to Piaget's theory of cognitive development.

Certainly, in organizing content into a productive sequence, we cannot totally disregard how individuals develop and learn. But neither can we neglect the substantive structure or logic of the content. Nor can we forget that learners have individual and group interests and needs and that these concerns must also be addressed.

Curricularists faced with sequencing content have drawn on some fairly well accepted learning principles. Smith, Stanley, and Shores introduced four such principles: simple to complex learning, prerequisite learning, whole to part learning, and chronological learning.

1. *Simple to complex learning* indicates that content is optimally organized in a sequence going from simple subordinate components or elements to complex components depicting interrelationships among components. It notes that optimal learning results when individuals are presented with easy, often concrete, content and then with more difficult, often abstract, content.

2. *Prerequisite learning* is similar to part to whole learning. It works on the assumption that bits of information or learning must be grasped before other bits of learning can be comprehended.

3. *Whole to part learning* receives support from cognitive psychologists. They urged that the curriculum be arranged so that the content or the experience is presented first in an overview (abstract) fashion to furnish students with a general idea of the information or situation.

4. *Chronological learning* is another organizer for sequencing content. Frequently, history, political science, and world events are organized in this manner. Curricularists refer to this type of organization as "world-related": The content is sequenced as it occurs in the world.[36]

Posner and Strike also furnished the field of curriculum with four other organizers for determining sequence: concept-related, inquiry-related, learning-related, and utilization-related learning.[37] The *concept-related* method draws heavily from the structure of knowledge. It focuses on the interrelationships of concepts rather than on knowledge of the concrete; it overlaps with the ideas of Hilda Taba and today's curriculum theorists such as Alan Bloom and Philip Phenix. The *inquiry-related* sequence is derived from the nature of procedures employed by scholars. The steps they would take in processing a sequence of concepts or principles in their investigations would become the sequence of topics in the curriculum. It coincides with the idea of teaching the syntactical structure of a subject, popularized by Bruner and Schwab. The *learner-related* sequence concerns how individuals learn or should experience content and activities; this is nothing more than old-fashioned progressivism. *Utilization-related* learning draws on how people who use some knowledge or engage in a particular activity in the world actually proceed through it. It closely resembles the "activity analysis" proposed by Bobbitt and Charters many years ago.

Continuity. Continuity deals with the vertical manipulation or repetition of curriculum components. Tyler indicated that if, for example, reading skills is an important objective, then "it is necessary to see that there is recurring and continuing opportunity for these skills to be practiced and developed. This means that over time the same kinds of skills will be brought into continuing operation."[38]

Continuity accounts for the reappearance in the curriculum of certain major ideas or skills about which educators feel students should have increased depth and breadth of knowledge over the length of the curriculum. It assures that students will have opportunities to revisit crucial concepts and skills as many times as necessary.[39] For instance, becoming a skilled reader requires numerous encounters over time with reading various types of materials. One does not learn how to conduct experiments unless one engages in such activities at various points in the curriculum, with each experiment providing opportunities to become more sophisticated in the processes. One learns to think deeply be having myriad instances in which thinking and questioning are continually enriched.[40]

Continuity is most evident in Bruner's notion of the "spiral curriculum." Bruner noted that the curriculum should be organized according to the interrelationships between the structure of the basic ideas of each major discipline. For students to grasp these basic ideas and structures, "they should be developed and redeveloped in a spiral fashion"—in increasing depth and breadth, as the pupils advance through the school program.[41]

Integration. Integration refers to the linking of all types of knowledge and experiences contained within the curriculum plan. It is essentially a design feature to bring into close relationship all the bits and pieces of the curriculum in ways that enable the individual to comprehend knowledge as unified, rather than as atomized.[42] It emphasizes horizontal relationships among various content topics and themes involving all domains of knowledge recognized.

Integration allows the learners to obtain a unified view of knowledge and an in-depth meaning of the subject matter. In fact, Saylor, Alexander, and Lewis went so far as to say that integration only occurs within the learner. "Although curriculum planners can organize opportunities for learning in such a way as to facilitate integration, it is the learners who integrate what they are learning through various educational experiences."[43] Taba also advanced a similar view, defining curriculum integration as "something that happens in an individual, whether or not the curriculum is organized for that purpose." This conception leads to a concern with the integrative process "in which students organize in a meaningful fashion knowledge and experiences which at first seem unrelated."[44] However, Taba did not just limit integration to that which was happening in the student. She realized that it was also an attempt to interrelate the content components with learning experiences and activities in ways that would facilitate learning. Goodlad and Su more recently expressed the same view that integration is of the learners and their subject matter.[45]

Of all the design dimensions, integration currently is receiving disproportionate attention from curriculum theorists and practitioners alike. It is as if many people have just discovered this aspect of design. Many appear unaware that Taba over thirty years ago noted that integration of knowledge was an important issue because of the knowledge explosion, increasing specialization in society, and expanding technology.

In the 1960s, Taba was concerned that much of the curriculum was disjointed, fragmented, segmented, and detached. In schools today, many argue that the curriculum still is arranged in bits and pieces that prevent students from seeing knowledge as unified. Certainly, in thinking about the next century and the education appropriate for it, we might well follow Taba's advice that there is a need to develop common knowledge by dealing with ideas that transcend and connect fields of study. We need to move to broader organizations of knowledge. We need, as Eisner points out, to attain an expanded view of knowledge.[46] He argues for a knowing that depends on direct experience that engages the learner in actual contact with the qualities of the environment or in touch with experiences conceived by the individual's imagination. Eisner's view is a demand that, when considering curriculum integration, we arrange curricular phenomena such that the individuals' intellects and hearts, and perhaps their souls, are addressed.

While one can easily obtain a definition of integration, there is a variety of current interpreta-

tions. Despite this we need to accept that integration serves to connect whatever it is that we are discussing. This is true whether we are discussing designing curricula into global clusters of content linked together by relational threads, whole language, or reading and writing across the curriculum. It is true in secondary programs such as STS, meaning science–technology–society, in which science is combined with social sciences in attempts to solve practical, everyday problems. Here the integrated approach takes the student outside the lab and away from the textbook into the local community, where the action is and where solving problems involves integration and application of subject matter.

The increased attention to integration results in part from the ongoing discussion of postmodernism, constructionism, and poststructuralism. These movements, which were discussed in more depth previously, all advance the idea that knowledge is not separated from its reality, that people cannot really disconnect themselves from their inquiry, and that the curriculum really cannot exist as separate bits. Things are connected and reconnected. Indeed, dynamism among the world and its players and therefore among the players and the phenomena of the curriculum serves to connect and integrate. Knowledge is dynamic, not static; knowledge cannot be separated, objectified, and then quantified with precision. One cannot separate the known from the knower. Everything is integrated and interconnected. Life is a series of emerging themes.[47]

The active life is full of surprises. So is the integrated curriculum. Our view of curriculum cannot be static. One cannot integrate or create themes or related clusters in the curriculum and think that the job is done. Also, one should realize that it is not possible to integrate totality. Totality cannot be completely grouped; it is ever expanding and emerging. As Pratt states, "We will never achieve total integration of knowledge." However, we do need to realize that "our knowledge is never completely disintegrated."[48] To attain what is essentially partial integration, we must be mindful of this design dimension. For science and the humanities to be connected and integrated, we must consciously plan it. If mathematics and art are to be linked, informed effort is demanded of us. It is likely that this design dimension will continue to be center stage in the dialogue of those concerned with curriculum.

Articulation. Articulation refers to the interrelatedness of various aspects of the curriculum. The relation can be either vertical or horizontal. Vertical articulation depicts the relationships of certain aspects in the curriculum sequence to lessons, topics, or courses appearing later in the program's sequence. For instance, a teacher might design introductory or ninth-grade algebra so that concepts in the algebra class are related to key concepts in a geometry course. When viewed vertically, we usually are referring to the sequencing of content from one grade level to another. The key reason for addressing vertical articulation is to assure that students receive those learnings that are prerequisite to later learnings in the curriculum. Horizontal articulation refers to the association between or among elements occurring simultaneously. Horizontal articulation takes place, for instance, when curriculum designers attempt to develop interrelationships between eighth-grade social studies and eighth-grade English courses.

When considering articulation horizontally, we are equating it with what some have called correlation. In horizontal articulation, curriculum decision makers are striving to meld those contents in one part of the educational program with those contents that are similar or have a logical or educational link. In those curricula where thinking is being stressed across the curriculum, we are making horizontal linkages dealing with thinking in, say, mathematics with thinking in science. Much of the present-day emphasis on "integrating the curriculum" is really an effort at horizontal articulation.

Articulation is difficult to achieve, and few school districts have developed procedures by which the various interrelationships within and among subjects are clearly defined. One reason for the difficulty is that it is sometimes a difficult task to determine just what these interrelationships are. Curricula arranged by subjects often pay no attention to connections with any other subject matter.

Another reason for the difficulty in attaining articulation is that we are not as far along in cooperative curriculum development as our educational talk might indicate. For example, within school districts, it is sometimes difficult to achieve articulation from one school to another school. Also, we could argue that there is need for articulation among school districts as well as within school districts. This is especially important at a time when the population is mobile. Students new to a school district sometimes experience a repeat of information they had in their former school at a previous grade level. Other times, they experience gaps; that is, they miss a particular concept or topic because it was offered the year prior to their arrival.

Balance. When designing a curriculum, educators are also concerned that appropriate weight be given to each aspect of the design so that distortions do not occur. In a balanced curriculum, students have opportunities to master knowledge and to internalize and utilize it in ways that are appropriate for their personal, social, and intellectual goals. To say that the components must be balanced is easier said than done. John Goodlad argues that the curriculum should be balanced in terms of subject matter and the learner. However, he comments, "The prospect of stressing one to the exclusion of the other appears scarcely worthy of consideration. Nonetheless, the interested observer has little difficulty finding school practices emphasizing one component to the impoverishment of the other."[49]

Adding to the complexity of attaining balance in the curriculum is the fact that what might be interpreted as balance today might well be imbalance tomorrow. The times in which schools find themselves are always changing, and what should be emphasized is in a state of flux. Also, Doll points out that balance is problematic because we are striving to localize and individualize the curriculum in its content and experiences while at the same time addressing a tradition that plans schooling for the masses of students.[50] Thus there is a balancing problem between the needs and interests of the individual students and a common content that all students should know.

It behooves curriculum specialists to maintain a balance in the curriculum despite pressures and fads. Oliva has listed a set of points to consider that can provide guidance in attaining balance in the curriculum:

1. The child-centered and subject-centered curriculum.
2. The needs of the individual and those of society.
3. The needs of common education and specialized education.
4. Breadth and depth of curriculum content.
5. Traditional content and innovative content.
6. The needs of the unique range of pupils regarding their learning styles.
7. Different teaching methods and educational experiences.
8. Work and play.
9. The community and school as educational forces.[51]

Following these suggestions may not make the task of attaining balance easier, but it may increase the probability of attaining it. Keeping the curriculum "in balance" requires continuous fine-tuning of the curriculum as well as balance in one's view of philosophy and psychology of learning so as not to fall prey to a particular drummer or popular tune. See Curriculum Tips 8-2.

REPRESENTATIVE CURRICULUM DESIGNS

Curriculum components can be organized in numerous ways. However, despite all the discussion about postmodern views of knowledge and creating curricula for social awareness and emancipation, most curriculum designs are modifications and/or interpretations of three basic designs: (1) subject-centered designs, (2) learner-centered designs, and (3) problem-centered designs. Each category comprises several examples. Subject-centered designs include subject designs, discipline designs, broad field designs, correlation designs and process designs. Learner-centered designs are those identified as child-centered designs, experience designs, romantic/ radical designs, and humanistic designs. Problem-centered designs consider life situations, core designs, and social problem/reconstructionist designs.

Subject-centered Designs

Subject-centered designs are by far the most popular and widely used curriculum designs. This is because knowledge and content are well accepted as integral parts of the curriculum. Schools have a strong history of academic rationalism; furthermore, the materials available for school use also reflect content organization.

The category of subject-centered designs has the most classifications of any of the designs. This richness may result from our greater understanding of knowledge or from the very strong tradition knowledge or content has in our culture. Concepts central to a culture are more highly elaborated than peripheral ones. In our culture, content is central to schooling; we thus have many concepts to depict our diverse organizations.

Subject Design. The subject design is both the oldest school design and the best known—to both teachers and laypeople. It is so well known because teachers and laypersons are usually educated and/or trained in schools employing it. It is also popular because it corresponds to textbook treatment and how teachers are trained as subject specialists.[52] This design is based on a belief that what makes humans unique and distinctive is their intellect; the searching for and the attainment of knowledge are the natural fulfillment of that intellect.

An early spokesperson for the subject curriculum was Henry Morrison, who was the state superintendent of public instruction in New Hampshire before he joined the University of Chicago. Morrison argued that the subject matter curriculum contributed most to the literacy of the individual and that literacy skills should be the focus of the elementary curriculum. This orientation to subject matter reflected a mental discipline approach to learning and a perennialist orientation to subject matter. Morrison also felt that such a design could allow a student at the secondary school level to develop interest and competence in one subject area. However, he believed that a variety of courses should be offered to cater to the diverse needs of students.[53]

William Harris, superintendent of the St. Louis schools in the 1870s, also receives credit for fostering this curriculum design. Under Harris's guidance, the St. Louis schools established a subject-oriented curriculum that took firm hold there well into this century. Indeed, some would argue that the subject design is still alive and well. One educator notes that most Americans would

---

========== *Curriculum Tips 8-2* ==========

Guidelines for Curriculum Design

The following guiding statements will help to clarify some of the steps involved in curriculum design. These statements, according to the authors, are based on school practice and apply to all curriculum models.

1. The curriculum design committee should include teachers, parents, and administrators; some schools might include students, too.
2. The committee should establish a sense of mission or purpose in the early stages or meetings.
3. Needs and priorities should be addressed in relation to students and society.
4. School goals and objectives should be reviewed, but they should not serve as the guiding criteria upon which to design the curriculum. Such criteria usually connote a broad educational philosophy to guide curriculum development.
5. Alternative curriculum designs should be contrasted in terms of advantages and disadvantages, such as cost, scheduling, class size, facilities and personnel required, and existing relationship to present programs.
6. To help teachers gain insight into the new or modified design, the design should reveal expected cognitive and affective skills, concepts, and outcomes.
7. Principals have significant impact on curriculum design through their influence on school climate and their support of the curriculum process.
8. District administrators, especially the superintendent, have only a peripheral impact on curriculum design, since their outlook and concerns center on managerial activities. While their curriculum role is minor, their support and approval are essential.
9. State education officials have even less impact on curriculum design, although various departments publish guides, bulletins, and reports that can be used for purposes of information. However, these educators establish policies, rules, and regulations that affect curriculum and instruction.
10. The influence of special-interest groups and local politics should not be underestimated. Polarization or conflict has frequently obscured reasonable efforts for reform and meaningful dialogue between educators and parents in regard to educational matters.

Source: Francis P. Hunkins and Allan C. Ornstein, "Designing the Curriculum: A Challenge for Principals," *NASSP Bulletin* (September 1988), pp. 58–59.

---

recognize this curriculum design, which he classifies as the conservative liberal arts design, as the type they experienced in school. In the mid-1930s, Robert Hutchins indicated what subjects would comprise such a curriculum design: (1) language and its uses (reading, writing, grammar, literature); (2) mathematics; (3) sciences; (4) history; (5) foreign languages.[54]

Today's emphasis on a common core curriculum, exemplified by Boyer, Goodlad, and Sizer and the theme of educational excellence, exemplified by the national task force reports since the mid-1980s reflects a subject orientation. The current attention on standards reflects the subject design, and the discipline design which is discussed next.

In the subject matter design, the curriculum is organized according to how essential knowledge has been developed in the various subject areas. With the explosion of knowledge and the resulting specializations in the various fields of knowledge, subject divisions have increased in number and sophistication. For instance, history has been divided into cultural history, economic history, and geographic history. English can be divided into literature, writing, speech, reading, linguistics, and grammar as major subject divisions.

This organization of curricular content also assumes that subjects are best outlined in textbooks. The teacher usually assumes the active role. Lecture, recitation, and large group discussion are major instructional techniques utilized with this design. Usually, discussion proceeds from simple to complex ideas. Logic is emphasized.

Advocates of this design defend the emphasis on verbal activities. They argue that knowledge and ideas are best communicated and stored in verbal form. Many educators today, in fact, agree that learning is primarily a verbal activity. Advocates also note that a prime advantage of the design is that it introduces students to the essential knowledge of society. Also, the design is easy to deliver because complementary textbooks and support materials are commercially available. Tradition, too, is on its side. People are familiar with this format, having gone through schools using it.

Critics, however, say that the design prevents individualization of the program and deemphasizes the notion of the learner. Some argue that the design disempowers students by taking away their rights to choose the content that is most meaningful to them.[55] Other critics contend that stress on subject matter fails to foster social, psychological, and physical development and to some extent fosters a scholarly elite, a ruling class based on knowledge. Another drawback of this design is that learning tends to be compartmentalized and to stress mnemonic skills. A serious problem is that this design stresses content and neglects students' needs, interests, and experiences. Another problem is that, in delivering such a curriculum, the teachers tend to foster in students a passivity for learning.

Dewey was concerned about isolating subject matter from the learner's reality—knowledge divorced from the learner's experiences, essentially second-hand knowledge and other persons' knowledge. Such knowledge tends to be merely verbal, and learning primarily becomes remem-

bering other peoples' ideas.[56] For Dewey, the curriculum did not need to emphasize subject matter or the learner. It should do both. From the analysis of the current scene, it seems that Dewey's and others advice to combine subject matter and pupils' experiences has gone unheeded. For instance, while following much of Tyler's advice on creating curriculum, educators have not reflected on his point that overemphasizing subject matter results in a curriculum that is "too technical and too specialized" for most students. What is needed is a common education that integrates content with the learner's prior experiences; this leads to meaningful, new experiences.[57]

Discipline Design. The discipline design that appeared in the post-World War II era evolved from the separate-subject design. This new design grew rapidly in popularity during the 1950s and reached its zenith during the mid-1960s. Like the separate-subject design, the discipline design's basis is the inherent organization of content. However, whereas the subject design does not make clear the foundational basis upon which it is organized or established, the discipline design's orientation does specify its focus on the academic disciplines.

King and Brownell, proponents of this design, indicate that a discipline is specific knowledge that has the following essential characteristics: a community of persons, an expression of human imagination, a domain, a tradition, a mode of inquiry, a conceptual structure, a specialized language, a heritage of literature, a network of communications, a valuative and affective stance, and an instructive community.[58]

This stress on disciplined knowledge can be likened to a "command" to only teach the disciplines—science, mathematics, English, history, and so on. The assumption used by advocates to support their advice is that the school is a microcosm of the world of intellect and that the disciplines reflect that world.[59] This means that the manner in which the content is to be learned is suggested by the methods scholars employ to study the content of their fields. Students in history would approach the subject matter as would a historian, and students in biology would investigate biological topics following procedures advocated by biologists.

This point is important. Even though proponents of the discipline design view as necessary experiencing the disciplines in the school, they stress understanding the conceptual structures and the processes of the disciplines. This is perhaps the essential difference between the discipline design and the subject matter design. In the discipline design, students experience the disciplines so that they can comprehend and even conceptualize, whereas in the subject matter design the students are considered to have learned if they just acquire knowledge and information. Sometimes, it is difficult to determine whether in fact a classroom has a subject matter or a discipline design. The key distinguishing characteristic seems to be whether students are involved in actually using some of the methods of the discipline to process information.

In the discipline design, students are encouraged to see the basic logic or structure of each discipline—the key relationships, concepts, and principles—what Joseph Schwab called the "substantive structure" and Phil Phenix called the "realms of meaning."

Considering structure or meaning allows a "deep" understanding of the content and a realization of ways in which such knowledge can be applied to generate additional meaning. This is what Harry Broudy calls "applicative knowledge,"[60] knowledge we can directly use, or apply, such as knowledge of problem-solving procedures.

The student who cultivates fluency with the modes of inquiry really attains mastery of the content area and is able to continue independently his or her learning in the field. The student need not always require the teacher to present information. Ideally, supporters of this design wish students to function as "little" scholars in the respective fields of the school curriculum. When learning mathematics, students would be neophyte mathematicians. When engaged in studying history, the students would employ the methods of historiography.

The emphasis on disciplines and structure eventually leads to Jerome Bruner's classic book, *The Process of Education.* The very title suggests that education, more precisely learning, should emphasize process or procedural knowledge. Bruner states that the "curriculum of a subject should be determined by . . . the underlying princi-

ples that give structure to that subject."[61] Organizing the curriculum according to the structure of the discipline will cause relationships to be made clear, indicate how elementary knowledge is related to advanced knowledge, allow individuals to reconstruct meaning within the content area, and furnish the means for advancing through the content area.

A most attractive notion of the disciplines approach expounded by Bruner was that "any subject can be taught in some effectively honest form to any child at any stage of development."[62] Contrary to what many persons had held, Bruner argued that students are able to comprehend the fundamental principles of any subject at almost any age. And children can thus understand the structure and operations of a discipline at any age—such understanding does not need to await adolescence or adulthood.

Bruner has been criticized as having a romantic notion of students as scholars. Developmentalists have disagreed with his thesis that "intellectual activity anywhere is the same," and point out that the processes of the young child, for example, differ in kind and in degree from the thinking processes of adolescents and adults. There are also differences between sexes in the early grades in terms of how children process cognitive information. The current deliberation about postmodernism is related to this design. The discussion about whether modernism is dead, passed, or reborn or whether postmodernism is being born or is itself losing life is really related to how people perceive the nature of disciplined knowledge. The reader might want to return to Chapter 6 to refresh his or her understanding of modernism and postmodernism. Presently, most teachers who accept the discipline design are really not that engaged in the dialogue. But, eventually, what theoreticians and philosophers are positing about the nature of knowledge and how knowledge is or is not constructed will influence what makes up the substantive structure of the disciplines and the procedures by which knowledge is constructed and deconstructed.

We do not see an early end to this dialogue. Those who favor this design and consider themselves modernists will think that we can formulate some consensus as to what comprises the structure of knowledge. They will argue that this design should enable students to become skilled in enacting systematic procedures for investigating reality by knowing the rules of the game. Those who consider themselves postmodernists will purport that discipline knowledge is not static and that the rules of the games, the procedures that we employ, are emergent. We cannot really come to agreement as to conclusions. We need to recognize that there will be new ideas and conceptions of knowledge that will upset previously held convictions.[63]

In some ways, the arguments between modernists and postmodernists are illusionary. Few scholars assume knowledge to be static. Most believe that new knowledge socially constructed will upset previously held views and understandings. Those who write about chaos theory recognize that reality is dynamic and emergent and that our understanding of it and even the rules by which we construct and critique knowledge of it are ever changing.[64]

However, it appears that most critics of this curriculum design are not really engaged in such discussions. They are not critiquing the design on the basis that it appears to accept a grand narrative, such as furthering the development of the rational mind, but on less esoteric features. For instance, some educators argue that the design seems only to address the interests of students who are college bound.[65] Many others have criticized the design for assuming that students must adapt to the curriculum, rather than the curriculum adapting or being modified to meet students' requirements.[66] Additionally, the design was attacked for assuming that all students have a common or at least a similar type of learning style.

Perhaps the greatest shortcoming of the design was that it caused the schools to ignore the vast amount of information that could not be classified as disciplined knowledge. Such knowledge, dealing with aesthetics, humanism, personal-social living, and vocational education, is difficult to categorize as a discipline, although Phil Phenix would argue that it can be achieved.[67]

Broad Fields Design. The broad fields design, which may also go by the name of interdisciplinary design, is another variation of the subject-centered design. It appeared as an effort to correct what many educators considered the fragmentation and compartmentalization caused by the sub-

ject design. It was an attempt to integrate content that appeared to fit together logically. Thus the separate social sciences of geography, economics, political science, anthropology, sociology, and history were fused into social studies. Linguistics, grammar, literature, composition, and spelling were collapsed into language arts. Biology, chemistry, and physics were integrated into general science. Because of this fusion of subjects, educators sometimes assign the fused subjects design to this organization. Others say that the fused subject design is a design unto itself.[68] However, we find that there really is no difference in kind between what some call the fused design and others call the broad fields design. It is only a matter of degree as to how many subject areas are related and collapsed into a curricular focus.

The idea for this design was both bold and simple. Educators essentially had only to meld two or more related subjects, already well known in the schools, into a single broad or fused field of study. However, it was a change from the traditional subject pattern of the perennialists and essentialists. While the design first appeared shortly after the first decade of this century at the college level, it gained its most popularity at the elementary and secondary levels of schooling. This continues to the present day. Its use today at the college level really is only seen in introductory courses, but it is widespread with the K-12 curriculum.

Harry Broudy et al. offered a unique broad fields design during the Sputnik era. They suggested that the entire curriculum be organized into the following categories: (1) symbolics of information—English, foreign language, and mathematics; (2) basic sciences—general science, biology, physics, and chemistry; (3) developmental studies—evolution of the cosmos, evolution of social institutions, and evolution of human culture; (4) exemplars—modes of aesthetic experience that would include art, music, drama, literature; and (5) molar problems that would address typical social problems.[69] This last category would have a yearly variety of courses depending on the social problems of the times.

The broad fields design allows students to discern relationships among the various aspects of the curriculum content, as well as wholeness of meaning. In this connection, one educator has referred to this design as the wave of the future, whereby subject matter "is less compartmentalized and more integrated and holistic. Although traditional subject boundaries will remain, there will be increased cross-subject material." Knowledge will no longer be fragmented or linear, "but multidisciplinary and multidimensional."[70]

One might go even further in reflecting on the nature of this design in the future. Currently, the broad fields design is still the bringing together of well-accepted content fields of subjects or disciplines. Some might argue that the current emphasis on constructivism in schools suggests that, rather than subjects or disciplines coming together in interdisciplinary organization, we will have broad fields made up of related conceptual clusters. These clusters can be connected by some type of theme. Some educators are calling for the organization of curriculum as integrated thematic units.[71] Others are using the term *holistic curriculum* for the future progression of this design.[72]

Broad fields design draws heavily on the design dimension of integration. It is very much a design that can be interpreted to be saying that the separate subject is dead.[73] No metanarrative should stand. Rather, we should have a design that draws on emergent clusters of problems and questions, which will engage students in constructing and reconstructing information.[74]

In broad fields design, students are invited to actually participate through the construction of meaning in grasping the meaning or meanings of the whole.[75] Students are engaged in creating webs and putting their own spin on webs created by the teacher. Much talk about integrated curriculum, which is really discussing the broad fields design, celebrates curriculum webs. Often these webs are loosely connected avenues of thematic content.[76] At other times, the webs are connections between and among related concepts. Many years ago, Taba discussed the concept of web when urging teachers to create cognitive maps in constructing curriculum.[77] Today, such cognitive map webs are identified as conceptual clusters.[78]

Of all the subject matter designs, the broad fields design may be the most active in the future. It may be the design that allows for hybrid types of content and knowledge to be created and incorporated into the curriculum in ways that are dynamic and emergent and allow students to participate in their own personalized constructions and reconstructions of knowledge. It is possible that this broad field design will meld with the learner-centered designs that are discussed later.

Like any design, this one has its problems. One is the issue of breadth versus depth. Having students spend a year studying social studies teaches them a greater and more varied range of social science concepts than they would learn if they just took a year of history. But is their knowledge of the various social sciences superficial? Certainly, a year of history will furnish more historical knowledge than a year of social studies. But then the question arises, at least at the elementary level, is it necessary to have great depth? Is not the purpose of the curriculum to have students understand the entire field of social science knowledge? How this question is answered depends in part on the particular philosophical posture of the school.

The issue of depth is even more central when one expands this design so that it is classified as an integrated curriculum. Just how much depth will students get following or constructing various webs of related concepts. Just how much depth does one get in science by following the theme of dinosaurs or holidays? In whole language, will students attain sufficient depth of understanding of reading, writing, and listening? Again, the philosophical postures of schools and educators will influence their responses. Also, where one places oneself regarding being modern or postmodern will shape one's response.

Correlation Design. Correlation is a design employed by those who do not wish to go as far as creating a broad fields design, but who realize that there are times when separate subjects require some linkage in order to reduce fragmentation of curricular content. Existing as a midpoint between separate subjects and total integration of content, it attempts to identify ways in which subjects can be related to one another while still maintaining their identity as subjects.

Perhaps the two most frequently correlated subjects are English literature and history at the secondary level and language arts and social studies at the elementary level. While studying a period in history, students in their English class read novels that relate to the same time period. Science and mathematics are also courses frequently correlated. Students in a chemistry course may have a unit in mathematics that deals with the mathematics required to conduct an experiment. However, the content areas remain distinct, and the teachers of these courses retain their subject matter specialties.

The notion of a correlated design was attractive to many. Alberty and Alberty were famous for their discussion of the correlated curriculum at the secondary level. They presented a variant of this design that employed an "over-arching theme." This version of core retained the basic content of the subjects, but the content was selected and organized with reference to broad themes, problems, or units.[79]

This variation of core required that classes be scheduled in a block of time. So scheduled, teachers of the various content areas to be correlated could work together and have students working on assignments that drew from the correlated content areas. Combining various subjects with other subjects is only limited by our imagination. It is possible to relate literature and art that depicts similar issues in verbal or pictorial form. Science is now being taught through literature. It is conceivable that courses in computer science can be correlated with separate courses in art, music, or economics.

Currently, few teachers are actually using the correlated design, possibly because it requires that they plan their lessons cooperatively. This is somewhat difficult to accomplish because teachers have self-contained classes at the elementary level and often do not have time for such collaboration. At the secondary level, teachers are organized into separate departments that tend to encourage isolation. Teachers must also meet time schedules dictated by specified classes and so may have little time to work with other teachers in team-teaching arrangements. Furthermore, most class schedules do not allow a sufficient block of time for students to meaningfully study correlated subjects. Modular scheduling and flexible scheduling, which would allow for this, really never received wide acceptance.

Process Designs. As indicated when discussing discipline-centered designs, attention is often given to the procedures and processes by which individuals advance knowledge. Thus, students in biology would learn the methods for dealing with biological knowledge; history students would learn the ways of historiography, and students studying anthropology would learn the various ethnographic procedures appropriate for the study of culture and society.

While advocates of the disciplines design urge students to learn process, other educators are suggesting curricular designs that stress the learning of general procedures, general processes not specific to any particular discipline, but applicable to all. The numerous curricula for teaching critical thinking exemplify this procedural design.[80]

Educators have always suggested that students be taught to think in schools. Curricular designs need to address process, or how learners learn, and the application of process to subject matter. Barry Beyer has written extensively on strategies of thinking. His curriculum would be organized around three key thinking strategies: problem solving, decision making, and conceptualizing. Accompanying these thinking strategies are micro-thinking skills such as analysis and synthesis of data necessary for engaging the major thinking strategies.[81]

Francis Hunkins has urged educators to engage students in learning how to question, to construct meaning through particular questioning strategies. These strategies are central to the student who is to challenge, construct, deconstruct, and reconstruct knowledge so as to obtain the essences of meaning requisite for effective functioning in an information age.[82] Process designs require educators to reflect on what it means to be educated within such a dynamic, emerging age. This design celebrates the fact that we are all, students and educators, in the knowledge business and that we all must create, manage, and utilize information so as to gain knowledge and, ultimately, wisdom. "The good thinker, possessing attributes enabling him or her to create and use meaning . . . possesses a spirit of inquiry, a desire to pose questions central to the world. The good thinker ponders the world, actual and desired, querying things valued and desired."[83] Process designs focus on the student as meaning maker.

Marilyn Adams points out that the fundamental assumption motivating all curricula on thinking is that there exists a certain set of skills or processes that are common to thinking in general, regardless of subject, domain, or purpose. The common goal of the curricula is to teach those processes and, in that sense, fall under the general rubric of process-oriented curricula.[84] It is this emphasis on processes that is applicable to all fields of knowledge that distinguishes this curriculum design from the discipline design in which the procedural knowledge is specifically related to the specialized discipline. Thinking critically is not unique to history or physics. Neither is thinking creatively the sole domain of art or literature. Thinking curricula can be organized so that procedural knowledge is integrated throughout the total curriculum.

Adams played a significant role in the development of a curriculum entitled, "Odyssey: A Curriculum for Thinking."[85] The curriculum was designed by the collaborative effort of Harvard University and the Venezuelan Ministry of Education and was influenced by two basic thinking components: information and interpretion. Thus the curriculum included special types of information and various strategies for interpreting such information or thinking about it. The processes provide the central structure for this curriculum design. Table 8-1 presents the total curriculum. By studying the table, it is evident that the process is not subject or discipline specific. But it is important to note that there is more than procedural knowledge in this curriculum. The units in this thinking series engage students in learning how to process content across subjects. For instance, in learning the content regarding analysis or reasoning, students are acquiring approaches for studying content in any subject. But in reality there is no content-free curriculum; it is the nature of the content that receives a different emphasis. Many of the processes are specific to a subject, or tend to be common in one more than in another, but the examples and exercises tend to be rich in diverse content areas. Instead of recalling knowledge in one subject, students are asked to think, react, and/or explore—to learn processes they can use in many subjects.

Another example of cognitive processing which is generic involves computer programming. Because there are so many programs available in many subject areas and grade levels, it is not essential to have program knowledge. Nonetheless,

TABLE 8-1 Odyssey: A Curriculum for Thinking

Theme 1: Foundations of Reasoning
  Unit 1: Observation and classification
  Unit 2: Ordering
  Unit 3: Developing hierarchy
  Unit 4: Employing analogies
  Unit 5: Spatial reasoning and strategies

Theme 2: Understanding Language
  Unit 1: Word relations
  Unit 2: Language,, its structure
  Unit 3: Gathering and interpreting information

Theme 3: Verbal Reasoning
  Unit 1: Assertions
  Unit 2: Arguments

Theme 4: Problem Solving
  Unit 1: Linear representations
  Unit 2: Tabular representations
  Unit 3: Simulating representations
  Unit 4: Engaging in trial and error
  Unit 5: Reflecting on implications

Theme 5: Decision Making
  Unit 1: Introduction to decision making
  Unit 2: Gathering and evaluating information
  Unit 3: Analyzing decision contexts

Theme 6: Inventive Thinking
  Unit 1: Design
  Unit 2: Processes as designs

Source: Adapted from Marilyn J. Adams, "Thinking Skills Curricula: Their Promises and Progress," *Educational Psychologists* (Winter 1989), pp. 50–51.

according to one educator, computer programming is an active mental endeavor, which fosters critical thinking, rational thinking, and problem-solving skills. Programming may be the only generic subject that succeeds in teaching students about things as a process. Writing and debugging a program force students to think logically and carefully about a subject. In addition, students can learn a repertoire of *templates,* that is, patterns of code using more than a single feature, to perform common tasks and complex mental activities.[86]

Templates can be likened to cognitive schema among teachers—methods for processing information. An analysis of the program can also tell the user about the quality of the thinking that went into the solution. When students master computer programming, it becomes possible for teachers to teach in different ways, and students to think in multiple ways, ways that indirectly foster achievement in traditional subject matter. For these reasons, students should be encouraged to learn how to program.

Seymor Papert argues that the computer is a medium of expression and should be used to build a sense of inquiry to "mess about," to explore, and to improve thinking. He also argues that the main impact of computers on learning is not teaching students practical uses of the computer such as word processing or data filing; the real impact will only come when students are taught how to program.[87] Hence they must process information, think logically, and problem solve.

It is likely that, with the knowledge explosion continuing to explode, as well as the increase in computers and computer programming, curricula with a process design, that is, designs emphasizing procedural knowledge, are going to receive increasing attention. These ways of knowing or processing are essentially "learning how to learn" designs.

The process designs emphasize those procedures and dispositions to act that enable students to analyze their realities and create frameworks by which the knowledge derived can be arranged. Often the organizational frameworks differ from the way the world appears to the casual observer.[88] Currently, there is much dialogue about involving students in their learning and empowering them to be the central players in the classroom. Present discussion on constructivism stresses process designs. However, much debate occurs as to the nature of the process to be stressed. Many process designs that privilege the scientific method are challenged by some as not appropriate for a postmodern world. Often the modern process design teaches students that they can use procedure to uncover a reality that exists "out there." The postmodern view challenges that. Students must realize that the methods employed in inquiry result in a world constructed, a world we can and must remake and reconstruct, as the need arises.[89]

In those process designs that reflect a modern orientation, the purpose of having students learn the process, the procedural knowledge, is to arrive at conclusions or to come to some degree of consensus. However, people like Lyotard argue that we engage in process, in the raveling and unraveling of our understandings, not to come to consensus but to search for instabilities. This postmodern posture realizes that the process design curriculum stresses new statements and new ideas that themselves are open to challenge. Curriculum process designs are organized so that students can make their understandings continually new.[90]

In a postmodern process design curriculum, students would even be encouraged to unravel and deconstruct the very processes by which they investigate. Nothing is certain, not even the manner in which we question. Processing reality to gain understanding and, one hopes, the wise use of knowledge is essentially a language game. In this game, according to some postmodernists, the individual employs language not to represent reality, but rather to construct it.[91] Certainly, this language game follows rules or procedures, but for some these rules will emerge from the actual playing, rather than being set prior to the game. Teaching process within this framework may prove difficult; the more appropriate approach may be to set up situations in which the process or the procedures emerge in the actual making or constructing of meaning.

Process designs may be the most dynamic in the future. Much discussion, disputation, is occurring. It is not likely that this dialogue, indeed confrontation, will diminish. Some postmodernists would probably celebrate the fact that there can be no final agreement. They hold that there can never be a permanent consensus as to the optimum process by which to organize the curriculum. We can only arrive at various temporary points of agreement, along the way to discovering, inventing, and constructing new ideas as to how to generate sense of our world and our participation in it. It is quite likely that process designs will meld increasingly with those designs identified as learner centered.

Learner-centered Designs

All curricularists are concerned with creating curricula that are valuable to students. In response to those educational planners who valued subject matter, educators early in this century asserted that students are the center or focus of the program. Supporters of this posture, largely progressives, advocated what have come to be called learner-centered designs. These designs are found more frequently at the elementary school level where teachers tend to stress the whole child. At the secondary level, the emphasis is more on subject-centered designs largely because of the influence of textbooks and the colleges and universities at which the discipline is a major organizer for the curriculum.

Child-centered Designs. Advocates of the child-centered or student-centered design believed that if we are to optimize learning then the student must be active in his or her environment. Learning should not be separated from the ongoing lives of students, as is often the case with the subject-centered designs. Indeed, it should be based on students' lives, their needs and interests. Taba noted that the rationale for this design was that "people learn only what they experience. Only learning that is related to active purposes and is rooted in experience translates itself into behavior changes."[92]

The shifting of emphasis from the tradition of subject matter to the needs and interests of children was part of Rousseau's educational philosophy demonstrated in his book on the education of Emile first published in 1762. Rousseau believed that children should be taught in context with their natural environment, drawing on their needs and interests in creating an educational program. However, Rousseau did not believe in just letting children run free. They required guidance from the teacher. But the manner in which the teacher stimulated the student's curiosity had to be appropriate for the particular developmental level of the child. In a very real sense, Rousseau was the first to advocate a developmental approach to teaching and learning.

Proponents of this design also drew on the thinking of some other early pedagogical giants. Heinrich Pestalozzi and Friedrich Froebel argued that children would attain self-realization through social participation; they voiced the principle of learning by doing. Their social approach to education furnished a foundation for much of the work of Francis Parker.

The child-centered design, often attributed to John Dewey, was really conceived by Parker, who laid the foundations for this movement. Parker had studied pedagogy in Germany, and he knew well the work of Pestalozzi and Froebel. Like Rousseau, Parker believed that effective education did not require strict discipline. Rather, the approach to instruction should be somewhat free, drawing on the child's innate tendency to become engaged in things that interested him or her. Teachers who involved children in conversations would find that students could effectively participate in their own learning. Parker took his views of teaching into practice in developing school curricula in science and geography. In the teaching of geography, he urged teachers to have children experience the content as would a geographer out in the field, doing observations and recording them in sketch books and later analyzing them. Parker was superintendent of schools in Quincy, Massachusetts, and his approach to curriculum was called the Quincy system.[93]

Dewey deduced similar notions in his early thinking. In 1896, he had a chance to put some of his ideas into action in his laboratory school at the University of Chicago. The curriculum was organized around human impulses: the impulse to socialize, the impulse to construct, the impulse to inquire, to question, to experiment, and the impulse to express or to create artistically.[94]

The emphasis on the child displaced the emphasis on subject matter. In addition, when subject matter was presented, it was no longer separated into narrow divisions, but was integrated around units of experience or social problems. The idea that a solution to a problem required using methods and materials from several subject fields was inherent in the child-centered, experience-centered curriculum. This new emphasis on the learner also led to "life needs," "life-adjustment education," "persistent life situations," "common learnings," and "core"[95] methods for organizing bodies of knowledge and subject matter. Here the idea was to integrate subject matter from various fields as needed for the understanding and solution of social problems, as well as to meet the developmental needs of students.

The child-centered design of curriculum flourished in the 1920s and 1930s, primarily under the work of the progressives such as Ellsworth Collings, who introduced the child-centered curriculum in the public schools of McDonald County, Missouri, and William Kilpatrick who created the "project method" which engaged children in their learning at the Lincoln School in New York City.[96] Although the "Project Method" was written up and discussed extensively in the literature, it only gained limited acceptance.

Certainly, today, in some schools the child-centered design is employed. However, as Goodlad and Su point out, such designs are often found to be a contradiction to a view of curriculum as primarily content driven.[97] Child-centered designs celebrate students' interests. There are attempts to have more educators accept this design under the guise of negotiated curriculum. Here students along with teachers negotiate what interests will be addressed with what content. Teachers and students participate in planning the unit, its purposes, the content focuses, the activities, and even the materials to be employed.[98]

Having students negotiate the curriculum enables them to gain ownership of their knowledge. It empowers them. Students so involved also fit into the current stress of constructivism. If we accept that constructivism is a way of coming to know one's world, as noted by Brooks and Brooks, then it makes sense to tune into students' needs and interests and give them opportunities to construct their own curricula and learning.[99] It may well be that this design will gain more favor in the future.

Experience-centered Designs. Experience-centered curriculum designs closely resembled the child-centered designs in that they used the concerns of children as the basis for organizing the children's school world. However, they differed from child-centered designs in their view that the interests and needs of children cannot be anticipated and, therefore, a curriculum framework cannot be planned for all children.

This notion—that a curriculum could not be preplanned, that everything had to be done "on the spot" by each teacher reacting to each child—made this design almost impossible to implement. It also put people in a posture of ignoring the vast amount of information they had about children's growth and development—cognitively, affectively, emotionally, and socially.

Those favoring the child-centered or experience-centered curriculum placed heavy emphasis on the learners' interests. Pupils' interests have received much attention throughout this century. However, cautions about relying solely on children's interests have been made frequently. Harold Rugg and Ann Shumaker wrote in 1928, "We do not dare leave longer to chance—to spontaneous, overt symptoms of interest on the part of occasional pupils—the solution of this important and difficult problem of construction of a curriculum for maximum growth."[100]

In the beginning of this century, Dewey noted that the spontaneous power of the child, his demand for self-expression, cannot by any possibility be suppressed. For Dewey, interest was purposeful; it had to be taken into consideration. In *Experience and Education,* he noted that education should commence with the experience learners already possessed upon entering school. Experience was essentially the starting point for all further learning.[101] He further noted that the child exists in a personal world of experiences. His or her interests are those of personal concern, rather than relating to the total body of knowledge with its myriad facts, concepts, generalizations, and theories.

While Dewey believed that experience was a starting point for further learning and that pupils' interests had to be considered, he was never an advocate of making the child's interest actually the curriculum or placing the child in the role of curriculum decision maker. On the child and the curriculum, he noted that "the easy thing is to seize upon something in the nature of the child, or upon something in the developed consciousness of the adult, and insist upon that as the key to the whole problem."[102] If we do this, we get into either/or thinking. We begin to see the situation as the child versus the subject or the nature of the individual versus the social environment.

Ideally, what Dewey wished educators to do was to analyze the experience of children and to see where in their natural experiences there were already existing ideas regarding organized knowledge of facts and truths. One searched for starting points, for places where the child's natural interests and concerns could be linked with more formalized knowledge. Dewey wanted educators to think of the child's experience as vital and fluid, dynamic as opposed to static. Thus, the curriculum would be ever changing in addressing the needs of students.[103]

Dewey contended that the very subjects studied in the curriculum are themselves the results of experience. They are the formalized learnings that have resulted from children's experiences. The content is not just mere clustering of information; rather, the information is organized systematically as the result of careful reflection.

The current postpositivist view supports this belief that individuals are part of their own experience and knowledge production. Individuals are not isolated from the world. Rather, they are dynamic players influencing their world and in turn being influenced by it. As Dewey indicated, subject matter and an individual's experiences are really parts of one's reality.[104] The child interacts with and modifies knowledge through his or her experiences.

Several curricularists have translated the ideas of the experience movement into courses emphasizing touching, feeling, and imagining. Some have emphasized life experiences and career-based activities intended to prepare students for adult responsibility.

Romantic (Radical) Designs. The view of the child as central has been stressed in more recent times by reformers who advocate radical school modification. Many of these individuals essentially adhere to Rousseau's posture on the value of attending to the nature of individuals and Pestalozzi's thinking that individuals can find their true selves by looking to their own nature. While their thinking has a particular progressive ring, they also are drawing on the views of more recent philosophers: Jurgen Habermas, a German philosopher and Paulo Freire, a Brazilian educator. The radical school reformers are eloquent proponents of learner-centered designs.

An underlying assumption of the radicals appears to be that the current society is corrupt, repressive, and unable to cure itself. Schools have used their curricula to control and to indoctrinate individuals into a particular cultural view rather than to educate and emancipate them. McLaren has gone so far as to state that capitalist schooling is generally perverse. Schooling and its curriculum are organized to solicit from students a belief

in and a desire for a common culture that in reality does not exist.[105] The curriculum is organized so that students develop intolerance for difference. McLaren is perhaps the most extreme current voice in the critical camp.

Paulo Freire, in his book *Pedagogy of the Oppressed,* was influential in shaping the thinking of some present-day radicals. Freire noted that the purpose of education is to enlighten the masses about their present state of being denied their rights, to design situations in which they recognize their state of being and feel dissatisfied with it, and finally to gain those skills and competencies requisite for correcting the identified inequities.[106]

Many radicals draw on critical theory, which has been explained in great detail by Habermas, who emphasizes that emancipation is the goal of education. This emancipation refers to individuals gaining those awarenesses, competencies, and attitudes to enable them to take control of their lives. No longer are they under the control of others; no longer must they follow social conventions without any thought or reflection. In writing about Habermas and his critical theory of education, Robert Young notes that the theme of emancipation has a rather long history, dating back to Roman times and keenly expressed by many philosophers during the Age of Enlightenment. Students must accept the responsibility for educating themselves, and they must garner the courage to resist indifference to freedom.[107]

Radical curricularists believe that individuals must learn those ways of engaging in a critique of knowledge. Learning is reflective; it is not externally imposed by a person in power. Education leads to freedom and emancipation. In the radical curriculum design, knowledge is not a finished product that sits in a unit plan or course syllabus. Such a document is a curriculum that indoctrinates. Learning is something that results from the interaction between and among people. It comes by challenging content and permitting different views about the content, as well as from critiquing the purposes of the information presented in the curriculum.

One need not be a critical theorist to accept the value of engaging students in active construction of their worlds of knowledge. Indeed, most educators urging a constructivist approach to the curriculum are not citizens of the critical political camp. Persons who value a postmodern posture to living, learning, and schooling might take issue with the narrowness of many critical theorists blinded by their ideology.

Hunkins has argued that curricula can be designed in ways that "disrupt" the status quo of students' understanding. Focuses of curricula can be presented that enable students to see the dynamic emergence of content and engage students in the very process of constructing their knowledge realities.[108] "Genuine thought only begins with a disturbance that impinges on thought, with a perplexing and paradoxical question that forces thought."[109] It is possible to create a design that celebrates the postmodern, poststructuralist views that focus study on open systems, local determinism, and methods classified as antimethod without accepting a particular political ideology.[110] Indeed, having a postmodern or postpositivist view should cause one to hold suspect any ideology suggested as metanarrative.

Perhaps the biggest difference between mainstream educators and radicals is that the latter view the general society as flawed and that education indoctrinates students to fit into those roles that the controlling groups in society wish youth to enter. According to radicals, the curriculum must be overhauled. But traditional curricularists argue that the content does not indoctrinate. For example, curriculum designs based on disciplines emphasize procedural knowledge: students actively involved with the content engage in a dialogue with teachers and fellow students, raise questions, and evaluate knowledge. Much of what the traditional curriculum is doing is in agreement with the demands of radicals. It certainly is not in conflict with many of the views of postmodernism and poststructuralism.

Humanistic Designs.   This design gained prominence in the 1960s and 1970s, partly in response to the excessive emphasis on the disciplines during the 1950s and the early 1960s. It was this perceived imbalance regarding attention to subject matter that caused humanistic education to appear in the 1920s and 1930s as part of progressive philosophy and the whole-child movement in psychology. After World War II, humanistic designs connected to existentialism in educational philosophy.

Much of the underpinning for humanistic designs has been associated with third-force psychology or humanistic psychology. Humanistic psychology developed in the 1950s in opposition to the then dominant psychological school of behaviorism. This new psychological orientation emphasized that human action was much more than a response to a stimulus, that meaning was more important than methods, that the focus of attention should be on the subjective rather than objective nature of human existence, and that there is a relationship between learning and feeling.

It was in this context that the Association for Supervision and Curriculum Development published its 1962 yearbook entitled, *Perceiving, Behaving, Becoming*.[111] It represented a new focus for education, an approach to curricular design and instructional delivery that would allow individuals to become fully functioning persons. Arthur Combs, the chairperson of the yearbook, noted some key questions. "What kind of person would it be who has truly achieved the ultimate in self-realization? How do they come about? What factors went into making this kind of person?" He suggested that the curriculum be designed to stress human potential and to enable the student to be involved in the process of becoming.[112] The emphasis was on empowering individuals—what today is called postpositivistic thinking, whereby a person is involved with his or her reality, participating in it, and is aware of the notion of becoming.

The 1977 yearbook of the Association for Supervision and Curriculum Development, entitled *Feeling, Valuing, and the Art of Growing*, also stressed the affective dimensions of humanistic educational designs. The yearbook made a case for the affective domain, indicating among other things that we need to harness human potential and to allow it to set itself free. It suggested that educators must permit students to feel, value, and grow.[113]

A key influence on this particular curriculum design has been Abraham Maslow and his theoretical concept of self actualization. His list of characteristics of such a person gave educators indicators that could serve as building blocks for this curriculum. A person who was self-actualized (1) was accepting of self, others, and nature; (2) possessed spontaneity, simplicity, and naturalness; (3) was problem-oriented; (4) possessed openness to different experiences beyond the ordinary; (5) possessed empathy and sympathy toward the less fortunate; (6) had mastered sophisticated levels of interpersonal relations; (7) believed in persons participating in decision making; and (8) possessed a philosophical sense of humor.[114] Maslow emphasized that an individual did not become self-actualized early in life. Rather, a person reaches this state sometime around or after age 40. But, to attain that stage, the individual has to start the process as a student. Some educators miss this point and think that their humanistic designs will have students attain self-actualization as an end product.

Carl Rogers's work has been another major force. He assumes that people can enhance self-directed learning by drawing on their own resources to improve self-understanding, to learn self-concepts and basic attitudes, and to guide their own behavior. The educators' task is to set the educational environment such that these personal resources can be tapped. Such an environment encourages genuineness of behavior, empathy, and respect for self and others.[115]

Individuals given such an environment will naturally develop into what Rogers termed a fully functioning person. Individuals able to take self-initiated actions and responsibility for those actions are capable of intelligent choice and self-direction. Furthermore, having acquired knowledge relevant to the solutions of problems, these persons are critical learners. They also are able to approach problem situations with flexibility and intelligence and to work cooperatively with others. They are internally guided with regard to their socialization process; they do not wait for or work for the approval of others.

Humanistic education in the 1970s absorbed the notion of *confluence*. Essentially, confluence education is a melding of the affective domain (feelings, attitudes, values) with the cognitive domain (intellectual knowledge and problem-solving abilities). This approach adds the affective component to the conventional subject matter curriculum that is already in place.[116] Those who support this design do not favor either content or experience or intellect or feeling; rather, they strive to blend the subjective or intuitive with the objective. They urge that the curriculum be so organized as to provide students with more alterna-

tives from which they can choose what to feel. Students are challenged to take responsibility for and to appreciate their choices and to feel comfortable knowing that they have the power to make choices.

Confluent education stresses participation; it emphasizes power sharing, negotiations, and joint responsibility. It is essentially nonauthoritarian. It also stresses the whole person and the integration of thinking, feeling, and acting. It centers on the relevance of subject matter in light of students' basic needs and lives. Throughout the curriculum, students are confronted with situations that make them realize that the development of self is a legitimate objective of learning.

Humanistic educators realize that the cognitive, affective, and psychomotor domains are interconnected and that the curriculum design should address these dimensions. Some educators in this camp—and in the subject-centered camp—would argue that, in addition to these three domains, the two domains of socialization and spirituality should also be addressed.[117]

Humanistic curriculum designs stress the development of positive self-concept and interpersonal skills. A related design, the transpersonal or transcendence orientation—the consciousness aspect of the humanistic design—takes this orientation a bit further. Here the stress, though still on the individual, encourages intuition and transcendence. Through intuition a person is able to access his or her creative thinking and to generate a holistic perception of reality. An individual's inner and outer worlds tie his or her inner self to the environment. This orientation suggests a curriculum that highly regards the uniqueness of the human personality.

This curriculum is open to human spirituality, which, as used by such curricularists, refers to the links between a person's inner life and the infinite. Transcendence and spirituality are experienced through quality experiences. As Phenix notes, in such a curriculum reality is experienced as a "single interconnected whole, such that a complete description of any entity would require the comprehension of every other entity."[118]

James Moffett suggests that a curriculum that emphasizes spirituality enables students to enter "on a personal spiritual path unique to each that nevertheless entails joining increasingly expansive memberships of humanity and nature." He cautions that if society is to foster knowledge and power without commensurate development of morality and spirituality then society is courting disaster.[119]

Transcendent education is lured by the concept of wholeness or comprehensiveness of experience. Certain content needs to be incorporated into the curriculum, but the stress is on giving the students the opportunity to take a journey, to contemplate on that journey, and to relate that journey to others—past, present, and future. It emphasizes the general dispositions of humans for hope, creativity, awareness, doubt and faith, wonder, awe and reverence.[120] See Curriculum Tips 8-3.

Humanistic curriculum designs have many of the same weaknesses as learner-centered designs. They require of the teacher great skill and competence in dealing with individuals. Moreover, available educational materials are often not appropriate.

One serious charge against this design is that humanists focus on their methods and techniques and do not adequately consider them in light of the consequences for learners. Another criticism leveled at the design concerns its apparently inconsistent emphasis on both the human as unique and on activities that all students experience. In contrast, some say that the design places far too much emphasis on the individual and ignores the needs of the overall society. A final criticism is really of third-force psychology itself. Critics charge that it does not integrate what we know about behaviorism and psychiatry or about cognitive developmental theory. Rather, it seems to splinter our knowledge base about human learning and development.

Problem-centered Designs

The third major type of curriculum design, which is problem-centered, focuses on the problems of living—on the perceived realities of institutional and group life—both for the individual and for society in general. Problem-centered curriculum designs are organized to reinforce cultural traditions and also to address those community and societal needs that are currently unmet. They address individuals' problems as well.

Even though these designs place the individual in a social setting, they are unlike learner-centered designs in a major way. Problem-centered designs are planned before the arrival of students. However, problem-centered curricularists realize that, because their concern is with genuine life problems, they will sometimes have to adjust or cater to the concerns and situations of learners.

How a curriculum is organized with this design depends in large part on the nature of the problem areas to be studied. The content selected must be relevant to the problem under consideration. For this reason, the content often cuts across subject boundaries. It must also be based, to a major extent, on the needs, concerns, and abilities of the students. This dual emphasis on both content and the development of learners distinguishes problem-centered designs from the other major types of curriculum designs.

Because problem-centered designs draw on social problems and the needs, interests, and abilities of learners, several variations exist. Some focus on persistent life situations, others center on contemporary social problems, others address areas of living, and some are even concerned with the reconstruction of society. What seems to distinguish these various types is the relative degree of emphasis they place on social needs as opposed to individual needs.[121]

Life-situations Design. Interest in this curriculum design emphasizing life functions or life situations can be traced to the nineteenth century and to Herbert Spencer's writings on a curriculum for complete living. His curriculum emphasized activities that (1) sustain life, (2) enhance life, (3) aid in rearing children, (4) maintain the individual's social and political relations, and (5) enhance leisure, tasks, and feelings.[122] This design, which draws its legitimation from society and its social challenges, was part of the recommendation of the Commission on the Reorganization of Secondary Education, sponsored by NEA in 1918. The commission outlined in its report a curriculum that would deal with the life situations of health, command of the fundamentals, worthy home membership, vocation, citizenship, leisure, and ethical character.

Fundamental to the design are three assumptions. The first is that persistent life situations are crucial to a society's successful functioning and that it makes educational sense to organize a

---

Curriculum Tips 8-3

The Curriculum Matrix

In designing a curriculum, keep in mind the various levels at which we can consider the content component of the curriculum. The following listing of curriculum dimensions should assist in considering content in depth.

1. Consider the intellectual dimension of the content. This is perhaps the most commonly thought dimension of curriculum. The content selected should stimulate the intellectual development of students.
2. Consider the emotional dimension of the content. We know much less about this dimension, but we are obtaining a better understanding of it as the affective domain of knowledge.
3. Consider the social dimension of the content. The content selected should contribute to students' social development. Content stressing human relations contributes to this dimension.
4. Consider the physical dimension of the content. This is commonly referred to as the psychomotor domain of knowledge. Content should be selected not only to develop physical skills, but also to allow students to become conscious of themselves as physical beings.
5. Consider the aesthetic nature of the content. People have an aesthetic nature, yet we currently have little knowledge of the place of aesthetics in education.
6. Consider the transcendent or spiritual dimension of the content. This dimension is almost totally excluded from our considerations. We tend to confuse this dimension with formalized religions. This dimension of content does not relate specifically to the rational. But we need to have content that causes students to reflect on the nature of their humanness and to strive to transcend their current levels of knowing and action.

Source: Adapted from Arthur W. Foshay, "The Curriculum Matrix: Transcendence and Mathematics," *Curriculum* (Autumn 1990), pp. 36–46.

---

curriculum around them. The second assumption is that students will see direct relevance to what they are studying if the content is organized around aspects of community life. Finally, by having students study social or life situations, they will not only study ways to improve society, but will be directly involved in such improvement.[123]

In 1947, this design was the focus of an entire curriculum textbook entitled *Developing a Curriculum for Modern Living.* The book, authored by Florence Stratemeyer, Hamden Forkner, and Margaret McKim, made the case that society could indeed be the basis upon which to develop a curriculum and that education had to function as a positive social force.

Stratemeyer and her coauthors based their argument for a life-situations design on the fact that the industrial age that was at full maturity had altered the traditional pattern of all aspects of life: economic, social, spiritual, even physical as it related to health. The curriculum had to enable students to function effectively in this new world, to process those life situations common in this highly industrialized society that was not only nationwide but worldwide. To address the challenge, she and her colleagues generated an extensive master list of persistent life situations that students would face and therefore needed to consider in school before entering the world of work and adult responsibilities. The key points of this curriculum are presented in Table 8-2.

Stratemeyer noted that "above everything else a curriculum developed in the manner described . . . depends on an understanding of indi-

TABLE 8-2   A Curriculum for Modern Living

I. GROWTH IN INDIVIDUAL CAPACITIES	II. GROWTH IN SOCIAL PARTICIPATION	III. GROWTH IN ABILITY TO DEAL WITH ENVIRONMENTAL FACTS AND FORCES

A. Situations calling for growth in ability to meet health needs
  1. Satisfying physiological needs
  2. Satisfying emotional and social needs
  3. Avoiding and caring for illness and injury
	A. Situations calling for growth in ability to act in person-to-person relationships
	  1. Establishing effective social relations with others
	  2. Establishing effective working relations with others
	  3. Using physical and chemical forces
		A. Situations calling for growth in ability to deal with natural phenomena
		  1. Dealing with physical phenomena
		  2. Dealing with plant, animal, and insect life
		  3. Using physical and chemical forces

B. Situations calling for growth in ability to use intellectual power
  1. Making ideas clear
  2. Understanding the ideas of others
  3. Dealing with quantitative relationships
  4. Using effective methods of work
	B. Situations calling for growth in ability to participate as a responsible group member
	  1. Deciding when to join a group
	  2. Participating as a group member
	  3. Taking leadership responsibilities
		B. Situations calling for growth in ability to deal with technological resources
		  1. Using technological resources
		  2. Contributing to technological advances

C. Situations calling for growth in the ability to take responsibility for moral choices
  1. Determining the nature and extent of individual freedom
  2. Determining responsibility to self and others
	C. Situations calling for growth in ability to act in intergroup relations
	  1. Working with racial and religious groups
	  2. Working with socioeconomic groups
		C. Situations calling for growth in ability to deal with economic, social, and political structures and forces
		  1. Earning a living
		  2. Securing goods and services
		  3. Providing for social welfare
		  4. Molding public opinion
		  5. Participating in local and national government

D. Situations calling for growth in ability to meet needs for aesthetic expression and appreciation
  1. Finding sources of aesthetic satisfaction in oneself
  2. Achieving aesthetic satisfaction through the environment		

Source: Adapted from Florence Stratemeyer, Hamden L. Forkner, and Margaret G. McKim, *Developing a Curriculum for Modern Living* (New York: Teachers College Press, Columbia University, 1947).

vidual learners. Their purposes must be sensed, their needs determined."[124] However, she pointed out that not all expressed needs and interests will become part of the curriculum. Some needs and interests would already be met adequately by other institutions in society: the family, the church, scouts, and other community organizations. The school would address those needs not met through these organizations.

One of the strengths of the life-situations design is its focus on the problem-solving procedures for learning. Process and content are effectively integrated into the curricular experience. Some critics point out that the students do not learn much subject matter. However, proponents are quick to counter that the design draws heavily from content, and from traditional content at that. What makes the design unique is that the content is organized in ways that allow students to clearly view problem areas.

Another strong feature of this design is that it utilizes the past and current experiences of learners as a means of getting them to analyze the basic areas of living. In this respect, the design is very different from the experience-centered design, which uses the learners' felt needs and interests as the sole basis for content and experience selection. The life-situations design uses students' existing concerns, as well as pressing immediate problems in the larger society, as a starting point.

The design has definite strengths. It presents subject matter in an integrated form by cutting across the separate subjects and centering on related categories of social life. Because it centers on social problems and personal concerns, it encourages students to learn and apply problem-solving procedures. The linking of subject matter to real situations increases the relevance of the curriculum.

But, like the previous designs, life-situation designs have deficiencies and challenges. Perhaps the greatest challenge is to determine what are the scope and sequence of the essential areas of living. Are the major activities of the current time also going to be the essential activities of future times?

Another criticism of this design has been that it does not adequately expose students to their cultural heritage. Moreover, it tends to indoctrinate youth into the existing conditions and thus perpet-uates the social status quo. However, if students are educated to be critical of their social situations, then intelligent processing of the social scene is fostered, rather than adherence to the status quo.

There are always some who point out that the life-situations design cannot be mounted by teachers for they lack adequate preparation for it. Others argue that textbooks and other teaching materials inhibit the implementation of this design. Furthermore, many teachers are uncomfortable with it because it departs too much from their training. Finally, this organization departs from the curricular tradition maintained by colleges and universities.

Core Design.   This particular curriculum design, sometimes called "social functions" core, is carefully planned. It centers on general education and is based on problems arising out of common human activities. There are several variations of core designs. Subject matter core designs, for example, would be classified as subject-centered designs. Areas-of-living core designs are rooted in the progressive education tradition. Indeed, Dewey argued that learning is part of living and, therefore, the experience of living should serve as the focus for the curriculum.[125] An authentic curriculum is life reflected upon intensely.

This type of core is problem centered rather than learner centered. It is carefully planned before the students arrive, but with the notion that adjustment can be made if necessary. This design is usually taught in a block-time format, whereby two or more normal periods for teaching the core component are scheduled together. One teacher assumes responsibility for this block of time and also manages a counseling function. Although content is part of this design, the common needs, problems, and concerns of learners comprise the central focus.

The focus on problems proceeds in different ways in each core class, but certain characteristics for problem solving are recommended by the advocates of core, as illustrated below. These recommendations make sense today, as they did when core was popularized by Faunce and Bossing.

1. The problem is selected by either the teacher or students.

2. A group consensus is made to determine important problems and interest of the class.
3. Problems are selected on the basis of developed criteria for selection.
4. The problem is clearly stated and defined.
5. Areas of study are decided, including dividing the class by individual and group interests.
6. Needed information is listed and discussed.
7. Resources for obtaining information are listed and discussed.
8. Information is obtained and organized.
9. Information is analyzed and interpreted.
10. Tentative conclusions are stated and tested.
11. A report is presented to the class on an individual or group basis.
12. Conclusions are evaluated.
13. New avenues of exploration toward further problem solving are examined.[126]

The advantages of the core design are that it unifies content, presents subject matter relevant to students, and encourages active processing of information. Furthermore, because it presents subject matter in a relevant form, it fosters intrinsic motivation in students. Alberty and Alberty state that this design makes it possible for students to attack directly problems they consider crucial in the contemporary society. It encourages students to view the community as a laboratory for learning.[127] Because the design encourages cooperative learning, its advocates claim it fosters democratic practices in the classroom.

But, the design has weaknesses, too. Perhaps the major one, which may also be its strength, is that it departs too significantly from the traditional curriculum. People attack it as ignoring the fundamentals. It also requires materials that are hard to find. Conventional textbooks, in fact, do not support this core design. Nor is it commonly used because many educators have not accepted the idea that general education is worthwhile. Furthermore, it requires an exceptional teacher, well versed in subject matter, problem-solving skills, and general knowledge.

Social Problems and Reconstructionist Designs.
Whereas some educators, such as Stratemeyer, have urged that children's interests should guide the selection of curriculum content and experiences, other educators still feel that the curriculum should address contemporary social problems and even social action projects aimed at reconstructing society. Many such educators consider themselves to be in the social orientation camp, or what some have called social reconstructionism. These individuals, interested in the relation of the curriculum to the social, political, and economic development of society, believe that through the curriculum educators will effect social change and ultimately create a more just society. Interestingly, even though many of the schools' current critics are of this opinion, aspects of reconstructionism actually first appeared in the 1920s and 1930s.

George Counts believed that society had to be totally reorganized to meet the common good. The times demanded a new social order and the schools should play a major role in such a redesign. Counts presented some of his thinking on this issue of new social order in a speech entitled "Dare Progressive Education Be Progressive?"[128] He challenged the Progressive Education Association to broaden its thinking beyond the current social structure. He accused its members of only advocating curricula that would continue the dominance of the middle class and its privileged positions. Counts expanded on his call for a reconstructed society in his classic book, *Dare the Schools Build a New Social Order.* He argued that if educators would accept the challenge they could involve students in a curriculum for participating in a more just and equitable society.[129]

Harold Rugg also believed that the school should engage children in a critical analysis of society in order to improve it. Rugg's criticisms were directed to those who favored child-centered schools. He stated that their laissez-faire approach to curriculum development only produced chaos, in which subjects were disjointed and unarticulated. "Rarely are they designed in the light of a review of a careful record of the program of earlier years and of the most probably effective year-programs to follow it in the school career of the child."[130] In the 1940s, Rugg observed that the Progressive Education Association still overemphasized the child. All seven purposes of the association referred to the child, and not one took into consideration "man's crucial social conditions and problems."[131]

Theodore Brameld, a spokesperson for the reconstructionists' view well into the 1950s, argued that the reconstructionists were committed to facilitating the emergence of a new culture. The times demanded a new social order; the existing society showed signs of decay: poverty, crime, racial conflict, unemployment, political oppression, and a wasting of the environment.[132] Brameld also believed that the school should help the individual to develop as a social being and as a skilled planner of the social reality. The individual must come to learn that he or she must satisfy his or her personal needs through social consensus. The group would be paramount. The schools not only had this obligation to educate children for the good of society; they also needed to point out the urgency for the change.

The fact that reconstructionists stress the notion of change and the needs to plan for tomorrow brings in mind a series of pressing questions raised by two other reconstructionists, Virgil Clift and Harold Shane, as they explore new directions for American educators and new decisions for curriculum specialists.

1. What policies shall govern our future use of technology?
2. At a global level, what shall be our goals, and how can we reach them?
3. What shall we identify as the "good life"?
4. How shall we deploy our limited resources in meeting the needs of various groups of people?
5. How shall we equalize opportunity, and how shall we reduce the gap between the "haves" and "have-nots"?
6. How can we maximize the value of mass media, especially television?
7. What shall be made of psychological, chemical, and electronic approaches to behavior modification?
8. What steps can we take to ensure the integrity of our political, economic, and military systems?
9. What, if anything, are we willing to relinquish, and in what order?
10. And, what honorable compromises and solutions shall we make as we contemplate the above questions?[133]

These questions deal with social issues that are generic—meaning they were relevant yester-

day, they are relevant today, and they will be relevant tomorrow, and they are relevant for most school subjects and grade levels. The way we deal with these issues or problems will make the difference about the society we are and will become.

The social reconstructionist curriculum has the primary purpose of engaging the learner in analyzing the many severe problems confronting humankind. However, the exact content and objectives are to be decided by those who actually create such a curriculum. The curriculum is to engage students in a critical analysis of the local, national, and international community. Also, attention is to be given to the political practices of the business and government groups and their impact on the economic realities of the workforce. Such a curriculum must propose industrial and political changes that will ultimately modify the social fabric of the nation and perhaps the world.

There are still curricularists who believe the society to be unjust, who presume that privilege is not equitably distributed. Few of these current individuals would call themselves reconstructionists, but they do consider that the curriculum and its design should address the key social problems of current society and impart in students a commitment for resolution of these problems. Michael Apple speaks of a curriculum that would address the issues of race, gender, and the poor. He speaks to the issue of the curriculum being designed so that the social inequities of society are not reproduced.[134]

Many current advocates focusing on social problems and the implied design identify themselves as reconceptualists. However, some say that we do not need to concern ourselves with such mundane things as curriculum development and design. We know all that. What should command our attention is understanding the phenomena of curriculum.[135] Certainly, we must understand curriculum and its purpose within social contexts. Education must engage real individuals in constructing meaning, social dialogue, and reflective comprehension of the social realities in which they find themselves.[136] But educators still want to know how you select the focuses for such questions. How do you organize the commonplaces of content, students, teachers, and environments? We need more than just a discounting of the value of the positivistic development and design of curriculum.

While the reconstructionists and the present-day reconceptualists both believe that the curriculum should provide students with those learnings requisite for adjusting the social, economic, and political realities, there are other curricularists who, while being less politically and philosophically motivated, are still interested in designing curricula that address social problems.

CONCLUSION

Curriculum design is more than just making sure that the parts of a curriculum are neatly organized in a document. Design is a complex phenomenon requiring of educators careful attention so that the curriculum conceived will have merit and will succeed in getting students to learn those concepts, attitudes, and skills considered worthwhile and essential.

The issue of design is likely to continue to draw the attention of curriculum specialists and generalists. Designing a curriculum is really dealing with a vision, which most educators have

but don't always apply. The concepts related to design help them put flesh on their visions and to increase their probability of becoming reality.

Various design options exist from which curricularists can select—subject centered, learner centered, and problem centered. Each of these, as has been noted in this chapter, has a history and philosophy associated with it. Each has its advocates. Each, when implemented, gives the school a particular character. However, many schools meld these designs, often so much that it is almost impossible to determine just what the curriculum design is. Table 8-3 presents an overview of the major designs.

Advocates of each design face the same design decisions as advocates of all the others. Regardless of the particular design, educators must be concerned with the scope and sequence of the curriculum elements. They must also pay attention to articulation, continuity, and balance. Overall, their understanding of curriculum design is necessary knowledge for the building of a curriculum.

ENDNOTES

1. George J. Posner and Alan N. Rudnitsky, *Course Design,* 2nd ed. (New York: Longman, 1990).
2. H. H. Giels, S. P. McCutchen, and A. N. Zechiel, *Exploring the Curriculum* (New York: Harper, 1942), p. 2.
3. Ralph W. Tyler, conversation with one of the authors, April 16, 1986.
4. Pinar referred to in Patrick Slattery, *Curriculum Development in the Postmodern Era* (New York: Garland Publishing, Inc., 1995).
5. William F. Pinar, William M. Reynolds, Patrick Slattery, and Peter M. Taubman, *Understanding Curriculum* (New York: Peter Lang, 1995).
6. Ronald C. Doll, *Curriculum Improvement: Decision Making and Process,* 9th ed. (Boston: Allyn and Bacon, 1996).
7. Hilda Taba, *Curriculum Development: Theory and Practice,* (New York: Harcourt Brace, 1962), p. 423.
8. Doll, *Curriculum Improvement.*
9. Ralph W. Tyler, *Basic Principles of Curriculum and Instruction* (Chicago: University of Chicago Press, 1949).
10. Elliott W. Eisner, "Aesthetic Modes of Knowing," in E. W. Eisner, ed., *Learning and Teaching the Ways of Knowing,* Eighty-fourth Yearbook of the National Society for the Study of Education, Part II (Chicago: University of Chicago Press, 1985), pp. 23–36.

11. William E. Doll, "Teaching a Post-Modern Curriculum," in J. T. Sears, and J. D. Marshall, eds., *Teaching and Thinking about Curriculum* (New York: Teachers College Press, Columbia University, 1990), pp. 39–47; Henry A. Giroux, ed., *Postmodernism, Feminism, and Cultural Politics* (Albany, N.Y.: State University of New York Press, 1991).
12. Pinar et al., *Understanding Curriculum.*
13. William A. Reid, *The Pursuit of Curriculum* (Norwood, N.J.: Ablex Publishing Corp., 1992).
14. John Naisbitt and Patricia Aburdene, *Megatrends 2000* (New York: William Morrow, 1990).
15. Doll, *Curriculum Improvement.*
16. Dwayne E. Huebner, "Spirituality and Knowing," in E. W. Eisner, ed., *Learning and Teaching the Ways of Knowing,* p. 163.
17. James Moffett, *The Universal Schoolhouse* (San Francisco: Jossey–Bass Publishers, 1994).
18. Pinar et al., *Understanding Curriculum.*
19. Ibid.
20. Francis P. Hunkins, *Curriculum Development: Program Improvement* (Columbus, Ohio: Merrill, 1980).
21. Jean-Francois Lyotard, "Foreward: Spaceship," in Michael Peters, ed., *Education and the Postmodern Condition* (Westport, Conn.: Bergin & Garvey, 1995, pp. xix–xx.

TABLE 8-3   Overview of Major Curriculum Designs

DESIGN	CURRICULAR EMPHASIS	UNDERLYING PHILOSOPHY	SOURCE	SPOKESPERSON
SUBJECT CENTERED				
Subject design	Separate subjects	Essentialism, perennialism	Science, knowledge	Harris, Hutchins
Discipline design	Scholarly disciplines (mathematics, biology, psychology, etc.)	Essentialism, perennialism	Knowledge, science	Bruner, Phenix, Schwab, Taba
Broad fields design	Interdisciplinary subjects and scholarly disciplines	Essentialism, progressivism	Knowledge, society	Broudy, Dewey
Correlation design	Separate subjects, disciplines linked while keeping identities of each	Progressivism, essentialism	Knowledge	Alberty and Alberty
Process design	Procedural knowledge of various disciplines; generic ways of information processing, thinking	Progressivism	Psychology, knowledge	Adams, Beyer, Dewey, Papert
LEARNER CENTERED				
Child-centered design	Child's interests and needs	Progressivism	Child	Dewey, Kilpatrick, Parker
Experience-centered design	Experiences and interests of child	Progressivism	Child	Dewey, Rugg and Shumaker
Radical design	Experiences and interests of child	Reconstructionism	Child, society	Freire, Habermas, Holt, Illich
Humanistic design	Experiences, interests, needs of person, and of the group	Reconstructionism, existentialism	Psychology, child, society	Combs, Fantini, Maslow, Rogers
PROBLEM CENTERED				
Life-situation design	Life (social) problems	Reconstructionism	Society	Spencer, Stratemeyer, Forkner, and McKim
Core design	Social problems	Progressivism, reconstructionism	Child, society	Alberty and Alberty, Faunce and Bossing
Social problems, reconstructionist design	Focus on society and its problems	Reconstructionism	Society, eternal truths	Apple, Brameld, Counts, Rugg, Shane

22. Arno A. Bellack, "What Knowledge Is of Most Worth?" *High School Journal* (February 1965), pp. 318–332.

23. Pinar et al., *Understanding Curriculum.*

24. John D. Bransford and Nancy J. Vye, "A Perspective on Cognitive Research and Its Implications for Instruction," in Lauren B. Resnick and Leopold E. Klopfer, eds., *Toward the Thinking Curriculum: Current Cognitive Research,* 1989 Yearbook (Alexandria, Va: Association for Supervision and Curriculum Development, 1989), pp. 173–205.

25. Mark Johnson, *The Body in the Mind* (Chicago: University of Chicago Press, 1987); James Pusch, "Metaphor and Teaching," *Educational Forum* (Winter 1992), pp. 185–192.

26. Moffett, *The Universal Schoolhouse.*

27. Jerome S. Bruner, *The Process of Education* (Cambridge, Mass.: Harvard University Press, 1959).

28. Robert S. Zais, *Curriculum: Principles and Foundations* (New York: Harper & Row, 1976).

29. Tyler, *Basic Principles of Curriculum and Instruction.*

30. John I. Goodlad and Zhixin Su, "Organization and the Curriculum," in Philip W. Jackson, ed., *Handbook of Research on Curriculum* (New York: Macmillan Publishing Company, 1992), pp. 327–344.

31. Ibid.

32. Doll, *Curriculum Improvement.*

33. Goodlad and Zhixin Su, "Organization and the Curriculum."

34. Taba, *Curriculum Development: Theory and Practice.*

35. Jean Piaget, *The Psychology of Intelligence* (Paterson, N.J.: Littlefield, Adams, 1960).

36. B. Othanel Smith, William O. Stanley, and Harlan J. Shores, *Fundamentals of Curriculum Development,* rev. ed. (New York: Harcourt, Brace, 1957).

37. Gerald J. Posner and Kenneth A. Strike, "A Categorization Scheme for Principles of Sequencing Content," *Review of Educational Research* (Fall 1976), pp. 401–406.

38. Tyler, *Basic Principles of Curriculum and Instruction,* p. 86.

39. Goodlad and Zhixin Su, "Organization and the Curriculum."

40. Francis P. Hunkins, *Teaching Thinking Through Effective Questioning* (Norwood, Mass.: Christopher–Gordon Publishers, 1995).

41. Bruner, *The Process of Education,* p. 52.

42. Goodlad and Zhixin Su, "Organization and the Curriculum."

43. J. Galen Saylor, William M. Alexander, and Arthur J. Lewis, *Planning for Better Teaching and Learning,* 4th ed. (New York: Holt, Rinehart, 1981), p. 251.

44. Taba, *Curriculum Development: Theory and Practice,* p. 223.

45. Goodlad and Zhixin Su, "Organization and the Curriculum."

46. Elliot W. Eisner, *Cognition and Curriculum Reconsidered* (New York: Teachers College Press, Columbia University, 1994).

47. Linda Crafton, *Challenges of Holistic Teaching: Answering the Tough Questions* (Norwood, Mass.: Christopher–Gordon Publishers, Inc., 1994).

48. David Pratt, *Curriculum Planning* (New York: Harcourt Brace College Publishers, 1994), p. 180.

49. John I. Goodlad, *Planning and Organizing for Teaching* (Washington, D.C.: National Education Association, 1963), p. 29.

50. Doll, *Curriculum Improvement.*

51. Peter Oliver, *Developing the Curriculum,* 4th ed. (New York: Longman, an imprint of Addison-Wesley, 1997).

52. Allan C. Ornstein, "Textbook Instruction: Processes and Strategies," *NASSP Bulletin* (December 1989), pp. 105–111.

53. Henry C. Morrison, *The Curriculum of the Common School* (Chicago: University of Chicago Press, 1940).

54. Robert M. Hutchins, *The Higher Learning in America* (New Haven: Yale University Press, 1936).

55. Moffett, *The Universal Schoolhouse.*

56. John Dewey, *Experience and Education* (New York: Macmillan, 1938).

57. Tyler, *Basic Principles of Curriculum and Instruction.*

58. Arthur R. King and John A. Brownell, *The Curriculum and the Disciplines of Knowledge* (New York: Wiley, 1966).

59. Taba, *Curriculum Development: Theory and Practice.*

60. Harry S. Broudy, "Becoming Educated in Contemporary Society," in K. D. Benne and S. Tozer, eds., *Society as Educator in an Age of Transition,* Eighty-sixth Yearbook of the National Society for the Study of Education, Part II (Chicago: University of Chicago Press, 1987), pp. 247–268.

61. Bruner, *The Process of Education,* p. 8.

62. Ibid., p. 33.

63. J. M. Fritzman, "From Pragmatism to the Different," in Michael Peters, ed., *Education and the Postmodern Condition* (Westport, Conn.: Bergin & Garvey, 1995), pp. 59–74.

64. M. Mitchell Waldrop, *Complexity: The Emerging Science at the Edge of Order and Chaos* (New York: Simon & Schuster, 1992).

65. Goodlad and Zhixin Su, "Organization and the Curriculum."

66. Elliot W. Eisner, *The Educational Imagination,* 3rd ed. (New York: Macmillan, 1993); Daniel Tanner and Laurel Tanner, *The History of Curriculum* (New York: Macmillan, 1990).

67. Philip Phenix, *Realms of Meaning* (New York: McGraw-Hill, 1964).

68. Evelyn J. Sowell, *Curriculum, An Integrative Introduction* (Upper Saddle River, N.J.: Merrill, and imprint of Prentice Hall, 1996).

69. Harry S. Broudy, B. O. Smith, and Joe R. Burnett, *Democracy and Excellence in American Secondary Education* (Chicago: Rand McNally, 1964).

70. Allan C. Ornstein, *Secondary and Middle School Teaching Methods.* (New York: Harper Collins, 1992).

71. Crafton, *Challenges of Holistic Teaching.*

72. Ibid.

73. Pinar et al., *Understanding Curriculum.*

74. Jacqueline Grennon Brooks and Martin G. Brooks, *The Case for Constructivist Classrooms* (Alexandria, Va.: Association for Supervision and Curriculum Development, 1993).

75. Eisner, *Cognition and Curriculum Reconsidered.*

76. Susanne Krogh, *The Integrated Early Childhood Curriculum* (New York: McGraw-Hill Publishing Co., 1990).

77. Hilda Taba, *A Teacher's Handbook to Elementary Social Studies* (Reading, Mass.: Addison-Wesley Publishing Co., 1971).

78. Brooks and Brooks, *The Case for Constructivist Classrooms.*

79. Harold B. Alberty and Elsie J. Alberty, *Reorganizing the High School Curriculum,* 3rd ed. (New York: Macmillan, 1962).

80. Allan A. Glatthorn, *Curriculum Leadership* (Glenview, Ill.: Scott, Foresman, 1987); Gene D. Shepherd and William B. Ragan, *Modern Elementary Curriculum,* 7th ed. (San Diego: Harcourt Brace Jovanovich, 1992).

81. Barry K. Beyer, *Practical Strategies for the Teaching of Thinking* (Boston: Allyn and Bacon, 1987); Beyer, *Teaching Thinking Skills* (Boston: Allyn and Bacon, 1991).

82. Hunkins, *Teaching Thinking Through Effective Questioning.*

83. Ibid.

84. Marilyn J. Adams, "Thinking Skills Curricula: Their Promise and Progress," *Educational Psychologist,* (Winter 1989), pp. 25–77.

85. Ibid.

86. Allan C. Ornstein, "Making Effective Use of Computer Technology," *NASSP Bulletin* (March 1992), pp. 27–33.

87. Seymor Papert, "Computer Criticism vs. Technocentric Thinking," *Educational Researcher* (January–February 1987), pp. 22–30.

88. William Bain, "The Loss of Innocence: Lyotard, Foucault, and the Challenge of Postmodern Education," in Michael Peters, ed., *Education and the Postmodern Condition* (Westport, Conn.: Bergin & Garvey, 1995), pp. 1–20.

89. Ibid.

90. Michael Peters, "Legitimation Problems: Knowledge and Education in the Postmodern Condition," in Michael Peters, ed., *Education and the Postmodern Condition,* pp. 21–39.

91. Pinar et al., *Understanding Curriculum.*

92. Taba, *Curriculum Development: Theory and Practice,* p. 401.

93. Francis W. Parker, *Talks on Pedagogics* (New York: E. L. Kellogg, 1894).

94. John Dewey, *The Child and the Curriculum* (Chicago: University of Chicago Press, 1902).

95. Frederick G. Bonser, *Life Needs and Education* (New York: Teachers College Press, Columbia University, 1932); Charles Prosser, *Life Adjustment Education for Every Youth* (Washington, D.C.: U.S. Government Printing Office, 1951); and Florence B. Stratemeyer et al., *Developing a Curriculum for Modern Living* (New York: Teachers College Press, Columbia University, 1947).

96. William H. Kilpatrick, "The Project Method," *Teachers College Record* (September 1918), pp. 319–335; Kilpatrick, *Foundations of Method* (New York: Macmillan, 1925).

97. Goodlad and Zhixin Su, "Organization and the Curriculum."

98. Garth Boomer, "Negotiating the Curriculum," in Garth Boomer, Nancy Lester, Cynthia Onore and Jon Cook, *Negotiating the Curriculum: Educating for the 21st Century* (Washington, DC: Falmer Press, 1992), pp. 4–14.

99. Brooks and Brooks, *The Case for Constructivist Classrooms.*

100. Harold Rugg and Ann Shumaker, *The Child-Centered School* (New York: World Book, 1928), p. 118.

101. John Dewey, *Experience and Education* (New York: Macmillan, 1938).

102. Reginald D. Archambault, ed., *John Dewey on Education* (Chicago: University of Chicago Press, 1964).

103. Daniel Tanner and Laurel Tanner, *Curriculum Development: Theory into Practice,* 2nd ed. (New York: Macmillan, 1980).

104. Dewey, *The Child and the Curriculum.*

105. Peter McLaren, "Education as a Political Issue: What's Missing in the Public Conversation about Education?" in Joe L. Kincheloe and Shirley R. Steinberg, *Thirteen Questions,* 2nd ed. (New York: Peter Lang, 1995), pp. 267–280.

106. Paulo Freire, *Pedagogy of the Oppressed* (New York: Herder and Herder, 1970); Freire, *The Politics of Education* (South Hadley, Mass.: Bergin and Garvey, 1985).

107. Robert Young, *A Critical Theory of Education* (New York: Teachers College Press, Columbia University, 1990).

108. Hunkins, *Teaching Thinking Through Effective Questioning.*

109. Giles Deleuze, *Nietzche and Philosophy* (New York: Columbia University Press, 1983), cited in Peters, ed., *Education and the Postmodern Condition.*

110. Michael Peters, "Introduction: Lyotard, Education and the Postmodern Condition," in Peters, ed., *Education and the Postmodern Condition.*

111. Arthur W. Combs, ed., *Perceiving, Behaving, Becoming* (Washington, D.C.: Association for Supervision and Curriculum Development, Yearbook, 1962).

112. Arthur W. Combs, "What Can Man Become?" in Combs, ed., *Perceiving, Behaving, Becoming,* pp. 1–8.

113. Louise M. Berman and Jessie A. Roderick, eds., *Feeling, Valuing, and the Art of Growing: Insights into the Affective* (Washington, D.C.: Association for Supervision and Curriculum Development, 1977). Also see Louise M. Berman, et al., *Toward Curriculum for Being* (New York: State University of New York Press, 1992).

114. Abraham H. Maslow, *Toward a Psychology of Being* (New York: D. Van Nostrand, 1962).

115. Carl Rogers, "Toward Becoming a Fully Functioning Person," in Combs, ed., *Perceiving, Behaving, Becoming,* pp. 21–33.

116. Gloria Λ. Castillo, *Left-Handed Teaching,* 2nd ed. (New York: Holt, Rinehart, 1970); Gerald Weinstein and Mario D. Fantini, *Toward Humanistic Education: A Curriculum of Affect* (New York: Praeger, 1970).

117. Ibid.

118. Philip H. Phenix. "Transcendence and the Curriculum," in Eisner and Vallance, eds., *Conflicting Conceptions of Curriculum,* p. 123.

119. Moffett, *The Universal Schoolhouse.*

120. Francis P. Hunkins, "Sailing: Celebrating and Educating Self," *Educational Forum* (Summer 1992), pp. 1–9.

121. Jacqueline C. Mancall, Erica K. Lodish, and Judith Springer, "Searching Across the Curriculum," *Phi Delta Kappan* (March 1992), pp. 526–528.

122. Herbert Spencer, *Education: Intellectual, Moral, and Physical* (New York: Appleton 1860).

123. Saylor et al. *Planning for Better Teaching and Learning.*

124. Florence B. Stratemeyer, Hamden L. Forkner, and Margaret G. McKim, *Developing a Curriculum for Modern Living* (New York: Teachers College Press, Columbia University, 1947), p. 300.

125. Goodlad and Zhixin Su, "Organization and the Curriculum."

126. Faunce and Bossing, *Developing the Core Curriculum.*

127. Alberty and Alberty, *Reorganizing the High School Curriculum.*

128. George S. Counts, "Dare Progressive Education Be Progressive?" *Progressive Education* (April 1932), p. 259.

129. George S. Counts, *Dare the Schools Build a New Social Order?* (Yonkers, N.Y.: World Book, 1932).

130. Harold Rugg, *Culture and Education in America* (New York: Harcourt, 1931), pp. 302–303.

131. Harold Rugg, *Foundations for American Education* (New York: Harcourt, 1947), p. 745.

132. Theodore Brameld, *Toward a Reconstructed Philosophy of Education* (New York: Holt, Rinehart and Winston, 1956).

133. Virgil A. Clift and Harold G. Shane, "The Future, Social Decisions, and Educational Change in Secondary Schools," in W. Van Til, ed., *Issues in Secondary Education,* Seventy-fifth Yearbook of the National Society for the Study of Education, Part II (Chicago: University of Chicago Press, 1976), pp. 295–315.

134. Michael W. Apple, "Conservative Agendas and Progressive Possibilities: Understanding the Wider Politics of Curriculum and Teaching," *Education and Urban Society* (May 1991), pp. 279–291.

135. Pinar et al., *Understanding Curriculum.*

136. Maxine Green, "Educational Visions: What Are Schools for and What Should We Be Doing in the Name of Education?" in Joe L. Kincheloe and Shirley R. Steinberg, *Thirteen Questions,* 2nd ed., pp. 305–313.

9

AIMS, GOALS, AND OBJECTIVES

Focusing Questions

1. How does the concept of intentionality relate to educational aims, goals, and objectives?
2. How can we distinguish educational aims from goals?
3. What are the major sources of educational aims?
4. What are the various types of educational objectives?
5. How do curriculum specialists formulate objectives?
6. How can the taxonomy of educational objectives be used for formulating educational objectives?
7. What are the differences between behavioral and nonbehavioral objectives?
8. How do behaviorists and humanistic educators differ in their formulation of objectives?
9. How do reconceptualists deal with objectives? To what extent do they accept objectives? Reject objectives?

While debates as to the purpose or purposes of education exist, few disagree that education is purposeful. We create curricula of various designs for both general and specific intents. Those who develop curricula, teach curricula, or discuss the nature of schools and their curricula have in mind some intent. Education is enacted for a reason. It may be emergent and random; nevertheless, it is intentional activity created to either allow students to attain certain understandings, skills, or attitudes or to gain a receptivity to participate in the world, current and future, in particular ways, and even to design their means of interactions.

Some of the intents of education are geared to the immediate. Being able to read a technical paper with understanding might be one. However, other intents are implied or hoped for, rather than immediate. While we may precisely indicate that a student after a unit in technical literacy would read with understanding a technical report, there is an implied intent that in the future the individual would take such a competency and apply it in ways as yet unknown and unspecified. Moreover, we hope that what the student does with this literacy skill will demonstrate knowledge wisely employed for personal and social benefit.

Since education is intentional activity, it makes sense to be clear as to purpose. As Pratt notes, the process of curriculum planning should exhibit clarification and articulation of meaning. Educators must be conscious of purpose.[1] However, educators in the technical camp of curriculum development conceptualize "being clear" differently from those in the nontechnical camp.

For advocates of the technical camp, being clear often means knowing or stating precisely the outcomes of students in regard to knowledge, skills, attitudes, and behaviors. One must articulate intentions and results to make the curriculum efficient and effective. Those in the nontechnical camp state that we can be clear as to our intentions to furnish students with definite types of curricular experiences, but we should not be so specific as to what outcomes will result that we prevent students from generating their own unique knowledge, skills, attitudes, and behaviors.

Whether educators, and curricularists in particular, view the outcomes of schooling as precisely defined and fixed terminal points or as points in a never-ending series of points, or an emergence of unanticipated points is influenced by the philosophies that educators hold. Because of the numerous philosophical positions, it is likely that the myriad ways to conceptualize, intentionalize, and deliver the curriculum will continue.

Intentionality of education is usually expressed at several different levels. The most general level is reflected in statements of aims; the most specific is exhibited in statements of objectives. And while the detail of these statements of intent will be influenced by educators' philosophical positions, all such statements serve to guide the development, implementation, and evaluation of educational programs.

Often people want educators to take a stand regarding key educational issues. However, it is not our purpose in this book to advocate a particular position. Rather, we wish to furnish the reader with a sense of the range of views regarding how to phrase intentionality within the curriculum context. We are not going to debate the various views of ends and means. Rather, we wish to point out the roles that philosophy and our views of the learner play in interpreting and responding to reality and to the task of creating educational programs. We need to be cognizant of the philosophical, psychological, and social–political underpinnings of our curricular actions. Such awareness is essential because our schools exist in a dynamic emergent society in which great waves of social and technical change are occurring.

In these dynamic times, John Dewey's argument that the ends to which people strive are not really ends, but waypoints on a continuous journey, is perhaps more significant than when Dewey first made the statement. Education is a journey, and our intentions, however phrased, must inform the learner that the attainment of a waypoint enables him or her to proceed to the next. Ends for a particular point are essentially the means for striving to another point, another destination, toward another intention. As Dewey commented, "Ends are, in fact, literally endless, forever coming into existence as new activities occasion new consequences."[2]

AIMS OF EDUCATION

In times of great change, society looks to its schools to help its citizens adjust. Society often demands that the schools modify their programs so that students will be able to function more effectively in current times. Few educators would dare respond to the many demands placed on the schools without some mention of educational aims. But often they are not precise in their use of educational language. The term aims is often used interchangeably with goals, ends, functions, general objectives, and purposes.[3] However, there are differences among the terms, and it is helpful to distinguish among them. Aims are general statements that provide both shape and direction to the more specific actions designed to achieve some future product or behavior. Aims are starting points that suggest an ideal or inspirational vision of the good.[4] They reflect value judgments and value-laden statements, and they furnish educators with guides for the educational process.

Educators of every age are challenged to interpret the aims of society. Because of their global quality, only a few aims are necessary to guide education. For example, Ralph Tyler summarized the aims of American schooling as (1) developing self-realization, (2) making individuals literate, (3) encouraging social mobility, (4) providing the skills and understanding necessary for productive employment, (5) furnishing tools requisite for making effective choices regarding material and nonmaterial things and services, and (6) furnishing the tools necessary for continued learning.[5] These all-encompassing aims reflect a progressive philosophy.

Ronald Doll notes that educational aims should address the intellectual or cognitive, the social-personal or affective, and the productive.[6]

1. Aims dealing with the *intellectual dimension* focus on the acquisition and comprehension of knowledge, problem-solving, skills, and various levels and methods of thinking.

2. Aims in the *social-personal dimension* are concerned with person-to-society, person-to-person, and person-to-self interactions. These aims also subsume the emotional and psychological aspects of individuals and their adaptive aspects with regard to home, family, church, and local community.

3. Aims relating to the *productive dimension* of schooling center on those aspects of education that allow the individual to function in the home, on the job, and as a citizen and member of the larger society.

To these dimensions, we would add four others: (1) *physical,* dealing with the development and maintenance of strong and healthy bodies; (2) *aesthetic,* dealing with values and appreciation of the arts; (3) *moral,* dealing with values and behavior that reflect appropriate behavior; and (4) *spiritual,* dealing with the recognition and belief in the divine and the view of transcendence.

Sources of Aims

During every period of contemporary history, society in general and educators in particular have formulated aims. These aims are usually developed by prestigious, nationwide commissions and task forces in the context of the overriding concerns and problems of a changing society. These commissions, which have been in existence since the turn of the twentieth century, usually include descriptive studies of society to guide program creation.

Spencer's Report.   We might denote the starting point for such reports as 1859, when Herbert Spencer published his essay "What Knowledge Is of Most Worth?" From his analysis of his contemporary society, Spencer concluded that for individuals to lead successful lives they needed preparation in five realms of activities: (1) direct self-preservation, (2) indirect self-preservation

(for example, securing food, shelter, and earning a living), (3) parenthood, (4) citizenship, and (5) leisure activities.[7] Since Spencer's time, hundreds of descriptive studies of all aspects of society, many conducted by blue-ribbon panels, have been utilized by educators to frame the aims of education.

The Cardinal Principles.   The National Education Association's Commission on the Reorganization of Secondary Education issued its report in 1918, when World War I ended. The report, called *Cardinal Principles of Secondary Education,* spoke to the role of education in our democratic society in the following manner: Education in a democracy, both within and without the school, should develop in each individual the knowledges, interest, ideas, habits, and powers whereby "he will find his place and use that place to shape both himself and society toward even nobler ends."[8]

Perhaps influenced by Spencer, the commission employed the organizational principle of important life activities to organize categories of curriculum aims. Seven major areas were presented:

1. Health
2. Command of fundamental processes
3. Worthy home membership
4. Vocational education
5. Civic education
6. Worthy use of leisure
7. Ethical character[9]

The Purpose of Education in American Democracy.   After the Great Depression, the Educational Policies Commission of the NEA issued a report entitled *The Purpose of Education in American Democracy.* The Commission noted that the definition of education needed to reflect the philosophy and practice of democracy. Education must cherish and inculcate its moral values, stress knowledge and information essential to its institutions and economy, and foster a creative and sustaining spirit.[10]

A comprehensive set of four aims, each with several corresponding goals (which the Commission called objectives) was delineated: (1) self-realization, (2) human relationships, (3) economic efficiency, and (4) civic responsibility. The aim of *self-realization* was to encourage inquiry, mental capabilities, speech, reading, writing, numbers, sight and hearing, health knowledge, health habits, public health, recreation, intellectual interests, aesthetic interests, and character formation. The aim of *human relationships* included humanity, friendship, cooperation with others, courtesy, appreciation of the home, conservation of the home, homemaking, and democracy in the home. The aims of *economic efficiency* encompassed work, occupational appreciation, personal economics, consumer judgment, efficiency in buying, and consumer protection. The aim of *civic responsibility* related to social justice, social activity, social understanding, critical judgment, tolerance, conservation of resources, social application of science, world citizenship, law of observance, economic literacy, political citizenship, and devotion to democracy.[11]

Education for All American Youth. In 1944, the Educational Policies Commission, still concerned about the purposes of education, formulated several aims of education. Influenced by World War II, it stressed the overriding aims related to democracy and world citizenship, as well as those related to the general needs of children and youth. Its report, *Education for All American Youth,* listed ten aims, or what it called the "Ten Imperative Needs of Youth." All youth needed to develop skills and attitudes that enhance the following:

1. *Salable skills and those understandings and attitudes that make them intelligent and productive participants in economic life.*
2. *Good health and physical fitness.*
3. *Understanding of the rights and duties of citizens of a democratic society, and those necessary to serve as members of the community and citizens of the state, nation, and world.*
4. *Understanding of the significance of the family for the individual and society, and the conditions conducive to successful family life.*
5. *Knowledge of how to purchase and use goods and services intelligently, understanding both the value received by the consumer and the economic consequences of their acts.*
6. *Understanding of the methods of science, the influence of science on human life, and the*

main scientific facts concerning the nature of the world and humanity.
7. *The development of capacities to appreciate beauty in literature, art, music, and nature.*
8. *The use of leisure time and the budgeting of it wisely, balancing activities that yield satisfaction to the individual with those that are socially useful.*
9. *Respect for other persons, insight into ethical values and principles, and the ability to live and work cooperatively with others.*
10. *Growth of their ability to think rationally, to express their thoughts clearly, and to read and listen with understanding.*[12]

The Central Purpose of American Education. Feeling the effects of Sputnik, the National Educational Association's Educational Policies Commission addressed the aims of education in 1961. It noted that in the modern world, an expanding role was accorded the rational power of humans. Using these powers, knowledge was increased to solve the riddles of life, space, and time.[13]

Educators were concerned that in a real sense we were losing excellence, especially in mathematics and science. Sputnik had caught us by surprise, and the schools were identified as the cause of our coming up second. America had to meet the demands of the space race and the Cold War. The Educational Policies Commission's 1961 report essentially stressed intellectual excellence and thinking competencies. We needed to challenge our gifted and talented students.

A Nation at Risk. In 1983, the Commission on Excellence in Education was directed to examine the quality of American education and to report its findings. The Commission concluded that our nation was at risk: Our educational system was delivering a mediocre performance and the schools had lost sight of the basic purposes of education. The Commission argued that "learning is the indispensable investment required for success in the 'information age' we are entering."[14]

The Commission made several recommendations that touched on the directions of education and how to address them. The first recommendation dealt with content. The commission stated:

We recommend that State and local high school graduation requirements be strengthened and that, at a minimum, all students seeking a diploma be required to lay the foundations in the Five New Basics by taking the following curriculum during their 4 years of high school: a) 4 years of English; b) 3 years of mathematics; c) 3 years of science; d) 3 years of social studies, and e) one-half year of computer science. For the college-bound, 2 years of foreign language in high school are strongly recommended.[15]

The Commission focused on the need for higher standards and expectations by urging educators to "adopt more rigorous and measurable standards, and higher expectations, for academic performance and student conduct, and that 4-year colleges and universities raise their requirements for admission . . . "[16] The Commission also made the recommendation that significantly more time be devoted to learning the New Basics. This would require more effective use of the existing school day, a longer school day, and a lengthened school year. Finally, the Commission urged that citizens hold educators and elected officials responsible for providing the leadership necessary to achieve these reforms and that citizens provide the fiscal support and stability required to bring about the reforms it proposed.

Challenge for Tomorrow. In looking at the broad sweep of American educational aims, you might ask yourself whether the schools are expected to do more than is feasible. The schools are often seen as ideal agencies to solve the nation's problems, but can they do so? Many people refuse to admit to their own responsibilities in helping children develop their potential and adjust to society.

The importance of various pressure groups also needs to be mentioned. As society changes, and as different groups seek to further their interests and promote their causes, the aims of education must change. Educators are confronted by new, vocal pressure groups—particularly ethnic groups, women's groups, homosexual groups, and the handicapped. These groups all define themselves as a minority. These groups have new power! Educators must process the needs and interests of these groups, along with traditional pressure groups such as the National Rifle Association, United Way, labor affiliates, and church groups. In processing the information, educators must both maintain and share professional con-

trol, yet address the demands placed on them. The educational aims must be relevant to the times—both the present and future—and furnish direction that is good for the overall society.

GOALS OF EDUCATION

Goals are statements of purpose with some outcome in mind. According to Sowell, goals furnish answers to the following question: "what destination do you have in mind for learners as far as a particular curriculum or subject is concerned?"[17] While goals suggest intended destinations, they do not specifically denote particular learning. Rather, goals address certain characteristics of the learner who attains the goals.[18] A curriculum with its aim that students be literate, functioning citizens would most likely have among it goals that the student be skilled in the processes of critical thinking, be sensitive to culturally diverse people, and have the disposition to assume responsibility for his or her learning.

When speaking of goals, we are addressing curriculum goals, or desired outcomes for students as a result of experiencing the curriculum. We are not addressing how teachers would instruct students to achieve these goals, although it is realized that instruction is related to curriculum and that particular methods of instruction are selected mindful of the demands of certain contents and also the demands of students and their abilities and interests.

By analyzing a school's goals, we can determine the scope of its entire educational program. Goals, in contrast to aims, are not open statements. They are specific statements written so that those responsible for program creation can use them as guidelines to achieve particular purposes. Goals are derived from various aims and thus provide teachers and curriculum decision makers with broad statements of what they should accomplish in terms of student learning as a result of a particular subject or educational program.

Levels of Goals

Goals can be written at several levels of generality. At one extreme, they can be written in such broad phrasing that they are similar to aims and reflect a philosophical base. At the other extreme, they can be written rather specifically to indicate a concern about a particular achievement.

The distinction between aims and goals of education is one of generality. Aims deal with the general process of education, such as "building worldmindedness" or "creating technological literacy." No particular program in the school will attain these aims; many aspects of the curriculum quite likely will address them. Aims become goals when they become more specific and refer to a particular school or school system and to a specific subject area of the curriculum. The aim of "building worldmindedness," for example, might become the social studies goal that "students will become aware of the various nations of the world and the roles that they play in the world community."

Much discussion regards the proper phrasing of educational goals. Some individuals prefer sentences, some phrases, some just a single word. The Association for Supervision and Curriculum Development identified ten major goals for youth that contain several words each: (1) learning self-conceptualization (self-esteem); (2) understanding others; (3) developing basic skills; (4) encouraging interest in and capability for continuing learning; (5) becoming responsible members of society; (6) developing mental and physical health; (7) enhancing creativity; (8) being informed about participating in the economic world of production and consumption; (9) using accumulated knowledge to understand the world; and (10) coping with change.[19] Each of these goals contained several subgoals.

Some educators are more comfortable with goal statements that start with infinitive verbs. These persons would rewrite the preceding list as follows: (1) to develop in students positive self-concepts; (2) to improve students' understanding of others; (3) to develop in students command of basic skills; (4) to stimulate students' interests and capabilities for continual learning, and so forth.

The Phi Delta Kappa honor society has distributed a list of goals; they are:

1. Learn how to be a good citizen.
2. Learn how to respect and get along with people who think, dress, and act differently.
3. Learn about and try to understand the changes that take place in the world.
4. Develop skills in reading, writing, speaking, and listening.
5. Understand and practice democratic ideas and ideals.
6. Learn how to examine and use information.
7. Develop skills to enter a specific field of work.
8. Develop a desire for learning now and in the future.
9. Practice and understand the ideas of health and safety.
10. Appreciate culture and beauty in the world.[20]

In 1990, President Bush and the governors of the United States generated a list of six goals for the nation's schools. During the same year, the National Goals Panel was established to determine just how the nation was progressing toward meeting these goals. The goals identified to lead the schools in the last decade of this century were:

1. *By the year 2000, all children in America will start schools ready to learn.*
2. *By the year 2000, the high school graduation rate will increase to at least 90 percent.*
3. *By the year 2000, American students will leave grades four, eight, and twelve having demonstrated competency in challenging subject matter (English, Mathematics, Science, History, and Geography).*
4. *By the year 2000, U.S. students will be first in the world in science and mathematics achievement.*
5. *By the year 2000, every adult American will be literate and will possess the knowledge and skills necessary to compete in a global economy and exercise the rights and responsibilities of citizenship.*
6. *By the year 2000, every school in America will be free of drugs and violence and will offer a disciplined environment conducive to learning.*[21]

These goals are still being advocated by the federal government. And the Governor's Council also attests to their worth. These Goals 2000 also are exerting influence on the current movement of raising the educational standards of American schools' curricula. It is both interesting and a bit disconcerting to note that these goals are very similar to those generated by various groups after the *Sputnik* scare in the late 1950s. The humanities appear not to be adequately addressed. The curriculum suggested by the goals also reveals a rather traditional emphasis on academics. With the exception of the last goal, there is little mention of the students' social, psychological, or moral development.

Formulating Goals

Goals, like aims, should have a degree of timelessness to them. That is, they should address the particular times in which educators find themselves, but should contain wording also appropriate for future times. While goals address endpoints, they leave a certain degree of freedom in identifying the particulars of the goal. Actually, the particulars are considered in the educational objectives.

Creating educational goals is really a continuing activity in which educators engage as they consider the philosophies of their schools and work to clarify their educational aims. The needs of society, of students, or of the particular community commonly give rise to initial statements of curriculum goals. When school districts have identified current students' learning and behaviors, they often match those with their views of what an educated person is. When persons analyze their philosophies and the aims of their schools, they come up with general statements of outcomes—results they expect to occur in consequence to educational activity. People then make a final match between students' learning and behavior and the goals they have generated. The goals are sometimes rank-ordered in light of importance or feasibility, or both. Persons involved in goal development—teachers, community members, and even students—are asked to decide if these are the goals they wish to address—if these are the end points toward which the program should strive. If they answer yes, then these goals are accepted by those who are creating and delivering the curriculum. See Curriculum Tips 9-1.

OBJECTIVES OF EDUCATION

Within the context of educational aims and goals, it is necessary to formulate objectives that will indicate in more specific terms the outcomes of the curriculum or project being considered. Through-

out much of our history objectives have been stated vaguely; they are often confused with goals and aims. To keep aims, goals, and objectives clearly separated, it is perhaps helpful to remind ourselves that in translating aims into goals and finally into objectives, we proceed from the very general, couched in a long-term framework, to the more specific, couched in a short-term time sequence. The sequence is illustrated as follows:

Philosophy $\rightarrow$ Aims $\rightarrow$ Goals $\rightarrow$ Objectives

For a particular science program or project, curriculum developers may state a goal like "improving students' skill in information processing when dealing with science material." Under this goal, they must have a series of more specific objectives. How specific the objectives are will be determined by the philosophies and conceptions educators have regarding curriculum.

Types of Educational Objectives

When proceeding from the most general statements to the more specific, as illustrated in the sequence above, some curriculum planners denote several levels or types of objectives. These begin with general objectives (which indicate general outcomes relating to specific areas of the curriculum, often courses or subjects and particular grade levels) and go to specific outcomes resulting from classroom instruction.

Hilda Taba asserted that educational objectives can be of two sorts: those that describe school-wide outcomes and those that are more specific and describe behaviors to be attained in a particular unit, a subject course, or a particular grade-level program.[22]

Ornstein identifies objectives as to the level for which they are written: (1) program objectives, addressing subjects (science or math) at particular grade levels; (2) course objectives (biology or algebra), relating to particular courses within grade levels; and (3) classroom objectives, which are further divided into unit objectives and lesson plan objectives. The first two types of objectives are usually developed by curriculum specialists working at the state or school district level; however, classroom objectives are designed by teachers in an attempt to achieve program and course objectives.[23]

Curriculum Tips 9-1

Developing Goals at the School District or School Level

Writing goals for a school district or school usually falls to a school committee consisting of curriculum specialists, teachers and administrators, and sometimes parents and students. If you are a member of a district or school committee intent on formulating goals, here are some suggestions to help you start. You need to read or be familiar with:

1. Federal and state mandates and legislation
2. National and state commission reports that identify aims and goals
3. Professional association reports that identify goals
4. Community concerns voiced by state and local organizations
5. Parental concerns expressed in parental advisory groups and teacher association meetings
6. Professional literature on theories of learning and child development
7. Professional literature on student needs and career choices
8. Books and reports on college and employee requirements
9. Teacher reports and comments
10. Subject specialist reports and comments
11. Evaluation reports about school programs and curriculum
12. Local needs assessments concerning students, teachers, the school, or school district
13. Reports from the state certification office and regional or national accrediting agencies
14. Reports and studies about social and economic trends in the local community, state, and nation

---

Source: Allan C. Ornstein, *Secondary and Middle School Teaching Methods* (New York: Harper Collins, 1992), p. 310.

George Posner and Alan Rudnitsky introduce another term for objectives: intended learning outcomes (ILOs), defining them as statements of precisely what the student is to learn. An ILO is a declaration about the specifics to be learned: facts, concepts, principles, process, techniques, generalizations, etc. Posner and Rudnitsky stress that the words *intended learning outcomes* require our reflection. *Intended* means that the statements are not referring to accidental learning. Learning that is intended is the result of reflecting on information judged to be of worth. Also, intended means that the educational process is under a type of control for particular purposes. While there may be many unintended learnings, in curriculum planning we are addressing those we *intend* to occur. The term *learning* is also important. As the authors point out, learning implies that the bottom line for planning is student performance. And *outcome* is also a crucial word. Curricular planners are concerned with the results from students interacting and experiencing the curriculum. What has the student achieved from taking a course?[24]

The outcomes of education are a topic receiving much current attention. Likely, this attention will continue. Outcome-based education is popular in most states in the Union. In Washington state, a commission was established to develop a list of essential learnings, outcomes that all students must attain to demonstrate learning success. And while these essential learnings appear more at the level of goals, teachers will be expected to translate them into specific learning outcomes, specific objectives at both the course and classroom level.

It perhaps rests with the educational professional, and that includes teachers, to decide just what to call objectives. But, whatever they are called, objectives are more specific than goals, and this specificity increases in the progression from general curriculum objectives (subject or grade level), to unit objectives (classroom level), to lesson objectives (also classroom level). Objectives are statements that enable curriculum decision makers—curriculum developers, teachers, and even students and members of the general public—to identify the particular intent of a particular action. Norman Gronlund and Robert Mager state that a meaningful objective is one that communicates effectively to the reader the instructional intent or behavior of the objective as well as specific learning outcomes.[25]

Behavioral Objectives. In our previous discussion, we referred to educational objectives as general or specific statements of expected learner outcomes. Advocates of both types of objectives have debated their value. But the general public and, so it seems, the majority of educators have accepted the view that specific statements are the most effective for educational objectives.

For an objective to be meaningful and therefore useful in guiding educators (whether or not it has been achieved), it should be measurable. To the extent that educators are unable to measure achievement, the meaningfulness of the objective is diminished. Put simply, this means that a behavioral objective is a precise statement of outcomes in terms of observable behavior expected of students after instruction. Such an objective responds to the following question: "What behavior can the learner engage in that will confirm that he or she grasps the knowledge or possesses the skills specified in the delivery of the curriculum?"[26]

Mager contends that an educational objective must describe (1) the *behavior* of the learner when demonstrating his or her achievement of the objective, (2) the *condition* imposed on the learner when demonstrating mastery of the objective, and (3) the minimum *proficiency* level that will be acceptable.[27] A behavioral objective in science following Mager's counsel might read as follows:

After studying the unit on energy, the student must complete a 100 item multiple-choice test on the subject. The student must answer correctly 75 items and respond to this exam within a 1-hour period.

An example for mathematics might be as follows:

Given a worksheet dealing with the process of multiplication, the pupil will be able to multiply sets of three-place numbers at the rate of one problem per minute with 80 percent accuracy.

Not all educators who favor such objectives follow Mager's counsel. While agreeing that the educational objective must describe the learner's behavior, which comprises the essential part of an action verb, these educators list condition and proficiency as optional parts. Additionally, they have an essential part not included by Mager, that of the subject content reference that addresses the content considered. A sample behavioral objective with the two essential parts (action verb and subject content reference) might be "The student will write a paragraph in English composition dealing with late twentieth-century literature." Another might be "The student in an economics class will compare data on a chart depicting gross national product for two years."

It is not always necessary to include level of achievement and conditions of performance. However, it is necessary to state the level of achievement when one is dealing with minimum requirements for some aspect of a course. This part of the objective answers the questions of how well, how much, and how accurate. The conditions of performance are only necessary when it is important to denote where and how the knowledge was demonstrated or the skill performed. What was the nature of the environment? With authentic learning being stressed, an educator might need to include the conditions of performance so that others can determine whether the conditions resembled those outside the school context. The following objective is an example of one that includes both essential and optional parts.

The student in a geographic field study exercise will arrange field notes in a way that meets the suggested guidelines stated in the geographic field study manual.

This above example reveals that the parts do not have to be organized in a particular order, such as the two essential parts first, followed by the two optional parts. The phrase "in a geographic field study exercise" refers to the *condition*. This is followed by the essential part of including an *action verb,* "will arrange"; "in a way that meets suggested guidelines" is the *level of achievement part.*[28]

Nonbehavioral General Objectives. Perhaps the greatest advantage of behavioral objectives is the clarity of communication they foster. People reading such objectives know precisely what they mean and can determine the extent to which they have been attained. But advocates of nonbehavioral objectives who use such words as "appreciate," "know," and "understand," contend that stating objectives too specifically restricts learning opportunities to those situations that require measurement. Objectives that address higher-order learning (for example, analytic thinking and appreciation of literature) are likely to be eliminated because they frequently do not lend themselves to precise measurement. Many opponents of behavioral objectives reject precise objectives as expressions of behaviorism. They insist that much learning can occur that does not result in overt, measurable pupil behavior. Learning in the affective domain is a more subtle form of learning.

Behavioral objectives are also criticized for not taking into account what Michael Polanyi has called *tacit knowing:* having knowledge that we are perhaps unable to verbalize or demonstrate specifically.[29] One example of tacit knowing is being able to recognize a familiar face in a crowd, yet not being able to describe in any detail the person's appearance.

Advocates of nonbehavioral objectives point out that educators must realize that there are many indicators of attainment of an educational outcome. With behavioral objectives, the educational outcome may be considered attained *if, and only if,* such a behavior is demonstrated. Knowledge of subtraction, for example, is attained if and only if a child completes eight out of ten subtraction examples in a 20-minute period. Are we willing to state that 80 percent is the only indicator of achieving this goal? What of the student who gets seven out of ten? Are curriculum designers really willing to enunciate such a narrow interpretation?

Over a decade ago, J. Galen Saylor et al. summarized the objections of many regarding behavioral objectives. They indicated that behavioral objectives only emphasize the teaching of facts (which are easy to measure) at the expense of the more complicated intellectual behaviors (which are difficult to measure). Such objectives place a sameness on the curriculum, assuming all must master identical material and do so almost in identical ways. Precise objectives nurture a rigidity in learning and tend to deny the unique learning outcomes of students, thus resulting in an assembly-like or factorylike educational process. Rigidly following objectives often dehumanizes individuals, overlooks individual outcomes, and stifles creativity and spontaneity. Finally, overemphasis on behavioral objectives negates that learning is much more than the gathering and hoarding of specific facts learned in isolation.[30]

Educators in the postmodern camp under no circumstances would advocate the use of behavioral objectives. Some of these educators would even balk at saying that we should have general objectives. Any objectives denote an end point, and in an emerging world, in an educational enterprise that advocates a process of development, dialogue, inquiry, and transformation, we cannot know at the outset what an objective would be. Some postmodern curricularists hold that educators, being external to the student, have no right to set what people should know, how they should behave, or what skills they should privilege.[31]

This does not mean that education is purposeless. Indeed, it has purpose, as a journey has purpose, but the exact waypoints are not preset or precise as to what will be done and the level of performance. We do state intents or perhaps, more importantly, invite students to set intents as to what they wish to do. The intents are such that students have options, that is, opportunities to negotiate their learnings and to judge their levels of performance. The intents of many of these curricularists are to allow for possibilities and encourage students to take pleasure in investigating and experiencing uncertainties. Most educators are not this extreme, just as most educators are not dyed in the wool advocates of behavioral objectives for every aspect of the curriculum.

As just stated, those who favor nonbehavioral objectives are concerned with being precise. All educational objectives should make clear what pupils are supposed to learn. The verbs "to know," "comprehend," "be able to," "enjoy," and "encounter" are all clear—they just are not behavioral! Words like "be familiar with" or "become aware of" or "have a feeling for" are vague and are rejected.[32]

Teachers who believe in nonbehavioral objectives sometimes prepare such objectives in broad general terms indicating what students are to do. Some examples follow:

As a result of this course, the learner will:

Be able to interpret the various map symbols found on the particular types of map projections.
Understand that a community is a place where people work and play together.
Understand the functions of nouns and verbs.
Be able to perform long division of numbers.
Demonstrate ability to do back flips.
Enjoy folk music.

Means and Ends. Much of the argument between behaviorists and nonbehaviorists revolves around the nature of language. Just how precise must the language in educational objectives be? Mauritz Johnson and David Pratt make an interesting and useful distinction between educational intent and the realization of the intent. They note that many educators fall prey to the belief that the objective is in reality the statement that indicates its measure of achievement.[33] They state that an educational objective is really a statement of intent, an expected end product, not an actual product.

Drawing on these arguments, consider the following objective: "The student will write three statements, three questions, three commands, and three exclamations within a 15-minute time period and will have at least ten of the sentences correct as to type and with regard to subjects, predicates, and punctuation."

A person charged with curriculum development should raise the question, "Why do I want the student to do this?" A likely response is that, by engaging in this activity, the student will show a basic understanding of the four types of sentences and punctuation. But does this answer the question? *Why* should a student need to understand these types of sentences? Johnson and Pratt would argue that the real reason is that a student will be able to apply such knowledge of sentence types and write what accurately and effectively expresses his or her feelings or interpretations of a subject. The real objective is not writing three

statements, three questions, three commands, and three exclamations; rather, it is writing effectively on subjects of the student's own choosing.

Guidelines for Formulating Educational Objectives

Because objectives indicate end points or expected outcomes or points that lead to other significant outcomes or points in the educational process, careful thought must be given to the creation of educational objectives. Indeed, giving careful thought to objectives increases the probability that a particular program will be judged successful. Educators should consider the following factors when creating objectives.

Matching. Objectives should relate to the goals and the aims from which they are derived. Many curriculum guides include objectives that, although perhaps having merit, are unrelated to the goals. An objective of students' "understanding" certain science contents, for example, is not in alignment with a goal that students be able to utilize particular information-processing approaches to uncover scientific understanding.

Worth. It is often debatable which educational objectives have worth and which do not. Many schools overemphasize detail, especially in the skills subjects such as reading and mathematics. As a result, many objectives are written that have little worth. Even in such subjects as social studies we see evidence of trivial objectives. "The student knows that the Mississippi River empties into the Gulf of Mexico." Does such an objective have value? Is it essential to know such information? Worth also relates to whether attaining an objective will have value to the student at present and in the future.

Wording. Objectives are only effective if the persons who are to use them as curriculum guides are able to understand from them the same intended outcomes as their writers. Objectives, brief and trimmed of excessive wordiness, are easy to understand and agree on. How appropriately an objective is worded also depends on its level and its scope. Some objectives are written as general subject or grade objectives, some are written as unit objectives, and some as lesson-plan objectives. Because lesson-plan objectives should be worded to indicate rather specifically the intended outcomes, they may include performance criterion statements. This type of precision is not necessarily needed at the first two levels (subject or grade level and unit plan level).

Appropriateness. Not all objectives need to be attained by all students. Curricularists must ask, What are the needs of the students? What type of learning outcomes do they need to achieve? To determine appropriateness, educators must consider the students who are to receive the instruction and the content within which the curriculum is to be delivered. Some objectives might not be appropriate because they demand of students behavior that they are incapable of performing. Some are not appropriate because they do not cater to the students' interests. Some objectives might be more suitable for students in a particular subject than for students interested in a general program. Some objectives might list outcomes that students have already attained.

Logical Grouping. Objectives should be grouped logically so as to make sense when units of instruction and evaluation are being determined. Frequently, statements of objectives lack organizational coherence. In many cases, objectives that address a general understanding of self, such as understanding the particular effects of lack of exercise on the body, are grouped with objectives that are more specific. Often such general objectives as students' understanding how to process information are listed alongside objectives of students knowing how to write complete sentences. The need is to group objectives according to some common thread or idea, what some observers call a "domain."[34]

Periodic Revision. No objectives should stand for all times; objectives require periodic revision. This is necessary because students change, society changes, the realm of knowledge changes, and instructional strategies change. Educators should occasionally analyze their objectives to determine if they are still of value to the program. See Curriculum Tips 9-2.

In general, an objective is useful if it exists not for its own purpose or end, rather if it exists as a means—as a pathway of educational activity or learning. We can judge whether our objectives are useful if they enable a student to proceed to the next step or to the next part of the unit plan or lesson plan. In this connection, the term *enabling objective* has appeared in the literature in recent years. This concept is worth noting, for most behaviors we wish students to engage in are not done primarily for their own sake. Students do not solve mathematical word problems just for their own sake. They work out these problems because doing so implies that such problems will assist students in the world outside of school.

TAXONOMIC LEVELS

When making curricular decisions, especially when generating objectives, educators ideally consider all domains of learning: The cognitive, the affective, and the psychomotor. Fortunately, several well-known classifications of learning exist for them to use. These classifications have organized various types of learning into taxonomies.

The Cognitive Domain

Of all the classifications of realms of objectives, Benjamin Bloom's *Taxonomy of Educational Objectives: Cognitive Domain* is perhaps the most familiar and certainly has the greatest influence on the formation of objectives.[35] The *Taxonomy* categorizes cognitive learning into six major divisions; each upper division subsumes the previous lower ones: (1) knowledge, (2) comprehension, (3) application, (4) analysis, (5) synthesis, and (6) evaluation.

1. *Knowledge.* This level includes objectives that are related to knowledge of (1) specifics, such as specific facts and terminology; (2) ways and means of dealing with specifics, such as conventions, trends and sequences, classifications and categories, criteria and methodology; and (3) universals and abstractions, such as principles, generalizations, theories, and structures. Example: The student will name the highest mountain range in Asia.

2. *Comprehension.* This level involves objectives that deal with (1) translation, (2) interpretation, and (3) extrapolation of information. Example: When given various geometric concepts in verbal terms, the student will draw the correct geometric form.

Curriculum Tips 9-2

Formulating Objectives

With all the various terms and suggested guidelines for writing objectives, Hilda Taba long ago provided us with some common principles that could and still can guide our creating of objectives. Her guidelines make sense for formulating objectives at both the school level and classroom level.

1. A statement of objectives should describe both the kind of behavior expected and the content or the context to which that behavior applies.
2. Complex objectives need to be stated analytically and specifically enough so that there is no doubt as to the kind of behavior expected or to what the behavior applies.
3. Objectives should be so formulated that there are clear distinctions among the learning experiences required to attain different behaviors.
4. Objectives are developmental, representing roads to travel rather than terminal points.
5. Objectives should be realistic and should include only what can be translated into curriculum and classroom experience.
6. The scope of objectives should be broad enough to encompass all types of outcomes for which the school is responsible.

Source: Hilda Taba, *Curriculum Development* (New York: Harcourt, Brace, 1962), pp. 200–205.

---

3. *Application.* This level includes objectives that are related to using abstractions in particular situations. Example: The student will be able to predict the effect on a container of exhausting its air contents.

4. *Analysis.* This level includes objectives that relate to the breaking of a whole into parts and distinguishing (1) elements, (2) relationships, and (3) organizational principles. Example: When given a document to read, the student will be able to distinguish facts from opinion.

5. *Synthesis.* This level includes objectives that relate to putting parts together in a new form such as (1) a unique communication, (2) a plan for operation, or (3) a set of abstract relations. Example: When confronted with a report on pollution, the student will be able to propose ways of testing various hypotheses.

6. *Evaluation.* This is the highest level in the cognitive taxonomy in terms of complexity. Objectives at this level would address making judgments in terms of (1) internal evidence or logical consistency and (2) external evidence or consistency with facts developed elsewhere. Example: The student will appraise fallacies in an argument.

The Affective Domain

David Krathwohl and others presented to the educational community a taxonomy of objectives, consisting of five major categories, in the affective domain.[36] Following is a brief listing, along with examples of objectives, of the categories of the affective domain:

1. *Receiving.* Objectives at this level refer to the learner's sensitivity to the existence of stimuli. This includes (1) awareness, (2) willingness to receive, and (3) selected attention. Example: From studying various cultures of the Eastern world, the student develops an awareness of aesthetic factors in dress, furnishing, and architecture.

2. *Responding.* Objectives at this level refer to the learner's active attention to stimuli such as (1) acquiescence, (2) willing responses, and

(3) feelings of satisfaction. Example: The student displays an interest in the topic of conversation by actively participating in a research project.

3. *Valuing.* Objectives in this level refer to the learner's beliefs and attitudes of worth. They are addressed in the form of (1) acceptance, (2) preference, and (3) commitment. Example: The student will take a viewpoint on advantages or disadvantages of nuclear power.

4. *Organization.* Objectives at this level refer to internalization of values and beliefs involving (1) conceptualization of values and (2) organization of a value system. Example: The student forms judgments about his or her responsibilities for conserving natural resources.

5. *Characterization.* This is the highest level of internalization in the taxonomy. Objectives at this level relate to behavior that reflects (1) a generalized set of values and (2) a characterization or philosophy of life. Example: The student develops a regulation of his or her personal and civic life based on ethical principles.

The Psychomotor Domain

The psychomotor domain has received much less emphasis than either the cognitive or affective domains. Also, fewer persons have worked on delineating it. Anita J. Harrow has, however, developed a psychomotor taxonomy with several categories:[37]

1. *Reflex movements.* Objectives at this level include (1) segmental reflexes (involving one spinal segment) and (2) intersegmental reflexes (involving more than one spinal segment). Example: After engaging in this activity, the student will be able to contract a muscle.

2. *Fundamental movements.* Objectives in this category address behaviors related to (1) walking, (2) running, (3) jumping, (4) pushing, (5) pulling, and (6) manipulating. Example: The student will be able to jump over a 2-foot hurdle.

3. *Perceptual abilities.* Objectives in this division address (1) kinesthetic, (2) visual, (3) auditory, (4) tactile, and (5) coordination abilities. Example: The student will categorize by shape a group of building blocks.

4. *Physical abilities.* Objectives included at this level are related to (1) endurance, (2) strength, (3) flexibility, (4) agility, (5) reaction-response time, and (6) dexterity. Example: The student will do at least five pushups more at the end of the year.

5. *Skilled movements.* Objectives at this level of the domain are concerned with (1) games, (2) sports, (3) dances, and (4) the arts. Example: The student can correctly perform a series of somersaults.

6. *Nondiscursive communication.* Objectives at this final level of the taxonomy relate to expressive movement through (1) posture, (2) gestures, (3) facial expressions, and (4) creative movements. Example: The student will be able to create his or her own movement sequence and perform it to music.

The categories of the three taxonomies are arranged in a hierarchy in which the levels increase in complexity from simple to more advanced. In the cognitive domain, levels 2 through 6 connote various problem-solving skills and abilities. Each level depends on the acquisition of the previous level. For example, for a student to analyze an issue, he or she must be able to apply information, must comprehend information, and must have some level of knowledge. For a student to express a value preference, he or she must be able to respond to situations and must be willing to receive information; that is, he or she must be sensitive to a particular situation. For a child to be skilled at the level of perceptual abilities, he or she must have mastered fundamental movements and reflex movements.

The taxonomies are useful for developing educational objectives and for grouping sets of objectives. One difficulty educators may have is making decisions identifying objectives between adjacent categories. This is particularly true if the objectives are not clearly stated. But, if educators carefully reflect on their objectives, they should find the taxonomies valuable tools for creating objectives. See Table 9-1.

A Totalizing Taxonomy

We humans like to categorize; however, students are not machines, are not bits and pieces that can be attended to separately. The taxonomies are indeed useful guides; however, real people are not separately organized into cognitive, affective, and

TABLE 9-1   Overview of Aims, Goals, and Objectives

EDUCATIONAL STATEMENT	FEATURES	SOURCE	SAMPLES	CURRICULUM IMPLICATIONS
Aims	A general statement that provides direction or intent to educational action.	From national commissions, task forces, and panels.	Cardinal Principles of Secondary Education; The Purpose of Education in American Democracy; A Nation at Risk	Identifies the overall direction of the curriculum.
Goals	Statements of purpose. More specific than aims.	From professional associations, government agencies, state departments of education, and school districts.	ASCD, Measuring and Maintaining the Goals of Education; PDK, Phase III of the Educational Planning Model; National Goals for Education	Identifies specific content areas of the curriculum.
Objectives	Specific statements that indicate either general or specific outcomes. Behavioral objectives indicate the specific behavior the student is to demonstrate to indicate learning. Nonbehavioral objectives use more general words to denote the learning desired, such as to know, to understand.	From school districts, schools, and individual writers.	Taxonomy of Educational Objectives; Posner, Gronlund, Mager	Behavioral objectives tend to make curriculum more sequenced, precise, and compartmentalized. Nonbehavioral objectives allow for a more open ended curriculum and integration of subject matter.

psychomotor realms. Humans are a meld of these and even other phenomena about which we still know little. The ethical, moral, and spiritual aspects of individuals are essential dimensions of human complexity.

Objectives or waypoints that involve many dimensions of human action are more powerful in the curricular game than those objectives with a narrow focus. Ideally, we want objectives or waypoints or intents that address knowledge acquisition and construction, skill development or creation, attitude formulation, value formulation and understanding. We want objectives that deal with declarative knowledge and procedural knowledge (process) and direct students toward enriching, enlightening, uplifting experiences. We want objectives that denote waypoints that indicate, or at least suggest, that individuals are being transformed in ways beneficial to both them and to the general society.

APPROACHES TO EDUCATIONAL OBJECTIVES

Objectives, stated more specifically than goals, are designed to communicate to involved parties—students, teachers, laypersons—the intents of particular actions. However, diverse views exist regarding approaches to curriculum objectives. Some attention was given to defining these approaches in Chapter 1.

Behavioral Approach

In the last two decades, much attention has been given to behavioral objectives. Although such objectives are rather new to educational dialogue, the theoretical basis for them is not; it has been borrowed from behaviorist learning theory in psychology and from the concept of operationalism in science (by which people operationalize or give a tangible or observable condition to a particular learning or disposition of a human being). For example, you may wish to indicate that a person appreciated good art; however, no one has ever seen an "appreciation." What you need to do is to indicate those tangible or observable ways of behaving that comprise "appreciation." Armed with such a tangible definition of appreciate, you have a better indication of what you are looking for or intending with your objective.

In this connection, B. F. Skinner views the curriculum as being formulated according to behavioristic objectives.[38] To Skinner, the teacher's role is primarily a mechanical one of arranging contingencies of reinforcement, in a sequenced and step-by-step procedure, under which the students are automatically conditioned toward specific terminal ways of behaving. Taking this approach to objectives, we view method as the scheduling of reinforcement contingencies established by the teacher or the curriculum developer.

The concern for high levels of behavioral specificity has some history in American business and education. It is tied closely to the notion of curriculum as a production system in which the student is a product to be acted on. This view of the curriculum received attention during the early decades of this century, when educators were attempting to relate scientific management to education.[39] This push for precision in planning and then stating what one intended to do or have students do has continued to the present time.

Popham and Baker defined the curriculum as "all planned learning outcomes for which the school is responsible."[40] They viewed curriculum as the ends and instruction as the means. This separating of curriculum and instruction as ends and means continues to affect behavioral objectives. Popham argued, "Measurable instructional objectives are designed to counteract what is to me the most serious deficit in American education today, namely a preoccupation with the process without assessment of consequences." He lists three areas in which "measurable objectives have considerable potential—in curriculum (what goals are selected); in instruction (how to accomplish those goals); and in evaluation (determining whether objectives of the instructional sequence have been realized)."[41]

Gagné et al. made a similar point. They stated that greater precision in the definition of objectives meets two needs: the need for communication of the purposes of instruction and the need for evaluation of instruction.[42] They note that in achieving precision in stating objectives "one is said to be 'defining objectives in terms of human performance [or human behavior].' " When objectives are so stated, an individual is "informed as to what must be observed" in order to determine the achievement of the course's purpose.[43]

A central assumption of this approach to objectives is that one can identify all the essential learnings and behaviors that should result from the curriculum. Teachers who attempt to follow this approach sometimes generate lists of hundreds of objectives. However, the major limitation of this approach is that we really cannot denote all of the specific competencies and essential behaviors that should result from education. Even if we could, the fact that the teacher is doing it in a major way excludes the student from playing some role in determining the direction of his or her education. The approach is effective in addressing areas of the curriculum that deal with skills and the training of certain performances.

But it is deficient in furnishing guidance for showing appreciation and attitudes toward content and values.

Managerial and Systems Approaches

The managerial approach and the systems approach are closely related. Thus they are included here as essentially comprising one approach to the formulation of objectives. These approaches represent a way of thinking that has its roots in the early scientific movement and behavioral approaches to educational decision making. Both school managers and systems personnel rely on organizational theory and are sensitive to the interrelatedness of the units or departments of the organization. According to Roger Kaufman, they rely on problem identification and problem resolution as a means of identifying goals and objectives and implementing and evaluating programs.[44]

Problem identification centers primarily on determining the exact nature of the problem and then considering possible ways to address or solve the problem. Specifying the problem allows us to identify what the objectives should be. For instance, if the problem is poor reading performance, we may reflect on what behaviors need to be addressed for students to read effectively. Whereas problem identification is identifying the particulars of the problem and contemplating and generating possibilities, the second major stage, *problem resolution,* is the actual determining of the objectives to be addressed and selecting the teaching procedures appropriate for these objectives. Problem resolution also refers to the actual carrying out of those strategies selected and engaging in particular actions to evaluate the effectiveness of the strategies employed to teach the objective.

The managerial and systems person has various levels of activities in which to engage: mission analysis, function analysis, and task analysis. The mission analysis is very similar to delineating the aims of education, similar to Charter's discussion in his classic book. Function analysis relates to the general activities, which can be equated to some degree to the activities that Bobbitt discussed. Task analysis represents the end point of what is to be done, what, in our case, the pupil is

to do to obtain a particular learning. Gagné is a proponent of such an approach.

Sometimes managerial and systems approaches appear in educational institutions under the guise of management by objectives. Management by objectives (MBO) can be considered as a philosophical approach whereby all school personnel identify their common and uncommon goals as a basis for defining successful criteria for evaluating the degree of goal attainment. Some people call this approach behaviorist. MBO rests on the assumption that school operations can be conducted in a logical and effective pattern. One can identify directions, plot action, implement such action, and evaluate the success of such implementation.[45]

Although MBO is not a complex process, it still includes an acceptance of the managerial and systems posture. When the school functions as a system, it consists of a number of components, each differentiated from the others in terms of particular functions to be performed; all these components contribute in some way to the accomplishment of the organization's purpose. Furthermore, the term *system* implies that the relationships among the various components are characterized by interdependence, regularity, order, and predictability.[46]

Humanistic Approach

All educators realize that they are creating curricula for human beings. However, humanists believe that the function of the curriculum is to provide each learner with intrinsically rewarding experiences that will make for more complete living and more authentic lives. Humanists view the goals of education as personal growth, integrity, and autonomy. Goals and objectives stress the person in contrast to subject matter. Curricula resulting from the formulating of humanistic objectives contain experiences through which individuals can expand their awareness of being human, compassionate, and caring. These human expressions are considered more important than knowing the capital of Nigeria or the chemical formula for carbon monoxide.[47]

Humanists deal with such questions as what is real, what is human, and what is good. In processing such questions, educators can arrange educational objectives and experiences to allow students to attain personal dignity and self-worth. Weinstein and Fantini embrace the notion that education in a free society should have a broad human focus, which is best served by educational objectives resting on a personal and interpersonal base and dealing with students' concerns.[48]

The idea of self-actualization is central to the humanistic approach to education. Carl Rogers, a recognized spokesperson for this approach, indicates that the goals and objectives of such a curriculum should be geared to enabling the individual student to gain an openness to experience, to view living as a process, and to trust his or her own experiencing. The individual is thus able to view himself or herself as becoming a more fully functioning individual.[49]

Abraham Maslow, a major figure in the development of humanistic psychology, viewed self-realization as multidimensional, as relating to life achievement, as continually evolving. Thus the curriculum was constantly changing as well. Every learner is, in part, "his own project" and makes the curriculum fit his own needs.[50] The objectives and goals that humanists favor address openness and tend to be stated in humanistic rather than behavioral or rational terms. The prime criterion is that such objectives must encourage self-actualization; they must relate to peak experiences. For Maslow such experiences are those that give rise to love, hate, anxiety, depression, and joy. Maslow noted that the peak experiences of awe, mystery, and wonder are both the end and the beginning of learning.

Philip Phenix has expanded some of Maslow's thinking. Phenix believes that the curriculum must do more than concentrate on academic knowledge. It must stress transcendence—the limitlessness of experience. Stressing transcendence, the student will experience every event within a context of wider relationships and possibilities. Phenix indicated that certain qualities are associated with transcendence: hope, creativity, awareness, doubt and faith, wonder, awe, and reverence.[51] Focusing on these dimensions permits optimal individual development.

Objectives in the humanistic camp direct the teachers to furnish learners with opportunities to become their own persons, to gain control over their processes of learning, and to realize the complexity of existence. Thus teachers in this camp do not usually write explicit or precise objectives. They allow the objectives, if there are any, to "evolve" from the experiences that students have. If we were looking at a curriculum guide for a humanistic curriculum, for example, we might find such objectives as (1) students will have experiences that will help them become self-directed and involved in the learning process, (2) students will gain in self-confidence, and (3) students will become more considerate of others. Such objectives do not list specific behaviors that the students are to demonstrate, nor do they indicate any criteria of performance. But these so-called "vague" statements are still objectives, for they do present educational outcomes.

Reconceptualism

The concerns and questions asked by advocates of the above approaches to the formation of objectives are not considered by the reconceptualists to be important. Reconceptualists think that curricularists are preoccupied with the practical and technical modes of understanding and action. William Pinar asserts that the key question is not the purposes of the school, but rather why, as an individual, I identify with particular people or certain situations. Why do I read these authors and not others? Why am I fascinated with this play or movie and not others?[52]

In a sense, reconceptualists are like humanists; however, reconceptualists are much more critical of education and view the educational arena from an existential, aesthetic, and spiritual framework. For this reason, their objectives are open ended. Reconceptualism is essentially not an approach to objectives, but more of a political and social force offering a critique of current schooling. They urge the reorganization of schools to address the social problems of the times.

Henry Giroux argues that we need to overcome the objectives of schooling as they exist today. For him, the shortcomings of objectives coincide with the shortcomings of schools: narrow focus, standardization of behavior, instruction as one dimensional, oppressive demands, and a technical orientation toward ends. To Giroux, technical processes in curriculum suggest an emphasis on standardization, efficiency, and concrete outcomes, while neglecting questions such as why are we doing what we are doing, why is this knowledge being learned, or why is this type of pedagogical style being used to transmit information in the classroom. Giroux remarks that "While the behaviorists have generally avoided the question of ends [purposes], the humanists have limited questions concerning ends to the immediacy of the classroom setting and have ignored helping students bent on surpassing what is merely given, on breaking through the everyday experiences." [53]

Giroux approaches his critique of education from a neo-Marxist orientation. Thus, he faults curricularists for ignoring those barriers that prevent humans from grasping and discussing the relationship between socially constructed knowledge and how it is employed in the classroom. The ideology behind the knowledge of the curriculum and the manner of instruction is not addressed. Curricularists should develop objectives stressing the importance of critical analysis of subject matter and the politics of knowledge. If this link is established and made known to students, then students will be able to construct connections among themselves and others and the larger social reality. Giroux contends that having such theoretical frameworks allows students to employ them as filters in their viewing of information, in selecting of facts, in considering reality, in formulating problems, and in generating solutions to the problems.

Similarly, David Purpel notes that education should strive in ways that will foster the "cultivation, nourishment, and development of a cultural mythos that builds on a faith in the human capacity to participate in the creation of a world of justice, compassion, caring, love and joy."[54] Reconceptualists and the critical theorists within this camp are concerned with the cultivation and nourishment of those processes requisite for making learning meaningful. They would argue that learning needs to be taken beyond the classroom. Learning is getting students to move beyond the textbook or classroom defined by a particular subject. It is meaningful if it establishes connections between schooling and the sociopolitical forces that mold the dominant culture.

Most reconceptualists have not provided specific advice on creating objectives. However, they do seem to have at least acknowledged that we can take a blended approach to writing objectives, perhaps using behavioral objectives for specific parts of a lesson and more global, open-ended objectives for the macro emphasis on the lesson. Still, the major thrust of the reconceptualists has been to critique the field of curriculum and to reinterpret the sociopolitical framework of schooling. See Table 9-2.

CHALLENGES

Educators are challenged by these various approaches to objectives and to the resulting curricula. Although many will not have to decide among these approaches, they will need to know that such approaches to objectives do exist and that each makes various assumptions regarding the schools, education, the curriculum, the students, and the teachers. It is likely that those faced with making decisions about objectives will draw on different aspects of each approach. The idea is to process objectives in light of our assumptions.

Considering goals and objectives as statements of end points in students' learning raises the issue of how to determine whether the competency implicit or explicit in an objective is stated appropriately. Although behavioral objectives have the virtue of clarity, they usually only indicate the observable levels of learning—some would argue only the trivial or lowest outcomes of the curriculum.[55]

Expanding on the point that objectives tend to trivialize important issues, Joseph Schwab asserted that curriculum developers who overrely on endless strings of objectives tend to separate what should be held together. "They atomize, not only subject matter, but teachers' thoughts about it, the pattern of instruction used to convey it, the organization of textbooks, and the analysis and construction of tests."[56]

Many curriculum specialists are concerned that behavioral objectives do not seem to focus on higher-order tasks and skills. Other educators, however, are concerned that the focus on precise objectives is likely to cause educators to ignore the unintended consequences, either positive or negative, of the curriculum on the learners.[57]

All the approaches to creating objectives have shortcomings. The behavioral approach might be

TABLE 9-2   Overview of Major Approaches to Educational Objectives

APPROACH	APPROACH FOCUS	SPOKESPERSONS	CURRICULAR IMPLICATION
Behavioral	Technical-scientific emphasis; concern for specificity. Assumption: we can identify essential learnings.	Bobbitt, Charters, Gagné, Mager, Popham, Tyler	Compartmentalization of curriculum; defined scope and sequence. Convergent emphasis on curricular learnings.
Systems-managerial	Systems theory, organizational theory; interrelatedness of parts of the organization. Objectives are seen as part of the total process of decision making and curriculum implementation. Management by objectives.	Hunkins, Kaufman, Pratt, Saylor	Curriculum viewed as a system of related components.
Humanistic	Focus on the person: personal growth, respect for others, joy of learning.	Eisner, Maslow, Phenix, Purpel, Rogers	Curriculum seen as divergent; opportunities for students to explore to become self-directed.
Reconceptualists	More of a political and social posture with a theoretical critique. Focus on individual's being empowered to be more fully human, socially sensitive, and existential.	Apple, Giroux, Pinar, Purpel	Curriculum seen as emergent, as concerned with cultivation of those processes that allow for control of one's learning.

viewed as too structured and trivial. The managerial and systems approaches could be viewed as technocratic and an offshoot of behaviorism. The very strength of the humanistic camp is perhaps also its major weakness; the wording of such objectives is vague and open to interpretation and misinterpretation.

The reconceptualists' approach can also be criticized as not furnishing enough specific guidance about how to form objectives. We might also fault such objectives as being directed more toward political and social realities than educational concerns.[58]

Both the humanistic-aesthetic and the reconceptualist approaches are difficult to assess: When have we attained the end point, the expected outcome? Even though educators can agree that end points are only points that lead eventually to other points in a continuum of existence, they still need some indication that they are at least on the correct track with regard to their purposes. It is not likely that advocates of these approaches will come to any agreement in the near future, because persons in these camps are not just arguing about the wording of objectives, but are debating the basic purpose of education itself, and they are coming up with different answers as a result of their inherent philosophical orientations. See Curriculum Tips 9-3.

The challenges surrounding the nature, purpose, and means of creating objectives will continue and should do so. Education is a dynamic process that addresses life. Life in this information age is exciting, dynamic, emergent, and uncertain.

Curriculum Tips 9-3

Assessing the Current Situation

Schools belong to many constituents—students, parents, community members, and policy-making groups. Each constituent group wishes to have what it views as important reflected either in aims, goals, or objectives statements or in the actual content and educational experiences planned. To respond to the numerous demands, curriculum decision makers need to assess the current situation and the factors that affect the operation of the school program.

1. Obtain a global picture of the fundamental characteristics of the community.
2. Determine the factors that are potentially limiting to the operation.
3. Identify strengths in the community that should be maximized.
4. Identify weaknesses that must be addressed.
5. Identify the implied and stated needs and desires of the staff and community.
6. Determine what are realistic levels of staff and community member involvement in decision making.
7. Have a good understanding of the physical facilities available.
8. Identify what types of professional negotiations and administrative management might be necessary to address the aims, goals, and objectives selected.

Source: Adapted from Lawrence Rodes and David Pearlman, "Starting on the Right Foot," *NASSP Bulletin* (October 1989), pp. 76–77.

Educators and the general public view objectives, present and anticipated, from their various philosophical views, their various understandings of how people learn, and their various understandings of the social needs addressed by education. People thinking about objectives draw from political, economic, social, philosophical, spiritual, and artistic postures. We have individuals participating in the world with modern and postmodern mind-sets.

Education must be responsive to the times. Indeed, some would argue that education must participate in those activities requisite to the creation of the times. Objectives espoused as meaningful reveal what educators and others think worthwhile. Worth is influenced by how people view the world. We are at a time when diversity in every aspect of life is being celebrated. Diversity of approaches to objectives, diversity of objectives, and diversity of the functions of objectives will continue to require conversations among all affected parties as to how to create objectives of meaning

and value and then to relate them to goals and back to aims possessing human significance.

CONCLUSION

We have presented in great detail information on aims, goals, and objectives. The chapter began with a discussion of the nature of aims. We presented aims that have been created by various groups and commissions. Aims essentially guide and direct our educational efforts. They are generated in response to general societal concerns at particular times.

Goals are statements that are more specific than aims; they indicate end points or outcomes of education. It was pointed out that often goals are generated by professional associations, but that educators can take more active roles in creating goals. It was also mentioned that creating goals is a continuous activity.

The major portion of the chapter dealt with the objectives of education, giving much attention to both behavioral and nonbehavioral objectives. Discussion centered on the common components of the various types of objectives, which illustrate that objectives differ perhaps more in degree than in kind.

The diversity of levels of objectives was presented in a discussion of the various taxonomies that are available for guiding the creation of objectives. Such taxonomies help educators write objectives. The various philosophical approaches assist as well. We presented these to show the richness of the views that we really need to consider when formulating objectives.

ENDNOTES

1. David Pratt, *Curriculum Planning* (New York: Harcourt Brace College Publishers, 1994).

2. John Dewey, *John Dewey on Education; Selected Writings,* D. Archambault, ed. (New York: Random House, 1964), p. 74.

3. Allan C. Ornstein, "How Do Educators Meet the Needs of Society?" *NASSP Bulletin* (May 1985), pp. 36–47; George J. Posner, *Analyzing the Curriculum* (New York: McGraw-Hill, 1992).

4. Decker Walker and Toner F. Voltis *Curriculum and Aims* (New York: Teachers College Press, Columbia University, 1986).

5. Ralph W. Tyler, "Purposes of Our Schools," *NASSP Bulletin* (May 1968), pp. 1–12.

6. Ronald C. Doll, *Curriculum Improvement: Decision Making and Process,* 9th ed. (Boston: Allyn and Bacon, 1996).

7. Herbert Spencer, *Education: Intellectual, Moral and Physical* (New York: Alden, 1885).

8. Commission on the Reorganization of Secondary Education, *Cardinal Principles of Secondary Education,* Bulletin 35 (Washington, D.C.: U.S. Office of Education, 1918), p. 9.

9. Ibid., pp. 11–16.

10. Educational Policies Commission, *The Purpose of Education in American Democracy* (Washington, D.C.: National Educational Association, 1938), p. 89.

11. Ibid.

12. Educational Policies Commission, *Education for All American Youth* (Washington, D. C.: National Educational Association, 1944), pp. 225–226.

13. Educational Policies Commission, *The Central Purpose of American Education* (Washington, D.C.: National Educational Association, 1961), p. 11.

14. Commission on Excellence in Education, *A Nation at Risk* (Washington, D.C.: U.S. Government Printing Office, 1983), p. 1.

15. Ibid., pp. 13–14.

16. Ibid., p. 24.

17. Evelyn J. Sowell, *Curriculum: An Integrative Introduction* (Upper Saddle River, N.J.: Merrill, an imprint of Prentice Hall, 1996), p. 20.

18. George J. Posner, *Analyzing the Curriculum* (New York: McGraw-Hill, Inc., 1992).

19. ASCD Committee on Research and Theory, *Measuring and Attaining the Goals of Education* (Alexandria, Va.: Association for Supervision and Curriculum Development, 1980).

20. *Phase III of the Educational Planning Model* (Bloomington, Ind.: Phi Delta Kappa Educational Foundation, 1976).

21. *National Goals for Education* (Washington, D.C., U.S. Department of Education, 1990).

22. Hilda Taba, *Curriculum Development: Theory and Practice* (New York: Harcourt, Brace, 1962).

23. Allan C. Ornstein, *Strategies for Effective Teaching* (New York: Harper & Row, 1990).

24. George J. Posner and Alan N. Rudnitsky, *Course Design,* 2nd ed. (New York: Longman, 1990).

25. Norman E. Gronlund, *Stating Objectives for Classroom Instruction,* 2nd ed. (New York: Macmillan, 1985); Norman E. Gronlund and Robert L. Linn, *Measurement and Evaluation in Teaching,* 6th ed. (New York: Macmillan, 1990); and Robert F. Mager, *Preparing Instructional Objectives,* 2nd ed. (Belmont, Calif.: Fearon, 1984).

26. Jerrold E. Kemp, Gary R. Morrison, and Steven M. Ross, *Designing Effective Instruction* (New York: Merrill, an imprint of Macmillan College Publishing Co., 1994), p. 83.

27. Mager, *Preparing Instructional Objectives.*

28. Kemp, Morrison, and Ross, *Designing Effective Instruction.*

29. Michael Polanyi, *The Tacit Dimension* (New York: Doubleday, 1966).

30. J. Galen Saylor, William N. Alexander, and Arthur J. Lewis, *Curriculum Planning for Better Teaching and Learning* (New York: Holt, Rinehart and Winston, 1981).

31. William E. Doll, Jr., *A Post Modern Perspective on Curriculum* (New York: Teachers College Press, Columbia University, 1993).

32. David Pratt, *Curriculum Planning* (New York: Harcourt, Brace, 1994); Richard D. Kimpston, Howard Y. Williams, and William S. Stockton, "Ways of Knowing and the Curriculum," *Educational Forum* (Winter 1992), pp. 153–172; Allan C. Ornstein, "A Look at Teacher Effectiveness Research," *NASSP Bulletin* (October 1990), pp. 78–88.

33. Mauritz Johnson, "Definitions and Models in Curriculum Theory," *Educational Theory* (April 1967), pp. 127–130; Pratt, *Curriculum Planning.*

34. Saylor, Alexander, and Lewis, *Curriculum Planning for Better Teaching and Learning.*

35. Benjamin S. Bloom, ed., *Taxonomy of Educational Objectives, Handbook I: Cognitive Domain* (New York: McKay, 1956).

36. David R. Krathwohl, ed., *Taxonomy of Educational Objectives, Handbook II: Affective Domain* (New York: McKay, 1964).

37. Anita J. Harrow, *A Taxonomy of the Psychomotor Domain* (New York: McKay, 1972).

38. B. F. Skinner, *The Technology of Teaching* (New York: Appleton, 1968).

39. Raymond E. Callahan, *Education and the Cult of Efficiency* (Chicago: University of Chicago Press, 1962).

40. W. James Popham and Eva L. Baker, *Systematic Instruction* (Englewood Cliffs, N.J.: Prentice-Hall, 1970), p. 48. Also see Merlin C. Wittrock and Eva L. Baker, *Testing and Cognition* (Boston, Mass.: Allyn and Bacon, 1991).

41. W. James Popham, "Practical Ways of Improving Curriculum via Measurable Objectives," *NASSP Bulletin* (May 1971), p. 48; also see Popham, *Modern Educational Measurement,* 2nd ed. (Boston, Mass.: Allyn and Bacon, 1990).

42. Robert M. Gagné, Leslie J. Briggs, and Walter Wagner, *Principles of Instructional Design,* 3rd ed. (New York: Holt, Rinehart, 1988).

43. Ibid., p. 56.

44. Roger A. Kaufman, *Educational System Planning* (Englewood Cliffs, N.J.: Prentice-Hall, 1972).

45. Robert V. Carlson and Gary Awkerman, *Educational Planning: Concepts, Strategies and Practices* (New York: Longman, 1991); Gerald C. Ubben, *The Principal: Creative Leadership for Effective Schools,* 2nd ed. (Boston, Mass.: Allyn and Bacon, 1992).

46. Max G. Abbott and Terry L. Eidell, "Administration Implementation of Curriculum Performance," *Educational Technology* (May 1970), pp. 62–64. See also

Robert G. Owens, *Organizational Behavior in Education,* 2nd ed. (Englewood Cliffs, N.J.: Prentice Hall, 1981).

47. Gerald G. Duffy, "Let's Free Teachers to Be Inspired," *Phi Delta Kappan* (February 1992), pp. 442–447.

48. Gerald Weinstein and Mario D. Fantini, *Toward Humanistic Education: A Curriculum of Affect* (New York: Praeger, 1970).

49. Carl R. Rogers, "Toward Becoming a Fully Functioning Person," in Combs, ed., *Perceiving, Behaving, Becoming,* pp. 21–33.

50. Abraham H. Maslow, "Some Basic Propositions of a Growth and Self-actualization Psychology," in Combs, ed., *Perceiving, Behaving, Becoming,* pp. 34–49.

51. Philip H. Phenix, "Transcendence and the Curriculum," in E. W. Eisner and E. Valance, eds., *Conflicting Conceptions of the Curriculum* (Berkeley, Calif.: McCutchan, 1974), pp. 117–135.

52. William Pinar, "Currere: Toward Reconceptualization," in Pinar, ed., *Curriculum Theorizing: The Reconceptualists* (Berkeley, Calif.: McCutchan, 1975), pp. 396–414.

53. Henry A Giroux, *Teachers as Intellectuals* (Granby, Mass.: Bergin & Garvey, 1988), p. 45.

54. David Purpel, *The Moral and Spiritual Crisis in Education* (New York: Bergin & Garvey, 1989), p. 150.

55. Gail Delicio, "Teaching Alliteration Inductively: Taba's Deductive Thinking Model in Practice." Paper presented at the annual meeting of the American Educational Research Association, San Francisco, April 1986.

56. Joseph Schwab, "The Practical Four: Something for Curriculum Professors to Do," *Curriculum Inquiry* (Fall 1983), pp. 239–266.

57. Bruce W. Tuckman, *Educational Psychology: From Theory to Application* (San Diego: Harcourt Brace Jovanovich, 1992); Wittrock and Baker, *Testing and Cognition.*

58. James T. Sears and J. Dan Marshal, eds., *Teaching and Thinking About Curriculum* (New York: Teachers College Press, Columbia University, 1990).

10

CURRICULUM IMPLEMENTATION

Focusing Questions

1. Why is implementation considered a restructuring activity?
2. How does planning relate to implementation?
3. What role does communication play in the implementation activity?
4. To what extent does the nature of change coincide with curriculum implementation?
5. What stages are common to the various implementation models?
6. Why do people tend to resist change?
7. How can we improve people's receptivity to change?
8. What factors influence the implementation process?
9. What roles can people assume in the educational change process?

The most appropriate and valued school curriculum will go for naught if it is left on the shelves after its development. A curriculum with optimal designs for students must get delivered; it must be implemented throughout a school district if it is to make any impact on student learning. Much that is planned and developed often does not get implemented due to a lack of a plan for dispersal throughout a school system. Frequently, new and innovative programs are blunted at classroom doors.

One reason that a new curriculum may miscarry is that implementation has not been considered critical in curriculum development. Frequently, schools have felt that the curriculum effort is complete once a new plan is developed or new materials purchased, even with much discussion about change and restructuring of schools. In fact, such discussion has often pushed curriculum talk off the discussion table. Attention is given more to organization and management problems than to curriculum change. Many individuals responsible for curriculum do not possess a macro view of the process or realize that innovations need careful planning and monitoring. Individuals often think that implementation is a clear-cut yes or no process; one either uses the new program or not.

Successful implementation is a process that should have some novelty. In fact, it should encourage those involved to be creative. Just how much play is in implementation depends on one's general approach to curriculum and curriculum development. Persons in the technical camp believe that successful implementation, regardless of curricular designs, rests on delineating precise steps at the outset of the development process. Individuals in the nontechnical and postmodern camps consider implementation as more uncertain and unpredictable. These individuals might even resist using the term implementation, thinking that the term suggests a technical rationality. Some have substituted *enacting,* which suggests a more fluid nontechnical approach to development and design. Some hold that curriculum enactment is less complicated than implementation since the curricula enacted have been created within a school or classroom.[1]

We think that adding the term enactment to the lexicon of curriculum terms is unnecessary. Implementation can be viewed along a continuum from very technical in nature to very fluid and very aesthetic. The central point is that it is a component in the curriculum action cycle that cannot be neglected. This step involves extensive actions by many parties, not just, for example, a solitary workshop for staff. Implementation attempts to alter individuals' knowledge, actions, and attitudes. It is an interaction process between those who have created the program and those who are charged to deliver it.

THE NATURE OF IMPLEMENTATION

Leslie Bishop stated that implementation requires restructuring and replacement. It requires adjusting personal habits, ways of behaving, program emphases, learning spaces, and existing curricula and schedules. It means getting educators to shift from the current program to the new program, a modification that can be met with great resistance. The ease with which a curriculum leader can trigger such behavior changes in staff depends in part on the quality of the initial planning and the precision with which the steps of curriculum development have been carried out up to this point.[2]

Although experienced leaders of curriculum activities have realized that implementation is an essential aspect of curriculum development, only in the last 15 or 20 years has implementation become a major educational concern. Such interest has evolved partly because even though millions of dollars have been spent developing curriculum projects, especially for reading and math, many of these projects have not succeeded.

There are numerous reasons for the failure of innovative curricula to be implemented successfully. Perhaps the key reason is one advanced by Seymour Sarason. He posits that much educational reform has failed because those in charge of the efforts had little or a distorted understanding of the culture of schools.[3] Many innovative programs are designed by experts outside the schools. However, such ignorance of school culture is also present among educators. Perhaps, innovations have not been implemented because educators have been impatient, wanting quick results to please legislators and a public conditioned to expect quick fixes.

Sarason notes two kinds of basic understandings essential to implementation. The first is theoretical information, which relates both to the theory of organizational change and to the theory of knowledge and how ideas fit into a real–world context. The second category of understanding relates to change in particular social–institutional contexts. Successful implementors of innovative curricula grasp the nature of the context into which new curricula are to be introduced. They comprehend the structure of the organization, sacred traditions, and power relationships, and how members define themselves and their roles. Skilled implementors realize that all these factors exist in an emerging and continuing dynamic.

One's views of this social–institutional context are influenced by whether one perceives the world of education through technical or nontechnical lenses. Some individuals believe that this stage of curricular activity can be outlined specifically; others hold that it is a fluid and emergent activity that is less to be understood and managed than to be appreciated and encouraged.

When discussing implementation, we must consider the various assumptions that we bring to the process or cluster of processes. We can assume that implementation is simply another step in curriculum planning or creation and that we can expect to proceed with relative ease, or we can assume the process to be fluid, with unexpected complexities emerging over time. Whatever our stance, and it may well be a combination of the two just presented, we must realize that for implementation to occur or enactment to emerge, we have to address the behaviors of all players in the curriculum game. Curriculum creators, administrators, teachers, and supervisors must be clear about the purpose or intent, the nature, and the real and potential benefits of the innovation. Even if we balk at stating specific outcomes, we must at least agree with the intent of the innovation. Fullan and Pomfret provide us with some sobering comments:

Effective implementation of . . . innovations requires time, personal interaction and contacts, in-service training, and other forms of people-based support. Research has shown time and again that there is no substitute for the primacy of personal contact among implementers, and between implementers and planners/consultants, if the difficult process of unlearning old roles and learning new ones is to occur.[4]

Implementation takes time, for at this stage in curricular activity we are attempting to win over people to influence their attitudes sufficiently so that people will alter their ways. To win over people, we must assure them that there is some recognition and/or reward in making the effort to change, that is, to implement or enact the new curriculum. That which we value, we do. Some state that we do not value what teachers do. Others say we do not pay teachers enough to be innovators, to implement or enact truly novel curricula.

Certainly, we do need to pay teachers and other professionals for their extra efforts. However, Kouzesa and Posner note that educational leaders have cause for concern if their staff justifies its involvement in a new program solely on economic bases.[5] Involvement in curriculum change and implementation solely for financial reasons only contributes minimum effort to the venture. To be institutionalized, an innovation must elicit internal motivation. Too much reliance on external incentives actually constrains people. Individuals contribute their best talents when they accept the new program, when they derive a good feeling from being involved, and when they view their contributions as adding to the quality of students' education.

Relationship of Implementation to Planning

Successful implementation of curricula results from careful planning. Planning processes address needs and resources requisite for carrying out intended actions. It involves establishing and determining how to administer policy that will govern the planned actions. Planning takes place prior to program creation and/or delivery.

Matthew Miles and Karen Louis note that for planning to occur there must be vision building. In their research, they found that those schools successful in implementing change and improving

their programs had staff who passionately held similar images of what the school should become. Teachers were committed to the new program and had developed enthusiasm about the innovation. Implementing the new program afforded an opportunity to make vision reality, to give vision form.[6] Ideally, from the outset of curriculum development curriculum leaders have furnished those involved with occasions for such an attitude.

Only recently has vision become part of the management lexicon. Previously, managers discussed purpose, but not vision. Today, vision is receiving attention, as opposed to purpose, for vision suggests images and pictures. It suggests a dynamic future.[7] Indeed, vision can distinguish technicians from nontechnicians. Persons advocating the use of the term enactment rather than implementation seem to be drawing on the concept of vision existing within a dynamic framework.[8] This new thinking has many people excited not so much for the particulars of what is there, but for the potential of the curriculum.

Whatever one's orientation to the curriculum, there is no denying that implementation and/or enactment requires planning, and planning focuses on three factors: people, programs, and processes. Although these three factors are inseparable, some individuals consider that dealing primarily with only one factor will facilitate implementation. Some persons feel, for example, that to facilitate implementation of a major change educators must deal primarily with people. If the people change, so does the program and/or process. Others consider that the primary focus should be the program. People will adapt if they are furnished with different ways to meet the objectives of the schools' programs.[9] Still others think that attention should center on the organizational processes within which the people work. If departments are reorganized, if spaces are remodeled, then people will adjust in the directions necessary for successful implementation.

A leader may wish to stress one factor more than another, but no skillful leader will ignore any one factor altogether. Many school districts have failed to implement their programs because they ignored the people factor and spent time and money modifying only the program or process. One reason why many curriculum projects fail is that the curriculum innovators, especially from universities, center most of their energies on changing the program but pay scant attention to the needs of teachers and minimal attention to the organization of their own schools.[10]

Incrementalism

People want to change; yet they are also afraid of change, especially if it comes quickly or if they feel they have little control or influence over it. People become accustomed to the status quo and prefer to make modifications in new behavior in small and gradual steps. Most people, when they talk about change, and say they welcome it, often would prefer that other people within the organization change.

The world of the teacher does not allow for much receptivity to change. Both Fullan and Goodlad have described the teacher's daily routine as presenting little opportunity for interaction with colleagues. This isolation results partly from the school's organization into self-contained classrooms and partly from the teaching schedules.[11] Seymour Sarason has also commented on the isolation of teachers in the school organization and on how that isolation negatively impacts change. He contends that the reality of the school has made teachers feel that, professionally, they are on their own. It is their responsibility, and theirs alone, to solve their problems.[12] This posture causes teachers to view change introduced into the program as an individual activity. Viewing their struggles as solitary, teachers often develop a psychological loneliness that results in hostility to administrators and outside change agents who seem insensitive to the teachers' plight.

Sarason has even predicted the failure of efforts at educational reform, primarily because many reform efforts really do not address changing the educational system.[13] He notes that remedies for educational reform, and we include curriculum revision here, are essentially statements that "we will do what we have been doing, or what we ought to be doing, only we will now do it better."[14] If teachers only continue to be involved in curriculum implementation in a manner identical to that which has occurred in the past, it is not likely that new curricula that will actually alter the character of schools in the next century will be developed and implemented. The system, or context within which we take curriculum from planned document to living encounter perhaps needs a major overall. It just may be too difficult to play "new games" of curriculum in traditional spaces with traditional time frames.

We need to think of new ways to engage teachers and curriculum creators (and in most cases these should be the same individuals) in the "writing of new educational plays." How do we engage teachers to assume new roles and be responsible to that which is to be implemented or enacted.

In an investigation of maturation during adulthood, one investigator noted that several principles can guide changing adults' behaviors. These principles include fostering multiple perspectives, allowing time for integration of ideas, and creating a supportive environment in which learning becomes more autonomous.[15] Drawing on these principles, the curriculum implementor facilitates the active involvement of teachers to allow for experiential learning, fosters the creation of an environment that encourages openness and trust, and gives feedback so that participants realize that their contributions are appreciated and their talents considered worthwhile.

Teachers need time to "try" the new program to be implemented. They need time to reflect on new goals and objectives, to consider new contents and learning experiences, and to try out new tasks.

Teachers also need time to reflect on the new program in relation to the mission of the school. For any new program to be successfully implemented, it must be perceived as central to the mission of the school. This congruence is especially important in turbulent times: "The more . . . change . . . is related or linked to [the] central . . . mission the more likely its survival in the face of shifting, but less central priorities."[16]

Implementation, therefore, does not occur all at once with all teachers. Ideally, an implementation process allows sufficient time for certain groups of teachers to try out the new curriculum in pieces. Loucks and Lieberman have found that teachers go through levels of use with a new curriculum. First, they orient themselves to the materials and engage in actions that will prepare them to deliver the curriculum. Their beginning use of the new curriculum is mechanical. They follow the guide with little deviation. Planning is largely day by day. Their delivery of the curriculum becomes rather routine, and they take little initiative to make any changes in the curriculum. As they become more comfortable with the curriculum, they may begin to modify it, either to adjust it to their own educational philosophies or to better meet students' needs.[17]

Communication

It is almost an axiom that whenever a new program is being designed, communication channels must be kept open so that the new program comes not as a surprise. Frequent discussion about a new program among teachers, principals, and curriculum workers is a key to successful implementation.[18]

But communication is a complex phenomenon. It has been defined as the transmission of facts, ideas, values, feelings, and attitudes from one individual or group to another. Put simply, communication deals with message processing between the sender and the receiver of a message. The receiver can either accept or reject the message. Communication is not a one-way street; rather, it is a two-way channel.

Knowing that communication deals with message sending and receiving is not sufficient to ensure that communication will be effective or that messages sent will be accurate or of high quality. To assure that the communication network is comprehensive and the message sending avenues are in place, the curriculum specialist must understand both the formal and informal channels of communication within the school or school system. Formal channels of communication follow the established arrangement of the levels of organization. Communication can flow throughout these levels of organization both vertically (upward or downward) or laterally (horizontally) among peers. See Curriculum Tips 10-1.

Lateral communication is perhaps the wave of the future. Horizontal networking among peers is being encouraged in many school restructuring efforts. Communication flows more easily among persons who consider themselves equals and equally involved in some change or curriculum implementation. There is much attention to teamwork within organizations. Also, many curricular activities involving combining of subject areas or integrating of major segments of the curriculum presuppose effective lateral communication.

While formal lines for lateral communication may exist in schools, much lateral message sending and receiving occurs informally. Ideally, effective curriculum leaders encourage the emergence of numerous channels of information communication. Informal communication networks result primarily from teachers' actions.

Whether the communication challenge is formal or informal, upward or downward or lateral, messages are relayed both orally and in written form. Information about new programs can be communicated by means of letters, memos, articles, books, bulletins, research reports, and speeches. The vehicles we use to communicate are only limited by our imaginations. With fax machines and electronic mail, messages can be delivered with a minimum of transit time. Interactive video allows meetings without individuals taking time to travel to meeting places.

There are still times when we wish face-to-face communication. Such communication is superior to other means of communication, for it allows the receiver of the message to raise questions and to furnish immediate feedback. Also, persons engaged in personal interaction can gain information from nonverbal aspects of the communication situation. Much can be learned from the tone of voice, the body language, and the facial expressions of the parties involved. The fact that people are brought together to discuss a new program gives testimony that the new program has significance. It also sends the message that feedback and input by faculty are crucial to the success of the new program and that people as individuals and professionals are valued.

Support

Curriculum designers need to provide the necessary support for their recommended programs or program modifications to facilitate their rapid implementation. They have to do this so as to build self-confidence among those affected. Educators often require in-service training or staff development time to feel comfortable with new programs. Research efforts have catalogued the characteristics of effective professional in-service

---

=== *Curriculum Tips 10-1* ===

Improving Upward Communication

Effective communication plays an important role in accomplishing the goals of the school. Below are methods to encourage upward communication so that those charged with implementing the curriculum, that is, teachers, are heard.

1. *Visit with teachers within the school.* Teachers in the school will more likely realize that the principal is open to suggestions and will receive information from them if the principal is not "stuck" in his or her office. Walking through the school hallways allows teachers to perceive that they are in a participatory culture.
2. *Keeping an open-door policy.* There are times when the principal or the school leader must close his or her office door. However, there is more upward communication in organizations where subordinates feel comfortable when interrupting the leader.
3. *Conduct attitude surveys.* Teachers want to know that their input is valued. Sending attitude surveys to faculty at various times allows teachers to realize that the curriculum leaders are interested in what they know, what they are feeling, what they are valuing, and what program aspects they are inclined to act on.
4. *Have suggestion boxes.* A simple suggestion box shows teachers that there is a way for information to be fed into the system. Responding to suggestions with notes of appreciation will assist in creating a professional community in which ideas can be freely exchanged.
5. *Have collegial staff meetings.* Communication involves talking, and staff meetings furnish time for talk. If such meetings are conducted in an atmosphere of trust, messages can more readily be delivered upward.

Source: Adapted from V. O. Jenks, *Human Relations in Organizations* (New York: Harper & Row, 1990).

---

programs. Such programs must be designed so that they can be integrated into and supported by the organizations within which they are designed to function. In-service programs that work have resulted from collaborative efforts and have addressed the needs of those who are to be affected by the new curricula.[19] Effective in-service training has the necessary flexibility to respond to the changing needs of the staff. Not all details of in-service training can be planned prior to implementation; nor can all problems and concerns be anticipated.

Because in-service programs must reach their intended audiences, they should be accessibly scheduled for curriculum implementors. Open discussions on the new programs should be scheduled throughout the implementation process. Such discussions allow implementors to voice their objections or concerns and consequently reduce opposition. Effective in-service programs must also evaluate whether they are achieving their objectives and whether they are in harmony with the underlying philosophy and approach of the district.[20]

Without adequate financial support, efforts to get a program going district-wide will fail. When federal monies were flowing, many school districts were quite innovative, but they failed to add funding for their innovations into their regular school budgets. When the federal monies ran out, which were essentially meant to be start-up monies, the districts discontinued their new programs, citing lack of necessary funds. If school districts, today, create new programs using federal or state grant money, called "soft money," they need to devise ways to support these programs once implemented with "hard money"—money that is part of the regularly allocated school budget.

Money is required for materials and equipment to institutionalize a new program. Money is also necessary to provide often-overlooked human support for the implementation effort. At the local level, five steps are involved in budgeting for new programs: preparation, submission, adoption, execution, and evaluation. The third step, adoption, involves the school board whereby it appropriates specific amounts for specific categories. The other four steps involve the superintendent at the district level and principal (or chair) at the school level.[21]

A trusting relationship must exist among all parties in the school, especially between the administration and the teachers. The principal is a key guarantor of successful innovation and implementation. Disagreement does exist, however, on how principals should furnish human support. Still, those considered to be successful principals are knowledgeable of and committed to the curriculum; they also view their role as providing encouragement for it, on one end of the continuum, and to serving as the curriculum leader, on the other end of the continuum.[22]

Implementation is a collaborative and emotional effort. Peer support is vital if implementation is to be successful. Dan Lortie points out that teachers spend the majority of their working time in individual classrooms with their students; therefore, they have minimal communication with their peers. By and large, they are left on their own with little input or assistance from colleagues or supervisors unless a crisis develops.[23] Opportunities for teachers to work together, share ideas, jointly solve problems, and cooperatively create materials greatly enhance the probability of successful curriculum implementation.

IMPLEMENTATION AS A CHANGE PROCESS

The purpose of curriculum development, regardless of level, is to make a difference—to enable students to attain the school's, the society's, and, perhaps most importantly, their own aims and goals. Implementation, an essential part of curriculum development, brings into reality anticipated changes. Simply put, curriculum activity is change activity.

But what happens when change occurs? What is the source of change? Can people predict the consequences of change? Can educators control those changes that directly affect them? Indeed, people can exert some control over the process of change, but to do so requires that they understand change. Understanding the concept of change and the various types of change allows individuals to determine sources of change. It also helps them realize that, even though they cannot really predict the consequences of change, they can make "best-guess" forecasts about its results.

In understanding the concept of change, educators must realize that people's attitudes toward change and implementation as a change process are influenced by their general view of reality. Those who accept the rational model of curriculum development will view change as something rather precisely managed and implementation as a predictable execution of a plan. Implementation is part of a linear process of change.[24]

Those in the nontechnical camp will perceive change as something impossible to tightly control. Although a phase in curriculum activity, implementation or enactment is not something that occurs in a linear fashion. Viewing implementation as interaction means that one cannot succumb to the demands of objectivity and quantification.[25] Indeed, this orientation to change celebrates a process enlightened by individuals and their beliefs and attitudes. Judgments made result from a meld of individuals' personal constructions of their realities and their attitudes toward life and the values that they hold sacred.[26]

Regardless of which camp one gives allegiance to, there is no denying that change can occur in several ways. The two most obvious ways are slow change (as when minor adjustments are made in the course schedule, when some books are added to the library, or when the unit or lesson plan is updated by the teacher) and rapid change (say as the result of new knowledge or social trends impacting on schools, such as computers being introduced into classrooms).

According to the research, for curriculum change to be successfully implemented, either slowly or rapidly, five guidelines should be followed to help avoid mistakes of the past.

1. *Innovations designed to improve student achievement must be technically sound.* This means that changes should reflect research about what works and what does not work, as opposed to whatever designs for improvement happen to be popular today or tomorrow.

2. *Successful innovation requires change in the structure of a traditional school.* By structural change, we mean major modification of the way students and teachers are assigned to classes and interact with each other.

3. *Innovation must be manageable and feasible for the average teacher.* We cannot innovate ideas concerning critical thinking or problem solving when students cannot read or write basic English or refuse to behave in class.

4. *Implementation of successful change efforts must be organic rather than bureaucratic.* Strict compliance, monitoring procedures, and rules are not conducive for change; this bureaucratic approach needs to be replaced by an organic or adaptive approach that permits some deviation from the original plan and recognizes grass-roots problems and conditions of the school.

5. *Avoid the "do something, do anything" syndrome.* The need is for a definite curriculum plan, to focus one's efforts, time, and money on content and activities that are sound and rational.[27]

The data indicate that the guidelines "are systematically interrelated, and that with the possible exception of the guideline regarding structural change, they apply equally well to all levels of education." Curricularists will benefit by "considering their applicability in the particular context of their own schools and school districts."[28]

A Theory of Change

Change results from new knowledge; however, the presence of new knowledge is not sufficient for change. People must recognize a need for change. And they are more likely to recognize that need if they understand change and how it works. Lovell and Wiles present a theory of change that incorporates five processes: (1) leadership, (2) communication, (3) release of human potential, (4) problem solving, and (5) evaluation. These processes can lead to system (school) tension and conflict or co-

operation and cohesion. Every system has this choice, and the choice depends on the participants involved in the change.[29]

Adding further complexity is the fact that the system's process for change, according to these two system experts, is affected by external forces. Indeed, those enacting curricular change must comprehend the environmental context within which they are operating. An external audit should be made in the initial phase of curriculum development to gather and assess information relating to the demographics of the community and its sociocultural, politicolegal, and economic aspects.[30] Data on such factors should be fed into the planning process so that the particular phases of implementation can be made sensitive to community attitudes and expectations. Information about the external environment, for instance, furnishes new information, identifies new expectations, and points to rewards or problems for those involved in the implementation process. Such data inputs regarding the external environment can generate tension within the educational system, thus creating a state of disequilibration among members within the school system. This condition often sets in motion an attempt by the players to achieve a new state of equilibrium.

Hence, change is achieved through the continuous process of disequilibration and reequilibration through problem-solving activities. Curriculum leaders, in short, must react to external factors, as well as internal factors, through the five change processes. Each one of these processes—leadership, communication, release of human potential, etc., will determine whether change is constructive or unproductive.

In contrast to Lovell and Wiles's theory, Kurt Lewin, considered to be the father of change theory, advanced a much simpler idea. His theoretical model appears in Figure 10-1.

Lewin considered that all persons find themselves in environments comprised of competing forces: driving forces and restraining forces. When these two groups of forces were equal, a balance or equilibrium existed enabling a steady state or status quo. This status quo is true regardless of whether we are discussing the actions of people or groups or the functioning of organizations. However, at times the driving forces begin to overpower the restraining forces, initiating change action. As long as these driving forces are

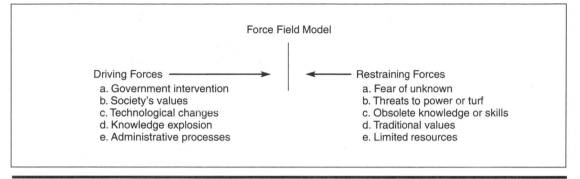

FIGURE 10-1 Force field model

the more powerful, the change activity will continue. When the restraining forces regain momentum, change will slow down. Once reestablished, restraining forces serve to inhibit change.[31]

Lewin conceptualized the change process as consisting of three stages. The first stage changes the current situation in which we find ourselves, an unfreezing, if you will, from a point A. This unfreezing actually means a decrease in the restraining forces in order to stimulate the driving forces. Lewin believed that to stimulate change, it was better to reduce the power of the restraining forces than to increase the driving forces. Such action allowed driving forces to act more naturally within the situation.

The second stage is getting the individual group or organization to move from the unfrozen point A to point B; the destination or goal point. Here the person or group or system engages in the actions necessary for attaining the change now desired. Upon successfully attaining point B, a refreezing occurs, the third stage of change. The process appears diagrammatically as follows:

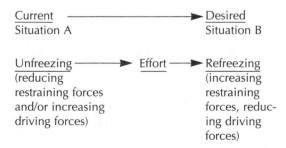

Lewin was instrumental in the development of laboratory training, also known as sensitivity training, T-groups, and encounter groups. The National Training Laboratories (NTL) refined these programs in the 1950s and 1960s—and they emerged as widely used strategies to stimulate change in organizations. Training sessions are carried out in small groups of 10 to 15 members. The main idea of these sessions is to get participants to better understand themselves and each other, and to become more aware of group processes, to facilitate constructive change.[32] By analyzing one's own behavior, and the behavior of others, communication, interpersonal relations, and subordinate–superior relations tend to improve within an organization; the atmosphere is thus conducive for constructive change.

Change Typologies

Persons with curriculum responsibilities, specifically those of implementation, need to understand the nature of change. With understanding, the change process can challenge and excite those who must be involved. Those who do not comprehend the complexities of change are likely to initiate actions that will result in discord within the school organization, either at the school level or district level or both.

Warren Bennis has identified several types of change:

1. *Planned change* is change in which those involved have equal power and function in a prescribed fashion. People identify and follow precise procedures for dealing with the activity at hand. Planned change is the ideal.

2. *Coercion* is characterized by one group determining the goals and intentionally excluding others from participating. The group in control has the major power and maintains the unequal power balance.

3. *Interaction change* is characterized by mutual goal setting and a fairly equal power distribution among groups. But those involved often lack a deliberateness of effort; they are uncertain how to follow through with the plans of development and implementation. Few procedures are carefully developed.[33]

The opposite of planned change is *natural* or *random change.* This type of change occurs with no apparent thought and no goal setting on the part of the participants. Often natural change is what occurs in schools. Curricula are adjusted or modified and implemented not as a result of careful analysis, but as a response to unanticipated events. For example, demands by legislatures or pressure groups that certain programs be implemented are inconsistent and based on whim or rhetoric.

Robert Chin has discussed three types of change strategies that can be considered as change typologies as well:

1. *Empirical-rational* strategies stress the importance of knowing the need for change and having the competence to implement it. Often schools lack this approach to change because they neither know they need a change nor have the skill to implement it.

2. *Normative-reeducative* strategies are based on the rationality and intelligence of humans. Humans will change if they are approached rationally and made to see that they need to modify their values, attitudes, understandings, and skills.

3. *Power strategies* require that individuals comply with the wishes of those who are in positions superior to theirs. Although outright strategies of coercion are rarely used in schools, it is not uncommon for those in power to "coerce" people into compliance by offering material and symbolic rewards in exchange for accepting new programs.[34]

We can also consider change according to its complexity. John McNeil has investigated the change process by using complexity as the organizer:

1. *Substitution.* This depicts alteration in which one element may be substituted for another. A teacher can, for example, substitute one textbook for another. By far, this is the easiest and most common type of change.

2. *Alteration.* This type of change exists when someone introduces into existing materials and programs new content, items, materials, or procedures that appear to be only minor and thus are likely to be adopted readily.

3. *Perturbations.* These changes could at first disrupt a program, but can then be adjusted purposefully by the curriculum leader to the ongoing program within a short time span. An example of a perturbation is the principal's adjusting class schedules, which would affect the time allowed for teaching a particular subject.

4. *Restructuring.* These changes lead to modification of the system itself, that is, of the school or school district. New concepts of teaching roles, such as differentiated staffing or team teaching, would be a restructuring type of change.

5. *Value-orientation changes.* These are shifts in the participants' fundamental philosophies or curriculum orientations. Major power brokers of the school or participants in the curriculum must accept and strive for this level of change for it to occur. However if teachers do not adjust their value domains, any changes enacted are most likely going to be short-lived.[35]

Although change that occurs in the schools cannot be fit into precise categories, curricularists need to realize that types do exist and that planned change is the ideal. But change is not synonymous with improvement. Education is a normative activity. A person's advocating and then managing change mean, in effect, making a statement about what he or she thinks is valuable.

Resistance to Change

A curriculum leader who accepts that people are the key to successful curriculum activity and implementation is cognizant of the barriers that people place between themselves and change efforts. Perhaps the biggest barrier is inertia—among the staff, the administration, or the community. Many people think it is just easier to keep things as they are. If we think of ourselves as systems, we realize that we like to maintain steady states. We have traditions to which we adhere and institutions that we cherish, and we do not wish to change them. Many people are happy with the current school setup as a bureaucracy.

Wanting to keep things as they are is often mixed with believing that things do not need to be changed or that the change being suggested is unwise and will thus be unproductive in meeting the objectives of the school. Educators themselves argue this point. Some say that the schools are fine and just need to be modified. Whereas others posit that the schools are not responsive to the times and require major modification. The status quo tends to be maintained if those suggesting change have not presented precise goals of the new program being suggested; that is, they have not planned adequately what the new program will look like or indicated ways in which the new program will be superior to the existing one.[36]

Status quo is supported also in schools when there is not a clear mission stated for the new program. Actually, how the new curriculum addresses the mission is considered at the commencement of curriculum development. At the phase of implementation, however, one must return to the mission, to the intent of the curriculum, to sell it to others in the educational organization. However, many schools phrase their mission statements as essentially bland general proclamations that do not really distinguish one new curriculum from another.[37]

Often, teachers have not been able or willing to keep up with scholarly developments. They have not stayed abreast of the knowledge explosion, which would allow them to feel committed to curriculum change and the implementation of new programs. Teachers frequently view change as just signaling more work—something else to add on to an already overloaded schedule for which little or no time is allotted. Usually, no extra money or reward is earmarked for the extra work either. Many educators, in fact, are overwhelmed by changes proposed and their implications. Often they view new curricular programs as requiring them to learn new teaching skills, develop new competencies in curriculum development, or acquire new skills in interpersonal relations.

While teachers have tremendous demands on their time, many do a remarkable job of keeping up with the literature. Even so, many teachers tend to disregard available evidence regarding new curricular or pedagogical practice if it challenges their current understandings and outlook.[38] They reject altering their programs and instructional strategies if this requires a change in outlook or practice. They engage in what is called "mind guarding" by discounting data that challenge current understanding.

Another reason curriculum leaders have difficulty getting teachers to accept innovation is, according to Edgar Friendenberg, that people who go into teaching tend to be conformist in nature, not innovative. These people have succeeded in the school system as it has existed. They have learned to play it safe and to keep a low profile in a bureaucratic system run by administrators who do not like to create "waves."[39] They have found success and fulfillment as students and now as teachers in this system, and for this reason many see no reason to change it. To many beginning teachers, the bureaucracy in place is a welcome and familiar support system, and they are often slow to change it.

Can educators cope with the demands for more change or for assuming new roles? Uncertainty fosters insecurity. Often educators who feel comfortable with the present are reluctant to change for a future they cannot comprehend or see clearly. People often prefer to stay with certain known deficiencies than venture forth to uncertain futures, even if the changes most likely would be improvements. Bringing new students or parents or content into the curriculum realm or organizing the program in new ways makes many teachers uneasy.

Another factor that causes people to resist change is the rapidity of change. Many people feel that if something is implemented this year, it will most likely be abandoned when another innovation appears and will thus make all their efforts useless. There have, in fact, been enough "bandwagons" in education to make educators "innovation shy."

Sometimes people resist innovation and its implementation because they lack knowledge. They either do not know about the innovation at all or they have little information about it. Curriculum leaders must furnish all affected parties—teachers, pupils, parents, community members—with information about the nature of the program and its rationale. Ideally, all affected parties should be informed either directly or indirectly by school representatives of the reasons for the new program.

People often resist change, too, if no financial or time support is given the effort. A project for which no monies are budgeted is rarely destined to be implemented. Often, school districts budget monies for materials but fail to allocate funds for the creation of the curriculum plan, its delivery within the classroom, or necessary in-service training.[40]

Thomas Harvey, writing on the nature of change, provides an analysis of the obstacles to getting people involved in change—and why they resist it.

1. *Lack of ownership.* Individuals will not accept change if they consider it alien or coming from outside their organization; interestingly, much of the current demand for reform and restructuring in the schools is coming from external sources, from national commissions or state legislatures.

2. *Lack of benefits.* If teachers are unconvinced that a new program will make things better for students (in terms of learning) or themselves (say, greater recognition, respect, or reward), they are likely to resist the suggested change.

3. *Increased burdens.* Often change just means more work, increased burdens; today, teachers are frustrated, even hostile, toward outside groups prescribing what needs to be done and lacking sensitivity to the issue of adding work to the teachers' already heavy schedule.

4. *Lack of administrative support.* People will not embrace change unless those officially responsible, often legally responsible, for the program have shown or guaranteed their support for the change.

5. *Loneliness.* Few people desire to innovate alone. Colleagual action is necessary for successful implementation of new programs.

6. *Insecurity.* People resist that which appears to threaten their security. The instinct to survive is strong and few will venture into programs with obvious threat.

7. *Norm incongruence.* The roles and assumptions of new programs must be congruent with the norms and expectations held by personnel in the system. Sometimes new programs represent philosophical orientations to education that are at odds with the staff's.

8. *Boredom.* No one accepts a new program believing that he or she is not going to enjoy the experience. Successful innovations are presented as alluring, enticing, and thought provoking.

9. *Chaos.* If a change is perceived as lessening control or of generating chaos, it is likely to be opposed. We desire changes that make things more manageable, allow for greater control, and enable us to function more effectively.

10. *Differential knowledge.* If we perceive those persons advocating change to have considerably more information than we, we may well consider those persons as having excessive power.

11. *Sudden wholesale change.* People tend to resist major changes, especially about-faces requiring a complete redirection.

12. *Unique points of resistance.* Sometimes, it is the unknown or the unexpected that surfaces and retards change. Not everything can be planned in advance; people or events outside the organization can dampen our innovative spirit.[41]

Considering the points raised in the above list may make it seem that curriculum specialists face insurmountable problems. But such need not be the case. Being mindful of these points and sensitive to the needs of persons involved in the change will greatly enhance the smoothness with which change can be introduced and curriculum can be implemented. Also, we should realize that resistance to change does have the benefit of requiring change agents to think carefully about the innovations and to consider the human dynamics involved in implementing programs. Having to fight for change protects the organization from becoming a proponent of random change and educational fads.

Improving Receptivity to Change

Curriculum activity involves people thinking and acting. Leaders of curriculum development, and especially implementation, realize that the human equation is of paramount importance and that, therefore, they must understand how people react to change. Often, people say they are willing to change, but act as though they are unwilling to adjust. A successful change agent knows how people react to change and how to encourage them to be receptive to change.

Curriculum implementation requires face-to-face interaction—person-to-person contact. Those persons charged with implementation must understand the interpersonal dimension of leadership. Curriculum implementation is also a group process involving individuals working together. Not only does the group enable certain actions to occur, it also serves to change its individual members.

Of course, if a group is to change individuals, it must be attractive to its members. The ideas and values the group expresses must be acceptable to them. This is why curriculum leaders need to make sure that the members of the group are clear about the platform upon which they are to build the curriculum. This is why members must understand the rationale for the various curriculum designs and the consequences of accepting a particular design. As groups talk about the need to change and the strategies for implementation, they create a pressure for change within the educational system.[42] Creating a well-formed group with a clear sense of mission and confidence that it can bring about change is one way to make individuals receptive to the notion of change.

Every individual who comes into a system plays a multitude of roles; each professional brings to his or her role his or her personality as well. Each person has certain needs he or she expects to fulfill within the system—in this discussion, the school—or the school district. Rarely is there absolute congruence between institutional roles and expectations and individual personality and needs. Misalignment can cause conflict. Curriculum leaders need to recognize that they cannot always avoid this conflict; they must manage it. The way they manage it is reflected in the social behavior of the individual.

Following the guidelines outlined next can help individuals increase their receptivity to curriculum innovations:

1. *Curriculum activity must be cooperative.* If a program is to be implemented and institutional-

ized, it should be perceived by all parties as their program. This sense of ownership is achieved by involving people directly and indirectly with the major aspects of curriculum development and implementation. When people participate in planning and implementing a program, they gain understanding of it and commitment to its goals and underlying philosophical basis.

2. *Some people like to change; some people do not like to change.* Resistance to any new idea is often natural. Curriculum leaders should anticipate it and should prepare procedures for dealing with it. They must also identify well in advance of the action questions that will arise about the innovation being implemented: How will people feel about the change? What worries will people have? What are some likely points of conflict? What can be done to lessen the anxiety levels of individuals who will be affected by the change?

3. *Innovations are subject to change.* Nothing should be viewed as permanent. A new curriculum is presented as a response to a particular time and context. As time passes and contexts change, other modifications, sometimes even new programs, will be required. Change is a constant, and people need to realize that all programs will be constantly reviewed to determine if they should be continued.

4. *Proper timing is a key to increasing people's receptivity to an innovation.* If the school community is demanding that a new program be created to respond to a perceived need, then a new program addressing that need is likely to meet with success and acceptance. However, if people are satisfied with the current program, and there is little demand for change from either the staff or community, then a major curriculum change should not be attempted. Also, if staff have just completed a major revision or created a major program, it is most likely not a good idea to involve the same people in another major curriculum development effort.[43] See Curriculum Tips 10-2.

CURRICULUM IMPLEMENTATION MODELS

We live in a time of overchoice not only of products, but also of orientations to action, as well as of models for guiding our actions. Considering the

---

======= *Curriculum Tips 10-2* =======

Checklist for Implementing Curriculum Change

Curriculum leaders, especially principals and supervisors, have concerns about change and how the school staff will react. People prefer the status quo when they are familiar with and satisfied with it. The checklist below consists of a number of questions that deal with decision making and process that curriculum leaders might wish to include in a presentation to the staff.

1. How will a teacher's personal day be changed by the innovation?
2. How much additional preparation time will the innovation require?
3. How much paperwork will be involved in implementing and monitoring the innovation?
4. How will the innovation "fit in" to the content to which learners have already been exposed?
5. What kinds of teacher resource materials will be provided?
6. Will resource materials be in each teacher's room, in a separate room in the school, at the central administration building, or at some other location?
7. What kinds of new learning materials will be provided for learners?
8. Are reading levels and other characteristics of these materials clearly appropriate for learners to be served?
9. What patterns of teacher–learner interaction will be demanded?
10. Will any required instructional procedures demand teaching techniques teachers have not already mastered?
11. What kinds of in-service training will be provided?
12. What is the relationship of the innovation to standardized tests learners must take?
13. What are the implications of the new program for classroom management?
14. How strong is the central district administration's commitment to the support of the new program?
15. Who, specifically, can be called on for help if there are problems regarding implementation of the innovation?
16. To what extent do parents know about and support the new program?

Source: Adapted from David G. Armstrong, *Developing and Documenting the Curriculum* (Boston: Allyn and Bacon, 1989), pp. 213–214.

---

total process of curriculum activity can help educators select a particular approach to implementation. Their views are often influenced by their overall curriculum approaches and philosophical preferences.

Ben Harris has pointed out that strategies for improving educational offerings are not easy to identify. But scholars and practitioners continue to dialogue about the need for effective means of improving the curriculum and its delivery. Harris observes that from the present dialogue we can ferret out common suggestions for possible strate-

gies of change: (1) clarifying lines of authority; (2) involving affected parties in goal setting, staff selection, and evaluation; (3) specifying roles and responsibilities of teachers; (4) training personnel in change strategies and conflict-resolution techniques; and (5) furnishing impacted parties with necessary support.[44]

Implementing change in any organization, and schools are no exception, requires a multitask approach. Regardless of the approach one takes, implementing has essentially three stages: initiation, implementation, and maintenance. *Initiation* of change refers to setting the stage for the implementation process, getting the school culture receptive to the planned innovation. At this stage, planners raise the essential questions about who will be involved, what the expected level of support is, and what is the state of readiness of persons for the innovation. Ideally, these questions relating to the initiation phase were asked when the parties were involved in the curriculum development activities.

The *implementation* stage involves presenting innovation and getting people to try it out in their classrooms or other appropriate educational spaces. It is the "doing" phase of implementation. It puts into action the various models or approaches to implementation, which will be discussed momentarily.

The third phase is *maintenance* or *institutionalization,* which essentially is the monitoring of the innovation after it has been introduced. If maintenance is not planned for, innovations that get introduced often fade or are altered to such degree that they cease to exist.[45] The innovation is never institutionalized. Teachers may either ignore it upon closing their classroom doors or change it to such extents that the new curriculum is no longer true to its initial intents. Some perceive this as good, for new programs should not be set in stone, but should emerge over time as students' and society's needs change. However, even if accepting this, there does need to be in effect some aspect of an implementation plan that will continue to provide the necessary pressure and support for the program. Many teachers feel left "holding the bag" when there is no continued support for the new curriculum. "Done that, been there" cannot be the posture of curriculum implementors. Instead, we need to say, "Done that, continue to be here."

Those involved in implementing new programs should be encouraged by the fact that much of the work of the last two decades has furnished tactics on how to effect change in schools. Indeed, Jon Snyder and others have indicated that the research on curriculum implementation has yielded findings about the conditions that either facilitate or inhibit the entire implementation process.[46] In fact, we know a lot about the implementation process, and some researchers are now less interested in implementation as a change process and more interested in how the implementation is enacted and experienced by teachers and students.[47] This focus seems to support Pinar's notion that we really know a lot about the procedural aspects of creating and implementing curricula, and now we should focus on attempting to understand how the key players experience the "educational play" we have written.[48] The emphasis perhaps should be on understanding curriculum, not just polishing well-known and well-understood models. Still, the players in the schools need to realize the particulars of various approaches to implementing the curriculum, for educational practitioners cannot avoid being engaged and affected by this stage of curriculum development.

Overcoming Resistance to Change Model

The overcoming resistance to change (ORC) model rests on the assumption, according to Neal Gross, that the success or failure of planned organizational change efforts is basically a function of the ability of leaders to overcome staff resistance to change that is present just prior to, or at the time of, the introduction of the innovation.[49]

To implement a new program, that is, to introduce change, we must gain advocates for the new program. Glatthorn talks of developing a constituency for the planned curriculum change. To get a program implemented, we need persons willing to engage in something new, to push boundaries, to explore new territories. And these advocates must be able to attract colleagues.[50] To establish a community of supporters for a new program, we must address their fears, misgivings, misapprehensions, and other factors that could inhibit the acceptance of change. We must convince all that their values, assumptions, beliefs, indeed visions, are included in the new program proposed.

One strategy to overcome resistance to change is power equalization between management and organizational members—school administrators and teachers in this case. The leaders of an innovation accept that subordinates will initially be negatively predisposed toward the innovation and will hence resist it. This resistance can be avoided if staff members are involved in the deliberations that initially create the program and in the deliberations to develop it. Curriculum leaders, mindful of this fact, share their power with subordinates by allowing them to participate in decisions about program change. When leaders adopt this strategy, staff members tend to view the innovation as self-imposed and thus express ownership of it and commitment to it. Power equalization has thus become a key concept in several theories of organizational change. It has been constructed as an initial subgoal, a necessary predecessor to creative change.

Curriculum leaders using the ORC model realize that they must identify and deal with the concerns of the staff. Indeed, some classify a model such as ORC as a concerns-based adoption model. An assumption of this approach is that individuals must change before organizations can be altered. Also, change is a very personal experience, and we must allow for individual personalities to shine through in the change or implementation process. Additionally, the change introduced must address the teachers' and other curriculum players' needs as interpreted by those players.[51]

In their research on the implementation of innovations in schools and colleges, Hall and Loucks have noted that concerns can be grouped into four broad developmental stages:

Stage 1: Unrelated concerns. At this level teachers do not perceive a relationship between themselves and the suggested change. For example, if a new science program is being created in a school, a teacher at this stage would be aware of the efforts, but would not consider that he or she would be affected by or concerned with the effort. The teacher would not resist the change, because he or she really does not perceive the change as affecting his or her own personal or professional domain.

Stage 2: Personal concerns. At this stage, the individual reacts to the innovation in relation to his or her personal situation. He or she is concerned with how the new program compares to the ongoing program—specifically, to what he or she is doing. In the science example, the teacher would perceive that he would have to be involved with the new program. The teacher would face the question of how well he could teach the innovation.

Stage 3: Task-related concerns. Concerns at this level relate to the actual use of the innovation in the classroom. Continuing the science ex-

ample, the teacher would now be concerned with how to actually implement the new program. How much time will be required for teaching this new program? Will adequate materials be provided? What are the best strategies for teaching the new program?

Stage 4: Impact-related concerns. When reacting at this stage, a teacher is more concerned with how the innovation will affect others—the total organization. The teacher is interested in how the new program might influence students, colleagues, and the community. The teacher might want to determine the program's impact, too, on what he or she is teaching. Will the new science program, for example, enable students to live in the future world?[52]

When working with the ORC model, educators must deal directly with the concerns at stages 2, 3, and 4. If they ignore them, then people will either not accept the innovation or will deal with it in ways that are not intended in the program's conception. Such concerns can be addressed by curriculum leaders' keeping all staff informed of the innovation and by their involving those persons who will be directly affected in the early decisions regarding the innovation. Often, faculty can be called together to share concerns and to map strategies for dealing with those concerns. Sometimes information can be gathered from questionnaires that allow for open-ended questions. When concerns are shared, often persons with some insecurity regarding the program find that they really have nothing about which to worry. This does not mean that they do not have to make changes. Perhaps teachers will find that they do have to change their strategies and that they do have to teach different content. By sharing concerns, they may realize, however, that they are capable of making any changes necessary in order to deliver the new program in its intended fashion.

Organizational Development Model

Schmuck and Miles hold the position that many approaches to educational improvement do not succeed because the leaders assume that adoption is a rational process. Taking such a view forces leaders to overrely on the technical aspects of innovation and diffusion. They assume that systematic properties of local school districts are constants. They do not perceive that the organizations need self-renewal or that various parts of the districts experience change as a result of interaction with the environment. Schmuck and Miles suggest organizational development (OD) as a better approach.[53] Organizational development has come to mean a rather specific approach for bringing about change and improvement in an organization. It is a long-range effort to improve an organization's problem-solving and renewal processes, particularly through collaborative diagnosis and management. The emphasis is on team work and organizational culture.

French and Bell depict seven characteristics that separate organizational development from more traditional ways of intervening in organizations.

1. Emphasis on the work team for addressing issues.
2. Emphasis on group and intergroup processes.
3. Use of action research.
4. Emphasis on collaboration within the organization as the dominant culture.
5. Realization that the culture must be perceived as part of the total system.
6. Realization that those in charge of the organization serve as consultants–facilitators.
7. Appreciation of the ongoing dynamics of the organization within a continually changing environment.[54]

Organizational development views the process of curriculum implementation as an ongoing interactive process. This emphasis might well place OD under what some currently consider curriculum enactment, a somewhat nontechnical approach to change. This dynamic, emergent aspect of OD could also identify the model as Type S Strategic Planning.[55] Kaufman notes that this type of strategic planning identifies both current and anticipated needs and opportunities for the curriculum, while also addressing the needs of individuals and the organization. The S stands for society. In employing this approach, planners not only raise the questions of "what is" and "what could be," but also "what is appropriate" for a dynamic, emerging future. It recognizes that implementation is or should deal with what ought to be done, rather than what is to be done.

A key assumption of this approach to curriculum implementation is that individuals care about the future. Thus they desire to be actively engaged in designing, developing, implementing, and evaluating the educational system. They want to implement an innovative curriculum that will allow students and teachers to attain their goals and objectives and encourage the key players to identify new missions that will lead ultimately to the betterment of society.[56]

Approaching curriculum implementation in this way celebrates the fact that curriculum knowledge is individualized for both the teacher and student.[57] Those involved in successful curriculum implementation or enactment understand and accept the subjective dimensions of people. Curriculum implementation, like curriculum development, is a human activity, not a machine-driven process engaging people as cogs in a wheel. Viewing curriculum as organizational development or as curriculum enactment requires accepting implementation as never finished. There are always new ideas to bring to the new program, new materials and methods to try out, new students to excite. Curriculum implementation is essentially educational theater in which the process of enacting the curriculum and acting the curriculum continually engages both teachers and students in growth by providing enriched learning that involves their total persons.[58] The various events of "teaching the new program" are organized so that optimal learning occurs.

Organizational Parts, Units, and Loops

The system of relations that forms the whole makes or defines an organization. If no system of relations draws the parts into a whole, then there is no organization, just free-floating parts. These parts, in our case people, work in such ways that their areas of responsibility overlap others within the organization. An interplay or overlap exists among these groups. According to Rensis Likert, persons in these overlapping work groups serve as "linking pins." The notion of linking pins coincides with the idea of team work and organizational development. The interplay of the dynamics of these work teams, as conveyed by the "linking pin" incumbents, has a powerful effect on the attitudes and behavior of people in both groups.[59]

This means that the manner in which those in the higher teams work with those in the lower teams will rub off on the lower teams. If persons responsible for a major portion of an innovation treat their team players with respect, support, and trust, it is likely that those team players when interacting with others throughout the organization will also exhibit a similar style. This central assumption applies to all people whether placed on standing or ad hoc committees. The entire culture is affected.

Educators are coming to realize that the school is actually an organization of loosely coupled units—departments, classrooms, and persons. Also, these parts have rather flexible relationships. Although a central administration is defined, most schools have little centralized control, especially over what occurs in the classroom. For this reason it is difficult for curricular change to be implemented as an edict from the central office.

Viewing implementation from an organizational stance, educators realize that organizations can create conditions that significantly influence how individuals will perceive the innovation and the ways in which they will be involved in implementing it. Chris Argyris addresses this point in a discussion of the concept of organizational learning. He notes that learning occurs when an organization achieves what it intended—a match between what it planned for action and the actual outcome of the implemented plans. He asserts that organizations can address learning, or what we can call effective action, by either a single- or double-loop approach.[60]

As depicted in Figure 10-2, single-loop learning takes place when an organization detects an error and corrects it without questioning or altering the underlying values of the system. It just asks whether it achieved its objectives in light of the problem defined. Single-loop learning is routine and repetitive. Argyris gives the example of a thermostat for a single-loop learner. The thermostat is programmed to detect states of "too cold" or "too hot" and to correct the situation by activating the furnace. If the thermostat were to ask itself *why* it was too cold or too hot, then it would be a double-loop learner. Double-loop learning is more advanced and complex than single-loop. It involves reasoning processes among people affected by the change.

Planned change within the organization, the school in our situation, should attempt to be perceived as "win-win" or match not "win-lose" or mismatch. In implementing change there will be the potential for conflict between people and groups, even departments. While conflict will occur, it must be managed so that people realize that everyone can win. The new program being implemented in the school presents an opportunity for all involved parties to gain: students, teachers, chairs, and principals. However, successful implementation requires energy, time, and patience. Implementation to be successful must be perceived as an effort requiring a long-range time frame and major involvement and cooperation among people and departments. See Curriculum Tips 10-3.

Educational Change Model

While there are numerous models of implementation at our disposal, our effectiveness in employing them depends in part on how well we grasp the

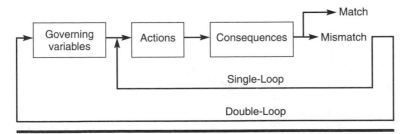

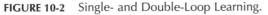

FIGURE 10-2 Single- and Double-Loop Learning.

Source: Chris Argyis, "How Learning and Reasoning Processes Affect Organizational Change," in P. S. Goodman, ed., *Change in Organizations* (San Francisco: Jossey-Bass, 1982), p. 50.

========================= *Curriculum Tips 10-3* =========================

Unconventional Wisdom for Promoting Change

The human equation is an important consideration for curriculum implementation. Agents of change and leaders of change must understand people and how they react to change. Here are some unconventional ideas to consider.

1. *Progress from certainty to ambiguity.* Rather than making sure that everything is in place before you begin implementation, realize that some unexpected things will happen.
2. *Allow for some chaos in your order.* In your implementation journey, allow time for serendipity, surprise, and a little chaos. In dealing with "planned chaos," we may stimulate creative modifications in our implementation order and bring into existence relationships that we never imagined possible.
3. *Look beyond the person to the behavior.* We will get people to try out new ideas if, instead of personalizing disagreement, we address the behavior or issue. Rather than state that a person is acting unprofessionally or resisting a change, indicate that the person has raised issues of concern that need to be addressed.
4. *Realize that people do not resist change, but victims do.* People do not want to be shaped up or made victims in the change process. Getting people to be partners in innovation can reduce this feeling of being victimized.
5. *Use your fallibility to build your credibility.* The effective manager of change realizes that he or she is human and therefore fallible. Those who come across as all knowing can bring smiles to wiser players who know otherwise. Worse yet, others may become angry at the omniscient person. People who admit their mistakes and even indicate that future mistakes will be made in the implementation process are likely to be accepted as strong leaders of innovation.
6. *Be sensitive.* People who realize their own fallibility are more likely to be sensitive to others. They operate with people in open, honest interaction, with a true sense of who they are. They have recognized their personal space and the personal boundaries of others.
7. *Upgrade permanent to temporary.* Any new program is only designed for a particular time period, a particular audience. Times and audiences will change, and even the best of programs will have to be modified, perhaps discarded.
8. *Have humor.* Remember that most plans carried out are not so crucial that a missed date or a few snags will cause lives to be lost. Yes, education is serious, but we can deal with ourselves and others with some degree of humor. People who can see humor in missed cues, who realize the need to laugh at themselves, are likely to be much more willing to be involved in implementation on a continuing basis.

Source: Adapted from Thomas L. Quick, *Unconventional Wisdom* (San Francisco: Jossey-Bass, 1989).

entire concept of implementation. Michael Fullan has discussed key factors that affect implementation, a list that curriculum workers would do well to keep in mind.[61] Table 10-1 lists these factors.

Persons who wish to implement the new curriculum *need* to understand the characteristics of the change being considered. Often people will resist the innovation because the need for the change is not made known or, if made known, not accepted by those persons to be affected by the change. Needs are influenced by the values we hold. When people view change to coincide with

TABLE 10-1   Factors Affecting Implementation

A. Characteristics of the change
   1. Need and relevance of the change
   2. Clarity
   3. Complexity
   4. Quality and practicality of program
B. Characteristics at the school district level
   5. History of innovative attempts
   6. Adoption process
   7. Central administrative support and involvement
   8. Staff development (in-service and participation)
   9. Time-line and information systems
   10. Board and community characteristics
C. Characteristics at the school level
   11. Principal characteristics and leadership
   12. Teacher characteristics and relations
   13. Student characteristics and needs
D. Characteristics external to the local system
   14. Role of government agencies
   15. External funds

Source: Adapted from Michael Fullan, *The New Meaning of Educational Change,* 2nd ed. (New York: Teachers College Press, Columbia University, 1991).

their values, they are more willing to accept the innovation being suggested.

What the program will do and what it will involve are two questions that persons raise regarding innovations. People want to know the purpose for the innovation and how it is going to be conducted. *Clarity* about goals and means is always an issue in any change activity.[62] If we are going to persuade others that the suggested innovation is worthwhile, then we must be clear at the outset as to what the goals are and specify the manner in which people will be involved. Often people are not clear as to why a particular innovation is actually different from what they are doing.

Complexity refers to the difficulty, which is relative to many factors. For staff experienced in curriculum development, extensive change can be rather easy. For inexperienced staff, the same change can be quite challenging. In most organizations, the idea is to remember the KISS theory: keep it short and simple. However, simple changes

may be less satisfying; simple changes often do not make much difference. We need to recognize our innovation for what it is and have a realistic perception of its difficulty level.

To accept an innovation people need to perceive its *quality, worth,* and *practicality.* While we would hope that any curriculum innovation would have evident quality, developers often miss the mark when it comes to practicality. The ideas are sound, but teachers just do not have the time to carry out the suggestions. Sometimes curricula are haphazardly implemented that could be practically implemented if those in charge had made sure that the necessary materials were available for teachers. Often teachers in new programs soon realize that technical or support staff are unavailable to answer questions.

Curriculum implementation is "putting the show on the road." We all want a "hit play." Recognizing the characteristics of change will not guarantee a hit, but it can make one more likely. We need to keep in mind the community in which the play will be performed, the characteristics of the school district and school, as well as the key players in Table 10-2.

For new curriculum to be successful depends largely on how well those who have planned its development and implementation have perceived the needs of students and teachers. In curriculum development, regardless of the approach taken, attention must be given to understanding students' needs to be addressed by the program being created. In curriculum implementation, one must also attend to what teachers require to accept the new curriculum.

Needs represent what is deemed essential for individuals to have or learn or understand in order for something of value to occur. Needs represent deficiencies that people find unacceptable. Some say that identifying needs as deficiencies is perhaps too negative. Perhaps it is better to define a need as a recognized and accepted discrepancy between a current state and desired state. A need is a statement that indicates what is and then compares it with what should be.[63] Pratt defines need as "a discrepancy between a present and a preferred state."[64]

Just as one never completely finishes developing a curriculum, neither does one ever totally complete its implementation. Since systems are dynamic and events and human actions emergent,

TABLE 10-2 Overview of Curriculum Implementation Models

MODEL	AUTHOR-ORIGINATOR	ASSUMPTIONS	KEY PLAYERS	RELATIONSHIP TO CHANGE TYPOLOGY
Overcoming resistance to change (ORC)	Neal Gross	Resistance to change is natural Need to overcome resistance at outset of innovation activities Must address concerns of staff	Administrators, directors, teachers, supervisors	Power strategy Empirical strategy Planned change
Organizational development	Richard Schmuck and Matthew Miles	Top-down approach (vertical organization) Stress on organizational culture Implementation an ongoing interactive process	Administrators, directors, supervisors	Empirical, rational Planned change
Organizational parts, units, and loops	Rensis Likert Chris Argyris	Parts, units, and departments of the organization compromise the whole Linkages between people and groups Implementations consist of corrective actions	Administrators, directors, teachers, supervisors	Normative, rational Planned change
Educational change model	Michael Fullan	Successful change involves need, clarity, some complexity, and quality of programs	Administrators, teachers, students, school board, community and government members	Centralized policies External/internal factors

one constantly gathers data for needs analyses to determine what to address, what to continue, or what to change. Although needs analysis comprises actions performed prior to curriculum development or implementation, it is also part of the evaluation process, which is discussed in the next chapter.

Needs assessment contributes to curricular renewal when it exists as an ongoing process, rather than an intermittent activity. Needs assessment is integral to planning and the change process. However, the quality of the data gathered is determined to some degree by how data are gathered and the types of data processed. Ideally, data should address both student and teacher performance. Needs assessment should furnish information on opinions, understandings, and desires. It should enable developers and implementors to generate a picture of the social context in which the new program will be brought to life.[65]

There are numerous ways to gather the data that allow program planners and implementors to make decisions. The analysis of test results is used in needs analysis during the initial phases of curriculum development. Questionnaires, telephone interviews, and hearings also furnish data at the initial stages of planning. These means of gathering data are also appropriate for the implementation phase.

In the piloting phase of implementation, one can utilize various tests, both commercial-made and teacher-made, to furnish data on how well students are interacting with the piloted new curriculum. As teachers teach the new curriculum, briefings can be conducted to obtain their ongoing reactions. These efforts are a part of short-term planning efforts. One can even use video cameras to furnish story lines that can be discussed and analyzed as a new program unfolds.

Needs assessment allows taking of the pulse of those involved in enacting the curriculum: the teachers, the students, the support staff, and even community members. Monitoring the pulses of the major players enables implementors to know the optimum heart rate to determine if the program is alive and well and responsive to both planned and unplanned events and actions. To advocate including needs analysis in the overall planning and enactment process of curriculum is not just being enamored with the technical approach. It simply means that in implementation we must have a sense of how things are going. In improvisational jazz, players need to listen to both themselves and the other players. They need to assess their performances against others in the band. Needs assessment can do that. It can allow us to be good jazz players, to make pleasing music that will address the intellect and excite the spirit.

ROLES OF THE KEY PLAYERS

Any attempt at change requires people playing key roles. These players may be students, teachers, administrators, consultants, state employees, university professors, parents, lay citizens, and political officials interested in education. Often such people can play different roles at different times in the change process, depending on their skills. Other persons are formally educated to assume particular roles as consultants, researchers, or systems experts. Often the job a person holds allows him or her to gain the expertise necessary to play that role in the change process.

Someone has to initiate the change process—or at least elicit a reaction to a demand. Almost anyone in the educational community can be an initiator. As we move up the administrative hierarchy, there is a greater chance for an individual, because of his or her role, to serve as an initiator.

Sometimes school districts pay one or more people to be internal initiators or change agents. These persons are charged with scanning the current scene to detect problems, demands, or deficiencies that require attention. These persons may get others to consider change by writing papers, forming ad hoc committees to analyze particular issues, submitting proposals, or simply sending memos to staff expressing concern for some action.

In some cases, an initiator stays with the change effort during its entirety. This frequently happens when the initiator is an internal member of the organization. Other times, the initiator is a catalyst and is not actively involved in any of the stages of curriculum change. The most successful change projects usually have an initiation phase with some person (or group) who is the initiator.

Students.   Rarely do educators think of students as agents of change. We are just beginning to realize that students, even in the elementary grades, can contribute to meaningful educational change. How much we involve them will not only depend on their maturity, but also on the complexity and scope of change we are considering. Just as teachers must accept a new program for it to be successful, so students must also be willing to participate in the program. If students see little relevance in the curricular activities planned, they are not going to be motivated to participate—or learn. Ideally, we want students to react with heightened interest, with enthusiasm.

While we have been discussing empowering students to be more in command of their own learning, we have perhaps been a bit slow in furnishing them with opportunities for gaining the competencies requisite for assuming a more active role in determining the nature of their school experiences. There is still limited research to guide us on how to involve students. We have little information that tells us how students react to innovation.

Involving students in the change effort is not suggesting that teachers and students working on change should take time off from the curriculum of the school. The act of being engaged in considering the "what" of their education and "how" they will experience it can be very much a part of the students' actual curriculum.

Teachers as Initiators. We are now in a period of reform where we are involving teachers in the change process. Until recently, we tended to only give lip service to the active participation of teachers. Now we realize that teachers with their knowledge and competencies are and must continue to be central to any curricular improvement effort. Regardless of which philosophical view one has of education, there is no doubting that teachers influence students' learning. And better teachers foster better learners.

Of course, teachers even when not formally involved in implementation are involved. They cannot be excluded because much of curriculum implementation is introduced in the classroom. But now we are involving them in the entire process of curriculum change.

For Henry Giroux, teachers are integral to the thinking that drives program creation and implementation. Teachers are reflective. They are aware of the assumptions behind the process, and they are involved in making the process of curriculum development and implementation even more effective. Many educators realize that, of all the people within the educational organization, teachers often are the most knowledgeable about the practice of teaching; teachers often represent the best clinical expertise available.[66] Of course, not all teachers are going to become actively involved in reform or change. But they can be involved in modifying and fine-tuning the work of their colleagues and outside professionals who have participated in curriculum development.

The key to getting teachers committed to an innovation is involvement. Good curriculum development is a cooperative venture. However, involvement means more than having teachers on the curriculum development advisory committee. For implementation to occur, many teachers will need to experience skill-training workshops. To truly have educational reform we must have professional development. Despite all the hoopla about educational reform, we do not have widespread efforts that promote teacher learning such that we have more effective curriculum and instruction. We are still very much involved in one-day workshops or training sessions. We often prefer the "expert" who provides the false promise of making us "experts" by the end of the day.

To get teachers to implement a new curriculum requires a paradigm shift. Currently, we seem to be enamored with the cognitive coaching model of getting teachers "up to speed." However, coaching suggests training; good education or effective pedagogy within a new curriculum is not training. Teachers must realize that the new game that they are playing is not a novel version of football. The educational game requires a professional stance of inquiry and creativity that enables one to process the uncertainties of changing practice, the systems breaks that emerge from engaging with the curriculum. Teachers need continuing opportunities within the educational system to develop different views of curriculum, teaching, and knowledge. They need to stretch intellectually, to play with ideas that challenge the nature, purpose, and scope of school curricula. We are entering a new century, and how we involve teachers in implementing new curricula must represent different ways of assuring that teachers are central to the total curriculum development and implementation processes.

Supervisors. The processes of curriculum development and implementation must be supervised. Someone must monitor what is occurring and determine whether these actions are appropriate. Frequently, the word *supervision* is associated with instruction. Certainly, instructional supervision is important, especially at the level of implementation, but, in fact, the entire process of curriculum development needs to be supervised. Moreover, during the implementation phase, not only the manner of teaching but also the content that is actually being addressed need to be supervised as well.

The supervisor provides direction and guidance and makes sure teachers have the skills to carry out the change. Those charged with supervising curriculum development and implementation are responsible for overseeing or directing the work of others. This requires making certain decisions, engaging in particular actions, and interacting with others involved in the change effort.[67]

Effective supervisors realize that they must alter their tactics depending on the situation and the participants. Supervisors can place much responsibility in the hands of seasoned and experienced teachers. However, they might have to provide beginning teachers with much more structure. They might need to schedule more supervisor–teacher conferences and more in-service training for such staff members to deliver the new curriculum.

Ronald Doll points out that supervisors have three major tasks: (1) assisting the total faculty in determining the purposes of education and monitoring the actions of professionals to see that these purposes are adhered to in the delivery of the program; (2) furnishing democratic instructional leadership; and (3) keeping channels of communications within the school organization and between the school and the community open.[68]

Supervisors can carry out their responsibilities in numerous ways. A few popular ways are classroom observation, demonstration teaching, supervisor–teacher conferences, staff development meetings, and grant funding.

If supervisors are effective, it is likely that the teachers within the system will feel committed to and comfortable with the new program being implemented. Teachers will be satisfied and thus the organization will run smoothly.

Principals as Initiators. Principals play a major role in program improvement. They can determine organizational climate and they support those persons involved in change. If a principal creates an atmosphere in which good working relationships exist among teachers, and teachers are willing to take the risks necessary to create and deliver new programs, then it is more likely that program changes will be implemented.

Effective principals orchestrate the interrelationships of educational environment. They foster the development of an atmosphere in which there occurs an increasing interest and excitement for the new program. Ideally, the principal nurtures a dynamic harmony among all teachers and support staff.[69]

While we have known that the principal is central to the success of having innovative programs delivered in schools, it is recently that we have asked principals to assume the role of curriculum leader as well as instructional leader. In their review of hundreds of innovative projects, Berman and McLaughlin point out the role of the principal:

> *The importance of the principal to both short- and long-run outcomes of innovative projects can hardly be overstated. When teachers thought that principals disliked a project, we rarely found favorable project outcomes. Some projects with neutral or indifferent principals scored well, particularly in the percentage of goals achieved; but these projects typically . . . had highly effective project directors who compensated for the lukewarm principals. Projects having the active support of the principal were the most likely to fare well.*[70]

In their survey of secondary-school principals, Barney Berlin et al. determined the top ten curriculum functions that principals contend they do as curriculum leaders. In rank order, they were: (1) develops an orientation program for new teachers, (2) develops a clear set of goals and objectives, (3) involves individual departments in curriculum development, (4) encourages communication among schools within the district, (5) handles controversial issues involving curriculum, (6) spends time visiting the teachers in the classroom, (7) plans staff development programs, (8) rewards curriculum innovation, (9) encourages use of library and media services by the teachers, and (10) modifies school environment to improve instruction.[71] To be sure, there are few who would contest that the principal is critical to the success of the change effort.

Curriculum Directors. The director of curriculum concentrates on the overall process of curriculum development, including implementation and evaluation. Large school districts have full-time centralized directors who oversee curriculum activities. Some directors oversee the entire K–12 program, whereas in other school districts there is a separate director of elementary education and a separate director of secondary education. In small school districts, the superintendent or associate (assistant) superintendent assumes responsibility over curriculum matters.

In schools where there has been successful change, the curriculum director assists teachers and principals in furnishing pedagogic and curricular knowledge. Teachers within the system expect these people to keep abreast of the latest research and theorizing about any particular innovation and to communicate these results to the school staff. Directors of curriculum can assist teachers, supervisors, and principals in the implementation process by inspiring and providing necessary support for the staff. For example, Edward Pajak points out that curriculum directors provide assistance to school people by (1) clarifying the district's goals and values, (2) conducting curriculum surveys, (3) communicating district policies and guidelines, (4) working cooperatively with local business groups to obtain funds, (5) coordinating federal/state programs, (6) organizing curriculum/instructional school teachers or committees, (7) coordinating staff development activities, and (8) assisting supervisors in the supervision of instruction.[72] Directors also serve as resource agents, information agents, and consultants for selected programs and schools. They serve as a "linking pin" between the central office and school site, between the superintendent's office and school principal (as supervisor). Directors should inspire change and implementation through personal conferences, participation in committees, and staff development activities.

Curriculum Consultants. There are times when a school district will wish to bring in an external

facilitator or coordinator. Often, in small school districts, there are no internal experts to consult regarding change or innovation. However, large school districts may also find that an outside facilitator is required. School districts do not usually employ curriculum consultants over extended periods of time. Rather, schools bring in consultants to do one- and two-day workshops. However, such workshops are not really effective—in curriculum development and implementation for such activities require a much longer time frame. Consultants are also used to analyze and/or assess programs, as well as to assist in grant funding. Most of these consultants are based at colleges and universities and have a specific skill that many small school districts lack in terms of central personnel who can do this particular job.

Joseph Murphy discovered from his research that when consultants were good, they were very good, and when they were bad, they were an obstacle. Good external consultants assisted by furnishing practical advice to teachers on how to utilize the materials. Often these persons conducted workshops to allow teachers to try out the innovation during the implementation stage. These consultants did not solve the teachers' problems; rather, they worked with teachers so that they could solve their own problems. Bad or ineffective consultants often furnished information that was far too abstract to be useful.[73]

Most consultants will not work with a school district throughout the entire curriculum development and implementation process; there is just not enough time. This problem can be addressed in part by having consultants establish peer support systems, peer coaching, and networks for working with internal facilitators and suggesting information that teachers can use to gain comfort and expertise with the innovation.

Parents and Community Members. We have known for some time, say since the 1960s when community control became a controversial issue in the big cities, that parents and community members want participatory influence in school matters and can be change agents. Certainly, school boards have always had a legal responsibility for approving and overseeing change efforts. But now we are witnessing the creation of temporary ad hoc committees comprised of community members and parents to assist in furnishing input into curriculum development and change efforts. After all, the schools belong to the community; they are not the possession of educators. Indeed, some critics argue that education is too important to be left just to the educators. Bringing in parents and members from the community should enable the change process to incorporate the diverse views of the community.

Just as we have not asked our students in past times what they thought about an innovation, so have we neglected to tap parents and other community members for their perceptions of new programs being considered for implementation. This is changing. More and more schools are involving parents in the stages of curriculum development from the formulation of goals to evaluation. This is all for the good, especially if we wish to promote participatory democracy, but many parents are unsophisticated and still others lack time or interest. In short, they are unable to provide us with much assistance in educational reform. But we have to start somewhere. We have to realize that we have a cadre of potential consultants who can furnish guidance in curriculum implementation, perhaps even contributing to the entire process of curriculum development.

CONCLUSION

Those who understand that implementation is much more than handing out new materials or courses of study realize that, if a new curriculum is to be successfully implemented, then those involved need to be able to visualize the purposes of the program, the roles people will play within the system, and the types of individuals who are to result from the interaction with the new curriculum. Such persons also realize that even though planning is central to the change and implementation process, the process cannot be rigidly planned. Human beings require plans that are flexible; we must be able to adapt the plans to unintended consequences of implementation efforts. Because change is a process—not an event that happens at a point in time—we are never really finished with the implementation task. Successful implementation of a program or procedure requires perpetual fine tuning.

Persons who have worked on creating a new curriculum or a new course are anxious to have it implemented and accepted with enthusiasm by all involved in the school or school district. However, new curricula often fail to become established in the schools because the importance and complexity of the implementation stage were not understood.

We have presented this chapter in hopes of making the case that curriculum implementation is crucial. We have shown that curricularists can bring various perspectives to implementation and that they can employ numerous strategies.

We have presented implementation as a change process. We have pointed out the complexity of change and that planned change is essential if innovation is to occur systematically in the school. Those in charge of change strategies must understand the relationship of change to planning and the interaction of individuals, groups, and systems.

ENDNOTES

1. Evelyn J. Sowell, *Curriculum: An Integrative Introduction* (Upper Saddle River, N.J.: Merrill, an imprint of Prentice Hall, 1996).

2. Leslie J. Bishop, *Staff Development and Instructional Improvement: Plans and Procedures* (Boston: Allyn and Bacon, 1976).

3. Seymour B. Sarason, *The Predictable Failure of Educational Reform* (San Francisco: Jossey–Bass Publishers, 1990).

4. Michael Fullan and Alan Pomfret, "Research on Curriculum and Instruction Implementation," *Review of Educational Research* (Winter 1977), pp. 391–392.

5. James M. Kouzes and Barry Z. Posner, *The Leadership Challenge* (San Francisco: Jossey–Bass, 1990).

6. Matthew B. Miles and Karen Seashore Louis, "Mustering the Will and Skill for Change," in *Educational Leadership* (May 1990), pp. 57–61.

7. Kouzes and Posner, *The Leadership Challenge.*

8. Sowell, *Curriculum: An Integrative Introduction.*

9. Ronald C. Doll, *Curriculum Improvement: Decision Making and Process,* 9th ed. (Boston: Allyn and Bacon, 1996).

10. Michael Fullan, *The New Meaning of Educational Change* (New York: Teachers College Press, Columbia University, 1991).

11. Fullan, *The Meaning of Educational Change*; John I. Goodlad, *The Dynamics of Educational Change* (New York: McGraw-Hill, 1975).

12. Seymour B. Sarason, *The Culture of the School and the Problem of Change,* 2nd ed. (Boston: Allyn and Bacon, 1981); Sarason, *Human Services and Resource Networks* (San Francisco: Jossey–Bass, 1988).

13. Sarason, *The Predictable Failure of Educational Reform.*

14. Ibid., p. 13.

15. David Heath, *Maturity and Competence: A Transcultural View* (New York: Gardner, 1977).

16. Thomas R. Harvey, *Checklist for Change* (Boston: Allyn and Bacon, 1990), p. 112.

17. Susan Loucks and Ann Lieberman, "Curriculum Implementation," in F. W. English, ed., *Fundamental Curriculum Decisions* (Alexandria, Va.: Association for Supervision and Curriculum Development, 1983), pp. 126–141.

18. David P. Crandall et al., *People, Policy and Practices: Examining the Chain of School Improvement* (Andover, Mass.: The Network, 1982).

19. Ann Lieberman and Lynne Miller, *Teachers— Their World and Their Work* (New York: Teachers College Press, Columbia University, 1991); Milbrey W. McLaughlin, Joan E. Talbert, and Nina Bascia, eds., *The Contexts of Teaching in Secondary Schools* (New York: Teachers College Press, Columbia University, 1990).

20. Bruce Joyce and Beverly Showers, *Student Achievement Through Staff Development* (New York: Longman, 1988).

21. Harry J. Hartley, "Budgeting," in R. A. Gorton, ed., *Encyclopedia of School Administration and Supervision* (New York: Oryx Press, 1988), pp. 40–41.

22. Laurence Iannaconne and Richard Jamogochian, "High Performing Curriculum and Instructional Leadership in a Climate of Excellence," *NASSP Bulletin* (May 1985), pp. 28–35; Allan C. Ornstein, "Curriculum, Instruction, and Supervision: Their Relationship and the Role of the Principal," *NASSP Bulletin* (April 1986), pp. 74–81.

23. Lortie, *Schoolteacher.*

24. Robert V. Carlson and Gary Awkerman, eds., *Educational Planning* (New York: Longman, 1991).

25. Ibid.

26. Ibid.

27. Daniel U. Levine, Rayna F. Levine, and Allan C. Ornstein, "Guidelines for Change and Innovation in the Secondary School Curriculum," *NASSP Bulletin* (May 1985), pp. 9–14.

28. Ibid., p. 14.

29. John T. Lovell and Kimball Wiles, *Supervision for Better Schools,* 5th ed. (Englewood Cliffs, N.J..: Prentice Hall, 1983).

30. Robert V. Carlson and Gary Awkerman, eds., *Educational Planning.*

31. Kurt Lewin, *Field Theory in Social Sciences* (New York: Harper & Row, 1951).

32. Chris Argyris, *Reasoning, Learning, and Action* (San Francisco: Jossey–Bass, 1982).

33. Warren Bennis, *Changing Organizations* (New York: McGraw-Hill, 1966); Bennis, *On Becoming a Leader* (Reading, Mass.: Addison Wesley, 1989).

34. Robert Chin, "Basic Strategies and Procedures for Effecting Change," in E. L. Morphet and C. O. Ryan, eds., *Planning and Effecting Needed Changes in Education* (Denver: Designing Education for the Future, 1967), pp. 39–57.

35. John D. McNeil, *Curriculum, A Comprehensive Introduction,* 4th ed. (Glenview, Ill.: Scott, Foresman, 1990).

36. Ronald F. Cambell et al., *The Organization and Control of American Schools,* 6th ed. (Columbus, Ohio: Merrill, 1990); John P. Miller and Wayne Seller, *Curriculum: Perspectives and Practice* (New York: Longman, 1985).

37. Carlson and Awkerman, eds., *Educational Planning.*

38. Sarason, *The Predictable Failure of Educational Reform.*

39. Edgar Z. Friendenberg, *Coming of Age in America* (New York: Random House, 1965).

40. Seymour B. Sarason, *The Predictable Failure of Educational Reform.*

41. Harvey, *Checklist for Change.*

42. Dorwin Cartwright, "Achieving Change in People," in W. Bennis, K. Benne, and R. Chin, eds., *The Planning of Change* (New York: Holt, Rinehart, 1976), pp. 36–67.

43. William W. Savage, *Interpersonal and Group Relations in Educational Administration* (Glenview, Ill.: Scott, Foresman, 1968).

44. Ben M. Harris, *Supervisory Behavior in Education,* 3rd ed. (Englewood Cliffs, N.J.: Prentice Hall, 1985); Harris, *Inservice Education for Staff Development* (Boston: Allyn and Bacon, 1989).

45. Francis P. Hunkins, *Curriculum Development, Program Improvement* (Columbus, Ohio: Charles E. Merrill, 1980).

46. Jon Snyder, Frances Bolin, and Karen Zumwalt, "Curriculum Implementation," in Philip W. Jackson, ed., *Handbook of Research on Curriculum* (New York: Macmillan Publishing Co., 1992), pp. 402–435.

47. Ibid.

48. William F. Pinar, William M. Reynolds, Patrick Slattery, and Peter M. Taubman, *Understanding Curriculum* (New York: Peter Lang, 1995).

49. Neal Gross, "Basic Issues in the Management of Educational Change Efforts," in R. E. Herriott and N. Gross, eds., *The Dynamics of Planned Educa-*

tional Change (Berkeley, Calif.: McCutchan, 1979), pp. 20–46.

50. Allan A. Glatthorn, *Curriculum Leadership* (Glenview, Ill.: Scott, Foresman, 1987).

51. Sowell, *Curriculum: An Integrative Introduction.*

52. Gene E. Hall and Susan Loucks, "Teacher Concerns as a Basis for Facilitating and Personalizing Staff Development," *Teachers College Record* (September 1978), pp. 36–53; Hall and Loucks, "The Concept of Innovation Configurations: An Approach to Addressing Program Adaptation." Paper presented at the annual meeting of the American Educational Research Association, Los Angeles, April 1981.

53. Richard S. Schmuck and Matthew Miles, eds., *Organizational Development in Schools* (Palo Alto, Calif.: National Press Books, 1971); Schmuck et al., *The Second Handbook of Organizational Development in Schools* (Palo Alto, Calif.: Mayfield, 1977).

54. Wendell L. French and Cecil H. Bell, *Organization Development,* 4th ed. (Englewood Cliffs, N.J.: Prentice Hall, 1990).

55. Roger Kaufman and L. W. Harrell, "Types of Functional Educational Planning Models," *Performance Improvement Quarterly,* 2(1), 1989, pp. 4–13, cited in Carlson and Awkerman, eds., *Educational Planning.*

56. Ibid.

57. Snyder, Bolin, and Zumwalt, "Curriculum Implementation."

58. Ibid.

59. Rensis Likert, *New Patterns of Management* (New York: McGraw-Hill, 1961), p. 113; Rensis Likert and Jane G. Likert, *New Ways of Managing Conflict* (New York: McGraw-Hill, 1976).

60. Chris Argyris, *Personality and Organization* (New York: Harper & Row, 1957); Argyris, *Increasing Leadership Effectiveness* (New York: Wiley, 1976).

61. Fullan, *The New Meaning of Educational Change.*

62. French and Bell, *Organizational Development.*

63. Belle Ruth Witkin, "Setting Priorities: Needs Assessment in a Time of Change," in Carlson and Awkerman, eds., *Educational Planning,* pp. 241–266.

64. David Pratt, *Curriculum Planning* (New York: Harcourt Brace College Publishers, 1994), p. 37.

65. Witkin, "Setting Priorities: Needs Assessment in a Time of Change."

66. Henry A. Giroux, *Teachers as Intellectuals* (Granby, Mass.: Bergin & Garvey, 1988).

67. Carl Glickman, *Supervision and Instruction,* 2nd ed. (Boston: Allyn and Bacon, 1990); Peter F. Oliva, *Supervision for Today's Schools,* 3rd ed. (New York: Longman, 1989).

68. Doll, *Curriculum Improvement: Decision Making and Process.*

69. Patrick Slattery, *Curriculum Development in the Postmodern Era* (New York: Garland Publishing, Inc., 1995).

70. Paul Berman and Milbrey W. McLaughlin, *Federal Programs Supporting Educational Change: Implementing and Sustaining Innovations* (Santa Monica, Calif.: Rand Corporation, 1980), p. 95.

71. Barney M. Berlin, Jack A. Kavanugh, and Kathleen Jensen, "The Principal as Curriculum Leader: Expectations vs. Performance," *NASSP Bulletin* (September 1988), 43–49.

72. Edward Pajak, "A View from the Central Office," in C. Glickman, ed., *Supervision in Transition* (Alexandria, Va.: Association for Supervision and Curriculum Development, 1992), pp. 126–140.

73. Joseph Murphy, *Restructuring Schools* (New York: Teachers College Press, Columbia University, 1991).

11

CURRICULUM EVALUATION

Focusing Questions

1. How can we define evaluation?
2. What important questions should be considered for evaluation?
3. How does measurement compare with evaluation?
4. Explain the differences between formative and summative evaluation.
5. Identify some of the evaluation models that follow each of the two major approaches.
6. Explain the major approaches to qualitative evaluation.
7. What is meant by alternative assessment? Why is this type of assessment receiving much attention?
8. How do positivists view evaluation?
9. How do naturalists view evaluation?
10. What are the major issues of evaluation?
11. In what ways can high-stakes assessment influence education?
12. What roles can educators play in evaluation?

Along with many definitions of curriculum are numerous interpretations of curriculum evaluation. However one defines such evaluation, few educators would dispute its importance. Evaluation is a necessary cluster of activities in which curriculum developers and implementors gather data to arrive at judgments about either individuals' experiencing the curriculum, which is usually considered assessment, or curricular programs in general, which is considered evaluation. Ideally, assessment and evaluation are concurrent activities. Assessment that focuses on gathering data to determine what people know or can accomplish feeds into the overall evaluation process and guides decisions regarding content topics, organi-

zation of content, teaching methods, and even the physical organization of the class.[1]

In the last four decades, evaluation and assessment have caught the attention of the general public. Many people consider evaluation crucial to the health of education and its programs. In the last two decades, the public has increasingly demanded that the results of curriculum activities be identified and communicated. Individuals and various funding agencies want evidence as to the effectiveness of programs. They wish to assess the content, materials, and teaching methods used. They wish to know what students are learning and what skills they can demonstrate. They also want to know the cost of new programs and whether they are cost effective. The general public wishes to know the quality of education at the local, state, and national levels—even how American school students compare with the rest of the world. These demands are likely to continue.

These demands are connected with a new realization of the importance of education and making the schools accountable. To meet such demands requires that educators conceive and carry out an effective evaluation and reporting process. It requires educators to possess an in-depth understanding of the nature and purpose of evaluation.

THE NATURE AND PURPOSE OF EVALUATION

Although a simple definition of the concept of evaluation can be misleading, it can nonetheless serve to clarify the term for our discussion. Evaluation is a process or cluster of processes that people perform in order to gather data that will enable them to decide whether to accept, change, or eliminate something—the curriculum in general or an educational textbook in particular. In evaluation people are concerned with determining the relative values of whatever they are judging. They are obtaining information that they can use to make statements of worth regarding the focus of the evaluation. They are interested in conducting evaluation to determine whether the expected or the planned for has occurred or is occurring in relation to the intended. Applied to curriculum, evaluation focuses on discovering whether the curriculum as designed, developed, and implemented is producing or can produce the desired results. Evaluation serves to identify the strengths and weaknesses of the curriculum before implementation and the effectiveness of its delivery after implementation.

The purpose of gathering such data about strengths and weaknesses is to allow curricularists to either revise, compare, maintain, or discontinue their actions and programs. Evaluation enables them to make decisions, to draw conclusions, and to furnish data that will support their decisions regarding curriculum matters.

As used here, evaluation focuses on the approval of the program and its components, as well as on the educators' delivery of such components.

This is in agreement with how most individuals interpret evaluation. However, at times in schools we evaluate individual students as to how they are succeeding in learning. When the focus is on individuals, many employ the term assessment. With assessment, one may not have any notion of changing the curriculum content. The purpose of gathering data is to determine how well a student is learning or behaving. However, at times we use assessment data to make changes in our teaching approaches. Some would classify this as *instructional evaluation.* However, to introduce this term along with curriculum evaluation seems to complicate the definitional issues. Suffice it to say that if we have judged a curriculum to be good we must also gather assessment data to inform us as to how students are doing.

Not all evaluation efforts, however, focus on securing data regarding the quality of the curriculum and/or making judgments regarding students' success in a program. Often, we investigate the appropriateness of a particular form of assessment or the procedure by which we are assessing students or evaluating the curriculum.[2] Frequently, evaluation efforts center on determining how to modify the staff's in-service education. Sometimes evaluation is directed toward making judgments on just how educators can communicate with and educate the community.

Evaluation Questions

Harriet Talmage has pointed out that a good part of educators' disillusionment with evaluation results because they misunderstand what it can and cannot do for them. We have perhaps been asking unrealistic or inappropriate questions of evaluation. Talmage discussed five types of value questions pertinent to evaluating curricula. An individual's approach to evaluation depends on which question or set of questions he or she poses.[3]

The Question of Intrinsic Value.   This question addresses the goodness and the appropriateness of the curriculum. It deals with the curriculum as it is planned and also with the finished curriculum as it is delivered. Essentially, if a school were dealing with a new language arts curriculum, it would ask whether the curriculum incorporates the best thinking to date on what is known about the content of language arts, the arrangement of that content, and the presentation of that content. Would specialists in linguistics, composition, grammar, and communication give the curriculum planned "high marks"?

But raising such questions is not a simple matter of getting experts to analyze the curriculum document. People bring to this question of intrinsic value their philosophical and psychological views. They perceive the curriculum in light of the purpose of education they see as paramount (Should we stress critical thinking, citizenship, or preparation for employment?) and what learning theory they prefer. (Behaviorists, cognitivists, and humanists have different views about content and methods for presenting it.)

The question of intrinsic value is difficult to process precisely, partly because there are subject areas in the school whose underlying principles are not carefully formulated. In science, there are underlying scientific principles about which most scientists and science educators agree. In contrast, bilingual educators would most likely express more diverse opinions about the underlying principles of their area of study.

The Question of Instrumental Value. This question posits, "What is the curriculum good for, and who is its intended audience?" Educators deal with the first part of this query by attempting to link up the curriculum planned with the goals and objectives stated for the program. Essentially, they judge whether what is planned in the program is going to address the goals and objectives stated. They can make this evaluation judgment by looking at the finished document; they also raise this question once the curriculum has been delivered.

The question of instrumental value also addresses whether what is planned in the curriculum will be attained, or to what extent, and by which students. In addition, this question concerns whether the philosophical or psychological orientation of the curriculum will be maintained, given the suggested contents, materials, activities, and methods. If a curriculum developer is a humanist, he or she might ask if the specifics planned for the curriculum are going to be instrumental in fostering in students a humanistic orientation toward

themselves and others. A behaviorist, on the other hand, might ask if the encounters planned in the program are such that students will attain the specific behavior at the intended level of competence.

The audience to be evaluated must be identified at the outset. The second part of the instrumental value question addresses this audience factor. Not all curricula planned may be of value to all students. Evaluation efforts should identify the types of students who are likely to benefit the most from the curriculum being planned.

The question of whom the curriculum serves, as well as the quality of students' experiences, is a key part of an approach to evaluation that comprises the critical–emancipatory emphasis of critical theorists. They believe that the curriculum must emancipate those students who have been oppressed by society in general and the curriculum in particular. Thus they are very interested in gathering evaluative data that indicate how effective the curriculum is in leading "oppressed" students to arenas of opportunity and freedom.[4]

The Question of Comparative Value. This question is often asked by those faced with possible new programs. Is the new program better than the one it is supposed to replace? Usually, new programs are created because people feel that the existing program is inadequate. Often, when dealing with the question, people get caught up in making comparisons between different programs with different goals. Is a program that stresses skill training better than a program that stresses contemporary issues of the world? Certainly, the two are different. Whether one is better than the other relates to the values people hold as educators. But, still, if the program being suggested for implementation is of the same type as the existing program, the question of comparative value should be considered.

Educators need to consider this question, in fact, more than just in terms of student achievement. They need to compare the two programs' ease of delivery, cost, demand on resources, role in the existing school organization, and responsiveness to expectations of the community.

The Question of Idealization Value. When dealing with evaluation, educators are not just concerned with determining whether what was planned actually happened. They are interested in engaging in actions that will furnish data that can help them decide how to make the program the best possible. They are concerned with taking their information on how the program is working and asking themselves if there are alternative ways to make the program even better—to heighten students' achievement or to involve students more fully in their own learning. This question requires continued action throughout the delivery of the new program. Educators must constantly ask themselves how they might fine-tune the program's content, materials, methods, and so on, so that students can derive optimal benefits from experiencing it.

The Question of Decision Value. If the previous four evaluation questions are addressed, the decisions made should be quality decisions. The evaluator and the curriculum decision maker should now have evidence documented in such a manner that they can decide whether to retain, modify, or discard the new program. Decisions have consequences, however. The question of decision value keeps the curriculum evaluator cognizant that the value of the decision or decisions made needs to be assessed as the curriculum is delivered in the school classrooms.

Definitions of Evaluation

The questions presented in the previous section suggest that evaluation is a process or group of processes by which evaluators gather data in order to make decisions. Like most concepts in education, there is no consensus as to the meaning of evaluation. Worthen and Sanders define evaluation as "the formal determination of the quality, effectiveness, or value of a program, product, project, process, objective, or curriculum." Evaluation includes inquiry and judgment methods: (1) "determining standards for judging quality and deciding whether those standards should be relative or absolute; (2) collecting relevant information; and (3) applying the standards to determine quality."[5]

Bruce Tuckman has defined evaluation as "the means of determining whether the program is meeting its goals: that is, whether . . . a given set of instructional inputs match the intended or prescribed outcomes."[6]

Ronald Doll defines evaluation as "a broad and continuous effort to inquire into the effects of utilizing content and process to meet clearly defined goals."[7] Somewhat similarly, Daniel Stufflebeam has defined evaluation as "the process of delineating, obtaining, and providing useful information for judging decision alternatives."[8]

What is the difference between research and evaluation? Stake and Denny point out that the difference deals with generalizability and application. "Almost always the steps taken by the researcher to attain generalizability tend to make his inquiries artificial or irrelevant in the eyes of the practitioner. The evaluator sacrifices the opportunity to manipulate and control but gains relevance to the immediate situation."[9]

Essentially, the researcher is interested in advancing knowledge by gathering data to enable the formulation of conclusions. These conclusions can guide the making of judgments as to the worth of the phenomenon being evaluated. Even this needs to be qualified, since many educators are engaged in action research in which the variables in a new program are manipulated so as to improve the program in question, rather than to produce some generalizable results.

Further enriching our discussion of just what is evaluation is the view of evaluation as critical inquiry. In some ways, this is related to evaluation as disciplined inquiry, that is, studying phenomena so as to make informed judgments. However, evaluation as critical inquiry emphasizes that most models of evaluation advanced in this century and their approaches to utilization have seemed to neglect the very concept central to the word evaluation, *value.* Many models discussed in this chapter share a common feature; they appear to be value free, that is, objective. What some evaluators want to do is to determine if the values implicitly or explicitly stated in the program are in fact attained. Does the program have worth or meaning? Is the program or curriculum valuable in the sense that its goals are attained? There is no attempt to judge the worth of the goals themselves or the social purposes to which the goals are employed in schools or society.

Kenneth Sirotnik and Jeannie Oakes expand on this concept of evaluation as critical inquiry. They argue that we should inquire into the assumptions undergirding the values we hold, the positions we advocate, the actions we undertake.[10] Many current evaluation models appear to fail to make explicit what the "good" is in evaluation activities. Most evaluators maintain that, while the presence and importance of values cannot be ignored, they can only be considered within a particular context. We judge whether the program attained its values and if those in charge of a curriculum have made their values explicit. Then what we evaluate is whether these goals have been attained. Thus, the evaluator approaches the task as a value neutral person. However, it can be argued that inquiry is not value free and evaluation cannot be value free.

Measurement versus Evaluation

Sometimes educators confuse measurement with evaluation. Other times they use the terms interchangeably to denote a general process of appraisal. Fred Kerlinger defines measurement as the assignment of numerals to objects or events according to rules. He points out that a numeral is a symbol of the form 1, 2, 3,. . . . It has no quantitative meaning unless someone chooses to give it such.[11] People use symbols to label objects, such as boxes of strawberries or learning packets. It is important to remember that they must also assign value and meaning to numerals. For example, an evaluation of 70 percent means nothing unless someone has stated that 70 percent means "passing" or "successful performance."

Measurement is really nothing more than the description of a situation or a behavior using numerical terms in order to avoid the value connotations that people can easily associate with words. A gym teacher can thus measure the number of times a student does pushups, a reading teacher can record the number of pages per hour a person reads, or a classroom teacher can indicate the score a child gets on a language skills test.

Measurement enables educators to record students' degrees of achieving particular competencies. Nonetheless, educators must do something with the data gathered; they must decide whether doing so many pushups is good, whether reading so many pages per hour indicates reading ability, whether a certain test score denotes success or failure. They must evaluate the data and make value judgments. Such judgments will be influenced by their understanding of the purposes of the program in particular and of education in general.

APPROACHES TO EVALUATION

Evaluation is a methodological activity that really is not content specific. The same procedures can be used to evaluate the effectiveness of any curriculum. Essentially, evaluation consists of gathering and combining data in relation to a weighted set of goals or scales so as to allow people to make judgments about worth. In determining the value of a curriculum plan, educators must eventually ask whether the results they expect to obtain are worth what the cost of delivering them is likely to be.[12]

How people specifically go about processing data is influenced by their philosophical and psychological postures. If they are behaviorists or if they believe in approaching evaluation from a prescriptive or sequenced orientation, they are likely to want to spell out specific entities of curriculum and instruction. They will want to have clearly stated objectives so that they can enact procedures that will furnish them with precise indicators of whether they—or, more precisely, their students—have achieved the intended outcomes of the program. If they are humanists, they are likely to be more interested in determining whether the situations planned have enabled students to improve their self-concepts. They may not pay as much attention to the students' specific achievements demonstrated by particular objective tests.

In general, evaluation focuses on and results in decisions in one of three areas: (1) decisions about course improvement; (2) decisions about individuals, teachers, and students; and (3) decisions about administrative regulation—actually judging how good the school system is and how good individual staff members are.[13]

Scientific and Humanistic Approaches to Evaluation

Lee Cronbach had identified the scientific and humanistic approaches to evaluation as opposite extremes on an evaluation continuum. Advocates of the scientistic end favor clinical or objective experiments; advocates of humanistic approaches consider experiments misinformative. Cronbach presented the *scientific* person as a believer in the true experiment:

> A true experiment . . . concentrates on outcome or impact and embodies three procedures: (1) Two or more conditions are in place, at least one of them being the consequence of deliberative intervention. (2) Persons or institutions are assigned to conditions in a way that creates equivalent groups. (3) All participants are assessed on the same outcome measures.[14]

Persons in this camp tend to concentrate their efforts on the learners. Data, frequently in the form of test scores, are employed to compare students' achievement in different situations. Information collected is quantitative, so it can be analyzed statistically. The decisions about the program or programs are made on the basis of the comparative information gained through the evaluation effort.

Most scientific approaches to evaluation draw on methods that have been utilized by physical scientists. Most schools still utilize these traditional procedures, despite much talk among curricularists of a need to change to procedures that furnish a more global view of the quality of curricula.[15] Objective tests, a hallmark of traditional approaches, are still major vehicles by which educators gather data. The quality of many curricular programs or the level of student understanding is still judged by a number or score on a standardized test.

Despite traditional evaluation methods still dominating school practice, there has been growing interest for the last three decades in what Cronbach categorizes as humanistic approaches. People are beginning to realize that to obtain more complete pictures of curricula, educators need to explore and then utilize alternatives to traditional evaluation procedures. Some of these alternatives are discussed later in this chapter.

As Cronbach has described, this increasingly popular approach is based on an ideal that is very different from the ideals that underly the scientific approach.

> Writers at the humanistic extreme find experiments unacceptable. For them, naturalistic case studies are the panacea. A humanist would study a program already in place, not one imposed by the evaluator. If persons are assigned to a treatment, that is because the policy under study calls for assignment; assignments are not made for the sake of research. The program is to be seen through the eyes of its developers and clients. Naturalistic investigators would ask different questions of different programs. Benefits are to be described, not reduced to a quality. Observations are to be opportunistic and responsive to the local scene, not prestructured.[16]

Those who approach evaluation from a humanistic or naturalistic posture analyze data collected in a way that differs significantly from that found in a scientistic evaluation. The data gathered in a naturalistic investigation are more qualitative than quantitative in nature. The evaluator relies more on impressions of what was observed. He or she engages in what are called "thick" descriptions of actual incidents that were observed during the evaluation effort. Data gained from interviews and discussions with participants are included in the evaluation. Patterns observed from the many observations form much of the data for analysis.

Today, the issue of approach to evaluation is not as clear cut. As Ernest House asserts, evaluation has moved from monolithic to pluralistic conceptions, to multiple methods, multiple criteria perspectives, and multiple audiences. Evaluators, who once for the most part viewed the methods of evaluation as primarily quantitative, are now coming to realize that qualitative methods are indeed appropriate means of processing data. Rather than viewing these two basic approaches as in conflict with each other, evaluators increasingly advocate mixed data collection methods.[17] A plurality of approaches seems to be the advice of the day.

However, some persons still consider quantitative and qualitative methods as essentially different ways of viewing the world. These people possess different senses of reality. Those firmly in the *quantitative* camp seem positivistic in their orientation to the world. Those favoring the *qualitative* approaches are perhaps post positivistic. According to House, most evaluators would not place themselves in either camp, but rather would attest to the fact that the qualitative and quantitative methods are complementary.[18] However, we maintain that most evaluators would still consider themselves as favoring one approach more than the other.

Although various models are employed in the traditional quantitative camp, most seem not to have particular names. Such is not the case with approaches to qualitative evaluation and research. Five major approaches in the qualitative camp have been identified: interpretive, artistic, systematic, theory driven, and critical–emancipatory.[19]

The *interpretive approach* requires that the evaluator consider the educational scene somewhat as a play with various actors. The evaluator must interpret the meaning and significance of the actors' actions. Attention to the social context of the play is essential. Also central is accepting the notion that not only is the evaluator interpreting the players' actions, but the actors within the educational drama are also socially constructing and subjectively interpreting meaning. The meanings that players give to their actions are modified through interpretive processes activated by the individual. The quality of reality for the curriculum program is created in the mind of the players. Essentially, the players are the evaluators, not people external to the curriculum. There is no objective world separate from personal perceptions.[20] With this approach the key judgments on the quality of curriculum or learning are primarily determined by the teachers and students engaged in the drama of curriculum.

In the *artistic approach,* the evaluator engages in aesthetic inquiry. Much as a connoisseur of fine wine tastes and observes, the individual observes and then announces publicly what is good or fine about the curriculum. This approach draws on an individual's intuition honed by experience.[21] The key advocate for this approach is Elliot Eisner, a professor of art and curriculum at Stanford University. Details of this approach are presented later in this chapter. Suffice it to say at this point that the evaluator's attention is focused primarily on the qualities of the relationships between teacher and students. Perception is key. The more classrooms and curricula experienced by the critic, the more meaningful are the judgments regarding the quality of the program.

Of the five approaches to qualitative research and evaluation, the *systematic approach* appears most familiar. Like traditional evaluators or researchers, persons in this camp accept the realistic epistemology that a real world exists. Reality is not within teachers' and students' minds. How-

ever, these qualitative researchers are not so positivistic as to claim that the external world is totally discoverable and, once discovered, reveals completely the truth of reality. The world is more than a machine that exists independently of the processes that we employ to view it.

Individuals try to be as objective as possible in their descriptions and base their judgments and their evaluations on fact. But these individuals, more often than not, employ descriptions and logical analyses of phenomena observed, rather than relying primarily on statistical techniques, the hallmark of the scientific, positivistic approach.

Numerous approaches can be clustered under the division of *theory driven.* Much current dialogue among curricularists gives ample evidence that many are evaluating curricula based on a theoretical or philosophical framework. Some individuals judge the quality of school programs by employing particular political theories. Others base their judgments on various social theories about class structure. Social structures and forces are considered as key influencing factors in the actions of individuals, in our case curriculum developers, teachers, and students.

Closely related to theory-driven approaches are those identified as *critical–emancipatory.* Advocates of this approach to evaluation are usually among the most radical curricularists. These individuals judge the quality and effectiveness by how well it rids individuals of those societal forces that constrain their development and fulfillment. These curricularists draw heavily on the work on Habermas dealing with the construction of knowledge and meaning. They also draw on critical theory, much of which has the imprint of Marx.[22]

Educators need not be tied to one or the other of these five major approaches. Indeed, there are several other ways to identify the approaches to evaluation. Evaluation can be classified as either utilitarian or intuitionist. The *utilitarian* is closely linked to the scientific, while the *intuitionist* is tied to the humanistic approach. The utilitarian evaluation operates under the premise that the greatest good is that which will benefit the greatest number of individuals.[23] This approach to evaluation looks at large groups such as an entire school or school district. Attention is on total group performances. Programs will be judged effective by considering how they affect the larger school student population. Those programs that allow the greatest number of students to attain the objectives will be judged of worth and appropriate to continue.

At the other end of the continuum is the intuitionist evaluation. Evaluators taking this approach are interested in gathering data to make judgments on the impact of the program on each individual. These approaches mirror those advocated by supporters of humanistic, qualitative evaluation. Persons taking this approach are interested in how individual students and subgroups of individuals are doing. Since attention is on individuals or small groups of individuals, there can be no one criterion of good. Rather, numerous criteria are employed to make judgments as to the worth of programs. Each person is the best judge of the quality of the program, not some outside evaluator. All those affected by the program can make judgments about the program; their opinion is considered more important than a clinical analysis of the program.[24]

Intrinsic and Pay-off Evaluation

In addition to looking at evaluation from a quantitative-qualitative or utilitarian-intuitionist continuum, we also can look at evaluation as either intrinsic or pay-off.

Evaluators can study the curriculum plan separately or they can study the effects of the curriculum after it is delivered to the students. Michael Scriven calls the first type *intrinsic evaluation.* The criteria for evaluation are not usually operationally formulated; evaluators are merely trying to answer the question: How good is the curriculum?[25] The criteria employed in such evaluation refer directly to the curriculum itself.

To evaluate curricula intrinsically, evaluators study the particular content included, the way in which the content is sequenced, the accuracy of the content, the types of experiences suggested for dealing with the content, and the types of materials to be employed. They might assume that if a curriculum plan has accurate content and a firm basis for its particular organization, it will be effective in stimulating particular student learning.

Although it may seem obvious that evaluators need to engage in intrinsic evaluation—that is, they must determine if the curriculum has value—some persons do neglect it. Rather than asking the

prior question, "How good is the curriculum?" they ask, "How well does the course or curriculum achieve its goals?" Unless educators have some judgment about the worth of the goals and objectives and the attendant content, they cannot be sure that attaining the goals through a particular course or curriculum is a good thing.

Once the basic worth of a curriculum has been evaluated, its effects when delivered must be examined. Scriven calls this *pay-off evaluation.* Often the outcomes are operationally defined. Evaluators can consider the effects not only on the students, but also on teachers, parents, and perhaps administrators. This approach to evaluation may involve making judgments regarding the differences between pre- and posttests and between experimental group tests and control group tests on one or more criterial parameters. Pay-off evaluation draws the most attention from educators. Its defenders assert that it is really the only one that counts, because it supplies information that allows them to determine the effects of the curriculum or course on learners.

Advocates argue that with their present state of knowledge, evaluators can only do "arm-chair" intrinsic evaluation. They cannot unequivocally defend the worth of some content or experience, but they can document whether in fact learners have attained a stated objective. Supporters of the intrinsic approach would counter that the important values do not really show up in the outcomes noted in a curriculum—outcomes to which pay-off people limit themselves. This is partly due, intrinsic people argue, to the deficiencies of present test instruments and scoring procedures. Also, the results reported in pay-off evaluation studies are usually short-term results of a curriculum. Little attention is given to the long-term outcomes of a particular program. If educators wish to have an idea of the relevance and perhaps elegance of a curriculum, they will best look at the materials directly, not at students' test scores.

Formative and Summative Evaluation

Another way to view evaluation is to distinguish between formative and summative evaluation. *Formative evaluation* encompasses those activities undertaken to improve an intended program. Evidence is sought so that decisions can be made about how to revise a program while it is being developed. That is, data are collected during the developmental phase of the program in order to modify the program before it is fully implemented in the school or district. During the developmental and early piloting stages of a curriculum, the evaluation effort provides frequent, detailed, and specific information to guide the developers. Formative evaluation takes place at a number of specified points during the curriculum development process. It provides the opportunity for the evaluator(s) to modify, reject, or accept the program as it is evolving.

How educators conduct formative evaluation varies widely. If they are evaluating only one unit plan, their manner of evaluation may be very informal, perhaps only involving those persons teaching the unit. However, if they are engaged in creating a new program for the entire school district, then the procedure of formative evaluation may be more formal and systematic.

Because curriculum development takes place over time, formative evaluation is especially well suited for guiding the creation and fine tuning of a curriculum. According to Gronlund and Linn, it allows the teacher and others involved in the evaluation not only to determine what intended effects are occurring, but also to record and examine the presence of unintended effects. It uses the process of feedback and adjustments and thus keeps the curriculum development process "open."[26]

Summative evaluation aims at getting the total picture of the quality of the produced curriculum. It is usually undertaken after the project has been completely developed and after it has been implemented school wide or district wide. It focuses on the effectiveness of the total course or total curriculum. Summative evaluation's major purpose is to enable the involved parties to draw conclusions about how well the curriculum or particular curriculum unit has worked. The name *summative* has been applied not because of any particular method employed, but rather because this type of evaluation obtains evidence about the "summed" effects of various components or units in a particular curriculum.[27]

SCIENTIFIC-POSITIVISTIC EVALUATION MODELS

Formal evaluation has a very long history. The ancient Chinese were giving civil service examinations to candidates as early as 2000 B.C. Early Greek teachers employed verbally mediated evaluation in their teaching. The first large-scale formal evaluation was reported in the United States in Joseph Rice's 1897 to 1898 comparative study of spelling performance of over 30,000 students in an urban school system. Also, Robert Thorndike's contributions to the issue of evaluation in the early 1900s cannot be ignored. Thorndike was instrumental in getting educators to measure human change.[28] Finally, the "Eight-Year Study," from 1933 to 1941, was a turning factor in educational evaluation.[29] In our view, it represented the beginnings of the modern era of program evaluation. The evaluation plan was organized in seven sequential steps: focusing on the goals and objectives of the program, classifying objectives, defining objectives in behavioral terms, finding situations in which achievements can be shown, developing or selecting measurement techniques, collecting student performance data, and comparing data against objectives.

Provus's Discrepancy Evaluation Model

A good example of a scientific–positivistic approach to evaluation is the model developed by Provus, which combines evaluation with systems-management theory; it consists of four components and five stages of evaluation. The four components are as follows: (1) determining program *standards,* (2) determining program *performance,* (3) *comparing* performance with standards, and (4) determining whether a *discrepancy* exists between performance and standards.[30] This is shown in Figure 11-1. Discrepancy information is reported to decision makers, who in turn must make a decision (or act) at each stage. The choice of decisions is to go to the next stage, recycle to a previous stage, start the program over, modify performance or standards, or terminate the program. It is the job of the evaluator to report to the decision maker and to identify problems and suggest what corrective actions are possible. When discrepancies exist, the decision maker is the key person in making decisions.

There are five stages in the Provus model, and they are described in Table 11-1. In all five stages, program performance is compared to program standards—criteria that have already been established.

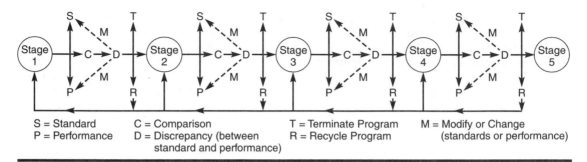

FIGURE 11-1   Components of Provus's Discrepancy Evaluation Model

Source: Malcolm Provus, "The Discrepancy Evaluation Model," in P. Taylor and D. M. Cowley, eds., *Readings in Curriculum Evaluation* (Dubuque, Ia.: Brown, 1972), p. 118; Provus, "Evaluation of Ongoing Programs in the Public School System," in R. W. Tyler, ed., *Educational Evaluation: New Roles, New Means.* Sixty-Eighth Yearbook of the National Society for the Study of Education, Part II (Chicago: University of Chicago Press, 1969), pp. 252–253.

1. *Design.* This involves a comparison of the program's design with a prescribed standard or criteria. The program is examined to determine if it is internally sound (adequacy of space, personnel, resources, materials, and so on) and externally sound (comparisons with similar programs that seem to work). The initial problems of the program are identified. Any discrepancy that exists between the program design and design standard is reported to the decision maker, who must decide whether the program should be rejected, modified, or accepted.

2. *Installation.* The actual operation of the program is compared with the installation standard or fidelity criteria. The characteristics of the program are evaluated, including facilities, media, methods, student abilities, and staff qualifications. Discrepancies between program installation and installation criteria are noted and reported to the decision maker for appropriate action.

3. *Processes.* Specific program processes are evaluated, including student and staff activities, functions, and communications. If the processes are inadequate, they should be reported to the decision maker who should make the appropriate adjustments.

4. *Products.* The effect of the whole program is evaluated in terms of the original goals. The products to be assessed can be in terms of student and staff products, as well as products related to the school and community. The information gained will assist decision makers about whether the program is worthwhile and should be continued as is, modified, or terminated.

5. *Cost.* The program products should be compared to products of similar programs; also, it should be evaluated in terms of cost-benefits. The methods of cost-benefit are not clearly explained. However, we must always ask whether the results are worth the cost—not only in terms of money but also morale and time taken away from other tasks. This answer has economic, social, and political implications.

TABLE 11-1   Stages of Provus's Discrepancy Evaluation Model

STAGES	PERFORMANCE	STANDARD
1	Design	Design criteria
2	Installation	Installation fidelity
3	Processes	Process adjustment
4	Products	Product assessment
5	Cost	Comparisons and cost-benefit

Source: From Malcolm Provus, "The Discrepancy Evaluation Model," p. 118; Provus, "Toward a State System of Evaluation," *Journal of Research and Development in Education* (September 1971), p. 93.

Provus claimed that his evaluation plan could be used to make evaluations of ongoing programs, in any stage, from the planning stage to the implementation stage. It could be used at the school level, school district level, and regional or state level.

Stake's Congruence-Contingency Model

In his discussion of evaluation, Robert Stake distinguishes between formal and informal evaluation procedures. While recognizing that educational evaluation continues to depend on casual observation, implicit goals, intuitive norms, and subjective judgment, he notes that educators should strive to establish more formal evaluation procedures. Formal procedures are objective rather than subjective and aim at furnishing data so that descriptions can be made and judgments rendered regarding the program being evaluated.[31]

Stake indicates that evaluation specialists seem to be, and rightly so, increasing their emphasis on providing full objective descriptions and on collecting and reporting hard data. Stake asks that evaluators collect and process more extensive types of data and that they consider the dynamics among the people involved in the curriculum process. Not only should evaluators assess the roles various people play, but they should be sure to allow those people more extensive participation in judging programs. Stake further maintains that those involved in curriculum evaluation must make judgments in addition to reporting data; they should even take positions on the worth of the program being evaluated.

Stake maintains that data can be organized into three bodies of information: antecedents, transactions, and outcomes. An *antecedent* is any condition that exists prior to teaching and learning that may influence outcomes. Antecedents are such things as the status or characteristics of the students prior to their lessons: their aptitudes, previous achievement scores, psychological profile scores, grades, discipline, and attendance. Antecedents also include teacher characteristics such as years of experience, type of education, and teacher behavior ratings. Antecedents are "entry behaviors," sometimes described as "inputs" by other evaluators.

Stake notes that *transactions* occur between and among students and teachers, among students and students, and among students and resource people. Transactions are interactions the students have with certain curriculum materials and classroom environments dealing with time allocation, space arrangements, and communication flow. Transactions comprise what is commonly called the "process" of teaching and instruction.

In our approach to evaluation, we have been concerned with *outcomes,* also called "products," of programs—particularly achievement, sometimes attitudes and motor skills. Evaluators also need to attend to such outcomes as the impact of a new program on teachers' perceptions of their competence. They need to evaluate the influence of a program's outcomes on the actions of administrators. They also need to consider outcomes that are not directly evident at the conclusion of a program. And they should attend to long-range effects, too. Stake contends that outcomes are the consequences of education—immediate and long-range, cognitive and affective, personal and community wide.[32]

Stake's model for planning an evaluation study provides an organizational framework that points out data to be considered and contrasts what is planned and what has occurred. This model arranges the three types of data into a matrix. Figure 11-2 shows the matrix. The model shows the antecedents, transactions, and outcomes—the elements of evaluation—both intended and observed.

The challenge to the evaluator is to identify contingencies, and later congruencies, among these antecedents, transactions and outcomes. *Contingencies* are the relationships among the variables in the three categories: antecedents, transactions, and outcomes. Ideally, it should be demonstrated that the outcomes are a result of antecedents and transactions. If it can be shown that transactions are related to prior antecedents, then the transactions are logically contingent on the antecedents. Similarly, the outcomes should be logically contingent from the transactions. In short, one category is expected to lead to observable and/or measurable variables in another category.

The model shows that the evaluator is also concerned with *congruence* between the intended and the observed outcomes. In dealing with congruency, he or she strives to match what is intended and what is observed. Did what

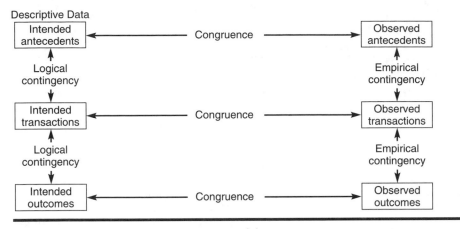

Descriptive Data

FIGURE 11-2   Congruence-Contingency Model

Source: From Robert E. Stake, "Language, Rationality, and Assessment," in W. H. Beatty, ed., *Improving Educational Assessment and an Inventory of Measures of Affective Behavior* (Washington, D.C.: Association for Supervision and Curriculum Development, 1969), p. 20. Used with permission.

intended actually happen? To be completely congruent, all the intended antecedents, transactions, and outcomes would have to occur.

Stufflebeam's Context, Input, Process, Product Model

Perhaps the most important contribution to a decision-management-oriented approach to educational evaluation has been that presented by Daniel Stufflebeam. His approach to evaluation is recognized as the CIPP (context, input, process, product) model.[33] This comprehensive model considers evaluation to be a continuing process.

Information is provided to management for the purpose of decision making. It is a three-step process: *delineating* the information necessary for collection, *obtaining* the information, and *providing* the information to interested parties. Any evaluation study must include these three steps. Corresponding to these decision types are four types of evaluation: (1) context, (2) input, (3) process, and (4) product.

Context Evaluation. Context evaluation involves studying the environment of the program. Its purpose is to define the relevant environment, portray the desired and actual conditions pertaining to that environment, focus on unmet needs and missed opportunities, and diagnose the reason for

unmet needs. Context evaluation is really a "situation analysis,"—a reading of the reality in which individuals find themselves and an assessment of that reality in light of what they want to do. This diagnosis stage of evaluation is not a one-time activity. It continues to furnish baseline information regarding the operations and accomplishments of the total system. See Curriculum Tips 11-1.

Input Evaluation. The second stage of the model, input evaluation, is designed to provide information and determine how to utilize resources to meet program goals.

Input evaluators assess the school's capabilities to carry out the task of evaluation; they consider the strategies suggested for achieving program goals, and they identify the means by which a selected strategy will be implemented. At this stage, we might consider alternative designs in terms of how they will contribute to the attainment of objectives in terms of resources, time, and budget. Here we are focusing on what is feasible.

Input evaluates specific aspects of the curriculum plan or specific components of the curriculum plan. It deals with the following questions: Are the objectives stated appropriately? Are the objectives congruent with the goals of the school? Is the content congruent with the goals and objectives of the program? Are the instructional strategies appropriate? Do other strategies

================= *Curriculum Tips 11-1* =================

Assessing the Curriculum Context

Most curricular actions occur within a socialized context and most all their delivery or enactment processes take place within a socialized context. Those in charge of the overall program need to evaluate the process by which they create and deliver curriculum. The following tips can assist in assessing the context of curricular action:

1. Determine the values, goals, and beliefs that drive the curriculum.
2. Obtain a reading of the community, noting the key players.
3. Determine the history of past curricular activity.
4. Get some indication of the physical facilities available and necessary for enactment of the curriculum.
5. Judge the pressures for actions, both for and against, generated from within and without the community and school district.
6. Determine the budget needed and the budget allocated.
7. Determine what performance outcomes are important for the school and community.
8. Get a fix on the perceptions, expectations, and judgments of teachers and administrators and what they expect out of the evaluation and how they intend to use it.

---

exist that can also help meet the objectives? What is the basis for believing that using these contents and these instructional strategies will enable educators to successfully attain their objectives?

Process Evaluation.   This stage addresses curriculum implementation decisions that control and manage the program. It is used to determine the congruency between the planned and actual activities. It includes three strategies. "The first is to detect or predict defects in the procedural design or its implementation stage, the second is to provide information for decisions, and the third is to maintain a record of procedures as they occur."[34]

In dealing with program defects, or the first strategy, it is important for educators to identify and monitor continually the potential sources of the project's failure. They must pay attention to the logistics of the entire operation, and they must maintain communication channels among all affected parties. The second strategy involves decisions to be made by project managers during the implementation of a project. For example, some decisions may require that certain in-service activities be planned and carried out before the program's actual implementation. The third strategy addresses the main feature of the project design, for example, the particular content selected, new instructional strategies, or innovative student–teacher planning sessions.

Process evaluation, which includes the three strategies, occurs during the implementation stage of curriculum development. It is a piloting process conducted to "debug" the program before district-wide implementation. From such evaluation, project decision makers obtain information they need to anticipate and overcome procedural difficulties and to make decisions.

Product Evaluation.   Product evaluators gather data to determine whether the final curriculum product now in use is accomplishing what they had hoped. To what extent are the objectives created being attained? Product evaluation provides evaluators with information that will enable them to decide whether to continue, terminate, or modify the new curriculum. It allows them to link actions at this stage of the model to other stages of the total change process. For example, a product evaluation might furnish data that show that the science curriculum planned for talented science students has successfully allowed students to attain the program objectives. The program is now ready to be implemented in other schools in the system.

Judicial Approach to Evaluation

Many educators still believe that the evaluator should judge in an impartial and nonvalue-laden manner. However, even within the scientific camp, individuals are coming to realize that evaluations are made by humans and humans have values. A rather new model being used in making evaluations sets up an encounter, rather than precisely spelling out steps to take. This model is the judicial model or what some call the adversary evaluation approach.[35]

This procedure encompasses numerous evaluation activities in which time is scheduled for opposing points of view to be heard. One evaluator or team member serves as the program's advocate, presenting the positive view of the program. Another evaluator or team member plays an adversial role, stressing problems in the program. The encounter is very much like a court trial. People to be affected by the new program have their day in court. By allowing individuals to present both sides or opposing views of the new program, a more accurate view of the new program is attained. The program stands or falls on the weight of the evidence furnished.

In addition to following judicial court proceedings, this adversary approach to evaluation can also be used in curriculum hearings, community town meetings, and formal debates. With the current emphasis on participant involvement in the evaluation process, this adversary approach may well serve to not only judge the value and effectiveness of a program, but give both the community within the school and outside the school a broad view of the program and also the underlying rationale. Not only are people apprised of the evaluation data, but the entire process can be considered educational for all parties. See Curriculum Tips 11-2.

HUMANISTIC AND NATURALISTIC EVALUATION MODELS

The previous models draw heavily on the quantitative and technical posture of evaluation. However, some evaluation theorists take issue with these scientific approaches to evaluation. They feel that evaluators have become much too concerned with observing or measuring specific behavioral objectives and generating elaborate evaluative schemes to measure program success.[36] In many ways, these critics reflect the growing awareness that educators have become obsessed with a positivistic paradigm, a mechanistic view of the world that consists of competencies, checklists, and tiny behaviors that can be assessed.

A new approach to evaluation has taken form, a thinking that places the evaluator in the center of things. Evaluators not only visit sites, but they are often personally involved in arguing their values and cases with colleagues. Evaluators are not separated from the system, looking on as disinterested parties; rather, they are viewed as integral parts of the very process they are evaluating. These persons believe in more humanistic or naturalistic methods of inquiry.

Numerous approaches to evaluation can be included under humanistic methods. However, all share the view that there are many realities and that the evaluator is influenced by his or her own values. In essence, these evaluators realize, accept, and even appreciate the "messiness" of the arena within which evaluation efforts are undertaken. Those urging use of humanistic or naturalistic procedures argue for a more holistic engagement that presents us with much more detail. With these methods, we get portraits of the situations we are evaluating. Evaluation reports are less lists of numbers than they are written descriptions of what was found or what occurred. The approach focuses more on human interactions than on outcomes and more on the quality than on the quantity of classroom or school life.

Scientific approaches may have revealed data that depicted what people did, but naturalistic approaches, while interested in that, are also concerned about delving into the *why* behind the *what* of performance. The stress is on interpretative understanding rather than on objective explanation.[37]

Where scientific evaluators might just ask what did students learn, humanistic or naturalistic evaluators might query the actual value of the knowledge that is known or presented in the curriculum. They observe the curriculum through political and social lenses. The pictures we get of

---

===== *Curriculum Tips 11-2* =====

Conducting Hearings and Court Encounters

Permitting hearing or court sessions allows the evaluation process to be public for both staff and community. It also encourages evaluators to look at more than just test scores to determine the success of a program. As the suggestions below indicate, these procedures can add a sense of drama to the evaluation process, which might well serve to encourage all those in the school to take an interest in the evaluation phase of curriculum activity.

1. Keep the rules for the proceedings flexible. Do not get into thinking that this is actually a court case.
2. Keep the rules of evidence simple. Again, this is not a court of law. We want to see if the evidence presented is relevant to the "court" hearing.
3. Be sure that all parties have presented the "hearing" office with all relevant materials (reports, test data, teachers' comments, names of witnesses to the use of the program).
4. Be sure that both sides have a copy of the changes or challenges to the program before court begins.
5. Conduct the session so that witnesses feel free to participate and to undergo cross-examination.
6. Include the testimony of expert witnesses, as well as outside consultants.
7. Schedule pretrial conferences so that the actual day or days in court are used to get a true picture of the effectiveness of the program.
8. Allow others to participate in the trial besides those who are the two key parties.

Source: Adapted from T. R. Owens, "Educational Evaluation by Adversary Proceeding," in E. R. House, ed., *School Evaluation: The Politics and Process* (Berkeley, Calif.: McCutchan, 1973).

---

programs are not only about content but also about the social significance of the content. We begin to judge the moral overtones of what we are doing with our programs, of what we are trying to accomplish. Such evaluation efforts are a far cry from the traditional position that inquiry is value free.

Eisner's Connoisseurship Evaluation Model

The previous models draw heavily on the quantitative, technical posture of evaluation. Elliot Eisner has recommended a process, called educational criticism and connoisseurship, that will supposedly produce more than hard data and outcomes. It will furnish a rich or qualitative description of educational life as a consequence of new programs.[38] Eisner notes that, to employ the procedure of educational criticism, evaluators

should ask such questions as "What has occurred during the school year at a particular school as a result of the new program? What were the key events? How did such events arise? How did students and teachers participate in these events? What were the reactions of the participants to these events? How might the events have been made even more effective? Just what do the students learn from experiencing the new program? These questions focus on process, on school life, and on school quality. They differ in kind from questions raised in the quantitative camp.

Eisner's case for educational criticism and connoisseurship draws heavily from the arts. If an individual is to be an illuminating critic of painting, opera, theater, film, or even wine, he or she must first be a connoisseur—that is, he or she must possess knowledge about and experience with the type of phenomenon he or she is to criticize. A good critic has an awareness and appreciation of the subtle qualities of the situation; he or she can detect and write about the nuances of the situation in ways that help others to become more aware of the phenomenon under consideration.

Eisner points out that educational connoisseurship is "the art of appreciating the educationally significant."[39] But such appreciation is made public through criticism—the description, interpretation, and assessment of the situation. In discussing his approach to evaluation, Eisner relies on personal observations, expert opinion, and group corroboration instead of scientific validity.

Eisner would have the evaluators engaged in such qualitative activities as being participant classroom observers and asking many questions about the quality of the school and the curriculum. An evaluator following Eisner's model would also engage in a detailed analysis of pupils' work. He or she would use films, videotapes, photographs, and audio tapes of both teachers and students in action; the person would also note what is done, what is said, and, perhaps more importantly, what is not done and not said. The evaluator would strive to describe the *tone* of the curriculum in action.

Additionally, an evaluator with this orientation might well employ evaluation by using portfolio analysis. Portfolios are collections of the students' works that exhibit their progress and achievement in one or more areas. The collection must include student participation in selecting contents and the criteria for judging merit.[40] Portfolios allow people to supply what they think is important for others to judge in order to make an evaluation as to the nature and degree of learning. They allow an educator to picture students in a broader context, in effect to get a more complete view about which to reflect and evaluate.

Eisner makes the point that evaluation should allow for some form of communication to some public—parent, school board, local or state agency—about what has been and is occurring in the school. The evaluator presents or describes the educational scene. To some extent, such evaluation takes on a subjective and aesthetic approach; for this reason, it is considered controversial by those who believe in objective and scientific documentation. Finally, the connoisseurship model has many characteristics of what is sometimes called responsive evaluation.

Stake's Responsive Evaluation Model

Responsive evaluation is a term popularized by Robert Stake and is more concerned with evaluating curriculum or program activities and processes than intents or outcomes; it relies more on informal and natural communication than formal and standard communication.[41] Like with the Eisner evaluation model, the responsive approach is more concerned with the portrayal of the program than standardized data, test scores, and goals—what some people might label as methodological or objective data. Responsive evaluation requires planning and development, but it relies less on formal statements and research-oriented information than do technical-scientific models of evaluation. Using the responsive approach, the evaluator tells the story of the program, presents its features, describes the clients and personnel, identifies major issues and problems, and reports the accomplishments. The evaluator assumes the posture of a critic reviewing a play or a painter depicting a landscape scene.

To conduct responsive evaluation, Stake maintains that the evaluator develop a plan that deals with the scope and activities of the program. He or she must arrange for people to make observations, prepare narratives and portrayals, and provide product displays. Because all of us have particular biases, the various audiences of the report must be identified; their feelings and expressions of what is worthwhile and important should be considered. The data reported must be analyzed in terms of the audience's biases, and they (as well as personnel of the program) must have a chance to react to the findings. To perform this task, the evaluator will probe and ask questions. Various participants and audiences may become defensive and seek to avoid or confront the evaluator. However, important questions about quality must be examined and processed.

Stake outlines the steps of responsive evaluation as applied to evaluating a curriculum. (Ten steps are listed; number four is the authors' based on interpretation of the entire model.)

1. Negotiate a framework for evaluation with the sponsors.
2. Elicit topics, issues, and/or questions of concern from the sponsors.

3. Formulate questions for guiding the evaluation.

4. Identify the scope and activities of the curriculum; identify the needs of clients and personnel.

5. Observe, interview, prepare logs and case studies, and so on.

6. Pare down the information; identify the major issues or questions.

7. Present initial findings in a tentative report.

8. Analyze reactions and investigate predominant concerns more fully.

9. Look for conflicting evidence that would invalidate findings, as well as collaborative evidence that would support findings.

10. Report the results.[42]

Many of these steps are related to goal-free evaluation, which is concerned with the biases of evaluation. In goal-free evaluation, the evaluator is expected to be objective, not influenced by the goals or objectives of the program or the values of the program developer or sponsors.

Illuminative Evaluation Model

Another naturalistic approach to evaluation is illuminative evaluation, sometimes called explication. It strives to furnish a complete picture of the educational program. Originally, developed by Parlett and Hamilton, this procedure illuminates problems and significant features of an educational program. The method allows the evaluator to discern the total program and to gather data about the particular workings of the program. There are three steps to the model: observation, further inquiry, and explanation.[43]

1. *Observation.* The first stage involves a general look at the program to orient oneself to the program and to describe the context within which the curriculum is being delivered. Attention is given to all factors that might influence the program. Thus, data can be gathered on the arrangement of school subjects, the types of teaching and learning styles evident, the materials being used, and even the types of evaluation methods employed by the teacher.

2. *Further inquiry.* Here the evaluator brings a focus to the evaluation, separating the significant from the trivial. During this second stage, the evaluator strives to get the individuals affected by the program to gain an understanding of it, not just to know if the program works, but also why it works. Further inquiry or progressive focusing emerges out of continually examining the program in action. This means that the evaluator spends extended time in the field. He or she also gathers data by examining school documents and portfolios of the students' work and from interviews and questionnaires with staff and parents.

3. *Explanation.* The evaluator using this model is not attempting to pass judgment on the program, but rather to furnish data on what is happening with the program and why. The evaluator's explanations are presented to those affected by the program. Upon receiving such information, these people can then engage in decision making.

The illuminative model assumes an artistic perspective, insisting that education is a complex and dynamic set of interactions. These interactions are to be observed and evaluated holistically and subjectively because they cannot be broken down into artificial ways or discrete categories for objective measurement. Illumination deals with the unintended categories and parts; it deals with the subtle aspects of the environment, the items that are often missed or discarded by the so-called objective observer.

Illuminative evaluators try to avoid taking sides, that is, which perspective is correct. They wish to accept the validity of both scientific and humanistic approaches to evaluation; they contend there are weaknesses and strengths in both approaches. Hence, other humanistic/naturalistic models become acceptable to the field.

Portraiture Model

While not strictly an evaluation model, portraiture can be used much like illuminative evaluation or Eisner's connoisseur model. Sara Lawrence Lightfoot developed this method, drawing from the field of anthropology.[44] In conducting a portraiture, an evaluator would go into a school, the field, and observe what was occurring regarding the curriculum. This individual would observe teachers and students in classrooms and look at school documents and students' work. He or she would conduct interviews and employ questionnaires. From these sources the evaluator would create a thin description. This description is basically a narrative in which what is actually occurring is recorded. If teachers teach a particular topic in the curriculum, or if teachers and students behave in particular ways, it is jotted down in the evaluator's journal.

Once the evaluator has completed a thin description, he or she then creates a "thick" description, which is an attempt to interpret what is recorded in the thin description. In creating this report, the evaluator engages in a process similar to that of explanation in illuminative evaluation. This thick description or portrait is then presented to the school or to those in charge of evaluating the curriculum.

A portrait is a compressed ethnography in which the evaluator attempts to capture the spirit of the school program, to not only tell what was done, but to offer some thought on the reasons behind actions. The portrait writer draws on his or her creative or aesthetic abilities in addition to his or her scientific abilities. There are usually five elements to a thick description: (1) description of the setting and activities, (2) recording and commentary about people in the systems, (3) inclusion of dialogue, (4) interpretation of the situation, and (5) impressionistic records.

When writing a portrait, the evaluator allows his or her feelings to enter into the document. However, the portrait should be such that those who receive it will recognize it as referring to them and their program. Ideally, the portrait is outlined in a manner that allows the emergence of themes or patterns to occur. Well-done portraits capture the insider's views of what is central to the conduct of the curriculum. Table 11-2 contrasts the scientific and humanistic approaches and Table 11-3 presents an overview of all the evaluation models.

PRACTICES AND ISSUES OF EVALUATION

The previous models involve a variety of practices. Although there is some disagreement about the precise steps that evaluation would take, some notion of how to proceed through the evaluation process is useful. Presented next are phases of evaluation that educators can follow. These steps draw heavily from the technical-scientific approach to curriculum. But, even a humanistic approach to evaluation would have to focus on the curricular phenomena being evaluated. Evaluators

TABLE 11-2 Contrasting Scientific-Positivist and Humanistic-Naturalist Approaches

AXIOMS	SCIENTIFIC-POSITIVIST PARADIGM	HUMANISTIC-NATURALIST PARADIGM
Nature of reality	Reality is single, tangible, and fragmentable	Realities are multiple, constructed, and holistic
Relationship of knower to the known	Knower and known are independent, a dualism	Knower and known are interactive, inseparable
Possibility of generalization	Time and context-free generalizations are possible	Time and context-bound working hypotheses are possible
Possibility of causal linkages	There are real causes, temporally precedent to or simultaneous with their effects	All entities are in a state of mutual simultaneous shaping, so it is impossible to distinguish cause from effect
Role of values	Inquiry is value free	Inquiry is value bound

Source: Yvonna S. Lincoln and Egon Guba, *Naturalistic Inquiry* (Beverly Hills, Calif.: Sage, 1985), p. 37. Used with permission.

TABLE 11-3   Overview of Evaluation Models

MODEL	AUTHOR	APPROACH	VIEW OF REALITY	POSSIBILITY OF GENERALIZATION	ROLE OF VALUES
Provus discrepancy model	Provus	Scientific	Reality is tangible, single	Yes	Value free
Congruence-contingency model	Stake	Scientific	Reality is tangible, single	Yes	Value free
Context, input, process, product model	Stufflebeam	Scientific	Reality is tangible, single	Yes	Value free
Judicial model	Wolf, Worthen, and Sanders	Scientific	Reality is tangible, single	Yes	Value free
Connoisseurship model	Eisner	Humanistic	Realities are multiple, holistic	No	Value bound
Responsive-evaluation model	Stake	Humanistic	Realities are multiple, holistic	No	Value bound
Illuminative model	Parlett and Hamilton	Humanistic	Realities are multiple, holistic	No	Value bound
Portraiture model	Lightfoot	Humanistic	Realities are multiple, holistic	No	Value bound

would also need some means, whether objective or subjective, of collecting the information.

Phases of Evaluation

As just mentioned, to carry out an evaluation, an evaluator must have a plan of action. Much has been written on what steps are necessary to accomplish this. The following steps seem to be common to most evaluators' discussions:

1. *Focusing on the curricular phenomena to be evaluated.* In this step, evaluators determine just what they are going to evaluate and also what design they will use. They determine the focus of the evaluation: Will it be the total school system or a particular school? Will it be one particular subject area or grade level within that school? In this con-

nection, evaluators spell out the objectives of their evaluation activity and identify the constraints and policies under which the evaluation will be conducted.

2. *Collecting the information.* In this step, evaluators identify the sources of information essential for consideration and also the means they can use to collect that information. They also map out stages for collecting the information in terms of their time schedule.

3. *Organizing the information.* Here evaluators organize the information so that it becomes interpretable and usable to the final intended audience. They note means of coding, organizing, storing, and retrieving the information.

4. *Analyzing the information.* At this stage, evaluators select and employ appropriate analysis techniques. The specific techniques they choose depend on the focus of the evaluation.

5. *Reporting the information.* Here evaluators decide the nature of the reporting, keeping in mind the audience for the report. They might engage in an informal reporting, such as giving opinions and making judgments based on general perceptions. They might, however, decide that their evaluation should more rigorously collect, treat, and report the data. The final report would have detailed statistical data.

6. *Recycling the information.* The need for current information involves continuous reevaluation and reassessment—a continuous attempt to improve the curriculum. Even if the curriculum appears to be viable, continuous feedback, modifications, and adjustments are necessary because forces affecting the schools are always changing.

In relaying information to the intended audience, the evaluators need to do more than just report—that is, tell the results. They should also relay their interpretations of the data, drawing from the analysis stage, and make recommendations for action. They need to help determine how the information and the results will be used. They need to make judgments. If they have been working for those responsible for the overall curriculum, then they may just submit their recommendations to the curriculum decision makers to do with as they wish. Sometimes, evaluators are also charged with ensuring that their recommendations are carried out. This is especially true when the evaluators are working directly for the central school office. In such instances, evaluators may indicate means by which their recommendations can be accomplished.

Of course, some person or persons must be in charge of these phases of evaluation. Schedules and budgets have to be determined. Ideally, the management aspects of evaluation should be carefully planned at the outset of the evaluation effort, whereby various stages of evaluation are outlined with timetables, divisions of labor (people assigned to tasks), and cost allocations per task and then totaled.

Alternative Assessment

In curriculum evaluation, educators are interested not only in the quality and value of the curriculum, but they also wish to gather data that will allow judgments to be made as to how students did with the curriculum experienced. This concern is the focus of assessment. Assessment cannot be divorced from curriculum evaluation. Certainly, we want to know the level of student attainment.

For most of this century, data were gathered on students by use of either teacher-made or standardized tests. These instruments are still very much a part of the total evaluation or assessment picture. However, one part of national and local efforts at educational reform is a move to alternative forms of assessment. This is a key issue that should continue well into the next century.

The movement to alternative forms of assessment attempts to address the shortcomings that have resulted from an overreliance on traditional standardized tests. Such tests have given us scores that only compare one group of students with another. We ended up with numbers that *really* did not enable us to say much about how students were doing or were affected by the curriculum. Furthermore, these tests assessed students in ways that little resembled how students would actually utilize the tested knowledge or skills in the world. In other words, the tests were not real or authentic situations. The move today, which should continue, is to employ methods that allow us to observe directly students' work and their skilled performances.[45]

These methods are known as alternative assessments. Like any term, there are variations of meaning and even arguments as to meaning. Many employ the term as synonymous with authentic assessment or performance assessment. Certainly any method that employs evaluative measures other than multiple-choice or like-developed objective tests is an alternative assessment. And almost all the alternatives engage the student in a performance or in a recording of a performance. However, Meyer argues that performance assessment and authentic assessment are not the same. For an alternative assessment to be authentic, it must engage students in tasks or activities that are real world or resemble the real world.[46] The tests cannot be contrived by the teacher.

An example of a performance assessment lacking authenticity is to have students engage in a writing assessment exercise. Students are informed that they will write a short story that will be used to judge writing skills. The teacher presents the students with a precise formula for preparing to write and for the actual writing of the short story. The students with this "manual" are given one fifty-minute period for three days. The first day is devoted to generating the topic for the story, the second day to creating a rough draft, and the final day to revising and preparing the final draft.[47] Certainly the students would be engaged in the process of writing, but few writers in the real world actually write short stories under such rigid time frames or following such a limiting manual, *for writing short stories.*

To make the writing of a short story authentic, the teacher might not present it as a summative activity to be done in a contrived context. In fact, teachers might not require students to write a short story. Rather, teachers might indicate that students are to engage in creative writing throughout the year and to file such writing in portfolios. Students would have opportunities to select the time for their writing, to share drafts with the teacher and other students, and to revise their writing according to an individualized schedule. In this case, students are engaging in writing activities that resemble more closely how professional writers actually create stories. This performance assessment is authentic.

Many alternative assessment approaches exist. Educators should strive to make all of them as authentic as possible. These approaches include real problem solving, designing and conducting experiments on real problems, engaging in debates, constructing models, creating videotapes of performances, doing actual fieldwork, creating exhibits, developing demonstrations, journal writing, creating new products, formulating computer simulations, and creating portfolios. This is not an exhaustive list. The key is to remember that authentic assessment employs strategies and approaches that connect students with real-life situations and conditions.[48]

Authentic assessment is more than the gathering of students' products. It also involves teachers' observations and inventories of students' work with accompanying commentary regarding the judgments made. It contains evaluative story lines about both individuals and groups within the school classroom.

Table 11-4 presents some points comparing alternative, authentic assessment and traditional paper-and-pencil test assessment.

Creating tables that compare approaches always triggers questions as to which is better. We would argue that both alternative assessment and traditional assessment be utilized. We sometimes tend too quickly to accept new practice. As Wolf and Reardon caution, "if new forms of assessment are to work, they require serious gestation."[49] Educators must reconceptualize their idea of intelligence, must rethink what it means to know something, must redefine excellence, and must rethink their measurement habits.

Glasser has suggested that with new assessment approaches we should utilize new criteria. The first criterion is "access to educational opportunity." Educators should design assessment so as to be able to gather data on the possibility for fostering student growth. Does the assessment approach contemplated allow us to realize possible ways to get students into a growth pattern regarding their learning? The second criterion is "consequential validity." The assessment we employ should allow us to see the consequences of instructional effects. Can we make statements that certain best practice is really positively influencing student learning and behavior? The third criterion is "transparency and openness." Here the assessment employed should be such that the processes and products of learning are clearly visible to the evaluator. The fourth criterion is "self-assessment," which means that individuals are able to judge their own achievement. Indeed, one of the new issues in assessment is making the student an active participant. The fifth criterion Glasser proposes is "social situation assessment." Alternative assessment should be an integral part of group activity. Assessment data should inform the educator not only about what a student knows, but also about how well the student works with others and adapts to group dynamics. The sixth criterion is "extended tasks and contexualized skills." This refers to having the assessment represent meaningful tasks. Essentially, alternative assessment activities are themselves learning opportunities. The activities tie into overall learning and have relevance to the knowledge implicit in the overall curriculum goals. The last criterion is "scope and comprehensiveness." Alternative

TABLE 11-4 Alternative Assessment versus Traditional Assessment

ALTERNATIVE ASSESSMENT	TRADITIONAL ASSESSMENT
Samples: student experiments, debates, portfolios, student products	*Samples:* multiple-choice tests, matching tests, true–false tests, completion tests
Evaluation judgment based on observation and subjective, yet professional, judgment	Evaluation judgment based on objective recording and interpretation of scores
Focus on individual student in light of his or her learning	Focus more on score of student as it compares with scores of other students
Enables evaluator to create an evaluation story regarding an individual or group	Enables evaluator to present student knowledge as a score only
Evaluation tends to be idiosyncratic	Evaluation tends to be generalizable
Furnishes data in ways that allow curricular action	Furnishes data in ways that inhibit curricular or instructional action
Allows students to participate in their assessment	Tends to place evaluation under the aegis of the teacher or external force

Source: Adapted from Dennis Palmer Wolf and Sean F. Reardon, "Access to Excellence through New Forms of Student Assessment," in Baron and Wolf, eds., *Performance-based Student Assessment: Challenges and Possibilities.* Ninety-fifth Yearbook of the National Society for the Study of Education (Chicago: University of Chicago Press, 1966), pp. 52–83.

assessment practices should address a range of learnings and performances. Such practices should not just be centered on a narrow understanding of a particular content.[50]

These criteria suggest that alternative assessment is a continuous activity that is integral to the enactment of the curriculum and the students experiencing it. It is not an activity solely done at particular times of the year to obtain information on student knowledge or progress. Alternative assessment is ongoing. Teachers and students continually generate questions as to how well things are being taught and learned. A paper trail is created that allows one to develop a picture of how well curricular actions are going and the quality of student learning.

Portfolios. The portfolio is perhaps the most popular technique of alternative assessment. It is a compilation of student work gathered over time that furnishes evidence of a student's understandings, skills, and even dispositions to act in particular ways.[51] The portfolio contains a sampling of student work and even written evidence of a student's thinking and feeling that is comprehensive

enough to provide a picture of how the student is doing. The sampling of materials in the portfolio covers an extended time period, usually the academic year. In this way, students, teachers, and parents can obtain concrete evidence of a student's growth over the time period. For instance, at the beginning of the year students can put in a term paper or composition. Another one can be included in the portfolio at the end of the school year. Students and teachers can view and critique the two papers to see if composition has changed for the better. Students can observe whether the sophistication of their writing has changed; they can consider evidence that will inform them whether process learning has occurred.

A key benefit of the portfolio is that it allows the student to present his whole person and the teacher to judge him or her in that fashion. Another benefit is that the student is forced by the very act of creating a portfolio to reflect on his or her work, his or her knowledge and understanding. The student has more than a list of scores or letter grades. He or she has the means to add evidence to the assessment of "How I did this year." Furthermore, the portfolio furnishes the student, teacher, and the parent with material for conversation. In discussing the contents of the portfolio, all parties develop a sense of the individual's achievement, progress, and development both as a person and student.[52]

What is contained in a portfolio should be negotiated by the teacher and student. There is no set list. Students can include summaries of their activities and research reports. They can use photographs that they have taken, videotapes that they have made, computer printouts that they have designed, drawings, and artwork. They can even include tests that they have taken. Homework assignments can be part of the document.[53] The central point is that the data included should foster the creation of a complete assessment picture of the student's abilities, understandings, dispositions to act, and affective stances.

High-stakes Assessment

Education is expensive, and the public is increasingly concerned with getting the best for their education dollar. The public has been for some time demanding that schools be held accountable. For successful schools, the public is suggesting rewards, sometimes in the form of additional monies. For schools that fail to measure up, sanctions are being mandated, often in the form of reduced funding or public notification of not performing well. Having the public look at performance-based assessment as a means of holding schools accountable gives schools incentives for doing well, but it also places educators at all levels under extreme pressure to perform. Most of the high-stakes discussion goes beyond or in many cases ignores the alternative means of assessment previously discussed. Often whether a school or school district performs well is tied to how the students score on standardized tests. These tests are still the dominant means by which assessment data are obtained. There is dramatic growth of high-stake testing of students. And while high-stakes testing programs are initiated with the goal of increasing educational quality and standards of achievement, they often have an opposite effect.[54]

Frequently, when teachers realize that their jobs and the reputation of their schools are on the line as the result of how well their students do on tests, the teachers actually teach to the test. Some argue that teaching to the test is not bad if the test is well constructed and valid. However, ideally tests should furnish data by which judgments can be made about student performance, the appropriateness of the curriculum, and the effectiveness of the instructional delivery system. With high-stakes examinations, many teachers teach to the goals and objectives of the test rather than to those of the curriculum. And the achievements of students align much more closely with examination objectives than with the objectives developed for the local curricula.[55] For this to happen, teachers actually teach the test, frequently using sample items from tests to coach their students to do well. And while scores are usually higher in such instances, one wonders if this is really evidence of students learning more and of higher-quality curricula.

Some individuals suggest that teacher pay be tied to students' test results. When students do well, teachers will get pay raises. If students fail to perform, teachers will have their pay adjusted accordingly. Faced with this prospect, it is most likely that teachers will take the safe way out and teach to the test. If this becomes common practice, it is likely that teacher-centered instruction will gain even more strength and innovative pedagogies will be inhibited.[56]

But high-stakes testing does not affect only teachers. Students are also affected by this practice when various tests and assessment procedures become the keys by which to open the doorways to diplomas. Currently, several states require students to pass competency exams in order to receive their diplomas. Students who fail receive only a certificate of attendance. Using exams to either give or withhold diplomas may run into legal challenges. It is possible that students might sue school districts for failing to "teach" them to pass such a high-stakes exam. Schools would have to defend their actions by arguing that they did provide students with opportunities to learn the skills, attain the competencies, and gain the understandings that the test assessed.[57]

As the information age matures, it is likely that demands for the assessment of teachers and students will likely increase. Already, we have companies that have designed materials that assist teachers and students in playing the high-stakes game with success. Commercially prepared materials have been developed that make students comfortable with test formats, scoring rules, and strategies for taking educated guesses. Materials have been created to coach students in ways of reducing test anxieties. By themselves such materials are not inappropriate. However, as students become more "test-wise," we may have a more difficult time interpreting the results of the test. Does a student do well because of a skilled test coaching situation or does the student really understand what the test is assessing? Will doing well on a high-stakes test give students a false sense of knowledge and skill that will not serve them well in the emerging, chaotic future of the twenty-first century? Whatever our reaction to such testing, it is certain that low-stakes testing, integrated to teacher-designed assessment procedures, will be overshadowed by high-stakes testing.

Intended Outcomes versus Goal-free Evaluation

Mauritz Johnson, who states that curriculum is a series of intended learning outcomes, argues that evaluators should indicate at the outset just what they want their program to accomplish in order to determine how to evaluate it.[58] Tyler has also, on occasion, told educators that they must define the objectives of a program and indicate the situations in which students would be given the opportunity to accomplish the objectives. Most evaluators favor using objectives for this purpose.

This seems logical, especially if evaluation is considered purposeful behavior—actions meant to determine the worth of the curriculum or whether the curriculum allowed students to attain the objectives stated. But for many years Scriven has been advocating a goal-free approach to evaluation.[59] Scriven argues that sometimes people wish to engage in evaluation just to examine the effects of an educational innovation and to judge the quality of the effects produced. He calls such evaluation goal-free evaluation; its purpose is to determine the actual effects of the program by recording and interpreting what occurred during and as a result of the program.

Taking this approach, an evaluator does not confine his or her energies to the stated objectives of the new program, but instead gathers data to assess and evaluate the outcomes, whatever they may be. The educator employs a wide variety of measures to do this. He or she uses both quantitative and qualitative measures to get a picture of the program in action and also a reading of what has happened to students from having experienced the program.

If educators employ goal-free evaluation measures, they may get a more accurate picture of both the intended and the unexpected results of how the curriculum functions. The trouble is, many educators are not goal free; they are compelled by strong views about schools and society and have already made up their minds about the worth of certain programs and curriculum before the outcomes are known.

Norm-referenced and Criterion-referenced Measurement

Two basic approaches to testing dominate curriculum evaluation. Norm-referenced measurement is the most common. In this approach, the student's performance on a particular test is compared with the performance of other students who also took the same test. The students as a group establish a norm. Student norms can be grouped by age, grade level, ethnicity, sex, geographical location, or any other easy to categorize factor.

Standardized achievement tests, probably the most well-known norm-referenced tests, identify persons of varying ability. They have, however, questionable value for measuring the quality of a curriculum or the instruction. Such tests do not relate specifically to the goals and content of a particular curriculum. These tests are designed to measure what a student knows in a particular subject (say reading or math) in relation to other students at a given time. However, they do not measure effectively what has been taught.[60] Despite their limitations, standardized tests are often administered to determine the success of the curriculum and for evaluating the effectiveness of teaching.

The alternative to the norm-referenced test is the criterion-referenced test. These tests are designed to report how a student performs or demonstrates a skill or task or understands a concept with respect to some fixed criterion. Such tests indicate a learner's performance that can be stated as some specific educational objective, such as the ability to identify longitude and latitude lines on a map or the ability to multiply two-digit numbers.[61] With these tests, students either attain mastery or nonmastery of each objective to which a test item refers. While the test produces a total score, it is the score on each item or related items that is of interest to the evaluator.

Criterion-referenced tests indicate what the students can and cannot do with regard to specific content, skills, and attitudes. In effect, they indicate changes in learning over time, compared to normative tests, which compare students and measure learning at a specific time. The student has either learned or not learned to do something, understands or does not understand something, or shows progress in understanding something as a result of experiencing the curriculum.

Criterion-referenced tests focus on the specific tasks and competencies that have been stressed in a particular curriculum. Because these tests are curriculum specific, they have special value to those who wish to evaluate a new curriculum in their school district. Evaluators can use such tests to gather data that will enable educators to determine what has been taught and the overall effectiveness of the curriculum.

Criterion-referenced tests can also reveal whether a student has mastered particular material. Thus, these tests can be used for student evaluation as well as program evaluation.[62] Educators can use the results of such tests to determine what specific remedies are necessary for particular students. Test results can be employed to indicate that students are ready to proceed to other stages in the curriculum.

Even though the criterion-referenced test enables educators to correct some of the shortcomings of the norm-referenced test, it does have some problems or disadvantages of which educators should be aware. One is that it addresses specific objectives. A great number of such tests, up to ten or fifteen, are thus necessary to get a thorough picture of the curriculum. Second, it is not easy to determine the standards for acceptable performance that criterion test items are supposed to measure. Just what is the cutoff score for mastery of an objective? However, educators usually get around this difficulty by setting the passing score arbitrarily; for instance, they may require the student to get three out of four correct. But, is three out of four really mastery?

Perhaps the most serious criticism of criterion-referenced tests is that most lack reliability

information; in fact, most of these tests are constructed without any attention to reliability. However, criterion-referenced tests have curricular validity (the items usually coincide with the objectives of the curriculum).[63] Table 11-5 presents a comparison of these two types of tests.

Human Issues of Evaluation

Many good evaluation reports, valid in all technical details, have failed because of interpersonal insensitivity, ethnic or racial considerations, or political naivete.[64] Educators increasingly realize that evaluation is not just a technical exercise set apart from people. Evaluation reports are presented to and received by important stakeholders. The manner of the presentation determines in part if the evaluation results will be buried or misused, or misinterpreted, or just ignored. Human, ethical, and political factors comprise many aspects of curriculum evaluation.

Ernest House has indicated that social conflict has placed the problems of values into prominence. If the evaluation process encapsulates the values, then where do the values come from and fit in an evaluation effort? Whose values are most worthwhile? In large part, programs have been evaluated in terms of goals and objectives, and whether they have been attained. However, increasingly we are being forced to ask if the goals and the objectives are of value. Just whose values are they? From where do the criteria of merit come?[65]

Different groups, jockeying for power and to have their views represented, point to the increasing politicalization of curriculum evaluation. Over the years, evaluation has come to be seen as part of the political process. Often schools release tests results not to improve programs but to impress various power groups within the community or to demonstrate to legislators that an educational program is effective. Sometimes, test results are broadcast to convince various minority groups that their children are experiencing equity within the school system.

Considering multiple interests and how they should be woven into the evaluation process places us within the realm of social justice. One educator states that the evaluation community to

TABLE 11-5 Comparison of Norm-Referenced Tests (NRT) and Criterion-Referenced Tests (CRT)

CHARACTERISTIC	NRT	CRT
1. Comparisons Made	Score to group average	Score to minimum standard
2. Purpose	Survey or achievement test	Mastery or performance test
3. Validity	Content, criterion or construct	Content *and* curricular
4. Degree of Validity	Dependent on instruction	Usually high
5. Reliability	Usually high	Usually unknown
6. Importance of Reliability to Test Model	Important	Unimportant
7. Traits Measured	Exist in varying degrees	Present or not present
8. Usability		
Diagnoses	Low general ability	Specific problems
Estimation of Performance	Broad area	Specific area
Basis for Decision Making	How much was learned	What has been learned
9. Item Difficulty	Medium	Easy items
10. Administration	Standardized	Variable
11. Size of Group Tested	Large	Small
12. Content Covered	Broad	Narrow
13. Skills Tested	Integrated	Isolated
14. Control of Content	Publisher	Instructor or School
15. Limitations	Inability of school personnel to interpret tests on local level	Difficulty of constructing quality tests
16. Versatility	Extensive	Limited
17. Comparison of Results Between Schools	Readily available	Not yet developed
18. Distribution of Scores	Normal (one)	Rectangular (two)
19. Range of Scores	High	Low
20. Repetition of Test if Test Is Failed	No, one test	Until mastery occurs
21. Basis for Content	Expert Opinion	Local Curriculum
22. Quality of Items	High	Varies, depending on ability of test constructor
23. Pilot Testing	Yes	No
24. Basis of Item Quality	High Discrimination	Content of items
25. Student Preparation	Studying for test does not help much	Studying for test should help
26. Teaching to Test	Difficult to do	Encouraged
27. Standards	Averages	Performance levels
28. Scores	Ranking, standard score, or number correct	Pass or fail
29. Type of Measure	Relative	Absolute
30. Purpose	Ranking students	Improving instruction
31. Revision of Test	Not possible	Often necessary
32. Student Information about Test Content	Little available	Known in advance
33. Motivation of Students	Avoidance of failure	Likelihood of success
34. Competition	Student to student	Student to criterion
35. Domain of Instruction	Cognitive	Cognitive or psychomotor

Source: Allan C. Ornstein and David A. Gilman, "The Striking Contrasts Between Norm-Referenced and Criterion-Referenced Tests," *Contemporary Education* (Summer 1991), p. 293.

some degree is reluctant to confront issues of social justice in the educational system. Part of this reluctance stems from a misunderstanding of what the evaluation process should accomplish and the reluctance to consider the politics of education.[66] Evaluators are hesitant to engage in conducting evaluation or in reporting results in ways that will alienate the numerous audiences. Evaluators often realize that reporting on certain data will only add fuel to discontented groups.

Placement of Evaluation and Assessment

The high-stakes testing discussed earlier has given rise to what is commonly called measurement-driven instruction (MDI). Advocates of measurement-driven instruction actually think that the test should drive the instruction and shape the curriculum. Tests can and should determine what is taught, how it is taught, and even what is learned and the manner of such learning. In this approach, achievement tests actually become the targets of instruction. Teachers organize their instruction so as to address the assessment focuses. Viewing evaluation and assessment in this matter actually makes the tests into a de facto curriculum.[67] What shall students learn, a key question in curriculum, is answered by "whatever is on the high-stakes tests." Actually, believers in measurement-driven instruction say that even low-stakes tests should determine the focus of instruction.

Measurement-driven instruction seems to be a part of much of the reform efforts currently in place. Educational policy makers have found that institutional resistance to educational change can be overcome by instituting external, high-stakes examinations. Advocates of this approach to assessment are found among the public, teachers, and even students.

As with any issue, some do not believe that measurement-driven instruction is appropriate. A key argument against it is that measurement-driven instruction puts tests designers and external policy makers, sometimes politicians, in the "driver's seat as to what is important to learn." Teachers and curriculum specialists are left out of the loop. Opponents of MDI are proponents of an opposite-stance, instruction-driven measurement (IDM). The curriculum should determine the appropriate means of assessment and evaluation. These people argue that measurement-driven instruction leads to cramming, narrows the curriculum, centers attention on those skills most easily measured by our current tests, dampens creativity among teachers and students, and essentially takes from teachers the opportunity to make professional judgments.[68] In contrast, when designing curriculum one should consider the appropriate means of judging the quality of the curriculum and assessing how well students do. The curriculum should define how evaluative and assessment data are gathered.

Many persons advocating alternative assessment procedures favor instruction-driven or influenced measurement. Certainly those who recommend that assessment should be authentic favor this. These individuals pose the question of what we want students to learn prior to asking the question of how we determine whether they have learned what we want.

ROLES PLAYED IN EVALUATION

Over three decades ago, Hilda Taba maintained that evaluation is a cooperative activity. This cooperation is as necessary to the process of evaluation as it is to the various activities of the total curriculum.[69] It is necessary in forming the overall evaluation plan, in selecting the instruments and evaluation model to be applied, and in carrying out all stages of evaluation.

In a school-wide evaluation effort, teachers, administrators, evaluators, and even students and parents need to cooperate to determine what is necessary to make judgments regarding the curriculum. They need to coordinate the gathering and formating of data. Evaluation decisions are not made by one teacher or one administrator in isolation, and they are not made about only one aspect of the curriculum. Usually, such decisions relate to the entire curriculum and all the people responsible for delivering it.

Taba indicated that perhaps the best reason for cooperative evaluation of the curriculum is that such a collective effort allows all involved to get a total curriculum picture. For example, teachers can work together to provide evidence of the effects of the curriculum on various types of students. If they work alone, teachers only realize how the program worked with their own students. If they collaborate, they can ascertain the program's effectiveness with all types of students.

Students

Mention has been made in several places in this book that students should be active learners. This being the case, students also should assume some responsibility for evaluating not only their own learning, but also for assessing the curriculum. Students can work with teachers in classrooms and curriculum committees in deciding the worth and effectiveness of various curriculum components. Of course, their involvement will be geared to their maturity and age levels.

Some educators hold that students are never too young to assume an active role. In a school district in Oregon, students from kindergarten are in charge of student-led parent conferences.[70] Student-led parent conferences not only allow parents to find out how well their child is doing, but also allow the student to reflect on what he or she is learning and how to share such reflections with his or her parents and teacher. Stiggins, head of the Assessment Training Institute based in Portland, has stated that "Student-led parent conferences may be the biggest breakthrough in communicating about student achievement in the last four decades. The level of responsibility it brings to students and the pride in accomplishment that it can engender when they succeed is unprecedented."[71]

Involving students is more extensive than just letting them lead a parent conference. Ideally, students participate in and in some cases are actually in control of assessing their own learning. Having students participate in their own assessment and evaluate the curriculum increases the students' agency, that is, their right to manage and perform in their own lives in socially acceptable and personally meaningful ways.[72] Self-assessment both provides students and teachers with valuable data and serves to nurture in students autonomy rather than dependency.[73] They grasp that as a learner they must also make judgments regarding the level and significance of learning.

Students should play increasing roles in determining what procedures of evaluation will be applied to judge how much learning is occurring.

Educators are now giving students responsibilities for creating portfolios containing their own work and their comments on how well they liked and how much they learned from particular curriculum units.[74]

And students are not just being asked to evaluate their own work. They are getting opportunities to work cooperatively to assess the quality of their peer's learning. In other schools, they participate in evaluating teachers—and these evaluations are sometimes considered for merit and tenure. It is likely that students will play increasing roles in evaluation to personalize their own learning and to work as a partner in the curriculum process.

Teachers

Teachers are perhaps the most obvious professionals who should assume evaluation roles. In some cases, they have worked alone in evaluating the curriculum, and in other cases, they have been shut off from the evaluation process. Indeed, teachers should be involved in cooperative curriculum work, and they should have partial responsibility for program evaluation. Today teachers realize that they can play several roles in evaluation.

As we employ more humanistic or naturalistic approaches to evaluation, teachers will play an involved, ongoing role in curriculum evaluation. They may well create journals or stories that record the successes and failures of various curricula being attempted. They may generate portraits of their class to compare how students have responded to the curriculum over time. Teachers may even evaluate their own and their students' feelings regarding a program in action. Eventually, teachers will become key players in an expanded conception of the evaluation process. They will likely determine the nature of their involvement in evaluation. The time is past when teachers only passed out tests or answered questionnaires designed by evaluators.

Evaluators

Cooperation among all parties engaged in curriculum development and delivery is necessary. Even though various people can play particular roles in an overall evaluation, it is wise to have one person in charge. This person, the evaluator, should work with the central school office, which administers the curriculum.

The evaluator can be a member of the school system. There are several advantages to this. The person knows the system and its goals. It is usually less expensive to conduct an evaluation if the evaluator is already on the school payroll. Because the person is an insider, the results of his or her evaluation may be accepted more easily. However, there are also disadvantages to having an insider as the key evaluator. An insider may not be willing to issue an evaluation report that is critical of the system. He or she may also have too many other responsibilities to be able to undertake a major evaluation effort. Furthermore, his or her expertise might not be considered to be at the same level as that of an outside expert.

The evaluator is one of the agents of the evaluation team and is usually an observer. He or she designs the means of gathering data so that knowledge can be supplied to decision makers. Note that the evaluator does not supply the values with which the data gathered will be used; rather he or she helps the decision maker to clarify his or her values so that they can be addressed.[75]

In theory, the evaluator serves as the eyes and the ears of the decision maker. In this role, he or she furnishes data gathered from observations about how the curriculum is functioning in the school. It is up to the curriculum coordinators, curriculum advisory committees, and the administrators to take the data gathered, to judge their value, and to then act on them. The evaluator is essentially a support person to the curriculum-development and implementation efforts.[76]

Consultants

It is sometimes wise for a school district to hire an outside consultant to conceptualize the evaluation approach and to coordinate the evaluation effort. Often small schools do not have any staff persons trained, especially for evaluation. When they require such activity, a common procedure is for them to bring in an outside person. In fact, some educators argue that the evaluator of a new program should always be an outsider.[77] Such a person, having no "professional turf" to guard, can be much more objective and truthful in reporting findings.

The resources of the school district, the extent of the evaluation effort, and the level of the staff's expertise should guide educators deciding whether to bring in an outside consultant for evaluation. An outside consultant should have expertise, but he or she may be viewed as an intruder from outside the system or as a representative of the central office, which would impede the evaluation process. The person in charge of the curriculum-development effort must take these factors into consideration.

Parents and Community Members

Unquestionably, education involves politics. Those affected by education should be involved in some aspects of decision making about education, including curriculum matters. Parents, and even community members without children, should be involved in curriculum evaluation efforts. The particulars in such involvement can be worked out with school officials. The point is that parents should not just be readers of evaluation reports or receivers of test results. Parents and community members should be contributing participants of curriculum teams engaged in all aspects of curiculum—and that includes evaluation.[78]

CONCLUSION

The nature and purpose of evaluation are associated with making decisions about curriculum matters. A number of questions dealing with the value of evaluation were examined, along with several definitions. Most scientific definitions involve inputs and outputs, or determining goals and then assessing results. Humanistic definitions deal with the values we hold and our biases within the evaluation process. We made the case that evaluation is an essential aspect of curriculum development; it requires expertise and resources, just as the other major stages in curriculum development.

Evaluation is a complex stage. This was keenly illustrated by the evaluation models that were examined. These evaluation models were divided into scientific and humanistic approaches. The field of curriculum evaluation is not without argument. To illuminate some of the dynamics of the field, we discussed methodological issues relating to evaluation. These ranged from selecting and forming objectives to choosing the types of tests to employ when gathering data. The chapter closed by pointing out various roles that people can play in the evaluation effort.

ENDNOTES

1. George F. Madaus and Thomas Kellaghan, "Curriculum Evaluation and Assessment," in Philip W. Jackson, ed., *Handbook of Research on Curriculum* (New York: Macmillan Publishing Company, 1992), pp. 119–154.
2. Ibid.
3. Harriet Talmage, "Evaluating the Curriculum: What, Why and How," *National Association for Secondary School Principals* (May 1985), pp. 1–8.
4. Madaus and Kellaghan, "Curriculum Evaluation and Assessment"; William F. Pinar, William M. Reynolds, Patrick Slattery, and Peter M. Taubman, *Understanding Curriculum* (New York: Peter Lang, 1995).
5. Blaine R. Worthen and James R. Sanders, *Educational Evaluation: Alternative Approaches and Practical Guidelines,* 2nd ed. (New York: Longman, 1987). pp. 22–23.
6. Bruce W. Tuckman, *Evaluating Instructional Programs,* 2nd ed. (Boston: Allyn and Bacon, 1985), p. 1.
7. Ronald C. Doll, *Curriculum Improvement, Decision Making and Process,* 8th ed. (Boston: Allyn and Bacon, 1992). p. 237.
8. Daniel L. Stufflebeam, *Educational Evaluation and Decision Making* (Itasca, Ill.: Peacock, 1971), p. 25.
9. R. E. Stake and T. Denny, "Needed Concepts and Techniques for Utilizing More Fully the Potential of Evaluation," in R. W. Tyler, ed., *Educational Evaluation: New Roles, New Means.* The Sixty-Eighth Yearbook of the National Society for the Study of Education, Part II, (Chicago: University of Chicago Press, 1969). pp. 370–390.
10. Kenneth A. Sirotnik and Jeannie Oakes, "Evaluation as Critical Inquiry: School Improvement as a Case in Point," in K. A. Sirotnik, ed., *Evaluation and Social Justice: Issues in Public Education* (San Francisco: Jossey-Bass, 1990), pp. 37–60.
11. Fred N. Kerlinger, *Behavioral Research: A Conceptual Approach* (New York: Holt, Rinehart and Winston, 1979).
12. Michael Scriven, "The Methodology of Evaluation," in J. R. Gress and D. E. Purpel, eds., 2nd ed. *Curriculum: An Introduction to the Field* (Berkeley, Calif.: McCutchan, 1988), pp. 340–412; Blaine R. Worthen and Vicki Spandel, "Putting the Standardized Test Debate in Perspective," *Educational Leadership* (February 1991), pp. 65–69.
13. Lee J. Cronbach, "Course Improvement through Evaluation," *Teachers College Record* (May 1963), pp. 672–683.
14. Lee J. Cronbach, *Designing Evaluations of Educational and Social Programs* (San Francisco: Jossey-Bass, 1982), p. 24.
15. Madaus and Kellaghan, "Curriculum Evaluation and Assessment."
16. Cronbach, *Designing Evaluations of Educational and Social Programs.*
17. Ernest R. House, "Trends in Evaluation," *Educational Researcher* (April 1990), pp. 24–28.
18. Ibid.
19. Madaus and Kellaghan, "Curriculum Evaluation and Assessment."
20. Ibid.
21. Ibid.
22. Pinar et al., *Understanding Curriculum;* Madaus and Kellaghan, "Curriculum Evaluation and Assessment."
23. Ernest R. House, "Assumptions Underlying Evaluation Models," in G. F. Madaus, ed., *Evaluation Models: Viewpoints on Educational and Human Services* (Hingham, Mass.: Kluwer Publishers, 1983), pp. 45–64; Worthen and Sanders, *Educational Evaluation: Alternative Approaches and Practical Guidelines.*
24. I. E. Seidman, *Interviewing as Qualitative Research* (New York: Teachers College Press, Columbia University, 1991); Worthen and Sanders, *Educational Evaluation: Alternative Approaches and Practical Guidelines.*
25. Scriven, "The Methodology of Evaluation."
26. Norman E. Gronlund and Robert L. Linn, *Measurement and Evaluation in Teaching,* 6th ed. (New York: Macmillan, 1990).
27. Robert M. Gagné, Leslie J. Briggs, and Walter W. Wager, *Principles of Instructional Design,* 3rd ed. (New York: Holt, Rinehart and Winston, 1988).
28. Robert L. Thorndike, *Applied Psychometrics* (Boston: Houghton Mifflin, 1982).
29. H. H. Giles, S. P. McCutchen, and A. N. Zechiel, *Exploring the Curriculum* (New York: Harper & Row, 1942); R. E. Smith and Ralph W. Tyler, *Appraising and Recording Student Progress* (New York: Harper & Row, 1942).
30. Malcolm Provus, *Discrepancy Evaluation for Educational Program Improvement and Assessment* (Berkeley, Calif.: McCutchan, 1971).
31. Robert E. Stake, "The Countenance of Educational Evaluation," *Teachers College Record* (April 1967), pp. 523–540.
32. Ibid.

33. Daniel Stufflebeam, *Educational Evaluation and Decision Making* (Itasca, Ill.: Prosuch, 1971).

34. Ibid, p. 229.

35. Robert L. Wolf, "The Use of Judicial Evaluation Methods in the Formulation of Educational Policy," in G. F. Madaus, ed., *Evaluation Models,* pp. 189–204; Worthen and Sanders, *Educational Evaluation: Alternative Approaches and Practical Guidelines.*

36. Sigrun Gudmundsdottir, "Story-maker, Storyteller: Narrative Structures in Curriculum," *Journal of Curriculum Studies* (May–June 1991), pp. 207–218; Gene I. Maeroff, "Assessing Alternative Assessment," *Phi Delta Kappan* (December 1991), pp. 272–281.

37. Sirotnik and Oakes, "Evaluation as Critical Inquiry: School Improvement as a Case in Point."

38. Elliot W. Eisner, *Educational Imagination: On the Design and Evaluation of School Programs,* 3rd ed. (New York: Macmillan, 1993).

39. Ibid., p. 226.

40. Linda Darling-Hammond, "Instructional Policy into Practice," *Educational Evaluation and Policy Analysis* (Fall 1991), pp. 233–242; F. Leon Paulson, Pearly R. Paulson, and Carol A. Meyer, "What Makes a Portfolio a Portfolio?" *Educational Leadership* (February 1991), pp. 60–64.

41. Robert E. Stake, *Evaluating the Arts in Education* (Columbus, Ohio: Merrill, 1975).

42. Robert E. Stake, *Program Evaluation: Particularly Responsive Evaluation* (Kalamazoo, Mich.: Evaluation Center of Western Michigan University, 1975); Robert E. Stake and James A. Pearsol, "Evaluating Responsively," in R. S. Brandt, ed., *Applied Strategies for Curriculum Evaluation* (Alexandria, Va.: Association for Supervision and Curriculum Development, 1981), pp. 14–28.

43. M. Parlett and D. Hamilton, "Evaluation as Illumination: A New Approach to the Study of Innovative Programs," in G. V. Glass, ed., *Evaluation Studies Review Annual* (Beverly Hills, Calif.: Sage, 1976).

44. Sara Lawrence Lightfoot, *The Good High School.* (New York: Basic Books, Inc. 1983).

45. Linda Darling-Hammond and Jacqueline Ancess, "Authentic Assessment and School Development," in Joan Boykoff Baron and Dennie Palmer Wolf, eds., *Performance-based Student Assessment: Challenges and Possibilities,* Ninety-fifth Yearbook of the National Society for the Study of Education, Part 1 (Chicago: University of Chicago Press, 1996), pp. 52–83.

46. Carol A. Meyer, "What's the Difference Between 'Authentic' and 'Performance' Assessment?" *Educational Leadership* (May 1992), pp. 39–40.

47. Ibid.

48. Bruce Frazee and Rose Ann Rudnitski, *Integrated Teaching Methods* (Albany, N.Y.: Delmar Publishers, 1995).

49. Dennie Palmer Wolf and Sean F. Reardon, "Access to Excellence through New Forms of Student Assessment," in Baron and Wolf, eds., *Performance-based Student Assessment: Challenges and Possibilities.*

50. Darling-Hammon and Ancess, "Authentic Assessment and School Development."

51. David J. Martin, *Elementary Science Methods, A Constructivist Approach* (Albany, N.Y.: Delmar Publishers, 1997); June R. Chapin and Rosemary G. Messick, *Elementary Social Studies,* 3rd ed. (New York: Longman, 1996).

52. Martin, *Elementary Science Methods, A Constructivist Approach.*

53. Ibid.

54. Madaus and Kellaghan, "Curriculum Evaluation and Assessment."

55. Ibid.

56. Ibid.

57. Northwest Report (Portland, Oreg.: Northwest Regional Educational Laboratory (Summer 1995).

58. Mauritz Johnson, "Definitions and Models in Curriculum Theory," *Educational Theory* (April 1967), pp. 127–139.

59. Scriven, "The Methodology of Evaluation."

60. Dale Findley and Robert Estabrook, "Teacher Evaluation: Curriculum and Instructional Considerations," *Contemporary Education* (Summer 1991), pp. 294–298; B. Worthen and V. Spandel, "Putting the Standardized Test Debate in Perspective."

61. W. James Popham, *Modern Educational Measurement,* 2nd ed. (Englewood Cliffs, N.J.: Prentice Hall, 1990).

62. Norman E. Gronlund, *Stating Objectives for Classroom Instruction,* 2nd ed. (New York: Macmillan, 1978); Gronlund, *How to Construct Achievement Tests,* 4th ed. (Englewood Cliffs, N.J.: Prentice Hall, 1988).

63. Allan C. Ornstein, "Comparing and Constructing Norm-Referenced and Criterion-Referenced Tests," *NASSP Bulletin* (1993); Allan C. Ornstein and David A. Gilman, "The Striking Contrasts Between Norm-Referenced and Criterion Referenced Tests," *Contemporary Education* (Summer 1991), pp. 287–293.

64. Worthen and Sanders, *Educational Evaluation: Alternative Approaches and Practical Guidelines.*

65. Ernest R. House, "Trends in Evaluation," p. 281.

66. David P. Ericson, "Social Justice, Evaluation and the Educational System," in K. A. Sirotnik, ed., *Evaluation and Social Justice: Issues in Public Education,* pp. 5–22.

67. Madaus and Kellaghan, "Curriculum Evaluation and Assessment."

68. Ibid.

69. Hilda Taba, *Curriculum Development: Theory and Practice* (New York: Harcourt, Brace, 1962).

70. Northwest Report (Portland, Oreg.: Northwest Regional Educational Laboratory (February 1997).

71. Ibid.

72. George J. Posner, *Analyzing the Curriculum* (New York: McGraw-Hill, Inc., 1992).

73. David Pratt, *Curriculum Planning* (New York: Harcourt Brace College Publishers, 1994).

74. Andy Paulson and Carol Meyer, " What Makes a Portfolio a Portfolio?" *Educational Leadership* (February 1991), pp. 60–64.

75. Stufflebeam, *Educational Evaluation and Decision Making.*

76. Rebecca K. Hawthorne, *Curriculum in the Making* (New York: Teachers College Press, Columbia University, 1992); Peter F. Oliva, *Developing the Curriculum,* 4th ed. (New York: Longmans, an imprint of Addison-Wesley, 1997).

77. James A. Beame, Conrad E. Toepfer, and Samuel J. Alessi, *Curriculum Planning and Development* (Boston: Allyn and Bacon, 1986); Ernest House, *Evaluating with Validity* (Beverly Hills, Calif.: Sage, 1980).

78. Warren Chapman, "The Illinois Experience: State Grants to Improve Schools Through Parent Involvement," *Phi Delta Kappan* (January 1991), pp. 355–358.

CURRICULUM ISSUES AND TRENDS

Focusing Questions

1. Should the federal government become more involved in setting national goals, academic subject matter, and/or standards of achievement? Why? Why not?

2. How can school people deal with censorship issues? How does one determine an appropriate school curriculum?

3. Why do textbooks play such a major role in determining the curriculum?

4. How can the curriculum be made more relevant to the needs and interests of students?

5. What are the major issues involving compensatory education? How has compensatory education influenced curriculum development?

6. Why is multicultural education a central issue of curriculum?

7. What major challenges face those concerned with school reform?

8. Why is moral education such a challenging issue for educators?

9. What issues are raised by the increasing presence of technology in the schools?

10. Why is curriculum likely to become more of a political issue in the future?

Given the rapidity of change in society, the volumes written about education, the exponential explosion of knowledge, the numerous conferences and conventions dealing with education and curriculum, certain trends and events have affected the field of curriculum. These events and trends are likely to continue well into the next century. One reason for the continuation of the events and their related issues is that they represent global ideas that have to be constantly juxtaposed against current contexts.

Schools exist within the emerging society. Educators are not only curriculum specialists and generalists, but they are also members of society and advocates of certain groups and ideas. As society changes and new forces and factors influence our lives, we are required to appraise the realities of the times and to determine whether the curricula within the schools need to be modified. The question as to whether the curriculum is appropriate is one that must be continually posed. As curriculum workers and theoreticians, we must exhibit constant alertness to trends and related issues.

When writing new editions, authors tend to strive to make issues chapters completely new to suggest currency. However, the issues that have been affecting the field of curriculum seem almost timeless; they are issues that must be constantly revisited. Several issues presented in this chapter have not changed as to kind, but rather in their degree of concern for members of general society and specifically the educational community. This chapter, as in the previous edition, deals with the issues of (1) national curriculum, (2) censored curriculum, (3) textbook curriculum, (4) compensatory education, and (5) multicultural education. However, new issues have emerged: school reform, moral education, the increasing technologization of the curriculum, and the continual rise of the politics of curriculum.

NATIONAL CURRICULUM

Starting in the 1980s under President Reagan and continued by President Bush, a new federalism evolved that called for a dramatic shift in federal policy and programs. Driven by a belief that the federal government was too meddlesome and involved in too many activities and regulations, Reagan and Bush reduced federal funds (vis-à-vis inflation), activities, and regulations in education as well as other social sectors of the economy.[1] In addition, monetary and program responsibilities had been shifted to state and local agencies. Federal rules and regulations governing education were revoked or more loosely enforced.

The new federalism, even continued under Clinton, can be viewed in terms of three policy moves by the executive branch of government: (1) deregulation, the reduction of federal bureaucratic rules and regulations; (2) consolidation, the reduction of government proliferation of agencies and programs; and (3) cutbacks, the move to reduce social and educational spending.[2] Similarly, the new federalism has been analyzed in terms of five policy shifts, or the "five D's" in education: (1) diminution, reduction of federal expenditures in education; (2) deregulation, revocation of federal enforcement of rules and regulations; (3) decentralization, the belief that the ills of education are related to federal intrusion into what should be a state or local responsibility; (4) disestablishment, limiting the powers of the Department of Education and other federal agencies; and (5) deemphasis, the sum of the preceding aspects or the narrowing of the focus and scope of the federal role in education.[3]

At the same time that the new federalism has been shaping education, another and seemingly opposing conservative trend at the federal level has been occurring, the move toward the nationalization of American education. This move is tied to national standards, which are perceived by many as necessary if American education is to regain and retain its competitive edge in the world marketplace. To many, there is continued concern for declining student scores on national and international achievement tests. There is a persistent decline in the quality of our teachers and a lowering of standards with regard to the curricula offered.

This drive for a national curriculum and national standards was made evident in President Bush's American 2000. President Clinton participated in the creation of American 2000 as an active member of a group of American governors. At the time, Clinton was governor of Arkansas. Clinton carried his interest in national standards into his administration and pushed for legislation that would make these goals official throughout the land. On March 31, 1994, Clinton was successful with the help of a bipartisan show of governors to have the Goals 2000: Educate America Act passed. This legislation codified the six national goals adopted by the governors' group during the Bush administration and added two new goals, one dealing with professional development (new goal 4) and parental involvement (goal 8).[4]

Goals 2000 now has the following eight goals: (1) By the year 2000, all children in America will start school ready to learn; (2) by the year 2000, the high school graduation rate will increase to at least 90 percent; (3) by the year 2000, all students will leave grades 4, 8, and 12 having demonstrated competency over challenging subject matter (English, mathematics, science, foreign languages, civics and government, economics, arts, history, and geography), and every school in America will ensure that all students learn to use their minds well, so they may be prepared for responsible citizenship, further learning, and productive employment in our nation's modern economy; (4) by the year 2000, the nation's teaching force will have access to programs for the continued improvement of their professional skills and the opportunity to acquire the knowledge and skills needed to instruct and prepare all American students for the next century; (5) by the year 2000, U.S. students will be first in the world in mathematics and science achievement; (6) by the year

2000, every adult American will be literate and will possess the knowledge and skills necessary to compete in a global economy and exercise the rights and responsibilities of citizenship; (7) by the year 2000, every school in the United States will be free of drugs, violence, and the unauthorized presence of firearms and alcohol and will offer a disciplined environment conducive to learning, and (8) by the year 2000, every school will promote partnerships that will increase parental involvement and participation in promoting the social, emotional, and academic growth of children.[5] Each of these goals has several sub-goals.

These goals have been likened to America's first moon walk. They aim high, suggesting that the American educational system will produce the best and the first.[6] They recommend that we need to have national standards if we are to attain these goals. However, these goals assume that there is a major crisis in American education, that people like Albert Shanker are correct when he states that American education's biggest problem was and is massive underachievement.[7] These goals give further testimony that our nation is still at risk as we near the next century. And we must fix the problem. There is also the belief that national needs and goals are more important than local or pluralistic needs and goals. There is a belief that we desperately need national standards for our teachers in order to correct the low achievement of our students. Also, there is the assumption that a common core of subjects, for example, a national curriculum at least in general content, will assure that we attain each and every one of the goals in Goals 2000.

Certainly, we would not be making all this effort toward national goals and curricular activity if things were perfect. However, we would argue that perfection in education or in any activity is an illusion. Some even purport that we have manufactured a crisis in education.[8] Berliner and Biddle have argued convincingly that many of our conclusions about the functioning of our schools and the achievement of our students are based on misinformation. Essentially, in the last two decades a disinformation campaign has been waged. Reports of the attainments of American education have actually been suppressed.[9] Berliner and Biddle note that many of us in the

general public and within the field of education have bought into fraudulent ideas.[10] These authors point out that it has not been an accidental set of events that has brought us to believe that the crisis is such that only a national curriculum with implied national standards will allow us to correct our educational ship. The campaign of school bashing has been an effort by many of "playing on people's worries, pandering to prejudices, and misreporting and misrepresenting evidence."[11]

Presently, the concerns raised by Berliner and Biddle have not been broadcast widely enough for people to challenge the basic premises on which the drive for a national curriculum and national standards gain nurturance. Many people, including sincere educators and policy makers, state that student achievement will not increase unless national goals, standards, and tests are introduced, whereby progress is monitored and teachers and schools are held accountable.[12]

While a national consensus of high standards and planned curricula continues to develop, orchestrated by the U.S. Department of Education, it is important to note that the control, special programs, and policies that produce the outcomes are being left up to the states. Goals 2000 permits each state to generate and manage its own reforms.[13] The basic change logic is a blend of top-down mandates with bottom-up planning and development. Basically, all states are working on ways to implement the law. Most states are taking into consideration the standards work of national organizations associated with particular content areas. Standards for mathematics were the first to get national attention. Presently, we have standards for the arts, civics, geography, physical education, U.S. history and world history, science, foreign language, and economics. Many of these standards are influencing major state efforts to define essential learnings for all students in both state and private schools. The standards movement has sufficient momentum to continue even if Goals 2000 were to be discontinued.[14]

As we continue to process this focus of concern, it seems evident that there has been a change in strategy by the federal government regarding education. Federal education policy makers have worked and continue to work to energize a national strategy for curricular change supported with money, technical assistance, and federal–state networks. This strategy is quite different from the traditional one, which is reform tied to increased federal spending for target students (such as the poor, minority, and handicapped) and in terms of special programs and personnel (such as compensatory education, bilingual education, and handicapped education).

The national curriculum seems driven by an essentialist philosophy, as opposed to the progressive and reconstructionist philosophy that drove the old idea of federal reform; it promotes the recent idea of a core curriculum, that is, a common curriculum that every student should be required to take, as opposed to the idea of a relevant and a student-centered curriculum; it puts emphasis on national assessment testing, framing high-stake tests, imposing and meeting standards for students and teachers, putting more emphasis on outputs (what criteria or outcomes students must meet) and not inputs (spending money), and comparing these outputs with other industrialized nations.

The competency movement in education, whereby the states are imposing "gatekeeping" tests for promotion, "exit" tests for high school graduation, and "certifying" tests for beginning teachers, is a spin-off of the national movement to establish standards and a common curriculum. By 1989, some twenty-five states had implemented competency tests for high school graduation and thirty-seven states had implemented it for certifying beginning teachers.[15]

Within the context of nationalization of standards, some critics are asking, why raise standards that students cannot meet to begin with? Why talk about a nationalized set of goals or curriculum when the focus has always been on local control of the schools and when there is little agreement on goals, standards, or requirements among the fifty states and 85,000 public schools? Why talk about a national commitment to education reform when the federal government is reducing education spending in real dollars?

On the other side of the coin is the fact that most industrialized nations already have a ministry of education in place at the federal or national level, supplemented by regional, state, or provincial agencies in education. The federal ministry creates a policy climate capable of fostering an integrated and organizationally coherent response to national problems and/or trends and makes it easier to restructure schools (a new trend shaping

American schools) in a focused manner by making marginal changes (such as adding new programs) or reshuffling organizational responsibilities.[16]

Similarly, most ministries of education (since they represent the federal government) work hand in hand with business and education groups. The result is that the roles and responsibilities of institutions connected with education are clarified and compliance regulations exist that force students and teachers to meet minimum standards or competency levels; in addition, an explicit curriculum exists with intended learning outcomes, and national employment needs are fine-tuned in conjunction with vocational and academic programs (including college admissions).

Clarifying the Federal Role in Education

The federal government's role in education is compelling, because how we educate our children and youth will determine the kind of nation we become. The issue is not whether we do or don't reduce the federal role or nationalize standards in education, but rather to clarify and determine how the federal government can and should use its resources and dollars to effectively promote schools and society. Federal leadership should support and work with state and local education agencies not for the purpose of promoting the needs of one group versus another group, but for the priorities of all of us, as a people or nation.

According to the National School Boards Association (NSBA), the future federal role in education should be ninefold: (1) define and clarify federal responsibility to education, (2) increase our competitive edge through education, (3) advance equal educational opportunity, (4) promote effective use of technology, (5) strengthen the quality of teaching, (6) serve special need students, such as the economically deprived, minorities, bilingual, and handicapped, (7) improve and fund rural schools, (8) continue to support urban schools, and (9) increase the federal interest in education.[17]

All these recommendations suggest increased federal presence and funding of education. Without a strong federal commitment, school effort will be sporadic and inconsistent, relying mainly on local and state wealth. The NSBA agenda suggested that we were at a critical period in our history, which required policies and actions in education by the federal government to enhance our national future. This is still the case. In fact, each emerging period that we experience as a nation requires the right action from both national and state governments regarding education. In 1997, President Clinton indicated in his state of the union message that education would be a primary focus of his second term. He renewed the call for continued work on national standards, especially in reading and mathematics.

The priorities noted for education suggest that federal leadership can and must work hand in hand with local school districts and that the focus should continue to be on enhancing academic achievement for all students and ensuring that students with special needs continue to have equal opportunity to succeed. The federal government's continued call for excellence in education and national standards does not foretell a push by the federal government for nationalized schools or for a national core curriculum. The federal government continues to view its role as assisting schools in dealing with the particulars, that is, in translating national standards into specific statements that guide the creation of curricula at the local level.

Actually, having the federal government assist schools in dealing with the particulars is as it should be. The federal role in education should be that of helping local schools and school districts build consensus and confidence in educating their clients. Many educational problems are national, state, and local. The problem is national because it occurs in many parts of the country and because world or national events help construct it. It is a state problem because states have legal responsibility for schools, and governors and state legislators are playing a much greater role in school reform. It is also local in the sense that the composition and needs of the student population differ from place to place, and local efforts and resources are needed to resolve the problem. If state and local efforts and resources are not available, then the services or personnel will not always be provided.

There seems to be continued agreement that a new federal strategy is needed—one that stimulates local school planning and reform and supplements local efforts and resources. Beyond that point there tends to be controversy as to whether the federal government should become involved in national minimum standards, national goals, national testing, or a national core curriculum. The concern over national activities regarding student achievement and subject matter is somewhat reminiscent of the post-Sputnik era when the perceived threat was from the USSR. Today the threat is more economic than military and has changed to those who are outproducing us. Indeed, our future jobs and standard of living will depend partially on the academic and work goals and standards that we establish, to the extent we track our progress, create conditions most likely to increase our output and produce quality, and support first-rate teachers and schools.

CENSORED CURRICULUM

A certain amount of curriculum censorship has always existed, not as a matter of policy or law, but rather as a customary practice. During the eighteenth and nineteenth centuries, content in curriculum was restricted to traditional American values that centered around the family, church, work, and nation. Textbooks portrayed, according to authorities, the Puritan morality, work ethic, individualism, achievement, American patriotism, and the melting pot theme.[18]

As late as the mid twentieth century, history, civics, and English literature textbooks barely included, or even excluded, such topics as poor people, immigrants, minorities, women, and organized labor. Many even ignored our Democratic presidents. In a strict sense, the curriculum was not censored. Rather, it only included information educators considered appropriate. Readers or textbooks presented an idealistic American society with traditional, patriotic, and majority core values. Information considered too sensitive or too controversial was simply excluded. This policy elicited no fanfare or controversy, only occasional criticism. The problem was, however, that some of the content in the textbooks was racist and sexist, at least by today's standards. It mirrored what some call the "established curriculum," the interests of dominant groups.

Today, publishers exercise self-censorship to appease dissenting factions and to avoid alienating pressure groups. As Elliott Eisner says, textbook editors "take no risks" and design textbooks the same way. Textbooks "alienate no one. They are usually models of the dull, the routine, and the intellectually feckless." In general, textbooks shape the curriculum and are stabilizing factors that serve "to resist change."[19] The need for publishers, and now textbook authors, is to be "politically correct," to reflect the cultures of all students. But some are willing to succumb to popular rhetoric, to the extent of showing contempt for the dominant culture and for nearly everything that is European or white. Some of the more ardent critics disparage the "common culture," as if it was a vehicle for sexism, racism, and oppression.[20]

As a matter of practical concern, textbook editors must have a keen sense of the educational marketplace and they must be highly cognizant of a variety of pressure groups. Like other businesspeople, publishers attend to what their customers want, and they are sensitive to the wishes of textbook selection committees. Current data show that all the major textbook companies conform to the preferences of the larger educational markets—the most populous states, such as California, Illinois, New York (which together accounted for more than 23 percent of the total national expenditure on curriculum materials in one recent year—or to the major adoption states—California, Texas, and Florida.[21] These few states greatly influence the books available for study in other states; most other school systems have little choice but to go along with the dictates, specifications, and price maintenance of a handful of school systems in a few states.

Recent Censorship

As the 1980s unfolded, covert censorship changed to overt censorship, and criticism began to mount. Widely publicized textbook battles and school library book battles fanned censorship flames in many parts of the country. Depending on the incident, the focus of controversy focused on one of six major issues: (1) the sanctity of the family, (2) criticism of the free enterprise system, (3) antiAmericanism or disrespect toward traditional American values, (4) obscene language, (5) racial bias or criticism, and (6) creationism versus evolution. By 1990, 244 censorship incidents were reported in 39 states, up 75 percent from the previous 3 years and 150 percent over 7 years.[22]

The ban on books, which has spread to school libraries, curriculum councils, and classrooms across the country, has involved all types of school districts: suburban and city, rich and poor, predominantly minority and predominantly white, and so on. Various community groups, parent groups, and taxpayer groups involved with censorship concerns have exhibited different "zones of tolerance," ranging from heated school-community conflicts and serious watch-dog committees to mild newspaper editorials and questions at PTA meetings.

Today, almost any book that contains strong political or economic messages, obscenity, sex, nudity, profanity, slang or questionable English, or ethnic or racially sensitive material or that is considered by a pressure group as antifamily, antireligious, or anti-American is subject to possible censorship. The list of books for potential censorship has included *Madame Bovary, Grapes of Wrath, Mary Poppins,* and *Catcher in the Rye* and even such classics as Shakespeare's *Hamlet* and Mark Twain's *Huckleberry Finn.* Even harmless nursery rhymes, such as "Mother Goose," "Muffin Man," and "Humpty Dumpty," are on the hit list in some states and banned from the primary grades because of so-called subliminal messages about sexism, drugs, or religion.

Caught in the middle of book-censoring controversies are publishers of school texts and materials, who are forced to compromise; boards of education, both state and local, who are pressed by special-interest groups to censor books; and librarians, teachers, and school administrators, who are afraid to stir citizen wrath. On one side are some parents and other community members, who contend that certain passages or pictures in textbooks or library books are warping traditional American or community values that should be inculcated in students; on the other side are advocates of intellectual freedom and most education associations, who say that schools and libraries should be forums for ideas that students can question and examine.

In general, the current community-school conflict over censorship has several causes. One is the schools' unwillingness to recognize the role of the community in selecting books. A second is the schools' inability to define or clarify the community's role in the selection process. A third cause is that certain community groups may be overzealous in pushing their ideas on other parents and public institutions.

One way to deal with this confrontation is to recognize the citizens' reasons for concern and their right to express views about the merit and appropriateness of the school curriculum and materials. Such concerns should be communicated to school authorities and responded to promptly and professionally. Censorship battles will continue, but appropriate selection policies with well-defined procedures worked out in advance by school and community representatives should alleviate some of the fury that has erupted in the past over curriculum materials and textbooks.

Censorship as a Condition

Censorship will always be with us in terms of what content is included and excluded, in terms of the pictures and diagrams we encourage or discourage. We must continually guard against censorship, "at least be alert to it," according to Anne Meek, "because it is always hanging around" under the guise of one slogan or another,"[23] and if we may add one ism or another. Even so-called "traditional" professional associations have impact and seek changes in what students learn. By advocating reform and embracing new ideas, the associations indirectly censor, or at least modify, subject boundaries. For example, the major subject areas, such as English, social studies, math, science, and foreign language, all have their professional associations that make basic recommendations for certain changes in content and influence the funding of programs.

In this connection, Michael Apple reinterprets Herbert Spencer's fundamental question about schooling, "What knowledge is of most worth?" to "Whose knowledge is of most worth?" This is simply not a theoretical question, but a practical and strikingly clear one that "calls for censorship and controversies over the values that our schools teach" or don't teach.[24] Apple asserts that the context of curriculum has become "a political football in school districts throughout the country" and is increasingly subject to legislative mandates and state reform measures.

Apple argues that conservative groups have gained the advantage and momentum in the reform movement in education, as characterized by tax credits for private schools, higher academic standards, mandated teacher and student compe-

tency tests, and the increased concern by parents and school officials for patriotism, discipline, moral character, free enterprise, and other content and values that suggest a western tradition. He concludes that curriculum scholars are considered irrelevant in the great debate involving reform or change in subject boundaries.

The issue of deciding what knowledge is appropriate for certain students will always be a central challenge for curriculum decision makers. In confronting this task, there will always be those persons who perceive that certain knowledge and information are not appropriate, are miseducative at least, and are morally damaging at most. There will always be those who wish to censor. With technology becoming more integral to schooling, the issues of access to information and knowledge and censorship may take on even greater significance. Already, schools are designing ways in which they can lock out certain types of material on the Internet. Likewise, parents are obtaining similar locking devices for their home personal computers.

However, with the increasing diversity of students and the general population, it will be more difficult to determine which material might be educationally or morally damaging and thus be locked out or censored. What is offensive to one group of individuals will often be educationally sound to another. Of course, this has always been the case. That is how a book like Mark Twain's *Huckleberry Finn* can be on the list to be removed from a school curriculum. As recently as 1997, this book was the target of censorship in a Washington state school district because it was determined to be offensive to a particular ethnic group. Also in 1997, it appeared that university professors at a respected institution would have to give students a special key to unlock Internet access to various museum art that contained nudes. Some people were concerned about allowing students access to material considered erotic. Making decisions about what and whose knowledge is of most worth will continue to become increasingly complex.

TEXTBOOK CURRICULUM

Textbooks for much of this century have been the linchpin of the curriculum. Indeed, despite demands for teacher involvement in determining the specifics of the curriculum and for curriculum reform, textbooks are the curriculum. Ask teachers and public alike what the curriculum is in a certain grade or area, and they most frequently will point to a textbook. This is not surprising, for textbooks have become stabilizing forces on the curriculum, along with standardized tests and college admission standards. What is emphasized by texts gets included in tests and taught by teachers. From a theoretical stance, teachers are in a position to influence the curriculum, but they really have little authority to recommend changes in the standard architecture of the curriculum. Teachers also have little time to plan the curriculum and even less time to interact with their colleagues about curriculum concerns. Few districts are prepared either philosophically or administratively to spend hundreds of thousands of dollars to design their own curricula. Most monies spent under the category of curriculum development are allocated for purchasing textbooks and related support materials.

Even given modern educational technology, it is unlikely that textbooks will be removed from the role of shaping the curriculum, determining its focus, and defining the core work of the school.[25] Tradition is on the side of keeping the textbook as the key influence on the curriculum. The textbook will continue as the most frequently used instructional material at all grade levels, from the primary grades through graduate school. In many cases, it will continue to be the only instructional resource used by the teacher. The power of the textbook to strongly influence and even dominate the nature and sequence of a course profoundly affects the learning experiences and knowledge of students.

Reliance on the textbook (as well as its companion, the workbook) is consistent with the stress on written words as the main medium of education and it is the way most teachers were educated. Print still remains supreme in this culture. Print will remain dominant in the information age, although there may be various ways in which print will be processed by students. Teachers have no desire nor do they have the background to engage in the publishing of this educational material. However, it is likely that teachers and other educational professionals will have to take more time to decide what are appropriate print materials to support the curriculum.

Advantages and Disadvantages

Textbooks represent authors' views on what knowledge is of most worth. Even for those authors who claim objectivity, the text includes and excludes information so that the author's biases are given primary focus. How the author develops the manuscript is slanted to reflect what the author deems important. All texts have subtext. If, in a class, the textbook becomes the only point of view, students may be left thinking that that is the only viewpoint, the only interpretation.

Of course, authors and their publishers try to be sensitive to their potential audience, their market. Publishers try to match their textbooks with the beliefs and intentions of those who are potential customers. The market influences the form of the textbook. To have wide application and to increase potential sales, textbooks tend to be general, noncontroversial, and bland. They are usually written for a national audience, so they do not consider local issues or community problems. Publishers really cannot address local issues, for the market for the textbook would not support the development costs. Because they are geared for the greatest number of students, textbooks may not meet the needs and interests of any particular group of students. Moreover, issues, topics and data that might upset potential audiences or interest groups are omitted.[26]

Textbooks summarize large quantities of data and in so doing become general and superficial and may discourage conceptual thinking, critical analysis, and evaluation. A key problem facing many textbooks is that, with the knowledge explosion, they become quickly outdated. This is especially true of social studies and science textbooks. It is less so with mathematics textbooks. But because textbooks are costly, they are often used long after they should be replaced. In the past, textbooks have been criticized as containing factual errors, although currently this is not a major problem. Of course, since information in textbooks results from an author's interpretation, we are becoming more aware that different authors can create different texts depending on their philosophical orientations. Even "facts" in textbooks are open to interpretation. Another criticism is that textbooks, especially those designed for the lower grades, are stilted in their writing, dull, and uninteresting. Much of this is because of publishers' concerns that their books have appropriate readability for the students. Reading formulas are employed to determine if the text material is suitable for specific student populations.

Reading formulas, first devised in the 1920s to estimate the reading difficulty of a text, have increased and are widely used by authors, publishers, teachers, reading consultants, and textbook adoption committees. Some reading formulas count the number of syllables or the number of letters in a word, some count the number of words not on a specific word list, others measure sentence length, and still others remove words in a passage and test whether students can fill in the exact words that were removed. Some formulas use graphs, regression statistics, and percentiles and range scores to calculate reading difficulty, and computer programs are now available for doing the counting and calculation chores involved in reading level determinations.

Critics of the various reading formulas say that (1) they fail to consider students' prior knowledge, experience, and interests, all of which influence reading comprehension; (2) they assume that words with fewer syllables and shorter, simpler sentences are easier to comprehend than words with more syllables and longer sentences with subordinate clauses, which is not always true; (3) publishers have reacted to these formulas by adjusting sentence and word length to give the appearance of certain levels of readability without necessarily providing them; and give (4) strict adherence to formulas robs prose of the connective words, vocabulary, and sentence structure that make it interesting and comprehensible and contribute to a style that makes the text worth reading.[27] In short, rigid following of reading formulas often results in a boring and bland text.

Considering these criticisms, you might ask why teachers, when they have access to other instructional materials, rely so heavily on textbooks. The answer is, of course, they do have many advantages. A textbook (1) provides an outline that the teacher can use in planning courses, units, and lessons, (2) summarizes a great deal of pertinent information, (3) enables the students to take home

in convenient form most of the material they need to learn for the course, (4) provides a common resource for all students to follow, (5) provides the teacher with ideas regarding the organization of information and activities, (6) includes pictures, graphs, maps, and other illustrative material, which facilitate understanding, (7) includes other teaching aids, such as summaries and review questions, and (8) relieves the teacher of preparing material for the course, thus allowing more time to prepare the lesson.[28]

Unless a curriculum committee or teachers can develop materials that are substantially better than a text in meeting evaluative criteria, there is little reason for them to spend much time, effort, and money on "homemade" materials that are sometimes put together for the sake of throwing away the textbook. Given the facts that textbooks take several years to write and revise and that publishers often spend considerable effort developing and refining them through market analysis, subject and method consultants, writing staffs, and copy editors, it makes little sense to condemn them as a whole as being ineffective or harmful to the educational process.

Good textbooks have many desirable characteristics. They are usually well organized, coherent, unified, relatively up to date, accurate, and relatively unbiased. They have been scrutinized by scholars, educators, and minority groups. Their reading level and knowledge base match the developmental level of their intended audience. They are accompanied by teacher's manuals, test items, study guides, and activity guides. The textbook is an acceptable tool for instruction as long as it is selected with care and is kept in proper perspective so that it is not viewed as the only source of knowledge and so that it does not turn into the curriculum. See Curriculum Tips 12-1.

Text Alternatives, Alternative Textbooks

The textbook's advantages of portability, rather low cost, essential role in teacher education, well-established production and marketing schemes, and the public's understanding of this educational material assure that textbooks will continue to be central to the structures and delivery of curriculum.[29] However, there are alternative formats to the standard textbook. One of these is computer-

======= *Curriculum Tips 12-1* =======

Appraising the Worth of a Textbook

Here are some questions to keep in mind in assessing the worth of a textbook for teachers and curriculum committees.

Content

1. Does the text coincide with the content and objectives of the course?
2. Is it up to date and accurate?
3. Is it comprehensive?
4. Is it adaptable to the students' needs, interests, and abilities?
5. Does it adequately and properly portray minorities and women?
6. Does it foster methodological approaches consistent with procedures used by the teacher and school?
7. Does it reinforce the type of learning (such as critical thinking and problem solving) sought by the teacher and school?
8. Does it provide the student with a sense of accomplishment because it can be mastered and is still challenging?

Mechanics

1. Is the size appropriate?
2. Is the binding adequate?
3. Is the paper of adequate quality?
4. Are the objectives, headings, and summaries clear?
5. Are the contents and index well organized?
6. Is there a sufficient number of pictures, charts, maps, and so on, appropriate for the students' level?
7. Does it come with instructional manuals and study guides?
8. Is it durable enough to last several years?
9. Is it reasonably priced relative to its quality? To its competitors?

Overall Appraisal

1. What are the outstanding features of the text?
2. What are the shortcomings of the text?
3. Do the outstanding features strongly override the shortcomings?

Source: Allan C. Ornstein, "Textbook Instruction: Processes and Strategies," *NASSP Bulletin* (December 1989), p. 110.

assisted instructional materials. Computer-assisted instruction (CAI) offers opportunities for teachers and students to experience variations from a fixed linear text. One way for this to happen is for the student using a personal computer to simply select from a menu the topics to read and study. This allows the student to be in control of the order in which text is read.

Text for students can be organized as hypertext. Hypertext refers to the arrangement of computer-based textual material in which a reader's progression through the material need not be sequential; it could rather be conceptual. A reader could navigate through the text material in an interactive manner that would satisfy his or her learning interests and needs. A reader could focus on one section of material, request examples of this focus from other text material, and ask for suggested linkages to further text material. In a sense, the student would be able to experience a customized program. Hypertext and other developments in information technology allow teachers to mass produce or mass access customized or personalized curricular material.[30]

Consider, for example, a student reading a text on a particular geographical region. The text material could be organized so that the reader can experience the material not only as a geographer, but also as an economist, a historian, an anthropologist, and a political scientist. Furthermore, the student might be able to read the material as if he or she were from a different cultural group. No longer would the student have to read the material from the author's imposed order or bias.

A key selling point here is that the student is empowered to control the text, to autoconstruct and autodeconstruct the material, to not only be part of the text but to get beyond the text.[31] Extending the concept of text and textbook even further is the combining of computers and video. Students will have even more dynamic ways to engage themselves with text and experience. Students will be able to be engaged interactively with a text that has fluidity.

As information technology develops, our concept of textbook will be challenged. Currently, customized publishing is increasingly popular, again a sign that we will be able to mass produce one-of-a-kind copies or texts to address students' and teachers' individual needs. In customized publishing, publishers using new printing machines can inexpensively select and edit material for a book and tailor the selections of the book to individual instructor's needs. Materials can be added or deleted to meet the purposes of the course. Levels of difficulty of the material can be adjusted to levels appropriate for particular classes. Customizing the publishing of books ushers in a time when a particular textbook may have a thousand variations.[32]

With such publishing, local decision makers are given a role in the actual writing and publishing of the text material. It empowers teachers by giving them a significant role in determining the nature of the educational materials to be employed in teaching the curriculum. In a sense, such pub-

lishing may make "the curriculum" a thing of the past; there will be numerous curricula within the classroom, all personalized as to text material and content and all done easily and quickly with the help of computers. In fact, students in classrooms may participate in designing their own personal textbooks. The textbook of the future may be essentially a skeleton to which schools and school districts and all the players in curriculum add curricular flesh.

COMPENSATORY CURRICULUM

A massive movement into compensatory education, begun in the 1960s and 1970s, was designed to overcome the educational (and to some extent social and psychological) deficiencies or disadvantages of lower-class and minority children. The movement was widespread and intense; it took on more than just bandwagon status.

The various programs and projects can be categorized by *target population* (kindergarten through college, student or teacher), *treatment* (remedial, enrichment, and therapeutic), *service* (curricular, instructional, counseling, school wide, and community), *setting* (urban and rural), and *policy* (local, regional, state, and national). Most compensatory programs were experimental or additive and were not designed for fundamental or system-wide reform. They operated from the theoretical premises that cognitive, social, and psychological development are mainly the consequence of environmental influences, and that improving the environment of the child can reverse whatever learning deficits exist. Beginning with the Johnson administration, special personnel and services were usually funded by the federal government, under Title I of the Elementary and Secondary Education Act (ESEA). Chapter I was introduced (to replace Title I) by the Reagan administration and continued by the Bush and Clinton presidencies.

The 1990s: New Concerns for "At-Risk" Students

Although the term "disadvantaged" has been replaced by "at-risk" and "special needs" students, concern for these children and youth has increased as the proportion of these students grows every year and is probably one major reason for our declining student achievement. This at-risk population tends to encompass the following major groups: poverty children (21 percent of student enrollments K–12); minority students (some 30 percent), especially immigrant children who speak a language other than English (15 percent); and handicapped students (12 percent).[33] Somewhat unnoticed is another group of at-risk students: hungry and/or malnourished, some 5.5 million under the age of twelve (and not necessarily all from poor home environments) and another 6 million considered borderline hungry.[34]

Although most at-risk students are poor (some 13.5 million in 1990), estimates were made at the outset of this decade that approximately 60 to 65 percent of our students, increasingly from the middle class, would be latchkey children or potentially at risk, that is, without adult supervision after school.[35] This estimate has been borne out. In addition, a category of the "new needy" has emerged, including some 250,000 to 500,000 homeless children, 250,000 to 300,000 crack-exposed babies born each year, and some 500,000 to 600,000 migrant children.[36]

Also, an increasing number of children are being raised in foster care centers, juvenile detention centers, and mental health facilities (in total projected to be over one million by 2000); the critical needs of these children go ignored to the extent that many are abused and the schools really have minimal programs to assist them. Although there is significant overlap between the old needy groups (poor, minority, non-English speaking, and handicapped) and the new needy groups, the full depth of our educational problems are just beginning to surface as we identify new at-risk groups.

In addition, some educators are expanding the notion of at-risk to include students who fall into one or more of these categories: (1) prematurely born, (2) abused or neglected, (3) substance addicted, (4) pregnant, (5) gang or cult members, (6) school-dropout parents, (7) teenage parents, (8) single-family parent, (9) AIDS children or parent, (10) divorced parents, (11) drug or alcohol-dependent parents, and (12) incarcerated parents.[37] Add these twelve groups to the traditional poor (minority, immigrant or bilingual, and handicapped categories) as well as the latchkey and

new needy, and more than 90 percent of the U.S. student enrollments may be at risk and can use some extra assistance in school.

Where is all the money going to come from? Given our shrinking tax base and that the elderly poor, a powerful political force, are vying for the same human-service dollars, the future is not promising for young Americans who cannot vote.

One way to put all these trends in perspective is as follows: the U.S. student population K–12 is expected to grow in this decade, from 46 million to 50 million by 2001.[38] But teaching in that year, and beyond, will be more difficult than today, especially in our big cities where the underclass (poor, minority, handicapped, and others) is growing rapidly. In more dramatic terms, our human capital is at stake; an increasing number of educationally disabled students are in part creating long-term American decline. All our new slogans and fuzzy buzzwords—"higher national standards," "restructuring schools," and "reforming education"—may be doomed before they get off the ground as a growing flood of at-risk children each year enters our classrooms, basically unprepared for school and later unprepared to enter our skilled workforce and information age.

Problems and Prospects

Much of the efforts during the early period of compensatory education has been raising the cognitive levels of disadvantaged students. Basically, four failure trends emerged:

1. In many of the best-known and heavily funded programs, such as Headstart and Follow-Through, no significant differences showed in learning between the target children and matched controlled groups.

2. In the early stages of compensatory funding, input increments had a discernible effect, but they gradually diminished until input was wasted because there was virtually no increase in output. The conclusion was that the programs had reached a "flat area"—less output in relation to input, or even worse, no return.

3. Longitudinal studies of several programs also revealed a "fade out" process; that is, the early gains made by these youngsters (if any) eventually leveled off and, after a few years of schooling, were equivalent to gains made by those without such funding.

4. Many so-called "successes" were generally based not on hard data, but on impressions and testimonies (in many cases suspect). When evaluated on the basis of measurable data, most of these programs proved to be ineffective. For example, of the more than 1200 projects evaluated in the 1970s and originally judged to be successful, only ten were found to be effective on the basis of statistical reanalysis.[39]

The same problems were exhibited in the 1980s, when several well-publicized and so-called outstanding early-childhood programs were analyzed and proved to have limited cognitive outcomes despite early claims of success. Some programs tended to be subject to fade-out within a few years; others had no data available with which to verify successes or to conduct critical reviews in scientific journals. What educators experienced in the early stages of compensatory programs was reality. Intervention efforts of a few hours a day in one or two school years could not compensate for several years of impoverishment, despite the claims of many environmentalists and behaviorists.[40]

In general, compensatory education has been criticized for (1) its hasty planning and piecemeal approach; (2) its mismanagement and misappropriation of funds; (3) its dependence on unethical grantspeople who justify their conduct on the basis that "everyone does it"; (4) the large consultant fees charged for unaccomplished or shoddy work; (5) its use of inadequately trained personnel at the state and local levels; (6) the high salaries it pays people at the administrative levels; (7) its disregard for and lack of teacher participation; (8) its vague objectives; (9) its poor evaluation procedures; and (10) the increased quantity of services it substitutes for change in the quality or content of the program.[41]

Advocates of compensatory spending claim that most of these problems can be remedied over time and that the real problem is the concern that disadvantaged children will not succeed. Americans are obligated to find solutions that will reach these children and provide them with the necessary equality of opportunities. Moreover, advocates contend that, in most instances, (1) money was made available in such haste that the quality

of planning and development was limited; (2) many programs have been operative for too brief a period to be effectively evaluated; (3) many programs were funded at insufficient levels; and (4) some student successes have been reported in the affective domain.[42]

MULTICULTURAL EDUCATION

America is a multicultural nation, a pluralistic society, a nation with many different ethnic groups and microcultures. For most of our history, we have perceived of our country as one where people from diverse backgrounds could come in and in time meld into or assimilate into Americans, a "new" race. This has come to be known as the melting-pot theory. And many, if not most cultural groups, have been successful in melting into a mainstream civic and common culture, which we call American or Anglo-American. Most European-Americans now get classed as white regardless of their particular ethnic–cultural backgrounds or the languages of their ancestral homes. There has been a price for such melting; most of these people have lost their histories, customs, and languages and have now accepted the common history of the United States as their own.

We expected the schools to contribute to this melting-pot process, this extinguishing of the cultures of immigrant students by socializing and acculturating them to American ways and by instructing them in English. Today, the melting-pot concept is held in disfavor by some groups, because it is perceived as stripping different ethnic groups of their cultures and identities. In contrast, cultural pluralism or cultural diversity has been suggested as the guiding concept for our nation. This concept calls for understanding and appreciating differences among people so that ethnic groups can maintain their customs, folk mores, and languages and still be able to participate in the common civic, mainstream culture. The cost of being an American should not be such that one must forget or deny one's ethnic and cultural roots. Ideally, cultural pluralism promotes a sense of wholeness within society, based on the strengths of each of its parts or groups, and maintains that ethnic group interests can coincide with the interests of the nation. In President Clinton's State of the Union address in January 1997, he stressed that we must always realize that the diversity of the peoples of the United States is indeed our greatest strength.

Multicultural education has become, for many people, the key approach for nurturing in all citizens an understanding of and acceptance of cultural pluralism or cultural diversity. Ideally, education cannot be anything other than multicultural. Many ethnic groups have contributed and continue to contribute to our national culture. And the microcultures within our national borders draw from the cultures of the world. This is a broad view of multicultural education.

However, many in this movement appear to take a narrow view of multicultural education. These individuals believe that multicultural education addresses those ethnic or cultural groups that have been marginalized by the major civic culture. Often these groups are identified as African Americans, Native Americans, Asian Americans, and Hispanic Americans. Women and people of various sexual orientations are frequently included. Hillis appears to support this view when he states that multicultural education has had the major goal of improving educational equity for female students who are marginalized, especially in mathematics and science, children of color, and poor children.[43] Grant and Sleeter also seem to have this narrow view of multicultural education when they state that the societal goals of multicultural education are to "reduce prejudice toward oppressed groups, to work toward equal opportunity and societal justice for all groups and to effect an equitable distribution of power among members of different cultural groups."[44]

They further state that the purpose of multicultural education is to "prepare future citizens to reconstruct society so that it better serves the interests of all groups, *especially* those who are of color, poor, female and/or disabled."[45] While these educators do state "the interests of all groups," the narrow focus becomes apparent with the words "oppressed groups" and "especially." This is not to say that schools should not address the needs of these students and celebrate their cultural diversity and their contributions to the national and world communities. Indeed, in its curriculum and pedagogy, the school must bring in those students who have been marginalized in the past and continue to be. However, in our zeal

to address these very real concerns, educators must realize that all peoples must be included and that the apparent invisibility of those ethnic groups that comprise the currently dominant civic culture must also be recognized and addressed. There is the danger that we will begin to stereotype all groups, assuming that, while we have pluralism within the national macroculture, each ethnic group is homogenous, and likewise for gender groups or disability groups. Erickson cautions that when considering and teaching about the cultural practices of other people there is a danger of stereotyping or misinterpreting them.[46]

Multicultural education grew as a reform movement out of the civil rights movement of the 1960s. Civil rights advocates organized people to fight for the end of discrimination in public accommodations, housing, jobs, and education. The civil rights movement was spearheaded by African Americans. Over the years, other groups have come into the movement and echoed the demands that schools reform their curricula and pedagogies to address and celebrate the groups' unique needs and heritages. As Banks notes, "The apparent success of the civil rights movement . . . stimulated other victimized groups to take actions to eliminate discrimination against them and to demand that the educational system respond to their needs, aspirations, cultures, and histories."[47] The women's rights movement voiced similar demands. Feminists posited that the ubiquitous textbook had made women and their contributions invisible. It is still argued that the curriculum and its materials are patriarchal. Over this past quarter-century, others have joined the chorus demanding that schools acknowledge the plurality that exists. People with disabilities and various sexual orientations have demanded attention.

When many educators reflect on multicultural education, perhaps because of the history of the movement, they think of curricula that relate to particular ethnic, racial, or cultural groups, usually those considered to be marginalized by the dominant macroculture. Banks points out that when teachers do this they tend to think of multicultural education as only dealing with certain subjects, usually social studies or literature. Other subjects, such as science and mathematics, are considered multicultural free. Likewise, some teachers think that these studies are only for those students who hold memberships in the marginalized groups.[48] It is for African American children or students of color so that they can gain cultural pride or self-esteem, so that they can be empowered to challenge oppression.[49] "We don't have those students in our school district" is sometimes heard.

Multicultural education is essentially an orientation to education, to curriculum and the teaching of it. It means that, when dealing with declarative knowledge (knowledge of facts, concepts, rules, generalizations, theories, principles, laws, and the like), we need to employ examples and content from the diversity of the human family. Our examples of key concepts, principles, and generalizations need to be drawn from a rich cultural base.[50] For instance, in teaching design in mathematics or in art, one can employ examples drawn from Native American, African, Danish, and East Indian design, and so forth. Students have the opportunity to see that there are many cultural ways to deal with design. Students develop what some call a polyfocality to design, viewing it from many vantage points through diverse cultural lenses. In essence, they have a rich educational experience. Teachers can use this polyfocality in the teaching of all subjects. For instance, in science, current knowledge about astronomy can be dealt with by describing the history of this disciplined area of study and revealing the contributions of many groups and individuals to our current knowledge. Even those areas of knowledge considered to be thoroughly western are collectives and meldings of contributions from diverse groups. Where appropriate, teachers must integrate ethnic and cultural content into their curriculum planning.

Multicultural education also deals with procedural knowledge and how we employ procedures to construct knowledge.[51] Furthermore, multicultural education strives to have students realize that how we engage the procedures or construct knowledge is influenced by our cultural assumptions, our frames of references, and the very procedures by which we construct meaning and process data. Knowing the procedure for solving a problem or developing a paper is important, but our knowledge of process is enriched if we understand why we privilege some ways of processing data and not others and that if we were to

employ different procedures, or take different vantage points, we might very well arrive at different conclusions.

Advocates of multicultural education strive for the curriculum to be totally transformed so that it truly represents the cultural diversity of all knowledge, the polyfocality of knowledge. Actually, this should be the goal of all curricularists. There are many views to take regarding knowledge. The more ways that individual students look at knowledge and process, the more complete their understanding. Also, students begin to appreciate the incompleteness of their knowledge. Such education allows students to immerse themselves in learning about the complexity of the worlds within which they live.

Advocacy for multicultural education has been and continues to be found in national professional associations, state and local education agencies, and colleges and universities. In general, they have emphasized curriculum materials and instructional techniques. They have specifically proposed (1) introducing materials that are multiracial, multiethnic, and nonsexist; (2) teaching values that promote cultural diversity and individuality; (3) incorporating various cultural and ethnic activities in the classroom and school-community program; (4) encouraging multilingualism and multiple dialects; and (5) emphasizing multicultural teacher education programs.[52]

Multicultural Instruction. Educators are also trying to identify effective instructional approaches for teaching students of various racial and ethnic backgrounds. Some of the more important approaches have been concerned with student learning, or what is called a "biocognitive" approach to student learning. For example, Ramirez and Castañeda concluded that Hispanic students tend to be more "field sensitive" than nonminority children.[53] Field sensitive children are described as being more influenced by personal relationships and by praise or disapproval from authority figures, including teachers, than are "field independent" students, who are more abstract thinkers. A field sensitive curriculum is "humanized through use of narration, humor, drama and fantasy and should be "structured in such a way that children work cooperatively with peers or with a teacher in a variety of activities."[54]

Another effort to identify instructional approaches suited to students' ethnic backgrounds has been provided by researchers who have worked with Native Americans.[55] These researchers conclude that schooling for Native American children would be most successful if the curriculum took better account of their "primary learning" patterns (learning outside the school) and organized instruction in a manner more compatible with these patterns. These researchers contend that primary learning tends to take place in personal communication with emotionally important individuals and in tutorial (face-to-face) situations in which learning is adaptive (linked to the concerns and needs of the community). Primary learning also includes verbal instruction, exploratory play, and concrete (as opposed to abstract) learning. It involves monitoring the activities of elders who are particularly important to the children, say, uncles or aunts.

Some caution is necessary. The value of field-oriented and primary learning approaches is not well documented. What appears to be as or more important, according to some observers, are the basic, old approaches—friendliness, understanding, democratic teacher behaviors, positive teacher expectations, English proficiency, and parental support for the students.[56]

Banks calls these various approaches to multicultural instruction equity pedagogy. Equity pedagogy means that teachers modify their teaching such that it enables students from diverse racial, cultural, gender, and social-class groups to be successful in academic achievement. It employs instructional approaches that are sensitive to ethnic students' ways of knowing and meaning making.[57] Some critical theorists are really talking about equity pedagogy when they are discussing ways of teaching marginalized groups so that they are empowered to fully participate in society.[58] Again, this seems to be just good pedagogy, that is, using the most appropriate instructional strategies with particular children.

Bilingual Education. Bilingual education, which provides instruction for non-English speaking students in their native languages, has been an expanding activity in public schools in the United States since the late 1960s. Although the federal and state governments fund bilingual projects for more than sixty groups speaking various Asian, Indo-European, and Native American languages, the large majority (70 percent) of children in these projects are Hispanics.

Bilingual education has been expanding for various reasons: (1) partly because of the United States Supreme Court decision in the *Lau* case, which requires that school districts initiate some type of bilingual program if they enroll more than twenty students of a given language group at a particular grade level; (2) partly because of the subsequent pressure of the federal Office of Civil Rights (OCR), which insists that educational opportunities be provided for limited-English speaking (LES) and non-English speaking (NES) students; and (3) partly because of the continuous federal funding of bilingual programs, even today, even though other categorical programs are being merged within block grants.

Bilingualism is intertwined with such sensitive issues as our attitudes toward immigrants, that is, our accepting or rejecting those legal and illegal immigrants who might work for less money and thus replace American-born citizens on the job and our deciding who can enter the United States: who is a political refugee or an economic refugee.

Controversies over bilingual education have become somewhat embittered emotionally as federal and state guidelines have led to the establishment of various programs. Those who would "immerse" children in an English-language environment argue with those who believe initial instruction will be more effective in the native language; and both of these groups argue with those who wish that a mixture of both English and the native language be taught in school. Ethnic and community leaders have engaged in bitter struggles over the establishment of bilingual programs in the public schools.

Educators and laypeople concerned with NES (no English speaking) and LES (limited English speaking) students also argue whether emphasis should be placed on teaching in the native language over a long period (maintenance) or proceeding to teach in English as soon as possible (transitional). On the one side are those who favor maintenance because they think it will help build or maintain a constructive sense of identity among ethnic or racial minorities.[59] On the other side are those who believe that cultural-maintenance programs are harmful because they separate groups from one another or discourage students from mastering English well enough to function successfully in the larger society.[60] The latter or transitional approach is reflected in current federal guidelines.

Another major controversy involving bilingual education concerns whether this approach is effective in improving the performance of low-achieving students. Most scholars who have examined the research agree that bilingual education has effected little, if any, improvement in the performance of participating students.[61] In fact, critics argue that multicultural and bilingual education is spearheaded not by current immigrants, but rather by black and (to a lesser extent) Hispanic educational leaders in big-city schools and universities to mask the academic failure of such students.

Other scholars partially disagree; they argue that well-implemented programs can result in significant individual and group self-esteem, achievement gains, and enriched cultural experiences.[62] In general, however, educators agree that much more than bilingual/bicultural education is needed to improve the performance of economically disadvantaged LES and NES students.[63]

In 1997 an event raised serious discussion about bilingual education all the way from a local school district in California to the halls of Congress. The event was the recognition of Black English, Ebonics, as a distinct language. Originally, the school board stated that teachers would be allowed to teach Ebonics in the classroom to those children for whom this language was their primary one. Furthermore, Ebonics would be the language of instruction for other courses. Controversy arose in the local district and received national attention, with people arguing whether Ebonics was a legitimate language or not and whether it should be employed as a language of instruction. The outcry was such in the school district that the school board rewrote its ruling to say that teachers must recognize that Ebonics is a language that many students come to school speaking, but that Ebonics would not be taught in the school nor would it be a language of instruction. The issue surrounding Ebonics was similar to many of the other arguments regarding languages

other than English. Ebonics is likely to become an issue in other school districts with a large percentage of African American children.

The discussion of language within bilingual education has been passionate at times. This is not too surprising since language is a key vehicle by which individuals express their cultural selves. Language is primary in their construction of meaning and sharing of visions. The centrality of language to the human spirit has also meant that many have felt their persons and their cultures attacked by the urging of languages other than English. In the 1980s, the English Only movement came into being as a way to counter the demand of many bilingualists, especially those who wished to maintain a second language in school. This movement, which is a national effort to pass a constitutional amendment making English the official language of the United States, is essentially a response to the rising political power of Spanish-speaking people, citizens and noncitizens alike.

Three states, California, Florida, and Illinois, have passed English Only resolutions. These three states are among the five states in the nation with the largest number of language minority students. Also, since the 1980s these states have been receiving great waves of immigration. One state, Arizona, amended its state constitution to make English the official state language. However, it was ruled unconstitutional in 1991.[64] It is likely that this issue will continue to be debated, especially as the numbers of linguistically diverse students continue to grow.[65]

Whether English becomes an official language or not, there is no denying that English is de facto the official language of the United States. Also, there is no denying that increasing numbers of children in school will have languages other than English as their primary language. Bilingual education will continue to exist in the future, as well it should. However, bilingual education is no panacea for changing the school success of these students. By itself, it cannot significantly change the learning experiences of children with a minority native tongue. Many other factors not related to language explain why such children achieve poorly in school. It should also be pointed out that not all language minority children are doing poorly in school or are mired in poverty.

Many factors relate to academic achievement, self-esteem, and economic outcomes. Many social–cultural factors influence how children perceive school and how education is valued and for what purposes. In dealing with language-minority children, we must realize that we require approaches that not only deal with language learning but also with appropriate curricular content and effective instructional approaches. Certainly, we need to celebrate diversity and nurture acceptance of all our citizens. The health of our society depends on such tolerance. We must recognize that in our discussion of bilingualism and curriculum in general there are many perspectives: an African American, Hispanic, and Asian American perspective, and also an Armenian, Croatian, and Iraqi perspective, and so on. The need is to legitimate these perspectives, especially when teaching students of these ethnic roots. But we must also remember that our diverse students must become functioning members of the macroculture, and English is required.

SCHOOL REFORM

Reform as a word means to form again, to reshape. It can be likened to a physical change in science, re-forming a solid into a liquid or a liquid into a gas. It seems to us that in reforming one really only changes appearances. In all the talk about reforming schools, we have not recognized that, as long as we talk reform, we are not likely to get major, significant change in the organization, instruction, or curricula in our schools. It is perhaps because we have thought of reform as only a remolding of the same parts or components of education that Goodlad's comments written a few years ago are still timely. "Throughout the century now drawing to a close, school reform has been driven by a theory that has produced models whose appeal has been little diminished by failure. The theory is a simple input/output model. If we wish to reform schools, we vary the inputs and check the outputs. The use of this theory in testing the power of any particular variable in educational research has produced a litany of 'no significant effects.' "[66]

We have been talking, doing, critiquing, and praising school reform for most of this century. We will end this century with a continuation of these dialogues and debates. The very issue of re-

form supplies employment for many professionals. Heaven forbid that we are successful in reforming the schools. Beymer, in a serious yet kidding way, cautioned us to be careful for what we pray, because our prayers just might be answered. He relates the story line of a movie entitled *The Man in the White Suit.* The movie dealt with a man who invented a cloth that would never wear out, never tear, and never soil. The invention of this marvelous material caused the textile, fashion, retail clothing, and laundry industries to mount means to destroy this person and his creation. Heaven forbid that we should be successful and truly reform our schools and have all students attain national standards. Beymer's tale is not to say we should not try to reform, but rather that you should "choose words carefully when composing your prayers, and think carefully about the possible consequences of the outcomes you demand of formal education."[67]

Actually, our prayers are not likely to be answered any time soon. And if it were possible, we should realize that that would not be a good thing, for once our prayers are answered, we might think ourselves saved, think we had arrived at the perfect curriculum, the perfect pedagogy, the perfect administrative arrangement for schools, the perfect staffing design, the perfect social arrangement with the community. Education is much too complicated to be fully comprehended, and it certainly cannot be controlled with any degree of precision. There are just too many people involved with and concerned about education to have any simple solution to adequately address the reform issue.

Perhaps one disturbing point about school reform is that most of reform talk is about the school as an administrative unit and not about curriculum. No one seems to be talking really about reforming the curriculum. Most seem to be talking about ways in which to more effectively manage schools. Clinchy challenges us to think what might be the result of reform efforts if we approached reform from the bottom up rather than from the top down.[68] It perhaps is too simplistic to assume that we can reform our schools and reform or reinvent our curricula by just having those who work daily with it in charge. Bottom-up or top-down management of education has been discussed for most of this century. Such talk is administrative talk, not curricular talk. We may reform or make more efficient the way that we decide what to teach, but we need to address the question of how we conceptualize what we teach, that is, reform or actually reconfigure curricular content and pedagogical delivery.

Much of the reform talk is rightly characterized as "on to the past."[69] Moffett argues that much school reform effort is wrong headed. He argues that much of the drive behind reform efforts is based on two assumptions that need to be challenged. The first is that, since schools teach to the test, we need to develop high-quality assessment devices. The second assumption is that business, and we would add government, knows best how to reform schools since public education is essentially just another business. We have government round tables with business executives indicating how to make education responsive and cost effective in its production of good citizens and workers. We have governors' councils as well to help shape or reshape education, to address those goals that should guide education.

One assumption behind thinking that business has the answer to the challenges of education is the belief that public schooling will reform and improve if schools operate by free-market competition. Businesses must compete in order to survive. They must be responsive to the marketplace and to their customers. Some districts are so enamored with this thinking that they are hiring individuals with business backgrounds—no educational backgrounds at all—to run their schools.

Accompanying this view that schools should function according to market principles is the increasing push for privatizing education. Allow schools to invent themselves, to reformulate themselves on a market mentality. The appearance of charter schools, discussed in Chapter 5, is one example of the move to a market mentality. Hill has gone even a bit further in suggesting that school be contracted out to various groups of people or organizations to address particular educational goals.

Hill indicates that contracting builds on the charter schools movement, allowing even more groups to gain permission from school districts to run public schools. "Under a contracting arrangement, every public school would have a charter. A school system would hold many different contracts, some for high schools and some for grade schools, some for highly distinctive schools (e.g., Montessori grade schools—or high schools focused on health careers, great books, multicultural curricula) and others for more conventional schools."[70] Only schools that were successful in meeting the goals of their contracts would have them renewed.

Any organization, any person really, could apply to enter into a contractual arrangement with the school district. Even a school district might contract for a school within a neighboring school district. Colleges and universities might contract for their own schools to experiment with novel curricula and pedagogy. Even the state and federal government might apply for contracts to run schools. And certainly there would be offers from businesses to contract to run a school.

The privatizing of education under the aegis of school reform can take more than the forms of charter or contract schools. Perhaps a more controversial type of privatizing is giving choice to parents in the form of scholarships or vouchers. Parents could take these scholarships or vouchers and apply them toward education in various types of schools, public or private. With vouchers, one can see school reform from at least two vantage points. One is the schools would reform in order to attract the parents with these vouchers. Another view is that schools would keep their curricula in place, and parents would "reform schools and the curriculum" for their children by placing them in schools where the curricula were suited to the goals of the parents and/or children.[71]

Bast and Walberg call this type of choice comprehensive choice. It is comprehensive because it goes beyond just giving parents a choice of public schools. In comprehensive choice, funds that now go to public schools would instead go to the parents in the form of certificates or scholarships. These are deposited into a type of educational savings account. When necessary, parents withdraw from this account and pay tuition at participating private and public schools. As Bast and Walberg point out, such a plan is not that new. Vermont has had a voucher program for over a century! Almost 95 percent of Vermont's 246 communities have no public high schools. Parents receive vouchers to pay for their children to attend either private high schools or public high schools in districts with such schools. Thirty-five towns offer a similar choice to parents of K–6 students. This program started in 1869. Thus this idea for school reform has a long history.[72]

Most of the actions taken for school reform appear to relate to changing the management or financing of the schools, rather than to changing the curriculum. Of course, it would indeed be foolish to reform schools to be more efficient in delivering a curriculum that has little relevance with regard to the next century. Much of the curriculum of schools has the imprint of the last century, which should cause some concern as we near the start of a new, information-rich century. We must not only challenge the structure and the administrative cultures of our schools, but we must also rethink what curriculum means in an information age. We must have a chemical change, not a physical change, in curriculum. We must continue to raise the question of school reform, realizing that it is a task that will never be completed; more than just tinkering with parts, reform requires bringing new visions and understandings to the concepts of curriculum, school, and education.

MORAL EDUCATION

In recent years, moral education and character formation have received increasing attention. This particular focus within the field of curriculum continues. We have gone beyond the question of how to get children to do what we want to asking what must be provided in the curricular experiences of children and youth that will enable them to engage in right action, to develop those competencies and dispositions to act that will advance not only the quality of their lives but also the well-being of the community.[73]

This particular trend does not stand alone nor is it caused by one particular event in society. However, it is safe to say that as a nation we all, educators and noneducators alike, realize that the challenges to our society are more than just economic or academic. Many of our problems relate to shortcomings in our morals and character or at least in our willingness to play what we essentially know as proper action. We can certainly raise test scores with new curricula. We can be more effective in the world economic theater with new courses with higher standards. However, we are beginning to realize that we must be as dedi-

cated to raising our moral standards as well. We must nurture those ethical ideas such as justice, faith, hope, and charity if we are to reach the heights of good character as individuals and members of the national and world community.

The issue of moral education and character development is not an easy one for educators to process. A key reason is the diversity in our country. Different ethnic groups have different views of what it means to have good morals or good character. As Foshay notes, people tend to agree that morality suggests following rules. However, the question paramount in many people's minds is "whose rules?"[74] Also, many people, in following rules, seem to mistake good behavior for good character.[75] They often wish to teach students those rules that result in good behavior. There is not much reflection on why these rules are appropriate. Kohn notes that many who stress moral education or character education are essentially advocating indoctrinating children in the ways of right behavior. Curricula with this orientation emphasize drilling students on desired behaviors, rather than engaging students in deep, critical reflection on what it means to be a moral individual, to act morally.[76] Kohn states that far too many published programs reflect this orientation to moral–character education. Also, what is moral is not easily answered, and educators as well as the general public have not spent much time reflecting on the moral dimension of learning and the purpose of such reflection. It is perhaps too easy to just say that moral education has as its purpose to transmit or have students become committed to the community's best values and most prized ethical ideas.[77] To be sure, moral education should enable students to understand and internalize those moral values and habits that they will require for "living the good life," for maintaining their well-being.

Selznick states that much depends on our understanding of well-being. "When well-being is taken to mean happiness, satisfaction, preference, or utility, we lose purchase on what is of genuine moral worth. It is not morally better to have more rather than less efficiency, more rather than less material goods, more rather than less fulfillment of desires. . . ." He notes that words like happiness and utility either mask essential meanings or refer to actions and outcomes that do not demand of persons a willingness to self-sacrifice, a concern for the interests of others, or a realization of our responsibilities to our fellow humans.[78]

A moral person is driven by more than warm feelings for herself and others. A moral person has awareness, understanding, and appreciation of those values and ideas that are essential for productive relations with others and for the meaningful and authentic construction of our own persons. As Selznick denotes, a moral person has both commitment and competence. It is here that a challenge exists for curricularists. We need, and more people are demanding, a curriculum that allows students to learn about moral values and ethics and the competence aspects and to experience such knowledge in ways that ignite in them a desire to put what they know into meaningful action. For curricularists to do this, they must become increasingly attuned to the notion that schools, by their very being, express moral significance and that what occurs within schools, that is, the curriculum and its nurtured experiences, serve as a crucible of human action.[79]

Jackson, Boostrom, and Hansen, realizing the moral dimension of schools and their curricula, set out to look for ways in which schools address the moral and character agenda. Using ethnographic procedures, they found that schools both consciously and unconsciously address moral action, getting students to come to know the good. They identified five explicit efforts that schools take to influence students morally: (1) specific curricular content that one would define as moral education, whether school developed or commercially prepared; (2) the direct introduction of moral topics into the curriculum, such as discussing the good character of some hero in literature; (3) the various rituals and ceremonies that emphasize right behavior or right action, for example, the giving of class awards for "best citizen"; (4) the signs and bulletin boards that are placed in the school environment, such as signs saying "Just say no!" or "Just wait"; and (5) the spontaneous interjection of moral talk by either teacher or students into classroom discussion.

These researchers also found in the schools that they studied three unintentional ways in which morals became part of the curriculum: (1) classroom rules and regulations governing student–student and teacher–student interactions;

(2) assumptions held by teachers that influence the scope and sequence of curricular topics (curricular substructures); and (3) expressive dimensions of the curriculum that have moral meanings that are not apparent unless one intentionally looks for them, a type of moral subtext.[80]

Through such means, both explicit and implicit, an individual comes to develop a morality. A moral person comes to know the good. It is important to note that the word "the" is not capitalized. It is perhaps not possible to know THE good. Theologians have debated the issue, and those of us in curriculum must realize that debating the issue may well take us away from our primary responsibilities as educators concerned with the well-being of our youth. Also, many would argue that with our diversity it may not be possible to even agree as to the good. Certainly, diversities exist among our various ethnic and cultural groups, each perceiving ethical ideas and values from its own vantage point. However, educators are challenged to teach all these diverse students and enable them to develop those moral beliefs and dispositions that will allow them to be effective members of the national and international community.

Despite our differences, few persons would contest the need for individuals to engage in right action, to make intelligent moral judgments. Indeed, it is because of our differences that individuals must possess sensitive moral values; the world is complicated and all actions have a moral undertone.[81] We previously made the point that all the curriculum of the school can be considered as possessing a moral text. We all need to query what the effects of employing certain knowledge are on our well-being and the well-being of others. How do our actions and the actions of others affect the social context? All personal acts have moral content. And the worth of our actions, the morality of them, must be assessed by considering their consequences on ourselves and the general society.

We want persons of good moral character. Selznick states that character has three united parts: moral knowing, moral feeling, and moral behavior. Character is a composite of habits, dependencies, interests, and values. Most of these are unconsciously developed. Such knowledge and actions have their beginnings in early life.[82]

Most of our habits are well learned before they are given names and descriptions. But habits, dependencies, interests, and values are not unalterable. Indeed, they are stretched or challenged when we realize that they are coming into conflict with moral rules.[83]

A purpose of the curriculum as moral text is to enable students to develop moral awareness and to replace unrecognized and unreflective development of their morals and character with more deliberate ways of forming their behavior. A person unaware of why he or she believes or behaves, even when such beliefs or behaviors are good, is not really a moral person. A moral person, a person of good character, knows the difference between right and wrong, knows the bases for his or her behavior, and chooses right over wrong, action that is of benefit to the person and society over that which is not. There is a difference between having a person engage in behaving rightly and behaving morally. The latter implies an awareness of the bases for action or nonaction. The moral person possesses moral competence that relates to a consciousness about action and the values that guide it. Moral competence also means that the person has those skills of procedural knowledge that give him or her the capacity for moral inquiry. A person with moral competence has the will and ability to seek goods that are genuine and enduring, not superficial and transitory.[84]

Many of the critical theorists discussed in other sections of this text are addressing the moral character of students and striving to empower them to attain and utilize that which is genuine and enduring. However, critical theorists are not the only persons urging a curriculum as moral text. Indeed, increasing numbers of educators are becoming more vocal in calling for a curriculum that allows students to inquire into morality and to consciously develop their own.

Of course, some might say that educators and thinking persons in general have always known the need for morality. The point was and is that we cannot agree as to whose morals or whose values should be privileged in the curriculum. It is essential for us all to realize that for societies to exist they must be bound by a core of powerful, shared beliefs. As Wynne and Ryan note, these beliefs and values should be such that citizens are motivated to make great personal sacrifices for the general good. Individuals must have goals that extend beyond immediate self-interest. But individuals should not have blind belief in the group.[85] Again, people are urging that the curriculum enable individuals to be morally competent, not led blindly into action. Those who create curricula need to realize, nevertheless, that if our nation fails to educate students to a commitment to a common morality it is likely to experience social chaos.

Wynne and Ryan present a list of moral facts to which most groups, if not all, in the United States would ascribe. Their list is drawn from the late C. S. Lewis's book, *The Abolition of Man.* And Lewis indicated that many of his ideas reflect the thinking of many cultures through time: Babylonian, ancient Egyptian, old Norse, Greek, Roman, Chinese, ancient Indian, Christian, Hebrew, Islamic, Anglo-Saxon, and American.[86] To the list of cultures, we can add myriad other cultures from Europe, Asia, and Africa. An adaptation of Wynne and Ryan's list follows:

- An effectively functioning society requires of its members human kindness.
- Individuals owe a special love and loyalty to their parents.
- Individuals owe a special love to and responsibility for their own families.
- For a society to prosper, its citizens must exhibit some degree of honesty.
- All members of society have an obligation to help the poor, sick, and less fortunate.
- An effective society requires its citizens to respect basic property rights.
- An effective society requires its citizens to respect the personal rights of others.
- The view of our own personal lives and our own mortality influences how we view life and its meaning.*

The curriculum can teach students these basic moral facts while still being sensitive to their ethnic and cultural diversity. While not all members of our society follow each of these principles to the same degree, we do have a high degree of consensus in the United States that these are impor-

*Adapted from Edward A. Wynne and Kevin Ryan, *Reclaiming Our Schools,* 2nd ed., Merrill, an imprint of Prentice Hall, Upper Saddle River, N.J., 1997.

tant. People could say that these guiding statements represent a national core of values.

It appears that much of the deliberations occurring with regard to moral education–character education are more directed at pedagogical issues than content issues. Certainly, there are those who debate "whose values, whose morals" are being presented. And many are concerned that the thinking of organized religions is creeping into the public schools under the guise of moral education. Also, some are challenging the moral stages of development as Kohlberg presented them as being much too concerned with the cognitive stages of moral development without attending to the particulars of what it means to be moral.

Kohn, in 1997, presented a critical look at character education. In an article entitled "How Not to Teach Values," he developed the case that too many of the commercially prepared moral–character education materials were drawing on behavioristic drill, external rewards, and indoctrination to get students to behave.[87] Kohn stated that the curricular materials present at that time were essentially a collection of exhortations and extrinsic inducements to get children to put forth more effort and to do what they were told. In a real way, these materials were more classroom management programs than moral education programs. Perhaps one of the reasons for their popularity was that they did indeed get children to behave by using teacher pressure, peer pressure, and external rewards to achieve the goals of the programs.[88]

Some of Kohn's critique of these character education programs comes from his challenge of the conservative view of this issue. Any program that focuses on conventional norms of good behavior is classified as conservative. And with this view there seems to be a dim view of human nature, focusing on the dark side of individuals. Children need fixing, and moral education is going to do the fixing. People are not by nature good; therefore we must condition them so that they do desire good behavior. Opponents of conservatism see any type of list for civic morality as trying to prevent individuals becoming thinking moral persons, that such programs want conformity of values and sameness of behavior. Kohn states that some programs are trying to sell virtues like cereal. Eat this "good for your soul" cereal and you too can be virtuous. Present heroes with particular virtues or moral actions and try to get students to mimic them. The talk of role models in multicultural education even has a "taste" of such cereal.[89]

Of course, there are those who do not accept that humans are essentially evil. People are inherently good and, if encouraged and nurtured, they will develop morals that will nurture both individual and community well-being. Taking this view, it is likely that the aims of their programs will differ in both purpose and pedagogy from programs driven by a dim view of human nature. Because of its essentialness to our well-being as individuals and as community, this issue must be continuously discussed and must be a part of our curricular dialogue.

Moral and character education seem to be increasingly a part of curricular dialogue. Perhaps it is because of the dynamic mix of our citizens that we are beginning to realize that to survive as a culture we must be morally caring and competent persons. Even at the political level, we are talking about being responsible for our fellow citizens and, further, that individuals must be responsible for themselves. With freedom comes responsibility, but a responsibility that is based on principles that contribute to society's well-being as well as the individual's.

TECHNOLOGY AND CURRICULUM

We live in a technological world, a world in which people come to expect that good things can only come from the increasing use of technology in our lives. As Kerr states, "We are fascinated with technology. We expect it to make a difference in our lives, and particularly in education. . . . We look for it to change and improve what has come before."[90]

In the early years of technology, we associated it primarily with science and to a lesser extent mathematics. We also thought that we should introduce the topic of technology into the curriculum. This view of technology as a subject of curriculum is still evident. And we still have the most computers in our math and science labs. But, today, the computer and related technologies are ubiquitous in the schools. We are urging that technology, especially computers, be our central learning tool in this expanding information age. In his inaugural address of 1997, President Clinton made it a goal to have every school connected to the Internet. Such a connection can only be good. In fact, many have come to believe that if something is possible then it should be done.[91] This is quite similar to the view held by some educators that if children are developmentally able to learn something then they should be taught it.

No doubt, schools will continue to get wired for technology. No doubt what Bill Gates states is true: "Information technology will not only bring mass-produced information to students, but all such information will be customized to their learning styles, their cultural backgrounds, their educational interests and their academic goals."[92] It is fast becoming possible for a teacher with the assistance of information technology to have essentially twenty-five curricula for twenty-five students.

However, curricularists and educators in general need to be thoughtful about how information technology is employed now and in the future. Certainly, we will continue to think of novel ways in which to employ technology in our classrooms. But education is fundamentally a human, not a technical, activity. We cannot become so enamored with the machine that we forget the child.[93] Talbott cautions us to temper our enthusiasm for the computer with a realization that if we unthinkingly embrace the computer and other information technology we may mold our students to be like the machines that they use and not like the unique individuals that they are.[94]

Talbott states that the challenge today is to discover how to make the computer an instrument of human ends. It is not to make ourselves fit the mold of the machine. A real danger lies in thinking that information technology can give us knowledge or enable us to attain wisdom. Information technology allows us to access information, tremendous amounts of information, through such things as the Internet. However, individuals must have strategies by which to make sense of and construct meaning from that information. Individuals must have ways in which to assess the validity and social worth of the information. They must realize that when using computers they are actually engaged in a human–human interface.[95] A person has programmed and organized the information in a definite way in order to influence

how one will react to and process the information. A student in a science experiment employing the computer as a tool must realize that the experimental method facilitated by the computer is the result of someone's approach (strategy) for solving the problem and processing the information. It is fine for the student to employ the method, but the student must be aware of this fact.

Talbott asserts, "Machines become a threat when they embody our limitations without our being fully aware of those limitations."[96] When computer programs allow the processing of information from one approach, they may actually prevent thinking about the problem in different ways. The language of the programmer gives us certain benefits, but it also presents limitations. There is a real danger in dealing with technology to have technology lead us where it will and to celebrate such leading as progress.[97] Do we want our students to think that the only way that they can organize their construction of meaning is to employ the method contained in a computerized program designed by one person or a particular team of computer scientists?

Bill Gates, certainly an advocate of information technology, states that computers on the information highway will have the capacities to present simulated worlds and to offer explanations of such worlds. Computers will also offer explanations of the real world.[98] But students must recognize that the explanation presented by the computer is not the only way to make sense. Also, with the computer presenting simulated worlds and eventually virtual worlds that are truly realistic, educators need to be careful lest they deny students experiences that foster awe and wonder. A student in a science experiment employing a computer program to determine the results of using some chemical on a particular plant may be handicapped by not having the opportunity to grow a real bean plant and to actually feel the soil and texture of the plant's leaves.

Certainly, the computer can introduce students to the study of any topic and bombard the student with dazzling detail and "mind-blowing" graphics. But if the student has been denied the opportunity to engage in his or her own creative participation, to experience a real field experience, to seek answers to his or her questions, then we may have misused the technology. We may have conditioned the student to want entertainment from this technology, rather than to seek engagement in an educational interaction.

The challenge of technology within the curriculum is *wise use*. Of course, wise use will be interpreted differently by different people at various times. Having students connected to e-mail does not automatically have value. Students can employ it to gossip rather than engage in reflective discourses.[99] Likewise, the Internet can furnish information that has relevance to the curriculum, or it can furnish information of little worth to the curriculum, information that is actually dangerous to the moral development of individuals. Having students engaged in interactive computer programs may be nothing more than conditioning them to expect to be entertained, rather than challenged. Of course, good education need not be lacking in entertainment value.

Technology is with us. Our future will see even more technology employed in our everyday lives. Students will come to school already skilled in using computers. Educators must constantly query themselves as to how to make use of the technology so that educational ends are addressed. Kerr has given us four qualities that we in education should consider when employing technology. First, technology should place human values and educational purposes over and above economic or other socially expedient ends for education. Second, educators must be clear as to the educational intents of employing technology. Software and hardware should be such that they encourage students to recognize that they are constantly challenged to engage themselves in education. Third, when considering the use of technology, it should not be viewed as a quick fix to instructional problems. If students do not know how to develop a research paper, that is no problem; get them a program that lays out the process. Writing papers is much too complicated for such an approach. Also, we need to realize that, as we employ more technology in our curriculum, teachers and students may well have to redefine their respective roles. Fourth, after careful reflection, we need to develop means on how information about school ought to be collected and shared. This last point is directed more to the teacher than to the student.[100]

As Gates commented, these are exciting times in the Information Age and exciting times to

be in education. There is much power to be had in the use of information technology. But, because of the power of such technology, we must be wise users of it. To determine what is wise use is perhaps our biggest challenge. We need to recognize that the information highway is really not in existence yet. Gates states that what we now have is more like the Oregon Trail than our superhighways. Just as our highways required that the majority of people have cars or access to them as well as instruction in proper driving, the majority of people must have "information vehicles" if the information highway is to develop. Gates notes that "information appliances won't become mainstream for publishing information until almost everyone is a user."[101] "The information highway is a mass phenomenon, or it is nothing."[102] This raises the question of who will pay for technology in the schools. Major software design for the most part has been supported to a large degree by federal and foundational support. If materials are to be produced for the entire curriculum, then novel and more effective ways of furnishing the monies are required. This is beginning to happen with school districts passing "technologies levies."[103]

Technology and curriculum will continue to be an issue, as well they should be. We will be constantly challenged to reconceptualize the use of technology and curriculum and technology as curriculum. We will be forced to ask ourselves how technology will affect our learning environments both within and outside the school. We will be dared to ask how this technology is shaping our very persons. Are we making our machines more like us or are we becoming more like our machines? Are our machines allowing us to interact with a broader human family or are we nurturing individuals who wish to isolate themselves, alone with their computers, detached from real human contact?

INCREASING POLITICALIZATION
OF THE CURRICULUM

We once thought, or at least told ourselves, that education was value neutral and apolitical. We now know differently. It is a normative enterprise, and it certainly is a political drama. This does not mean that the government is taking an increasing role in directing the curriculum, although one might conclude this from the federal and state governments' efforts at establishing higher standards.

Education is political in that there is much talk among curricular theorists, if not practitioners, about the curriculum being used as an instrument for advancing particular political ideologies and agendas. Much critical theorist talk is political talk. Indeed, many of the critical theorists are urging a politics of the left, although they realize that the left has essentially not been successful in reorienting the discussion of schooling, and of curriculum in particular, to the views of a socialized welfare state.[104]

There are increasing voices in opposition to the left, stating that the left has caused much mischief among the academic and educational community. Gross and Levitt have stated that the academic left dislikes science and, we would add, knowledge that comes from a modernist construction.[105] But even more crucial for people concerned with education to realize is that the left is actively hostile to the very social structures through which knowledge is created and utilized, to the system of education in which citizens are educated, and to the views actually held by many who oppose their views of the world. Gross and Levitt talk about the left's view of science and scientists in general. But we think it safe to extrapolate the comments to all knowledge.

However, in recognizing the increasing political nature of curriculum and curriculum talk, we are not essentially talking about the debates between those who favor a type of neo-Marxist socialism, or a democracy of the collective, and those who favor a democratic free-market capitalism; rather, we address the attempts of various groups within society to have their stories, their values, included in the curriculum text. Indeed, multicultural education, already discussed, is very political. Specific legislation has been passed protecting the rights of perceived marginalized groups. Also, with regard to bilingual education, political pressure groups have attempted to pass legislation to address their concerns.

As more groups find their identities, there will be more attempts to have their stories included in the curriculum. Formal and informal means will be employed to make their points. Here is the politics that will influence curriculum decisions. And this is good, for it is democracy in action. The move to involve more of the community in curriculum decision making is well established. This involvement will continue.

Academics will not be left out, but their influences are not likely to be directly heard at board meetings in school districts. Debate will continue as to whether there is a hegemony of the macroculture in the schools organized in such ways as to perpetuate what some perceive to be inequities in the society at large. Complaints will continue that the curriculum is patriarchal and serves to marginalize women and nonwestern culture. Most people who criticize the schools and the curriculum are insisting that the schools be responsive to their demands and include them, making these people a part of the macroculture, of the main body politic, and not giving them a separate status and story for their children.

People of diverse voices who also share a common voice of the mainstream culture are not going to be silenced. They will be heard. This politics will be with us increasingly in the future. Almost any issue that we can think of will be part of the politics of education. Issues of censorship will engage people in political action, either to resist such action or to have it applied to educational material that they think offensive or inhibiting to the advancement of their group.

Talk of nurturing global villages is political talk. So also is stressing the need to develop competent individuals who can see beyond themselves. As Lasley and Biddle note, the selfless disposition is essential in a democratic society that is characterized by increasing diversity and personal autonomy.[106] All the discussion of moral and character education can be considered political talk that relates to the notion of having concern, respect, and empathy for others.

Politics addresses power. Power is a hallmark of human endeavors; thus we cannot talk about human action without engaging in political talk. We cannot write down what students are to learn or reflect on without recognizing that curriculum is political text.[107] It appears that we think of power along with powerless, a duality perhaps generated by our language. Some of us think of those with power as oppressors and those without power as oppressed. Certainly, in our political talk, we wish all to have power over their own persons and power to contribute to the community. We do not wish to nurture in the curriculum and in our political dialogue a powerlessness among our students. What we desire and what people are requesting is the wise use of power, the power to have education nurture both the individual and the common good.

CONCLUSION

This chapter has been concerned with contemporary philosophical, social, cultural, and political issues in curriculum. Indeed, the search to improve school curricula is a continuing process that reflects the current issues and trends affecting schools and society. The curriculum trends noted in this chapter are controversial. Debate will continue over these trends in the near and most likely distant future.

The issues discussed have no clear solutions, no simple, all-inclusive answers. Curriculum workers must be willing listeners, alert to the social context within which they work and schools exist. We need to maintain a balance with subjects, programs, and projects, noting that at certain times specific subjects and programs may be more fashionable or deemed more crucial than others. But the constant regarding issues is that they are dynamic and ever changing. In a democracy, such change is encouraged. Groups and countergroups are recognized as necessary for a vibrant democracy. Issues come and go, one hopes with at least partial solutions.

Recognizing that in the United States we essentially have the world within our borders, curricularists should proceed on the basis that all cultures and groups have strengths and that there is worth in and something to be learned from the whole human population. We must be responsive to the needs and demands of our diverse groups. However, in our attempts to be responsive and caring, we must be sure we do not marginalize or demonize others. We must refrain from establishing a politically correct curriculum; such a curriculum is dangerous. The issues of curriculum demand a curriculum characterized by fluidity and a pedagogy that truly recognizes human complexity.

ENDNOTES

1. Norman Amaker, "Reagan Record on Civil Rights," *Urban Institute Policy and Research Report* (Fall 1988), pp. 15–16; Thomas R. McDaniel, "Demilitarizing Public Education: School Reform in the Era of George Bush," *Phi Delta Kappan* (September 1989), pp. 15–18.

2. Paul T. Hill, "The Federal Role in Education: A Strategy for the 1990s," *Phi Delta Kappan* (January 1990), pp. 398–402.

3. David L. Clark and Mary A. Amiot, "The Reagan Administration and Federal Education Policy," *Phi Delta Kappan* (December 1981), pp. 258–262; Larry Cuban, "Four Stories about National Goals for American Education," *Phi Delta Kappan* (December 1990), pp. 265–271.

4. American Association of Colleges for Teacher Education, Memorandum, Agenda Item III (Washington, D.C.: The Association (September 1995), pp. 1–35.

5. Northwest Regional Educational Laboratory, Northwest Report (Portland, Oreg.: The Laboratory (Summer 1995).

6. Ibid.

7. Albert Shanker, "National Standards," in Chester E. Finn, Jr., and Herbert J. Walberg, eds., *Radical Educational Reforms* (Berkeley, Calif.: McCutchan Publishing Corporation, 1994), pp. 3–20.

8. David C. Berliner and Bruce J. Biddle, *The Manufactured Crisis* (Reading, Mass.: Addison-Wesley Publishing Co., 1995).

9. Daniel Tanner, "A Nation 'Truly' at Risk," *Phi Delta Kappan* (December 1993), pp. 288–297.

10. Berliner and Biddle, *The Manufactured Crisis.*

11. Ibid., p. 9.

12. Diane Ravitch, "A Message from Assistant Secretary Diane Ravitch," *OERI Bulletin* (Winter 1991–92), p. 2; Theodore R. Sizer, "No Pain, No Gain," *Educational Leadership* (May 1991), pp. 32–34.

13. American Association of Colleges for Teacher Education, Memorandum, Agenda Item III.

14. Ibid.

15. Allan C. Ornstein, "National Reform and Instructional Accountability," *High School Journal* (October–November 1990), pp. 51–56.

16. Dale Mann, "Conditional School Deregulation," *Executive Educator* (January 1990), pp. 26, 28; Thomas Timar, "The Politics of School Restructuring," *Education Digest* (May 1990), pp. 7–10.

17. *A National Imperative: Educating for the 21st Century* (Arlington, Va.: National School Board Association, 1989).

18. Charles P. McFadden, "Author–Publisher–Educator Relationship. and Curriculum Reform," *Journal of*

Curriculum Studies (January–February 1992), pp. 27–42; Sandra Stotsky, "Whose Literature? America!" *Educational Leadership* (December–January 1992), pp. 53–56.

19. Elliott W. Eisner, "Who Decides What Schools Teach?" *Phi Delta Kappan* (March 1990), p. 523.

20. Diane Ravitch, "A Culture in Common," *Educational Leadership* (December–January 1982), pp. 8–11, 75; Sandra Stotsky, "Cultural Politics," *American School Board Journal* (October 1991), pp. 26–29.

21. *Fifty-state Survey of Textbook Adoption Procedures and Policies* (Washington, D.C.: Education Commission of the States, 1984); Ray Gerke, "American Textbooks: Perspectives on Public Controversies and Censorship," *High School Journal* (October–November 1983), pp. 59–64.

22. *Attack on the Freedom to Learn, 1989–90* (Washington, D.C.: People for the American Way, 1990).

23. Telephone conversation with Anne Meek, managing editor of *Educational Leadership.* September 4, 1990.

24. Michael Apple, "Is There a Curriculum Voice to Reclaim?" *Phi Delta Kappan* (March 1990), pp. 526–530

25. Ian Westbury, "Textbooks, Textbook Publishers, and the Quality of Schooling," in David L. Elliott and Arthur Woodward, *Textbooks and Schooling in the United States,* Eighty-ninth Yearbook of the National Society for the Study of Education, Part 1 (Chicago: University of Chicago Press, 1990), pp. 1–22.

26. Allan C. Ornstein, "Textbook Instruction: Processes and Strategies," *NASSP Bulletin* (December 1989), pp. 105–111.

27. Margret T. Bernstein, "The Academy's Contribution to the Impoverishment of America's Textbooks," *Phi Delta Kappan* (November 1988), pp. 193–198; Marily J. Chambliss and Robert C. Calfee, "Designing Science Textbooks to Enhance Student Understanding," *Educational Psychologist* (Summer 1989), pp. 307–322; Karen A. Shriver, "The Impact of Reader's Self-evaluations in Comprehending Poorly Written Instructional Text," paper presented at the annual meeting of the American Educational Research Association, Chicago, April 1991.

28. Ornstein, "Textbook Instruction."

29. Westbury, "Textbooks, Textbook Publishers, and the Quality of Schooling."

30. Bill Gates, *The Road Ahead* (New York: Viking, 1995).

31. Richard L. Venezky, "Textbooks in School and Society," in Philip W. Jackson, ed., *Handbook of Research on Curriculum* (New York: Macmillan Publishing Company, 1992), pp. 436–461.

32. Ibid.

33. *A National Imperative: Educating for the 21st Century* (Arlington, Va.: National School Boards Associa-tion, 1989); "Children of Poverty," *Phi Delta Kappan* (June 1990), pp. K1–K12.

34. Ellen Flax, "One in Eight Children in Households With Insufficient Food, Study Finds," *Education Week,* April 3, 1991, p. 13.

35. Lynette Long and Thomas J. Long, "Latchkey Adolescents: How Administrators Can Respond to their Needs," *NASSP Bulletin* (February 1989), pp. 102–108.

36. Martha R. Burt, "Roots and Remedies of Homelessness," *Urban Institute Policy and Research Report* (Summer 1991), pp. 1–5; *The Effects of Migrant Children* (Washington, D.C.: U.S. Office of Education, 1989); Marilee C. Rist, "The Shadow Children," *American School Board Journal* (January 1989), pp. 19–24.

37. Allan C. Ornstein, "Enrollment Trends in Big-city Schools," *Peabody Journal of Education* (Summer, 1989), pp. 64–71; David C. Smith and Edward E. Greene, "Preparing Tomorrow's Principals Today," *Principal* (September 1990), pp. 20–24.

38. *Projections of Education Statistics to 2001* (Washington, D.C.: U.S. Government Printing Office, 1990), Table 1, p. 4.

39. Richard L. Fairley, "Accountability's New Test," *American Education* (June 1972), pp. 33–35; Daniel Moynihan, *Coping On the Practice of Government* (New York: Random House, 1975). Also see Mary J. LeTendre, "Improving Chapter I Programs: We Can Do Better," *Phi Delta Kappan* (April 1991), pp. 576–581.

40. Arthur R. Jensen, "Compensatory Education and the Theory of Intelligence," *Phi Delta Kappan* (April 1985), pp. 554–558; A. Harry Passow, "Urban Schools a Second or Third Time Around," *Education and Urban Society* (May 1991), pp. 243–255.

41. Allan C. Ornstein and Daniel U. Levine, "Compensatory Education: Can It Be Successful?" *NASSP Bulletin* (May 1981), pp. 1–15.

42. Consortium for Longitudinal Studies, *As the Twig Is Bent* (Hillsdale, N.J.: Erlbaum, 1983); Jacqueline J. Irvine, *Black Students and School Failure* (Westport, Conn.: Praeger, 1991); and Nancey A. Madden et al., "Success for All," *Phi Delta Kappan* (April 1991), pp. 593–599.

43. Michael R. Hillis, "Multicultural Education as a Moral Responsibility," *Education Forum* (Winter 1996), pp. 142–148.

44. Carl A. Grant and Christine E. Sleeter, "Race, Class, Gender, and Disability in the Classroom," in James A. Banks and Cherry A. McGee Banks, *Multicultural Education: Issues and Perspectives,* 3rd ed. (Boston: Allyn and Bacon, 1997), pp. 61–83.

45. Ibid., p. 71.

46. Frederick Erickson, "Culture in Society and in Educational Practice," in Banks and Banks, *Multicultural Education: Issues and Perspectives,* 3rd ed., pp. 5–6.

47. James A. Banks, "Multicultural Education: Characteristics and Goals," in Banks and Banks, *Multicultural Education: Issues and Perspectives* 3rd ed., pp. 5–6.

48. Ibid.

49. Hillis, "Multicultural Education as a Moral Responsibility."

50. Banks, "Multicultural Education: Characteristics and Goals."

51. Ibid.

52. *Relating Knowledge to Teacher Education* (Washington, D.C.: American Association of Colleges for Teacher Education, 1989); *Toward High and Rigorous Standards for the Teaching Profession,* 2nd ed. (Washington, D.C.; National Board for Professional Teaching Standards, 1990.

53. Manuel Ramirez and Carlos Castañeda, *Cultural Democracy: Biocognitive Development and Education* (New York: Academic Press, 1974).

54. Ibid., p. 142.

55. Paul E. Greenbaum, "Nonverbal Differences in Communication Style between American Indian and Anglo Elementary Classrooms," *American Educational Research Journal* (Spring 1985), pp. 101–116. Lindra Grant, "Regenerating and Refocusing Research on Minorities and Education," *Elementary School Journal* (May 1988), pp. 441–448.

56. James A. Banks, *Multiethnic Education: Theory and Practice,* 4th ed. (Boston, Mass.: Allyn and Bacon, 1992); Pamela L. Tiedt and Iris M. Tiedt, *Multicultural Teaching,* 3rd ed. (Boston: Allyn and Bacon, 1990).

57. Ibid.

58. William F. Pinar, William M. Reynolds, Patrick Slattery, and Peter M. Taubman, *Understanding Curriculum* (New York: Peter Lang, 1995).

59. Jose A. Cardeñas, "The Role of Native Language Instruction in Bilingual Education," *Phi Delta Kappan* (January 1986), pp. 359–363; Henry A. Giroux and Paulo Freire, eds., *Culture and Power in the Classroom: A Critical Foundation for Bicultural Education* (Westport, Conn.: Praeger, 1991).

60. Noel Epstein, *Language, Ethnicity, and the Schools: Policy Alternatives for Bilingual-Bicultural Education* (Washington, D.C.: George Washington University Press, 1977); Joshua A. Fishman, *Language and Ethnicity in Minority Sociolinguistic Perspective* (Bristol, Pa.: Taylor & Francis, 1989).

61. Keith Baller, "The Effectiveness of Bilingual Education." Paper presented at the annual meeting of the American Educational Research Association, New Orleans, April 1988; Epstein, *Language, Ethnicity, and the Schools;* and Martin Ridge, *The New Bilingualism: An American Dilemma* (New Brunswick, N.J.: Transaction, 1990).

62. Joseph E. Barry, "Politics, Bilingual Education and the Curriculum," *Educational Leadership* (May 1983),

pp. 56–60; Asa G. Hillard, "Why We Must Pluralize the Curriculum," *Educational Leadership* (December–January 1992), pp. 12–15; and Ann C. Willig, "Examining Bilingual Education Research," *Review of Educational Research* (Fall 1987), pp. 363–376.

63. Joshua A. Fishman, *Reversing Language Shift* (Bristol, Pa.: Taylor & Francis, 1991); Christine H. Russell, "The Research on Bilingual Education," *Equality and Choice* (Winter 1990), pp. 29–36.

64. Ursula Casanova and M. Beatrice Arias, "Contextualizing Bilingual Education," in M. Beatrice Arias and Ursula Casanova, eds., *Bilingual Education: Politics, Practice, and Research,* Ninety-second Yearbook of the National Society for the Study of Education, Part II (Chicago: University of Chicago Press, 1993), pp. 1–35.

65. Walter G. Secada and Theodora Lightfoot, "Symbols and the Political Context of Bilingual Education in the United States," in Arias and Casanova, eds., *Bilingual Education: Politics, Practice, and Research,* pp. 36–64.

66. John I. Goodlad, "The National Network for Educational Renewal," *Phi Delta Kappan* (April 1994), p. 94.

67. Lawrence Beymer, "The School in the White Suit," *Phi Delta Kappan* (December 1993), p. 341.

68. Evans Clinchy, "Reforming American Education from the Bottom to the Top: Escaping Academic Captivity," *Phi Delta Kappan* (December 1996), pp. 268–270.

69. James Moffett, *The Universal Schoolhouse* (San Francisco: Jossey-Bass Publishers, 1994).

70. Paul T. Hill, "Reinventing Urban Public Education," *Phi Delta Kappan* (January 1994), pp. 396–401; Lynnell Hancock, "Bureaucracy Is Choking Public Education to Death. So Contract Out the Schools," *U.S. News and World Report* (December 1996–January 1997), pp. 40–41.

71. Joseph L. Bast and Herbert J. Walberg, "Free Market Choice: Can Education Be Privatized?" in Chester E. Finn, Jr., and Herbert J. Walberg, *Radical Educational Reforms* (Berkeley, Calif.: McCutchan Publishing Corporation, 1994), pp. 149–171.

72. Ibid.

73. Alfie Kohn, *Beyond Discipline, From Compliance to Community* (Alexandria, Va.: Association for Supervision and Curriculum Development, 1996).

74. Arthur W. Foshay, "Character Education: Some Observations," *Educational Forum* (Winter 1996), pp. 130–134.

75. Alfie Kohn, "How Not to Teach Values: A Critical Look at Character Education," *Phi Delta Kappan* (February 1997), pp. 428–439.

76. Ibid.

77. Edward A. Wynne and Kevin Ryan, *Reclaiming Our Schools,* 2nd ed. (Upper Saddle River, N.J.: Merrill, an imprint of Prentice Hall, 1997).

78. Philip Selznick, *The Moral Commonwealth* (Berkeley: University of California Press, 1992).

79. Philip W. Jackson, Robert E. Boostrom, and David T. Hansen, *The Moral Life of Schools* (San Francisco: Jossey-Bass Publishers, 1993).

80. Ibid.

81. Howard B. Radest, *Can We Teach Ethics?* (New York: Praeger, 1989).

82. Selznick, *The Moral Commonwealth.*

83. Radest, *Can We Teach Ethics?*

84. Selznick, *The Moral Commonwealth.*

85. Wynne and Ryan, *Reclaiming Our Schools.*

86. Ibid.

87. Kohn, "How Not to Teach Values: A Critical Look at Character Education."

88. Ibid.

89. Ibid.

90. Stephen T. Kerr, "Visions of Sugarplums: The Future of Technology, Education and the Schools," in Stephen T. Kerr, ed., *Technology and the Future of Schooling,* Ninety-fifth Yearbook of the National Society for the Study of Education, Part II (Chicago: University of Chicago Press, 1996), pp. 1–27.

91. Ibid.

92. Gates, *The Road Ahead,* (New York: Viking, 1995).

93. Kerr, "Vision of Sugarplums: The Future of Technology, Education and the Schools."

94. Stephen L. Talbott, *The Future Does Not Compute* (Sebastopol, Calif.: O'Reilly & Associates, Inc., 1995).

95. Ibid.

96. Ibid., p. 33.

97. Ibid.

98. Gates, *The Road Ahead.*

99. Gavriel Salomon and David Perkins, "Learning in Wonderland: What Do Computers Really Offer Education?" in Kerr, ed., *Technology and the Future of Schooling,* pp. 111–130.

100. Kerr, "Visions of Sugarplums: The Future of Technology, Education and the Schools."

101. Gates, *The Road Ahead.*

102. Ibid., p. 256.

103. Ibid.

104. Svi Shapiro, *Between Capitalism and Democracy* (New York: Bergin & Garvey Publishers, 1990).

105. Paul R. Gross and Norman Levitt, *Higher Superstition: The Academic Left and Its Quarrels with Science* (Baltimore: The Johns Hopkins University Press, 1994).

106. Thomas J. Lasley and James R. Biddle, "Teaching Students to See Beyond Themselves," *Educational Forum* (Winter 1996), pp. 165–173.

107. Pinar et al., *Understanding Curriculum.*

13

FUTURE DIRECTIONS FOR CURRICULUM

Focusing Questions

1. What is futurism?
2. How has the information age affected curricularists' thinking about education?
3. Identify some future trends that can affect the curriculum.
4. What procedures can educators employ in planning for the future?
5. Which constants in education are likely to continue in the future?
6. What new curricular areas are likely to evolve in the future?
7. How is future technology likely to affect the range of curriculum content?
8. What cautions should educators be mindful of as they contemplate the future?

We live in unique times characterized by a dizzying rate of diverse and extensive changes affecting all aspects of living. The rapidity and extensiveness of these changes have given our times a high degree of uncertainty. In trying to address these chaotic times, many curricularists realize that what the curriculum is and its purpose can never be set in stone. What the school does, even the nature of schooling, emerges from dynamic interactions between the school and various realms of society. There is no reason to believe that the energy of this century will lessen. Indeed, the future should be even more energetic, compelling all players in society, educators certainly included, to give careful thought to the nature and purpose of curriculum.

For some, the ultimate purpose of education is to present programs and thus opportunities for students to gain the knowledge, skills, beliefs, and values that will enable them to create productive lives for themselves and others. However, others

contend that this is still viewing education as the filling the heads of students with facts.[1] Even those who advocate empowering students view education as filling the head with objective knowledge. Only, with students empowered, they can do it themselves. Learning the curriculum is the filling the head with stuff. With this view, the sole challenge for the future curricularist is to determine or assist the student to determine what knowledge, skills, attitudes, and values are requisite for being an active player in future times.

Many are asking what kind of education program will achieve the aim of fostering effective future citizens. Although this is an important question, it is not the most critical. The central question is what it means to be human in an emerging, chaotic series of futures. This requires educators and others concerned with education to query the very nature of humanness. We must view humanness in a fluid context. Just what probable futures will or should emerge? How will such futures affect humans? How should humans shape their futures? Is the future to be experienced? Is the future to be invented?

All educators should reflect on these questions, for all educators are futurists. We do not create programs or engage students in them for the present, and certainly not for the past. For education to be relevant, it must address images of the future; it must actually mold these images. Curricular activity is a process of visioning, a type of foresight. However, some educators appear by their behavior to think of curricular visioning as hindsight. They are marching into the future walking backward, holding sacred past views of the curriculum and the school. For these people, the future is yesterday. The only difference is that the future has all its problems solved. Those who argue for a return to the basics of reading, writing, and arithmetic are "hindsighters." Just raise the standards, they argue. Even those who urge reconceptualizing the curriculum draw on past theories to guide actions toward the future. Other educators are "present sighters." To them, the future is a linear extension of current times, again with the current problems solved. Just create a time line, a simple extension of current happenings, and the future will be defined for you.

For people with either of these "sight impediments," the future appears predictive. However, Toffler notes that people cannot view their images of the future as totally predictive in the sense that what they see is what they will get. Possible futures, he points out, are not singular, but plural.[2] We would add that possible futures are not linear, but chaotic. Futures will result both from factors that people can control and from factors that they cannot.

FUTURE AND FUTURISM

Naisbitt asserted as recently as 1990 that we were a society caught between two eras: the age in which industry was the leader and an age built on information. He argued that industrial might was being swept aside by the age of the information industry. He suggested that we were in the early stages of the information age.[3] In the short time since Naisbitt uttered this proclamation, we have gone well into the information age. No longer are we between eras. With new technology and new

mind sets, we are well into a knowledge or at least an information society. Churchill's prophecy that the empires of the future would be empires of the mind has come to pass.[4]

It is essential that educators comprehend that a new era is here, that information and the capacity to process information with various technologies are exploding. Educators must realize that Moore's law, proclaimed in 1965, that there would be a doubling every year of the capacity of the computer chip to process data is essentially accurate. The implications for the curriculum and the ways in which students will experience it are awesome.

The question for educators, especially curricularists, is whether the schools are in the same information age. Schlechty asserts that much of the driving force behind recent and current school form results from educators realizing that schools must shift their focus so that students can function and compete in an emerging information-based world community. He argues that schools must contemplate and actualize redesigned curricula and school organizations to prepare students for life in the twenty-first century.[5] Curricularists must ask themselves what needs to be addressed in designing curricula for students who will spend their lives in a century in which information and the knowledge derived from such information are the ultimate resources.[6]

Curricularists must reflect on the implications for schools of existing in a age in which computers can process information at awesome speeds. Already, laboratories have computers with transistors that can switch circuits on the order of a femtosecond. A femtosecond is 1/1,000,000,000,000,000 of a second.[7] Will such speed in processing data lead to knowledge creation or just information overload? Will schools furnish students with ways to be fully conscious of the impact of computers on their thinking, their viewing and construction of reality? Or will students be lulled into depending entirely on machines to mold their human natures?[8]

In the information age, people are engaged in "knowledge work," the employment of ideas and symbols to produce meaning and some purposeful results. Knowledge work is mental work as compared to physical work, which was paramount in the industrial work age. In reading this book, in contemplating the questions and issues raised by this and previous chapters, you are engaged in knowledge work. Schlechty notes that "in an information-based society, knowledge is the primary mode of work, since information provides the primary means by which work is accomplished."[9]

Today, more individuals are involved in knowledge work than in physical work. The shift occurred in the mid 1950s when, for the first time in American history, white-color workers in technical, managerial, and clerical positions outnumbered blue-color workers. At this juncture, we experienced for the first time more people working with information than producing material goods.

The rate at which the information, or postindustrial age, has appeared has clouded people's images of the future. They have to generate new paradigms to organize their social and work worlds. This makes many people unclear about the roles they are to play. Indeed, many are finding that their secure jobs are being phased out and that they have to almost "start again."

Not only are people being informed that they must start again, they are being advised to be prepared to actually "keep starting again." There is no end in sight for change. Indeed, Thomas Quick has urged us to change the permanent to the temporary.[10] Those in education currently embracing notions on the restructuring of schools and the curriculum need to keep this caveat in mind; our organizations must be considered temporary in order to be responsive to a rapidly changing future, a future that is actually being managed for change and modification.

In discussing this temporary mode of thinking, Warren Bennis refers to adaptative organizations creating temporary systems to confront emerging problems quickly and effectively. In responsive organizations, there will be "task forces composed of groups of relative strangers with diverse professional backgrounds and skills organized around problems to be solved. The groups will be arranged on an organic rather than mechanical model, meaning that they will evolve in response to a problem rather than to represent, programmed expectations. . . . Organizational charts will consist of project groups rather than stratified functional groups."[11] The future requires that those designing curricula function similarly: groups of curricularists evolving in response to educational demands emanating from myriad sources.

Keeping our organizations temporary and our roles fluid points to the rapidity with which things are changing. The European shift from an agricultural to an industrial society took several centuries; the same shift evolved over a century in the United States. However, the shift from an industrial to an information society has occurred in only two or three decades! The times have not allowed us either the opportunities to reflect on the nature of the change or "breathing room" in which to react. And to heighten our discomfort, the rate of change currently is increasing.

Megatrends: Beyond 2000

The ten megatrends that Naisbitt reported are well established and yet continuing to evolve. We are ever deeper into an *informational society* (megatrend 1). We are embraced by a *high tech/high touch world* (megatrend 2). We are in a *world economy* in which changes in any part of the world almost immediately affect us (megatrend 3). We are becoming more comfortable in engaging in *strategic planning,* in going from *short term to long term* (megatrend 4). The school restructuring move is only part of the shift from *centralization to decentralization* (megatrend 5). The press for independent learners, to empower teachers and parents in the educational game, represents a move from *institutional help to self-help* (megatrend 6), a move to *participatory democracy* (megatrend 7) within our schools. Restructuring also is part of the move to *networking,* rather than the hierarchical arrangements of yesterday (megatrend 8). And we are beginning to plan options and programs that will emerge in our schools, reflecting the move from *either/or thinking to that of multiple options* (megatrend 9). Megatrend 10 refers to demographic shifts from north to south.[12]

In *Megatrends 2000,* Naisbitt identified additional trends that will also affect education and its offerings. The booming *global economy,* trends 1 and 2 in Naisbitt's list, certainly will mean that our students will have to possess an increasing global education expertise. Ideally, the *renaissance in the arts* will affect the curriculum, forcing educators to realize that we must educate the whole person, all those dimensions that address human spirit. New *lifestyles and cultural nationalism* should make students come to realize what it means to participate as a world citizen. The *expanding role of women* will further influence college environments and the job sector. The *age of biology* will affect what educators know about individuals. Biological discoveries may allow us all to participate in our evolution, or at least extend our life span. For this reason, life-long education and two or three different employment careers should become more common in the future.[13]

Perhaps key for educators to consider is that the individual changes himself or herself first before attempting to change society. More than ever, all of us need to be awake and fully conscious of our times and our actions within these times. As Talbott notes, "everything depends today on how much we can penetrate our activities with a full consciousness, deeply felt intention, leaving as little as possible to the designs that have 'escaped' us and taken up residence in the impersonal machinery of our existence."[14]

Talbott reasons that it is essential that individuals grasp the meanings inherent in their various activities within the information age. Individuals need to enter into action with imaginative thinking. Certainly, in this information age, individuals will use computers and other types of technology, but they cannot ignore the nature of this interaction. Individuals must apprehend the difference between viewing a two-dimensional, perspective image and participating in the world. They must realize the difference between interacting with a computer and interacting with a person.[15] We cannot ignore these distinctions, lest we become more machinelike and less humanlike. The challenge of the information age is to allow us to utilize this resource without bounds in a way that we can attain not only knowledge but wisdom. The challenge for educators as curriculum planners is to create programs that enable students to adapt to an evolving future, to participate in its planning, to maximize themselves for the benefit of all, and to realize increasingly their human nature.[16]

Dealing with the Future

Although educators may not have perfected the tools for dealing with all aspects of the future, they do have the means for viewing and creating futures. These tools partly comprise the field of *futuristics,* sometimes called *futurism* or *future studies.* Whatever it is called, it embraces both the science of forecasting and the art of imagining.[17] This discipline views both technological and social events not as separate and independent occurrences, but as twin components linked in a system or process. Reality and the events comprising it are holistic. Events affect other events, which in turn affect still other events. Knowing the strength and direction of an interaction allows people to "preview" what are the likely consequences of such interactions—to "visualize" the future. See Curriculum Tips 13-1.

Futurism is a systematic attempt to meld creative forecasting, planning, and action. Those engaged in this field, and curriculum leaders should be among them, are studying and developing alternative futures and generating supporting scenarios elaborating specific areas of society including its institutions. From the tentative futures, these professionals draw significant variables likely to influence events or behavior and then deduce the kinds of educational programs that have a high probability of meeting the projected conditions. Using the tools of educational futurism, educators can proact rather than react.

The majority of futures techniques are really types of forecasting. Note that *predictions* are statements about occurrences that are to happen in a specific future. *Forecasts* tell us not what will happen, but rather what can happen if certain conditions or certain events occur or continue. The accuracy and inclusiveness of forecasts depend on the data fed into the deliberations, the decision systems employed, and the diversity of the techniques utilized.

One researcher has provided a useful overview of the major approaches to future planning. These approaches involve either exploratory forecasting or normative forecasting.[18] *Exploratory forecasting* means processing data to discover possible capabilities, changes, opportunities, and problems that may or are likely to appear in the future, assuming the continuance of certain events. Attention is given to identifying likely futures. Often such forecasting expands various trends that have been identified. *Normative forecasting* deals with attending to various goals or norms to be ac-

```
================ Curriculum Tips 13-1 ================
```

Getting into a Futures Mode

Being a curriculum futurist requires an active futures orientation and a realization that the future is not something that must be coped with when it arrives, but rather phenomena that we can manage to varying degrees. We can proact.

1. Ask yourself what business you are really in. What is the nature and purpose of school? Are we to transmit knowledge or allow students to be in the knowledge production business?
2. Think of new metaphors that can give clarity to the concept of school. Recognize the need to employ new language to create new thoughtways.
3. Accept the idea that the future is a manageable concept. Yes, you can change the nature and direction of tomorrow. Seek out persons in the school organization who have similar thoughts.
4. Accept the idea that you as an educator are both an inventor and leader when it comes to education in general and curriculum in particular.
5. Recognize that the school organization is a culture run by values implicit in that culture. Identify those values central to the organization's success.
6. Schedule time for day dreaming; visions of schools take time.
7. Have a strategy or strategies for marketing your vision of the school to the local community.

Source: Adapted from Phillip C. Schlechty, *Schools for the 21st Century* (San Francisco: Jossey-Bass Publishers, 1990).

---

tualized in the future. Here forecasters are "inventing" the future of their choice. They actually set the norms for the future and then indicate what needs to be accomplished to attain such norms or goals.

Following is a listing of some major approaches to forecasting:

Simulation Forecasting. This technique generates the future by activating models of known physical, social, and environmental laws and determines how they will most likely impact the future. The models, designed and used to forecast future probabilities, denote sets of variables or entities and their interactions.[19] They allow forecasters to discover what can be or should be controlled, what can be or needs to be designed, and ultimately what needs to be forecasted.

For example, educators might create a model of the future school system denoting the key variables and then, using various mathematical formulas, design a computer program that will enable them to project results or alternative actions and thus make particular choices. Using this technique, educators might be able, for example, to accurately picture what might happen if all the students in a school experienced a particular curriculum. By obtaining a readout of possible consequences, educators can decide whether to enact their current plans.

Trend Forecasting. To use this procedure, an educator plots mathematically the path of discovered events and extends them into the future. Such forecasting assumes that the rate of change noted in the past and present will continue uninterrupted into the future. For example, educators may be interested in the amount of new knowledge that is being discovered in a subject or discipline. The number of discoveries can be either plotted on a graph or compared against specific points in time, such as decades, years, or months, and arranged in increasing order. Arranging the information in this manner, educators can see if the variable, for example, the number of discoveries in biology, is increasing or decreasing with time. A straight line may be fitted to the points and then extended beyond the most recent point. If the line denotes an increase, then educators can forecast that they will likely need to expand coverage in the biology curriculum.

Intuitive Forecasting. This procedure is something everyone can do. It relates to the images or feelings people have about the future. These perceptions of what is to come influence their decisions and actions, such that many of their views become reality. For example, someone may feel that in the future there will be a greater need for more science and mathematics courses in light of the increasing technological nature of our society. In other words, their intuition about the increasing technology becomes essentially a tool for their forecasting what will be a useful educational future.

Delphi Forecasting. Along with brainstorming, Delphi forecasting is perhaps the most well known futures procedure. It is a process of extracting "expert" opinions about the future and then furnishing the "experts" with the preliminary results. This process is repeated several times until the "experts" achieve consensus of opinion regarding the future. According to one observer, "Delphi . . . operates on the principle that several heads are better than one in making subjective conjectures about the future, and that experts . . . will make conjectures based on rational judgment and shared information rather than merely guessing, and will separate hope from likelihood in the process."[20]

Educators might use a Delphi technique to obtain a "reading" of what they believe the future will demand of the curriculum with regard to specific content to be covered. Each educator might be given a questionnaire that asks him or her to note ten major content areas that will be needed for future education. An analysis of the results of the first questionnaire is used to develop a second questionnaire. This second questionnaire is sent to the same group of educators with the results of the first questionnaire to indicate those areas considered essential for inclusion in the curriculum. Educators are asked to respond to this second questionnaire after considering the responses of

the "experts" to the first questionnaire. They are also asked to indicate why they revised their responses if they did so.

A third questionnaire is then created to summarize the previous responses and the reasons individuals changed those responses. As before, the educators are asked to consider the questionnaire items, to revise their responses if they think it necessary, and to explain their actions. Ideally, by this third round, educators have a fairly good consensus of how they and their colleagues "read" the future.

Scenario Forecasting. This procedure is also quite well known to the public. It involves creating a scenario, which is basically a well-thought-out story or description about how a possible future state of affairs might occur. The story must draw on current happenings and likely trends. Often it notes how people can go from the present reality to some possible future period.[21] Scenario writing puts into prose form innovative, imaginative, and plausible futures for people to contemplate.

There is really no one method for creating a scenario, but there are certain approaches to scenario forecasting. Usually, the general process requires those involved to begin with a checklist of the aspects of society that deserve attention. The scope of the checklist depends on the writer's definition of the system that is to be the focus of the scenario. If, for example, a teacher is going to write a scenario about the schools of the future, the list will be much more detailed than if he or she is writing a scenario about only one subject area in the curriculum.

The writer would then propose specific questions on the checklist items. For curriculum, they might include: What new contents might be produced? How will the new contents be organized? What old contents are likely to remain? How will these old contents be organized? What are some likely new teaching methods? How will computers interface with students? What new staff members will be needed? How will change agents, researchers, and instructional designers be used in formulating curriculum? The writer reviews the answers to these questions for accuracy and arranges them in chronological order or in a time period. This arrangement of the responses to the questions really forms the basis for the scenario.

In essence, the scenario writer has created an outline for his or her "story."

Force Analysis Forecasting. To use this procedure, educators note and analyze forces (sets of events, pressures, problems, and/or social events) and their probable impact on future events or areas. For example, people start out by selecting a topic, say, an area of the curriculum. Next, they define a force as a set of events, pressures, or technologies whose impact on the curriculum will impel those who design the curriculum to make modifications in it. Next, they ask persons knowledgeable about the curriculum to scan the present and immediately past environment for forces, as they have defined them. Recent discoveries in knowledge might be listed as one force, and the

public's increasing demands that certain contents be covered might be another. National needs might also be noted, as could the changing nature of students.

Once these forces have been selected, each is described. After descriptions have been written, the forecasting team draws upon data gathered and the inferential summaries made to describe the nature of each force and the impact it has previously had on, in this case, the curriculum. Last, the forecasting team uses the data gathered to forecast the nature of each force and how it will affect the curriculum in the time frame indicated.[22]

Although the preceding discussion has listed six types of forecasting (see Table 13-1), it is not all-inclusive. Nonetheless, it does indicate that educators have options. Rarely would they employ

TABLE 13-1   Overview of Futures Techniques

TECHNIQUE	FORECAST TYPE	POSSIBLE USES	POSSIBLE BENEFITS
Simulation	Exploratory, normative	To play out consequences of employing various curriculum designs	Permits educators more control over programs; introduces more creativity in school programs
Trend forecasting	Exploratory	To plot the path of events into the future	Gives curricularists insights into future demands and needs for planning curriculum
Intuitive forecasting	Exploratory, normative	To get a feel for what the future may hold for education	Provides educators a sense of readiness to deal with new events, demands
Delphi procedure	Exploratory, normative	To obtain conjectures regarding future needs in education, or to outline preferred future events	Allows educators to survey views of knowledgeable persons regarding future developments affecting education
Scenario writing	Exploratory, normative	To outline a future story of how curriculum will or should look	Gives educators a usable written document on possible future times for which the curriculum is designed
Force analysis	Exploratory	To plot those events that will affect each other and the school	Allows curricularists to design programs that will influence future events in society

just one technique; rather, they would usually combine various types of forecasts to obtain a useful reading of a possible future.

But forecasting the future is still challenging, because the future is the consequence of the dynamics between events current and events yet to happen. The future, in a real sense, is always evolving. For this reason, a curriculum that is to be responsive to the times must also be evolving. See Curriculum Tips 13-2.

Today, our awareness of the nature of chaos influences our thinking about methods of dealing with the future. No longer can we rely totally on using trend analysis that assumes that the future will be a straight-line extension of current events. Time and events are turbulent. As Briggs and Peat state, "Natures's systems will often undergo rigid, repetitive movements, and then, at some critical point, evolve a radical new behavior."[23]

In forecasting the future, we need to get away from just looking at events as particles in time. Rather, we need to observe the space between the particles, the relationships extant between the events, happenings, and natural and human reactions. According to Hayles, the fundamental assumption is that the individual, the unit, does not matter. What is important are the "recursive symmetries between different levels of the system."[24] What this means for curricularists attempting to forecast the future is that they must not just look at individual students, individual schools, or particular political or economic happenings; rather, they must observe the relationships between and among students, schools, and events with an ecological, holistic, and systemic mind set.[25] In looking at the relationships, which are actually abstractions that cannot be observed directly, one can see emerging patterns if the relationships are graphed. Plotting these relationships on graphs reveals patterns previously hidden. From the analysis of these patterns, one can then generate forecasts showing trends or pathways emerging from chaos, from turbulence. Here computers with their graphics can provide curricularists with views into possible futures.

FUTURE DIRECTIONS

We in this century have seen unprecedented change in every aspect of life. More change has occurred in this century, in fact, than has occurred in all the previous centuries of human existence. Harold Shane notes the rapidity of change. From a historical point of view, it seems reasonable to conclude that for the first time in human history, we have been propelled from yesterday into tomorrow with no familiar "today" during which we can become acclimated to change.[26]

Toffler states "at the rate at which knowledge is growing, by the time the child born today graduates from college the amount of knowledge in the world will be four times as great. By the time that same child is fifty years old, it will be 32 times as great and 97 percent of everything known in the world will have been learned since the time he was born."[27] Toffler's projection, however, assumes a linear extrapolation of current events. It does not consider changes in either rate or direction nor does it consider unseen variables or events, what some people call system breaks. It does not consider chaos theory.

Daniel Bell has noted that the world is becoming increasingly empirical, worldly, secular, humanistic, pragmatic, utilitarian, contractual, epicurean, and hedonistic. Bourgeois, bureaucratic, and meritocratic elites also seem to be forming. More and more decisions are being made by fewer and so-called highly qualified individuals. Scientific and technological knowledge is accumulating that leaves many areas of decision-making beyond the scope and participation of many people.[28]

Michael McDaniel has listed seven factors that have contributed to the rapidity and nature of change. They basically deal with social and cultural trends and the way society is undergoing change:

1. *Demographic change:* sex and age patterns death rates, lifespans, family size, balance of youth versus old, and so on.

2. *Technological innovation:* adaptive changes in existing machines and productivity.

3. *Social innovation:* new arrangements, systems, or styles in educational, political, economic, military, and other dimensions.

4. *Cultural-value shifts:* changes in cultural axioms or values and ideas.

5. *Ecological shifts:* changes in the natural ecology, catastrophic events, pollution of rivers.

===== *Curriculum Tips 13-2* =====

Curriculum Forecasting

Forecasting identifies and describes possible future developments or events pertinent to a particular topic. It also makes estimates about the probabilities that these developments or events will occur. Curriculum planners who proact engage in some forecasting activities. The following points should assist:

1. Identify the particular topic or event about which the forecast is to be made. Be sure that those involved actually are knowledgeable about the topic.
2. Be sure that the necessary data about the topic have been gathered in order to have a good reading of current and past situations.
3. Identify the continuities that exist in the topic considered. (Continuities refer to any observed relations among specific aspects of a topic or between topics.)
4. Identify or estimate discontinuities likely to affect the topic considered. (Discontinuities refer to any significant change in relations among identified aspects of a topic or between topics.) Determining discontinuities is a bit more challenging than identifying continuities, for discontinuities tend to be sudden and unanticipated.
5. Have the group estimate the timing of the event. When and under what circumstances might what is forecast occur? The rate of past and current change in the topic can be used to estimate the scheduling. Are the change rates likely to remain constant? How much confidence can we place in these change rates?
6. Determine the manageability of the topic in question. How well will people at some future time be able to regulate the various aspects of the topic?

Note: Some ideas for these tips came from David Miller and Ronald Hunt, *Survey of Future Studies,* Final Report, U.S. Department of Health, Education and Welfare, 1972.

6. *Information-idea shifts:* scope, quality, and manipulability of knowledge; new conceptions of how things work.

7. *Cultural diffusion:* transfer of ideas, values, or techniques from one culture to another through war, invasion, advertising, and increased travel.[29]

Certainty versus Uncertainty

While rapid change in all aspects of life has been and continues to be a hallmark of this century, this does not mean that individuals have accepted change with ease and grace. Indeed, much has been and still is traumatic. We realize that the times are uncertain. We increasingly grasp the difficulty of generating projections that are both accurate and on target. While appreciating that

making accurate projections is increasingly problematic, we also understand that the costs of failure to make such readings, to generate such forecasts, is indeed high. If we as educators misread the future, we may create curricula that do not address students' needs. We may even educate students in ways that may add to social problems, for example, by preparing students for obsolete jobs and thus unemployment.

One thing is certain: "Knowledge is power." Knowledge is the critical resource. Those individuals who develop new thoughtways to create understanding will indeed have meaningful roles in the future. The uncertainty as to how to create in our students new thoughts should not make us withdraw from the challenge. Rather, we should grasp that uncertainty will compel us to think of options and alternatives; uncertainty will challenge our creativity. Decisions made under uncertainty are different from those generated under certain conditions. When a situation is certain, we have only to decide to achieve whatever it is that we want to maximize and then focus our resources and schedule time to do it.[30] At other times, it is good procedure to leave options open and to denote contingency plans. Being unsure about what the future may demand, we should arrange for possible options; that is, we should suggest several avenues or programs that can be delivered in a multitude of ways. In this way, we anticipate future problems and ways to deal with them before they actually materialize.

In accepting uncertainty as a constant, we approach the concept of time, both present and future, in a somewhat different mind frame. Time is emergent; time is uncertain as to rate and duration. Huebner has spoken of time in this manner:

> Time is not a dimension in which we live—a series of "nows" some past and some in the future. Man does not have so many "nows" allotted. He does not simply await a future and look back upon a past. The very notion of time arises out of man's existence, which is an emergent. The future is man facing himself in anticipation of his own potentiality for being . . . human life is never fixed but is always emergent . . . [31]

In many instances, the futures perceived are nothing like the past. Answers currently considered correct will be frequently wrong in future times. Students who consider education as more than the gathering of answers will find themselves challenged by time. The explosion of knowledge has indeed furnished new information that has questioned the validity—even the occurrence—of previously held conclusions. A constant challenge for us all will be to abandon existing answers and perceptions. Distancing ourselves from current answers and indeed from the means of processing information is a crucial first step in dealing with unanticipated futures. From chaos theory, we realize that ways of processing information will often emerge from the very situations that demand our attention. The successful student of the future may be that person who can change his or her mind and identify those situations that require such change.

The successful person of the twenty-first century will certainly be that individual skilled in raising meaningful questions, rather than just being precise in finding answers. This individual will realize that the intent of inquiry is not to uncover certainty, but to bring into focus increasing numbers of uncertainties, which will require additional questions and novel means of questioning. To nurture such an individual, schools must present the curriculum as unfinished text, as cultural stories continually being created.

Human life as emergent makes individuals major players in their own lives. Empowering people means that we educators have a responsibility to assure that individuals, our students, gain those competencies to act so that they indeed can take control of their lives. If this is to be the age of the empowered individual, then schools must furnish opportunities so that students can be fully unique and in control of themselves and their destinies.

The times demand that individuals function autonomously and collaboratively. Technology is putting individuals in control of information. Students in our schools will not only be asked to receive information from teachers, but also to search out information of their own choosing and, perhaps even more importantly, to create information from their investigations. This stress on the individual does not mean that people will be duped into believing that they are indeed alone in the world and that they can function in isolation from their societies. Quite the opposite. Naisbitt states that the triumph of the individual does not mean that "the individual is condemned to face the world alone. Stripped down to the individual, one can build community, the free association of individuals. In community there is no place to hide either. Everyone knows who is contributing and who is not. Individuals seek community."[32]

Focusing on the individual, educators realize that the school curricula needs to be adjusted and created so that students do develop as individuals, as enlightened persons. Educators are now thinking of modifying the schools to fit the students rather than demanding that the students change to fit the schools. Increasingly, curricularists are creating specialized environments to meet individuals' needs, and they are contemplating requisite support services. We have new curricular designs to integrate content in more meaningful ways. In addressing the empowered individual, educators are creating varied program options and alternatives and multiple career programs. Furthermore, educators are recognizing and addressing the different forms of intelligence that individuals possess—not just in the cognitive domain—but also musical, artistic, spatial, kinesthetic, and interpersonal.

FUTURE INTELLIGENCE

Toffler believes that the intelligent environment that is so dramatically altering our info-sphere may indeed transform our minds. It may even alter the chemistry of our brains.[33] While that may be a bit extreme, students having access to various types of computers may actually think about problems, synthesize information, and generate options for actions in ways far different from current students. Students may indeed have different language forms and employ different types of symbols as yet unimagined. Certainly, our verbal messages will be affected by the available means of sending skills via technological links and electronic impulses.

In his book, *Power Shift,* Toffler discusses extra-intelligence. Our technological equipment can now create "added value" to our messages. Currently, businesses employ electronic networks to gather and even analyze data patterns. Toffler notes that companies are growing very dependent on their networks for billing, ordering, tracking data, and trading. Design information is exchanged, schedules are communicated, and even production is controlled from distant places.[34]

This networking occurring within the general community and the schools is actually creating a content revolution. This revolution relates both to the information being created and to the means by which people can access and manipulate it. Not too long ago, schools thought themselves current if their students had their own electronic mail or e-mail. Students were able to e-mail their teachers to inquire how the teacher "liked" their papers, which also had been sent electronically. Now students have access to the Internet, which enables them to access literally the world. They have access to electronic books. They can connect with textbooks and even encyclopedias. Students can

tune into the views of other students anywhere in the world regarding any conceivable school topic.

Gates points out that the real point of electronic documents is not simply access. The new technology of digital documentation is that we are undergoing a redefinition of the concept of a document itself.[35] This means that the curricular documents of old, the textbooks, pamphlets, worksheets, and curriculum guides, will also need to be redefined. Students in the very near future will have access to a complete line of digital documents. Students will be able to transmit information instantly by computer and retrieve it immediately upon demand. Students will be able to engage in worldwide searches for information and to obtain the context in which the information was produced. Students will not only have information as to what some author wrote, but will also have data on why the author has taken a certain position.

Certainly, the textbook will continue to be a mainstay of the curriculum, at least for the foreseeable future. For many teachers, it may well continue to be the curriculum. However, change is on the way and, in some cases, is already here. Gates talks of Microsoft Encarta, an electronic encyclopedia. Encarta comes on a single CD-ROM (compact disc, read-only memory) weighing only 1 ounce. Included on this disk are 26,000 topics containing 9 million words of text, 8 hours of sound, and 7,000 photographs and illustrations. It also contains 800 maps, 250 interactive charts and tables, and 100 animations and video clips. Unlike an encyclopedia, it costs less than \$100.[36]

Every student can have this curricular document now. In fact, students can access such documents in their own homes. This has implications for whether students will even need to come to school to access information. Hunkins is the author of a world geography book that comes with a video disk version in which students can access maps, photographs, and charts. And what makes such presentations of document content exciting is that students can "personalize how they actually use this information." No longer must students just read the material in a linear fashion. Learning and meaning making can reach a new height of personalization.[37]

Not only are we expanding the information base and arranging for creative interaction with information, but we are also seeing the rapid development of networks that have the quality of self-awareness. Such networks have "intelligence" built into them. They are like the double-loop systems that Argyris talked about in management systems. These networks now monitor the messages; they can even decide which routing of the message will be the most efficient. As Toffler notes, it is "as though a once-dead organism . . . [can] suddenly . . . [check] its own blood pressure, pulse, and breathing rate."[38] Such self-aware networks are crisscrossing the world in increasing density. Millions of computers are tied into them. Individuals taking notes with lap-top computers and fax machines are now able to tie into these networks and then communicate around the world in a matter of seconds. The current networks are what Toffler calls "second stage." Researchers are working on third-stage networks. The results will most likely give even more intelligence to our info-sphere. One thing is certain, however, the future is uncertain; it is this uncertainty that challenges our intelligence.

For schools, such networks used by students will certainly influence the manner in which students learn, process information, and experience school. Learning styles should be influenced as networks interact with the student using them, as networks carry on conversations and act as critics of the information being sent. Such networks will have students of the future thinking more multi-dimensionally and creatively—utilizing visual, computer, and communication tools to enhance the way they process and utilize information. Many students in the future will think and process information in ways that may challenge and even differ from their teachers, who might still rely on traditional thinking patterns. It is very possible that future students will think more future oriented than their teachers; youth should be able to adapt to the world of optical fibers, lasers, and electronics much easier than the older generation.

In the twentieth century, intelligence depended on and expressed itself in a print culture. More books and written documents were made available to the public than in all previous centuries. Currently, over 300,000 new titles are published each year. However, as Meyrowitz comments, just as print culture has come to its full power, the seeds of its destruction have been sown. Actually, print culture is not being destroyed, but rather reconstructed, by electronic media. Today, increasing numbers of people, certainly students, encounter print that is delivered by electronic media.[39]

As electronic media deliver messages through print and other imagery, our current culture becomes more like an oral one. We are gaining key aspects of oral societies: an immediacy and simultaneity of action, perception, and response.[40] We are having our intellectual responses and the processing of data augmented with sensory experience. However, this is not a return to the oral societies of old. In those societies, once a story was told that version was gone. Each retelling was a bit different. With the orality of electronic media, our communication is not limited by time and space. Our messages do not fade; they can be preserved and reuttered and, perhaps most importantly, experienced simultaneously by great numbers of people in places near and far. In fact, there is no "there" anymore; there is only "here." It is "we" in conversation, and we can repeat our conversation over and over. As Meyrowitz notes, "Electronic media bypass traditional 'literacy circles,' group association, and national boundaries and give us a new world view by thrusting us among people who have not read what we have read, have not shared our territory, and may not even speak our language."[41]

With electronic media, we are able to have new types of shared experience. And such sharing is most likely to alter our ways of thinking, perceiving, and feeling. Our very intelligence is bound to be affected by this expanded world conversation. From using this technology, what we think about and how we think about it will expand in amount and diversity. We will experience a new consciousness and what it means to be a thinking individual. We will also alter our notions of wisdom.

Electronic media should also bring about increased personal involvement with people who are actually separated by physical space and culture. People will change from world strangers to informed acquaintances. Conversations with others sharing the "here" of electronic space should affect our thinking, our ways of questioning, and our processing of information. Future questions will not be limited by a desire to know if something is true or false. Rather, we will ask more complete questions, such as How does it look?, How does it feel?, or What emotional response do I have?[42]

The previous questions point out that electronic media and other technology put to educational use should make the entire process of education more human. As Kerr cautions, we must remind ourselves "that education is fundamentally a human, not a technical or economic activity."[43] Education and its curricula should nurture human beings in ways that enhance their humanness and their connectedness to others in the human family. Our intelligence, nurtured by new technologies, should involve our emotions, our very spirits. Whether technologies and future curricula do this depends in part on how well they enable us all, students included, to have rich experiences with multiple realities, both near and far and both real and virtual.[44] Technologies and future curricula must allow us to experience our worlds as embryos. We are in the world, not of the world. We are part of the system, not outside the system. We are not manipulating the system, but engaged in a mutually interacting dynamic.

Some Constants

So much change. Nothing seems constant. What can one hang onto? Many, educators and curricularists included, are overwhelmed. However, we can take some comfort in the realization that the four commonplaces of the curriculum depicted by Schwab will remain: students, teachers, content, and context. Schools will not disappear despite the increasing demands for choice, regardless of the electronic media and the introduction of cyberspace, and not-withstanding the increasing sophistication of the Internet. Schools will continue as the most efficient means of bringing students into contact with their cultures and the cultures of the world. Schools will still be places where students can confront themselves, their colleagues, and other students of the world. Certainly, schools will have curricula, although the topics and delivery or experiencing of the topics will likely change. We may not recognize the content, but we will have content. We may not recognize the activities or the experiences, but students will still have "school experiences."

Schools are, however, likely to play a less important role, or at least a shared role, in learning. More learning will occur as a result of students' interacting with the mass media, especially television and tapes. But, the mass media will not be a few media sources presenting a rather common "picture." Rather the media is likely to be what Toffler calls demassified.[45] The media industry will create both written and visual materials for specialized markets. Already in the United States, mass magazines are no longer a powerful influence in national life. Such magazines as *Life* and *The Saturday Evening Post* have even been phased out as an explosion of minimagazines address particular audiences. The media also cover an expanded range of topics: addressing young children, teenagers, middle-aged persons, and senior citizens. These trends are likely to continue.

The Internet already has changed the nature of mass media. Students have an avalanche of material and ways to experience it. Curricular materials will be a constant, but what comprises curricular materials will continually be expanded and redefined. All the world's exploding knowledge and information are fast becoming only a "mouse click" away.

FUTURE CURRICULA

While this section addresses some possibilities regarding school curriculum content and also ways of organizing such content, it does not spell the demise of the traditional subject-centered design. Indeed, because it is the most pervasive design not only in the United States, but also in the rest of the world, it is unlikely to disappear in the near future.

At the elementary school level, the subject-centered design comprises such subjects as language arts, social studies, mathematics, science, and the arts. At the secondary level, the traditional academic subjects are English, mathematics, science, history, geography, and foreign language. These subjects, many would agree, will be part of the educational future of schools. Miller and Seller have noted that those who accept this as the most likely future, indeed the preferred future, believe that schools of tomorrow will be much like schools of today. Schools and their curricula will be organized to essentially transmit the general society.[46] This is not to say that schools will not be responsive to the times and evolving futures. Rather, those individuals who believe schools are primarily created for transmitting the culture will exert their energies to maintain and continue a relatively traditional curriculum.

New Curricular Designs

While traditional designs have served us fairly well in the past, we realize that the future demands of schools different curricular designs and novel curriculum content. Education is more than mere accumulation of facts and mastery of skills. As Schlechty states: "In this age, . . . it is not more facts that people need. Citizens need ideas, concepts, and refined sensibilities to make sense out of the facts that bombard them daily and overwhelm their instincts as well as their understanding."[47]

Much current talk on integration of the curriculum, even within the standard content areas, reflects a beginning realization that individuals need ideas, concepts, and refined sensibilities for making meaning of their world. We are at a threshold in our curricular thinking. We are realizing that our programs must be designed so that students not only transmit that which is good in society and world culture, but also can transform themselves and their cultures. Many of us are commencing to grasp that being alive is not only *being,* but *becoming.*[48]

Those suggesting new designs for curriculum appear to be accepting this notion of humans as becoming, rather than just humans as being. This is a major conceptual shift, a moving away from viewing the world as a giant mechanical clock with knowable or potentially knowable causes generating anticipated effects.[49] It is a departure from viewing the world, and the school for that matter, with a feeling of certainty and control.

This major shift in thinking is seeping into educational discourse, into new curriculum designs. Many of these new designs draw on the dynamics of reality and humans in action. These designs draw on existentialist, moral, and spiritual ideas, what some call "Third Force" psychology. Abraham Maslow, a pioneer in humanistic psychology, considered this type of psychology to be a transitional preparation for a higher Fourth Force or transpersonal psychology. Transpersonal psychology focuses on the cosmos, rather than on human needs and interests, and on intuition and transcendence.[50] Through intuition, an individual thinks creatively and views the world holistically.

Some curricularists, as indicated in Chapter 12, are suggesting that education and its curricula address the moral and even spiritual ideas of students. Although most educators find little problem with the moral dimensions of teaching and learning, they do with the spiritual dimension. We are not advocating the teaching of religion but trying to show via experiences within schools that human nature is more than intellect. We learn by our relationships with our world, with all peoples. Students also are learning that they need to go beyond their narrow self-centered views; they need to transcend themselves—at least to see themselves as part of a community (local, state, national, international) of people. What we do can affect others and often does, and what others do can affect our lives.

Arthur Foshay addresses the transcendent issue within the curriculum. He maintains that transcendence is the most ignored of all universal dimensions of human experience. Perhaps schools ignore it because educators think that the transcendent, also called the spiritual, suggests religion. Indeed, we are sensitive about maintaining the separation of church and state.[51] However, students are more than mere rational beings who can only grasp cognitive ideas. Both educators and students need to realize that reflecting on the purpose of being is essential in this highly complex world.

David Purpel speaks of the moral and spiritual crisis in education. He discusses liberation theology. While such theology is not taught directly in the schools, many are attending to the issue of poverty and oppression, which reflects this orientation. Bringing into the curriculum attention to compassion and justice for the less fortunate of the world is also part of the concern for the transcendent.[52]

While some might counsel resisting any semblance of incorporating the transcendent in the curriculum or drawing ideas from theology, most of us would accept the broad educational goals central to this orientation. Purpel presents these goals as an educational credo, as basic values and assumptions about education that are "nonnegotiable."

1. *The examination and contemplation of the awe, wonder, and mystery of the universe.*
2. *The cultivation and nourishment of the processes of meaning making.*
3. *The cultivation and nourishment of the concept of the oneness of nature and humanity.*
4. *The cultivation, nourishment, and development of a cultural mythos that builds on a faith in the human capacity to participate in the creation of a world of justice, compassion, caring, love, and joy.*
5. *The cultivation, nourishment, and development of ideals of community, compassion, and interdependence within the traditions of democratic principles.*
6. *The cultivation, nourishment, and development of attitudes of outrage and responsibility in the face of injustice and oppression.*[53]

These new designs of the curriculum, essentially humanistic, are currently more talk than reality. They emphasize putting the student more in control of his or her learning. In these designs the teacher acts as facilitator and catalyst rather than as transmitter of knowledge. These designs orient the curriculum to prizing the primacy of personal meaning; they include higher-level psychological and philosophical experiences.

New Curriculum Areas

The curriculum of the future will no doubt contain entirely new areas of information; these will not only enable the grasping of new information, but will also enable the human spirit to soar unfettered. Some critics of current education have noted that existing curricula have shackled individuals, limiting their dreams of things possible.[54] New areas of curriculum should break any such constraints. New curricula should reveal to participants that there are no limits to information, to knowledge, or to revelation. Curricular planners should draw on information and the resulting knowledge realizing that knowledge, in principle, is inexhaustible. Information processed begets knowledge; knowledge begets additional knowledge. There are no limits or boundaries. Even the naming of new curricular areas must be done with the realization that the realms of knowledge are fleeting, ever emerging. We only name them to have a flickering grasp of what to include in the curriculum. The challenge of the future is to real-

ize that although the energy of the fire of curriculum is continuous, the shapes of the flames, the particular subjects, are ever changing.

Informatics. Informatics deals with computers and their use. It has been described as a science for dealing with information. The computer, a central aspect of this new discipline, will afford students access to vast amounts of currently unattainable information. Students will be able, for example, to process documents written in other languages, because the computers will translate them. Computers will also enable students to network with other students in other schools, even in other countries. Joint investigations by students in different states or countries can become commonplace.[55]

As students think of ways to program their computers, they will begin to conceptualize different ways of organizing information. "Presenting" the computer to students will really give them power and control over the curriculum. If they control the machine, they can control the information; if they control the information, they may in effect gain increased influence in the classroom. This shift in classroom power from teacher to student could be a real system break in how school is "played." Learning could come to dominate teaching.[56]

Not all learning with the computer will occur in schools. Much of it will occur in the home or perhaps in public learning centers. Computerized call-up systems and intercontinental networks, as well as closed circuit and cable telecourses, should be commonplace by 2000, and video and/or auditory discs and tapes should replace many textbooks and written materials. Students may even have available a dial-access facility that permits access, via laser or a telephone, to a central learning center equipped with high-speed computers that can communicate with computers in any home or learning center anywhere in the world.[57]

The computer is fast becoming ubiquitous, an omnipresent extension of ourselves. Computers and their educational software programs will possess distinct personalities. They will possess social interfaces that will allow them through artificial intelligence to determine how best to present information or engage students with information in customized ways.[58] However, we must be cautious in our relationships with computers. We need to keep in mind that these machines are or should be extensions of us. We should not offer ourselves to be remade or reshaped by these marvelous mechanisms.[59]

Talbott has noted that we are spending much time deliberating the nature of the intelligence of our machines and how such intelligence can further evolve. However, Talbott posits that we are "less inclined to ask toward what goal we are evolving. Certainly if our computers are becoming ever more human like, then it goes without saying that we are becoming ever more computer like. Who, we are well advised to ask, is doing the most changing?"[60] Certainly, the marvels of technology and the computer will enable us to advance, but the advance should be in our humanness. We do not want to use the computer to entrap ourselves within a particular culture. We cannot have blind infatuation with computers, assuming that they will be the "all" of the future. We must realize that it is not just having access to information or objective content that matters. What matters is what we as humans do with such information, how we utilize information to increase the qualitative fullness of our thinking.[61] This is a key challenge for curricularists.

The Future as Curriculum Content. It would seem unusual if future curricula did not include courses on the future itself. Such courses already exist in a few secondary schools. Some objectives of future studies courses are to give students a more sophisticated approach to thinking about the future and to help students learn forecasting techniques. Such courses will most likely increase in number; they may also extend into elementary schools.

Draper Kauffman has presented six areas of competence that could comprise a possible future-oriented curriculum: (1) having access to information; (2) thinking clearly; (3) communicating effectively; (4) understanding humanity's environment; (5) understanding the individual and society; and (6) enhancing personal competence.[62]

As part of the future studies curriculum, students should learn about planning procedures, the nature of decision making, various types of heuristics for dealing with information, and procedures for handling stress caused by the rapidity of change. They should learn not only how to think critically about the future, but also perhaps how to distinguish between logic and nonlogic.

New Areas of Content. Whereas some courses on the future are predictable, other courses on the future are not so predictable. Nevertheless, we venture some predictions. Many courses may reflect hybrid fields of study—courses in biostatistics and molecular biology, for example.

Courses in dieting and exercise should increase as we become more health conscious. Research linking good nutrition and exercise for children with positive social behavior and academic achievement should encourage the schools to incorporate increased nutrition and exercise into the curriculum—and possibly lead to the elimination of junk food (especially excessive sugar and fats) from school vending machines and lunch counters.[63]

Some new courses may deal with the changing nature of society. Courses in aging, for instance, may become commonplace because students will be faced with an increasingly large "maturing" populace. Eventually the curriculum should treat many of the problems of aging as a form of discrimination, as another "ism." This emphasis should parallel changes in the curriculum concerning racism, "ethnicism," and sexism.[64] Special courses may offer students the opportunity to study about lifelong education and the ways in which it can be accessed.

As society continues to become more culturally and ethnically pluralistic, more courses will deal with cultural diversity and international and global education. Indeed, multicultural education will go from the current rather narrow political interpretation of courses to empower those few groups considered marginalized to truly dealing with the myriad cultures and subcultures of the national and world communities.

Associated with a more mature and sophisticated interpretation of curricula that deal with cultural diversity will be peace studies curricula. Rather than having history and political science curricula that highlight wars and violent conflicts, we will have curricula that celebrate those persons who have "fought" for peace.[65]

Such courses will not be idealistic exhortations to live with love toward others, but since conflict is bound to arise with diverse groups, they will deal with real means of processing conflict in nonviolent ways. Such curricula will stress efforts to get students to assume a selflessness, a willingness to see beyond themselves and their own needs. As Lasley and Biddle note, "social value, common good, or public well-being is only possible once individuals are willing and able to look beyond themselves."[66] Such peace curricula should nurture civic morality in students.

Not all new courses will be related to emerging fields in the public sector. Some new courses may deal with the brain and ways of thinking. Secondary schools may have courses entitled "Your Brain," "Metacognition," "Left-Brain/Right-Brain Thinking," and "Transductive Thinking." Specific courses in self-management of one's intellect, emotions, and stress are probable as well. Courses on inner awareness, T-groups, and encounter groups may reappear. See Curriculum Tips 13-3.

We should see increasing numbers of courses dealing with character education, with human virtue and what it means to be moral. Already, we have educators putting their concerns in these areas into their educational writing.[67] Courses should emerge that will deal with variations on being human. Certainly, being human must be defined continuously as individuals interact with the new century. Attention to what it means to be free in a dynamic century will find its way into the curriculum. Such courses will allow us in some ways to remake ourselves regarding mind, body, and spirit. The courses of the future will acknowledge that students are more than talking, thinking heads.

CURRICULUM CONSIDERATIONS AND CHOICE

Much current discussion of new content areas does not actually suggest particular courses for students. Rather, general areas of content or program focus are proposed. This globalness of proposals allows each of us concerned with curriculum to reflect on ways to make the curriculum unique to particular students, yet beneficial to the general society. Schools are knowledge-work organizations.

However, schools are much more than that. Schools are places for inventing, sculpting, and redesigning the human mind, body, and spirit. Future schools must invent knowledge and knowledge work for students so that they gain those competencies and attitudes requisite for living in an information age. But schools must also realize that they are engaged in fostering spirit work, ways of seeing, feeling, and acting. Educators need to realize that they must foster in schools clear visions and the means of generating them. Presently, most educators do not have a clue as to what courses to create to address such purposes.

The designs for curriculum as the raw material for the students' knowledge-work process are as diverse as our imaginations and are primarily influenced by our educational and world philosophies and the resultant visions we hold for the school. As mentioned earlier, there are many educators, indeed some argue that these persons make up the vast majority of educators, who think that the knowledge-related curriculum of the future will be essentially the one we currently have. The prime shift for the future school curriculum is seen in its delivery or in the ways in which students experience it rather than in a major change in content. The ways of dealing with the content of the curriculum comprise the new basics of the information age.

An Extreme Future Curriculum Design

While most schools will bring into the next century curricular organizations more like those of today than of some far-off future, some current curricularists suggest curricula that do push at the boundaries of possibility. The following curriculum represents a radical shift in what are considered appropriate raw materials with which students can interact. The curriculum centers on areas of emphasis rather than specific course content.[68]

Empowerment and transformation. In this curriculum component, students come to understand the power of knowledge; they are engaged in actions that unblock their minds. Students center on the relationships of various types of knowledge and how people interact with that knowledge and also with other people. Students come to realize that they are both producers and consumers of

---

Curriculum Tips 13-3

Guidelines for Curriculum Reform

Since the times are dynamic, we need to realize that the curriculum is never completed; it is ongoing. We never arrive at the perfect curriculum for the times. History is added to each day. Science makes new discoveries. The following guidelines can help us meet the ongoing challenge of curriculum for evolving futures.

1. Consider curriculum improvement as a continuous process.
2. View broadly what your school can contribute to your students and the general society.
3. Realize that there are numerous resources that can assist you in improving your curriculum.
4. Understand that attempts at change require time and will usually occur in small increments.
5. Realize that we must maximize the continued growth and professionalization of teachers and staff.
6. Be vigilant in monitoring your vision for your school regarding its curriculum and its practices.
7. Adopt a spirit of inquiry in your school; become students of education as well as deliverers of curriculum.
8. Realize that there will be a continued need to involve others from outside the school in curriculum activities.

Source: Adapted from Frances M. Klein, *Curriculum Reform in the Elementary School* (New York: Teachers College Press, Columbia University, 1989).

---

knowledge. It is their task to take knowledge and to make it their own, to personalize it.

Intellectual processes and forms. The central thrust of this curriculum organizer is to furnish students with opportunities to study the structures of the well-accepted disciplines and the new emerging disciplines. In their study, students will begin to grasp the ways in which knowledge is created, the ways in which meaning is developed, and the means by which people generate conclusions. They will study the nature of language, the essential character of modes of inquiry, and the different forms of evidence.[69]

Social Skills. Kenneth Benne states that rather than presenting a notion "of the self as passive, reactive, in continual need of motivation and socialization from outside itself—a self divided, with its intellect segregated from its feelings and emotions—and from the interpersonal community

that sustains it in being," we in education need to "apply a conception . . . of self as inherently active and creative, a self proactive, going out to select, to choose, to shape through its actions its environment toward a habitat more supportive of human living."[70]

In this rather radical curriculum, students learn requisite skills for functioning in an increasingly dynamic community. Students learn skills of doing, rather than skills of learning about. Students learn to develop commitment to act, to utilize their skills within the community arena.[71]

Historical sense. Dwayne Huebner notes that human life is anticipatory, never fixed, but always emergent.[72] In this suggested curriculum, content and experiences are arranged so that students come to truly understand the relationship of past, present, and future. Students come to realize that events in time, at least human events, are or can be under our control. We have created our histories and our views of past events. We are currently managers of our present time, and we have the power to manage our futures.

Critical awareness and competence. Few would argue against students today being active thinkers. This segment of the curriculum relates to developing in students both a disposition to question and process information and the competence to actually do so. In the present and future world, students must possess critical awareness and know how to process their questions in order to deeply comprehend their world.[73] Critically aware students realize their potential to create their own knowledge; they grasp the richness and diversity of the world, and they accept their responsibility for being active in contemplating the world and their places within it. Critical consciousness makes individuals aware of their presence in the world in an existential sense.[74]

Imagination and visioning. Imagination and creativity are central to meaning making. Indeed to develop meaning requires imagining, visioning, and dreaming. Such creative processes partly define our humanness. In this curriculum, time is given to individuals to imagine schemata and their metaphorical and qualitative projections of life. Students learn to think creatively.[75]

These content areas are not to be presented separately. Rather, they serve as markers of encounters designed to integrate all these contents into events in which students can participate and from which they can generate meaning.

A More Traditional Curriculum Model

We need not change the curriculum as dramatically as suggested in the previous model in order to attain a curriculum responsive to a dynamic future. We can have a curriculum divided into three rather familiar categories: academic curriculum, creative curriculum, and socialization curriculum.[76]

The academic curriculum would embrace the traditional school subjects such as language arts, social studies, mathematics, biology, and chemistry. The courses could stand alone or could be integrated. The courses could also be presented as a required core or offered as options for student selection. But the academic curriculum would not

be delivered in a traditional way. Students would have opportunities to work both alone and collaboratively.

The creative curriculum, scheduled alongside the academic curriculum, would contain contents from the arts and also from areas not traditionally included in the curriculum: courses such as cooking, dance, and graphic design. Here the emphasis would be on students satisfying their creative urges, perfecting their aesthetic ways of knowing.

The socialization curriculum would furnish students with opportunities to learn about problem solving, health maintenance, interpersonal communications, and purpose in life.[77] Students would develop their social intelligence and their social competence. Social intelligence is knowing oneself and knowing other people. Social competence is the ability to act on one's knowledge so that a desire to interact among self and others is achieved.[78] In a world that is becoming globalized, both social intelligence and social competence are essential.

THE CHALLENGE OF DEALING WITH THE FUTURE

To create the extreme curriculum design would indeed be a challenge. It would call for bold reconceptualization of the curriculum and the manner in which students experience it. The extreme design is no superficial rearrangement. Yet, it is really not advocating departing from those things that all educators consider essential for a fully functioning individual—to be in control of oneself, to have command of intellectual processes, to have a sense of one's history, to be socially literate, to possess essential knowledge, to be a critical thinker, and to be imaginative and creative.

We cannot leave behind everything. If we do we are merely engaged in curricular substitution, substituting what we previously had with something entirely new. We do not need substitution; we require transformation of our curricula and of ourselves in turn. We do bring our past, however reconceptualized, into our evolving futures.

The key concepts are transformation, modification, redefining, and seeing anew. Even the more traditional model just noted comprised of the academic, the creative, and the social divisions would require some modification of our thinking.

It is not just bringing a static past and present into the future. Perhaps the design demands less stretch of vision, but some stretch is present, nevertheless. Being realistic, we think that the future curricula of schools might well indeed look more like this design than the extreme one.

Although most traditional designs maintain the basic curriculum organizations of the current time, they can be taught in ways that get students active in their learning and committed to participating in their local, state, and national societies. No design can remain totally static.

Curriculum designs, whether traditional or radical, will have to exhibit polyfocality in their pedagogical treatment. As noted by Hills, "multifocality" or polyfocality brings to the curriculum varied ways of looking at the world. It allows individuals to acquaint themselves with various viewpoints. It enables people to discern the interconnectedness of all things, of ideas, actions, and beliefs.[79] While Hills was discussing polyfocality with regard to bringing various views to multicultural education, we are employing the term much more broadly. Future curricula must be polyfocal by bringing not only various viewpoints to one area or subject of study, but also by melding various traditional and new conceptions of subject matter into educational focus. We cannot study history as just history. We must include the philosophy of history, the sociology of history, the ethics of history, the technology of history, and the geography of history so that students can construct and reconstruct a more complete understanding of events in time, which is what history is. Additionally, future educators must realize that each of these additions to the study of history is not monolithic. There are sociologies of histories, there are philosophies of histories, and so forth. And each of these focal points or viewpoints influences history as curricular text. The same is true with all the curriculum.

We view such melding of viewpoints and subject matter to be in the distant future, for few of us have the breadth of knowledge to engage students in such study of curricula. However, students must realize that they only receive a very small part of the content and from only a few viewpoints. Expressed awareness can certainly be fostered with the expansion of the Internet and World Wide Web.

Well, what curriculum or curricular design do we advocate for the future? While we do have philosophical and theoretical positions, we have not presented these designs with any particular preference. Rather, these designs are offered as grist for our thinking. We mentioned at the beginning of this chapter that all education springs from some image or vision of the future. It is important to remember that dealing with visions is not a casual activity; it requires careful planning, intense reflection, and deliberate action. We educators must assume the posture of futurists to deal with anticipated visions, even to create and manage those visions, those future directions of schools and their curricula. Being futurists will allow us to design curricula that are responsive to students' needs not only in the practical sense of application to job situations but also in the totally humanistic sense of allowing them to understand, manage, and appreciate their realities.

Toffler pointed out several years ago that no educational institution can address the challenges placed on it until all its members, including students, subject their views of the future and related challenges to critical analysis. Toffler cautioned "to design educational systems for tomorrow . . . we need not images of a future frozen in amber, as it were, but something far more complicated: sets of images of successive and alternative futures, each one tentative and different from the next."[80]

Our invitation to curriculum designers and developers is to create programs so that all students will function optimally in future societies that exhibit justice. The challenge is made more complicated in that we will never know precisely what optimal functioning is, for the times will not stand still. Neither can we assume that there will be only one just society. Justice must be viewed as having multiple interpretations.

As Gates points out, "It isn't easy to prepare for the next century, because it's almost impossible to guess the secondary effects of even the changes we can foresee, much less those we can't."[81] We cannot say what will be the results of teaching a new curriculum. We can say that students will have skills and some content that is necessary for gaining a job. But, realistically, we cannot denote how having certain knowledge will mold the spirit or attitude of selflessness of an individual. Yet we know that there must be secondary effects of having such knowledge and skills.

The tasks confronting us are difficult and complex and perhaps at times unmanageable. However, those persons with curriculum responsibilities must rise to the occasion. They must fully appreciate that, in a dynamically changing, chaotic world, education is the only means by which individuals will gain the understandings, competencies, attitudes, and dimensions of spirit that will allow them to be players and to adapt to the evolving times and influence the very nature of the times and the quality of all things, both human and natural. Society, viewed globally, depends on our rising to these challenges.

CONCLUSION

In this chapter we have attempted to define what futurism is and to relate it to the field of curriculum. Futurism was presented as a systematic attempt to meld creative forecasting, planning, and action. In using futurism, educators can proact rather than react to events. Certainly, educators have past habits to break, because it has been their posture to react to events affecting the schools and their programs. Often educators are unaware of how to influence the future, how to modify public or client demands to more manageable dimensions, or how to be more in tune with accepted purposes of education.

We live between eras, and we have uncertainty in our lives. Nonetheless, we need to approach this uncertainty as a plus rather than a minus. Uncertainty forces people to engage in decision making that is liquid, flexible, and adaptable. This should encourage the creation of more diverse curricular offerings.

In this chapter we discussed various directions of the future that appear likely for our schools and society. We discussed procedures that we can muster that will enable us not only to react to directions but also to play a role in their creation. We presented various forecasting procedures for consideration. We presented, too, a general overview of some of the developments within the curriculum field. We mentioned what might be expected in new curricular areas and we outlined possibile future curricula.

The challenge for curricularists is to generate images of the future and then to fit schools and their programs into those images so that the curriculum that is actualized serves the needs and desires of all those within the school and society. To attain this is no small task. The health and vitality of society depend to a significant degree on how well curricularists meet this challenge.

ENDNOTES

1. Stephen L. Talbott, *The Future Does Not Compute* (Sebastopol, Calif.: O'Reilly & Associates, Inc., 1995).
2. Alvin Toffler, "The Psychology of the Future," in Toffler, ed., *Learning for Tomorrow: The Role of the Future in Education,* (New York: Vintage Books, 1974), pp. 3–18.
3. John Naisbitt, *Megatrends* (New York: Warner Books, 1982), John Naisbitt and Patricia Aburdene, *Megatrends 2000* (New York: William Morrow, 1990).
4. Alvin Toffler, *Powershift* (New York: Bantam Books, 1990).
5. Phillip C. Schlechty, *Schools for the 21st Century* (San Francisco: Jossey-Bass, 1990).
6. Toffler, *Powershift.*
7. Bill Gates, *The Road Ahead* (New York: Viking, 1995).
8. Talbott, *The Future Does Not Compute.*
9. Schlechty, *Schools for the 21st. Century.*
10. Thomas Quick, *Unconventional Wisdom* (San Francisco: Jossey-Bass, 1989).
11. Warren Bennis and Paul Slater, *The Temporary Society* (New York: Harper & Row, 1968); W. Bennis, *Why Leaders Can't Lead* (San Francisco: Jossey-Bass, 1989), p. 155.
12. Naisbitt, *Megatrends.*
13. Naisbitt and Aburdene, *Megatrends 2000.*
14. Talbott, *The Future Does Not Compute.*
15. Ibid.
16. Ibid.
17. Harold L. Strudler, "Educational Futurism: Perspective or Discipline?" in Toffler, ed., *Learning for Tomorrow,* pp. 173–180.
18. Earl C. Joseph, "An Introduction to Studying the Future," in S. P. Henley and J. R. Yates, eds., *Futurism in Education* (Berkeley: McCutchan, 1974), pp. 1–26.

19. Roy Amara, *Some Methods of Future Research* (Menlo Park, Calif.: Institute for the Future, 1975); Elizabeth Vallance, "Ways of Knowing and Curricular Conceptions," in E. Eisner, ed., *Learning and Teaching the Ways of Knowing,* Eighty-fourth Yearbook of the National Society for the Study of Education, Part II (Chicago: University of Chicago Press, 1985), pp. 199–217.

20. John W. Sutherland, "Architecturing the Future: A Delphi-based Paradigm for Normative System Building," in H. Linstone and M. Turoff, eds., *The Delphi Method* (Reading, Mass.: Addison-Wesley, 1975), p. 467.

21. Robert V. Carlson and Gary A. W. Kerman, *Educational Planning: Concepts, Strategies and Practices* (New York: Longman, 1991); Department of Defense, *Military Standard: Human Engineering Design Criteria for Military Systems* (Washington, D.C.: U.S. Government Printing Office, 1988).

22. Joseph, "An Introduction to Studying the Future."

23. John Briggs and David Peat, *Looking Glass Universe: The Emerging Science of Wholeness* (New York: Simon & Schuster, 1984), p. 33; cited in William E. Doll, Jr., *A Post Modern Perspective on Curriculum* (New York: Teachers College Press, Columbia University, 1993).

24. Katherine Hayles, *The Cosmic Web* (Ithaca, N.Y.: Cornell University Press, 1984), p. 170; cited in Doll, *A Post Modern Perspective on Curriculum.*

25. Doll, *A Post Modern Perspective on Curriculum.*

26. Harold G. Shane, "Future-Planning as a Means of Shaping Educational Change," in R. M. McClure, ed., *The Curriculum: Retrospect and Prospect,* Seventieth Yearbook of the National Society for the Study of Education, Part I (Chicago: University of Chicago Press, 1971); Shane, "Improving Education in the Twenty-first Century," *Educational Horizons* (Fall 1990), pp. 10–15.

27. Toffler, *Future Shock,* pp. 157–158.

28. Daniel Bell, "The Year 2000—The Trajectory of an Idea," *Daedalus* (Summer 1967), pp. 642–644.

29. Michael A. McDaniel, "Tomorrow's Curriculum Today," in Toffler, ed., *Learning for Tomorrow,* pp. 103–131.

30. Kenneth E. Boulding, "Predictive Reliability and the Future: The Need for Uncertainty," in Lewis Rubin, ed., *The Future of Education: Perspectives on Tomorrow's Schooling* (Boston: Allyn and Bacon, 1975), pp. 57–82.

31. Dwayne Huebner, "Curriculum as Concern for Man's Temporality," in W. Pinar, ed., *Curriculum Theorizing, The Reconceptualists* (Berkeley, Calif.: McCutchan, 1975). p. 362.

32. Naisbitt and Aburdene, *Megatrends 2000,* p. 300.

33. Alvin Toffler, *The Third Wave* (New York: Bantam Books, 1980), p. 168.

34. Alvin Toffler, *Power Shift* (New York: Bantam Books, 1990).

35. Gates, *The Road Ahead.*

36. Ibid.

37. Richard G. Boehm, David G. Armstrong, and Francis P. Hunkins, *Geography: The World and Its People* (videodisc edition) (New York: Glencoe, McGraw-Hill, 1998).

38. Toffler, *Powershift.*

39. Joshua Meyrowitz, "Taking McLauhan and 'Medium Theory' Seriously: Technological Change and the Evolution of Education," in Stephen T. Kerr, ed., *Technology and the Future of Schooling,* Ninety-fifth Yearbook of the National Society for the Study of Education, Part II (Chicago: University of Chicago Press, 1996), pp. 73–110.

40. Ibid.

41. Ibid., p. 97.

42. Ibid.

43. Stephen T. Kerr, "Visions of Sugarplums: The Future of Technology, Education, and the Schools," in Kerr, ed., *Technology and the Future of Schooling.*

44. Talbott, *The Future Does Not Compute.*

45. Alvin Toffler, *Previews and Premises* (Boston: Sound End Press, 1983).

46. John P. Miller and Wayne Seller, *Curriculum: Perspectives and Practice* (New York: Longman, 1985).

47. Schlechty, *Schools for the 21st Century,* p. 32.

48. Ilya Prigogine and Isabell Stengers, *Order Out of Chaos* (New York: Bantam Books, 1984).

49. Toffler, *Power Shift.*

50. Jerry L. Patterson, Steward C. Purkey, and Jackson V. Parker, *Productive School Systems for a Nonrational World* (Alexandria, Va.: Association for Supervision and Curriculum Development, 1986); Donald Vandenberg, *Education as a Human Right: A Theory of Curriculum and Pedagogy* (New York: Teachers College Press, Columbia University, 1990).

51. Arthur Foshay, untitled paper presented at Professors of Curriculum Meeting, Chicago, 1988.

52. David Purpel, *The Moral and Spiritual Crisis in Education* (New York: Bergin & Garvey, 1989).

53. Ibid., pp. 113–118.

54. Patrick Slattery, *Curriculum Development in the Postmodern Era* (New York: Garland Publishing, Inc., 1995).

55. Harlan Cleveland, "Educating Citizens and Leaders for an Information-Based Society," *Educational Leadership* (March 1986), pp. 62–63; M. Francis Klein, "Beyond the Measured Curriculum," *Theory into Practice* (Winter 1986), pp. 1–17.

56. Daniel Barron and Timothy J. Bergen, "Information Power," *Phi Delta Kappan* (March 1992); Cleveland, "Educating Citizens and Leaders for an Information-Based Society."

57. Paul E. Merril et al., *Computers in Education,* 2nd ed. (Boston: Allyn and Bacon, 1992); Decker F. Walker, "Computers and the Curriculum," in J. A. Culbertson and L. L. Cunningham, eds., *Microcomputers and Education.* Eighty-fifth Yearbook of the National Society for the Study of Education, Part I (Chicago: University of Chicago Press, 1986), pp. 22–39.

58. Gates, *The Road Ahead.*

59. Talbott, *The Future Does Not Compute.*

60. Ibid., p. 340.

61. Ibid.

62. Draper Kauffman, *Teaching the Future* (Palm Springs, Calif.: ETC Publications, 1976).

63. Judith Herr and Winifred Morse, "Food for Thought: Nutrition Education for Young Children," *Young Children* (November 1982), pp. 3–11: Allan C. Ornstein, "Controversy and Trends in Curriculum for the 1980s," *Contemporary Education* (Summer 1985), pp. 242–251.

64. Allan C. Ornstein, "Emerging Curriculum Trends: An Agenda for the Future," *NASSP Bulletin* (February 1989), pp. 37–48.

65. Thomas J. Lasley and James R. Biddle, "Teaching Students to See Beyond Themselves," *Educational Forum* (Winter 1996), pp. 158–164.

66. Ibid., p. 160.

67. *Note:* The entire Winter 1996 issue of *The Educational Forum* was devoted to character education.

68. Purpel, *The Moral and Spiritual Crisis in Education.*

69. Ibid.

70. Kenneth D, Benne, *The Task of Post-Contemporary Education* (New York: Teachers College Press, Columbia University, 1990), p. 170.

71. Purpel, *The Moral and Spiritual Crisis in Education.*

72. Huebner, "Curriculum as a Concern for Man's Temporality."

73. Vandenberg, *Education as a Human Right: A Theory of Curriculum and Pedagogy.*

74. Maxine Green, *The Dialectic of Freedom* (New York: Teachers College Press, Columbia University, 1988).

75. Purpel, *The Moral and Spiritual Crisis in Education.*

76. Timothy D. Evans, Raymond J. Corsini, and George M. Gazda, "Individual Education and the 4Rs," *Educational Leadership* (September 1990), pp. 52–55.

77. Ibid.

78. Ellen Berscheid, "Interpersonal Modes of Knowing," in Elliot Eisner, ed., *Learning and Teaching the Ways of Knowing,* Part II. Eighty-fourth Yearbook of the National Society for the Study of Education, 1985), pp. 60–76.

79. Michael R. Hillis, "Multicultural Education as a Moral Responsibility," *Educational Forum* (Winter 1996), pp. 142–148.

80. Alvin Toffler, "The Psychology of the Future," in Toffler, ed., *Learning for Tomorrow,* p. 5.

81. Gates, *The Road Ahead.*

Theory *(continued)*
   metaphors and theoretical
      camps, 182–89
   at mid-century, 179–82
   overview of, 184
   sources of, 174
   theoretical perspectives, 172–74
   machine, 3, 84, 85, 196
   philosophical and humanistic, 175
   scientific, 175, 179
   translated into practice, 21–24,
      183
Theory-driven approach to
   evaluation, 325
Therapeutic learning, 125–26
Thinking, 111–16
   constructivism and, 115–16
   convergent, 112, 116, 132
   creative, 116–17, 120–22
   critical, 117–20, 132
   curricula for, 249–51
   divergent, 112, 116, 132
   intuitive, 121–22
   learning styles and, 113–14
   major shift in, 394
   multiple intelligences, 112–13
   ordinary, 118
   postpositivistic, 255
   reflective, 117, 132
   strategies, 249
   structure of intellect and, 111–12,
      113
   systematic, 6
"Third Force" psychology, 394
Thomism, 35
Time, concepts of, 141, 390
Timing, receptivity to change and,
   303
Title I of ESEA, 361–63

Top-down approach, 199, 200,
   368–69
Total quality control, 6
Town school, 64
Tracks, tracking, 80, 83
Traditional approach, 7–8
Traditionalists, 183–85
Training, 71, 295–96, 299
Transactions, 329
Transcendence, 256–57, 285, 394
Transfer of learning, 102
Transformation, 110–11, 397–98
Transitional period (1893–1918),
   78–84
Transparency of assessment, 339
Transpersonal orientation, 256–57
Transpersonal psychology, 394
Trend forecasting, 385–86, 387
True experiment, 324
Twenty-Sixth Yearbook (NSSE), 13,
   88–89, 91
Type S Strategic Planning, 307

Uncertainty, certainty vs., 389–91,
   392
Unit of analysis, 190
Universal core, 51–52
Universal education, rise of
   (1820–1920), 72–78
University of Chicago, 83, 91
Upward communication, improving,
   296
U.S. Department of Education, 353
U.S. Supreme Court, 158, 366
Utilitarian education, 71–72
Utilitarian evaluation, 325–26
Utility, 39
Utility, content selection and, 216
Utilization-related learning, 240

Validity, 215–16, 339
Valuational theory, 179
Value clarification, 126, 127, 132
Value-orientation changes, 300
Value questions, types of, 320–22
Values, 37, 154, 343, 371–73
Valuing, objectives related to, 281
Variation, theory of, 6
Verbal and concrete learning, 123
Verbal association, 104
Vertical articulation, 242
Vertical organization, 237
Vertical relationships, 239–40
Vision building, 293
Visioning, 399
Volume of environment, 222
Vouchers, 369–70

Webs, curriculum, 248
White House Conference on
   Education (1955), 156
Wholeness of curriculum
   experiences, 217
Whole to part learning, 240
William and Mary College, 67
Windows, 221
Wisdom, 121
Women, expanding role of, 384
Women's rights movement, 364
Wording of objectives, 278–79
Work ethic, belief in, 141
World curriculum, 51–52
Worldwide systems, 52
Worth, curriculum implementation
   and, 310
Worth of objectives, 278

Yale College, 65

416